P9-DWJ-748

The New Bungalow

Essays by Matthew Bialecki, AIA

Christian Gladu

Jill Kessenich, Associate AIA

Jim McCord, AIA

Su Bacon

Salt Lake City

First Edition

05 04 03 02 01 4 3 2 1

Copyright © 2001 Gibbs Smith, Publisher

Essays © 2001 Matthew Bialecki, Christian Gladu, Jill Kessenich, Jim McCord, Su Bacon

Photograph copyrights as noted throughout

All rights reserved. No part of this book may be reproduced by any means whatsoever without written permission from the publisher, except brief excerpts quoted for purpose of review.

Published by

Gibbs Smith, Publisher

PO Box 667

Layton, UT 84041

Orders: (800) 748-5439

www.gibbs-smith.com

Cover design and production by Traci O'Very Covey

Interior design and production by FORTHGEAR, Inc.

Edited by Suzanne Taylor and Madge Baird

Library of Congress Cataloging-in-Publication-Data

Bialecki, Matthew.

The new bungalow / essays by Matthew Bialecki, Christian Gladu, Jill Kessenich, Jim McCord, and Su Bacon.—1st ed.

p. cm.

ISBN 1-58685-042-3

1. Bungalows—United States—History. 2. Architecture—United States—20th century. 3. Arts and Crafts Movement—Influence. I. Gladu, Christian. II. Kessenich, Jill. III. McCord, Jim. IV. Bacon, Su. V. Title.

NA7571.B53 2001

728.'373—dc21

2001002766

Contents

Acknowledgments

Our deepest thanks to the following individuals and companies who helped us round out our understanding of the bungalow in today's architecture and who shared information, philosophy, leads, and photographs, and some of whom opened their homes for photographing:

Tim Ashmore
Su Bacon
Matthew Bialecki
John Brinkmann
Marshall Compton
Mikel Covey
Traci O'Very Covey
Brett Gee
Curtis Gelotte
Christian Gladu
Kristin Gladu
Lee Hershberger
Don Hensman
Ted Houseknecht
Valerie Johnson
Jill Kessenich
Lis King
Lynn King
Robert Lidsky
Johan Luchsinger
Randell L. Makinson
John Malick
Michael and Jane Mangelson
Jim McCord
Alex Moseley
David Papazian
Voorhees Craftsman
Robert Winter

Introduction

For three decades, Gibbs Smith, Publisher, has been exploring the works of Greene & Greene, Bernard Maybeck, and Frank Lloyd Wright. But the truth is that very few of us can own a masterpiece like the Greenes' ultimate bungalow, or a house of the quality of Wright—but we can afford a home in a style that moves beyond nationwide suburban and tract homes and condominium complexes that all look the same. Where can the sameness end and individual expression begin? It begins with *The New Bungalow.*

We have watched American taste for retro style and antiques move old-home renovation to an unprecedented level of popularity and taste, and have witnessed a marked demand for information on remodeling and decorating bungalow homes. They fit right in with a taste for things of the past; their smallness appeals for its manageability. Even though most people have never lived in one, they long for the neighborhood homes like those in which their parents and grandparents lived.

To many Arts & Crafts enthusiasts, bungalows are about a narrowly defined style, a certain look. The truth of the matter is that bungalows exist throughout the country in a variety of different styles. This book shows examples of homes that run the gamut from pure classical to the more interpretive designs. Yet all of them exude the true spirit of the bungalow—architectural expressions of a philosophy that took hold a century and a half ago.

Homes showcased within also run the gamut in affordability. Some of them focus on simplicity and efficient use of space. Others are high-end dwellings with thousands of square feet and utilizing pricey materials. At both ends of the spectrum—whether the house is in the $80 or $800-per-square-foot range—builders and owners have treated themselves to details that will last for generations, such as tile fireplace surrounds, doors and windows with character and class, and attractive and functional built-in cabinets and benches. Whether your budget is $80 or $800 a square foot, there are ideas and creative solutions here that will expand and enrich your understanding of the bungalow as a housing type for today's lifestyle.

After having read architects' and historians' educated opinions on the bungalow and its place in the past and today, foremost in our minds were the questions "What is a bungalow?" "What is its appeal?" "Why are we drawn to this style of house?" "In what ways is it appropriate for today's lifestyle?" To get some answers, we looked to the architects and builders who are creating new bungalows, to some who are remodeling old bungalows, and to the past for the principles underlying the original Arts & Crafts movement.

In our research, we called upon some experts: Randell L. Makinson, Hon. AIA, scholar and author of numerous books on Greene and Greene, their homes, and their distinctive architectural style; Robert Winter, art and architectural historian and author of books on the American bungalow as well as Batchelder tiles and architectural guidebooks to Los Angeles and San Francisco. Both Makinson and Winter led us to people whose philosophies and works are featured in this book. We also searched the Internet and were elated to find a number of architects in various regions of the country offering new plans for bungalow homes and bungalow neighborhoods.

Then we began dialogues with the architects and designers themselves. It was exhilarating to learn firsthand their various approaches to the modern bungalow, their interpretations of its elements, style, and materials. Their enthusiasm made it obvious that each of the professionals whose writings, photographs, and designs appear in this book is fully engaged in developing a house style for people today. They are keen on quality and allocation of space; they are tuned in to the environment both aesthetically and from an ecological standpoint; they are champions of the bungalow revival and are steadily enlisting disciples.

Matthew Bialecki, AIA, of Matthew Bialecki Associates, New Paltz, New York, has possibly the broadest interpretation of those architects and designers whose essays are included in this book. He analyzes the philosophy of the original Arts & Crafts movement that started in the mid-1800s in England and shows how the American Arts & Crafts proponents carried the tenets along. He strongly advocates nature-based design as the answer for twenty-first-century residential architecture.

Christian Gladu of The Bungalow Company in Bend, Oregon, has developed bungalow neighborhoods with life and vitality on Bainbridge Island, Washington, and other locations. His designs integrate the style and timeless charm of the past with a modern point of view. Gladu helps us understand the quality of life that can be achieved through bungalow living and illustrates how the bungalow style has adapted to fit the needs of today's homeowners.

Jill Kessenich, Associate AIA, is a partner with Tim Ashmore in Ashmore/Kessenich Design with offices in Madison, Wisconsin, and Portland, Oregon. They specialize in house designs inspired by the early twentieth century. Kessenich shares professional advice on restoring old bungalows, and examples of their designs provide fresh options for new-home construction in the classic style.

Jim McCord, AIA, of Monterey, California, shares some practical advice on ways to achieve a bungalow look and feel in a remodel or spec home, detailing construction elements that can be upgraded or simply selected with prudence by the homeowner to achieve a bungalow look.

Su Bacon, interior and lighting designer and co-owner of Historic Lighting in Monrovia, California, has outfitted historic remodels of Greene & Greene, new homes in the style of the Greenes, and many other historic residences and businesses with period-appropriate lighting. She shares her design professional's perspective on the function of lighting in today's homes and addresses each aspect: sconces, ceiling lights, lamps, and makes a case for the use of the newer recessed lighting technology in the bungalow.

Numerous additional architects, interior designers, and homeowners have opened their archives and homes, lending photographs for this book and allowing new photography as well. To them, we are deeply appreciative. A few architects who we wished to include were unable to participate for one reason or another, some having to do with privacy wishes of the homeowners. Nevertheless, we have listed their firms in the Resources, as we recognize their driving efforts in the bungalow revival.

We have been enlightened through our interaction with each individual and firm that is represented in this book. We trust that you will be inspired as well. —*The Editors*

: Origins of the Bungalow :

Matthew Bialecki, AIA

New bungalows can be made, new objects created; but if they are to be as valued and treasured as the originals we admire, they need to do more than copy the look: they need to interpret the original spirit and objectives for our time and place.

Matthew Bialecki, AIA

Could anyone have predicted in the early 1920s, when the original Arts & Crafts movement died out, that it would enjoy a revival that would start some fifty years later and last longer than the original movement? Arts & Crafts has evolved into a national style phenomenon. It is now possible to live in Arts & Crafts–themed developments, work in Arts & Crafts–inspired office parks, eat in Arts & Crafts–styled restaurants and, of course, buy most any Arts & Crafts–style furniture at your local mall, big-box retailer,

Maclucas house in Pacific Palisades, California. This craftsman remodel was first done in the mid-1980s. Courtesy of Historic Lighting.

The tall tree-like posts blend the house with the surrounding woods. Gundlach House, New Paltz, New York, Matthew Bialecki, architect.

or Web site. What happened to our obscure, little, cognoscente-only art movement that turned it into a multimedia merchandising juggernaut?

With the revival now well into its fourth decade, it is time to pause and critically ask what is fueling this great interest in a minor hundred-year-old art movement. Where is the bungalow revival going, and, more importantly, will it support a new architecture and a new way of living?

Front elevation, Studley residence, Gardiner, New York, Matthew Bialecki, architect.

The answer lies in understanding the principles of the original architects and artists who founded the movement in the nineteenth century. To be sure, there will always be a market for the fine and rare artifacts of any notable period, but that audience is limited and the marketing activity is ultimately commercial, not creative. New bungalows can be made, new objects created; but if they are to be as valued and treasured as the originals we admire, they need to do more than copy the look: they need to interpret the original spirit and objectives for our time and place. A review of those principles will lay the groundwork for interpreting the bungalow for our time.

A Brief History

Many people who are just becoming acquainted with the style today would be astonished at how quickly the original American Arts & Crafts and bungalow movement came and went. It was barely sixteen years from Stickley's introduction of his first craftsman furniture (1900) and the first printing of his magazine, *The Craftsman.*

An early California bungalow shows the typical overhanging eaves and exposed structure. It is blended nicely with the landscape for a unified design.

An early rear view of the Blacker House, designed by Charles and Henry Greene.

Charles and Henry Greene, the greatest architects of the bungalow movement and designers of the finest bungalows, didn't fare much better. They started their practice in Pasadena in 1894, gradually developing their art and business until reaching the apex of their careers in 1910, when they completed the last of their five "ultimate bungalows." They built significant work for another eight years but, nevertheless, from that pinnacle they slowly but steadily faded until in 1922 they dissolved their firm. A mere twenty-five years had elapsed from tentative beginnings to acknowledged masterworks to professional obscurity.

Were design tastes so fickle? How could something that now seems so timeless and enduring have faded so quickly?

In the early 1900s, companies made the style available to anyone by delivering bungalow kits to one's doorstep.

The great bungalow building boom of the 1910s and '20s was the popular acknowledgement of Stickley's and the Greenes' accomplishments, but it eventually became a victim of its own success. With factories delivering bungalow kits to your doorstep and builders creating bungalow heavens coast to coast by the score, the original qualities that made them so popular got lost. By the late '20s and '30s, the bungalow had became a synonym for "cheap little house."

But what cheap little houses! Porches, woodwork, built-ins, windows—who could resist? It is easy to see why the bungalows were so popular: they provided a traditional sense of craftsmanship in a fundamentally contemporary home. Simply, bungalows were America's first popular example of modern architecture, and we loved it. In fact, bungalows and their progeny—the ranch house of the 1940s–60s—were the dominant housing type for the twentieth century.

Bungalows in all varieties of shapes and sizes were advertised across the country as the answer to housing needs after World War II.

What elements made them so popular?

- The compact plan merged front hall and parlor, creating an open, flowing space.
- The homes were mostly one story and volumetrically horizontal.
- The windows were large and mostly horizontally proportioned, making bungalows bright and transparent.
- The wood structure was exposed and celebrated, even exaggerated, with beams, rafter tails, and structural framing details highlighted as decorations.
- The bungalow house was linked to the yard and garden.

In the finest examples of American Arts & Crafts architecture—Greene and Greene's ultimate bungalows—the houses are inseparable from the gardens. The entire scope of house and environment is conceived as one intrinsic design. Terraces embrace porches, which flow into living spaces filled with materials and images from the garden. Sleeping porches, balconies, and courtyards dissolve the "built" architecture into the landscape. With the doors open on a summer night, you don't know if you are inside or out. The ultimate bungalows are much more a pavilion in the landscape than a house next to a garden. Even at the most modest scale, the bungalows have the porch and the garden that maintain the feel of a pavilion.

The bungalow was the design for America's new millennium. A new plan, a new look, a new lifestyle. Yes, it's heretical to say anything about contemporary architecture among history-soaked, fumed-oak, clinker-bricked, open-beamed bungalow fanatics, but it's true: bungalows were America's first widely available modern architecture and we have never looked back. The bungalow craze of the teens and '20s never really ended. It was just given a different name—the ranch.

One reason bungalows became popular was that they celebrated their wood structure by using structural framing details as decorations.

Art historians have long recognized that significant artistic movements follow an almost predictable trajectory from discovery ➢ achievement ➢ gradual decline into obscurity ➢ eventual rediscovery and reinvention. Clearly, the current bungalow revival is our rediscovery and reinvention phase. This is truly a renaissance of ideas and not just images with origins in the English Arts & Crafts movement. The fundamental principles of the American bungalow were developed in England in the mid-nineteenth century, and the aspirations of those original artists and architects are the basis for the ideals of the new bungalow renaissance.

England 1840–90

While the American bungalow movement followed the historical cycle of discovery through decline from 1900–30, the Arts & Crafts movement in England began its trajectory about fifty years earlier.

Up until that time, English architecture was centered completely on accepted historical styles—Greek, Roman, French Renaissance, Baroque, Gothic, Romanesque, Moorish, and so forth. Debates among architects became increasingly narrow and the issues more obscure: Parish churches should definitely be Gothic! Government buildings can only be Greek! Meanwhile, the industrial revolution had developed new technologies (steel frames, glass walls, mass production of components) that were rarely acknowledged.

The leading English architects were filled with uncertainty about the practicality of the historical styles. Buildings other than palaces and churches were needed—train stations, offices, warehouses—to which historic styles often didn't conform. By mid-century, the stage had been readied for the two great struggles of twentieth-century architectural theory: Nature and the Machine, or "bungalow vs. Bauhaus."

Designed by architect John Malick, the Cereghino home recalls the charming, unpretentious homes of nineteenth-century British architect C. F .A. Voysey.

PUGIN, RUSKIN, MORRIS: NATURE-BASED ARCHITECTURE

By the time of his premature death in 1852 at the age of forty, Augustus Welby Pugin was already recognized as the savior of English architecture. His work on the Houses of Parliament with Charles Barry had crowned an extraordinary career as an architect and designer. Although he was primarily considered for his work in the Gothic Revival, he was widely read and praised for his advocacy of a return to the craft traditions of the medieval guilds and to an expressive, straightforward approach to exposing structural elements such as beams, stone walls, and hardware.

Pugin turned away from the debate over historical styles and found his own unique expression. His principle of truthfulness—handcrafted materials used honestly and showing the structure of a building directly—would become fundamental principles of the first Arts & Crafts architects two decades later.

Indeed, it is difficult to imagine Pugin's contemporaries—the great critic and theorist John Ruskin, and William Morris, the grandfather of the English Arts & Crafts movement—able to support their theories without having Pugin's work as an example. Ruskin, Morris, and their followers were active critics against the injustices of the industrial revolution. And, like Pugin, they believed that art and architecture had the capacity to redeem and reform society. They lived and wrote in favor of a simple life rejuvenated by the handcrafting of art. Morris rejoiced in the wonders and restorative power of nature, and representations of the natural world filled his art.

The main body of the Cereghino residence has a heavy stucco finish and is detailed to create the appearance of an old stone building.

The Hoelter residence boasts a new garden design, inspired by the English gardens of Gertrude Jekyll, which creates a clearly recognizable pathway from the street to the front entry. John Malick, architect.

Wooden framing in the high ceilings of the Cereghino residence brings warmth and spaciousness to the living room. John Malick, architect.

From the founding of Morris & Company in London in 1861 until Morris's death in 1896, he and his circle were the leading decorative artists and theoretical leaders of the growing Arts & Crafts movement. He redefined art to include traditional crafts such as stained glass, weaving, wallpaper and pattern making, bookbinding, tiles, murals, and furniture design. His designs were not merely objects to admire; they were an integral part of a philosophy that proposed a new lifestyle of self-reliance that celebrated an artistic life. "Have nothing in your houses which you do not know to be useful or believe to be beautiful," he said.

Morris inspired all the great architects of the English Arts & Crafts movement: Webb, Voysey, Lethaby, Lutyens, Ballie Scott, and others. It

Malick redesigned this home with many gardens, gates, and trellises to integrate the house and garden.

was these architects who most successfully implemented Morris's ideals and developed three of the most important aspects of the future bungalow movement: the celebration and use of vernacular architecture (using local natural materials), the unifying of a building's architecture with its interior fixtures and furnishings, and the integration of the house and garden. For example, Lethaby's Melsetter House on Orkney is as vernacular as a group of massive boulders; a home so completely part of the island's building tradition and landscape that it would flounder anywhere else; Voysey's Bormley and Moorcrag houses in Cumbria, with their slate roofs like piles of rocks hovering over whitewashed walls, both contrast with the lush green hills and fit in like a strong crag.

The Cereghino residence's staircase is the masterwork of the home.

The interiors were equally radical. Rejecting the fixtures and furnishings produced at the time as hopelessly garish and inappropriate, the English Arts & Crafts architects simply made their own. The Red House by Webb and Morris was considered shockingly bare, a neutral background for the hand-painted furniture and elegantly crafted furnishings they designed for it. Voysey, Scott, and Lutyens were masters at designing and fabricating the hardware, glass, textiles, and furniture that fused the interior with the architectural expression.

The last other major achievement by the English Arts & Crafts architects that would have a profound influence on the bungalow movement was the emphasis on integrating the garden with the home. No one did this better than Ballie Scott, whose small gardens show a practicality and beauty.

Traditional Craftsman construction methods create well-above-average life expectancy for the Hoelter residence. John Malick, architect.

In just over fifty years, the English Arts & Crafts movement had broken from the tired stylistic formulas of the past and developed a new architectural language. They created new forms based on nature and the indigenous, vernacular architecture. They defined a whole new integrated approach to the decorative arts and interior design of their buildings. They linked the house with the landscape and the rooms with the garden directly as one element. They promoted a new lifestyle of living and working artistically with nature as guide and muse.

The Hoelters' breakfast room and terrace surrounded by nature is part of the Arts & Crafts ideal.

William Morris's work was eagerly read and discussed on both sides of the Atlantic, especially by an idealistic American furniture maker from upstate New York named Gustav Stickley.

The Hoelter design emphasizes exposed post-and-beam construction and hand-assembled wainscots, casework, doors, and windows.

Craftsman Houses in America, 1898–1928

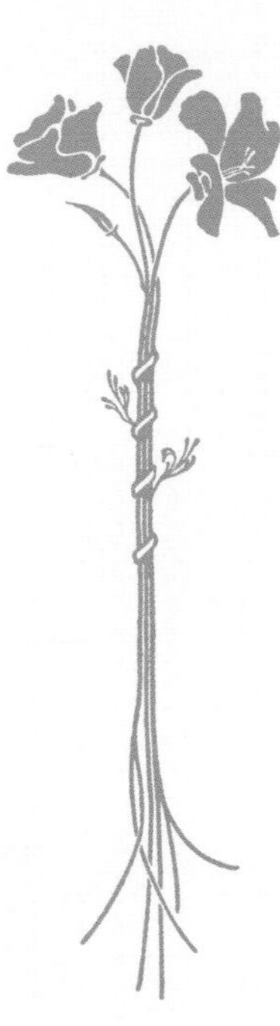

This home in Salt Lake City was designed and constructed in the Arts & Crafts style through the collaborative effort of John Shirley (exterior), Juidiith Clawson (interior), and Steve Dubell, project foreman for Doug Knight construction. The overriding desire was to build a new house that would blend with the style of an older bungalow neighborhood.

"We do not believe in large houses with many rooms elaborately decorated and furnished, for the reason that these seem so essentially an outcome of the artificial conditions that lay such harassing burdens upon modern life. . . . That is why we have from the first planned houses that are based on the big fundamental principles of honesty, simplicity and usefulness. . . ."

—Gustav Stickley

If William Morris can be considered the grandfather of the bungalow movement, certainly Gustav Stickley must be the father. Deeply impressed after his meetings with Voysey and

Stickley's traditional designs merged common sense with good design.

Ashbee in England in 1898, Stickley returned to America a disciple. By 1900, he had introduced his soon-to-be-famous craftsman furniture, and a year later, he began publication of *The Craftsman,* the magazine that brought the designs and lifestyle of the bungalow movement to America.

Stickley was more than a furniture maker. His studio produced over two hundred house plans, offered consulting and design services, and claimed by 1913 that several thousand of his Craftsman homes had been built for a total value of over $20 million! As the apostle of the Arts & Crafts bungalow, Stickley brought the virtues of affordability and practicality to the ideals of the English Arts & Crafts homes. His designs embraced indigenous building types, extolled the virtues of the garden and outdoor spaces, praised simple, honest materials crafted beautifully, and advanced the necessity of convenience and practicality in a home. Kitchens were designed and discussed with as much care as living rooms. Gardens were for recreation and growing fruits and vegetables.

Furnishings were durable and dignified, made of oak, leather, and hammered copper. He brought the Arts & Crafts ideals to the American middle class, merging common sense and good design.

Of the many styles featured in *The Craftsman,* Stickley clearly embraced the wood-shingled, heavy timbered bungalows of California as the ideal expressions of the bungalow movement. He visited there in 1904 and was deeply impressed by the work of the Greenes.

The meticulous woodwork of this contemporary craftsman home is an enduring tribute to the legacy of Greene & Greene. Studley residence, Gardiner, New York, Matthew Bialecki, architect.

The Blacker house was designed as a seamless extension of its gardens and landscape.

Greene is so clearly the high-water mark of the bungalow movement that discussion of other architects and designers almost seems superfluous. Their five ultimate bungalows—the Blacker, Gamble, Thorsen, Pratt, and Ford Houses—are the best examples of the fusion of architecture, landscape architecture, and the decorative arts America has produced. The ultimate bungalows were designed as seamless extensions of their gardens and the landscape, with the interior furnishings and fixtures complementing the garden and architecture perfectly. The homes embodied the bungalow lifestyle with thoughtful and practical kitchens and domestic conveniences while providing the poetic luxuries of sleeping porches, inglenooks, and terraces. Quite simply, they were masterpieces.

With the completion of the ultimate bungalows and the conclusion of Stickley's *Craftsman* in 1916, the artistic and theoretical development of the bungalow and the Arts & Crafts movement stopped. The masterworks had been achieved, the philosophy written, the recognition given.

The bungalow craze, however, was in full swing. Fueled by the great Florida and California land speculations of the twenties, the economic boom, the growth of the middle class, and the mass-marketing of prefabricated bungalow building kits, companies such as Sears, Alladin, Lewis, and others sold by some estimates more than 100,000 homes by the late 1920s. Bungalows had become big business that would take the Great Depression to it slow down, and, in 1932, a little architectural exhibition called International Style to finish it off.

Bungalows like this one were mass marketed by companies such as Sears, Alladin, Lewis, and others.

By the late 1920s, more than 100,000 bungalows had been built.

The Bungalow vs. the Bauhaus, 1930–70

"Frank Lloyd Wright? Why he was the greatest architect of the 19th Century. . . ."—*Phillip Johnson*

With the opening of the now-famous "International Style" exhibition at the Museum of Modern Art in 1932, the Bauhaus made a grand entrance into the American design and architectural world. Homes were, as architect Le Corbusier stated in 1925, "machines for living."

In fact, the entire modern movement was enthralled with the machine and all its aesthetic possibilities. Use factory manufacturing methods and components! Make walls of glass and steel! Abolish the sloped roof! Buildings should express their machine origins and become abstract sculpture. Buildings should contrast with nature, not blend with it.

This was not an architecture that accepted the romantic, the quaint, or the cozy. The bungalow was yesterday's style, at least if you wanted to graduate from architecture school in the 1950s and '60s.

However, a small group of architects kept developing the concepts that were central to the original bungalows. Led by Frank Lloyd Wright, Rudolph Schindler, Harwell Harris, William Wurster, and others, architects in the '30s, '40s and '50s talked about architecture inspired by nature, using natural materials. This was the next evolution of the Arts & Crafts movement.

Now, it is true that these new bungalows didn't quite resemble the Stickley/Greene & Greene craftsmans of the 1910s–20s. They were lighter and architecturally more dynamic, but the principles were there— integrating the landscape with the building, exposing the structure, composing the building with horizontal volumes and glass, an overreaching practicality for solving domestic solutions, and a love for wood.

The post-war period was a fertile one for architecture in America. Frank Lloyd Wright's Usonian houses, William Wurster and Joseph Eshrick's emerging Bay Area style, and Harris's many buildings all showed a new way of building with nature. The movement was growing, and it attracted its share of critics.

In 1948 Jean Bangs, Harris's wife and an architectural historian, wrote a series of articles on Greene & Greene and Bernard Maybeck (their contemporary in the Bay Area) that are credited with the "re-discovery and recognition of these [at the time] forgotten architects." At the same time, the debate between the Bauhaus-trained architects and the naturalists reached a boiling point. The famous modernist Marcel Breuer summed up the modernists' disdain for the emerging group of regional, nature-based architects: "I don't feel too much impulse to set 'human' [in the best sense of the word] against formal. If human is considered identical with redwood all over the place, or if it is considered identical with camouflaging architecture with planting, with nature, with romantic subsidies, I am against it."

The debates of the late '40s and early '50s clearly didn't change much among the practitioners. However, it did get a lot of press at *House Beautiful,* where the influential editor Elizabeth Gordon championed Wright and the whole movement. She published and promoted the nature-based designers and moved readers toward a natural, humanized modernism. The final model of the bungalow was now at hand: the post-war ranch house.

Like the mass-produced bungalows of the '20s had broken the hearts of Greene & Greene, so did the mass-produced versions of Wright's and Harris's houses grieve them. Fueled by the post-war boom, developers stripped the wood, the glass, the nature, and the detail and built the ranch house coast to coast: suburbia was born.

The Arts & Crafts Revival: A New Beginning

By the mid-1970s architects rarely designed work that required a lot of detailed craftsmanship. "They just don't make them like they used to," was the resigned shrug. But fortunately, the historic preservation of the movement's great masterworks and the publication of scholarship, notably Randell Makinson's Greene & Greene monographs, fueled the current Arts & Crafts revival, and hasn't lost steam since.

The current revival has brought to the fore a new generation of craftspeople to the professions: architects, designers, woodworkers, metal smiths, glass artists, tile makers, textile artisans, and building contractors trained in the restoration of historic buildings. The craftspeople and trades needed for restoring old bungalows and designing new ones are well established, and homeowners have beat paths to their doors. But to what end? The restoration and preservation of the historic homes, of course, must continue. What are the inspirations for new work? Will the revival be a studied re-creation of turn-of-the-century bungalows, or will it result in fresh new house design based on the original principles of bungalow design?

posite) Glass crystal nightstand designed for the Studley residence, with fundamental materials—cast glass, hammered copper, and carved ne—expressed in a direct way. Matthew Bialecki, architect.

This magnificent stairway in the Studley house is one of the finest examples of design and craftsmanship in the Arts & Crafts revival.

: Elements of :

Bungalow

Jill Kessenich, Associate AIA

One of the great things about a bungalow is that it's most often a one-story house, which makes it a viable retirement home.

Jill Kessenich, Associate AIA

Ask anyone in Milwaukee, Wisconsin, what a bungalow is and nine times out of ten, they can simply point to one on their street. It is a clapboard or brick home with a hipped or jerkin-head roof and a three-season front porch. It is a story and a half tall, and the upper level has an open attic, or maybe has one bedroom with a dormer window. As a kid, that attic was a great place to play, but to the designer and builder, it was ready-made for expansion. Milwaukee is just one of many cities that came of age dur-

This contemporary home, designed by Curtis Gelotte Architects, is built in the spirit of Greene & Greene.

Typical bungalow of the mid-1900s from a Boise Payette Lumber Co. plan book.

ing the industrial era, when housing was needed for a growing population and growing families. The bungalow seemed to fit most everyone's requirements.

Most bungalows in America were built in the early 1900s on narrow city lots, grouped in neighborhoods near a local industry. The American bungalow of the mid-1900s typically has a prominent front porch, a low roof pitch, and wide eaves. The narrow end usually faces the street, and the first floor has six rooms, stacked side-by-side: a living room, formal dining room, kitchen on one side, and two bedrooms and a bath on the other side.

The Qualey family home in Santa Monica, vintage 1950s, was remodeled in 1998 to a Greene & Greene–style beauty. This classy new bungalow is complemented with lighting design by Historic Lighting.

3236

Vintage Bungalows: Space

Upon entering a vintage bungalow from the spacious porch, you see there's a built-in bench or boot box in the front hall. You immediately feel the house envelop you with its warmth. Most likely, it's the woodwork, maybe a natural redwood, or Douglas fir, or a richly stained white oak. Even if the woodwork is painted, it's usually abundant, and still gives the rooms a rich quality. The floors will also be wood, maybe a natural maple or vertical-grain fir, but typically oak. In the living room there's almost always a fireplace, and it may be flanked by bookcases and piano windows. It's the perfect place to relax on a chilly evening with a good book and a blazing fire.

In the dining room there will most likely be a built-in china hutch, often with a beveled mirror and, if you're lucky, some stained art glass. This may even have a pass-through to the kitchen. The hutch provides a lot of storage space and doesn't clutter up the room like free-standing furniture can. Maybe there's a window seat, or a bay window that lets in more natural light and gives the room a spacious quality.

The kitchen might still have its original cabinets, which are probably painted white or at least a light color. Perhaps there is a wall-mounted sink or a wood-burning or gas stove. There might even be some funky old linoleum on the floor. Some bungalow kitchens might still have the old icebox and compressor, or at least the cabinet.

The bathroom may have its own set of treasures. If it's in original condition, it will most likely have white hexagonal floor tile, maybe with a colored accent. There could be a tiled wainscot on the walls, or plaster scored to look like tile.

(Left) A small window seat on the second-floor stair landing makes good use of space that would otherwise be relegated to pass-through territory. Courtesy of Historic Lighting.

A spacious entryway in the Maclucas house is warmed by a beautiful collection of Oriental rugs and a gallery of photographs. Courtesy of Historic Lighting.

(upper left) Dark wainscoting sets off the pedestal sink in the Qualey powder room. Courtesy of Historic Lighting.

(Above) Built-in benches in the fireplace nook take less space than freestanding furniture would. Design by David M. Schwarz / Architectural Services Inc.

Juidiith Clawson of Simply Fetched took a Wrightian approach to this stairway design. Mahogany and lacewood below the banister pop the grain. The whole look is artistic, making an attractive transition between the open space of the main floor and the private family area upstairs. Architectural detailing and space planning by Juidiith Clawson of Simply Fetched; Michael and Jane Mangelson, owners.

A pedestal sink and claw-foot tub would be the norm, and the toilet might have a wooden tank mounted high on the wall, or even a round tank. The original shower could have a sunflower-shaped head surrounded by a round or curved curtain rod. The bedrooms will most likely be small and cozy.

One of the great things about a bungalow is that it's most often a one-story house, which makes it a viable retirement home for when negotiating stairs can be a problem. It's also a good first home that can be expanded upstairs as the need arises. Sometimes staircases are narrow and steep, or hidden behind a door. These can often be opened up or reworked to make a more natural transition between first- and second-floor living spaces.

The rich wood from the main floor of the Qualey house continues up the stairway, for a smooth blending of two living areas. This kind of wood detailing is reminiscent of the brothers Greene. Courtesy of Historic Lighting.

A NEIGHBORHOOD HOUSE

In larger terms, vintage bungalows are ideal for today's living because of where they were built. They are most often in first-ring suburbs of major cities, or just blocks from the downtown in smaller towns. That makes them close to shopping, entertainment and other services, often within walking distance.

The trees that were planted when the houses were built are now mature, and provide welcome shade from the summer heat. Their towering canopies give the streetscape an inviting quality.

The houses themselves also provide a neighborly quality. The front porches are a place where children can play, or a parent can watch from a distance. This promotes interaction with neighbors.

Many people living in vintage bungalows are attracted to them for the same reasons: they're affordable, they're close to the city, and the houses are built with character. These homeowners also have something else in common. With the value of these houses on the rise, they all have some ideas for restoring, remodeling, or adding onto their houses. Any improvements they make will add to their equity.

Midcentury bungalow designs usually incorporated porches, where neighborly interchanges were stimulated as people spent time outdoors.

A CHANGING HOUSE

Whether you own a modest kit bungalow or one that was designed by a local architect, chances are that your house has gone through a few changes over the years. The rooms most likely remodeled were the kitchen and the bathroom, as the advent of amenities like refrigerator/ freezers and stand-up showers were seen as modern advances, and most people wanted to obtain them. Later on, items such as pre-manufactured cabinets, built-in ovens, and fiberglass shower surrounds began to appear.

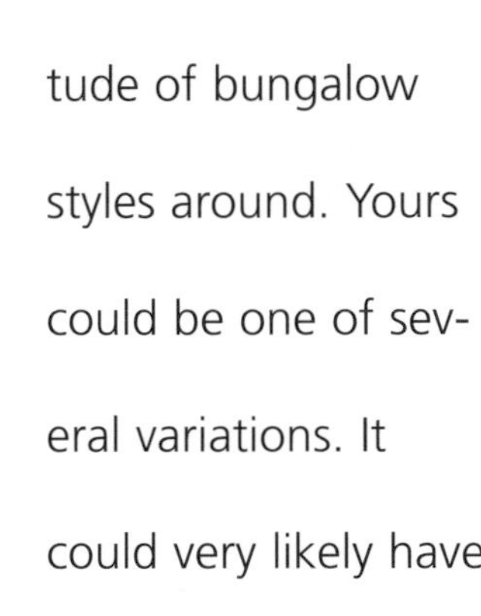

Unfortunately, most of these new innovations were not built in styles that complemented the old-fashioned bungalow and, to our eyes, might clash with the original built-ins and furniture. One of the first steps in restoring these spaces to their original charm, while maintaining modern functions, is to identify the style, or styles, of your bungalow. Then, when you plan a larger project such as a major remodeling or addition, you can know what to look for in products and designs.

There are a multitude of bungalow styles around. Yours could be one of several variations. It could very likely have Craftsman detailing on the outside yet be Colonial Revival on the inside. There are some identifying features of the different styles. And since the bungalow is eclectic by nature, styles can be interpreted and applied in various ways.

The more one knows about the history of the bungalow one lives in, the easier it is to make renovations and updates in keeping with the character of the house.

VERNACULAR STYLES

QUEEN ANNE (1890–1905)

Queen Anne cottages or bungalows sprang up on the East Coast and quickly spread to the West as a more simple and economical alternative to the grander Queen Anne two-storied houses.

- Typically clad in clapboards or shingles
- Medium-pitched roof
- Porch with a small amount of gingerbread ornamentation
- Interiors typically Victorian, with wallpapered walls
- A picture molding a foot or two below the ceiling
- Non-typical drawing room/parlor configuration of same-era houses; rooms merged into one living room

CRAFTSMAN (1905–25)

Sometimes called Arts & Crafts, this style is most often associated with the state of California.

- Most prominent element is the low-pitched roof with wide, overhanging eaves
- Triangular gable ends often feature substantial wood brackets, or knee-braces
- Sometimes has massive beams without brackets
- Beams and other structural elements often appear larger than necessary
- Replaces mere decoration with elements that suggest strength and substance
- Often has more than one front-facing gable
- Porch columns always prominent but can be of various styles
- Materials like river rock, cobblestone, and clinker brick incorporated for contrast into piers, chimneys, and retaining walls
- Brick used in a variety of ways, for instance rough-textured style on the chimney exterior, contrasting with a smoother, often glazed, style for the mantel
- Interiors usually of natural or darkly stained wood, e.g., redwood or Douglas fir
- Plaster walls often painted deep natural shades, such as terra-cotta, gold, or green
- Walls might be covered in burlap or grass cloth

California Style

Sometimes this reference is used to describe vernacular variations of what we call Craftsman style.

- A simplified, usually stucco version of the Craftsman or Arts & Crafts style
- Relates indoors to outdoors with large windows, south-facing sun porch, or open courtyard

Airplane

Another variation on the California Craftsman style.

- Distinctive raised second level with four separate side walls rising up in the center of the main roofline, creating a sort of cockpit

Oriental, Japanese, and "Japo-Swiss"

A natural offshoot of the Craftsman style. Many western architects were influenced by Asian architecture, and the bungalow lent itself particularly well because of its structural emphasis. Some versions are subtle, while others are exaggerated and almost cartoon-like.

- Upsweeping gable peaks and pagoda-derived forms

Chicago Style (1920–30)

Chicago style is considered a melding of Craftsman and Prairie School influences.

- Almost always of brick construction
- Built narrow and long for city lots
- Typically steeper-pitched roof, often hipped or jerkin-head
- Often has leaded art-glass windows
- Small three-season porch or sunroom
- Designed and materials selected to accommodate snow loads and colder climates; hence, most popular in the Midwest

PRAIRIE SCHOOL (1900–1920)

This style is heavily associated with Chicago and the work of Frank Lloyd Wright and other architects especially in the area of Oak Park, Illinois.

- Low-pitched, hipped roof and wide eaves
- Horizontal lines and low foundations
- Usually brick or stucco
- Entrances commonly asymmetrical to the center of the house, often hidden from view

REVIVAL STYLES (1890–1940)

These bungalows were starting to be referred to as "cottages" in plan books and other publications, as the popularity of the term bungalow was waning in the 1930s. One plan book company, W. W. Dixon, cleverly created three exterior "cottage" styles for the same bungalow plan.

English Tudor/English Cottage (1890–1930)

Also referred to as British or English Arts & Crafts.

- Rooflines suggest the original thatched roofs of their predecessors
- Typically brick or a combination of brick and stucco
- Half-timbering details
- Casement windows sometimes leaded in a diamond pattern
- A flattened "Tudor arch" might be added to the fireplace

Mission, Spanish Colonial, and Pueblo (1890–1930)

Though not limited to the southern states, most often seen in places with a Spanish past.

- Mission or Mediterranean styles drew on Hispanic church architecture
- Spanish Colonial drew influences from Mexico and Spain
- Pueblo Revival drew on Southwest Native American style
- All similar in their use of stucco walls that resemble adobe bricks
- Clay-tile roofs
- Rounded or stepped arches, often in an arcade
- Simple ornamentation of trellis or pergola outside, fireplace or tile-accented floor inside

Colonial (1910–40)

The end of World War I seemed to spawn an interest in most of these revival styles, Colonial Revival being the most popular.

- Classical details include rounded columns and porch roofs with flat arches
- Entrances are symmetrical with painted white moldings and the occasional dentil
- Clad in either brick (usually red) or narrow clapboard siding
- Simple interiors
- Woodwork usually painted white

SWISS CHALET & LOG CABIN (1900–30)

Both styles are heavily associated with the Arts & Crafts movement and rustic furniture. The log cabin bungalow's popularity is attributed to the rise of rustic lodges and distinctive national park architecture. In the Adirondacks, wealthy weekenders built camps for themselves that resembled Swiss chalets.

- Often have cutout moldings and railings, or those made with rough-hewn branches
- Chalet or chateaux: front-facing gable
- Cabin: side-facing gable with dormer windows

MODERNE (1930–40)

The last early-twentieth-century bungalow style, and the one with the shortest run. Often called Art Deco, now referred to as Streamline Moderne.

- Styling inspired by clean lines of current industrial design, such as Airstream trailers and Frigidaire refrigerators
- Queen Mary-inspired porthole windows and metal trim
- Glass brick and terra-cotta for ornamental accent

: Renovation: Where

TO START?:

Jill Kessenich, Associate AIA

We have had fifty or more years to reflect on early-twentieth-century housing, and we have watched the charming and efficient bungalow become what we are seeing in new developments today.

Jill Kessenich, Associate AIA

Now that you have a good foundation of the history and distinctive styles of the bungalow, you can actually start to prioritize the work that you want to do on your bungalow. Most successful renovation projects are the result of careful planning. Even if the project is to be completed in stages, a master plan that coordinates current and future activities will ensure a smooth transition from one project to another. Architects or other design professionals can help to develop the "big picture" as well as provide valuable insight into the possibilities for your bungalow.

Antique tin ceiling tiles make a classy backsplash for a period sink and stove. Everything about this kitchen is reminiscent of the 1940s bungalow, right down to the tablecloth.

Before starting any major remodeling project, it is a good idea to update any systems that are worn out or even dangerous. Most vintage bungalows are at least sixty years old and some are more than a hundred. The oldest ones were the first houses to have indoor plumbing. In these older bungalows, electricity was still in its infancy and often accompanied coal gas lighting. Central heating systems consisted of large inefficient wood or coal-fired boilers and furnaces. Home inspectors and professional electricians and plumbers can help you to evaluate the condition of your current mechanical systems and assess the impact that future renovations will have on them. Although this can be the least-glamorous and rewarding work you do on your house, updating these mechanical systems serves as the foundation for much of the work to follow. Here are some things you should address.

• Will your electrical system handle all the appliances, lighting, and other amenities you want to incorporate into your remodel? Fuse boxes and three or four circuits of knob-and-tube wiring (wax- and cloth-wrapped wires with porcelain insulators and sleeves) were standard in most bungalows. Upgrading with modern circuit breakers and properly sized and grounded wiring networks will help safeguard against an electrical fire and will make future modifications easy and safe.

• The plumbing systems in many bungalows are in need of upgrading. Most cast-iron drain systems continue to work well and have some advantages over plastic piping, particularly sound transmission and inadvertent perforation. Their disadvantage lies in the difficulty of attaching additional drains and possible leaks around connections. Water-supply piping is often in need of replacement for a variety of health and safety reasons. Iron or steel pipes corrode from

Built-in cabinets, cupboards, and shelves are classic elements of bungalow style. They allow for personal expression by providing space for collectibles such as the lamps, animals, and helicopter fleet that brighten the perimeters of this room.

RESCUE

the inside, gradually constricting or closing off the pipe. This decreases water pressure, adds impurities to the water, and can produce an occasional leak. Some supply pipes in older houses and neighborhoods are made of lead that leaches into the water. Replacement with copper or plastic tubing and the proper solders and connections will provide a long-lived and safe water supply.

Two panels of three-over-one windows meeting in the corner of the room take advantage of the sun through most of the day, providing heat in winter and letting in plenty of light under the overhanging eaves. Designed and interiors by Highland Group.

•Most bungalows had some type of solid fuel (wood or coal) heat, relying on natural convection currents to distribute it around the house. This system, while quiet, heated only a short distance from the source and required oversized ducts and pipes to overcome friction. The development of fan or pump-assisted, high-efficiency, gas-fired furnaces and boilers distributed heat evenly throughout the house. A giant steel "octopus" furnace in the basement can be replaced by a suitcase-sized model and vented directly through the foundation wall with PVC tubing. Other advantages of this upgrade range from lower heating bills to an increase in useable space through the removal of the furnace and utility chimney.

• A renovation project may also be a good time to add insulation or replace windows. Depending on the climate in your area and the price of fuel, these improvements may or may not make economic sense. Local weatherization specialists can advise you in this matter. Attic insulation is generally easy to do and almost always makes sense. Wall insulation is much more difficult and will require removing at least some of the siding to drill holes in the sheathing and blow in the insulation. The siding is then replaced. Some contractors will drill through the siding and patch the hole with a plug. As you can imagine, this technique is a visual compromise, and insulation done by this method is spotty at best, as it tends to get hung up on wires, pipes, and blocking within the wall and may not be worth the effort.

• Windows may be upgraded with storm windows or replacement sashes with insulated glass. Often a large part of the character of a bungalow is derived from its windows. Muntin or leaded patterns are difficult and expensive to replicate, so careful attention should be paid to the construction and proportions of the replacement components to maintain the original character.

Many fine books have been devoted to bungalow restoration. After some serious homework, a restorer can decide what kind of restoration or renovation is feasible for their budget and appropriate for their lifestyle.

Living rooms and dining rooms are usually the easiest to restore since they are the most likely to be in original condition, as the way we use them today

This restored living room is trimmed out in the Arts & Crafts style, including dark wood trim, a high-back craftsman-style settee, and plentiful period-look lighting.

A small pantry off the kitchen helps keep some of the clutter out of view. The refrigerator as well as dishes and foodstuff can be hidden behind a closed door but are easily accessible. Bead board is used for both the wainscoting and the cabinet fronts below.

isn't all that different from the way they were used eighty or ninety years ago. If they have been modified, the changes were usually cosmetic; carpeting and inappropriate wallpaper are pretty easy to tear out.

However, because we have changed the way we use kitchens and bathrooms, these are most likely the rooms that have been remodeled. Originally built to be very utilitarian, and with one user, these rooms have become an extension of the recreational parts of our houses and lives. Entertaining today often involves both partners cooking dinner for friends or family, who are often looking on from a family room or eating area.

Even the bathroom has become a place for relaxation, with whirlpool tubs, steam showers, and spas. These luxury items

This classic California bungalow with airplane roof was home to Tom Mix, cowboy hero of the silver screen.

might even be desired in a home gym, which could include a current pool or full-size hot tub. On a more practical note, bathrooms have grown bigger, with more than one sink and other fixtures to accommodate two working adults.

Most of the original bungalows never anticipated a need for these extra spaces, so their original footprints (the shape on the lot) often don't accommodate them. If you are one of the lucky bungalow owners who still have an unfinished attic, an extra bathroom or master suite may be able to fit into that sort of space. But for first-floor additions, building back is usually your best bet, since that is usually where most of the buildable room is on your lot.

Add a Space

• One common design problem is expanding the kitchen and possibly creating an adjacent room. This might be a simple nook for eating breakfast, a larger sunroom, or a full-size family room. Kitchen expansions often involve enlarging the work triangle (sink, range, and refrigerator) to accommodate another cook, a worktable, or island. Larger or additional appliances may also be the reason for expansion; there weren't dishwashers or refrigerator/freezers in the early bungalows. Maybe a walk-in pantry can be dismantled, creating more room for appliances and cabinets or an eating area with a view into the backyard.

• Another common desire is to create a home office or designated workspace. This could be as simple as working a desk or computer area into the kitchen-cabinet layout, or it may require devoting an entire room to a private office. Sometimes a small bedroom can be converted, but it may require an addition.

• Expanding out the side of the house is often difficult, as local zoning codes restrict owners to minimum side yard setbacks (the distance from the house to the lot line). Even adding a dormer can be difficult. Until recently in some cities, second-story dormers were only built with a variance, as they infringed on the "light and air" rights of neighbors. Perhaps at one time this law was necessary to control overcrowding of neighborhoods, but now it discourages inner-city property improvements. These laws are slowly being modified to accommodate and encourage people to improve existing city properties rather than force them to build yet another suburban home.

If you live in a city that allows this kind of expansion, adding a dormer or two is often a great solution. It doesn't change the size of the footprint of the house, so no additional foundation work is required. It simply allows for useable headroom where there was only floor space. Many larger dormer additions house master bedroom suites or additional bedrooms, while smaller ones can contain bathrooms or a little nook for reading or a desk.

An L-shaped addition is one way to add space. The private outdoor nook created by the L is a side benefit.

Adding a dormer or two is a great solution for growth because no foundation work is required. It simply adds headroom where there was only floor space before.

The Bungalow Revived

We have had fifty or more years to reflect on early-twentieth-century housing, and we have watched the charming and efficient bungalow become what we are seeing in new developments today. We cherish our cozy bungalows, on tree-lined streets within walking distance of a little business district in our favorite city. We love their quirky charms: built-in benches or china hutches; clothes chutes or pass-throughs.

If you own a bungalow, you are probably aware that the style is in a revival, as can be seen in magazines like *American Bungalow* and *Old House Journal* and a number of books on their history and restoration. You might also have begun to notice that a few new bungalows are cropping up here and there, designed by people who have long respected the original ones and don't feel the need to reinvent the wheel.

The stage is set for a revival of bungalow neighborhoods that can equal the manageability and charm of earlier decades.

: The New Bungalow :

REVIVAL

by Christian Gladu

The site, the craftsmanship, the materials, and the design executed correctly will equal a sum much greater than its parts—we call it the bungalow.

Christian Gladu, The Bungalow Company

With its emphasis on handcrafted beauty, quality workmanship, and respect for natural materials, today's bungalow style offers friendly streetscapes and sensible, ecologically oriented homes that nurture twenty-first-century families.

Most homes built today contain space that is poorly utilized, consume far more energy than is reasonable, and are often built from inferior materials that just don't stand the

New bungalows, like this one built by The Bungalow Company, integrate the style and timeless charm of the past with a modern point of view.

test of time. As we move from the industrial age to the information age, the bungalow revival is a natural transition. The bungalow stands strong as an icon of simpler times and is responding to the increasing complexity of land development and the harsh reality of urban sprawl. New urbanism and other planning concepts have provided more homes in less space while at the same time developing more community-oriented neighborhoods. This development style also results in less commuting and the preservation of our undeveloped lands. As we return to traditionally planned neighborhoods, we recognize the bungalow as a philosophy first and a building style second. As such, it offers the following:

- A proactive approach to community through design.
- A tool to transition our culture to a simpler way of life.
- A future that embraces environmental challenges.

For the Jacobs residence in Pasadena, architect Gilbert Lee Hershberger created a friendly streetscape that blends the house with the yard.

Planning

Densely planned neighborhoods, if properly designed and executed, evolve into thriving communities for generations to enjoy.

In the best bungalow neighborhoods,such as this one designed by The Bungalow Company, all facades of the house are designed with the attention to detail as if they faced the street.

SQUARE FOOTAGE

Since the 1920s, the average family has decreased in size, while the square footage of the average home has doubled, increasing the amount of space that is poorly utilized. The new bungalow is modest in size by today's standards, and includes floor plans that are designed for a more casual lifestyle—floor plans that are more open and informal than their predecessors.

Determining a house's value by the square foot is similar to buying an automobile by the pound. Ironically, smaller older homes in established neighborhoods bring a premium cost per square foot, supporting the theory that bigger is not necessarily better and that homebuyers are willing to pay for design and neighborhood character. The challenge in traditionally planned neighborhoods is to encourage the building, real estate, and banking communities to divorce themselves from their preconceptions of how to value homes and realize that square footage is not always the be-all and end-all of building. The truer concept is how that square footage is utilized.

The temptation to build larger is twofold: first, the larger home will typically cost less per square foot and, secondly, for builders, more square footage typically elevates the asking price. The downsides to this are both visual and environmental. Visually, the more space a home requires, the less opportunity there is to develop outdoor spaces. This also makes it hard to maintain a comfortable level of personal and private spaces.

Environmentally, bungalows not only use space wisely, but they also take advantage of the common natural materials indigenous to their particular area of the country.

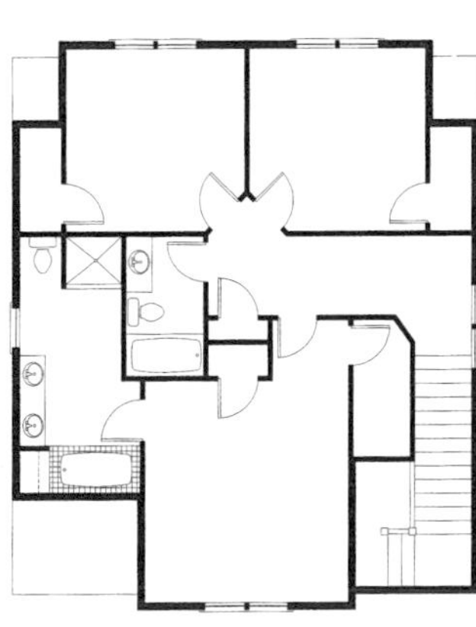

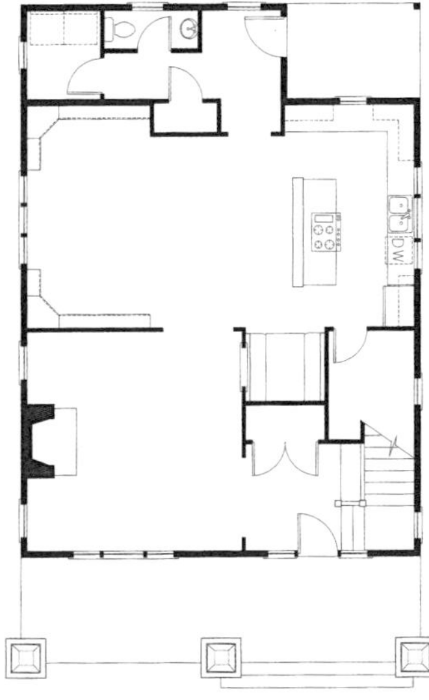

These plans by The Bungalow Company are modest in size by today's standards but more open and informal than their predecessors.

NORTH TOWN

North Town Woods is a community neighborhood of craftsman-style bungalows on Bainbridge Island, Washington. It is centrally located near schools, shopping, and public transportation. It is a revival of simple, well-crafted designs from the past, a community with a look that recalls a bygone era. Designed by The Bungalow Company, built by Reese Construction, and developed by Madison Avenue Development, these bungalow-style homes feature traditional craftsmanship and design. Careful attention to historic details from tile fireplaces to period lighting gives these homes a truly authentic style. They blend modern amenities with nostalgic themes, providing the best of both worlds.

NEIGHBORHOODS

Traditionally planned neighborhoods are most successful when they are located within walking distance of schools, work, parks, transportation hubs, and shopping. Basic real estate economics would suggest that bungalow properties should be more expensive than land thirty miles from town without local amenities. Building denser communities in these urban areas gives the inhabitants the ability to reduce their reliance on the automobile. However, in dense neighborhoods, the ability to build expansively is limited by the actual size of the lot. Bungalows in new neighborhoods should be built to last in order to have the community appreciate in both actual dollar value as well as social desirability. Consistency in design and detailing is always important but is imperative when designing for a neighborhood; views are often territorial. To create visual value and character, all elevations of a home must be designed as if they were the front door. The pursuit of desirable neighborhoods and communities is a collective effort and requires cooperation of all parties, including neighborly etiquette in co-developing beautiful homes with a true sense of place.

Bungalows in new neighborhoods should be built to last a hundred years or more. This requires attention to selection of materials, as well as heating and cooling systems and fixtures.

Merging Yesterday With Today

The goal of new bungalows is to synthesize original exterior design and details while adapting the interior plans to reflect lifestyles of today—essentially, to take off from where the first builders and designers of the American bungalows left off, and bring these homes and communities to the next level by meeting the needs of today's families. Designing the new bungalow is truly a cooperative effort, shared by the designers, craftsmen, and clients.

Designing the new bungalow transcends individual designs and requires one to look closely at the renaissance that is redefining our culture: Families are rediscovering their past and are searching for nostalgic connections to unite them with their history and their modern community. They are also looking to create a comfortable, functional home. The following are basic elements that help capture the bungalow spirit and meet the needs of today's homeowners.

Designing the new bungalow is truly a cooperative effort, shared by the designers, craftsmen, interior designers, and clients. Here a contemporary paint technique by Lisa Lacaden and Mary Jane Papazian complements traditional craftsmanship.

VITAL SIGNS

8966

PORCHES

The bungalow porch serves as a visual break from the street, softening the contrast between street, landscape, and architecture. It draws from agrarian life and reinforces a connection with nature and community. The porch and front entry also serve as a physical portal from public space to the privacy of the home, including setting the stage for the interior with details and scale.

NOOKS

Bungalow designs have always been synonymous with traditional living space augmented by intimate spaces with specific uses. The use of inglenooks and breakfast nooks give the home extra space without over-scaling the floor plan. These spaces also provide opportunities to use quality materials with more detail to create memorable spaces. When using intimate spaces, homeowners are often more aware of the details, and the use of superior materials drives the experience home. These elements often create visual breaks in or between rooms.

The bungalow porch serves as a physical portal from public space to the privacy of the home, including setting the stage for the interior details and scale.

NATURAL LIGHT

One of the key factors is to develop spaces with natural light from two or more directions while being sensitive to the views and privacy that are created. An example would be the use of high windows flanking a fireplace or the use of decorative art glass to obscure entry doors or bathroom views.

DEFINING SPACE

Defining space without overuse of walls is what makes the bungalow "live big." Delineating areas with dropped and cased doorways or archways sends a clear message to inhabitants that they are changing spaces. Framed doorways are opportunities to direct views to other areas and give focus to outdoor scenes. The focusing of views gives the bungalow the ability to bring the outside in and the inside out, reinforcing our connection with nature. There is also great opportunity to create changes in color, material, and details.

In the Michael and Jane Mangelson house, designer Juidiith Clawson designed a quiet receiving area just off the front entrance. The formal dining area shares space with a sitting room, separated not by doors but simply by an arch with pillars on either end. This area of the home has a formal look without being ostentatious.

KITCHENS

Today's bungalow kitchens have been transformed from isolated work centers to the heart of the home. Kitchens offer plentiful workspaces while serving as hubs for the home. They are also areas to express craftsman detailing and workmanship. Additionally, the more centrally featured kitchen has brought the ability to introduce more natural light into the home.

Stainless-steel finishes of industrial-grade ranges and refrigerators are a good fit. Other items like apron sinks and wall-mounted faucets give newly done spaces vintage charm. Courtesy Ashmore/Kessenich.

Custom cabinetry designs by Juidiith Clawson are based on craftsman but with an edgy look. Under-cabinet windows bring light and openness to an area that is usually ignored

New bungalows have answered today's call for master bedroom suites. This room, tastefully painted in period style by Lisa Lacaden and Mary Jane Papazian, creates a private retreat that is an antidote for a hectic schedule.

Multipaned windows with broad casing act almost like a work of art on this bedroom wall. Paint colors were selected to maintain peacefulness in this master suite. Design by Juidiith Clawson of Simply Fetched.

MASTER BEDROOMS

New bungalows have adjusted to the trends of master bedrooms by applying the principles of creating private retreats that serve as an antidote to hectic schedules. As such, the bedrooms are designed with large attached baths and ample closet space. The goal is to make rooms that reflect their owners' lifestyles.

Incorporating some "today" elements in an Arts & Crafts design, Juidiith Clawson of Simply Fetched created a bath alcove in the master suite that is as beautiful as it is functional. A rustic cedar liner bears a tree motif modeled on a Frank Lloyd Wright Oak Park design. Michael and Jane Mangelson house.

Classic bathroom elements such as pedestal sinks, honeycomb tile, and wainscoting make this bathroom clean and spacious. Courtesy Ashmore/Kessenich.

BATHROOMS

Simply put, new bungalows incorporate more bathrooms into their floor plans than were there traditionally. Bathrooms are also utilitarian in their use of space and components. They are designed with classic elements such as pedestal sinks, built-in medicine cabinets, and careful details in tile work and trim but also incorporate some of today's luxuries, such as larger tubs.

WORKSPACES

Work-at-home spaces have transitioned well into the bungalow, but they do not need to be expansive. It is more important that they are properly located to either provide adequate privacy for concentration or to be more public for facilitating interaction among family members. Many of the more traditional spaces can actually double quite effectively as work and living spaces. Example: a breakfast nook

At-home workspaces do not have to be expansive to work well. This design by John Malick integrates the workspace into the kitchen area, creating a unique family hub.

A home office at the front of the house overlooks the goings-on in the neighborhood. Juidiith Clawson designed the space to be multifunctional. Built-ins (the desk with drawers, and book cases lining the wall behind (unseen) make this room comfy for reading or working. Dark bronze roller screens at the windows allow maximum light with minimum intrusion. Another nice feature is a restored tin ceiling (unseen). The same tin was used on the ceiling and as wainscoting in the guest bathroom.

with an Internet connection serves not only as a place of communication, but may also support household, family, and financial record keeping. It may also provide an area for parental guidance of children using the Internet or completing homework assignments while still allowing for meal preparation.

THE NEW "VINTAGE" BUNGALOW

The proper detailing for climate and the correct heating, cooling, and ventilation are the backbone of building longevity. Conservation is a holistic approach: build smaller, more energy-efficient homes on less land and in locations that will reduce the amount of miles driven per year. All homes shown are by The Bungalow Company.

Building footprints dimensioned in modules of four-foot increments is a smart way to save on materials in the framing stages, according to Ashmore/Kessenich Design. All homes shown here are from their plan book.

How to Get "the Look" in New Construction

Jim McCord, AIA

Let's assume for a moment that you wanted to recapture a part of the Arts & Crafts philosophy and introduce some level of calmness, beauty, and simplicity into your lifestyle. Or perhaps you are one of those individuals who is seeking a cozy abode that better expresses the way you live. No matter what you might be looking for—whether it is an Arts & Crafts–style lamp or a new bungalow-style home filled with interior enhancements such as wood trim, copper and iron hardware, period-looking light fixtures, stenciled draperies, and a full contingent of new craftsman furniture—the Gustav Stickleys, Elbert Hubbards, and Sears of the new century offer plenty of choices. (See Resources.)

It is appropriate that today's market offers various levels of quality, design, and fabrication. As such, individuals of all economic levels are able to enjoy the Arts & Crafts lifestyle to the degree they feel is appropriate.

Interior enhancements such as this copper lamp, windows, and furniture are being created by today's Stickleys and Hubbards. All of the accessories seen here were made by the homeowner, Audel Davis.

Once you have decided you want to live in a home styled like a new bungalow, one of the first things you need to decide is what kind of home you are seeking. Do you want a small urban, single-family home on a small lot, or a more spacious suburban-type home with a significant yard and square footage to match? Or do you want to buy your dream site and select a plan from one of the designers capable of providing bungalow plans reminiscent of the period but interpreted to meet the needs of contemporary living? Another option is to acquire land and hire an architect to custom design your new bungalow within the parameters you define and the level of detail and period harmony that you feel is appropriate.

This John Malick interior was custom-designed to fit the parameters of the owners' desire for detail and period harmony. Plentiful natural light and ample artificial lighting make this room comfortable at all times of the day. Note how the area rug delineates the use of space in an open setting.

CHOOSING A DEVELOPER

Because "bungalow" can be defined in a number of different ways, developers who specialize in new bungalow houses come from different experiences and mind-sets. Some are sensitive to the bungalow style as a representation of a historic building type and carry their commitment to the style as far as possible within the scope of the residential development as the sales price allows. Others simply reflect the bungalow style as an exterior architectural expression and leave the interior to the devices of the new owner. Making the most of your bungalow before you close escrow will diminish the scope of work required to make your house a home once you take occupancy.

For this location in the Colorado Rockies, David M. Schwarz / Architectural Services Inc. designed the house to suit a mountain landscape. Its orientation takes optimal advantage of both sun and shade.

(Below) Highland Group designed this exterior using natural materials consistent with its locale near the mountains. Soffits, fascias, and exposed rafters maintain the authenticity of craftsman styling.

THE WELL-DESIGNED BUNGALOW

The well-designed bungalow respects the land on which it is built by optimizing sun orientation or shade as best suits the climatic requirements, considering prevailing winds, and providing protection or cooling as needed. The building is formed from materials that are consistent with its locale, such as natural stone, common wood species, or clay bricks. These make a harmonious transition to the land, both physically and visually, capturing the feeling of comfort and harmony that are the hallmarks of the bungalow style.

UPGRADES

Following is an overview of some relatively simple choices you can make to enhance a new bungalow-style home built on speculation. It is possible to extrapolate some of these methods as topics of discussion for use when sitting down with a designer or an architect to plan your new bungalow. These suggestions just scratch the surface of considerations that should be taken into account when doing a significant remodeling or engaging in construction of a new bungalow. This information, coupled with review of the products and services itemized in the Resources, will enable you to begin your mission toward ownership of a new bungalow with a clear frame of reference and initial direction.

Wood Trim

If you buy a home during the initial framing process, you may have an opportunity to add some upgrades or more-appropriate interior finish selections prior to completion of the home. One upgrade, installing simple rectilinear stain-grade wood trim at doors, windows, and other openings can be handled with a materials and finish-up charge without significant additional labor. Many times, the simplicity of the detail fabrication of Arts & Crafts–inspired wood trim eliminates some of the mitered corners and detailed coping transitions that exist in many new homes today. The change in the look and feel is significant.

Light fixtures such as this one from Historic Lighting can be chosen to enhance the Arts & Crafts feel of a conventionally constructed home.

Ashmore/Kessenich upgraded this design to include an atmospheric fireplace with a tile fireplace surround. The built-in bookcases on either side are enviable.

No element can change the character of a home more dramatically than paint. This ceiling (opposite and above) was detailed by Lisa Lacaden and Mary Jane Papazian to complement the reproduction light fixtures and built-in cabinetry.

The designer-painted surface makes a classy background for this simple wall arrangement. Courtesy of Historic Lighting.

Paint

No inexpensive element can change the character of a home more dramatically than paint. Since it needs to be painted anyway, making the right color selections can be an important part in realizing your vision. Fortunately, a few paint manufacturers offer their versions of historic colors. Sherwin Williams's Preservation Palette is recommended: they call their colors by names such as Bungalow Blue, Studio Blue Green, Roycrofters Arts & Crafts colors, etcetera. Some manufacturers offer preselected combinations of colors for body, window sash, and trim. Interior colors, as well as exterior colors, can be harmonized by using these period palettes.

If you want help selecting colors, you may want to engage a design service that specializes in historic restorations. A few resources pop up on the Internet when you search the key words "historic paint colors."

Caution: When it comes to period colors, subtle variations can sometimes result in disaster. Color selections should be made from period color renditions and oftentimes "close" is not good enough.

Walnut trim on this oak flooring adds definition to the simplistic design of this living room. The decor is a personalized melding of contemporary with Arts & Crafts. Courtesy of Historic Lighting.

Floor Coverings

Floor coverings can be handled in much the same manner. Whether using carpet, ceramic tile, or wood, make choices that reflect the bungalow style. Often a selection can be made within the products that the contractor would normally use that would better suit the Arts & Crafts palette. Ask yourself what material suits the other features of the house.

This high-end home designed by architect Gilbert Lee Hershberger displays a richness of craftsmanship associated with the original Arts & Crafts movement.

The most common floor materials that mimic the style are softwoods (pine or fir), hardwoods, and vinyl or linoleum. Softwoods that are put together using a tongue-and-groove method are quite costly today—consider the savings you may have accrued in other areas and if it is still affordable, this would be a great place to splurge. If it is not feasible, oak or maple flooring is an equally wonderful, but less-expensive, alternative.

If linoleum is preferred, look for companies that offer some vintage-looking patterns that would complement the Arts & Crafts look you are trying to achieve.

VIKING
PROFESSIONAL

Kitchens and Bathrooms

Due to the changes in technology and needs (for instance, we now like spas and big open kitchens that weren't part of the original bungalow movement), these rooms are difficult to design in a manner absolutely consistent with an original bungalow, but plumbing and hardware manufacturers are offering some period-style fixtures that are appropriate for early or late bungalow styles. Pedestal sinks and tubs, claw-foot tubs, period faucets, pull-chain toilets—all these can bring

The twentieth century meets the twenty-first: stainless-steel appliances fit right in with clean lines of the cabinetry in this home. Both photos courtesy of Historic Lighting.

bungalow charm into your new house or into your remodeled rooms. Brand-name items are available at big-box outlets and could be traded for the standard plumbing fixtures that were destined for your house, and some pricier versions are available through the trade. Your contractor should be able to purchase from any of these exclusive sources.

There are excellent references for original period kitchens and bathrooms, two of which are *Bungalow Kitchens* and *Bungalow Bathrooms,* both by Jane Powell and photographed by Linda Svendsen. The examples pictured in these books are of vintage and remodeled homes, and there are both period-true examples and compromise interpretations. Studying these books will surely help you decide what you want your rooms to look like.

"Contemporary materials give this Arts & Crafts look a contemporary edge," says interior designer Valerie Paoli-Johnson. Slate lines the tub surround and covers the floor. Custom cabinetry throughout the house, in cherry and oak, evokes a period feeling as well. Plumbing and hardware manufacturers offer fixtures appropriate for early or late bungalow styles, such as these from Kohler. Design by Highland Group.

Fixtures from Historic Lighting complement the Greene and Greene-style cabinetry and tile flooring.

Historic Lighting brings period-style lighting into the twenty-first century in this craftsman-inspired bathroom.

Hardware

A variety of hardware styles can be appropriate for your new bungalow, based upon fabrication type and materials. Hammered black iron, hammered copper, and wooden knobs matching the species of the wood in the cabinet when stained, are common accessory finishes of the period that are still available today. This hardware is available in all price ranges, the most expensive being that which faithfully reproduces the period. There are a variety of lesser-cost hardware choices that provide the look without the price, such as bin pulls made famous on the Hoosier cabinets of the period. In black iron, brushed nickel, unlacquered brass, or possibly chrome, they add a period touch to a kitchen, especially if painted-wood cabinet surfaces are used. Nickel or chrome in the kitchen can provide a link with range trim, plumbing, and other typical kitchen finishes.

Door hardware can go through a similar metamorphosis. Bungalow doors were generally equipped with hardware that was an alternative to the bright brass of Victorian homes. Antique brass that is currently available is much like bright brass in that it acquires an uneven tarnish through normal use in a manner that is inconsistent with the durable type of finishes adopted by the bungalow style.

Although the general layout of a traditional bungalow kitchen is vastly different from contemporary layouts, care can be taken in the selection of cabinets and appliances to diminish the level of contrast. John Malick, architect.

Finishes should be oil-rubbed bronze (either base metal or over steel) and black iron. These two finishes are standard with many manufacturers and can be acquired with a slight up-charge, again looking at the installation cost as being identical with the hardware sets that the general contractor originally had in mind. These finishes are consistent with the patinated copper, black iron, and other metal tones of Arts & Crafts interiors, and blend better with stained door finishes than do bright brass fixtures.

Bin pulls, made famous by the Hoosier cabinets of the period, are lesser-cost hardware choices that provide the look without the price. Photo courtesy of Historic Lighting.

The tone of this home is established at the front door with an entry hardware set by Hugh Culley and a Pewabic tile inset above. Inside, a stained-glass lamp and ceiling lanterns by Bob Baird extend a warm welcome in the Arts & Crafts style. Design by Highland Group.

When building a new bungalow, make sure that the contractor installs cabinets in period style. These are in the Shaker style, and match the woodwork used on the ceiling and walls. John Malick, architect.

Cabinetry

Take a close look at the kitchen and bathroom cabinetry. Although the general layout of a traditional bungalow kitchen is vastly different from contemporary layouts, care can be taken in the selection of cabinets and appliances to diminish the level of contrast between your new kitchen and that of the period. Try to keep the cabinet layout as basic as possible and augment it with kitchen furniture, if that option is available to you. For instance, if a kitchen plan has an island counter or a peninsula that does not include an appliance or sink, see if the built-in can be deleted and replaced with a piece of furniture such as a butcher block, enamel-top table, or cabinet. Hoosier cabinets and kitchen dressers are appropriate furnishing pieces. Should you be able to eliminate a section of kitchen counter and replace it with one of these fine storage units, you would make a significant change in the look of your kitchen without sacrificing function. There should be a credit involved in removing some of the cabinetry if the changes do not involve a lot of electrical and plumbing reconfiguration.

One step you can take, in general, is making sure that the contractor installs cabinets in the style of this period. Many cabinet manufacturers offer mission- or Shaker-style cabinets. In general, these cabinets, whether they are painted or stained, have a single, flat-panel door framed with rectangular wood and top and bottom rails. The space between the panel and the frame elements is usually either an inside square corner or contains

Mangelson house cabinet detail. Throughout the house, cabinets were designed by Juidiith Clawson using an artistic mix of alderwood and Honduras mahogany with an inlay of ebony and bird's-eye maple. To subdue the wood colors and tie them together, Clawson developed a green wash to paint over all of the cabinet surfaces.

(Above) The divided-pane motif is a classic element of Arts & Crafts style. Marshall Compton chose to accent these panes with a color darker than the surrounding wood.

Glass doors on built-in cabinetry—the craftsman answer to hutches—is a boon for displaying collectibles or vintage dishes. Su Bacon, designer.

(Facing) This built-in unit designed by David M. Schwarz / Architectural Services Inc. combines spaces for both storage and display. The clean look says "quality" all the way.

simple molding, such as quarter-round or an ovoid sticking variety. These doors are fairly straightforward and are consistent with the cabinetry styles of built-in casework of the period, as well as much of the kitchen furniture produced. Selecting one of these alternative patterns usually results in a minimal extra cost and the effect is worth it.

Countertops, Sinks, and Walls

Ceramic tile was one of the most common bungalow materials, followed by wood and galvanized steel. These materials are readily available today, though they cost considerably more than standard-issue Formica coverings.

Most early sinks were white enameled cast-iron units, many of which had a drain board built into one side. There are kitchen sinks today made with ceramic fronts and splashes to emulate these earlier periods. Or if you

A farmhouse-style sink gives a period look to a contemporary kitchen.

Craftsman-style cabinets topped with concrete countertops mix old and new design to create a classic contemporary look. Lighting design by Historic Lighting.

Ceramic tile was one of the most common bungalow materials that is readily available today. (Above) Photo courtesy David Papazian. (Right) Photo courtesy Marshall Compton.

want to spare the expense, a simple white rectangular one- or two-compartment sink should do the trick.

Kitchen walls and countertop backsplashes were often carried out in ceramic tile, which is often beyond the scope of work in new residential construction. The incorporation of the tile accents brings the bungalow spirit into your home.

White plumbing fixtures will fit the bill, but keep an eye out for new models in the old colors. Accents were chrome or nickel and plumbing fixtures and fittings were either oxidized brass (uncoated and shiny for only the first few months) or polished nickel or chrome, which is readily available in the marketplace today.

A Jack and Jill bathroom connecting two children's rooms features a twig mirror in the Adirondack style by Troy Poulson of Millcreek Furniture. Photo courtesy of Highland Group.

Borrowing a touch from the tradition of Gustav Stickley, encouraging words remind those entering the master suite that this is a place to slow down and enjoy the comfort of a safe haven. The door is of vertical-grain fir. Design by Highland Group.

One way to upgrade a spec house is to choose a bungalow-style door. This one is on a Bungalow Company house.

Stained-glass art , designed by Juidiith Clawson for the Mangelson house and executed by Sandy of Excell, is in the Arts & Crafts tradition but is clearly contemporary. Throughout the house, transom windows atop all the doors (unseen) bear sand-blasted glass.

Doors

For early period homes, five-flat-panel doors, single-flat-panel doors, and many other upgrade styles are available for painting or staining at a variety of quality levels. Early involvement in spec houses may afford the owner opportunity to select doors—even if they are factory-hung mass-market units—that can create a level of quality and warmth consistent with the bungalow image. The additional cost then lies in the quality of the materials used by way of a markup in the value of the door unit rather than in additional installation or finish charges.

The dining room and adjacent kitchen in this home designed by Baylis Architects of Bellevue, Washington, open onto a great room. The dining room features a built-in cherry buffet with slate backsplashes; the slate's natural edges echo the mountains of the Pacific Northwest. A dining table and chairs manufactured by Stickley are in a more contemporary craftsman style. Seen beyond the doorway is a water wall in the home's entry. Photo courtesy Baylis Architects.

Lighting

It is possible to buy various versions of a period lamp, obviously with vast differences in materials and fabrication techniques, that vary in price from under $100 to $15,000.

Interior and exterior light fixtures, including ceiling-hung and bracket types, are readily available in today's market. Most broad-market light fixture manufacturers offer some mission-style or Arts & Crafts–style lighting lines. As with all styles of light fixtures, the quality of design as well as materials and methods of manufacture vary greatly. If well selected, light fixtures can last a lifetime. Finish choices are limited on lower-cost lamps, but flat black, oxidized brass, and patinated brass are generally available. Higher-quality

A built-in bench at the bottom of the stairway, gives the entry an inglenook feeling. The stair railing is cherry wood; the floor is Brazilian cherry. Design by Highland Group.

fixtures are typically of heavier gauge, equipped with porcelain sockets consistent with earlier fixtures, and offered in finishes that can handle the level of intended use. For example, oxidized copper fixtures tend to continue to age quite nicely outdoors and do not rust or otherwise degrade over the years. If some natural patination is desired, natural brass fixtures can be ordered unlacquered. The installer should wear soft gloves so that the natural patination evolves over the years to create a rich, honest, mottled antique finish that no manufacturing process can replicate.

If well selected, light fixtures can last a lifetime. John Malick, Hoelter residence.

Embracing the contemporary craftsman, this light fixture by Sam Mossaedi honors those of Greene & Greene. Lighting design by Historic Lighting.

Su Bacon, Historic Lighting

A contemporary lantern by Arroyo Craftsman combines with the rocks and brick to create a warm front porch welcome. Courtesy Historic Lighting.

When looking at the revival of Arts & Crafts lighting, it is important to understand what the original craftsmen were trying to accomplish with their art. Their focus was to reach back to nature and hand craftsmanship. Working with the available technology and using copper, bronze, mica, hand-blown glass, pottery, and wood, their creations were born. The work of Gustav Stickley, Dirk Van Erp, and Roycroft came alive with the use of hammered copper and mica. To create their beautiful lamps, Lewis C. Tiffany, Frank Lloyd Wright, and Charles and Henry Greene used glass to bring nature's landscape inside. The scenic panels and lamps set the tone for the main structure, and the wood artistry of Greene & Greene added one more of nature's elements to the lights.

As it did at the turn of the twentieth century, lighting plays an important design role in today's revival. However, lighting is not meant to stand alone but rather to blend with colors, textures, furnishings, and art to set the mood and accentuate the architecture. It is also designed as to not take away from a setting but to complete the picture, just as one would experience nature.

Sam Mossaedi takes his inspiration from the Gamble House living room lanterns in his mahogany and art glass light fixture. Courtesy Historic Lighting.

As the old saying goes, "times have changed" and so have our lifestyles. Formal living and dining rooms have almost become extinct, replaced by family rooms that are structured to be adjacent to the kitchen areas, which have evolved into being part of the social gathering. This is where lighting becomes critical, because the room is not only a work area but also a space to socialize and relax.

Bedrooms have now become suites, with sitting rooms and personal libraries. Master bathrooms are mini spas, with fireplaces, Jacuzzi tubs, shower and steam combinations and two sinks. Powder rooms have become small galleries where art can be displayed.

Libraries have turned into in-home offices with computers, entertainment centers with stereo and sound systems and video/DVD players, multiple telephone lines, and intercoms.

Family entertaining has also moved outdoors, with decks, pools, barbecues and cooking areas, along with outdoor fireplaces. All of this necessitates the addition of unique and tasteful lighting that reflects the style of the home.

With all of this change comes a diversification of lighting needs. By working with what is available today and remembering that form follows function, it is possible to bring rooms together with light. Whether using originals or reproductions, there are still some traditional design concepts that can be incorporated in today's new bungalows.

(Above) Lighting should blend with colors, textures, furnishings, and art to set the mood and accentuate the architecture. David M. Schwarz / Architectural Services Inc.

Working with the home's architecture, these lanterns bring light—not glare—to the space. Fixture from Historic Lighting.

Sconces either act as art or they work with the art in wall arrangements.

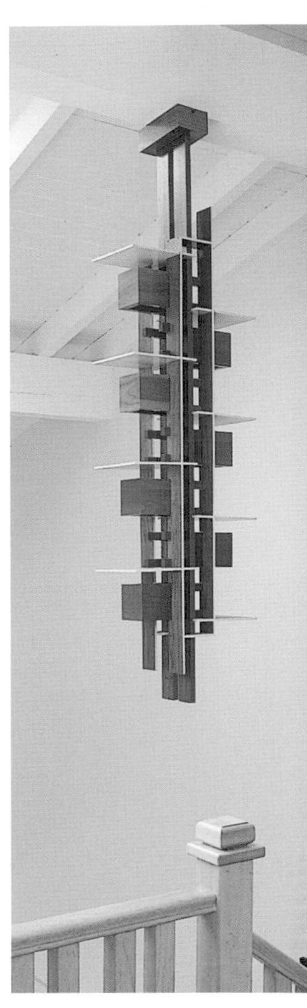

Ceiling-hung lighting runs the gamut between decorative and task lighting. A variety of styles are suitable for the bungalow, from Frank Lloyd Wright or Tiffany-type designs to much simpler forms. All lighting on this page is from Historic Lighting.

SCONCES

Sconces are often considered directional lighting. They are meant to greet people in the entry or grand hall and then lead them into the living room, where sconces often frame the fireplace over the mantel. In the dining room they draw attention to the server or sideboard. They are also used in stairwells and halls. They are often the first light you turn on once you enter the bedroom. In bathrooms they frame the mirror over the sink area.

PENDANTS, CHANDELIERS, AND CEILING MOUNTS

Pendants, chandeliers, or ceiling mounts run the gamut between decorative and task lighting. Entries, parlors, and dining rooms are wonderful venues to decorate with Tiffany-style chandeliers or table and floor lamps. Pendants are also used in hallways and kitchen work areas. There is also the infamous plain bulb fixture, the turn-of-the-twentieth-century's answer to today's recess canned lighting. The works of Tiffany and Greene & Greene add another dimension to recessed lighting by disguising them beautifully with glass panels framed with carved wood or metal.

The great room updates the use of traditional bungalow materials and details for a contemporary living style. The custom cabinets in quarter-sawn oak are by Peppertree. Note the inset tile in the river rock fireplace. The painting over the mantel is by Kirk Randle. Design by Highland Group.

Exquisite details give this contemporary great room in the Mangelson house the warm feeling of an Arts & Crafts–era bungalow. A fireplace of Vernal flagstone is the central focus while a stained-glass window (design by Juidiith Clawson, production by Sandy of Excell) set in an interior wall shows some Wrightian influence. Architectural detailing and space planning by Simply Fetched.

RECESSED AND TRACK LIGHTING

Although their appropriateness for historic-model bungalows is often controversial, these contemporary light sources can be used in new bungalow–style homes and offices. It is important to remember that their roles are to take the eyes away from these sources of light and direct them toward what is decorative. One of the ways to accomplish this is with period light fixtures, originals, or reproductions.

Recessed and track lighting play an important part in fulfilling the demands that our lifestyles require. They provide lighting under, over, and within cabinetry to bring ambiance to the setting. Strip lighting, as it sometimes is referred to, can be used along beams or within soffits, again bringing indirect light into a room.

TODAY'S ADVANCES

There is nothing wrong with the advances we have made in lighting. The problems occur when taste and design are sacrificed. It is this author's opinion that if Morris, Stickley, Wright, Tiffany, Van Erp, and Charles and Henry Greene were here today, they would embrace what is presently available and find more to work with to enhance their creations.

The passion for this revival is strong. The craftsmen and artisans of this century have embraced the work of this period's original craftsmen and artisans and are adding to it. Their attention to detail, return to simpler designs, and commitment to the art are what fuel this renaissance.

Whether you want to go with a full-out bungalow period-style home, or whether you just want to incorporate some elements that would give you the feeling of a bungalow and make your house unique, these ideas and examples have shown how you can do it.

: Interpreting : the Spirit

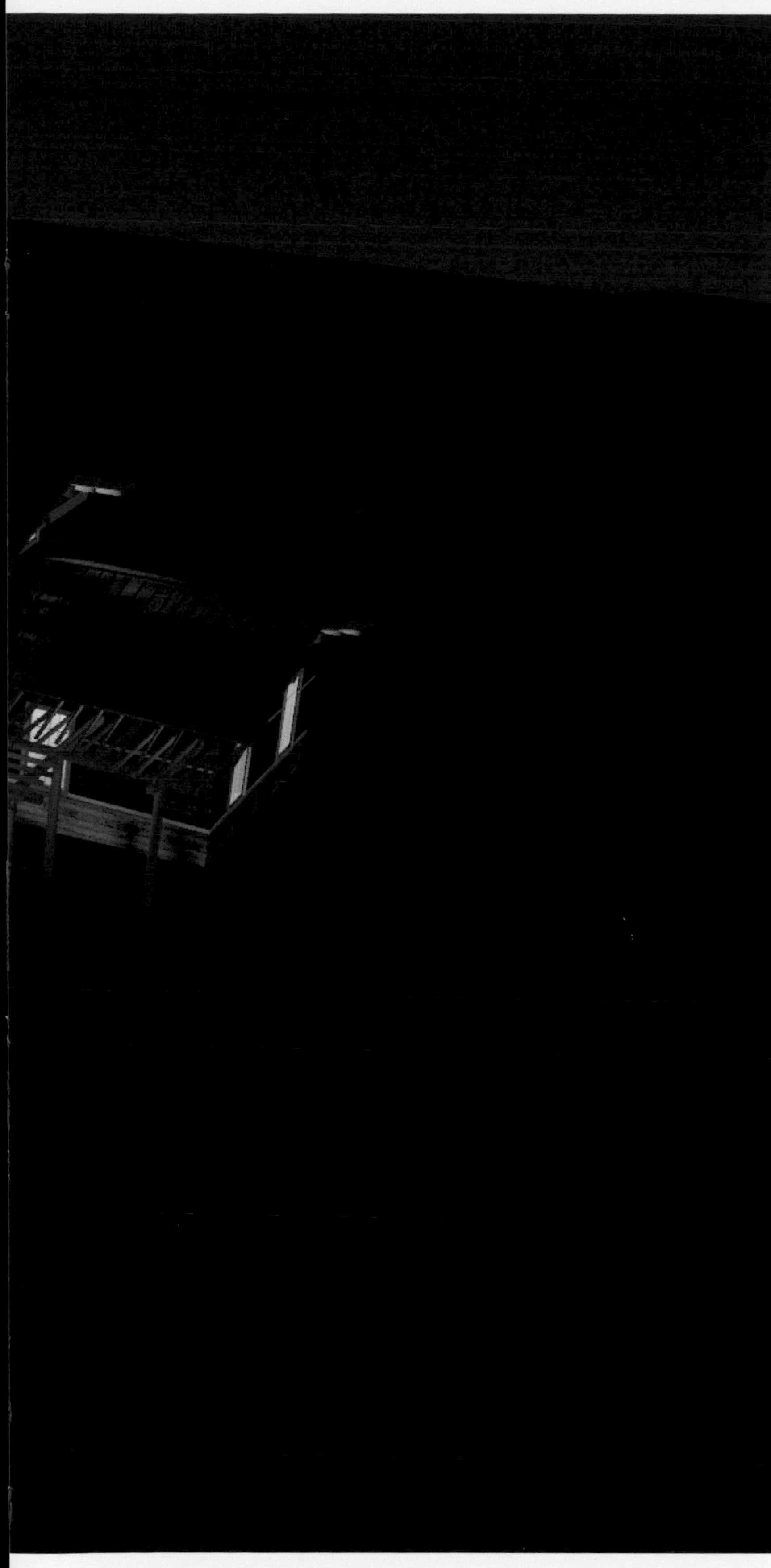

Matthew Bialecki, AIA

Arts & Crafts is so young . . . let's learn what the masters did, learn how they did it, and then adapt it to the landscape and your own expression. That will make it new and exciting, every time.

—*Matthew Bialecki, AIA, quoted in* Period Homes

The new bungalow, the residential design that will take us happily to the doors of the next millennium, is not a copy of a Stickley craftsman or a Greene & Greene masterwork. Pieces of it, however, are to be seen here and there, giving glimmers of hope that show a growing awareness of new problems that need new solutions while embracing the fundamentals of the bungalow movement: honest straightforward design ✦ unrefined natural materials used directly ✦ exposed structure as a primary design

Aerial view of the courtyard and gardens of the Vidich-Stein house in High Falls, New York. Matthew Bialecki, architect.

element ✦ a direct relationship to the landscape ✦ affordability and practicality for our lives today. Nature-based design is an appropriate label because its fundamental statement is about a harmony with the land, our communities, and our place in them.

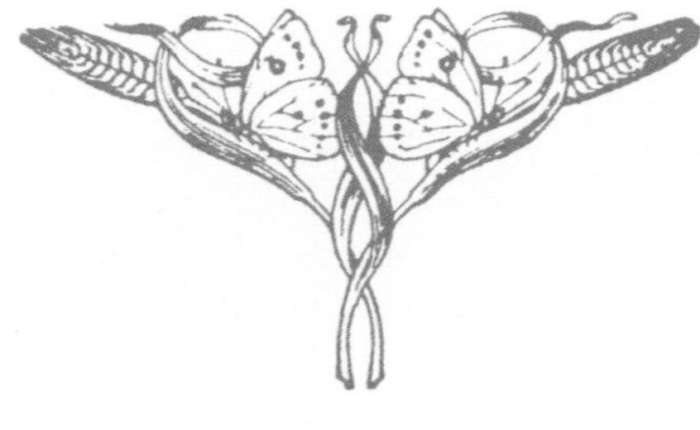

View from pool showing breakfast room, sun room, and master bedroom of the Vidich-Stein house. The rooms are arranged informally about the pool area. Matthew Bialecki, architect.

Southwest elevation showing pergola intersecting glass wall of the living room, Vidich-Stein house.

The northwest elevation of the Vidich-Stein house shows the front entry courtyard.

South elevation, Knecht residence, Matthew Bialecki, architect. A screened porch transitions between outdoors and indoor living space.

East view of the Knecht house reveals a pergola that extends living space to the outdoors.

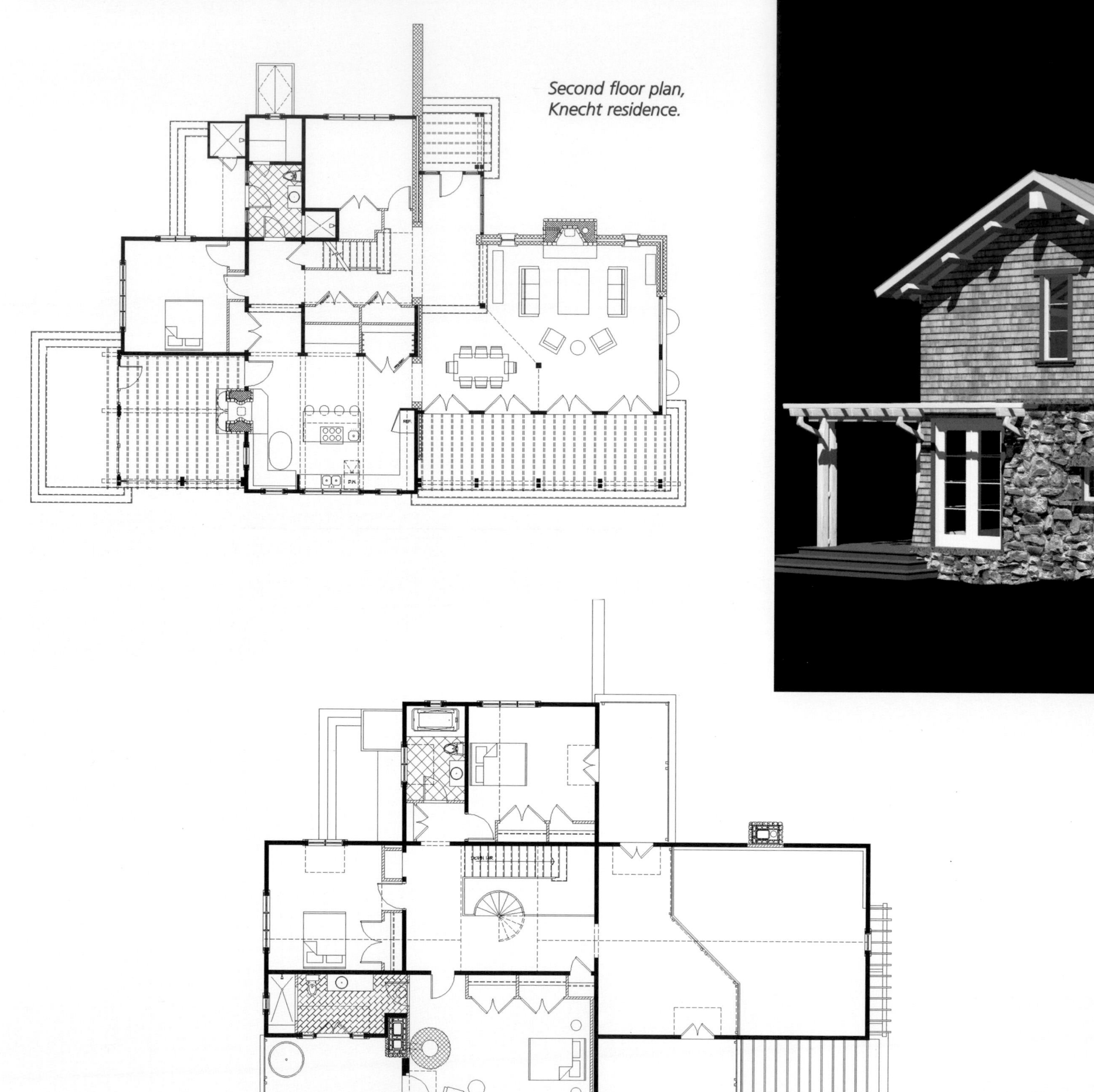

Second floor plan, Knecht residence.

First-floor plan, Knecht residence.

The northwest elevation of the Knecht residence shows another entry porch. An eroded stone wall blends the materials of the house into the landscape.

What are some of today's problems that need innovative solutions? Sustainability heads the list. There wasn't a lot of concern for managing our resources or saving energy back in the early bungalow days. Photovoltaic panels (BIPV's) integrated as roof shingles, strict solar orientation for maximum passive-energy efficiency, earth berming and green roofing for a new type of volumetric massing for the architecture are some workable solutions. Using local sustainable-yield woods, indigenous materials like rammed earth, adobe, straw bale, and other regionally based construction systems are opening new chapters for bungalow design.

One of my favorite architects of all, the San Francisco Bay Area regionalist Bernard Maybeck (1862–1957) was always experimenting with different materials—concrete as finished walls, plywood panels and burlap dipped in plaster for interior wall panels. His work was constantly changing as he tried new forms and nontraditional materials. With the vast range of materials available, the only thing limiting the possibilities of the new bungalow movement is our imagination and willingness to take the risks.

Affordability is a problem that needs addressing. In many regions, nicely built "new" bungalows cost an average of $250–300 per square foot in construction costs alone. This means these homes are affordable to the very few. To be true to its roots, the new bungalow movement needs builder, developer, and architect to team up and develop affordable, nature-based, sustainable designs that can implement the fundamental concepts of a new bungalow for a wider audience. These homes will never be low-income housing, but as historical revival (including some Arts & Crafts revival developments and bungalow developments featured in this book) and as interpretations of the underlying principles, new bungalows have the potential to not only enhance the look of our homes but to unite us in communities around some life-impacting causes.

A major part of affordability is the size and scale of a house. Greene & Greene's ultimate bungalows look positively small next to the typical high-end mansions that fill our well-off neighborhoods today. One of the enduring qualities of the bungalow is its modesty of scale. Big is not beautiful and the unattractiveness of some overblown "mansionettes" is appalling.

Finally, building locally and embracing indigenous materials will help us celebrate the qualities of the regions where we live. In the Southwest, adobe, or rammed earth, or autoclaved concrete are sustainable indigenous materials. In the Northwest, salvaged or recycled woods can fill the bill. Each region has its own characteristic materials and techniques that bring a unique quality to any new nature-based home.

(Opposite) Designs by Matthew Bialecki utilize earthy materials as well as visual representations of nature to augment a nature-based design in an urban space.

FOUR GOOD SIZE
LEMONS GRATED
AND JUICED, ONE
QUART SUGAR,
MORE IF NEEDED,
AND EIGHT EGGS.
ONE LB. FLOUR,
ONE LB. SUGAR, ONE
LB. RAISINS, 3/4 LB.
BUTTER, FOUR EGGS,
ONE CUP CREAM,
GLASS BRANDY

There are award-winning architects practicing whose work embodies many of the principles of the bungalow movement. James Cutler and Miller/Hull Architects in the Seattle area do beautifully detailed homes that capture the essence of their region and a new bungalow ideal.

In the Southwest, William Bruder merges raw materials and a strong integration with the landscape to stunning effect. In Texas, Lake/Flato architects have developed a regional courtyard style based on Texas vernacular that incorporates sustainable and recycled materials. In Maine, Peter Forbes has elevated the small gabled structure to high art. In Pennsylvania, Bohlin Cywinski Jackson architects have interpreted historic Adirondack traditions in a way that is not sentimental or coy.

Furniture is integrated into the architecture at 108 Fifth Avenue. Matthew Bialecki, architect.

Ultimately, using nature and landscape as inspiration continues the tradition that began when A. W. Pugin commenced his quest for an honest expression of materials and craftsmanship. The design of the new bungalow will always be fresh and vital if it responds to its site and the particular conditions surrounding it. Don't chop the tree down; build a building around it. Don't remove the boulders; build the fireplace with them. Above all, bring the sun in—east, west, south, country or urban sites. Use the light and celebrate it.

Study and learn from the local building traditions and available materials. These principles are as valid today as they were 150 years ago; we just have to keep applying them to problems we face today. The solutions we find will keep the bungalow unique and fresh for the next millennium.

A cast-aluminum basin sits atop the counter in a design by Matthew Bialecki.

: Home Show : Of Details

In an effort to honor the Arts & Crafts ideal of fusing architecture with nature, Highland Group incorporated local river rock in the construction of this new bungalow. Shawn Wright was the mason. The roofing is natural cedar shakes, and the walls are cedar shingles laid in a pattern specified by Tim and Tim of Highland Group. Copper rain gutters and fascias are in keeping with the bungalow tradition.

Tin ceiling tiles bring old style and new character to this dining area. Photo courtesy David Papazian.

These Greene & Greene–style staircase details were fashioned by owner/builder Pat Qualey. Courtesy of Historic Lighting.

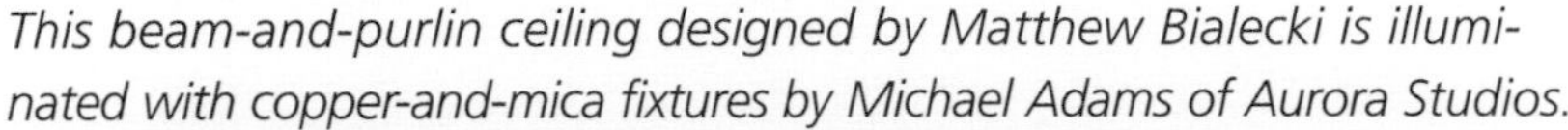

This beam-and-purlin ceiling designed by Matthew Bialecki is illuminated with copper-and-mica fixtures by Michael Adams of Aurora Studios.

Natural elements like this fireplace stonework bring a softer feel to the contemporary style of this home. Courtesy of Historic Lighting.

The Wrightian tree motif seen in these ceramic fireplace tiles was repeated throughout the house. Tiles designed by Simply Fetched.

These Frank Lloyd Wright–inspired lines are brought to life with a Tiffany-style chandelier from Historic Lighting.

This adventurous mahogany bed designed by Matthew Bialecki for the Studley house is held together with iron straps that are locked with clasps and opposing wedges while the feet sit on slabs of granite.

Fine Arts & Crafts-style reproduction furniture is a viable alternative to expensive period originals. This chair, side table, and lamp are by Voorhees Craftsman.

(Far left) The exquisite design and woodwork in the Jacobs house are comparable to the quality of Charles and Henry Greene. Gilbert Lee Hershberger, architect.

Painting detail on a door designed by Matthew Bialecki, AIA.

(Right) This pergola by Curtis Gelotte and Associates is a romantic blending of the outside and inside.

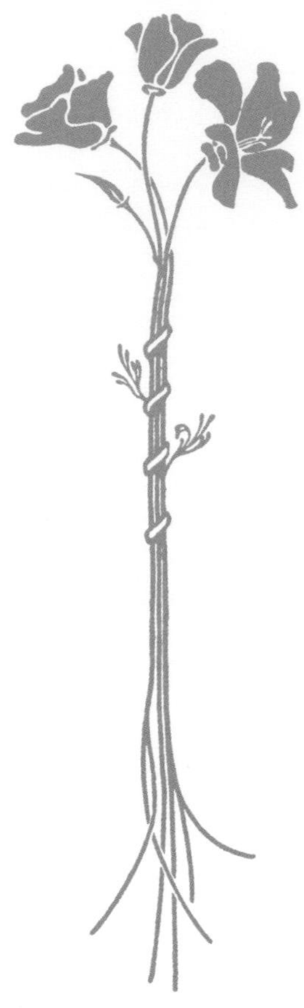

A mahogany end table in the Studley house is designed by Matthew Bialecki and reflects his goal of transforming furniture into small works of architecture. Lamp design by Michael Adams.

Two-tone paint applied to the columns throughout the Mangelson house accentuates the details. Ambient lighting reflects off the ceiling and lifts the structure.

: RESOURCES :

ARTS & CRAFTS STYLE

Organizations/Places

Arts & Crafts Society
1194 Bandera Dr
Ann Arbor MI 48103
(734) 665-4729
(734) 661-2883 fax
Info@arts-crafts.com

Craftsman Farms
2352 Rte 10-West #5
Morris Plains NJ 07950
(973) 540-1165
(973) 540-1167 fax
Craftsmanfarms@att.net

The Gamble House
4 Westmoreland Pl
Pasadena CA 91103
(626) 793-3334
gamblehs@usc.edu

Books from Gibbs Smith, Publisher

Baca, Elmo. *Romance of the Mission,* 1996.

Cigliano, Jan, and Walter Smalling Jr. (photos). *Bungalow: American Restoration Style,* 1998.

Ewald, Chase Reynolds. *Arts and Crafts Style and Spirit: Craftspeople of the Revival,* 1999.

Heinz, Thomas A. *Frank Lloyd Wright's Stained Glass & Lightscreens,* 2000.

Makinson, Randell L. *Greene & Greene: Architecture as a Fine Art* (1977) / Greene & Greene: Furniture and Related Designs (1979), 2-in-1 pb, 2001.

Makinson, Randell L., Thomas A. Heinz, and Brad Pitt (photo essay). *Greene & Greene: The Blacker House,* 2000.

Makinson, Randell L. *Greene & Greene: The Passion and the Legacy,* 1998.

Powell, Jane, and Linda Svendsen (photos). *Bungalow Bathrooms,* 2001.

Powell, Jane, and Linda Svendsen (photos). *Bungalow Kitchens,* 2000.

Smith, Bruce, and Yoshiko Yamamoto. *The Beautiful Necessity: Decorating with Arts & Crafts,* 1996.

Varnum, William Harrison. *Arts & Crafts Design,* reprint 1995.

Wallace, Ann, and Phil Bard (photos). *Arts & Crafts Textiles,* 1999.

Yamamoto, Yoshiko, Bruce Smith, and Gail Yngve. *Arts & Crafts Ideals: Wisdom from the Arts & Crafts Movement in America,* 1999.

ARCHITECTS, BUILDERS & PLANNING CONSULTANTS

Tim Andersen, Architect
Seattle, WA
(206) 524-8841
Pasadena, California
(626) 793-4914
timsen@seanet.com

Ashmore/Kessenich Design
6336 NE Garfield Ave
Portland OR 97211
(503) 286-6258

Ashmore/Kessenich Design
Madison, WI
(608) 233-0354

Su Bacon
Historic Lighting, Inc.
114 East Lemon Ave
Monrovia CA 91016
(626) 303-4899
(626) 358-6159 fax
www.historiclighting.com

Bainbridge Island Bungalow Company
4890 Taylor Ave
Bainbridge Island WA 98110
(206) 842-7910
(206) 727-6352 fax

Baylis Architects
10801 Main St, Ste 110
Bellevue, WA 98004
(425) 454-0566

BC Mountain Homes
501-622 Front St
Nelson BC
Canada V1L 4B7
(250) 352-2502 ph/fax

Kurt Beckmeyer
Beckmeyer Carver Architects
1151 El Centro, Ste E
South Pasadena, CA 91030
(626) 799-2277

Matthew Bialecki Associates
108 Main St
New Paltz, NY 12561
(914) 255-6131
(914) 255-6276 fax

Blankemeyer & Blankemeyer
1409 W Third Ave
Columbus OH 43212
(614) 488-7263
(614) 488-7264 fax
Amerfurn@aol.com

The Bungalow Company
550 SW Industrial Way, Ste 37
Bend OR 97702
(541) 312-2674
(877) 785-7512 fax
thebungalowcompany.com

Castlerock Homes, Inc.
347 NW 83rd Pl
Portland, OR 97229
(503) 292-2819
www.castlerock-home-inc.com

Circa Design
1376 Yosemite Ave
San Jose CA 95126
(408) 998-1906
(408) 998-2545 fax

Juidiith Clawson
Simply Fetched
2257 South 1100 East
Salt Lake City, UT 84105
(801) 468-0526
www.simplyfetched.com

Michael Colombo, AIA
JTS Architects
101 Schelter Rd
Lincolnshire, IL 60069-3603
(847) 634-8100
www.jtsarch.com

Marshall Compton
4980 Miami Rd
Cincinnati OH 45243
(513) 784-1234
(513) 561-2312 fax

Charles Cook
Myefski Cook Architects
Glencoe, IL
(847) 835-7081

Michael Corcoran, Architect
Corcoran & Corcoran
2240 University Dr, Ste 120
Newport Beach, CA 92660
(949) 650-0600

Eagan & Associates, Architects
8116 Old York Rd
Elkins Park, PA 19001
(215) 635-2600

Felhandler, Steeneken, and Wilk, Architects
151 West 85th St #4
New York NY 10024
(800) 791-9522
(212) 874-6277 fax
Info@fswarchitects.com

Curtis Gelotte
150 Lake St South, Ste 208
Kirkland WA 98033
(425) 828-3081
(425) 822-2512 fax

Genesis Architecture
6929 Mariner Dr, Ste C
Racine WI 53406
(262) 886-6656
(262) 886-6657 fax

Greene & Proppe Design Inc.
1209 West Berwyn Ave
Chicago IL 60640
(773) 271-1925
(773) 271-1936 fax

William East Hamilton Designs
6701 Mallards Cove Rd #39F
Jupiter FL 33458
(561) 743-7657
(561) 746-6429 fax

David Heide Design
301 4th Ave S, Ste 663
Minneapolis, MN 55415
(612) 337-5060
www.davidheidedesign.com

Gilbert Lee Hershberger
1471 Indiana Ave
South Pasadena, CA 91030
(323) 256-2526

Highland Group
Tim Wyatt and Tim Furner
4471 South Highland Dr
Salt Lake City, UT 84124
(801) 277-4433
(801) 277-1450 fax
Tims@highland-group.com
www.highland-group.com

Hoyle, Doran & Berry, Inc.
38 Newbury St
Boston, MA 02116
(617) 424-6200
(617) 424-7762 fax

The Johnson Partnership
1212 NE 65th St
Seattle WA 98115-6724
(206) 523-1618

JSA
John Shirley, Architect
3115 Lion Ln #300
Salt Lake City, UT 84121
(801) 278-8151
(801) 278-8661 fax

A. Kitsinger, AIA
1665 Overton Park Ave
Memphis TN 38112
(901) 272-0155

Robert Lidsky
The Hammer & Nail
232 Madison Ave
Wyckoff, NJ 07481
(201) 891-5252

Johan Luchsinger
Baylis Architects
10801 Main St, Ste 110
Bellevue, WA 98004
(425) 454-0566

John Malick and Associates
1195 Park Ave, Ste 102
Emeryville, CA 94608
(510) 595-8042

Marcus and Willers, Architects
415 First St West, Ste 3
Sonoma CA 95476
(707) 996-2396 ph/fax

Alan Mascord Design
Associates
1305 NW 18th Ave
Portland, OR 97209
(800) 411-0231
(503) 225-0933 fax
www.mascord.com

Jim McCord
503 Wave St
Monterey, CA 93940-1426
(831) 375-7800
(831) 655-3259 fax

New Urbanist Homes
St. Charles, MO
(636) 688-7111
info@newurbanist.com

Prairie Architects, Inc.
103 South Third St
Fairfield IA 52556
(515) 472-9981

Preservation + Planning
1382 Perry Ave
Salt Lake City UT 84103
(801) 814-5405
(801) 355-8611 fax

Princeton Plans Press
PO Box 622
Princeton NJ 08540
(609) 924-9655
(800) 566-9655 toll-free

Spencer Ruff Associates, Inc.
732 East Woodlawn Dr
Sioux Falls SD 57105
(605) 331-5413
(605) 331-2101 fax

SALA Architects, Inc.
43 Main St SE, Ste 410
Minneapolis MN 55414
(612) 379-3037
(612) 379-0001 fax
www.salaarch.com

Salmon Falls Architecture
56 Industrial Park Road, Ste #7
Saco MA 04072
(207) 283-4247
(207) 284-4546 fax

Les Schulz, Architect
1664 East Grand
Springfield MO 65804
(417) 863-8448
(417) 863-0131 fax

David M. Schwarz /
Architectural Services Inc
1701 L St NW, Ste 400
Washington, DC 20036
(202) 862-0777
Fax (202) 331-0507
www.dmsas.com

Simply Fetched
Juidiith Clawson
2257 South 1100 East
Salt Lake City, UT 84105
(801) 468-0526
www.simplyfetched.com

Spellman Construction
8509 Ferncliff Ave
Bainbridge Island, WA 98110
(206) 842-2786
spellcon@jps.net

CRAFTSMEN

Associations

Western Red Cedar Lumber
Association
1200 - 555 Burrard St
Vancouver BC
Canada V7X 1S7
(604) 684-0266
(604) 687-4930 fax
wrcla@wrcla.org

Window and Door
Manufacturers Association
1400 East Touhy Ave, Ste 470
Des Plaines IL 60018
(800) 223-2301
(847) 299-1286 fax
admin@wdma.com

Building Links

Energy & Environmental
Building Association
10740 Lyndale Ave S, Ste 10W
Bloomington MN 55420-5615
(952) 881-1098
(952) 881-3048 fax
info@eeba.org

National Association of
Home Builders
400 Prince George's Blvd
Upper Marlboro MD 20774
(301) 249-4000
(800) 638-8556 toll-free
(301) 430-6180 fax

Building Products

American Timbers LLC
PO Box 430
Canterbury CT 06331
(800) 461-8660
(860) 546-9334 fax

Artwood Design
10-755 Vanalman Ave
Victoria BC
Canada V8Z 3B8
(250) 727-3100
(250) 727-7887 fax

Custom Hardwoods
1030 Wild St
Sycamore IL 60178
(815) 895-9519
(815) 895-7493 fax

Dowd Stonemasonry
RR1 Box 108
Barre MA 01005
(978) 355-6396

Eco-Timber Ltd.
175 Pitt St
Saint John NB
Canada E2L 2W8
(506) 642-9663
(506) 657-5100 fax

Extraordinary Doors
953 C Tower Pl
Santa Cruz CA 95062
(831) 465-1470
(813) 465-1471 fax

Grabill Inc.
Windows and Doors
7463 Research Dr
Almont MI 48003
(810) 798-2817
(810) 798-2809 fax

Historic Home Supply
Corporation
213–215 River St
Troy NY 12180-3809
(518) 266-0675
(518) 266-0810 fax

Livos Natural Wood Finishes
PO Box 1740
800 Falmouth Road
Mashpee MA 02649
(508) 477-7955
(508) 477-7988 fax

McGrory Glass, Inc.
100 Commerce Dr
Aston PA 19014
(800) 220-3749 toll-free
(610) 364-1071 fax

Prairie Woodworking
343 Harrison St
Oak Park IL 60304
(708) 386-0603 ph/fax

Remanufactured Hardwoods
2630 Loop 35
Alvin TX 77511
(281) 331-7838
(381) 331-6467 fax

Superior Water-Logged Lumber
2200 East Lakeshore Dr
Ashland WI 54806
(715) 685-9663
(715) 685-9620 fax

Talarico Hardwoods
RD 3, Box 3268
Mohnton PA 19540
(610) 775-0400
(610) 775-1456 fax

Woodshed
2505 - 12th Ave South
Moorhead MN 56560
(218) 236-0009

Fireplaces

The Chimney Pot Shoppe
Michael Bentley Enterprise
Avella PA 15312
(724) 345-3601
bentley@chimneypot.net

Heat-N-Glo—A Division of
Hearth Technologies
20802 Kensington Blvd
Lakeville MN 55044
(888) 743-2887

Vermont Castings
Majestic Products
410 Admiral Blvd
Mississauga ON
Canada L5T 2N6

Market Places

The Craftsman Home
3048 Claremont Ave
Berkeley, CA 94705
(510) 655–6503
lee@craftsmanhome.com

The Craftsman Homes
Collection
PMB 343
2525 East 29th, Ste 10B
Spokane, WA 99223
(509) 535-5098
(509) 534-8916
Elvis@crafthome.com

Siding

Builder Online
One Thomas Circle NW
Ste 600
Washington DC 20005
(202) 452-0800
(202) 785-1974 fax
www.builderonline.com

Cedar Shake & Shingle Bureau
PO Box 1178
Sumas WA 98295-1178
(604) 820-7700
(604) 820-0266 fax

Tile

Claystone
547-B Constitution Ave
Camarillo CA 93012
(805) 388-5248
(805) 388-7298 fax
brahma@claystone.com

Ephraim Faience
Bookfield, WI
(800) 704-POTS [7687]
toll-free

Motawi Tile Works
33 North Staebler, Ste 2
Ann Arbor, MI 48103
(734) 213-0017
(734) 213-2569 fax
motawi@bizserve.com

Norberry Tile
207 Second Ave South
Seattle WA 98104
(206) 343-9916
(206) 343-9917 fax

Tile Restoration Center
3511 Interlake North
Seattle WA 98103
(206) 633-4866
trc@wolfenet.com

Windows

Andersen Commercial Group
PO Box 12
100 Fourth Ave North
Bayport MN 55003-1096
(800) 299-9029
(U.S. and Canada)
(651) 264-5279 fax
commercialgroup@
andersenwindows.com

Efficient Windows
Collaborative Alliance
to Save Energy
1200 -18th St NW, Ste 900
Washington DC 20036
(202) 530-2245
(202) 331-9588
www.ase.org

Excell
(stained glass)
via Juidiith Clawson
Simply Fetched
2257 South 1100 East
Salt Lake City, UT 84105
(801) 468-0526
www.simplyfetched.com

Wood Products

Bear Creek Lumber
PO Box 669
Winthrop WA 98862
(800) 597-7191 toll-free
(509) 997-2040 fax

Boise Cascade
Engineered Wood Products
Corporate Headquarters
PO Box 50
Boise ID 83728-0001
(800) 232-0788 toll-free
(208) 384-7455 fax
info@BCEWP.com

Crosscut Hardwood—Eugene
2344 West 7th Pl
Eugene OR 97402
(541) 349-0538

Crosscut Hardwood—Portland
3065 NW Front Ave
Portland OR 97210
(503) 224-9663
(503) 227-4670 fax

Crosscut Hardwoods—Seattle
4100 First Ave South
Seattle WA 98134
(206) 623-0334
(800) 756-0334 toll-free
(206) 623-0556 fax

TimberGrass LLC
9790 Murden Cove Dr
Bainbridge Island WA 98110
(206) 842-9477
(800) 929-6333 toll-free
(206) 842-9818 fax
www.timbergrass.com
info@timbergrass.com

HOME CONTRACTORS & RENOVATORS

Artwood Design (Canada) Ltd.
10-755 Vanalman Ave
Victoria BC
Canada V8Z 3B8
(604) 727-3100

Screen Scenes
PO Box 3625
Quincy CA 95971
(530) 283-4366
(530) 283-4675 fax
Scrnscns@inreach.com

GARDENS & LANDSCAPING

Arto Brick/California Pavers
3751 Durango Ave
Los Angeles CA 90034
(940) 591-0518 ph/fax

W. D. Bosworth Woodworking
59 Luther Warren Dr
St. Helena Island SC 29920
(843) 838-9490
(843) 838-1187 fax
Woodwork@hargray.com

Copper Forge
2148 Inner Circle Dr
Rockford IL 61101
(815) 965-5314

Rick Darke
526 Chambers Rock Rd
Landenberg PA 19350
(610) 255-0432
(610) 255-0439 fax

Richard Liberto
1907 Lowrie St
Pittsburgh PA 15212-3224
(412) 321-4427 ph/fax

Old House Gardens
536 West Third St
Ann Arbor MI 48103-4957
(734) 995-1486
(734) 995-1687 fax

INTERIOR DECORATORS & DESIGNERS

Juidiith Clawson
Simply Fetched
2257 South 1100 East
Salt Lake City, UT 84105
(801) 468-0526
www.simplyfetched.com

Distinctions Interior
Consultation Services
235 Summit View Cove
Collierville TN 38017
(901) 484-2397

Highland Group
Valerie Paoli-Johnson and
Rebecca Osborne
4471 South Highland Dr
Salt Lake City, UT 84124
(801) 277-4433
(801) 277-1450 fax
www.highland-group.com

Interior Vision in the
Craftsman Style
PO Box 867
Port Townsend WA 98368
(360) 385-3161
(888) 385-3161 toll-free
(360) 385-4874 fax

INTERIORS

Cabinetry

Acorn (Forged Iron)
Mansfield, MA
(800) 835-0121

Crown City (Arts & Crafts)
Pasadena, CA
(800) 950-1047 toll-free

Crownpoint Cabinetry
153 Charlestown Road
Claremont NH 03743
(800) 999-4994
toll-free phone
(800) 370-1218 toll-free fax
www.crown-point.com

Crystal
Princeton, MN
(612) 389-4240

Designer Doors Inc.
283 Troy St
River Falls WI 54022
(715) 426-1100
(800) 241-0525 toll-free
info@designerdoors.com

Gainsborough
(Turn of the Century)
Norcross, GA
(800) 845-5662 toll-free

International Door & Latch
191 Seneca Rd
PO Box 25755
Eugene OR 97402
(541) 686-5647
(888) 686-3667 toll-free
(541) 686-4166 fax
www.internationaldoor.com

Notting Hill
Lake Geneva, WI
(414) 248-8890

William Russell Doors
31 Doornang Rd
Scoresby, Victoria
3179 Australia
(03) 9763 1544
(03) 9764 2250 fax
www.wrusselldoors.com

Rutt of Seattle
Seattle, WA
(206) 762-2603

Furniture & Frames

CRAFTSMEN

Holton
Emeryville, CA
(800) 250-5277 toll-free

Troy Poulson
Millcreek Furniture
via Simply Fetched
2257 S 1100 E
Salt Lake City, UT 84105
(801) 468-0526
www.simplyfetched.com

Sandhill Designs
Morrisonville, Wisconsin
(608) 846-2717

Voorhees Craftsman
Rohnert Park, CA
(888) 982-6377 toll-free

REFINISHING & REPAIR

Restoration & Design Studio
249 East 77th St
New York NY 10021
(212) 517-9742

Hardware

Chown Hardware
PO Box 2888
333 NW 16th Ave
Portland, OR 97208
(503) 243-6500
(800) 547-1930 toll-free
(503) 243-6519 fax
(800) 758-7654 toll-free fax
www.chown.com

Craftsmen Hardware Co., Ltd.
PO Box 161
Marceline MO 64658
(660) 376-2481
(660) 376-4076 fax

Crown City Hardware
1047 North Allen Ave
Pasadena CA 91104-3292
(626) 794-1188
(626) 794-0234 catalog direct
(800) 816-8492
toll-free/orders only
questions@
crowncityhardware.com

Hahn's Woodworking
Company, Inc.
109 Aldene Rd, Bldg #8
Roselle NJ 07203
(908) 241-8825
(908) 241-9293 fax
info@hahnswoodworking.com

Hippo Hardware
1040 East Burnside St
Portland OR 97214
(503) 231-1444
www.hipponet.com

Lighting

Brass Light Gallery
Milwaukee, WI
(800) 243-9595 toll-free

Historic Lighting, Inc.
114 East Lemon Ave
Monrovia CA 91016
(626) 303-4899
(626) 358-6159 fax
www.historiclighting.com

Luminaria Lighting
South 154 Madison
Spokane WA 99201
(509) 747-9198
(800) 638-5619 toll-free
info@luminarialighting.com

Old California Lantern
Company
975 North Enterprise
Orange CA 92867
(714) 771-5714
(800) 577-6679 toll-free

Rejuvenation House Parts
Portland, Oregon
(888) 3GETLIT [343-8548] toll-free

Rejuvenation Lamp
& Fixture Co.
2550 NW Nicolai St
Portland OR 97210
(503) 231-1900

(888) 401-1900 toll-free
(503) 230-0537 fax
(800) 526-7329 toll-free fax
info@rejuvenation.com

Plumbing & Faucets

Affordable Antique
Baths & More
San Andreas, CA
(209) 754-1797

Ann Sacks
5 East 16th St
New York, NY 10003
(212) 463-8400
(212) 463-0067 fax
www.annsacks.com

Restoration Hardware
104 Challenger Dr
Portland TN 37148-1703
Home office:
Corte Madera CA 94925
(800) 762-1005
toll-free customer service
(888) 243-9720
toll-free information
www.RestorationHardware.com
—Sinks, tubs, faucets, lighting, Mission-style furniture.

Sign of the Crab
Chicago Faucet
A-Ball Plumbing
Portland, OR
(503) 228-0026

The Sink Factory
2140 San Pablo Ave
Berkeley CA 94702
(510) 540-8193
(510) 540-8212 fax
TheCrew@sinkfactory.com
www.sinkfactory.com
—Pre-1940s reproduction sinks, tubs, and faucets.

Textiles: Drapes/Carpeting

Dianne Ayers
Arts & Crafts Period Textiles
5427 Telegraph Ave, Ste W2
Oakland, CA 94709
(510) 654-1645
—Finished textiles, custom embroidery, applique/embroidery, kits, yardage, hardware.

J. R. Burrows and Company
PO Box 522
Rockland MA 02370
(800) 347-1795 toll-free
www.burrows.com
—Candace Wheeler reproduction textiles, net and jacquard lace curtains, also carpets.

Ann Chaves
Inglenook Textiles
240 North Grand Ave
Pasadena CA 91103
(mail contact only)
—Custom embroidery.

Heartland House Designs
741 North Oak Park Ave
Oak Park IL 60302
(708) 383-2278
—Frank Lloyd Wright and Charles Rennie Mackintosh designs in counted cross-stitch.

JAX Arts & Crafts Rugs
Berea, KY
(606) 986-5410

Liberty Valances
782 North Fair Oaks Ave
Pasadena CA 91103
(949) 766-7505
(949) 766-3287 fax
Bernie@LibertyValances.com
Attn: Sharon Robinson
or Bernie Ennis

Michael Fitzsimmons
Decorative Arts
311 West Superior St
Chicago IL 60610
(312) 787-0496
—Reproduction and antique/finished textiles, applique/embroidery, also rugs.

Sanderson and Sons
979 Third Ave
New York NY 10022
—William Morris textiles (to the trade).

Schumacher and Company
939 Third Ave
New York NY 10022
(212) 415-3909
—Frank Lloyd Wright textiles and carpets (to the trade).

Textile Art Artifacts
1847 Fifth St
Manhattan Beach CA 90266
(310) 379-0207
—Specialist in antique Arts & Crafts textiles, applique/embroidery.

Textile Artifacts
12589 Crenshaw Blvd
Hawthorne CA 90250
(310) 676-2424
—Antique and reproduction fabrics.

Trustworth Studios
Box 1109
Plymouth MA 02362
(508) 746-1847
—Custom needlepoint/kits.

United Crafts
127 West Putnam Ave
Greenwich CT 06830
(203) 869-4898
www.ucrafts.com
—Finished textiles, also rugs.

Ann Wallace & Friends
Prairie Textiles
Box 2344
Venice CA 90294
(213) 617-3310
www.webmonger.com/
annwallace/
—Custom window treatments, finished textiles, yardage, hardware, applique/embroidery.

Wall Finishes

Faux Finishes
Lisa Lucaden and
Mary June Papazian
Portland, Oregon
(503) 335-3131
(503) 291-1415

Fulper Glazes
New Hope, Pennsylvania
(215) 862-3358

WALLPAPER—HANDPRINTED

Bradbury & Bradbury
Benecia, CA
(707) 746-1900

J. R. Burrows and Company
PO Box 522
Rockland MA 02370
(800) 347-1795 toll-free
www.burrows.com
—Candace Wheeler reproduction textiles, net and jacquard lace curtains, also carpets.

STENCILS/PAINT

Helen Foster Stencils
Sanford, ME
(207) 490-2625

Old-Fashioned Milk Paint
Broton, MA
(508) 448-6336

RESTORATION & PRESERVATION

Consultants

JM Young Furniture Research & Consulting
376 West 4th St
Elmira NY 14901-2471
(607) 734-3664

Contractors & Services

Burma Design Antique Restoration
285 Washington St
Union Square
Somerville MA 02143
(617) 628-2666 ph/fax

Custom Cushions
76 Lively Road
Middle Sackville NS
Canada B4E 3A9
(902) 864-3221

FRW Inc.
1550 Richmond Terrace
Staten Island NY 10310
(718) 442-3781
(718) 273-2239 fax

Hyland Studio
650 Reed St
Santa Clara CA 95050
(408) 748-1806
(408) 748-0160 fax
Mfg@jphc.com

Keith's Furniture Stripping
1108 Hazel Rd
Burlington NC 27215
(336) 229-1290

Noordzee Construction Company
7-1888 Maple St
Vancouver BC
Canada V6J 3S7
(604) 880-1175
(604) 736-8069 fax

Post Manufacturing
343 Harrison St
Canandaigua NY 14424
(716) 396-1570 ph/fax

Robert Schweitzer
3661 Waldenwood Dr
Ann Arbor MI 48105
(734) 668-0298
robs@umich.edu

Stonehedge Restoration & Antiques
PO Box 32094
Route 863
Highwater St
Hillsboro VA 20134
(540) 668-6985

Wallpaperguru
PO Box 491243
Los Angeles CA 90049
(310) 281-6298

Rudolph Waros Glass
PO Box 678
#17 South Park Row
Waterford PA 16441
(814) 796-3933
(814) 866-6079 fax

Winterburn Group
PO Box 99
Duntroon ON
Canada L0M 1H0
(705) 445-5911 ph/fax

Photo Credits

Key: T=Top, B=Bottom, R=Right, L=Left

Courtesy of Ashmore/Kessenich Design, photography by Steven Ashmore: 74–79, 84–85, 93

Courtesy of Matthew Bialecki: 6, 25, 30, 31, 128, 131–41, 145, 147–50

Courtesy of The Bungalow Company: 54–55, 58–59, 62–63, 65, 66–67, 70, 82, 83, 117
© Kim Carey of Michael Seidl Photography: 54, 58–59, 62–63, 66–67, 70, 80, 83 TR
© Randy Allbritton: 83 L and BR

Courtesy of Marshall Compton; © Kit Morris: 110, 114

Mikel Covey: 22–23, 38, 73, 75, 77–78, 81, 109, 117, 127, 145, 150

Charles Didcott, Didcott Visions (for David M. Schwarz / Architectural Services Inc.) 38 TR, 90–91, 111, 124 T

Curtis Gelotte Architects, Leavitt Contruction Co., © Land Image: 32–33

© Doug Hill: 60–61, 97, 146

Courtesy of the Highland Group; © Pete Houdeshel, photographer: 38, 48, 90, 100, 107, 115, 116, 119, 126, 140

Courtesy of Historic Lighting, © Jon Edwards, photographer (for Su Bacon and Historic Lighting): 4–5, 35–39, 92, 95, 96, 98, 99, 102, 103, 106, 110, 111, 113, 121, 122, 123, 124, 125, 145, 146

Courtesy Douglas Keister: 8–9, 10, 12, 24, 26, 27, 34, 53, 56-57

Courtesy of John Malick: 14–21, 80, 88, 104, 108, 120

Courtesy of Jim McCord: 54–55

© David Papazian: 69, 76, 94, 95, 114, 144

© Pro Image Photography (for Baylis Architects): 118

Durston Saylor (for Matthew Bialecki Associates): 25, 30, 31, 137, 138, 139

© Linda Svendsen: 13, 45, 47, 50–52, 87

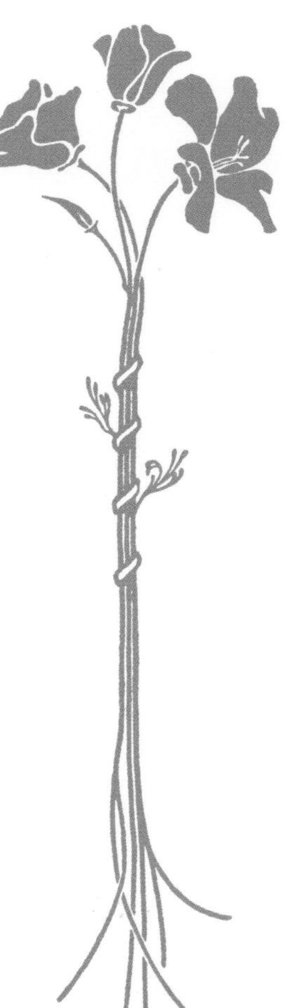

P9-DXJ-330
INDIANAPOLIS MOTOR SPEEDWAY

BY RICK POPELY
WITH L. SPENCER RIGGS

Publications International, Ltd.

Copyright © 1998 Publications International, Ltd. All rights reserved. This book may not be reproduced or quoted in whole or in part by any means whatsoever without written permission from:

Louis Weber, C.E.O.
Publications International, Ltd.
7373 North Cicero Avenue
Lincolnwood, Illinois 60646

Permission is never granted for commercial purposes.

Manufactured in U.S.A.

8 7 6 5 4 3 2 1

ISBN: 0-7853-2798-3

Acknowledgements

Front cover:
The front cover art is the work of Indianapolis artist David Taylor. It depicts the Marmon Wasp in which Ray Harroun won the first Indianapolis 500; Parnelli Jones's Watson roadster and Jim Clark's rear-engine Lotus, which finished 1-2, respectively, in 1963 and clearly defined the line between racing eras; and the G Force-Aurora that Arie Luyendyk drove to victory in 1997, the first 500 run under the Indy Racing League's distinctive chassis/engine formula. Also shown are the Borg-Warner Trophy, which bears the likeness of each race winner, and the "yard of bricks" at the finish line, a lasting reminder of the surface that gave the Indianapolis Motor Speedway its nickname: "the Brickyard."

Photography:
The vast majority of photographs in this book were provided by the Indianapolis Motor Speedway Photography Operations staff, Ron McQueeney, director. Other photos were taken or otherwise provided by Bob Stolze (*Pg. 79, top right*), W. A. Moore (*Pg. 205, top box*), Rick Whitt (*Pg. 277, second from top, left*), Bob Scott (*Pg. 351, top*), and John Biel (*Pg. 407, top left*).

Special thanks:
The author and editors wish to express their gratitude to Donald Davidson, Speedway historian, and Steve Ellis, IMS staff photographer and lab technician, for their invaluable assistance in verifying the accuracy of the contents of this book. Thanks are also extended to Jim Hoggatt, formerly of the Indianapolis Motor Speedway Hall of Fame Museum library staff, for his help in gathering research materials.

CONTENTS

FOREWORD

I've often thought that when Carl G. Fisher went out to view the old Pressley Farm on the outskirts of Indianapolis, he must have heard the same disembodied voice depicted in the movie *Field of Dreams*. The hero is told: "If you build it, they will come." Certainly, Fisher must have heard a similar muse when he surveyed the rundown, overgrown 320 acres where the Indianapolis Motor Speedway would stand. But even the visionary Fisher couldn't have imagined the stature his dream would attain.

Not long after its sale to former racer and World War I flying ace Eddie Rickenbacker in the Twenties, the Speedway, stricken by the Depression, doggedly staggered its way forward. Spurred on by the exploits of drivers, who won fame and glory on the stubborn old oval, the "Brickyard" became known as the proving ground for man and machine alike. But just when the track seemed about to fully gain its proper and deserved place of prominence alongside other major sporting events, World War II sent Fisher's and Rickenbacker's dream crashing to the ground.

Perhaps the most important 500 miles ever run at the Speedway were covered by a lone machine during the war. Taking part in a tire test, Wilbur Shaw—a three-time winner of the Indianapolis 500—realized the once-proud racing facility was ripe for demolition. Had it not been for Shaw's solitary run over the hallowed bricks, we might not be enjoying the Indy 500 today. The very sight of his beloved Brickyard crumbling away gave Wilbur a cause. Thereafter, he went to work trying to find a way to rescue America's most famous automobile race course.

After many weeks, Shaw convinced Terre Haute, Indiana, businessman Anton "Tony" Hulman to purchase the dilapidated track. Through Hulman's unstinting efforts, the Speedway came back to life like the Phoenix of myth rising once more from its ashes.

As they say, the rest is history. But, it's also the future. Since then, the same dream has continued through the auspices of Hulman's daughter, Mari Hulman George, and her son, Tony George.

Through the years, the Indianapolis 500 has evolved from a curiosity into one of the world's most eagerly awaited annual sporting events. If you've ever wondered how it all came about, you've come to the right place: The spellbinding events that shaped auto racing as we know it are contained here.

Whether you're a casual observer or a hard-core racing enthusiast, *Indianapolis 500® Chronicle* will give added meaning to the legend of the 500. Lead author Rick Popely has struck a happy balance between sterile statistics and hyperbolic rhetoric, both of which sometimes cloud the real facts. His detailed, thorough research provides a clear, concise report of every 500 from 1911 to the present.

You'll read of the thundering Edwardian monsters wheeled by Barney Oldfield and Ralph DePalma, as well as the jewel-like designs of Harry Miller and the Duesenberg brothers. You'll ride with the rumbling Depression-era two-man cars dominated by the likes of three-time winners Shaw and Louie Meyer. You'll relive the postwar years, when owner Lou Moore's Blue Crown Spark Plug Specials captured the imagination of fans worldwide. Read about Bill Vukovich and the emergence of the roadsters that overwhelmed the competition in the Fifties. Learn about Jack Brabham's underpowered—but slick-handling—Cooper-Climax and Jim Clark's Lotus-Ford, cars that established the rear-engine racer as the vehicle of choice in open-wheel racing.

Meanwhile, this writer has been asked to provide a smattering of inside anecdotes and human-interest stories to let you in on who, how, when, and why. There's the story of the Louis Chevrolet design that foreshadowed Colin Chapman's Lotus and the tale of how a casual acquaintance led to Louis Meyer's first Indy victory. Learn how lost radiator caps, stuck throttles, and borrowed parts changed Indy history.

Be our guest. Turn the page and enjoy all the drama and excitement that has surrounded every Indianapolis 500 classic.

L. Spencer Riggs

1909-1910

Carl G. Fisher

Though the first 500-mile race that makes the Indianapolis Motor Speedway world renowned won't be held until 1911, the track opens for business in 1909.

Carl G. Fisher, co-owner of Indianapolis-based Prest-O-Lite Company, is the mover and shaker behind the Speedway, which he builds on a 320-acre site northwest of the city limits.

The Indiana capital is an appropriate place for such a facility. Early in the 20th century, Indianapolis—not Detroit—is the Motor City, and Fisher's co-founders are a who's who of the area's burgeoning auto industry: James Allison, Fisher's partner in Prest-O-Lite; Arthur Newby, of National Motors; and Frank Wheeler, of Wheeler-Schebler Carburetor.

Fisher, a former race driver himself, envisions the Speedway as a proving ground where auto manufacturers test their products and race against competitors from around the world.

When the track opens on August 19, 1909, the basic configuration is as it is today: a 2.5-mile oval with four corners banked at nine degrees, 12 minutes. The 50-foot-wide front and back straightaways are five-eighths of a mile each, and the four turns are 60 feet wide and a quarter-mile long. The turns are connected at the north and south ends of the track by one-eighth-mile straights—the "short chutes."

The original surface of crushed stone and tar proves unable to withstand the pounding of high-speed automobiles. Fisher has the Speedway repaved late in 1909 with paving bricks, 3.2 million in all, grouted with cement. Thus, the "Brickyard" is born.

Two races are held in 1909, the second on December 17 after the bricks are laid. In 1910, there are three-day race meets held on three holiday weekends: Decoration Day (now Memorial Day), Independence Day, and Labor Day. The next year, the Speedway is home to just one race—a 500-miler on Memorial Day.

Lewis Strang (*top*), who would go on to start from the pole in the first Indianapolis 500, looks over a model of the proposed Indianapolis Motor Speedway. The pegs in the ground were pivot points for nails attached to strings that carved the four identical turns into the dirt. Carl G. Fisher, one of the four co-founders of the Speedway and its first president, is at the wheel of his Stoddard-Dayton during a press tour of the track while it is under construction (*above*) on May 1, 1909. Note the grandstand being erected in the distance. The front row lines up for one of the first auto races held at the Speedway on August 19, 1909 (*left*). Balloon races had been the track's first competitive events.

A tightly packed field of cars lines up for the main event at the August 19, 1909, opening of the track (*top left*). Loose engine tolerances made for excessive oil consumption, so there was as much smoke as noise in the early days of racing (*top right*). Louis Chevrolet, a native of Switzerland, was one of the first foreign-born drivers to compete at Indianapolis, though it is a Buick he is behind the wheel of (*above left*), not a Chevy. Buick supported a racing team that featured some of the top drivers of the day. Ray Harroun (*second from top, right*), the 1910 national champion, was another of the drivers active at the Speedway in the pre-500 years. Harroun wrestles with a tire at a 1909 event under the guidance of mechanic Harry Goetz (*above*). Drivers regularly got their hands dirty in those days helping to keep the car running. Nine cars squeeze across the start-finish line (*left*) for a heat race during one of the three-day meets held in 1910. These racing fests included as many as 42 races on the Speedway's 2.5-mile ribbon of bricks.

1st Race • May 30, 1911

A record racing purse of $27,550 draws 46 cars from the U. S. and Europe for the first Indianapolis 500-Mile International Sweepstakes. Forty qualify by sustaining 75 mph for a quarter mile, though order of entry determines starting positions. Rules include a minimum weight of 2300 pounds and a maximum engine size of 600 cid.

The cars line up in rows of five before a crowd of more than 80,000, and Carl G. Fisher, a co-founder and the president of the Speedway, paces the field to a flying start in a Stoddard-Dayton passenger car.

Amid clouds of smoke and the roar of 40 engines, American Johnny Aitken grabs the lead in a National and holds it until lap five, when Spencer Wishart takes over in a Mercedes. David Bruce-Brown's Fiat dominates the race until Ray Harroun passes him near the halfway point.

Harroun, the only driver competing without a riding mechanic, keeps an eye on his pursuers with a cowl-mounted rear-view mirror. This is the first recorded use of a feature that eventually becomes standard on passenger and race cars alike.

While others falter during the grueling race of nearly seven hours, Harroun averages 74.602 mph in a six-cylinder Marmon Wasp with Firestone tires, beating second-place Ralph Mulford's Lozier by one minute, 43 seconds. Harroun designed the winning car, which is narrower and lighter than most others in the field, and is marked by a sharply pointed, wasp-like tail.

Though he is relieved by Cyrus Patschke for about 100 miles, Harroun leads 88 of the 200 laps, the most among seven leaders, and earns $10,000 first-place prize money. Harroun, the defending AAA national champion, retires after the race.

Twenty-six cars are running at the end. Riding mechanic Sam Dickson is the lone fatality, killed when driver Arthur Greiner smacks the Turn 2 wall on lap 12.

Lewis Strang's Case started from the pole next to the Stoddard-Dayton pace car (*above*), but Johnny Aitken's No. 4 National led the first lap in Indianapolis 500 history. Harry Knight's No. 7 Westcott crashed on the 90th lap (*below*).

STARTING LINEUP

Qualifying Speed: Minimum of 75 mph for a quarter mile

Numbers in flags indicate finish position

POLE POSITION
Determined by order of entry

Johnny Aitken

Will Jones

Arthur Chevrolet

Howdy Wilcox

Ernest Delaney

Harry Endicott

Joe Jagersberger

Fred Belcher

Charles Merz

Jack Tower

Ralph DePalma

Harry Knight

W. H. Turner

Harry Grant

Harry Cobe

Lewis Strang

Frank Fox

Spencer Wishart

Eddie Hearne

Fred Ellis

PACE CAR POSITION

Louis Disbrow

Gil Anderson

Charles Basle

Mel Marquette

RESULTS

NO.	DRIVER	CAR	ENTRANT	ENGINE	CYL.	DISP.	CHASSIS	COLOR	START	FINISH	LAPS / SPEED / REASON OUT
32	Ray Harroun	Marmon "Wasp"	Nordyke & Marmon Co.	Marmon	6	477	Marmon	yellow, black	28	1	200-74.60
33	Ralph Mulford	Lozier	Lozier Motor Co.	Lozier	4	544	Lozier	white	29	2	200-74.29
28	David Bruce-Brown	Fiat	E. E. Hewlett	Fiat	4	589	Fiat	maroon, white	25	3	200-72.73
11	Spencer Wishart	Mercedes	Spencer Wishart	Mercedes	4	583	Mercedes	gray	11	4	200-72.65
31	Joe Dawson	Marmon	Nordyke & Marmon Co.	Marmon	4	495	Marmon	yellow, black	27	5	200-72.34
2	Ralph DePalma	Simplex	Simplex Automobile Co.	Simplex	4	597	Simplex	red, white	2	6	200-71.13
20	Charlie Merz	National	National Motor Vehicle Co.	National	4	447	National	blue, white	18	7	200-70.37
12	W. H. "Jack" Turner	Amplex	Simplex Automobile Co.	Amplex	4	443	Amplex	red	12	8	200-68.82
15	Fred Belcher	Knox	Knox Automobile Co.	Knox	6	432	Knox	brown	13	9	200-68.63
25	Harry Cobe	Jackson	Jackson Automobile Co.	Jackson	4	559	Jackson	maroon, white	22	10	200-67.90
10	Gil Anderson	Stutz	Ideal Motor Car Co.	Wisconsin	4	390	Stutz	gray, white	10	11	200-67.73
36	Hughie Hughes	Mercer	Mercer Motors Co.	Mercer	4	300	Mercer	yellow, blue	32	12	200-67.73
30	Lee Frayer	Firestone-Columbus	Columbus Buggy Co.	Firestone-Col.	4	432	Firestone-Col.	scarlet, gray	26	13	flagged
21	Howdy Wilcox	National	National Motor Vehicle Co.	National	4	589	National	blue, white	19	14	flagged
37	Charles Bigelow	Mercer	Mercer Motors Co.	Mercer	4	300	Mercer	yellow, blue	33	15	flagged
3	Harry Endicott	Inter-State	Inter-State Automobile Co.	Inter-State	4	390	Interstate	gray, black	3	16	flagged
41	Howard Hall	Velie	Velie Motors Corp.	Velie	4	334	Velie	gray	36	17	flagged
46	Billy Knipper	Benz	E. A. Moross	Benz	4	444	Benz	white	40	18	flagged
45	Bob Burman	Benz	E. A. Moross	Benz	4	520	Benz	white	39	19	flagged
38	Ralph Beardsley	Simplex	Simplex Automobile Co.	Simplex	4	597	Simplex	red	34	20	flagged
18	Eddie Hearne	Fiat	Edward A. Hearne	Fiat	4	487	Fiat	red, white	16	21	flagged
6	Frank Fox	Pope-Hartford	Pope Manufacturing Co.	Pope-Hartford	4	390	Pope-Hartford	red, white	6	22	flagged
27	Ernest Delaney	Cutting	Clark-Carter Auto Co.	Cutting	4	390	Cutting	gray, black, white	24	23	flagged
26	Jack Tower	Jackson	Jackson Automobile Co.	Jackson	4	432	Jackson	maroon, white	23	24	flagged
23	Mel Marquette	McFarlan	Speed Motors Co.	McFarlan	6	377	McFarlan	lead, white	20	25	flagged
42	Bill Endicott	Cole	Cole Motor Car Co.	Cole	4	471	Cole	green	37	26	flagged
4	Johnny Aitken	National	National Motor Vehicle Co.	National	4	589	National	blue, white	4	27	125-con. rod
9	Will Jones	Case	J. I. Case T. M. Co.	Wisconsin	4	284	Case	red, gray	9	28	122-steering
1	Lewis Strang	Case	J. I. Case T. M. Co.	Wisconsin	4	284	Case	red, gray	1	29	109-steering
7	Harry Knight	Westcott	Westcott Motor Car Co.	Westcott	6	421	Westcott	gray	7	30	90-wrecked FS
8	Joe Jagersberger	Case	J. I. Case T. M. Co.	Wisconsin	4	284	Case	red, gray	8	31	87-wrecked FS
35	Herbert Lytle	Apperson	Apperson Bros. Auto. Co.	Apperson	4	546	Apperson	vermillion, white	31	32	82-wrecked in pits
19	Harry Grant	Alco	American Locomotive Co.	Alco	6	580	Alco	black	17	33	51-bearings
17	Charles Basle	Buick	Buick Motor Co.	Buick	4	594	Buick	white, red	15	34	46-mechanical problem
5	Louis Disbrow	Pope-Hartford	Pope Manufacturing Co.	Pope-Hartford	4	390	Pope-Hartford	red, black	5	35	45-wrecked FS
16	Arthur Chevrolet	Buick	Buick Motor Co.	Buick	4	594	Buick	white, red	14	36	30-mechanical problem
39	Caleb Bragg	Fiat	Caleb S. Bragg	Fiat	4	487	Fiat	maroon	35	37	24-wrecked in pits
24	Fred Ellis	Jackson	Jackson Automobile Co.	Jackson	4	355	Jackson	maroon, white	21	38	22-withdrawn
34	Teddy Tetzlaff	Lozier	Lozier Motor Co.	Lozier	4	544	Lozier	white, red	30	39	20-wrecked FS
44	Arthur Greiner	Amplex	Simplex Motor Car Co.	Amplex	4	443	Amplex	red, white	8	40	12-wrecked BS

Winner Ray Harroun's Wasp (*opposite bottom*) was the only single-seater in the field.

Ralph Mulford

Ralph Beardsley

Bob Burman

Ray Harroun

Charles Bigelow

Arthur Greiner

Joe Dawson

Hughie Hughes

Bill Endicott

Lee Frayer

Herb Lytle

Howard Hall

David Bruce-Brown

Teddy Tetzlaff

Caleb Bragg

Billy Knipper

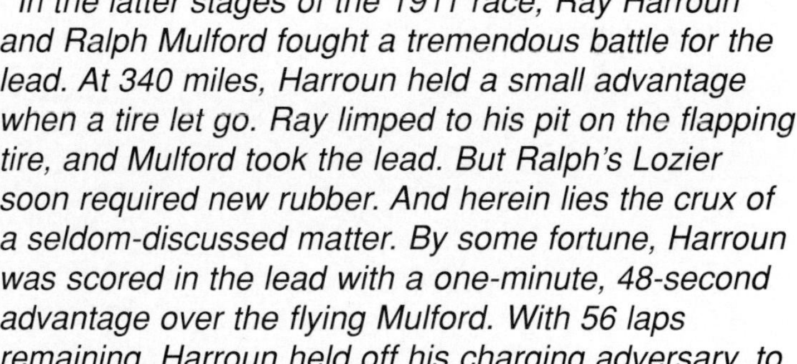

In the latter stages of the 1911 race, Ray Harroun and Ralph Mulford fought a tremendous battle for the lead. At 340 miles, Harroun held a small advantage when a tire let go. Ray limped to his pit on the flapping tire, and Mulford took the lead. But Ralph's Lozier soon required new rubber. And herein lies the crux of a seldom-discussed matter. By some fortune, Harroun was scored in the lead with a one-minute, 48-second advantage over the flying Mulford. With 56 laps remaining, Harroun held off his charging adversary, to become the first Indianapolis 500 winner.

Mulford quickly filed a protest of the official finish, contending he lapped Harroun when the Wasp limped in on the blown tire. While this seemed feasible to some, the chief scorers noted that it had taken several minutes for the Lozier crew to change a wheel that stuck on the hub during Mulford's pit stop. The protest was denied, but Mulford always contended he had beaten Harroun's Wasp to Indy's first checkered flag.

1912

2nd Race • May 30, 1912

New rules require riding mechanics, making obsolete single-seaters like Ray Harroun's 1911 race-winning Wasp. From 29 entries, 24 qualify for the $50,000 race by completing a full lap at a minimum 75 mph.

David Bruce-Brown qualifies fastest at 88.45 mph, but starting positions are determined by entry date. The field lines up in five rows, with four cars in the last and five in the others.

Teddy Tetzlaff's Fiat leads the first two laps, but Italian-born Ralph DePalma jumps in front on lap three and stays there the next 196 laps. DePalma's grey Mercedes builds a four-lap cushion, and he has victory in sight until a heartbreaking mechanical problem on lap 197.

DePalma's Mercedes misfires and slows on the front straight. He nurses it another lap at reduced speed, but his car finally quits on the back stretch as a broken connecting rod tears a hole in the crankcase. Cheered by the crowd of 80,000, DePalma and riding mechanic Rupert Jeffkins push the car to the pits, just one lap short of victory.

Indianapolis driver Joe Dawson, running second most of the day in his blue and white National, flashes past the crippled Mercedes for the lead on lap 199. Dawson finishes more than 10 minutes ahead of Tetzlaff, but, fearing a scoring miscue, he completes another two laps for good measure. It is the only victory for French tire-maker Michelin in 500 history.

Dawson's American-built National averages 78.72 mph, and his winning time of six hours, 21 minutes is 21 minutes faster than the 1911 race.

Only the top 12 finishers earn prize money, and Speedway rules require that drivers complete the 500-mile distance to collect. Ralph Mulford takes umbrage at the rule and takes his sweet time complying. Mulford and his mechanic reportedly enjoy a dinner-on-the-run while finishing the 500 miles—two hours and 32 minutes after Dawson—to collect $1200 for 10th place. Dawson earns $20,000 plus contingency prizes.

STARTING LINEUP

Average Field Qualifying Speed: 81.76

Numbers in flags indicate finish position

POLE POSITION
Determined by order of entry

20 Eddie Hearne

13 Bert Dingley

5 Bill Endicott

24 Len Ormsby

11 Ralph DePalma

23 Harry Knight

17 Billy Liesaw

19 Mel Marquette

18 Louis Disbrow

2 Teddy Tetzlaff

9 Howdy Wilcox

21 Lee Frayer (for Rickenbacker)

8 Joe Horan

22 David Bruce-Brown

6 Len Zengel

1 Joe Dawson

12 Bob Burman

3 Hughie Hughes

4 Charles Merz

16 Gil Anderson

15 Spencer Wishart

7 Johnny Jenkins

10 Ralph Mulford

14 Joe Matson

RESULTS

NO.	DRIVER	CAR	ENTRANT	ENGINE	CYL	DISP	CHASSIS	COLOR	QUAL SPD	START	FIN	LAPS / SPEED / REASON OUT
8	Joe Dawson	National	National Motor Vehicle Co.	National	4	491	National	blue, white	86.13	7	1	200-78.72
3	Teddy Tetzlaff	Fiat	E. E. Hewlett	Fiat	4	589	Fiat	red	84.24	3	2	200-76.75
21	Hughie Hughes	Mercer	Mercer Motors Co.	Mercer	4	301	Mercer	yellow	81.81	17	3	200-76.13
28	Charlie Merz	Stutz	Ideal Motor Car Co.	Wisconsin	4	390	Stutz	gray	78.88	22	4	200-76.00
18	Bill Endicott	Schacht	Schacht Motor Car Co.	Wisconsin	4	390	Schacht	red	80.57	15	5	200-74.25
2	Len Zengel	Stutz	Ideal Motor Car Co.	Wisconsin	4	390	Stutz	gray	78.85	2	6	200-73.83
14	Johnny Jenkins	White	White Indianapolis Co.	White	6	490	White	white	80.82	11	7	200-73.25
22	Joe Horan	Lozier	Dr. W. H. Chambers	Lozier	4	545	Lozier	white, red	80.48	18	8	200-71.50
9	Howdy Wilcox	National	National Motor Vehicle Co.	National	4	590	National	blue, white	87.20	8	9	200-69.30
19	Ralph Mulford	Knox	Ralph Mulford	Knox	6	597	Knox	white, red	87.88	16	10	200-56.29
4	Ralph DePalma	Mercedes	E. J. Schroeder	Mercedes	4	583	Mercedes	white	86.02	4	11	198-con. rod
15	Bob Burman	Cutting	Clark-Carter Auto Co.	Cutting	4	598	Cutting	white, red	84.11	12	12	157-wrecked T2
12	Bert Dingley	Simplex	Bert Dingley	Simplex	4	597	Simplex	red, white	80.77	10	13	116-con. rod
25	Joe Matson	Lozier	O. Applegate	Lozier	4	545	Lozier	white, red	79.90	21	14	110-crankshaft
7	Spencer Wishart	Mercedes	Spencer Wishart	Mercedes	4	583	Mercedes	gray, black, red	83.95	6	15	82-water connection
1	Gil Anderson	Stutz	Ideal Motor Car Co.	Wisconsin	4	390	Stutz	gray, white	80.93	1	16	80-wrecked T3
17	Billy Liesaw	Marquette-Buick	Will Thomson	Buick	4	594	Marquette	tan, red	77.51	14	17	72-caught fire
5	Louis Disbrow	Case	J. I. Case T. M. Co.	Case	6	450	Case	white, red	76.54	24	18	67-differential pin
23	Mel Marquette	McFarlan	Speed Motors Co.	McFarlan	6	425	McFarlan	gray	78.08	19	19	63-broken wheels
6	Eddie Hearne	Case	J. I. Case T. M. Co.	Case	6	450	Case	white, red	81.85	5	20	55-burned bearing
16	Eddie Rickenbacker	Firestone-Columbus	Columbus Buggy Co.	Firestone-Col.	4	345	Firestone-Col.	crimson, black	77.30	13	21	43-intake valve
29	David Bruce-Brown	National	National Motor Vehicle Co.	National	4	590	National	blue, white	88.45	23	22	25-valve trouble
10	Harry Knight	Lexington	Lexington Motor Car Co.	Lexington	6	422	Lexington	brown, white	75.92	9	23	6-engine trouble
24	Len Ormsby	Opel	I. C. Stern & B.C. Noble	Opel	4	450	Opel	gray, red	84.09	20	24	5-con. rod

Bob Burman (*opposite*), who finished 12th, has on his leather driving suit and race-day face. Five cars started from the front row, and Gil Anderson had the pole position in a Stutz (*right*). The pace car also was a Stutz. Wooden grandstands along the front stretch were a Speedway fixture for decades. The Brickyard was a severe proving ground for tire companies, as a shredded Palmer cord tire (*below*) shows. No wall separated the pits from the front straight (*bottom left*), and drivers simply steered in and out of traffic during the race. *Bottom right:* Speedway President Carl Fisher (right) congratulates winner Joe Dawson.

Hampered by serious clutch trouble and numerous stops with his huge Knox, Ralph Mulford was running long after all other contestants had been flagged off in 1912. As a result, Carl Fisher and starter Fred Wagner got into a tiff. Wagner wanted to give Mulford the checkered flag without his completing 500 miles; Fisher contended he should go the distance. Long after Fisher and Wagner had left the grounds, Mulford slogged on. By one account, he stopped to have fried chicken and ice cream, and to change shock absorbers for a softer ride.

And so, with the sun beginning to set, Mulford finally finished eight hours, 53 minutes after the start. His average speed of 56.29 mph is still a record: the slowest finishing speed in 500 history.

3rd Race • May 30, 1913

A new five-story pagoda-style timing and scoring tower on the inside of the front straight gives the Speedway an enduring landmark. Its styling reflects Speedway President Carl Fisher's apparent interest in Oriental design.

Maximum engine size drops from 600 cubic inches to 450 to attract more European competitors. French automaker Peugeot responds by entering a pair of cars with 160-horsepower four-cylinder engines that boast dome-shaped combustion chambers, dual overhead camshafts, and four valves per cylinder, features still used on modern engines.

Despite Peugeot's substantial horsepower advantage, Jack Tower is the fastest qualifier at 88.23 mph in a Mason. The 27 qualifiers draw for starting positions the night before the race.

An intense sun and 90-degree temperatures heat the track, shredding tires and forcing several drivers to make unscheduled stops. Peugeot driver Jules Goux, meanwhile, runs at the front with apparent ease. Goux coasts through the corners, saving his tires, and then taps the abundant power of his sophisticated engine to blow by other cars on the straights.

Still, even Goux suffers from the heat. The Frenchman requests champagne to refresh himself and his mechanic at his first pit stop—and five subsequent stops, according to Speedway legend. Goux cruises to a 13-minute, eight-second victory over Spencer Wishart's Mercer, the biggest margin in history. He averages about 10 mpg of fuel—and an unknown amount of champagne per pit stop.

Goux is the first rookie winner (apart from the "all-rookie" 1911 field), the first foreign winner, and the first to go 500 miles without a relief driver. He also is the first to win with wire wheels instead of wooden-spoke wheels.

Charles Merz finishes third, completing the last lap with his mechanic, Harry Martin, precariously perched on the hood of their Stutz, beating out the flames of an engine fire.

STARTING LINEUP

Average Field Qualifying Speed: 81.518

Numbers in flags indicate finish position

POLE POSITION
Determined by pre-race drawing

Robert Evans

Teddy Tetzlaff

Ralph DePalma

Charles Merz

Howdy Wilcox

Billy Liesaw

Jules Goux

Billy Knipper

Willie Haupt

Spencer Wishart

Albert Guyot

Harry Grant

Harry Endicott

Gil Anderson

Vincenzo Trucco

Caleb Bragg

Don Herr

Bill Endicott

Theodore Pilette

John Jenkins

RESULTS

NO.	DRIVER	CAR	ENTRANT	ENGINE	CYL	DISP	CHASSIS	COLOR	QUAL SPD	START	FIN	LAPS / SPEED / REASON OUT
16	Jules Goux	Peugeot	Peugeot	Peugeot	4	448	Peugeot	blue, white	86.03	7	1	200-75.933
22	Spencer Wishart	Mercer	Mercer Motors Co.	Mercer	4	300	Mercer	yellow	81.99	19	2	200-73.49
2	Charlie Merz	Stutz	Ideal Motor Car Co.	Wisconsin	4	400	Stutz	white, red	84.46	16	3	200-73.38
9	Albert Guyot	Sunbeam	Sunbeam Motor Car Co.	Sunbeam	6	368	Sunbeam	gray	80.75	2	4	200-70.92
23	Theodore Pilette	Mercedes-Knight	E. C. Patterson	Knight	4	251	Mercedes	gray, white	75.52	13	5	200-68.15
12	Howdy Wilcox	Gray Fox	Frank Fox	Pope-Hartford	4	390	Pope-Hartford	gray	81.46	20	6	200-67.65
29	Ralph Mulford	Mercedes	E. J. Schroeder	Mercedes	4	449	Mercedes	gray	80.79	22	7	200-66.95
31	Louis Disbrow	Case	J. I. Case T. M. Co.	Case	4	449	Case	gray, red	82.76	23	8	200-66.80
35	Willie Haupt	Mason	Mason Motor Co.	Duesenberg	4	350	Duesenberg	dark tan	80.72	15	9	200-63.48
25	George Clark	Tulsa	Tulsa Auto Mfg. Co.	Wisconsin	4	340	Tulsa	red, black	75.91	27	10	200-62.99
4	Bob Burman	Keeton	Keeton Motor Co.	Wisconsin	4	449	Keeton	green, white	84.17	21	11	—-flagged
3	Gil Anderson	Stutz	Ideal Motor Car Co.	Wisconsin	4	400	Stutz	white, red	82.63	14	12	187-camshaft gears
5	Robert Evans	Mason	Mason Motor Co.	Duesenberg	4	350	Duesenberg	dark tan	82.01	4	13	158-clutch
17	Billy Liesaw	Anel	Will Tompson	Buick	4	318	Buick	orange, black	78.02	3	14	148-loose rods
19	Caleb Bragg	Mercer	Mercer Motors Co.	Mercer	4	424	Mercer	yellow	87.34	1	15	128-pump shaft
10	Billy Knipper	Henderson	Henderson Motor Car Co.	Duesenberg	4	350	Knipper	azure blue	80.26	11	16	125-clutch
27	Teddy Tetzlaff	Isotta	Isotta	Isotta	4	444	Isotta	red, green	81.30	8	17	118-drive chain
32	Joe Nikrent	Case	J. I. Case T. M. Co.	Case	4	449	Case	gray, red	78.89	24	18	67-burned bearing
6	Jack Tower	Mason	Mason Motor Co.	Duesenberg	4	350	Duesenberg	dark tan	88.23	25	19	51-wrecked T1
28	Vincenzo Trucco	Isotta	Isotta	Isotta	4	444	Isotta	red, green	81.94	18	20	39-loose gas tank
1	Harry Endicott	Nyberg	Nyberg Auto Co.	Nyberg	6	377	Nyberg	red	76.35	10	21	23-transmission
15	Paul Zuccarelli	Peugeot	Peugeot	Peugeot	4	448	Peugeot	blue, white	85.83	26	22	18-main bearing
21	Ralph DePalma	Mercer	Mercer Motors Co.	Mercer	4	340	Mercer	yellow	76.30	12	23	15-burned bearing
26	Harry Grant	Isotta	Isotta	Isotta	4	444	Isotta	red, green	75.96	6	24	14-gas tank
18	Johnny Jenkins	Schacht	Schacht Motor Car Co.	Schacht	4	299	Schacht	red, white	82.84	17	25	13-crankshaft
8	Don Herr	Stutz	Ideal Motor Car Co.	Wisconsin	4	400	Stutz	white, red	82.84	5	26	7-clutch shaft
33	Bill Endicott	Case	J. I. Case T. M. Co.	Case	6	448	Case	gray, red	85.70	9	27	1-drive shaft

Cars lined up in rows of four this year (*opposite top*); Caleb Bragg drew pole position in Mercer. Indianapolis-based Stutz entered a three-car team (*opposite bottom*). Drivers included, from left, Charlie Merz, Gil Anderson, and Don Herr. Merz finished third behind Jules Goux and Spencer Wishart. Ralph DePalma inspects the engine in his No. 21 Mercer (*right*), which lasted just 15 laps. The 23rd-place finish would be the lowest of DePalma's storied Indy career. The Case team (*below right*) prepares for the race in the garage area.

Joe Nikrent

Louis Disbrow

George Clark

Ralph Mulford

Paul Zuccarelli

Bob Burman

Jack Tower

During practice for the 1913 event, Jules Goux was having problems getting everything together for a good run at winning the Indianapolis 500. Carl Fisher set the diminutive Frenchman straight. "Go see Johnny Aitken," Fisher advised. "He knows as much about what it takes to win this race as any man in the world." The French ace never forgot the favor.

In 1919, when Fisher needed someone to prepare the Speedway-owned Peugeots and Premiers, Goux answered the call. Under his guidance, Howdy Wilcox won the 500. "I also do this in the memory of our friend," Goux told Fisher. Johnny Aitken had died in the great influenza epidemic of 1918.

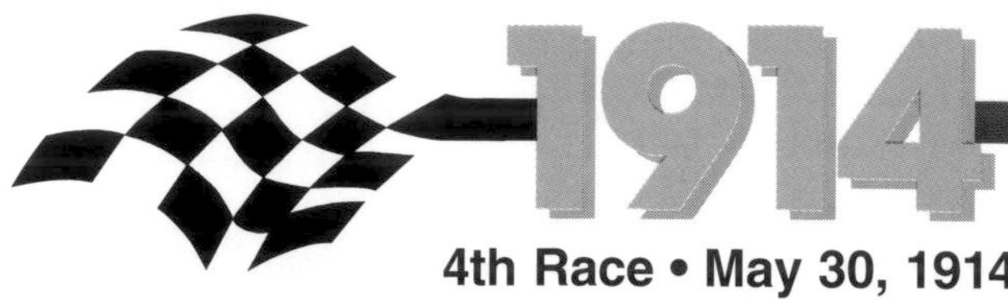

4th Race • May 30, 1914

The 1914 race fulfills the need for speed, but European cars and drivers dominate the fourth 500, which attracts 46 entries fighting for 30 starting positions.

Frenchman Georges Boillot qualifies his Peugeot at a stunning 99.86 mph, more than 11 mph faster than the previous record of 88.45. Fifteen others top the old record in qualifying. Drivers again draw for starting positions the night before the race. Ralph DePalma, scheduled to start 20th, withdraws his Mercedes race day morning because of excessive vibrations during warmup.

American Howdy Wilcox starts from the front row and leads the first lap before an estimated crowd of 100,000, but the rest of the day belongs to the Europeans.

French drivers and cars sweep the first four positions, led by newcomer Rene Thomas in a Delage, who leads 102 laps to win at a record 82.47 mph. Thomas takes the lead for good on lap 147 when Boillot blows a tire, and finishes seven minutes ahead of second-place Arthur Duray. Thomas pockets $20,000 in prize money and $17,000 more in contingency awards.

Maximum engine displacement is 450 cubic inches, but Duray's Peugeot uses a dual-camshaft 183-cid four-cylinder, the smallest in the race.

Barnstormer Barney Oldfield takes fifth place in a Stutz as the highest finishing American. Inaugural 500 winner Ray Harroun, now in charge of the Maxwell team, develops a fuel-sipping carburetor that runs on kerosene. Willie Carlson's Maxwell uses just 30 gallons over 500 miles and finishes ninth. With kerosene going for six cents a gallon, the fuel bill is a mere $1.80 for the day.

Eddie Rickenbacker places 10th despite blowing a tire on lap 199, and stalls in the pits for several minutes until his Duesenberg restarts.

STARTING LINEUP

Average Field Qualifying Speed: 90.125

Numbers in flags indicate finish position

POLE POSITION
Determined by pre-race drawing

22 — Howdy Wilcox

6 — Josef Christiaens

3 — Albert Guyot

1 — Rene Thomas

4 — Jules Goux

28 — Teddy Tetzlaff

11 — Ralph Mulford

2 — Arthur Duray

18 — Earl Cooper

15 — Ernst Friedrich

29 — Jean Chassagne

9 — Billy Carlson

19 — Caleb Bragg

23 — George Mason

25 — Joe Dawson

PACE CAR POSITION

21 — William Chandler

20 — Art Klein

13 — Billy Knipper

26 — Gil Anderson

RESULTS

NO.	DRIVER	CAR	ENTRANT	ENGINE	CYL	DISP	CHASSIS	COLOR	QUAL SPD	START	FIN	LAPS / SPEED / REASON OUT
16	Rene Thomas	Delage	L. Delage Co.	Delage	4	380	Delage	blue, white	94.54	15	1	200-82.47
14	Arthur Duray	Peugeot	Jacques Munier	Peugeot	4	183	Peugeot	blue, white	90.00	10	2	200-80.99
10	Albert Guyot	Delage	Albert Guyot	Delage	4	380	Delage	blue, white	89.15	11	3	200-80.20
6	Jules Goux	Peugeot	Jules Goux	Peugeot	4	345	Peugeot	blue, white	98.13	19	4	200-79.49
3	Barney Oldfield	Stutz	Stutz Motor Car Co.	Stutz	4	434	Stutz	white, red	87.25	30	5	200-78.15
9	Josef Christiaens	Excelsior	Josef Christiaens	Excelsior	6	446	Excelsior	yellow	91.21	7	6	200-77.44
27	Harry Grant	Sunbeam	Sunbeam Motor Car Co.	Sunbeam	6	273	Sunbeam	blk, red, white	86.46	26	7	200-75.69
5	Charles Keene	Beaver Rullet	Charles Keene	Wisconsin	4	449	Keene	blue	86.87	27	8	200-74.82
25	Billy Carlson	Maxwell	United States Motor Co.	Maxwell	4	445	Maxwell	black, white	93.36	5	9	200-70.97
42	Eddie Rickenbacker	Duesenberg	Duesenberg Bros.	Duesenberg	4	361	Duesenberg	red, wht, blue	88.14	23	10	200-70.83
23	Ralph Mulford	Mercedes	E. J. Schroeder	Peugeot	4	448	Mercedes	white, blue	88.21	6	11	200-69.55
43	Willie Haupt	Duesenberg	Duesenberg	Duesenberg	4	361	Duesenberg	red, wht, blue	89.39	28	12	200-66.66
31	Billy Knipper	Keeton	Keeton Motor Co.	Wisconsin	4	449	Keeton	red	89.57	12	13	200-65.79
7	Georges Boillot	Peugeot	Georges Boillot	Peugeot	4	345	Peugeot	blue, white	99.86	29	14	141-broken frame
34	Ernst Friedrich	Bugatti	Ettore Bugatti	Bugatti	4	390	Bugatti	white	87.73	18	15	134-drive pinion
1	Louis Disbrow	Burman	Bob Burman	Wisconsin	4	449	Burman	blue, white	86.79	24	16	128-con. rod
19	Spencer Wishart	Mercer	Mercer Motors Co.	Mercer	4	445	Mercer	red, black	92.69	25	17	122-camshaft
2	Earl Cooper	Stutz	Stutz Motor Car Co.	Stutz	4	343	Stutz	white, red	88.02	14	18	118-broken wheel
21	Caleb Bragg	Mercer	Mercer Motors Co.	Mercer	4	445	Mercer	red, black	92.97	9	19	117-camshaft
15	Art Klein	King	Arthur H. Klein	Wisconsin	4	449	King	yellow, blue	86.87	8	20	87-valve
38	William Chandler	Braender Bulldog	Braender Rubber Co.	Duesenberg	4	449	Mulford	white, black	87.54	4	21	69-con. rod
4	Howdy Wilcox	Gray Fox	Frank Fox	Pope-Hartford	4	432	Fox	gray	90.76	3	22	67-valve
13	George Mason	Mason	Mason Motor Co.	Duesenberg	4	361	Duesenberg	green, red	87.10	13	23	66-piston
17	Bob Burman	Burman	Bob Burman	Wisconsin	4	449	Burman	blue	90.41	22	24	47-con. rod
26	Joe Dawson	Marmon	Charles E. Erbstein	Marmon	4	445	Marmon	yellow, black	93.55	17	25	45-wrecked BS
24	Gil Anderson	Stutz	Stutz Motor Car Co.	Stutz	4	416	Stutz	white, red	90.49	16	26	42-loose cylinder bolts
49	Ray Gilhooley	Isotta	G. M. Heckschew	Isotta	4	375	Isotta	green	84.20	20	27	41-wrecked BS
8	Teddy Tetzlaff	Maxwell	United States Motor Co.	Maxwell	4	445	Maxwell	black	96.36	2	28	33-rocker arm
12	Jean Chassagne	Sunbeam	Sunbeam Motor Car Co.	Sunbeam	6	273	Sunbeam	green	88.31	1	29	20-wrecked T4
48	S.F. Brock	Ray	—	Wisconsin	4	449	Mercer	gray, red	87.83	21	30	5-camshaft

Drivers and mechanics gathered on the front straight before the start of the fourth 500 (*opposite page*). Jean Chassagne drew pole position. A wooden scoreboard (*above left*) kept fans abreast of standings. *Above:* Three Peugeots were in the field. Arthur Duray finished second in one. The others were driven by Georges Boillot, left, and Jules Goux, right.

Eddie Rickenbacker

Charles Keene

Bob Burman

Harry Grant

Barney Oldfield

S. F. Brock

Spencer Wishart

Georges Boillot

Ray Gilhooley

Louis Disbrow

Willie Haupt

Perhaps the most advanced car to appear at Indianapolis in 1914 was the Hughes-Rayfield Special. The brainchild of veteran racer Hughie Hughes and carburetor magnate William Rayfield, the narrow-hooded, streamlined machine carried its radiator in the cowl behind a powerful six-cylinder 442.6-cid engine with inclined valves.

The car wasn't ready until May 20, when Hughes drove it from Chrisman, Illinois, to Indianapolis. Hughes reportedly turned practice laps at more than 95 mph—easily enough to make the field. But on the eve of his qualification run, Hughes was either showing off for the press or for a young lady when he over-revved the engine, destroying the crankcase. The car never turned a lap in competition.

Two years later, when Rayfield filed bankruptcy, the special racer was sold to an amateur sportsman named Thompson. It was never heard from again.

1915

5th Race • May 29-31, 1915

This is a year of change at the Brickyard, which adopts the AAA standard of one car for every 400 feet of track, limiting the field to the 33 fastest cars.

The minimum qualifying speed climbs from 75 mph to 80, and drivers make one-lap qualifying runs instead of drawing for starting position. Car numbers are assigned according to qualifying speed. Maximum engine displacement drops from 450 cubic inches to 300, and no more than three cars of the same make can start the race.

The 41 entries include 10 European cars, down from the previous year because of World War I. Only 24 cars qualify, with Howdy Wilcox posting the top speed—98.9 mph—in a Stutz. Ralph DePalma's Mercedes (98.58) and Dario Resta's Peugeot (98.47) are close behind.

Rain postpones the race for the first time, delaying the 500 from Saturday, May 29, to Monday, May 31. (At this time Speedway policy was to not race on Sunday).

The race quickly becomes a fierce struggle between Resta and DePalma. Resta is faster on the straights; DePalma quicker through the corners as they duel for the lead lap after lap.

Resta leads by a lap when his right rear tire blows on lap 137, forcing him to pit. DePalma takes over and pulls away from Resta.

With just three laps to go, a puff of smoke signals trouble for DePalma. A broken connecting rod punches two holes in the crankcase—the same mechanical problem that denied him victory in 1912. This time, oil spewing from the engine, DePalma coaxes his crippled Mercedes the distance to beat Resta by three minutes, 32 seconds.

DePalma's average speed of 89.84 is more than seven mph faster than the previous record, and his time of 5:33.55 is 30 minutes quicker.

DePalma and the next 10 finishers ride on B.F. Goodrich Silvertown tires, giving Goodrich its first win.

STARTING LINEUP

Average Field Qualifying Speed: 88.388

Numbers in flags indicate finish position

POLE POSITION
Qualifying Speed: 98.90

Earl Cooper

Art Klein

Jack LeCain (for Babcock)

Billy Carlson

John A. Mais

Dario Resta

Bob Burman

Eddie O'Donnell

Joe Cooper

Eddie Rickenbacker

Ralph DePalma

Jean Porporato

Harry Grant

Noel Van Raalte

Ralph Mulford

Howdy Wilcox

Gil Anderson

Tom Alley

John DePalma

Tom Orr

RESULTS

NO.	DRIVER	CAR	ENTRANT	ENGINE	CYL	DISP	CHASSIS	COLOR	QUAL SPD	START	FIN	LAPS / SPEED / REASON OUT
2	Ralph DePalma	Mercedes	E. C. Patterson	Mercedes	4	274	Mercedes	cream, red, blk	98.58	2	1	200-89.84
3	Dario Resta	Peugeot	Peugeot Auto Import Co.	Peugeot	4	274	Peugeot	blue, white	98.47	3	2	200-88.91
5	Gil Anderson	Stutz	Stutz Motor Car Co.	Stutz	4	296	Stutz	white, red	95.14	5	3	200-87.60
4	Earl Cooper	Stutz	Stutz Motor Car Co.	Stutz	4	296	Stutz	white, red	96.77	4	4	200-87.11
15	Eddie O'Donnell	Duesenberg	Duesenberg Bros.	Duesenberg	4	299	Duesenberg	white, red	88.93	11	5	200-81.47
8	Bob Burman	Peugeot	Bob Burman	Peugeot	4	296	Peugeot	blue, white	92.40	7	6	200-80.36
1	Howdy Wilcox	Stutz	Stutz Motor Car Co.	Stutz	4	296	Stutz	white, red	98.90	1	7	200-80.11
10	Tom Alley	Duesenberg	Duesenberg Bros.	Duesenberg	4	299	Duesenberg	white, red	90.00	9	8	200-79.33
19	Billy Carlson	Maxwell	United States Motor Co.	Maxwell	4	298	Maxwell	blk, white, red	84.11	16	9	200-78.96
7	Noel Van Raalte	Sunbeam	Sunbeam Motor Car Co.	Sunbeam	4	271	Sunbeam	green, red	86.87	14	10	200-75.87
28	Willie Haupt	Emden	R. E. Donaldson	Emden	4	298	Emden	red, white	80.36	24	11	200-70.75
14	Harry Grant	Sunbeam	Fortuna Racing Team, Inc.	Sunbeam	6	278	Sunbeam	maroon, grn	89.29	10	12	184-loose mud apron
21	Tom Orr	Maxwell	United States Motor Co.	Maxwell	4	298	Maxwell	blk, white, red	83.55	17	13	168-axle bearing
6	Jean Porporato	Sunbeam	Sunbeam Motor Car Co.	Sunbeam	4	271	Sunbeam	green, red	94.74	6	14	164-piston
18	Joe Cooper	Sebring	E. E. Miles & J. W. Gwin	Duesenberg	4	299	Duesenberg	white, red	85.55	15	15	154-wrecked SS
22	Ralph Mulford	Duesenberg	Duesenberg Bros.	Duesenberg	4	299	Duesenberg	white, red	82.72	18	16	124-con. rod
12	George C. Babcock	Peugeot	Peugeot Auto Import Co.	Peugeot	4	188	Peugeot	blue, white	89.46	12	17	117-broken cylinder
9	Art Klein	Kleinart	Art Klein	Duesenberg	4	299	Duesenberg	white, red	90.45	8	18	111-disqualified smoking
23	E. Rickenbacker	Maxwell	United States Motors Co.	Maxwell	4	298	Maxwell	blk, white, red	81.97	19	19	103-con. rod
27	Louis Chevrolet	Cornelian	Louis Chevrolet	Sterling	4	103	Cornelian	white, red	81.01	23	20	76-valve
17	John DePalma	Delage	James E. Wilson	Delage	4	299	Delage	blue, red, wht	87.04	13	21	41-loose flywheel
24	John A. Mais	Mais	John A. Mais	Mercer	4	298	Mais	white, red	81.97	20	22	23-left course
26	George Hill	Bugatti	C. W. Fuller	Bugatti	4	300	Bugatti	white, black	81.52	22	23	20-water pump gear
25	G. C. Cox	Cino-Purcell	Edward D. McNay	Mercer	4	299	Cino	white, red	81.52	21	24	12-timing gears

Opposite page: Even a damaged engine couldn't stop Ralph DePalma (left, with mechanic Louis Fontaine) from winning this year. A jocular group of Speedway denizens (*above*) includes August Duesenberg (second from left). *Below:* Rookie Dario Resta (left) poses with Johnny Aitken. *Bottom:* Future Speedway owner Eddie Rickenbacker (right) and mechanic Eric Shroeder at speed.

Willie Haupt

Louis Chevrolet

George Hill

G. C. Cox

The 1915 race was scheduled for Saturday, May 29, but it rained and rained. Roads were flooded, hotels were overcrowded, and when it was announced the 500 would be postponed until the 31st, even more people flocked to Indianapolis. People went door to door looking for a place to stay. The estimated 100,000 extra visitors caused a shortage of food in the community. When the rain subsided on the 30th, people roamed the streets looking for something to do. If a distraction wasn't found, a riot or some other trouble seemed inevitable.

As usual, Carl Fisher knew what to do. Word passed through the community that a race between aviator DeLloyd Thompson's biplane and Gil Anderson's Stutz (with Barney Oldfield at the wheel) would take place at the Speedway on Sunday afternoon. Thompson also performed stunts over the enthusiastic crowd. Ralph DePalma and some of the other competitors put on a sort of early-days "pit-stop competition." And crowd trouble was averted.

Not until 1967 would weather postpone another Indy 500.

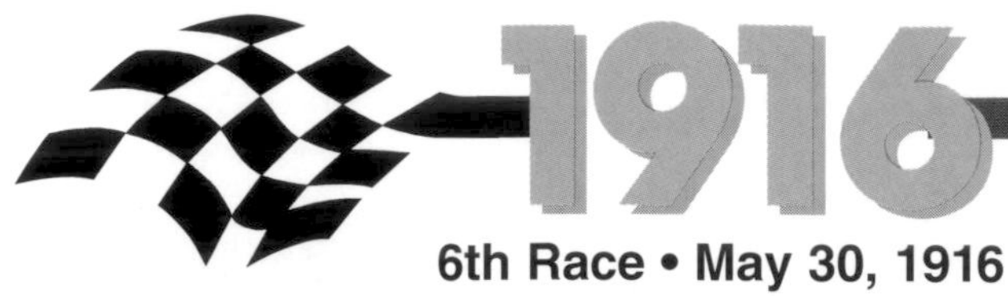

1916

6th Race • May 30, 1916

With war raging in Europe and draining resources, auto manufacturers pare their racing programs and entries drop to 30. The cars include three Premiers, clones of Peugeots built by the Speedway to fill the field. The race is cut to 300 miles, the only time the scheduled distance is less than 500 miles.

Only 21 cars qualify, the smallest field in history, and Johnny Aitken is fastest at 96.69 mph in a Peugeot.

Crowd favorite Eddie Rickenbacker starts on the front row and leads the first nine laps before a broken steering knuckle sidelines his Maxwell. Aitken takes over for the next seven laps, but Dario Resta charges to the front on lap 18. Resta leads the rest of the way in his Peugeot, the same car in which he placed second in 1915.

Resta, an Englishman of Italian ancestry, makes one pit stop and finishes two minutes ahead of Wilbur D'Alene's Duesenberg. Ralph Mulford is third in a Peugeot. The race draws a crowd of about 80,000 and Resta earns $12,000 prize money, both smaller than in previous years.

Before Aitken drops out on lap 69 with valve trouble, he makes an emergency stop for a fresh rear tire. Aitken gets the new rubber in just 20 seconds, according to press reports, showing that quick pit stops are already an important factor in race strategy.

Rickenbacker and teammate Pete Henderson wear steel helmets, the first crash helmets in American racing. Shortly after the race, Rickenbacker leaves for Europe, where he gains international fame as a World War I flying ace.

Louis and Arthur Chevrolet finish 12th and 18th, respectively, in their American-built Frontenacs, which use 300-cid, single-camshaft four-cylinder engines that are unique for their use of weight-saving aluminum.

STARTING LINEUP

Average Field Qualifying Speed: 89.77

Numbers in flags indicate finish position

Dario Resta

Charles Merz

Jules DeVigne

Aldo Franchi

Ralph Mulford

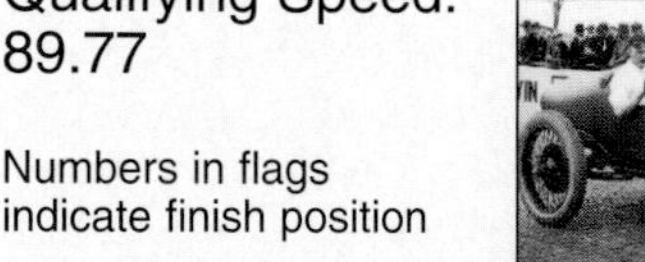

Gil Anderson

Tom Rooney

Arthur Chevrolet

William Chandler

Tom Alley

Eddie Rickenbacker

Howdy Wilcox

Wilbur D'Alene

Josef Christiaens

Dave Lewis

POLE POSITION
Qualifying Speed: 96.69

Johnny Aitken

Barney Oldfield

Pete Henderson

Ora Haibe

Art Johnson

RESULTS

NO.	DRIVER	CAR	ENTRANT	ENGINE	CYL	DISP	CHASSIS	COLOR	QUAL SPD	START	FIN	LAPS / SPEED / REASON OUT
17	Dario Resta	Peugeot	Peugeot Auto Racing Co.	Peugeot	4	274	Peugeot	blue, white	94.40	4	1	120-83.26
1	Wilbur D'Alene	Duesenberg	Duesenberg Bros.	Duesenberg	4	299	Duesenberg	white	90.87	10	2	120-83.15
10	Ralph Mulford	Peugeot	Ralph Mulford	Peugeot	4	274	Peugeot	blue, white	91.09	20	3	120-82.60
14	Josef Christiaens	Sunbeam	Sunbeam Motor Car Co.	Sunbeam	6	299	Sunbeam	green (frame)	86.08	14	4	120-79.96
15	Barney Oldfield	Delage	Barney Oldfield	Delage	4	275	Delage	blue	94.33	5	5	120-79.20
4	Pete Henderson	Maxwell	Prest-O-Lite Racing Team	Maxwell	4	298	Maxwell	white	91.33	9	6	120-78.30
29	Howdy Wilcox	Premier	Ind. Speedway Team Co.	Premier	4	274	Premier	green, white	93.81	6	7	120-76.80
26	Art Johnson	Crawford	William Chandler	Duesenberg	4	298	Crawford	orange, black	83.69	17	8	120-74.40
24	William Chandler	Crawford	William Chandler	Duesenberg	4	298	Crawford	orange, black	84.84	15	9	120-74.20
9	Ora Haibe	Osteweg	S. Osteweg	Wisconsin	4	296	Osteweg	blue	87.08	13	10	120-74.00
12	Tom Alley	Ogren	Ogren Motor Car Co.	Duesenberg	4	299	Duesenberg	blue	82.04	19	11	120-73.55
8	Louis Chevrolet	Frontenac	Chevrolet Bros.	Frontenac	4	300	Frontenac	maroon, white	87.69	21	12	82-con. rod
28	Gil Anderson	Premier	Ind. Speedway Team Co.	Premier	4	274	Premier	green, white	95.94	3	13	75-oil line
25	Dave Lewis	Crawford	William Chandler	Duesenberg	4	298	Crawford	orange, black	83.12	18	14	71-loose gas tank
18	Johnny Aitken	Peugeot	Ind. Speedway Team Co.	Peugeot	4	274	Peugeot	blue, white	96.69	1	15	69-valve
21	Jules DeVigne	Delage	Harry Harkness	Delage	4	274	Delage	yellow, black	87.17	12	16	61-wrecked NS
27	Tom Rooney	Premier	Ind. Speedway Team Co.	Premier	4	274	Premier	green, white	93.39	7	17	48-wrecked SS
7	Arthur Chevrolet	Frontenac	Chevrolet Bros.	Frontenac	4	300	Frontenac	maroon	87.74	11	18	35-magneto
19	Charles Merz	Peugeot	Ind. Speedway Team Co.	Peugeot	4	274	Peugeot	blue, white	93.33	8	19	25-lubrication
5	E. Rickenbacker	Maxwell	Prest-O-Lite Racing Team	Maxwell	4	298	Maxwell	white	96.44	2	20	9-steering
23	Aldo Franchi	Peusun	Aldo Franchi	Sunbeam	4	299	Peugeot	orange, black	84.12	16	21	9-engine trouble

With World War I already raging in Europe and diverting the attention of many foreign drivers and manufacturers, the Speedway entered a three-car Premier team (*opposite*) to help fill the field. Drivers included, from left, Tom Rooney in his first start and veterans Howdy Wilcox and Gil Anderson. Indianapolis-based Premier also provided the pace car (*right*). The Premier racers were copies of Peugeot's successful design, the dominant car of the era. The Speedway also entered two of the French flyers, including the one Johnny Aitken qualified on the pole. Aitken led early, but dropped out with engine problems. After that, the race belonged to Dario Resta, who started on the outside of the front row in a Peugeot.

With entries for 1916's "Indianapolis 300" pouring in, fans and officials alike looked forward to a renewal of the great battle waged between popular winner Ralph DePalma and Dario Resta in the 1915 classic. Such was not to be, however.

DePalma tried to negotiate a deal for appearance money from the Speedway. Carl Fisher adamantly opposed such financial maneuverings. "If we pay Ralph to come here, eventually, we'll have to pay every name driver to appear in the race," Fisher maintained. "Nobody will ever get appearance money at the Speedway as long as I'm running it."

But as the deadlines approached, DePalma was still a holdout. Two days after entries officially closed, Ralph sent a telegram, asking permission to file. Fisher denied the request. The defending 500 winner was not allowed to partipate in the event. Many critics contended this was the reason Resta won such an easy victory.

Louis Chevrolet

The affable Johnny Aitken was an outstanding driver and strategist. To his credit, he led the first lap of the first 500, managed the National team and Joe Dawson to victory in 1912, and helped Jules Goux get the most from his Peugeot in the Frenchman's triumph in '13. In 1916, when Aitken returned to the cockpit, he took the pole position for the race and appeared to be the only real threat to Resta until his Peugeot dropped a valve. Johnny wanted to win the 500 so badly he could taste it.

On September 9,1916, with World War I already raging for two years, the Speedway held a day of short racing events known as the "Harvest Classic." It would be the last event held there prior to America's entry into the hostilities and no one could foresee when racing would return to the huge course.

Aitken was at his hard-charging best that day. He made a clean sweep of the program, wheeling his Peugeot to wins in the 20-, 50-, and 100-mile events. "Now, why couldn't I do that in May?" Aitken wondered. "Well, at least I finally won at the Speedway."

7th Race • May 31, 1919

With the war in Europe having ended the year before, the race returns in 1919 after a two-year hiatus. Prerace excitement heightens when 1914 winner Rene Thomas, driving a Ballot, becomes the first pole winner to post a speed faster than 100 mph. Thomas's mark of 104.78 is nearly five mph faster than the old record. Six others top 100 mph in qualifying.

In another first, opening-day qualifiers line up ahead of drivers who qualify on subsequent days, regardless of speed, establishing a practice that continues today.

Car numbers are assigned the morning of the race to foil "bootleggers" trying to sell counterfeit programs.

A full field of 33 cars takes the green flag. Ralph DePalma's Packard leads most of the first 250 miles, but suffers wheel-bearing problems and finishes sixth. Thomas battles a variety of mechanical woes and struggles to an 11th-place finish.

Howdy Wilcox starts second in a Speedway-owned Peugeot and dominates the second half of the race, winning by nearly four minutes over Eddie Hearne's Durant. Wilcox is the first American-born driver to win since 1912 and gives French automaker Peugeot its third victory in the last five races. Goodyear Tire celebrates its first 500 victory.

Three deaths mar the race. Driver Arthur Thurman dies when his car hits the northeast wall and overturns. His riding mechanic, Nicholas Molinero, suffers a fractured skull. Driver Louis LeCocq and mechanic Robert Bandini die when their Roamer explodes and burns on the south short chute.

After the race, Speedway President Carl Fisher announces a reduction in engine displacement from 300 cubic inches to 183 for 1920 to lower speeds. The same 3.0-liter standard already exists in Europe.

STARTING LINEUP

Average Field Qualifying Speed: 92.85

Numbers in flags indicate finish position

Ralph DePalma

Eddie Hearne

Louis Chevrolet

Gaston Chevrolet

Cliff Durant

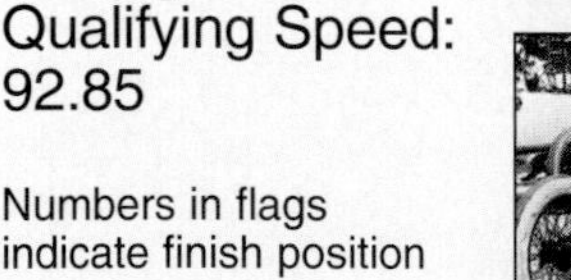

Albert Guyot

Art Klein

Charles Kirkpatrick

Ralph Mulford

Roscoe Sarles

Howdy Wilcox

Paul Bablot

Ira Vail

Joe Boyer

Arthur Thurman

POLE POSITION
Qualifying Speed: 104.78

Rene Thomas

Eddie O'Donnell

Earl Cooper

Louis Wagner

W. W. Brown

RESULTS

NO.	DRIVER	CAR	ENTRANT	ENGINE	CYL	DISP	CHASSIS	COLOR	QUAL SPD	START	FIN	LAPS / SPEED / REASON OUT
3	Howdy Wilcox	Peugeot	Ind. Motor Speedway	Peugeot	4	275	Peugeot	blue, white	100.01	2	1	200-88.05
14	Eddie Hearne	Durant	R. Cliff Durant	Stutz	4	299	Stutz	gray	94.50	8	2	200-87.09
6	Jules Goux	Peugeot	Ind. Motor Speedway	Premier	4	275	Peugeot	blue, white	95.00	22	3	200-85.93
32	Albert Guyot	Ballot	Ernest Ballot	Ballot	8	296	Ballot	blue, white	98.30	3	4	200-84.44
26	Tom Alley	Bender	Ahlberg Bearing Co.	Bender	4	289	Bender	—	92.20	28	5	200-82.18
4	Ralph DePalma	Packard	Packard Motor Car Co.	Packard	12	299	Packard	cream	98.20	4	6	200-81.04
7	Louis Chevrolet	Frontenac	Frontenac Motors	Frontenac	4	300	Frontenac	maroon	103.10	12	7	200-81.03
27	Ira Vail	Hudson	Hudson Motor Car Co.	Hudson	6	289	Hudson	blue, white	94.10	10	8	200-80.49
21	Denny Hickey	Stickle	A. C. Stickle	Hudson	6	289	Hoskins	blue, white	92.50	27	9	200-80.22
41	Gaston Chevrolet	Frontenac	Frontenac Motors	Frontenac	4	300	Frontenac	maroon, white	100.40	16	10	200-79.50
31	Rene Thomas	Ballot	Ernest Ballot	Ballot	8	296	Ballot	blue, white	104.78	1	11	200-78.75
8	Earl Cooper	Stutz	Earl Cooper	Stutz	4	299	Stutz	white, red	94.25	9	12	200-78.60
23	Elmer T. Shannon	Mesaba	Elmer T. Shannon	Duesenberg	4	299	Shannon	white	91.70	29	13	200-76.75
17	Ora Haibe	Hudson	Hudson Motor Car Co.	Hudson	6	289	Hudson	blue	92.80	26	14	200 —
37	Andre Boillot	Baby Peugeot	Jules Goux	Peugeot	4	275	Peugeot	blue, white	89.50	32	15	195-wrecked BS
48	Ray Howard	Peugeot	A. G. Kaufman	Peugeot	4	275	Peugeot	blue, white	95.00	21	16	130-lost oil pressure
22	Wilbur D'Alene	Duesenberg	Duesenberg Bros.	Duesenberg	4	299	Duesenberg	white	94.20	23	17	120-axle
15	Louis LeCocq	Roamer	Roscoe Sarles	Duesenberg	4	299	Duesenberg	gray, blue	92.90	25	18	96-wrecked T2
29	Art Klein	Peugeot	Arthur H. Klein	Peugeot	4	275	Peugeot	blue, white	94.90	7	19	70-oil line
19	Chas. Kirkpatrick	Detroit	Frank P. Book	Mercedes	4	274	Mercedes	silver	90.00	11	20	69-con. rod
33	Paul Bablot	Ballot	Ernest Ballot	Ballot	8	296	Ballot	blue, white	94.90	6	21	63-wrecked
10	Eddie O'Donnell	Duesenberg	Duesenberg Bros.	Duesenberg	4	299	Duesenberg	brown	97.30	5	22	60-piston
12	Kurt Hitke	Roamer	Roscoe Sarles	Duesenberg	4	299	Duesenberg	gray, blue	93.50	24	23	56-rod bearing
1	Cliff Durant	Chevrolet	R. Cliff Durant	Stutz	4	299	Stutz	tan	96.50	20	24	54-steering
9	Tommy Milton	Duesenberg	Duesenberg Bros.	Duesenberg	4	299	Duesenberg	brown	89.90	31	25	50-con. rod
34	Louis Wagner	Ballot	Ernest Ballot	Ballot	8	296	Ballot	blue, white	101.70	13	26	44-broken wheel
18	Arthur Thurman	Thurman	Arthur Thurman	Duesenberg	4	299	Duesenberg	gray	98.00	18	27	44-wrecked T3
43	Omar Toft	Darco	Omar Toft	Miller	4	289	Miller	white	91.50	30	28	44-con. rod
2	Ralph Mulford	Frontenac	Ralph Mulford	Frontenac	4	300	Frontenac	maroon	100.50	15	29	37-driveshaft
36	J. J. McCoy	McCoy	J. J. McCoy	—	4	293	McCoy	white, red	86.50	33	30	36-oil line
39	Joe Boyer	Frontenac	Frontenac Motors	Frontenac	4	300	Frontenac	maroon	100.90	14	31	30-rear axle
5	W. W. Brown	Richards	C. L. Richards	Hudson-Brett	6	288	Brown	yellow	99.80	17	32	14-con. rod
28	Roscoe Sarles	Oldfield	Barney Oldfield	Miller	4	289	Miller	gold	97.70	19	33	8-rocker arm

A Packard Twin Six paced the 33 starters who lined up for the first 500 after World War I (*opposite top*), and former winner Ralph DePalma qualified a V-12 Packard on the outside of the front row. DePalma led 93 laps, raising his career total to 425, but he was slowed by wheel bearing problems. Howdy Wilcox, making his seventh straight start, dominated the last half of the race to give Peugeot its third win in the last five events. Three-time national champion Earl Cooper finished 12th in a four-cylinder Stutz (*opposite bottom*). Jules Goux, the 1913 winner, came in third in a Peugeot. Goux's riding mechanic offers him a drink during a break in his driving duties (*right*).

Official Program INDIANAPOLIS MOTOR SPEEDWAY Saturday MAY 31 1919 PRICE 10¢

LIBERTY SWEEP STAKES

Kurt Hitke

Tom Alley

Andre Boillot

Wilbur D'Alene

Denny Hickey

Tommy Milton

Jules Goux

Ora Haibe

Omar Toft

Ray Howard

Louis LeCocq

Elmer T. Shannon

J. J. McCoy

The fact that Howdy Wilcox won the 1919 classic in a French Peugeot didn't matter to the adoring fans, who flocked around him in the winner's circle. After all, Wilcox was the first American-born driver to win at Indianapolis since Joe Dawson in 1912. And like Dawson, Wilcox was a local native.

When Howdy roared down the stretch and saluted the checkered flag, the crowd went into an absolute frenzy. Spectators came over the barriers and fences, chasing after the blue machine. As Wilcox coasted silently past the "Massed Band," it struck up a tune and followed him off the track. The spectators even started to sing the song to Wilcox.

No one realized it then, but this impromptu event sparked an occurrence that would take place prior to every Indianapolis 500 held since: the playing and singing of Back Home Again In Indiana.

1920

8th Race • May 31, 1920

New rules require four-lap qualifying runs, and each car gets up to three attempts to make the field. Another new wrinkle that later becomes tradition is a bonus for lap leaders, who earn $100 for each lap they are in front.

With the new engine displacement limit of 183 cubic inches, qualifying speeds drop. Crowd favorite Ralph DePalma wins the pole at 99.15 mph in a Ballot, more than five mph slower than the record set in 1919.

Only 21 cars qualify, but the Speedway adds two starters. Frenchman Jean Porporato, whose Gregoire barely falls below the 80-mph qualifying minimum, starts 22nd. Veteran Ralph Mulford fails to qualify through a misunderstanding, but lines up 23rd to continue his record of starting every race.

Joe Boyer starts from the front row and leads 93 laps in a Frontenac before giving way to DePalma, who recovers from a flat tire on the pace lap to take command of the second half.

DePalma builds a two-lap cushion, but with 13 laps to go, his engine catches fire. DePalma keeps going as his riding mechanic, Pete DePaolo, crawls onto the hood to extinguish the flames. The car stalls on the backstretch, and DePaolo dashes for the pits on foot, thinking they are out of gas. DePalma manages to restart the crippled Ballot, picks up DePaolo enroute, and limps home to fifth place running on four of eight cylinders.

That gives the lead to Gaston Chevrolet, who runs out of gas on lap 197, but coasts into the pits for a splash-and-go stop and beats Rene Thomas by six minutes. Chevrolet's Monroe chassis is identical to the Frontenac and powered by a four-cylinder Frontenac engine. It is the first American car to win since 1912.

Chevrolet rides on Firestone-built Oldfield tires and is the first winner to go the distance at the Brickyard on a single set of tires. Chevrolet dies seven months later in a race at Beverly Hills.

STARTING LINEUP

Average Field Qualifying Speed: 89.401

Numbers in flags indicate finish position

POLE POSITION
Qualifying Speed: 99.15

Louis Chevrolet

Roscoe Sarles

Tommy Milton

Jimmy Murphy

Joe Thomas

Joe Boyer

Gaston Chevrolet

Ray Howard

John Boling

Rene Thomas

Ralph DePalma

Art Klein

Eddie Hearne

Willie Haupt

Pete Henderson

PACE CAR POSITION

Jean Chassagne

Bennett Hill

Eddie O'Donnell

Andre Boillot

RESULTS

NO.	DRIVER	CAR	ENTRANT	ENGINE	CYL	DISP	CHASSIS	COLOR	QUAL SPD	START	FIN	LAPS / SPEED / REASON OUT
4	Gaston Chevrolet	Monroe	William Small Co.	Frontenac	4	183	Frontenac	green, white	91.55	6	1	200-88.16
25	Rene Thomas	Ballot	Ernest Ballot	Ballot	8	181	Ballot	blue, white	93.95	18	2	200-87.47
10	Tommy Milton	Duesenberg	Duesenberg Bros.	Duesenberg	8	181	Duesenberg	yellow	90.20	11	3	200-86.52
12	Jimmy Murphy	Duesenberg	Duesenberg Bros.	Duesenberg	8	181	Duesenberg	yellow	88.70	15	4	200-85.10
2	Ralph DePalma	Ballot	Ralph DePalma	Ballot	8	181	Ballot	cream	99.15	1	5	200-82.12
31	Eddie Hearne	Duesenberg	Duesenberg Bros.	Duesenberg	8	182	Duesenberg	yellow	88.05	9	6	200-80.15
26	Jean Chassagne	Ballot	Ernest Ballot	Ballot	8	181	Ballot	blue, white	95.45	4	7	200-79.94
28	Joe Thomas	Monroe	William Small Co.	Frontenac	4	181	Frontenac	green	92.80	19	8	200-78.60
33	Ralph Mulford	Mulford	Ralph Mulford	Duesenberg	8	182	Mulford	brown	Did not qualify	23	9	200-68.33
15	Pete Henderson	Revere	Revere Motor Car Corp.	Duesenberg	4	181	Duesenberg	white, red	81.15	17	10	200-67.93
32	John Boling	Richards	C. L. Richards	Brett	6	179	Brett	yellow	81.85	14	11	199-flagged
6	Joe Boyer	Frontenac	Frontenac Motor Co.	Frontenac	4	183	Frontenac	red	96.90	2	12	192-wrecked T3
9	Ray Howard	Peugeot	Peugeot Auto Racing Co.	Peugeot	4	182	Peugeot	blue, white	84.60	10	13	150-camshaft
29	Eddie O'Donnell	Duesenberg	Duesenberg Bros.	Duesenberg	8	182	Duesenberg	yellow	88.20	12	14	149-oil line
16	Jules Goux	Peugeot	Jules Goux	Peugeot	4	182	Peugeot	blue, white	84.30	21	15	148-engine trouble
34	Willie Haupt	Meteor	Meteor Motors Co.	Duesenberg	8	182	Duesenberg	maroon	85.48	13	16	146-con. rod
7	Bennett Hill	Frontenac	Frontenac Motor Co.	Frontenac	4	183	Frontenac	red	90.55	8	17	115-wrecked T4
3	Louis Chevrolet	Monroe	William Small Co.	Frontenac	4	183	Frontenac	green	96.30	3	18	94-steering
18	Howdy Wilcox	Peugeot	Jules Goux	Peugeot	4	182	Peugeot	blue, white	88.82	20	19	65-engine trouble
5	Roscoe Sarles	Monroe	William Small Co.	Frontenac	4	183	Frontenac	green	90.75	7	20	58-wrecked T4
8	Art Klein	Frontenac	Frontenac Motor Co.	Frontenac	4	183	Frontenac	red, white	92.70	5	21	40-wrecked
19	Jean Porporato	Gregoire	Jean Porporato	Gregoire	4	182	Gregorie	blue, white	79.98	22	22	23-car fell apart
17	Andre Boillot	Peugeot	Jules Goux	Peugeot	4	182	Peugeot	blue, white	85.40	16	23	16-engine trouble

Tommy Milton was one of the "hot shoes" of the early Twenties. In 1920 alone he piloted the streamlined 16-cylinder Duesenberg Special (*opposite*) to seven speed records in two days on the sands of Daytona Beach, Florida; won the first of two consecutive AAA national championships (he was the first driver to pull off that feat); and drove a Duesenberg to third place in the Indianapolis 500. Popular Barney Oldfield, a pioneering racing hero who competed in two 500s, drove the Marmon 34 pace car (*right*). Gaston Chevrolet (*below*) started sixth in a Frontenac prepared by his brothers, Louis and Arthur, and inherited the lead when mechanical problems slowed Ralph DePalma. Chevrolet's path to victory was traversed on a single set of tires, but he would be killed racing later in the year.

Ralph Mulford

Jean Porporato

Jules Goux

Howdy Wilcox

9th Race • May 30, 1921

With most major auto manufacturers sitting out this year, only 25 cars enter, and all but two qualify. Ralph DePalma is the first to win back-to-back poles, pushing his Ballot to 100.75 mph in his four-lap qualifying run.

On race day, cars line up in rows of three for the first time, launching one of the 500's enduring traditions.

DePalma bolts in front at the start and sets a blistering pace, averaging over 93 mph as he leads 109 of the first 110 laps. The perennial hard luck driver of the time, DePalma holds a three-lap lead when he throws a connecting rod and suffers another disappointing finish.

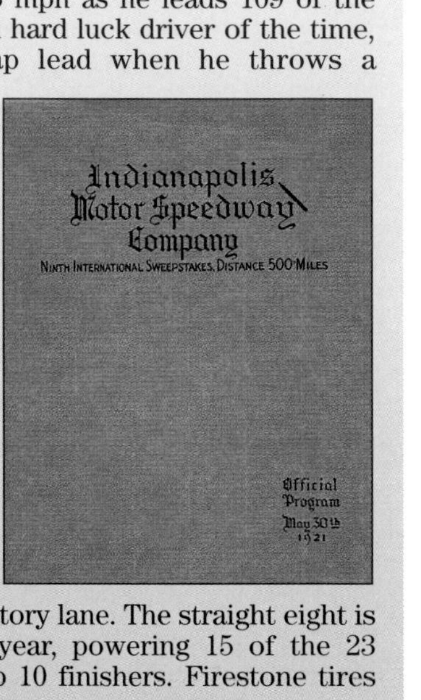
Indianapolis Motor Speedway Company
Ninth International Sweepstakes, Distance 500 Miles
Official Program May 30th 1921

Tommy Milton, filling a vacancy on the Frontenac team created by the death of Gaston Chevrolet, inherits the lead and cruises to an easy two-lap victory over Roscoe Sarles' Duesenberg.

A Frontenac engine wins for the second year in a row, but this time it is a dual-camshaft straight eight instead of a four, the first eight-cylinder in victory lane. The straight eight is the engine of choice this year, powering 15 of the 23 starters and nine of the top 10 finishers. Firestone tires win for the second year in a row.

Three other Duesies finish in the top 10, giving the American company a growing presence at the Speedway.

There are no serious injuries, but a close call occurs on lap 34 when Louis Fontaine spins his Junior Special exiting Turn 4, locks the brakes, and skids into the outside wall. His car comes to rest on top of the wall with the rear wheels on the spectators' side. No one is hurt.

DePalma leads the most laps in the race to raise his career total to 612, an incredible record that lasts more than six decades. Though he competes in three more 500s, he never leads another lap.

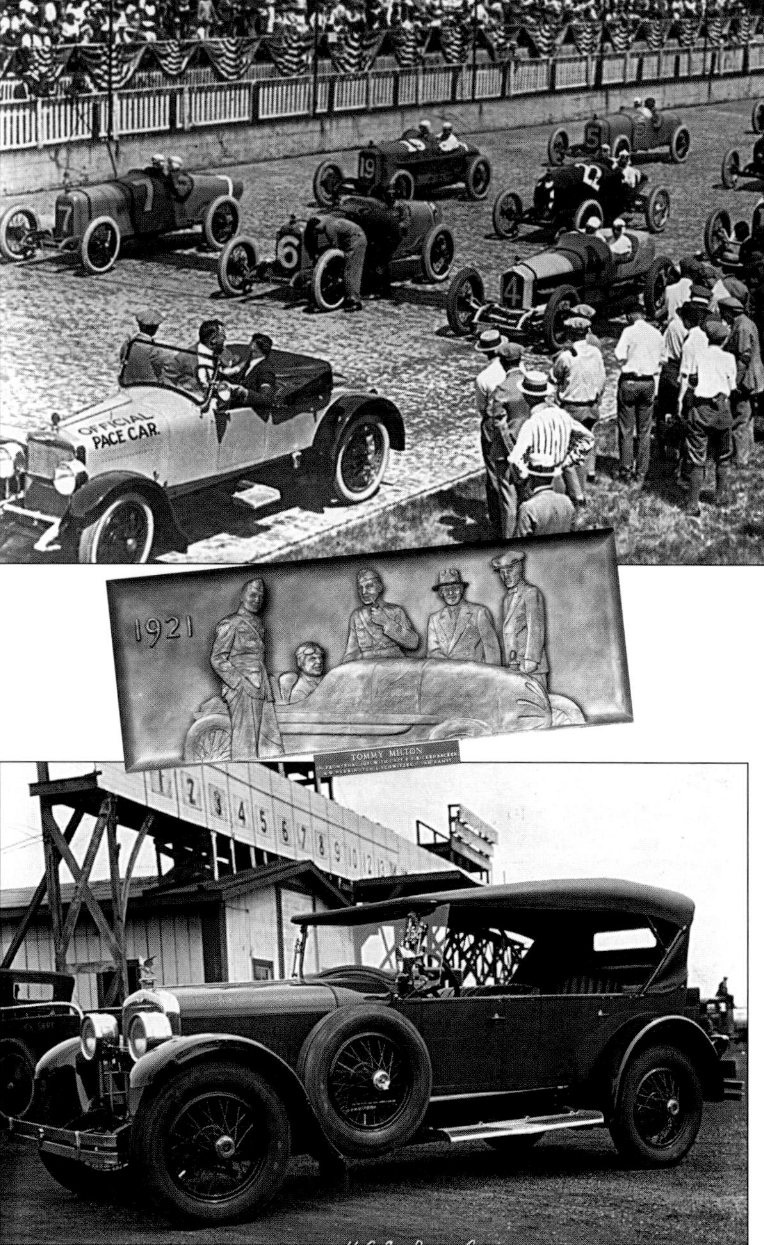

STARTING LINEUP

Average Field Qualifying Speed: 91.194

Numbers in flags indicate finish position

Joe Boyer

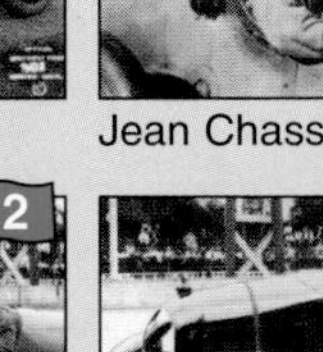

Jean Chassagne

Eddie Miller

Howdy Wilcox

Bennett Hill

Roscoe Sarles

Jules Ellingboe

Percy Ford

Andre Boillot

Albert Guyot

POLE POSITION
Qualifying Speed: 100.75

Ralph DePalma

Eddie Hearne

Joe Thomas (for Fontaine)

Ira Vail

Ora Haibe

RESULTS

NO.	DRIVER	CAR	ENTRANT	ENGINE	CYL	DISP	CHASSIS	COLOR	QUAL SPD	START	FIN	LAPS / SPEED / REASON OUT
2	Tommy Milton	Frontenac	Louis Chevrolet	Frontenac	8	178	Frontenac	plum, white	93.05	20	1	200-89.62
6	Roscoe Sarles	Duesenberg 8	Duesenberg Bros.	Duesenberg	8	184	Duesenberg	gray	98.35	2	2	200-88.61
23	Percy Ford	Chicago Frontenac	Stanley Kandul	Frontenac	4	182	Frontenac	red, white	87.00	8	3	200-85.02
5	Eddie Miller	Duesenberg 8	Duesenberg Bros.	Duesenberg	8	184	Duesenberg	gray	83.85	9	4	200-84.65
16	Ora Haibe	Sunbeam	Sunbeam Motor Car Co.	Sunbeam	8	182	Sunbeam	silver	93.50	13	5	200-84.28
9	Albert Guyot	Duesenberg 8	Duesenberg Bros.	Duesenberg	8	183	Duesenberg	gray	87.78	14	6	200-83.03
3	Ira Vail	Leach	Ira Vail	Miller	8	181	Leach	unpainted	82.35	10	7	200-80.15
21	Bennett Hill	Duesenberg 8	John Thiele	Duesenberg	8	183	Duesenberg	gray	87.75	15	8	200-79.13
8	Ralph Mulford	Frontenac	Louis Chevrolet	Frontenac	8	183	Frontenac	red, white	91.70	21	9	177-flagged
15	Rene Thomas	Sunbeam	Sunbeam Motor Car Co.	Sunbeam	8	181	Sunbeam	silver	83.75	17	10	144-water connection
27	Tom Alley	Frontenac	L. L. Corum	Frontenac	4	182	Frontenac	red, white	80.50	18	11	133-con. rod
4	Ralph DePalma	Ballot	Ralph DePalma	Ballot	8	176	Ballot	cream	100.75	1	12	112-con. rod
1	Eddie Hearne	Revere	E. A. Hearne	Duesenberg	8	182	Duesenberg	white	96.18	4	13	111-oil line
24	Jimmy Murphy	Duesenberg 8	Duesenberg Bros.	Duesenberg	8	184	Duesenberg	gray	93.60	19	14	107-wrecked FS
17	Riley J. Brett	Junior	George L. Wade	Brett	6	179	Brett	cream	87.80	16	15	91-hit wall, damaged
28	C. W. Van Ranst	Frontenac	C. W. Van Ranst	Frontenac	4	183	Frontenac	green, white	88.35	23	16	87-water connection
7	Joe Boyer	Duesenberg 8	Duesenberg Bros.	Duesenberg	8	184	Duesenberg	gray	96.65	3	17	74-rear axle
19	Jean Chassagne	Peugeot	Jean Chassagne	Peugeot	4	182	Peugeot	blue	91.00	6	18	65-lost hood
22	Jules Ellingboe	Frontenac	Jules Ellingboe	Frontenac	4	182	Frontenac	red, white	95.40	5	19	49-steering
14	Andre Boillot	Talbot-Darracq	Louis Coatalen	Sunbeam	8	181	Sunbeam	silver	97.60	11	20	41-con. rod
18	Louis Fontaine	Junior	George L. Wade	Brett	6	179	Brett	blue	88.30	7	21	33-wrecked FS
25	Joe Thomas	Duesenberg 8	Duesenberg Bros.	Duesenberg	8	184	Duesenberg	gray	96.25	22	22	25-steering
10	Howdy Wilcox	Peugeot	Jules Goux	Peugeot	4	176	Peugeot	blue	96.00	12	23	22-con. rod

Harry C. Stutz drove his own H.C.S. pace car (*opposite top*) for the ninth running of the 500. As is the practice today, H.C.S. also provided other cars, such as this touring car (*opposite bottom*), to shuttle the press and dignitaries around Indianapolis. A commemorative plaque (*opposite middle*) shows Tommy Milton in his winning Frontenac. Flying ace and future Speedway owner Capt. Eddie Rickenbacker is in uniform at the left, and the chief engineer for the Chevrolet brothers, Cornelius Van Ranst, is on the right. Milton takes the checkers (*right*) from a flagman precariously perched on a suspension bridge over the finish line, and then is mobbed in victory lane by crew members and well-wishers (*below right*). Louis Chevrolet is the dapper gent in the straw hat and Barney Oldfield is chomping his trademark cigar on the right. The death of Gaston Chevrolet in 1920 left open a spot on the Frontenac team that Milton had been invited to fill.

Tom Alley

Ralph Mulford

Rene Thomas

Tommy Milton

C. W. Van Ranst

Riley J. Brett

Jimmy Murphy

Eddie Pullen (for Joe Thomas)

1922

10th Race • May 30, 1922

The Duesenberg brothers square off against the Chevrolet brothers this year, the last for the 183-cid limit. A starting field of 27 cars includes nine Duesies and nine Chevrolet-built Frontenacs and Monroes. Two Fronty-Fords in the lineup are based on the Model T chassis and use Ford engines with Frontenac heads.

Californian Jimmy Murphy takes the pole in a Murphy Special—the Duesenberg chassis he drove to victory in the 1921 French Grand Prix at LeMans but with a new Miller engine.

Murphy's car earns attention not only for its speed, but its stopping ability. He is the first to compete with brakes on all four wheels, a feature that eventually becomes standard on passenger cars.

Murphy dominates the race and is the first driver to win from the pole. He leads 154 laps and averages a record 94.48 mph, becoming the first to average more than 90 mph over 500 miles. He earns $28,075 before an estimated crowd of 135,000.

Harry Hartz, one of 11 first-time starters, finishes second, two laps back in a Duesenberg. It is a big day for Indianapolis-based Duesenberg; eight of the top 10 finishers are Duesenberg chassis, which lead all but five of the 200 laps. Eddie Hearne finishes third in a French Ballot and Tom Alley ninth in a four-cylinder Monroe. Alley's car is the only one in the top 10 that doesn't have a straight-eight.

Four former winners start, but one finishes. Ralph DePalma places fourth, and Tommy Milton, Jules Goux, and Howdy Wilcox all drop out by the 44th lap.

The winning engine, built by Harry Miller, is the first of a family of racing engines that rules the Speedway for decades. Over the years, this dual-cam, multi-valve straight-eight evolves into the Offenhauser, the Meyer-Drake, and the four-cylinder turbocharged Drake.

The 1922 field pulls away from the grid amid clouds of smoke (*above*). Jimmy Murphy won from the pole in a Duesenberg (*top*) powered by a Miller eight, the first in a long line of Miller-based winners. The Speedway's original pagoda (*opposite left*), built in 1913, housed timing and scoring facilities. Specialized machines kept track of lap times mechanically (*opposite, middle top*). Drivers performed mechanical duties in this period; Jerry Wonderlich works on the chassis of his No. 24 Duesenberg (*opposite, middle bottom*). The dual-camshaft Frontenac straight-eight (*opposite right*) powered the 1921 winner, but could do no better than 11th in '22.

STARTING LINEUP

Average Field Qualifying Speed: 93.783

Numbers in flags indicate finish position

Ralph DePalma

Roscoe Sarles

Ira Vail

Tom Alley

L. L. Corum

Harry Hartz

Ralph Mulford

Frank Elliott

Cliff Durant

Ora Haibe

POLE POSITION

Qualifying Speed: 100.50

Jimmy Murphy

Leon Duray

Jerry Wonderlich

Peter DePaolo

I. P. Fetterman

RESULTS

NO.	DRIVER	CAR	ENTRANT	ENGINE	CYL	DISP	CHASSIS	COLOR	QUAL SPD	START	FIN	LAPS / SPEED / REASON OUT
35	Jimmy Murphy	Murphy	Jimmy Murphy	Miller	8	181	Duesenberg	white	100.50	1	1	200-94.48
12	Harry Hartz	Duesenberg 8	Duesenberg Bros.	Duesenberg	8	182	Duesenberg	white	99.97	2	2	200-93.53
15	Eddie Hearne	Ballot	Jules Goux	Ballot	8	180	Ballot	blue	95.60	23	3	200-93.04
17	Ralph DePalma	Duesenberg 8	Ralph DePalma	Duesenberg	8	181	Duesenberg	cream	99.55	3	4	200-90.61
31	Ora Haibe	Duesenberg 8	Duesenberg Bros.	Duesenberg	8	177	Duesenberg	gray	92.90	14	5	200-90.58
24	Jerry Wonderlich	Duesenberg 8	Duesenberg Bros.	Duesenberg	8	182	Duesenberg	buff, red	97.76	7	6	200-88.79
21	I. P. Fetterman	Duesenberg 8	Duesenberg Bros.	Duesenberg	8	180	Duesenberg	gray	93.28	13	7	200-87.99
1	Ira Vail	Disteel Duesenberg	Disteel Flyers, Inc.	Duesenberg	8	183	Duesenberg	white	96.75	9	8	200-86.15
26	Tom Alley	Monroe	William Small Co.	Frontenac	4	182	Frontenac	green, white	94.05	12	9	200-84.20
10	Joe Thomas	Duesenberg 8	Duesenberg Bros.	Duesenberg	8	181	Duesenberg	gray	88.80	17	10	200-82.50
3	"Cannonball" Baker	Frontenac	Louis Chevrolet	Frontenac	8	183	Frontenac	red	89.60	16	11	200-79.25
34	Cliff Durant	Durant	R. Cliff Durant	Miller	8	181	Miller	blue	95.85	11	12	200-77.75
22	W. D. Hawkes	Bentley	Bentley	Bentley	4	182	Bentley	silver	81.90	19	13	200-74.95
18	Jack Curtner	Fronty-Ford	Jack Curtner	Fronty-Ford	4	181	Ford T	red	Did not qualify	21	14	160-flagged
25	Wilbur D'Alene	Monroe	William Small Co.	Frontenac	4	182	Frontenac	green, white	87.80	18	15	160-flagged
9	Frank Elliott	Leach	Ira Vail	Miller	8	181	Miller	grn,whte,yellow	97.75	8	16	195-axle
27	L. L. Corum	Monroe	William Small Co.	Frontenac	4	183	Frontenac	green, white	89.65	15	17	169-engine trouble
19	C. Glenn Howard	Fronty-Ford	Chevrolet Bros. Mfg. Co.	Fronty-Ford	4	181	Ford T	red	83.90	27	18	165-engine trouble
5	Ralph Mulford	Frontenac	Louis Chevrolet	Frontenac	4	182	Frontenac	red	99.20	5	19	161-con. rod
7	Peter DePaolo	Frontenac	Louis Chevrolet	Frontenac	8	183	Frontenac	red	96.20	10	20	110-wrecked T3
6	Art Klein	Frontenac	Louis Chevrolet	Frontenac	4	183	Frontenac	black	87.15	25	21	105-con. rod
4	Leon Duray	Frontenac	Louis Chevrolet	Frontenac	4	183	Frontenac	red, white	99.25	4	22	94-broken axle
2	Roscoe Sarles	Frontenac	Louis Chevrolet	Frontenac	4	183	Frontenac	red	98.00	6	23	88-con. rod
8	Tommy Milton	Leach	Tommy Milton	Miller	8	181	Milton	red	94.40	24	24	44-loose gas tank
14	Jules Goux	Ballot	Jules Goux	Ballot	8	180	Ballot	blue	96.95	22	25	25-broken axle
23	Jules Ellingboe	Duesenberg 8	Duesenberg Bros.	Duesenberg	8	182	Duesenberg	gray	95.50	20	26	25-wrecked
16	Howdy Wilcox	Peugeot	Howdy Wilcox	Peugeot	8	177	Peugeot	blue	86.10	26	27	7-valve spring

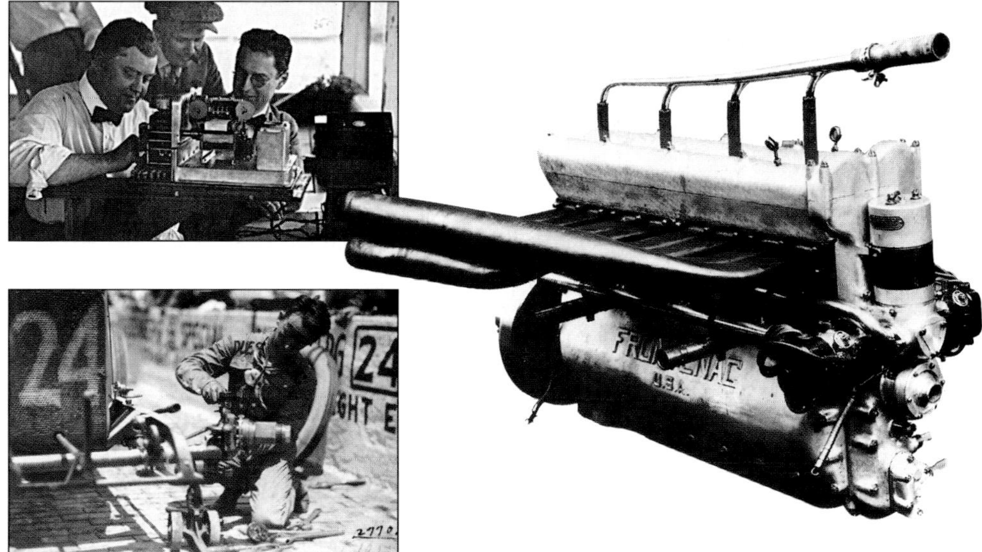

Wilbur D'Alene

C. Glenn Howard

Tommy Milton

Jack Curtner

Joe Thomas

Jules Ellingboe

Eddie Hearne

Howdy Wilcox

Cannonball Baker

W. Douglas Hawkes

Jules Goux

Art Klein

Following his 500 victory in 1921, Tommy Milton worked to get the bugs out of a car he and Cliff Durant had put together. Milton drove the Miller-powered Durant Special to the AAA national championship. But in early 1922, when Milton won a series of races at the Beverly Hills Boards, an overzealous car dealer advertised the Durant Special as a passenger car. The AAA suspended the machine from competition. The only way it could be reinstated was if Durant drove it.

Forced to drive the hastily completed Leach Special in the '22 Indianapolis 500, the champ dropped out after 44 laps. Meanwhile, Durant tooled the Miller along well off the pace. Not until Dave Lewis relieved him, did the racer start to climb, eventually finishing 12th.

To the very last, Milton believed AAA politics kept him from winning in '22.

11th Race • May 30, 1923

New rules drastically alter the landscape. The AAA makes two-man cars optional instead of mandatory, and maximum engine size drops from 183 cubic inches to 122 to match the international 2.0-liter formula.

The new rules attract more European entries, including a five-car Bugatti team (with a prince and a count among its drivers) and three Mercedes with the first supercharged engines to compete in the 500.

Despite the smaller engines, speeds are higher, helped by the advent of octane-boosting ethyl gasoline. Tommy Milton, the 1921 winner, captures the pole at a blistering 108.17 mph, 7.42 mph faster than the old record. Milton drives a Miller-powered H.C.S. entered by Harry C. Stutz. Four others top 100 mph in qualifying.

Howdy Wilcox, also in an H.C.S., is the slowest at 81 mph. Wilcox qualifies in a driving rain on the first day. Duesenberg, which dominated the year before, struggles to make the show. Phil Shafer finally qualifies a Duesie at 5:45 A.M. on race day, but suffers blistered hands and steps aside for Wade Morton. Morton, Shafer, and two others combine to place 10th.

The Mercedes of Christian Lautenschlager and riding mechanic Jacob Krause is the only two-man car in the race, and it crashes on lap 15. Cliff Durant, millionaire son of General Motors founder William Durant, owns eight of the 24 cars in the field.

Milton beats them all in his H.C.S., winning by more than three minutes over the Durant of Harry Hartz, the bridesmaid two years in a row. Milton is the first two-time winner, the first since 1911 to win without a riding mechanic, and the second in a row to win from the pole. Tight gloves give Milton painful blisters, and Wilcox relieves him while his hands are bandaged. They lead a combined 179 laps.

Tom Alley, driving in relief of Earl Cooper, crashes through the backstretch fence on lap 22, killing one teenager and injuring two others watching the race through a knothole.

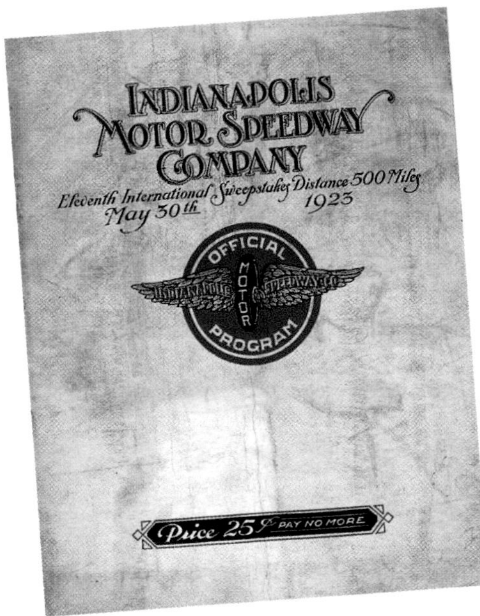

STARTING LINEUP

Average Field Qualifying Speed: 94.642

Numbers in flags indicate finish position

Dario Resta

Pierre de Viscaya

Jimmy Murphy

Earl Cooper

Christian Werner

Harry Hartz

Count L. Zborowski

Howdy Wilcox

Ralph DePalma

Eddie Hearne

POLE POSITION
Qualifying Speed: 108.17

Tommy Milton

Martin De Alzaga

L. L. Corum

Cliff Durant

Joe Boyer

RESULTS

NO.	DRIVER	CAR	ENTRANT	ENGINE	CYL	DISP	CHASSIS	COLOR	QUAL SPD	START	FIN	LAPS / SPEED / REASON OUT
1	Tommy Milton	H.C.S.	H.C.S. Motor Co.	Miller	8	121	Miller	white, red	108.17	1	1	200-90.95
7	Harry Hartz	Durant	R. Cliff Durant	Miller	8	121	Miller	yellow, red	103.70	2	2	200-90.06
5	Jimmy Murphy	Durant	R. Cliff Durant	Miller	8	121	Miller	yellow, red	104.05	9	3	200-88.08
6	Eddie Hearne	Durant	R. Cliff Durant	Miller	8	121	Miller	yellow, red	97.30	14	4	200-86.65
23	L. L. Corum	Barber-Warnock Ford	Barber-Warnock	Fronty-Ford	4	122	Ford T	orange	86.65	7	5	200-82.58
31	Frank Elliott	Durant	R. Cliff Durant	Miller	8	121	Miller	yellow, red	93.25	16	6	200-82.22
8	Cliff Durant	Durant	R. Cliff Durant	Miller	8	121	Miller	yellow, red	102.65	10	7	200-82.17
15	Max Sailer	Mercedes	Daimler Motoren Gesellschaft	Mercedes	4	121	Mercedes	white	90.55	20	8	200-80.68
19	Prince de Cystria	Bugatti	Prince de Cystria	Bugatti	8	122	Bugatti	blue	88.90	22	9	200-77.64
34	Wade Morton	Duesenberg	Duesenberg Bros.	Duesenberg	8	121	Duesenberg	gray	88.00	24	10	200-74.98
16	Christian Werner	Mercedes	Daimler Motoren Gesellschaft	Mercedes	4	121	Mercedes	white	95.20	15	11	200-74.65
18	Pierre de Viscaya	Bugatti	Martin de Alzaga	Bugatti	8	122	Bugatti	blue	90.30	6	12	166-con. rod
28	Leon Duray	Durant	R. Cliff Durant	Miller	8	121	Miller	yellow, red	89.90	21	13	136-con. rod
3	Dario Resta	Packard	Packard Motor Car Co.	Packard	6	122	Packard	blue	98.02	3	14	88-head gasket
2	Ralph DePalma	Packard	Packard Motor Car Co.	Packard	6	122	Packard	blue	100.42	11	15	69-head gasket
26	Harlan Fengler	Durant	R. Cliff Durant	Miller	8	121	Miller	yellow, red	90.75	19	16	69-gas tank
25	Howdy Wilcox	H.C.S.	H.C.S. Motor Co.	Miller	8	121	Miller	white, red	81.00	8	17	60-clutch
4	Joe Boyer	Packard	Packard Motor Car Co.	Packard	6	122	Packard	blue	98.80	13	18	59-differential
35	Bennett Hill	Miller	Harry A. Miller	Miller	8	120	Miller	—	91.20	18	19	44-crankshaft
27	Count L. Zborowski	Bugatti	Count L. Zborowski	Bugatti	8	122	Bugatti	blue	91.80	5	20	41-con. rod
29	Earl Cooper	Durant	R. Cliff Durant	Miller	8	121	Miller	yellow, red	99.40	12	21	21-wrecked BS
22	Raul Riganti	Bugatti	Martin de Alzaga	Bugatti	8	122	Bugatti	blue	95.30	23	22	19-gas leak
14	C. Lautenschlager	Mercedes	Daimler Motoren Gesellschaft	Mercedes	4	121	Mercedes	white	93.20	17	23	14-wrecked T1
21	Martin de Alzaga	Bugatti	Martin de Alzaga	Bugatti	8	122	Bugatti	blue	92.90	4	24	6-con. rod

A Duesenberg Model A paced the field (*opposite*), but only one Duesie racer made the show, and it struggled to a 10th-place finish credited to Wade Morton, who started in place of Phil Shafer, who was injured in qualifying. A month before the 1923 race, a Duesenberg much like the pace car made a record-setting non-stop run of 3155 miles at the Speedway (*below*). Though Goodyear wasn't yet in the blimp business, the Akron-based tire company provided aerial views of the 1923 race from hot-air balloons (*left*). Rival Firestone, however, rolled into victory lane for the fourth year in a row. In his only start as a driver, Harlan Fengler finished 16th in the No. 26 Durant (*above left*). Fengler later became a Brickyard fixture as USAC's chief steward. The eight Durant cars on the grid used the potent Miller straight-eight (*above right*), a dual-camshaft engine that powered the first four finishers, including Tommy Milton's race-winning H.C.S. Durants finished second through fourth.

Bennett Hill

Leon Duray

Phil Shafer (qualifier)

Christian Lautenschlager

Max Sailer

Raul Riganti

Frank Elliott

Harlan Fengler

Prince de Cystria

Tommy Milton's qualifying run of 108.17 mph was a new record. But the time trial of his teammate, former winner Howdy Wilcox, barely made the grid. His 81-mph run was the slowest in the 24-car starting field. Even so, in fewer than 60 laps, Wilcox charged through the pack to lead 10 circuits. Thereafter, he was eliminated by clutch trouble.

When Milton asked for relief after 103 laps, Wilcox took over. Of the 48 laps Howdy drove, he led another 41. This not only made him the second-highest lap leader of the race, but the only driver in history to set the pace in the slowest and fastest car in the Indy classic.

12th Race • May 30, 1924

Carl G. Fisher steps down as president to pursue other interests and turns control of the Speedway over to James Allison, one of his co-founders. A new flag stand at the start-finish line replaces a suspension bridge that had spanned the front straight.

For the first time, the Speedway posts $10,000 consolation money for those who finish outside the top 10. All 32 entries are single-seat cars.

Duesenberg bounces back from its poor showing the previous year to place four cars in the field, including the first three American cars with superchargers. Naturally aspirated Miller engines, however, power 14 of the 22 starters, including the three fastest qualifiers. Jimmy Murphy, the 1922 winner, sits on the pole with a non-record speed of 108.037 mph.

At the start, Joe Boyer dashes to the front from the second row in his Duesenberg and leads the first two laps. Duesenberg's fortunes quickly turn bad. Ernie Ansterburg, Boyer's teammate, crashes in Turn 2 on the second lap and Boyer develops supercharger problems a lap later. Boyer pits, giving the lead to Murphy, who engages in a see-saw battle with Earl Cooper until late in the race.

L. L. Corum starts 21st and runs fourth in the remaining supercharged Duesie until he pits on lap 110. Car owner Fred Duesenberg replaces him with Boyer, who steadily gains ground on the Miller-powered cars of Cooper and Murphy.

The hard-charging Boyer grabs the lead on lap 178 when Cooper pits for tires and pulls away to a one-minute, 24-second victory, winning at a record 98.23 mph. Boyer and Corum are the 500's first co-winners.

Miller-powered cars take eight of the first 10 spots, and Duesenberg the other two. Peter DePaolo finishes sixth in a naturally aspirated Duesie.

Wealthy owner-driver Cliff Durant, who reportedly spends millions trying to win the 500 during the 1920s, drives a strong race but runs out of gas half a lap from the checkered flag to finish 13th.

STARTING LINEUP

Average Field Qualifying Speed: 97.922

Numbers in flags indicate finish position

Tommy Milton

Earl Cooper

Antoine Mourre

Frank Elliott

Ira Vail

Harry Hartz

Bennett Hill

Cliff Durant

Jerry Wonderlich

Eddie Hearne

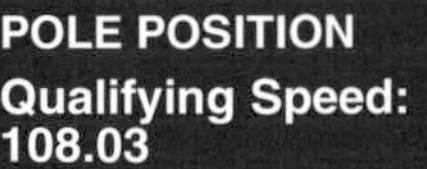
POLE POSITION
Qualifying Speed: 108.03

Jimmy Murphy

Joe Boyer

Jules Ellingboe

Ernie Ansterburg

Peter DePaolo

RESULTS

NO.	DRIVER	CAR	ENTRANT	ENGINE	CYL	DISP	CHASSIS	COLOR	QUAL SPD	START	FIN	LAPS / SPEED / REASON OUT
15	L. Corum-J. Boyer	Duesenberg	Duesenberg	Duesenberg	8	121	Duesenberg	maroon	93.333	21	1	200-98.23
8	Earl Cooper	Studebaker	Earl Cooper	Miller	8	121	Miller	green	103.900	6	2	200-97.79
2	Jimmy Murphy	Miller	Jimmy Murphy	Miller	8	121	Miller	gold	108.037	1	3	200-97.27
4	Harry Hartz	Durant	R. Cliff Durant	Miller	8	121	Miller	gray, blue	107.130	2	4	200-96.55
3	Bennett Hill	Miller	Harry A. Miller	Miller	8	121	Miller	red	104.840	5	5	200-96.46
12	Peter DePaolo	Duesenberg	Duesenberg Bros.	Duesenberg	8	121	Duesenberg	maroon	99.280	13	6	200-94.30
14	Fred Comer	Durant	R. Cliff Durant	Miller	8	121	Miller	gray, blue	92.880	16	7	200-93.43
6	Ira Vail	Ira Vail	Ira Vail	Miller	8	121	Miller	yellow	96.400	15	8	200-92.45
32	Antoine Mourre	Mourre	Antoine Mourre	Miller	8	121	Miller	red	99.490	9	9	200-91.76
19	Bob McDonogh	Miller	Harry A. Miller	Miller	8	121	Miller	red	91.550	18	10	200-90.51
18	Jules Ellingboe	Miller	Harry A. Miller	Miller	8	121	Miller	silver	102.600	7	11	200-90.47
7	Jerry Wonderlich	Durant	R. Cliff Durant	Miller	8	121	Miller	yellow	99.360	11	12	200-85.48
16	Cliff Durant	Durant	R. Cliff Durant	Miller	8	121	Miller	silver	101.610	8	13	199-out of gas
26	Bill Hunt	Barber-Warnock Ford	Barber-Warnock	Fronty-Ford	4	122	Ford T	red	85.040	19	14	191-flagged
31	Ora Haibe	Schmidt	Albert Schmidt	Mercedes	4	120	Mercedes	dark gray	92.810	17	15	182-flagged
28	Alfred E. Moss	Barber-Warnock Ford	Barber-Warnock	Fronty-Ford	4	122	Ford T	red	85.270	20	16	177-flagged
27	Fred Harder	Barber-Warnock Ford	Barber-Warnock	Fronty-Ford	4	122	Ford T	red	82.770	22	17	177-flagged
9	Joe Boyer	Duesenberg	Duesenberg Bros.	Duesenberg	8	121	Duesenberg	maroon	104.840	4	18	176-hit wall T1
1	Eddie Hearne	Durant	R. Cliff Durant	Miller	8	121	Miller	silver	99.230	14	19	151-fuel line
21	Frank Elliott	Miller	Frank R. Elliott	Miller	8	121	Miller	silver	99.310	12	20	149-gas tank
5	Tommy Milton	Miller	Tommy Milton	Miller	8	121	Miller	red, blue	105.200	3	21	110-gas tank
10	Ernie Ansterburg	Duesenberg	Duesenberg	Duesenberg	8	121	Duesenberg	maroon	99.400	10	22	1-wrecked BS

Bob McDonogh

L. L. Corum / Joe Boyer

Ora Haibe

Alfred E. Moss

Fred Comer

Bill Hunt

Fred Harder

Opening ceremonies had already become a major part of the event. A marching band follows the military procession for the posting of the colors on Memorial Day, 1924 (*opposite*). Drivers, crew members, and race officials pose for the traditional pre-race group photograph on the front straight (*above*). Although a V-8-powered Cole—another of the Indianapolis autos favored by Speedway management—was selected for pace-car honors, that didn't stop other manufacturers from trying to have their cars seen at the track. Lincoln supplied a phaeton for official use (*below*).

1925

13th Race • May 30, 1925

Harry Miller, after finishing second the previous year behind a supercharged Duesenberg, develops a supercharger of his own for 1925. The supercharged Miller that is the buzz of the garage area is the blue Junior 8 entered by Cliff Durant, the first front-drive car to compete in the May classic.

Built by Miller, the front-drive Junior 8 is low-slung, measuring just 36 inches tall at the top of the windshield, and features a low center of gravity. It is built for 1922 winner Jimmy Murphy, but Durant acquires it after Murphy dies in a racing accident.

Dave Lewis qualifies the front-drive Junior 8 at a record 109.061 mph. However, that is only fifth fastest, as five others shatter the old record of 108.17 on pole day. Leon Duray is fastest in a Miller at 113.196, nipping Peter DePaolo's Duesenberg by about one-tenth mph. Miller engines, 11 of them supercharged, power 16 of the 22 starters.

Firestone introduces the "balloon" tire, which requires just 30 pounds of pressure and inflates laterally as well as vertically to put a larger rubber patch on the track, making the cars faster in the turns.

The race is as fast as qualifying promises. DePaolo, the nephew of Ralph DePalma, gets the jump on Duray and leads at a record clip. Lewis takes over when DePaolo pits for relief to get his blistered hands bandaged.

An exhausted Lewis pits on Lap 173 for relief by Bennett Hill. DePaolo, now back in the No. 12 Duesie, regains the lead and puts the Junior 8 a lap down. Hill passes DePaolo once to get back on the lead lap, but runs out of time to mount a challenge. Duesenberg wins its second in a row.

DePaolo wins at a record 101.13 mph, the first to top 100 and finish in less than five hours. His 54-second margin is the narrowest to date.

Fire destroys the pagoda-style scoring and timing tower the day after the race.

The Rickenbacker Eight pace car, driven by its celebrated namesake, Capt. Eddie Rickenbacker, lines up at the head of the pack (*above*). Fire destroyed the Speedway's timing and scoring pagoda the day after the '25 race (*below*). Peter DePaolo won in a Duesenberg (*opposite top*) with Firestone's new low-pressure "balloon" tires. The inside of the front straight was a popular fan vantage point (*opposite bottom*).

STARTING LINEUP

Average Field Qualifying Speed: 104.488

Numbers in flags indicate finish position

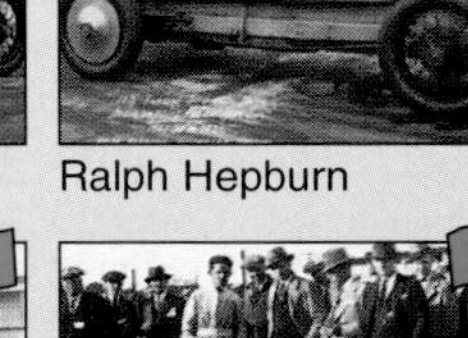

Harry Hartz (4) · Ralph Hepburn (16) · Peter Kreis (8) · Fred Comer (11) · Earl DeVore (13)

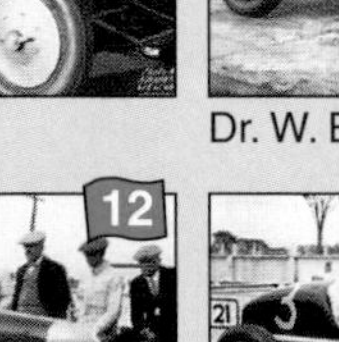

Peter DePaolo (1) · Dave Lewis (2) · Pietro Bordino (10) · Tommy Milton (5) · Dr. W. E. Shattuc (9)

POLE POSITION
Qualifying Speed: 113.196

Leon Duray (6) · Earl Cooper (17) · Jules Ellingboe (22) · Frank Elliott (12) · Bennett Hill (18)

RESULTS

NO.	DRIVER	CAR	ENTRANT	ENGINE	CYL	DISP	CHASSIS	COLOR	QUAL SPD	START	FIN	LAPS / SPEED / REASON OUT
12	Peter DePaolo	Duesenberg	Duesenberg Bros.	Duesenberg*	8	122	Duesenberg	banana, black	113.083	2	1	200-101.13
1	Dave Lewis	Junior 8	R. Cliff Durant	Miller**	8	121	Miller	blue	109.061	5	2	200-100.82
9	Phil Shafer	Duesenberg	Duesenberg Bros.	Duesenberg*	8	122	Duesenberg	green	103.523	22	3	200-100.18
6	Harry Hartz	Miller	Harry Hartz	Miller*	8	121	Miller	gray	112.433	3	4	200-98.89
4	Tommy Milton	Miller	Tommy Milton	Miller*	8	121	Miller	red, blue	104.366	11	5	200-97.26
28	Leon Duray	Miller	Harry Hartz	Miller*	8	121	Miller	maroon, gold	113.196	1	6	200-96.91
8	Ralph DePalma	Miller	Ralph DePalma	Miller*	8	122	Miller	cream	108.607	18	7	200-96.85
35	Peter Kreis	Duesenberg	Duesenberg Bros.	Duesenberg*	8	122	Duesenberg	maroon	106.338	9	8	200-96.32
15	Dr. W. E. Shattuc	Miller	Dr. W. E. Shattuc, M.D.	Miller*	8	121	Miller	red	102.070	14	9	200-95.74
22	Pietro Bordino	Fiat	Pietro Bordino	Fiat*	8	121	Fiat	red	107.661	8	10	200-94.75
5	Fred Comer	Miller	Harry Hartz	Miller*	8	121	Miller	lilac	104.296	12	11	200-93.67
27	Frank Elliott	Miller	Richard G. Doyle	Miller*	8	121	Miller	green, yellow	104.910	10	12	200-92.23
24	Earl DeVore	Miller	Bancroft & Pope	Miller*	8	121	Miller	silver	97.799	15	13	198-flagged
14	Bob McDonogh	Miller	Tommy Milton	Miller*	8	121	Miller	red, blue	101.931	20	14	188-truss rod
23	Wade Morton	Duesenberg	Duesenberg Bros.	Duesenberg*	8	122	Duesenberg	blue	95.821	16	15	156-wrecked T4
17	Ralph Hepburn	Miller	Earl Cooper	Miller	8	121	Miller	green, jade	108.489	6	16	144-gas tank
2	Earl Cooper	Miller	R. Cliff Durant	Miller	8	121	Miller	green	110.487	4	17	127-wrecked T1
3	Bennett Hill	Miller	Harry A. Miller	Miller*	8	121	Miller	red, silver	104.167	13	18	69-rear spring
29	Herbert Jones	Jones	Herbert Jones	Miller	8	121	Miller	white	89.401	17	19	69-wrecked SS
19	Ira Vail	R. J.	R. J. Johnson	Miller	8	121	Miller	blue	104.785	19	20	63-con. rod
17	M. C. Jones	Skelly	H. J. Skelly	Fronty-Ford	4	122	Ford T	unpainted	88.478	21	21	33-transmission
10	Jules Ellingboe	Miller	Jerry Wonderlich	Miller	8	121	Miller	brown	107.832	7	22	24-steering key

*Supercharged **Supercharged & Front Drive

Ralph DePalma

Harold Skelly (for M. C. Jones)

Herbert Jones

Bob McDonogh

Norman Batten (for Morton)

Ira Vail

Phil Shafer

Prototypes of anything seldom are as near perfection as Harry Miller's Junior 8. It represented the first successful application of the front-wheel-drive concept. Built for Jimmy Murphy, the light blue machine carried the number one, emblematic of Murphy's posthumously awarded 1924 national championship. In the 1925 Indianapolis 500, the Junior 8 carried Dave Lewis and Bennett Hill to a sensational second-place finish.

Front-drivers nearly crowded the conventional car off the nation's dangerous, wickedly fast board tracks in the Twenties. However, at Indianapolis, where Miller debuted his promising machine, the "pullers" won only six times in their long run at the Brickyard.

14th Race • May 31, 1926

Maximum engine displacement drops again, this time to 91.5 cubic inches from 122, as the Speedway tries to slow the cars. The minimum four-lap qualifying speed increases to 90 mph from 80 to tighten the field. A new pagoda on the front straight replicates the one that burned the previous year.

Rookie Frank Lockhart, an unknown 23-year-old dirt tracker from California, becomes a Cinderella story. Lockhart arrives at Indy as a relief driver for Peter Kreis, who becomes ill and withdraws.

Lockhart, in his first race on a paved track, guides Kreis's Miller to a one-lap qualifying record of 115.488 mph but shreds a tire before he completes four laps. One more attempt fails, and Lockhart makes the field on his final qualifying run at just 95.780 mph, good for 20th on the grid.

Earl Cooper earns the pole at a non-record 111.735 in a front-drive Miller, and Dave Lewis qualifies fourth in an identical car. These are the only front-drive cars, but all 28 starters are supercharged. Two Duesenbergs make the show, defending 500 winner Peter DePaolo and rookie Ben Jones with a two-cycle engine. Both are well off the pace.

A record crowd of 140,000 watches Lewis lead 43 laps and lap the field in his front-drive Miller before he drops out with valve trouble. Lockhart charges through the field and is fifth by lap four, second by lap 32. When rain halts the race on lap 72 for more than an hour, Lockhart is in front.

After the race resumes, Harry Hartz leads six laps in another Miller but can't keep pace with Lockhart, who pulls away and is two laps ahead when it rains again. Officials call the race at 400 miles.

Lockhart is the first rookie winner since 1914. His victory comes in the first race to be suspended by rain and the first to be shortened by rain. Hartz is runner-up for the third time in five years.

STARTING LINEUP

Average Field Qualifying Speed: 100.196

Numbers in flags indicate finish position

Leon Duray

Jules Ellingboe

Bon McDougall

Tony Gulotta

Ralph Hepburn

Harry Hartz

Phil Shafer

Frank Elliott

Cliff Durant

Cliff Woodbury

POLE POSITION
Qualifying Speed: 111.735

Earl Cooper

Dave Lewis

Bennett Hill

Dr. W. E. Shattuc

Fred Comer

RESULTS

NO.	DRIVER	CAR	ENTRANT	ENGINE	CYL	DISP	CHASSIS	COLOR	QUAL SPD	START	FIN	LAPS / SPEED / REASON OUT
15	Frank Lockhart	Miller	Peter Kreis	Miller*	8	90	Miller	white	95.780	20	1	160-95.885
3	Harry Hartz	Miller	Harry Hartz	Miller*	8	90	Miller	gray	109.542	2	2	158-94.481
36	Cliff Woodbury	Boyle	Cliff R. Woodbury	Miller*	8	90	Miller	red, silver	105.109	14	3	158-94.131
8	Fred Comer	Miller	Harry Hartz	Miller*	8	90	Miller	gray	100.612	13	4	155-92.323
12	Peter DePaolo	Duesenberg	Duesenberg Bros.	Duesenberg*	8	90	Duesenberg	cream	96.709	27	5	153-91.544
6	Frank Elliott	Miller	Frank Elliott	Miller*	8	91	Miller	grn,whte,yellow	105.873	8	6	152-90.917
14	Norman Batten	Miller	Norman Batten	Miller*	8	91	Miller	cream	101.428	16	7	151-90.275
19	Ralph Hepburn	Miller	Ralph Hepburn	Miller*	8	91	Miller	brown	102.517	15	8	151-89.882
18	John Duff	Elcar	Al Cotey	Miller*	8	91	Miller	blue	95.546	28	9	147-87.551
4	Phil Shafer	Miller	Phil Shafer	Miller*	8	90	Miller	yellow, red	106.647	5	10	146-87.096
31	Tony Gulotta	Miller	Harry Hartz	Miller*	8	91	Miller	gray	102.789	12	11	142-flagged
16	Bennett Hill	Miller	Harry A. Miller	Miller*	8	90	Miller	mroon,red,whte	105.876	7	12	136-flagged
33	Thane Houser	Abell	George G. Abell	Miller*	8	90	Miller	maroon, gold	93.672	21	13	102-flagged
27	W. Douglas Hawkes	Eldridge	E. A. D. Eldridge	Anzani	4	91	Eldridge	silver	94.977	17	14	91-frozen camshaf
1	Dave Lewis	Front Drive Miller	Harry A. Miller	Miller **	8	90	Miller	red, white	107.009	4	15	91-broken valve
5	Earl Cooper	Front Drive Miller	Harry A. Miller	Miller**	8	90	Miller	green	111.735	1	16	73-transmission
9	Cliff Durant	Locomobile Jr. 8	R. Cliff Durant	Locomobile*	8	90	Fengler	blue, white	104.855	11	17	60-gas tank leak
29	Ben Jones	Duesenberg 2-Cycle	Duesenberg Bros.	Duesenberg*	8	90	Duesenberg	mroon,crm,blk	92.142	18	18	54-wrecked
26	E. A. D. Eldridge	Eldridge	E. A. D. Eldridge	Anzani	4	91	Eldridge	green	89.777	23	19	45-tie rod
23	L. L. Corum	Schmidt	Albert Schmidt	Argyle*	6	91	Schmidt	light blue	88.849	24	20	44-shock absorbers
24	Steve Nemish	Schmidt	Albert Schmidt	Argyle*	6	91	Schmidt	light blue	92.937	22	21	41-transmission
7	Jules Ellingboe	Miller	F. P. Cramer	Miller*	8	90	Miller	mroon,red,crm	106.376	6	22	39-supercharger
10	Leon Duray	Locomobile Jr. 8	R. Cliff Durant	Locomobile*	8	90	Fengler	blue, white	109.186	3	23	33-broken axle
17	Fred Lecklider	Nickel Plate	Earl DeVore	Miller*	8	91	Miller	silver	100.398	26	24	24-con. rod
28	Jack McCarver	Hamlin Front Drive	Chevrolet Bros.	Fronty-Ford*	4	90	Ford T	red, white	86.418	25	25	23-con. rod
34	Bon McDougall	Miller	R. G. McDougall	Miller*	8	91	Miller	brown	105.180	9	26	19-valve
22	Dr. W. E. Shattuc	Miller	Dr. W. E. Shattuc, M.D.	Miller*	8	91	Miller	red	104.977	10	27	15-valve
39	Albert Guyot	Guyot	Albert Guyot	Argyle*	6	91	Schmidt	light blue	88.580	19	28	8-steering knuckle

*Supercharged **Supercharged & Front Drive

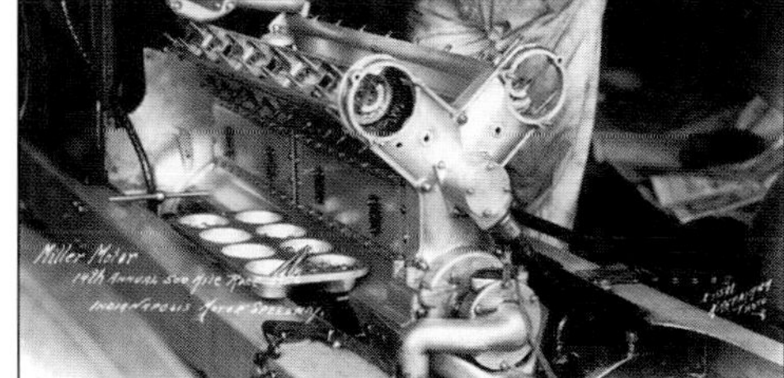

Using cars, ladders, and even utility poles, the infield crowd was resourceful in trying to get a clear view of the action (*opposite top*). The 500 was a marketing bonanza for car companies, including Willys-Knight, which touted its "Great Six" that was used as a police car at the track (*opposite middle*). A new five-story pagoda towers over the front straight and pit lane (*opposite bottom*). Three-time national champ Earl Cooper (*far left, top*) hit the wall in his front-drive Miller in practice (*top left*), but still made the race. With its bodywork removed, security guards survey the innards of E. A. D. Eldridge's car (*far left, bottom*). The supercharged Miller eight, shown without its cylinder heads (*bottom left*), powered 12 of the first 13 finishers, including winner Frank Lockhart.

Ben Jones

Thane Houser

L. L. Corum

Peter DePaolo

W. Douglas Hawkes

Frank Lockhart

E. A. D. Eldridge

Fred Lecklider

Norman Batten

Albert Guyot

Steve Nemish

Jack McCarver

John Duff

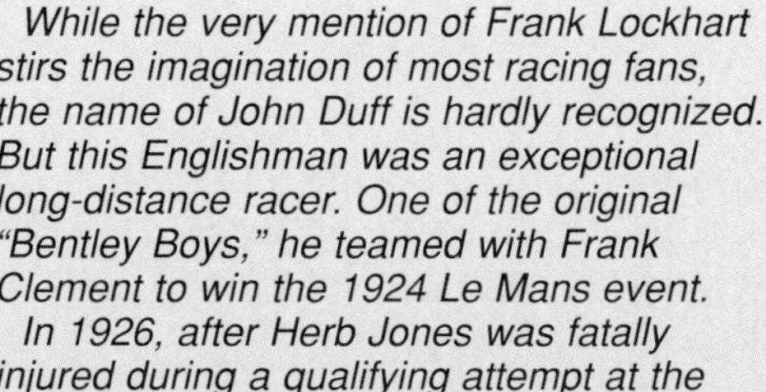

While the very mention of Frank Lockhart stirs the imagination of most racing fans, the name of John Duff is hardly recognized. But this Englishman was an exceptional long-distance racer. One of the original "Bentley Boys," he teamed with Frank Clement to win the 1924 Le Mans event.

In 1926, after Herb Jones was fatally injured during a qualifying attempt at the Speedway car owner Al Cotey hired Duff to drive his rebuilt Miller Special. Starting dead last, Duff ran a surprisingly consistent race, finishing an outstanding ninth.

Duff next drove the car to a third at the dangerously fast Altoona board track. But on July 5, he barely escaped with his life when his car pitched into the rail at the Rockingham board track. Badly injured, he never raced again.

15th Race • May 30, 1927

Frank Lockhart picks up where he left off in 1926. The defending 500 champ again sets a new qualifying mark, only this time he sustains it for the full four laps. Lockhart's rear-drive Miller averages 120.1 mph, nearly seven mph faster than the old record, set by Leon Duray in 1925.

Ralph Hepburn, Harry Hartz, and 1925 winner Peter DePaolo—the latter two in front-drive Millers—also top the old record in qualifying. From 41 entries, 33 cars qualify, the most since 1919. All average more than 100 mph for the fastest field in 500 history to date.

The number of front-drive cars in the field grows to 10, and all starters have supercharged straight eights. Two-time winner Tommy Milton starts 25th with a Miller engine that features the first use of an intercooler, which cools the air fed to the engine for more efficient combustion.

Lockhart charges ahead of the pack at the start and burns up the track in the early laps. Then on lap 24, it's Norman Batten's Miller that catches fire—literally. With flames and smoke pouring from his gas tank, Batten drives the length of the front straight and safely steers away from the pits and other cars before bailing out.

Lockhart leads until he pits on lap 82. Dutch Baumann takes over for 10 laps, but drops out with a broken pinion gear. Lockhart charges back to the front only to suffer a broken connecting rod. He leads 110 of the first 120 laps before retiring. DePaolo, in relief of Bob McDonogh, leads 30 laps in a front-drive Miller until he slows with a misfiring engine.

Newcomer George Souders, a dirt track star who starts 22nd, inherits the lead and builds a two-lap cushion in the same Duesenberg DePaolo drove to victory in 1925.

Babe Stapp is running second in relief of Benny Shoaff when he loses the drive gear on his Duesenberg two laps from the end. Souders cruises to an easy eight-lap victory over Earl DeVore, who finishes the 500 miles 12 minutes later, the widest margin since 1913.

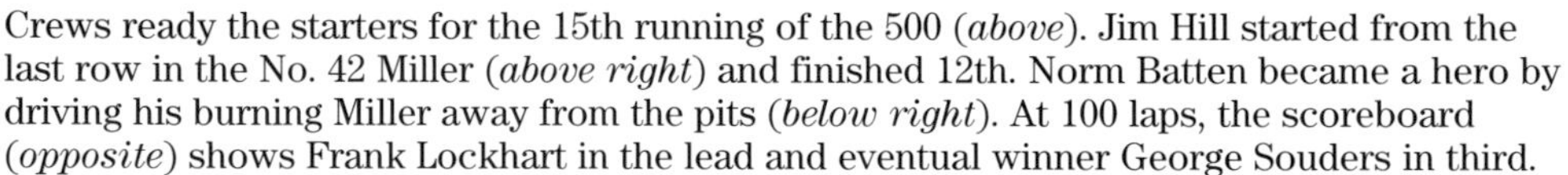
Crews ready the starters for the 15th running of the 500 (*above*). Jim Hill started from the last row in the No. 42 Miller (*above right*) and finished 12th. Norm Batten became a hero by driving his burning Miller away from the pits (*below right*). At 100 laps, the scoreboard (*opposite*) shows Frank Lockhart in the lead and eventual winner George Souders in third.

STARTING LINEUP

Average Field Qualifying Speed: 110.183

Numbers in flags indicate finish position

Leon Duray

Cliff Woodbury

Bennett Hill

Peter Kreis

Earl DeVore

Peter DePaolo

Ralph Hepburn

Dave Lewis

Jack Petticord

Cliff Bergere

POLE POSITION
Qualifying Speed: 120.100

Frank Lockhart

Harry Hartz

Bob McDonogh

Norman Batten

Frank Elliott

RESULTS

NO.	DRIVER	CAR	ENTRANT	ENGINE	CYL	DISP	CHASSIS	COLOR	QUAL SPD	START	FIN	LAPS / SPEED / REASON OUT
32	George Souders	Duesenberg	William S. White	Duesenberg*	8	90	Duesenberg	gray, black	111.551	22	1	200-97.545
10	Earl DeVore	Miller	F. P. Cramer	Miller*	8	90	Miller	red, white, blk	107.497	15	2	200-93.868
27	Tony Gulotta	Miller	Anthony Gulotta	Miller*	8	90	Miller	blue, white	107.765	27	3	200-93.139
29	Wilbur Shaw	Jynx	Fred Clemons	Miller*	8	90	Miller	gold	104.465	19	4	200-93.110
21	Dave Evans	Duesenberg	David E. Evans	Duesenberg*	8	91	Duesenberg	red, blue, wht	107.360	28	5	200-90.782
14	Bob McDonogh	Cooper	Cooper Engineering Co.	Miller**	8	90	Cooper	yellow, black	113.175	7	6	200-90.410
16	Eddie Hearne	Miller	Harry Hartz	Miller*	8	90	Miller	gray, blue	105.115	18	7	200-90.064
6	Tommy Milton	Detroit	Tommy Milton	Miller**	8	90	Detroit	gray, silver	108.758	25	8	200-85.081
25	Cliff Bergere	Miller	Muller Bros.	Miller*	8	91	Miller	green	108.820	14	9	200-79.929
5	Frank Elliott	Junior 8	Frank Elliott	Miller**	8	91	Miller	red, white	109.682	13	10	200-78.244
31	Fred Frame	Miller	O. B. Dolfinger	Miller*	8	90	Miller	blue	106.859	33	11	199-flagged
42	Jim Hill	Nickel Plate	Earl DeVore	Miller*	8	90	Miller	silver	107.392	32	12	197-flagged
24	Benny Shoaff	Perf. Circle Dsnbrg.	Duesenberg Bros.	Duesenberg*	8	91	Duesenberg	red, blue	110.152	31	13	198-rear end gears
41	Wade Morton	Thompson Valve	Duesenberg Bros.	Duesenberg*	8	91	Duesenberg	red, blue	108.075	26	14	152-wrecked (Winnai)
44	Al Melcher	Miller	Charles Haase	Miller*	8	90	Miller	green	102.918	20	15	144-supercharger
43	Louis Schneider	Miller	Fred Lecklider	Miller*	8	91	Miller	tan	109.910	23	16	137-timing gears
9	Peter Kreis	Cooper	Cooper Engineering Co.	Miller**	8	90	Cooper	yellow, black	109.900	12	17	123-bent front axle
2	Frank Lockhart	Perfect Circle Miller	Frank S. Lockhart	Miller*	8	90	Miller	white	120.100	1	18	120-con. rod
15	Cliff Woodbury	Boyle Valve	Cliff Woodbury	Miller*	8	90	Miller	wht, blue, red	113.200	6	19	108-supercharger
26	"Dutch" Baumann	Miller	Harry S. Miller	Miller*	8	90	Miller	yellow	106.078	17	20	90-pinion shaft
35	Al Cotey	Elcar	Al Cotey	Miller*	8	91	Miller	—	106.295	29	21	87-universal joint
17	Dr. W.E. Shattuc	Miller	Dr. W. E. Shattuc, M.D.	Miller*	8	91	Miller	red, white	107.060	16	22	83-valve
23	Fred Lecklider	Elgin Piston Pin	Henry Kohlert	Miller*	8	91	Miller	black, white	105.729	30	23	49-wrecked T1 (Kohlert)
19	Ralph Hepburn	Boyle Valve	Cliff Woodbury	Miller*	8	91	Miller	white	114.209	5	24	39-leaking fuel tank
1	Harry Hartz	Erskine Miller	Harry Hartz	Miller**	8	90	Miller	gray, blue	116.739	4	25	38-crankshaft
3	Peter DePaolo	Perfect Circle Miller	Peter DePaolo	Miller**	8	90	Miller	banana, black	119.510	2	26	31-supercharger gears
12	Leon Duray	Miller Front Drive	Leon Duray	Miller**	8	90	Miller	black, white	118.788	3	27	26-leaking fuel tank
4	Bennett Hill	Cooper	Cooper Engineering Co.	Miller**	8	90	Miller	yellow, black	112.013	9	28	26-rear spring shackle bolt
18	Jules Ellingboe	Cooper	Earl Cooper	Miller**	8	90	Miller	yellow, black	113.239	21	29	25-wrecked
8	Norman Batten	Miller	Norman K. Batten	Miller*	8	90	Fengler	red, silver	111.940	10	30	24-caught fire
38	Babe Stapp	Duesenberg	Duesenberg Bros.	Duesenberg*	8	91	Duesenberg	brown, white	109.555	24	31	24-universal joint
22	Jack Petticord	Boyle Valve	Cliff Woodbury	Miller*	8	91	Miller	wht, blue, red	109.920	11	32	22-supercharger
7	Dave Lewis	Miller Front Drive	Dave Lewis	Miller**	8	90	Miller	white, red	112.275	8	33	21-front spring pad

*Supercharged **Supercharged & Front Drive

When Lafayette, Indiana, native George Souders won the Indianapolis grind in '27, it was the greatest surprise in 500 history. A product of local dirt track racing, the first-time entrant ran among the top 10 most of the way. On a sweltering day, Souders was the only driver in the top 17 finishers to make the trip solo. When he took the checkered flag, the young Hoosier held a better than 12-minute advantage over second place Earl DeVore.

Crowd control was not what it is today. While still seated in his car in Victory Lane, frenzied fans plucked buttons and other souvenirs from the exhausted driver's coveralls and the winning car. When officials asked Souders what they could do for him, George mumbled that he wanted to send a telegram. They figured he wanted to inform a prospective sponsor or some oil company of his success.

"Who shall we send the telegram to?" they asked. "There's nobody but mother," Souders replied. "And I'll send that myself pretty soon."

Eddie Hearne

Jules Ellingboe

Babe Stapp

Tony Gulotta

Fred Lecklider

Fred Frame

Dutch Baumann

Al Melcher

Louis Schneider

Wade Morton

Al Cotey

Jim Hill

Dr. W. E. Shattuc

Wilbur Shaw

George Souders

Tommy Milton

Dave Evans

Benny Shoaff

1928

16th Race • May 30, 1928

The Speedway is under new management. World War I flying ace Eddie Rickenbacker, a veteran of four 500s, buys out the original owners before the 1928 race and becomes the new president. Notably absent is popular 1926 winner Frank Lockhart, who dies a month before the race at Daytona Beach.

Leon Duray earns his second pole, driving a front-drive Miller to a 122.391-mph average for four laps and 124.018 for one lap, both records. Cliff Woodbury also breaks the previous record and lines up second.

A qualifying crash injures 1925 winner Pete DePaolo. His crew fixes the front-drive Miller in time for Wilbur Shaw to qualify. DePaolo watches the race from a stretcher, and Shaw places 25th, dropping out with a bad timing gear.

Clarence Belt qualifies the first V-8-powered car, entered by the Green Engineering Co. He lasts just 32 laps before dropping a valve. Dutch Baumann and 1924 co-winner L. L. Corum wreck their Duesenbergs in practice on race-day morning and are unable to start.

Duray's Miller is fastest in the early going. He leads 59 laps, but develops overheating problems and parks on lap 134. Jimmy Gleason in a Duesie and Tony Gulotta in a Miller swap the lead in a fierce battle until Gulotta stalls with fuel problems with about 20 laps to go.

Gleason appears to have the race won when he stops for water on lap 195. A crew member aims for the radiator, but stumbles and douses the magneto instead. This knocks a frustrated Gleason out of the race and hands the lead to Louis Meyer.

Driving a two-year-old rear-drive Miller, Meyer runs a steady race and hangs on to beat a closing Lou Moore by 44 seconds, the closest finish yet.

Meyer, a 23-year-old dirt track star, wins in his first start. (He drove in relief of Shaw in 1927, however.)

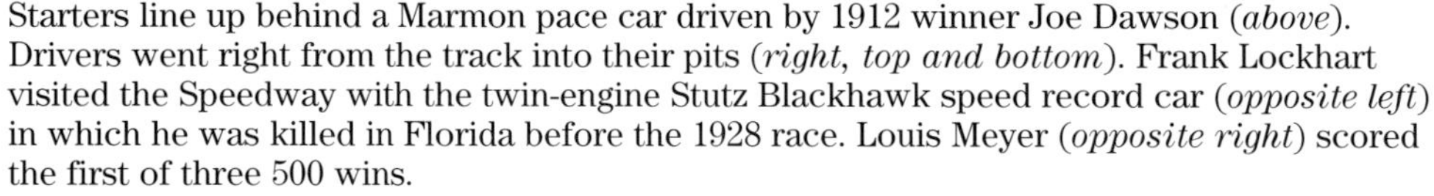

Starters line up behind a Marmon pace car driven by 1912 winner Joe Dawson (*above*). Drivers went right from the track into their pits (*right, top and bottom*). Frank Lockhart visited the Speedway with the twin-engine Stutz Blackhawk speed record car (*opposite left*) in which he was killed in Florida before the 1928 race. Louis Meyer (*opposite right*) scored the first of three 500 wins.

STARTING LINEUP

Average Field Qualifying Speed: 109.841

Numbers in flags indicate finish position

Cliff Bergere

Ralph Hepburn

Fred Comer

George Souders

Norman Batten

Cliff Woodbury

Babe Stapp

Lou Moore

Johnny Seymour

Fred Frame

POLE POSITION
Qualifying Speed: 122.391

Leon Duray

Tony Gulotta

Louis Schneider

Ray Keech

Lou Meyer

RESULTS

NO.	DRIVER	CAR	ENTRANT	ENGINE	CYL	DISP	CHASSIS	COLOR	QUAL SPD	START	FIN	LAPS / SPEED / REASON OUT
14	Lou Meyer	Miller	Alden Sampson II	Miller*	8	90	Miller	gold, black	111.352	13	1	200-99.482
28	Lou Moore	Miller	Charles Haase	Miller*	8	90	Miller	red, white	113.826	8	2	200-99.241
3	George Souders	State Auto Ins.	William S. White	Miller*	8	90	Miller	blue, white	111.444	12	3	200-98.034
15	Ray Keech	Simplex Piston Ring	M. A. Yagle	Miller*	8	90	Miller	white, blue	113.421	10	4	200-93.320
22	Norman Batten	Miller	Norman K. Batten	Miller*	8	90	Fengler	red, silver	106.585	15	5	200-93.228
7	Babe Stapp	Miller	Phil Shafer	Miller**	8	90	Miller	gold, blk, wht	116.887	5	6	200-92.638
43	Billy Arnold	Boyle Valve	Boyle Valve Co.	Miller*	8	90	Miller	wht, blue, red	111.926	20	7	200-91.111
27	Fred Frame	State Auto Ins.	William S. White	Duesenberg*	8	91	Duesenberg	blue, white	107.501	14	8	200-90.079
25	Fred Comer	Boyle Valve	Boyle Valve Co.	Miller**	8	90	Miller	wht, blue, red	113.690	9	9	200-88.889
8	Tony Gulotta	Stutz Blackhawk	J. R. Burgamy	Miller*	8	90	Miller	white, black	117.031	4	10	200-88.888
24	Louis Schneider	Armacost Miller	Louis F. Schneider	Miller*	8	91	Miller	red, silver	114.036	7	11	200-87.964
12	Dave Evans	Boyle Valve	Boyle Valve Co.	Miller*	8	90	Miller	wht, blue, red	108.264	23	12	200-87.401
29	Henry Kohlert	Elgin Piston Pin	Elgin Piston Pin Co.	Miller*	8	91	Miller	red, white	93.545	28	13	180-flagged
23	Deacon Litz	Miller	A. B. Litz	Miller*	8	91	Miller	cream, black	106.213	17	14	161-flagged
39	Jimmy Gleason	Duesenberg	H. C. Henning	Duesenberg*	8	91	Duesenberg	maroon	111.708	21	15	195-magneto
5	Cliff Durant	Detroit	Tommy Milton	Miller**	8	90	Detroit	blk, red, white	99.990	18	16	175-supercharger
33	Johnny Seymour	Marmon	Cooper Engineering Co.	Miller**	8	90	Cooper	yellow, black	111.673	11	17	170-supercharger
6	Earl DeVore	Chromolite	Metals Protection Co.	Miller*	8	90	Miller	chrome, red	109.810	24	18	161-wrecked T1
4	Leon Duray	Miller	Leon Duray	Miller**	8	90	Miller	black, white	122.391	1	19	133-overheating
38	Sam Ross	Aranem	Reed & Mulligan	Miller**	8	90	Miller	red, black	106.572	16	20	132-timing gears
26	Ira Hall	Duesenberg	Henry Maley	Duesenberg*	8	91	Duesenberg	blue, red	96.886	27	21	115-wrecked T1
32	Peter Kreis	Marmon	Cooper Engineering Co.	Miller**	8	90	Cooper	yellow, black	112.906	19	22	73-rod bearings
10	Cliff Woodbury	Boyle Valve	Boyle Valve Co.	Miller**	8	90	Miller	wht, red, blue	120.418	2	23	55-timing gears
16	Ralph Hepburn	Miller	Harry A. Miller	Miller**	8	90	Miller	drk. blue, wht	116.354	6	24	48-timing gears
1	Wilbur Shaw	Flying Cloud	Peter DePaolo	Miller**	8	90	Miller	banana, black	100.956	29	25	42-timing gears
18	Benny Shoaff	Duesenberg	Duesenberg Bros.	Duesenberg*	8	91	Duesenberg	blue, red	102.409	26	26	35-wrecked T1
41	C. W. Belt	Green	Green Engineering Co.	Green*	8	91	Green	—	96.026	25	27	32-valve
21	Cliff Bergere	Miller	Cliff Bergere	Miller**	8	90	Miller	red, white	119.956	3	28	7-supercharger
34	Russ Snowberger	Cooper	Cooper Engineering Co.	Miller**	8	90	Miller	yellow, black	111.618	22	29	4-supercharger

*Supercharged **Supercharged & Front Drive

Cliff Durant

Jimmy Gleason

Earl DeVore

Ira Hall

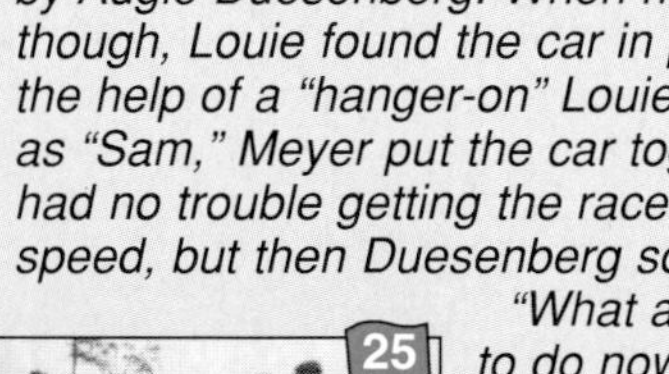

Rookie Louie Meyer was promised a car by Augie Duesenberg. When he came for it, though, Louie found the car in pieces. With the help of a "hanger-on" Louie only knew as "Sam," Meyer put the car together. He had no trouble getting the racer up to speed, but then Duesenberg sold the car.

"What are we going to do now?" Sam asked. "I'm looking around to see who this 'we' is," said a disgruntled Meyer.

Then Phil Shafer's Miller came up for sale. "Sam" revealed himself to be Alden Sampson II, one of the richest young men in America. He bought the car, and Meyer won the 500 with it.

Deacon Litz

Billy Arnold

Dave Evans

Benny Shoaff

Wilbur Shaw

Sam Ross

Peter Kreis

Russell Snowberger

C. W. Belt

Henry Kohlert

1929

17th Race • May 30, 1929

Front-drive Millers occupy the entire front row. Cliff Woodbury is on the pole, the fastest of 33 qualifiers at a non-record 120.599 mph. Leon Duray and Ralph Hepburn line up alongside in cars Duray owns. In all, 12 front-drive cars start the 17th Memorial Day classic.

Duray bolts in front of Woodbury to lead the first lap, and it goes downhill from there for the polesitter. Woodbury crashes in Turn 3 on the fourth lap and is out of the race.

Bill Spence's Duesenberg hits the Turn 2 wall six laps later, and he is thrown from the car when it flips over. Spence dies of a fractured skull.

Duray loses the lead after seven laps. Deacon Litz, who is running third, reaches for his handbrake only to find it has fallen off. He steers down to the inside of the track and, unable to slow down, skids sideways past Duray and Hepburn into the lead. Litz stays in front until a burned rod sidelines him on lap 57.

Louis Meyer and Lou Moore, the previous year's 1-2 finishers, battle for the lead over the next 200 miles. Meyer leads 65 laps and is well ahead when he makes his final pit stop on lap 157 for oil. He stalls, and it takes seven minutes to restart his Miller, handing the lead to Ray Keech.

Moore is the only serious threat to catch Keech, but he breaks a rod two laps from the finish. Keech coasts to a six-minute, 24-second victory over Meyer, who recovers from his disastrous pit stop to finish second.

A Miller engine wins for the second straight year and three of the last four. Firestone tires win for the 10th time in a row, and rear-wheel drive triumphs over front-wheel drive again.

Keech, competing in his second 500, drives a Miller designed and built by the late Frank Lockhart, the 1926 winner. Keech dies just two weeks later in a racing accident in Altoona, Pennsylvania.

Leon Duray jumps out to the lead as the Studebaker President pace car exits the track at the start of the 1929 race (*above*). *Below:* Drivers (from left) Ralph Hepburn, Leon Duray, Fred Winnai, and (far right) Babe Stapp take time out for a smoke and a bite to eat with mechanic Cotton Henning (center) and two unidentified race-team members. French automaker Delage, which won the 1914 race, returned to the Brickyard with a twin-cam straight-eight (*opposite left*). Maintaining correct tire pressure was critical to "balloon" tires (*opposite right*).

STARTING LINEUP

Average Field Qualifying Speed: 110.954

Numbers in flags indicate finish position

Ralph Hepburn

Ray Keech

Deacon Litz

Bill Spence

Jules Moriceau

Leon Duray

Peter DePaolo

Lou Meyer

Tony Gulotta

Louis Chiron

POLE POSITION
Qualifying Speed: 120.599

Cliff Woodbury

Babe Stapp

Billy Arnold

Russell Snowberger

Lou Moore

RESULTS

NO.	DRIVER	CAR	ENTRANT	ENGINE	CYL	DISP	CHASSIS	COLOR	QUAL SPD	START	FIN	LAPS / SPEED / REASON OUT
2	Ray Keech	Simplex Piston Ring	M.A. Yagle	Miller*	8	90	Miller	white, blue	114.905	6	1	200-97.585
1	Lou Meyer	Miller	Alden Sampson II	Miller*	8	90	Miller	white, black	114.704	8	2	200-95.596
53	Jimmy Gleason	Duesenberg	A. S. Duesenberg	Duesenberg*	8	91	Duesenberg	blue, red	110.345	23	3	200-93.699
43	Carl Marchese	Marchese	Marchese Bros.	Miller*	8	92	Miller	white	108.440	25	4	200-93.541
42	Freddy Winnai	Duesenberg	A. S. Duesenberg	Duesenberg*	8	91	Duesenberg	maroon	113.892	21	5	200-88.792
48	"Speed" Gardner	Chromolite	F. P. Cramer	Miller*	8	90	Miller	black	105.985	28	6	200-88.390
6	Louis Chiron	Delage	Louis Chiron	Delage*	8	90	Delage	blue	107.351	14	7	200-87.728
9	Billy Arnold	Boyle Valve	Cliff R. Woodbury	Miller*	8	90	Miller	white, red	114.752	7	8	200-83.909
25	Cliff Bergere	Armacost Miller	Cliff Bergere	Miller**	8	90	Miller	red, silver	103.687	32	9	200-80.703
34	Fred Frame	Cooper	Cooper Engineering Co.	Miller**	8	90	Cooper	yellow, black	111.328	22	10	193-flagged
28	Frank Brisko	Burbach	Frank Brisko	Miller*	8	89	Miller	white	105.857	29	11	180-flagged
17	Phil Shafer	Miller	Phil Shafer	Miller **	8	90	Miller	black, silver	111.628	18	12	150-flagged
3	Lou Moore	Majestic Miller	Charles Haase	Miller*	8	90	Miller	green, white	110.677	13	13	198-con. rod
36	Frank Farmer	Miller	William Albertson	Miller*	8	91	Miller	red, silver	107.972	26	14	140-supercharger
49	Wes Crawford	Miller	Marian Batten	Miller*	8	90	Fengler	red	108.607	24	15	127-carburetor
4	Peter Kreis	Detroit	Tommy Milton	Miller**	8	90	Detroit	black, white	112.528	17	16	91-engine seized
23	Tony Gulotta	Packard Cable	Leon Duray	Miller*	8	90	Miller	violet, yellow	112.146	11	17	91-supercharger
5	Bob McDonogh	Miller Front Drive	M. R. Dodds	Miller**	8	90	Miller	blue, white	111.614	19	18	74-oil tank
46	Bill Lindau	Pittsburgh Miller	Painter & Hufnagle	Miller*	8	88	Miller	orange	102.509	33	19	70-valve
31	Herman Schurch	Armacost Miller	Fred Schneider	Miller*	8	91	Miller	red, white	107.477	27	20	70-gas tank split
38	Johnny Seymour	Cooper	Cooper Engineering Co.	Miller**	8	90	Cooper	yellow, black	114.307	16	21	65-rear axle
21	Leon Duray	Packard Cable	Leon Duray	Miller**	8	90	Miller	violet, yellow	119.087	2	22	65-carburetor
29	Rick Decker	Miller	Rickliffe Decker	Miller*	8	91	Miller	cream	105.288	30	23	61-supercharger
26	Deacon Litz	Rusco Durac	A. B. Litz	Miller*	8	90	Miller	white, black	114.526	9	24	56-con. rod
27	Albert Karnatz	Richards Bros.	Reed & Mulligan	Miller**	8	91	Miller	red, white	104.749	31	25	50-gas leak
47	Ernie Triplett	Buckeye Duesenberg	C. H. Cunard	Duesenberg*	8	91	Duesenberg	brown	114.789	20	26	48-con. rod
12	Russ Snowberger	Cooper	Cooper Engineering Co.	Miller**	8	90	Cooper	yellow, black	113.622	10	27	45-supercharger
32	Babe Stapp	Spindler Miller	William S. White	Miller*	8	90	Duesenberg	wht, blue, red	115.618	4	28	40-universal joint
35	Jules Moriceau	Thompson Prod.	Thompson Products, Inc.	Amilcar*	6	78	Amilcar	yellow, black	105.609	15	29	30-wrecked T4
37	Peter DePaolo	Boyle Valve	Cliff R. Woodbury	Miller**	8	90	Miller	wht, red, blue	115.093	5	30	25-steering
18	Ralph Hepburn	Packard Cable	Leon Duray	Miller**	8	90	Miller	violet, yellow	116.543	3	31	14-transmission
10	Bill Spence	Duesenberg	A. S. Duesenberg	Duesenberg*	8	91	Duesenberg	lavender, blk	111.649	12	32	14-wrecked T2
8	Cliff Woodbury	Boyle Valve	Cliff R. Woodbury	Miller**	8	90	Miller	wht, red, blue	120.599	1	33	3-wrecked T4

*Supercharged **Supercharged & Front Drive

In 1927, Norman Batten became an instant hero when he piloted his flaming racer past the pit area before jumping to safety. The photo of his daring deed went round the world.

A veteran of America's board and dirt tracks, Batten was a talented, intensely brave driver. He'd finished seventh in the rain-shortened '26 Indy classic, and with relief help from Zeke Meyer, brought his Miller home fifth in 1928. In the latter event, he was treated for burns on his right foot and leg. This resulted from a persistent oil leak, which began almost from the outset of the event. Most drivers would have given up, but not Batten.

At various times, his red Miller was entered under his wife's name. And so, to the casual fan, when his racer was entered at Indianapolis in 1929, they never noticed when Wes Crawford drove Marian Batten's Miller to 15th place. But that was because the hero of 1927 was already dead.

On November 12, 1928, Batten and fellow driver Earl DeVore were lost in the sinking of the SS Vestris. *It was believed both men were the victims of shark attacks. Batten was helping pull survivors from the shark-infested waters when the end came. No one would have expected any less from him.*

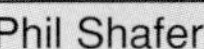

Phil Shafer

Fred Winnai

Wesley Crawford

Herman Schurch

Rick Decker

Bill Lindau

Peter Kreis

Ernie Triplett

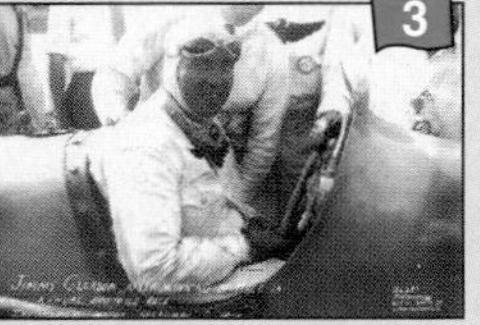

Jimmy Gleason

Frank Farmer

Frank Brisko

Cliff Bergere

Johnny Seymour

Bob McDonogh

Fred Frame

Carl Marchese

W. H. "Speed" Gardner

Albert Karnatz

18th Race • May 30, 1930

The Depression brings a new era to the Speedway. New rules require two-man cars and riding mechanics again, and engines of up to 366 cubic inches with two valves per cylinder. Superchargers are allowed only on two-cycle engines. Minimum qualifying speed drops to 85 mph from 90, and the number of starting positions increases to 40.

Critics call it the "Junkyard Formula," but the Speedway makes the changes to lower the cost of racing and promote the use of production cars and engines. Instead of $15,000 purpose-built race cars with exotic engines, there are entries such as Chet Miller's Fronty-Ford, a nearly stock four-cylinder Model T that sells for $2300.

Qualifying speeds drop and 38 cars start, the most since 1911. Nineteen drivers make their debuts, tying the 1919 record. No cars are supercharged, but two use 16-cylinder engines: a Maserati that lasts just seven laps before ignition problems set in and a Miller that 1928 winner Louis Meyer drives to fourth place. Meyer qualifies second with his 201-cid 16-cylinder—two Miller straight eights linked to one crankshaft—and leads the first two laps.

Polesitter Billy Arnold passes Meyer on the third lap and leads the remaining 198 laps, a record that still stands. He finishes more than seven minutes ahead of Shorty Cantlon's Miller four-cylinder. Arnold earns a record $50,300 of the $96,250 purse, including lap money.

Arnold's eight-cylinder Miller, built for racing and owned by former driver Harry Hartz, is the first front-drive car to win.

Mishaps mark this year's race. Chet Gardner spins his Duesenberg on the first lap and retires, becoming the first driver to exit before completing a lap. A multi-car wreck in Turn 3 on the 23rd lap knocks seven cars out of the race, though there are no serious injuries.

Seven laps later, riding mechanic Paul Marshall dies when his brother, Cy Marshall, crashes through the Turn 3 wall.

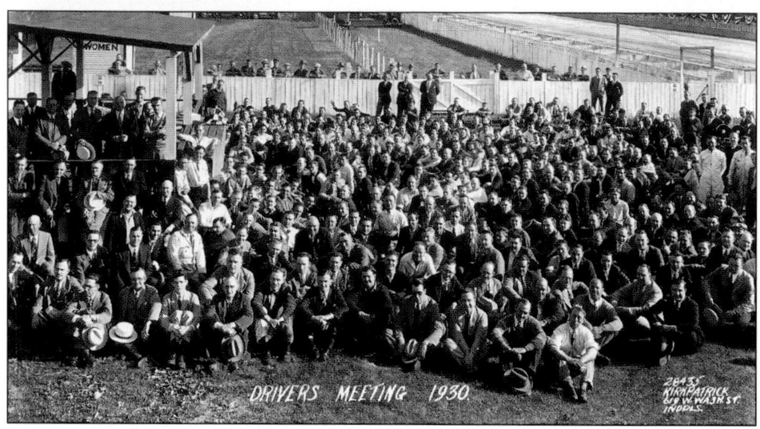

The Cord L-29 pace car, driven by Wade Morton, leads the 38 starters to the green flag (*top*). Chet Gardner, in the middle of the second row, spun in Turn 1 on the opening lap and was out of the race. Drivers, car owners, and crew members gather for the annual pre-race meeting in the infield (*above*). A victorious Billy Arnold, with riding mechanic Spider Matlock (*opposite*), led a record 198 laps. Car owner Harry Hartz is hatless and happy standing behind the number 4 car. Hartz finished second three times as a driver.

STARTING LINEUP Average Field Qualifying Speed: 98.989 Pole Position Qualifying Speed: 113.268

Numbers in flags indicate finish position

Shorty Cantlon

Ernie Triplett

Leslie Allen

Lou Moore

Chet Miller

Johnny Seymour

Peter DePaolo

Lou Meyer

Chet Gardner

Phil Shafer

Frank Farmer

Joe Caccia

L. L. Corum

Tony Gulotta

Billy Arnold

Louis Schneider

Russell Snowberger

Cy Marshall

J. C. McDonald

Claude Burton

Charles Moran

RESULTS

NO.	DRIVER	CAR	ENTRANT	ENGINE	CYL	DISP	CHASSIS	COLOR	QUAL SPD	START	FIN**	LAPS / SPEED / REASON OUT
4	Billy Arnold	Miller-Hartz	Harry Hartz	Miller*	8	152	Summers	gray, blue	113.268	1	1	200-100.448
16	Shorty Cantlon	Miller Schofield	William S. White	Miller	4	183	Stevens	white, red, blk	109.810	3	2	200-98.054
23	Louis Schneider	Bowes Seal Fast	Louis F. Schneider	Miller	8	121	Stevens	white, blk, red	106.107	4	3	200-96.752
1	Lou Meyer	Sampson	Alden Sampson, II	Miller	16	201	Stevens	white	111.290	2	4	200-95.253
6	Bill Cummings	Duesenberg	Peter DePaolo	Duesenberg	8	244	Stevens	banana, black	106.173	22	5	200-93.579
24	Dave Evans	Jones & Maley	David E. Evans	Miller*	8	138	Stevens	cream	97.342	33	6	200-92.571
15	Phil Shafer	Coleman Frnt Drive	Coleman Motors Corp.	Miller*	4	183	Coleman	black	102.279	8	7	200-90.921
22	Russ Snowberger	Russell "8"	Russell Snowberger	Studebaker	8	336	Snowberger	tan	104.577	7	8	200-89.166
25	Leslie Allen	Allen Miller Prod.	Leslie Allen	Miller	4	183	Miller	black, red	101.919	9	9	200-85.749
27	L. L. Corum	Stutz	Milton Jones	Stutz	8	322	Stutz	blue, white	94.130	17	10	200-85.340
38	Claude Burton	V8	Ira Vail	Oakland	8	251	Oakland	white, black	95.087	16	11	196-flagged
42	Letterio Cucinotta	Maserati	Letterio Piccolo Cucinotta	Maserati	8	122	Maserati	red	91.584	30	12	185-flagged
41	Chet Miller	Fronty	Thomas J. Mulligan	Fronty-Ford	4	176	Ford T	grn, blk, wht	97.360	15	13	161-flagged
46	Harry Butcher	Butcher Bros.	Harry M. Butcher	Buick	6	332	Buick	orange	87.003	38	14	127-flagged
10	Mel Keneally	MAVV	J. Talbot, Jr.	Miller	4	150	Whippet	black	103.327	23	15	114-valve
21	Zeke Meyer	Miller	Zeke Meyer	Miller	8	138	Miller	—	95.357	34	16	115-con. rod
17	Ernie Triplett	Guiberson	Allen Guiberson	Miller	4	183	Whippet	white	105.618	6	17	125-piston
35	J. C. McDonald	Romthe	William H. Richards	Studebaker	8	336	Studebaker	blue, wht, blk	98.953	13	18	112-leaking fuel tank
28	Roland Free	Slade	Julius C. Slade	Chrysler	6	268	Chrysler	white, black	89.639	37	19	69-clutch
9	Tony Gulotta	MAVV	J. Talbot, Jr.	Miller	4	150	Whippet	black	100.033	20	20	79-valve
33	Frank Farmer	Betholine Miller	M. A. Yagle	Miller	8	101	Miller	—	100.615	11	21	69-wrecked
44	Bill Denver	Nardi	Gabriel Nardi	Duesenberg	8	260	Duesenberg	black, white	90.650	35	22	41-connecting rod
34	Joe Huff	Gauss Front Drive	Herman N. Gauss	Miller*	8	100	Cooper	yellow, black	101.178	26	23	48-valve
3	Wilbur Shaw	Empire State	Empire State Motors	Miller	8	152	Smith	blk, white, red	106.132	25	24	54-wrist pin
29	Joe Caccia	Alberti	William Alberti	Duesenberg	8	260	Duesenberg	blue	97.606	14	25	43-wrecked (Decker)
36	Cy Marshall	Duesenberg	George A. Henry	Duesenberg	8	262	Duesenberg	green	100.846	10	26	29-wrecked T3
32	Charles Moran	du Pont	du Pont Motors, Inc.	du Pont	8	322	du Pont	cream	89.733	19	27	22-wrecked T3
7	Jimmy Gleason	Waverly Oil	Thomas J. Mulligan	Miller	8	125	Miller	white	93.709	24	28	22-wrecked T3
14	Lou Moore	Coleman Frnt Drive	Coleman Motors Corp.	Miller*	4	183	Coleman	white	99.867	12	29	23-wrecked T3
12	Deacon Litz	Duesenberg	Henry W. Maley	Duesenberg	8	150	Duesenberg	cream, gold	105.755	31	30	22-wrecked T3
8	Babe Stapp	Duesenberg	A. S. Duesenberg	Duesenberg	8	143	Duesenberg	blue, silver	104.950	32	31	18-wrecked T3
39	Johnny Seymour	Gauss Front Drive	Herman N. Gauss	Miller*	8	100	Cooper	yellow, black	93.376	18	32	21-wrecked T3
5	Peter DePaolo	Duesenberg	Peter DePaolo	Duesenberg	8	244	Stevens	banana, black	99.956	21	33	19-wrecked T3 (R. Roberts)
45	Marion Trexler	Trexler	M. M. Lain, Jr.	Lycoming	8	298	Auburn	silver	92.978	29	34	19-wrecked T3
19	Speed Gardner	Miller Front Drive	W. H. Gardner	Miller*	8	151	Miller	orange, silver	95.585	27	35	14-loose main bearing
26	Baconin Borzachini	Maserati	Alfieri Maserati	Maserati	16	244	Maserati	red	95.213	28	36	7-magneto, plugs
48	Rick Decker	Hoosier Pete	Clemons Motors, Inc.	Clemons	4	197	Mercedes	white	92.293	36	37	8-oil tank
18	Chet Gardner	Buckeye	James H. Booth	Duesenberg	8	150	Duesenberg	green	105.811	5	38	0-spun T1

*Front drive **Positions scored in the order in which cars left the track

During the race, Chet Miller's Fronty-Ford broke a front spring. The crew had no spare, so Chet and a mechanic ran to the parking lot, where they discovered a spectator's Ford Model T with just what they were seeking. The Fronty, borrowed spring and all, finished 13th. After the race, Chet put the part back on the fan's Model T and offered to pay for its use. "No sirree," the fan said. "It's enough for me to be able to say part of my car ran in the 500."

Jimmy Gleason

Speed Gardner

Letterio Cucinotta

Dave Evans

Rick Decker

Mel Keneally

Joe Huff

Marion Trexler

Babe Stapp

Bill Denver

Harry Butcher

Bill Cummings

Wilbur Shaw

Baconin Borzachini

Deacon Litz

Zeke Meyer

Roland Free

19th Race • May 30, 1931

A record 70 entries fill Gasoline Alley for practice and qualifying, as the rules instituted the previous year attract new contestants. Exotic Millers and Duesenbergs built for racing now compete for starting spots against production chassis with "stock-block" engines from car companies such as Studebaker, Hudson, Chrysler, Buick, and Ford.

Russ Snowberger wins the pole at 112.796 mph with a Studebaker eight. Defending 500 champ Billy Arnold later posts the fast time of 116.080 in his front-drive Miller.

Forty cars start the race, tying the record set in 1911. Rain delays the start two hours and forces part of the race to run under caution. Only one supercharged car is in the show, a two-cycle 16-cylinder driven by veteran Leon Duray. He parks after six laps because of overheating.

Arnold is a jackrabbit. He starts 18th, zips to the front by the seventh lap, and leads 155 laps.

Wilbur Shaw, driving a Duesenberg in relief of Phil Pardee, loses control on lap 60 and goes over the Turn 3 wall. Unhurt, he walks back to the pits and later relieves Jimmy Gleason, who finishes sixth.

On lap 162, Arnold is five laps ahead when his rear axle breaks. As he spins, he is hit by another car, sending him over the Turn 4 wall. A wheel flies off his car and kills an 11-year-old boy on Georgetown Road. Arnold breaks his pelvis and riding mechanic Spider Matlock breaks a shoulder.

Louis Schneider, in a rear-drive Miller, leads the last 34 laps to beat Fred Frame's Duesie by 43 seconds.

Dave Evans is the tortoise of the race. He qualifies the first diesel engine, a 361-cid Cummins four-cylinder, at 96.871 mph, slowest in the field. With his fuel-sipping diesel, Evans is the first to complete 500 miles non-stop. He averages 16 mpg, compared to about 10 for most gas engines, and finishes 13th.

STARTING LINEUP

Average Field Qualifying Speed: 106.673 Pole Position Qualifying Speed: 112.796

Numbers in flags indicate finish position

Paul Bost

Babe Stapp

Stubby Stubblefield

Luther Johnson

Chet Miller

Billy Arnold

Francis Quinn

Bill Cummings

Ernie Triplett

Fred Frame

Phil Pardee

Cliff Bergere

Dave Evans

Jimmy Gleason

Russell Snowberger

Deacon Litz

Speed Gardner

Ralph Hepburn

Louis Schneider

Joe Russo

Tony Gulotta

RESULTS

NO.	DRIVER	CAR	ENTRANT	ENGINE	CYL	DISP	CHASSIS	COLOR	QUAL SPD	START	FIN	LAPS / SPEED / REASON OUT
23	Lou Schneider	Bowes Seal Fast	B. L. Schneider	Miller	8	151	Stevens	wht, blk, red	107.210	13	1	200-96.629
34	Fred Frame	Duesenberg	Harry Hartz	Duesenberg	8	150	Duesenberg	blue, white	109.273	8	2	200-96.406
19	Ralph Hepburn	Harry Miller	Ralph Hepburn	Miller	8	230	Miller	brown	107.933	10	3	200-94.224
21	Myron Stevens	Jadson	Louis Meyer	Miller	8	230	Stevens	cream	107.463	35	4	200-94.142
4	Russ Snowberger	Russell "8"	Russell Snowberger	Studebaker	8	336	Snowberger	tan	112.796	1	5	200-94.090
33	Jimmy Gleason	Duesenberg	Denny Duesenberg	Duesenberg	8	243	Duesenberg	orange, white	111.400	20	6	200-93.605
25	Ernie Triplett	Buckeye	James H. Booth	Duesenberg	8	151	Duesenberg	black, red	111.034	5	7	200-93.041
36	Stubby Stubblefield	Jones-Miller	Milton Jones	Miller	4	183	Willys-Knight	black, white	108.797	9	8	200-92.424
28	Cliff Bergere	Elco Royale	Elco Grease & Oil Co.	Reo	8	358	Reo	blue, wht, red	106.781	14	9	200-91.839
27	Chet Miller	Marr	R. G. "Buddy" Marr	Hudson	8	234	Hudson	blue, silver	106.185	15	10	200-89.580
44	George Howie	G.N.H.	George N. Howie	Chrysler	8	356	Dodge	beige	102.844	30	11	200-87.651
12	Phil Shafer	Shafer "8"	Phil Shafer	Buick	8	270	Rigling	red, blk, silver	105.103	23	12	200-86.391
8	Dave Evans	Cummins Diesel	Cummins Engine Co.	Cummins	4	361	Duesenberg	white, blue	96.871	17	13	200-86.107
72	Al Aspen	Alberti	William Alberti	Duesenberg	8	266	Duesenberg	black, white	102.509	31	14	200-85.764
59	Sam Ross	Miller	William M. Yahr	Miller	4	158	Rigling	white	104.642	37	15	200-85.139
69	Joe Huff	Goldberg Bros.	S. C. Goldberg	Miller*	8	100	Cooper	brown	102.386	40	16	180-flagged
5	Deacon Litz	Maley	Henry Maley	Duesenberg	8	151	Duesenberg	rust, black	111.531	4	17	177-wrecked T1 (Cummings)
37	Tony Gulotta	Hunt	D. A. "Ab" Jenkins	Studebaker	8	337	Rigling	green, gold	111.725	19	18	167-wrecked T4
1	Billy Arnold	Miller-Hartz	Harry Hartz	Miller*	8	151	Summers	gray, blue	116.080	18	19	162-wrecked T4
57	Luther Johnson	Bill Richards	William H. Richards	Studebaker	8	336	Studebaker	orange, black	107.652	12	20	156-wrecked T4
55	Billy Winn	Hoosier Pete	F. E. Clemons	Clemons	8	226	Rigling	silver	105.405	36	21	138-flagged
16	Frank Brisko	Brisko-Atkinson	Frank Brisko	Miller	8	151	Stevens	white, red	106.286	27	22	138-steering arm
26	Gene Haustein	Fronty-Ford	Fronty-Ford Sales of Mich.	Fronty-Ford	4	219	Ford T	grn, blk, white	108.395	34	23	117-lost wheel
41	Joe Russo	Russo	George A. Henry	Duesenberg	8	260	Rigling	white	104.822	16	24	109-oil leak
17	Speed Gardner	Nutmeg State	C. E. Ricketts	Miller*	8	151	Miller	red	109.820	7	25	107-frame
14	Lou Moore	Boyle Valve	M.J. Boyle	Miller	8	230	Miller	cream, blk, red	103.725	38	26	103-differential
2	Shorty Cantlon	Harry Miller	William S. White	Miller	16	301	Miller	white, red	110.372	26	27	88-con. rod
3	Bill Cummings	Empire State	Empire State Gas Motors	Miller	8	215	Cooper	black, red	112.563	2	28	70-oil line
24	Freddy Winnai	Bowes Seal Fast	B. L. Schneider	Miller	8	122	Stevens	white, blk, red	105.899	28	29	60-wrecked NS
32	Phil Pardee	Duesenberg	Phil Pardee	Duesenberg	8	243	Duesenberg	orange, white	107.772	11	30	60-wrecked T3 (Shaw)
31	Paul Bost	Empire State	Empire State Gas Motors	Miller	8	215	Rigling	blk, red, silver	112.125	3	31	35-crankshaft
35	Frank Farmer	Jones-Miller	Milton Jones	Miller	4	183	Willys-Knight	maroon	108.303	22	32	32-rod bearing
58	George Wingerter	Wingerter	George Wingerter	Duesenberg	8	266	Duesenberg	dark red	100.139	32	33	29-fuel tank
7	Lou Meyer	Sampson	Alden Sampson II	Miller	16	200	Stevens	white	113.953	25	34	28-oil leak
39	Babe Stapp	Rigling & Henning	Rigling & Henning	Duesenberg	8	260	Rigling	black	110.125	6	35	9-oil leak/clutch
48	John Boling	Morton & Brett	Grapho Metal Packing Co.	M & B	8	226	M & B	white	102.860	24	36	7-con. rod
54	Leon Duray	Duray	Leon Duray	Duray**	16	230	Stevens:Whippet	black, white	103.134	29	37	6-overheating
49	Harry Butcher	Butcher Bros.	Harry H. Butcher	Buick	8	273	Buick	orange	99.343	33	38	6-wrecked T4
10	Herman Schurch	Hoosier Pete	F. E. Clemons	Clemons	8	226	Rigling	gold	102.845	39	39	5-transmission
67	Francis Quinn	Tucker Tappett	James H. Wade	Ford A	4	221	Miller	black, red	111.321	21	40	3-rear axle

*Front drive **Supercharged, 2-cycle engine

Paul Bost jumps into the lead from the outside of row one at the start (*opposite top*). The scoreboard (*opposite bottom*) shows Billy Arnold leading after 20 laps, Bill Cummings in second, and Bost third. Pre-race events included the band performance in front of the main grandstand (*opposite, middle left*). Anyone who wanted to play an instrument could join in. The infield (*opposite, middle right*) as seen from the pagoda looking toward Turn 4. Lou Schneider's Bowes Seal Fast Special (*right*) cruised to victory after Arnold crashed on lap 162.

John Boling

Frank Brisko

George Howie

Harry Butcher

Billy Winn

Herman Schurch

Phil Shafer

Shorty Cantlon

Leon Duray

George Wingerter

Myron Stevens

Lou Moore

Frank Farmer

Lou Meyer

Freddy Winnai

Al Aspen

Gene Haustein

Sam Ross

Joe Huff

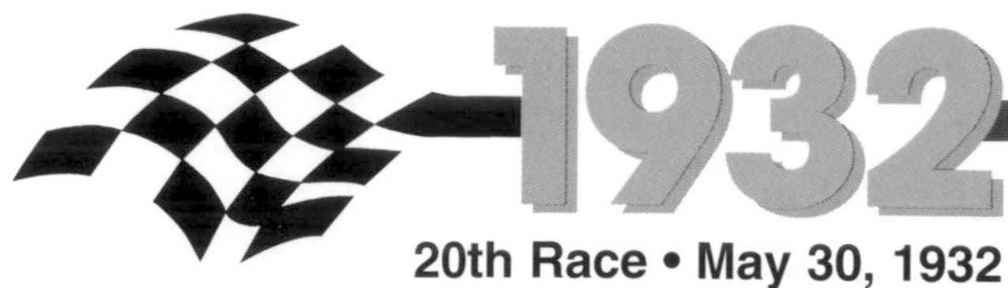

1932

20th Race • May 30, 1932

With a record 72 entries and new minimum qualifying speed of 100 mph, there is more competition for the 40 starting positions this year.

Lou Moore earns the pole in a rear-drive Miller eight at 117.363 mph, the fastest time in three years. Kelly Petillo, in a Whippet powered by a Miller four-cylinder, is the slowest of the starters at 104.645.

Moore leads the first lap, but 1930 winner Billy Arnold, who starts second, charges to the fore on the second lap. Arnold leads at a record clip until disaster strikes on lap 59.

Arnold spins to avoid another car and goes over the Turn 3 wall. Just as in the previous year, both Arnold and riding mechanic Spider Matlock are hurt. This year, Arnold suffers a broken shoulder and Matlock a broken pelvis, the opposite of 1931. After this, Arnold retires from racing.

After Arnold's wreck, rookie Bob Carey leads until lap 90, when he spins and hits a wall. He limps to the pits for repairs and manages to finish fourth.

Four others work their way up to first place, but can't hold it as attrition mounts. On lap 143, Fred Frame becomes the eighth different driver to lead the grueling race, breaking the previous record of seven set in three races.

Frame starts 27th (furthest back for any winner except Ray Harroun) in a front-drive Miller and averages 104.144 mph, breaking Pete DePaolo's 1925 record speed by nearly three mph. He cruises home 44 seconds ahead of rookie Howdy Wilcox II (no relation to the 1919 winner) to give the car owner, Harry Hartz, his second victory in three years.

Wrecks and mechanical failures claim 26 cars. Among the survivors, Cliff Bergere finishes third in a factory Studebaker and Russell Snowberger is fifth in a Hupmobile. Two of the early dropouts, Gus Schrader and Bob McDonogh, are in the first four-wheel-drive cars to compete in the 500, Miller chassis with Miller V-8 engines.

The crowd presses in for a close look at the field prior to the race start (*above left*). The five cars of the Studebaker factory team (*above right*) were easily identified by their distinctive grilles. Cliff Bergere (second from left) drove the highest-finishing Studebaker, coming in third. Hudson also made the show; its race car is dwarfed by a Hudson Greater Eight sedan (*left*). Wilbur Shaw, with mechanic Dean DuChemin (*opposite left*), led 27 laps before a broken rear axle knocked out the No. 3 Miller, owned by Ralph Hepburn, who is on the right. *Opposite right:* Henry Ford, left, with Speedway official Gar Wood and Barney Oldfield, was a visitor even though his company's cars weren't in the race this year. (A Lincoln was the '32 pacesetter, however.)

STARTING LINEUP

Average Field Qualifying Speed: 111.269 Pole Position Qualifying Speed: 117.363

Numbers in flags indicate finish position

Bryan Saulpaugh

Howdy Wilcox II

Billy Winn

Bill Cummings

Joe Huff

Al Miller

Joe Russo

Billy Arnold

Ira Hall

Paul Bost

Luther Johnson

Bob Carey

Peter Kreis

Tony Gulotta

Lou Moore

Russell Snowberger

Lou Meyer

Cliff Bergere

Frank Brisko

Wes Crawford

Deacon Litz

RESULTS

NO.	DRIVER	CAR	ENTRANT	ENGINE	CYL	DISP	CHASSIS	COLOR	QUAL SPD	START	FIN	LAPS / SPEED / REASON OUT
34	Fred Frame	Miller-Hartz	Harry Hartz	Miller*	8	182	Wetteroth	gray, blue	113.856	27	1	200-104.144
6	Howdy Wilcox II	Lion Head	William Cantlon	Miller	4	220	Stevens	crm, red, blue	113.468	6	2	200-103.881
22	Cliff Bergere	Studebaker	The Studebaker Corp.	Studebaker	8	337	Rigling	maroon, white	111.503	10	3	200-102.662
61	Bob Carey	Meyer	Louis Meyer	Miller	8	249	Stevens	cream	111.070	14	4	200-101.363
4	Russ Snowberger	Hupp Comet	Russell Snowberger	Hupmobile	8	361	Snowberger	tan	114.326	4	5	200-100.791
37	Zeke Meyer	Studebaker	The Studebaker Corp.	Studebaker	8	337	Rigling	green, white	110.745	38	6	200-98.476
35	Ira Hall	Duesenberg	G. B. Hall	Duesenberg	8	243	Stevens	blue	114.206	5	7	200-98.207
65	Freddy Winnai	Foreman Axle Shaft	Henry Maley	Duesenberg	8	151	Duesenberg	gray	108.755	35	8	200-97.437
2	Billy Winn	Duesenberg	Fred Frame	Duesenberg	8	151	Duesenberg	wht, blue, blk	111.801	9	9	200-97.421
55	Joe Huff	Highway Parts	S. C. Goldberg	Cooper*	16	183	Cooper	black, silver	110.402	15	10	200-87.586
33	Phil Shafer	Shafer "8"	Phil Shafer	Buick	8	272	Rigling	black, silver	110.708	26	11	197-flagged
36	Kelly Petillo	Jones-Miller	Milton Jones	Miller	4	190	Whippet	green, blue	104.645	40	12	189-flagged
25	Tony Gulotta	Studebaker	The Studebaker Corp.	Studebaker	8	337	Rigling	gray, blue	108.896	20	13	184-flagged
15	Stubby Stubblefield	Gilmore	Sparks & Weirick	Miller	4	220	Adams	cream, red	112.899	25	14	178-flagged
18	Peter Kreis	Studebaker	The Studebaker Corp.	Studebaker	8	337	Rigling	blue	110.270	17	15	178-wrecked T1
46	Luther Johnson	Studebaker	The Studebaker Corp.	Studebaker	8	337	Rigling	steel, silver	111.218	11	16	164-lost wheel FS
3	Wilbur Shaw	Miller	Ralph Hepburn	Miller	8	230	Miller	cream, red	114.326	22	17	157-rear axle
24	Deacon Litz	Bowes Seal Fast	John Rutner	Duesenberg	8	151	Duesenberg	white, blk, red	109.546	19	18	152-con. rod
10	Bill Cummings	Bowes Seal Fast	B. L. Schneider	Miller	8	151	Stevens	white, blk, red	111.204	12	19	151-crankshaft
57	Malcolm Fox	Richards	William H. Richards	Studebaker	8	336	Studebaker	blue, black	111.149	32	20	132-spring
9	Chet Miler	Hudson	R. G. "Buddy" Marr	Hudson	8	255	Hudson	blue, silver	111.053	29	21	125-engine trouble
7	Ernie Triplett	Floating Power	William S. White	Miller	4	220	Miller	orange, black	114.935	31	22	125-clutch
1	Louis Schneider	Bowes Seal Fast	B. L. Schneider	Miller	8	151	Stevens	white, blk, red	110.681	30	23	125-frame
41	Joe Russo	Art Rose	George A. Henry	Duesenberg	8	261	Rigling	white	108.791	21	24	107-con. rod
8	Lou Moore	Boyle Valve	M. J. Boyle	Miller	8	268	Miller	wht, red, blue	117.363	1	25	79-timing gear
14	Juan Gaudino	Golden Seal	Juan Gaudino	Chrysler	8	358	Chrysler	green	107.466	36	26	71-clutch
29	Al Miller	Hudson	R. G. "Buddy" Marr	Hudson	8	255	Hudson	blue, silver	110.129	18	27	66-engine trouble
42	Doc MacKenzie	Brady	Ray T. Brady	Studebaker	8	337	Studebaker	lavender, wht	108.154	39	28	65-engine trouble
32	Frank Brisko	Brisko-Atkinson	F. Brisko & D. Atkinson	Miller*	8	151	Stevens	cream, red	111.149	13	29	61-clutch
72	Ray Campbell	Folly Farm	E. D. Stairs, Jr.	Graham	8	245	Graham	blue	108.969	34	30	60-crankshaft
5	Billy Arnold	Miller-Hartz	Harry Hartz	Miller	8	151	Summers	gray, blue	116.290	2	31	59-wrecked T3
27	Bryan Saulpaugh	Harry Miller	William S. White	Miller	16	303	Miller	cream	114.369	3	32	55-oil line
16	Lou Meyer	Sampson	Alden Sampson II	Miller	16	220	Stevens	white, black	112.471	7	33	50-crankshaft
21	Al Aspen	Brady & Nardi	G. Nardi & Ray Brady	Studebaker	8	340	Duesenberg	black, red	108.008	23	34	31-con. rod
49	Johnny Kreiger	Consumers Petrol.	Fred P. Duesenberg	Duesenberg	8	138	Duesenberg	—	109.276	33	35	30-con. rod
48	Wes Crawford	Boyle Valve	M. J. Boyle	Duesenberg*	8	137	Miller	wht, red, blue	110.396	16	36	28-crankshaft
17	Paul Bost	Empire State	Paul B. Bost	Miller*	8	215	Cooper	red	111.885	8	37	18-crankshaft
58	Bob McDonogh	Miller FWD	Four Wheel Drive Auto Co.	Miller**	8	308	Miller	cream, red	113.276	24	38	17-oil line
45	Gus Schrader	Harry Miller	William Burden	Miller**	8	308	Miller	red, cream	112.003	28	39	7-wrecked T4
26	Al Gordon	Lion Tamer	G. D. Harrison	Miller	4	220	Miller	blue, white	111.290	37	40	3-wrecked T4

*Front drive **Four-wheel drive

At 225 miles, young Bob Carey had taken a long lead when he spun in some oil and hit the wall twice. Although records show him in the pits for 10 minutes, many claim it took at least 12 to 15 minutes to remove a damaged wheel and replace a broken spring clip.

Driving like a man possessed, Carey came back to finish a sensational fourth. "That spin through the oil was the second wildest ride I ever took in a race car," said Carey's veteran mechanic, Lawson "Useless" Harris. When asked what the wildest ride had been, Harris said: "The last 100 laps, when Bob tried to come back and win it!"

38 Bob McDonogh

1 Fred Frame

23 Louis Schneider

35 Johnny Kreiger

26 Juan Gaudino

28 Doc MacKenzie

34 Al Aspen

11 Phil Shafer

21 Chet Miller

20 Malcolm Fox

8 Freddy Winnai

6 Zeke Meyer

17 Wilbur Shaw

14 Stubby Stubblefield

39 Gus Schrader

22 Ernie Triplett

30 Ray Campbell

40 Al Gordon

12 Kelly Petillo

21st Race • May 30, 1933

The number of starting positions increases to 42, the most ever. New rules call for 10-lap time trials instead of four, and cars must have on-board starters for the first time.

Bill Cummings wins the pole at 118.53 mph in a rear-drive Miller eight-cylinder, nipping Frank Brisko's four-wheel-drive Miller four-cylinder by just .142 mph.

Howdy Wilcox II, the previous year's runner-up, qualifies sixth fastest, but is disqualified when officals discover he has diabetes. The other drivers protest, and the Speedway agrees at the 11th hour to let Mauri Rose substitute for Wilcox. Rose starts 42nd and works his way up to fourth before retiring with a bad timing gear.

At the start, Cummings leads from the pole and gets a strong challenge from Fred Frame, who starts on the outside of row one. Frame leads 37 laps, but exits on lap 85 with a broken valve. Brisko's four-wheel-drive car drops out of contention early with oil problems.

Cummings sets the pace for 32 laps before he retires on lap 136 with a leaky radiator. Teammate Babe Stapp charges from his 29th starting spot and runs in front for 60 laps. Cars can carry only 15 gallons of fuel this year (most carried 40 gallons previously), and Stapp runs out of gas on lap 157 while running fourth.

Louis Meyer starts sixth, bides his time as other front runners drop out, and leads 71 laps enroute to a three-lap victory over Wilbur Shaw. Meyer joins Tommy Milton as the only two-time winners and is the first to guzzle milk in victory lane. His winning speed of 104.162 breaks the record set in 1932 by .018 mph.

Three men die in the race. A single-car crash on lap 80 kills newcomer Mark Billman and seriously injures his riding mechanic. On lap 133, Lester Spangler, also a rookie, rides over a wheel on Malcolm Fox's spinning car. Spangler flips, and both he and mechanic G. L. Gordon die.

When heavy rains doused Indy, canoes set the fastest lap times (*top left*). FWD trucks towed swamped cars (*top right*). Kids competed in a "pushmobile" race (*middle*). Track owner Eddie Rickenbacker rests on an Oldsmobile provided to the Speedway (*above*). *Opposite:* Lou Meyer gets to victory lane (left). Firestone technicians pose for a portrait (middle). Bill DeVore and Wilbur Shaw enjoy a "cold one" (right).

STARTING LINEUP

Average Field Qualifying Speed: 112.426 Pole Position Qualifying Speed: 118.530

Numbers in flags indicate finish position

Fred Frame

Louis Meyer

Cliff Bergere

Tony Gulotta

Chet Gardner

L. L. Corum

Louis Schneider

Frank Brisko

Ernie Triplett

Ira Hall

Peter Kreis

Deacon Litz

Russell Snowberger

Luther Johnson

Bill Cummings

Lou Moore

Lester Spangler

Stubby Stubblefield

Shorty Cantlon

Zeke Meyer

Bennett Hill

RESULTS

NO.	DRIVER	CAR	ENTRANT	ENGINE	CYL	DISP	CHASSIS	COLOR	QUAL SPD	START	FIN	LAPS / SPEED / REASON OUT
36	Lou Meyer	Tydol	Lou Meyer	Miller	8	258	Miller	cream, red	116.977	6	1	200-104.162
17	Wilbur Shaw	Mallory	Leon Duray	Miller	4	220	Stevens	black, white	115.497	23	2	200-101.765
37	Lou Moore	Foreman Axle	Maley & Scully	Miller	4	255	Duesenberg	gray, red	117.843	4	3	200-101.599
21	Chet Gardner	Sampson Radio	Alden Sampson II	Miller	16	201	Stevens	white, black	112.319	15	4	200-101.182
8	Stubby Stubblefield	Shafer "8"	Phil Shafer	Buick	8	284	Rigling	black	114.784	10	5	200-100.762
38	Dave Evans	Art Rose	Arthur E. Rose	Studebaker	8	260	Rigling	rose, silver	109.448	36	6	200-100.425
34	Tony Gulotta	Studebaker	Studebaker Corp.	Studebaker	8	336	Rigling	white, blue	113.578	12	7	200-99.071
4	Russ Snowberger	Russell "8"	Russell Snowberger	Studebaker	8	336	Snowberger	tan, black	110.769	17	8	200-99.011
9	Zeke Meyer	Studebaker	Studebaker Corp.	Studebaker	8	336	Rigling	blue, silver	111.099	16	9	200-98.122
46	Luther Johnson	Studebaker	Studebaker Corp.	Studebaker	8	336	Rigling	black, silver	110.097	20	10	200-97.393
6	Cliff Bergere	Studebaker	Studebaker Corp.	Studebaker	8	336	Rigling	maroon, silver	115.643	9	11	200-97.286
47	L. L. Corum	Studebaker	Studebaker Corp.	Studebaker	8	336	Rigling	green, silver	110.465	18	12	200-96.458
49	Willard Prentiss	Jack O. Carr	J. W. Kleinschmidt	Duesenberg	8	365	Rigling	black, red	107.776	40	13	200-93.595
14	Raul Riganti	Golden Seal	Raul Riganti	Chrysler	8	305	Chrysler	green	108.081	27	14	200-93.244
29	Gene Haustein	Martz	Lawrence J. Martz	Hudson	8	235	Hudson	orange	107.603	28	15	197-flagged
26	Deacon Litz	Bowes Seal Fast	A. B. Litz	Miller	4	220	Miller	white, blk, red	113.138	14	16	197-flagged
18	Joe Russo	Wonder Bread	F. P. Duesenberg	Duesenberg	8	275	Duesenberg	wht, red, blue	112.531	31	17	192-flagged
51	Doc MacKenzie	Brady	Ray T. Brady	Studebaker	8	340	Duesenberg	black, red	108.073	39	18	192-rear axle
27	Kelly Petillo	Yahr-Miller	William M. Yahr	Miller	4	213	Smith	cream, red	113.037	25	19	168-spun and stalled
28	Chet Miller	Marr	R. G. "Buddy" Marr	Hudson	8	255	Hudson	blue, silver	112.025	32	20	163-con. rod
19	Al Miller	Marr	R. G. "Buddy" Marr	Hudson	8	255	Hudson	blue, silver	109.799	24	21	161-con. rod
68	Bennett Hill	Goldberg Bros.	S. C. Goldberg	Cooper*	16	190	Cooper	blue, red	110.264	19	22	158-con. rod
45	Babe Stapp	Boyle Products	M. J. Boyle	Miller*	4	221	Miller	wht, blue, red	116.626	29	23	156-out of gas
32	Wesley Crawford	Boyle Products	Frank Brisko	Miller*	8	151	Stevens	cream, red	109.862	26	24	147-wrecked T1 (Winn)
5	Bill Cummings	Boyle Products	M. J. Boyle	Miller	8	270	Miller	white, red	118.530	1	25	136-leaking radiator
15	Lester Spangler	Miller	Harry Hartz	Miller	4	255	Miller	gray, blue	116.903	7	26	132-wrecked T1
65	Freddy Winnai	Kemp	James Kemp	Duesenberg	8	154	Duesenberg	white, purple	110.018	35	27	125-engine trouble
57	Malcolm Fox	Universal Service	William Richards	Studebaker	8	337	Studebaker	blue, black	112.922	30	28	121-wrecked T1
12	Fred Frame	Miller-Hartz	Harry Hartz	Miller	8	182	Wetteroth	gray, blue	117.864	3	29	85-valve
64	Mark Bilman	Kemp-Mannix	James Kemp	Duesenberg	8	265	Duesenberg	white, red	112.410	22	30	79-wrecked T2
53	Johnny Sawyer	Lencki-Madis	Lencki & Unger	Miller	4	220	Miller	blue, red	110.590	34	31	77-clutch
2	Peter Kreis	Frame-Miller	Fred Frame	Miller	8	151	Summers	blue	114.370	11	32	63-universal joint
16	Ernie Triplett	Floating Power	William S. White	Miller	4	220	Weil	red, white	117.685	5	33	61-piston
25	Shorty Cantlon	Sullivan & O'Brien	William Cantlon	Miller	4	220	Stevens	tan, silver	113.384	13	34	50-con. rod
3	Mauri Rose	Gilmore	Joe Marks	Miller	8	248	Stevens	red, silver	117.649	42	35	48-timing gears
58	Frank Brisko	F.W.D.	F.W.D. Auto Co.	Miller**	8	308	Miller	cream, red	118.388	2	36	47-oil too hot
10	Ira Hall	Denny Duesenberg	Denny Duesenberg	Duesenberg	8	249	Stevens	blue	115.739	8	37	37-piston
23	Ralph Hepburn	Highway Truck Parts	S. C. Goldberg	Cooper*	16	330	Cooper	blue, white	110.001	41	38	33-con. rod bearing
59	Ray Campbell	G & D	Tulio Gulotta	Hudson	8	244	Hudson	maroon, white	108.650	37	39	24-oil leak
24	Paul Bost	Frame-Miller-Duesenberg	Fred Frame	Miller	4	220	Duesenberg	gray	111.330	33	40	13-oil line
61	Rick Decker	Miller	Bessie Decker	Miller*	8	167	Miller	white	108.280	38	41	13-manifold
22	Lou Schneider	Edelweiss	W. R. Blackburn	Miller	8	151	Stevens	red	109.850	21	42	1-stalled

*Front drive **Four-wheel drive

Cotton Henning was one of the most respected mechanics in 500 history. He took pride in using only the best parts. But in 1933, this came back to haunt him. Bill Cummings, in the Boyle-Henning entry, looked like the one to beat until his engine began overheating. By lap 136, he was out of the race with what was called a radiator leak. However, Cotton had chosen a special radiator cap; it fell off on the course, and there was no replacement available.

Al Miller

Raul Riganti

Malcolm Fox

Paul Bost

Dave Evans

Doc MacKenzie

Howdy Wilcox II (for Rose)

Wilbur Shaw

Wesley Crawford

Babe Stapp

Chet Miller

Freddy Winnai

Rick Decker

Ralph Hepburn

Mark Billman

Kelly Petillo

Gene Haustein

Joe Russo

Johnny Sawyer

Ray Campbell

Willard Prentiss

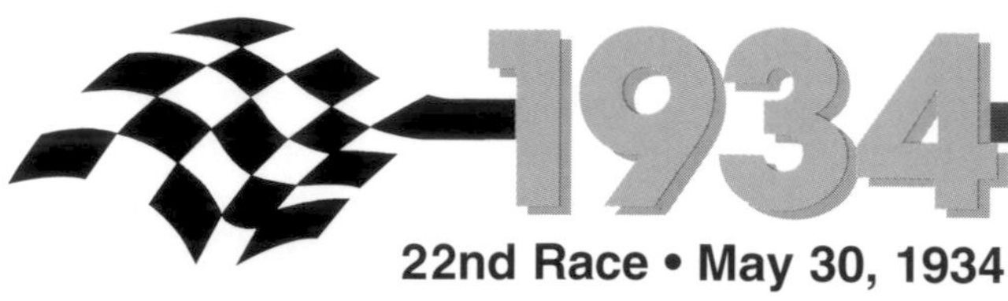

1934

22nd Race • May 30, 1934

Safety and fuel economy are big concerns this year as the Speedway tries to reduce fatalities and injuries. This includes reverting to a 33-car starting field to reduce race-day traffic. To reduce speeds, cars are limited to 2.5 gallons of fuel for the 10-lap qualifying runs and 45 gallons for the race, which requires averaging more than 11 mpg to complete 500 miles.

Two drivers are disqualified for exceeding the fuel limit in time trials, Babe Stapp and Charles Tramison, the latter in a car called the Economy Gas Special. Fred Frame, the 1932 winner, crashes in practice and misses the race. Louis Meyer, the only former winner in the field, shoots for a record third win, but drops out on lap 92 with oil problems.

Despite the fuel restrictions, qualifying speeds are faster. Kelly Petillo sits on the pole at 119.329 mph, and he leads six laps before he has to pit.

Frank Brisko, who starts from the front row in a four-wheel-drive Miller for the second straight year, takes over. Brisko leads 69 laps before falling back.

The race turns into a duel between Mauri Rose in a rear-drive Miller and "Wild Bill" Cummings in a front-drive Miller, one of only four front-drive cars in the race. Cummings passes Rose for the last time on lap 175 and wins by 27 seconds, the closest victory margin to date.

Cummings, an Indianapolis native, wins at a record 104.865 mph, the third record speed in a row, while averaging nearly 14 mpg. His 220-cid Miller is the first four-cylinder engine to win since 1920.

Two Cummins diesels compete. Dave Evans, driving a four-cycle version, quits after 81 laps with a busted transmission, and Stubby Stubblefield, driving a two-cycle diesel, goes the distance and places 12th, the last car running at the finish.

The slick Hulbert Special (*top*) didn't make the field, but predicted the future. Chet Miller started 32nd with a Ford V-8 (*middle left*); he survived an early crash in No. 46 (*middle right*). The field gets up to speed at the start (*above*). "Wild Bill" Cummings and mechanic Earl Unversaw (*opposite*) won in a four-cylinder, front-drive Miller.

STARTING LINEUP

Average Field Qualifying Speed: 112.645

Numbers in flags indicate finish position

Frank Brisko

Phil Shafer

Russell Snowberger

George Barringer

Shorty Cantlon

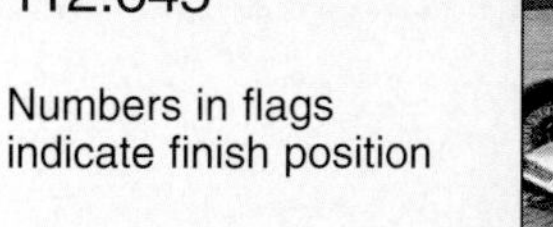

Wilbur Shaw

Chet Gardner

Al Miller

Ralph Hepburn

Herb Ardinger

POLE POSITION
Qualifying Speed: 119.329

Kelly Petillo

Mauri Rose

Tony Gulotta

Bill Cummings

Lou Meyer

RESULTS

NO.	DRIVER	CAR	ENTRANT	ENGINE	CYL	DISP	CHASSIS	COLOR	QUAL SPD	START	FIN	LAPS / SPEED / REASON OUT
7	Bill Cummings	Boyle Products	H. C. Henning	Miller*	4	220	Miller	wht, red, blue	116.116	10	1	200-104.865
9	Mauri Rose	Leon Duray	Leon Duray	Miller	4	220	Stevens	black, white	116.044	4	2	200-104.697
2	Lou Moore	Foreman Axle	California Racers, Inc.	Miller	4	255	Miller	gray, red	113.442	20	3	200-103.625
12	Deacon Litz	Stokely Foods	A. B. Litz	Miller	4	220	Miller	white, blue	113.731	19	4	200-100.749
16	Joe Russo	Duesenberg	Joe E. Russo	Duesenberg	8	275	Duesenberg	orange, white	113.115	24	5	200-99.893
36	Al Miller	Shafer "8"	Phil Shafer	Buick	8	286	Rigling	black, white	113.307	8	6	200-98.264
22	Cliff Bergere	Floating Power	William S. White	Miller	4	220	Weil	red, white	115.243	18	7	200-97.818
10	Russ Snowberger	Russell "8"	Russell Snowberger	Studebaker	8	336	Snowberger	blue	111.428	9	8	200-97.297
32	Frank Brisko	F.W.D.	F.W.D. Auto Co.	Miller	4	255	Miller	cream	116.894	3	9	200-96.787
24	Herb Ardinger	Lucenti	Angelo Lucenti	Graham	8	265	Graham	blue, gold	111.722	14	10	200-95.936
17	Kelly Petillo	Red Lion	Joe Marks	Miller	4	255	Adams	cream, red	119.329	1	11	200-93.432
5	Stubby Stubblefield	Cummins Diesel	Cummins Engine Co.	Cummins**	4	364	Duesenberg	red, white	105.921	29	12	200-88.566
49	Charles Crawford	Detroit Gskt & Mfg.	Detroit Gasket & Mfg.	Ford V8	8	221	Ford	black	108.784	28	13	110-in pits
31	Ralph Hepburn	Miller	Ralph Hepburn	Miller	8	254	Miller	cream, red	114.321	11	14	164-con. rod
18	George Barringer	Boyle Products	H. C. Henning	Miller	8	270	Miller	white, red	113.859	12	15	161-bent front axle
26	Phil Shafer	Shafer "8"	Phil Shafer	Buick	8	292	Rigling	green	113.816	6	16	130-crankshaft drive
8	Tony Gulotta	Schroeder	Floyd Smith	Studebaker*	8	250	Cooper	black, silver	113.733	7	17	94-con. rod
1	Lou Meyer	Ring Free	Lou Meyer	Miller	4	255	Stevens	yellow, red	112.332	13	18	92-oil tank
6	Dave Evans	Cummins Diesel	Cummins Engine Co.	Cummins	4	364	Duesenberg	white, red	102.414	22	19	81-transmission
15	Shorty Cantlon	Sullivan & O'Brien	William J. Cantlon	Miller	4	220	Stevens	tan	117.875	15	20	76-crankshaft
4	Chet Gardner	Sampson Radio	Alden Sampson II	Miller	16	201	Stevens	white, black	114.786	5	21	72-con. rod
51	Al Gordon	Abels & Fink	Paul Weirick	Miller	4	239	Adams	blue, silver	116.273	17	22	66-wrecked T1
35	Rex Mays	Frame-Miller-Duesenberg	Fred Frame	Miller	4	220	Duesenberg	gray, blue	113.639	23	23	53-front axle
42	Dusty Fahrnow	Superior Trailer	Irving Goldberg	Cooper*	16	330	Cooper	blue, red	113.070	25	24	28-con. rod
41	Johnny Sawyer	Burd Piston Ring	Lencki & Unger	Lencki	4	183	Miller	green, black	109.808	21	25	27-con. rod
33	Johnny Seymour	Streamline Miller	Fred Frame	Miller	4	200	Adams	gray, blue	108.591	33	26	22-pinion gear
45	Rick Decker	Carter Carburetor	Rickliffe Decker	Miller*	8	171	Miller	white	110.895	27	27	17-clutch
3	Wilbur Shaw	Lion Head	Joe Marks	Miller	8	249	Stevens	red, silver	117.647	2	28	15-lost oil
73	Doc MacKenzie	Cresco	Mikan & Carson	Studebaker	8	337	Mikan-Carson	silver, orange	111.933	26	29	15-wrecked NS
29	Gene Haustein	Martz	Lawrence J. Martz	Hudson	8	257	Hudson	orange	109.426	31	30	13-wrecked T4
63	Harry McQuinn	DeBaets	Michel DeBaets	Miller	4	220	Rigling	blue	111.067	30	31	13-con. rod
58	George Bailey	Scott	Roy Scott	Studebaker	8	360	Snowberger	tan, blk, white	111.063	16	32	12-wrecked T3
46	Chet Miller	Bohnalite Ford	Bohn Alum & Brass Corp.	Ford V8	8	221	Ford	gold, black	109.252	32	33	11-over T1 wall

*Front drive **Two-cycle engine

Among the estimated 140,000 fans on hand to see Bill Cummings's victory was a man who made a habit of hiding in plain sight. Many who knew the so-called "Modern-day Robin Hood" of the Thirties claimed he was in the crowd. Some contend he actually had a grandstand seat, and just before the race ended, he made his presence known to those seated near him. One fan even had a ticket stub with an autograph that matched the stealthy individual's signature.

Though lawmen put little credence in such stories, notorious bank robber John Dillinger may well have attended the 500 in 1934.

Cliff Bergere

Johnny Sawyer

Joe Russo

Rick Decker

Harry McQuinn

Johnny Seymour

Al Gordon

Lou Moore

Rex Mays

Doc MacKenzie

Stubby Stubblefield

Chet Miller

George Bailey

Deacon Litz

Dave Evans

Dusty Fahrnow

Charles Crawford

Gene Haustein

1935

23rd Race • May 30, 1935

The roar of the Offenhauser engine signals a new era at the Brickyard. The "Offy," an offspring of a Miller four-cylinder originally built for marine use, will be competitive at the Speedway for nearly three decades.

Californian Kelly Petillo qualifies an Offy at 121.687, less than one mph slower than the track record and fastest ever for a two-man car. After tech inspection, his time is thrown out because he exceeds the 2.5-gallon fuel limit by 10 ounces. He blows an engine on his second attempt, and finally makes the field on his third try at 115 mph.

Rex Mays qualifies for his second 500 at 120.736 mph to earn the pole with a Miller four-cylinder. Mays leads until he pits after 60 laps, and Petillo charges to the front from 22nd starting position to take over.

Mays battles back into the lead for a while, but Petillo has the upper hand on Lap 123 when Mays pulls into the pits, a broken spring shackle ending his day. Petillo loses the lead briefly to Wilbur Shaw when he pits, but regains it for good when Shaw has to stop. Shaw's pursuit is slowed by a caution flag for 14 laps late in the race because of light rain, and he finishes 40 seconds back. Offenhauser engines finish 1-2.

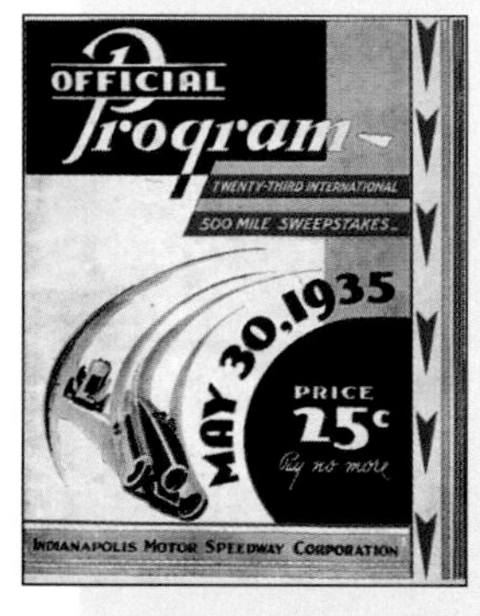

The speed record for 500 miles falls for the fourth year in a row, with Petillo averaging 106.24 mph.

Crash helmets are required for the first time, and green and yellow traffic lights are installed around the track. Under yellow, drivers must slow to 75 mph and hold their positions.

Despite these changes, four men die at the speedway. Rookie Johnny Hannon dies in a crash on his first practice lap at speed. Veteran driver Stubby Stubblefield and riding mechanic Leo Whittaker are killed on the eighth lap of a qualifying run. Clay Weatherly dies when he plows through the Turn 4 wall on the ninth lap of the race, ironically in the same car as Hannon.

STARTING LINEUP

Average Field Qualifying Speed: 114.846

Numbers in flags indicate finish position

POLE POSITION
Qualifying Speed: 120.736

Floyd Roberts

Tony Gulotta

Chet Gardner

Babe Stapp

Doc MacKenzie

Al Gordon

Bill Cummings

Fred Frame

Russell Snowberger

George Connor

Rex Mays

Lou Meyer

Ralph Hepburn

Mauri Rose

Deacon Litz

RESULTS

NO.	DRIVER	CAR	ENTRANT	ENGINE	CYL	DISP	CHASSIS	COLOR	QUAL SPD	START	FIN	LAPS / SPEED / REASON OUT
5	Kelly Petillo	Gilmore Speedway	Kelly Petillo	Offy	4	260	Wetteroth	red, cream	115.095	22	1	200-106.240
14	Wilbur Shaw	Pirrung	Gil Pirrung	Offy*	4	220	Shaw	blue, white	116.854	20	2	200-105.990
1	Bill Cummings	Boyle Products	H. C. Henning	Miller*	4	221	Miller	wht, red, blue	116.901	5	3	200-104.758
22	Floyd Roberts	Abels & Fink	Earl Haskell	Miller	4	255	Miller	blue, silver	118.671	3	4	200-103.228
21	Ralph Hepburn	Veedol	Ralph Hepburn	Miller	8	258	Miller	cream, red	115.156	7	5	200-103.177
9	Shorty Cantlon	Sullivan & O'Brien	William J. Cantlon	Miller	4	220	Stevens	tan, silver	118.205	19	6	200-101.140
18	Chet Gardner	Sampson Radio	Alden Sampson II	Miller	4	220	Stevens	white, black	114.556	9	7	200-101.129
16	Deacon Litz	Sha-litz	A. B. Litz	Miller	4	220	Miller	red, blk, wht	114.488	13	8	200-100.907
8	Doc MacKenzie	Pirrung	Gil Pirrung	Miller	4	220	Rigling	blue, silver	114.294	15	9	200-100.598
34	Chet Miller	Milac Front Drive	Fred Frame	Miller*	8	151	Summers	blue	113.552	17	10	200-100.474
19	Fred Frame	Miller-Hartz	Harry Hartz	Miller*	8	183	Wetteroth	blue, yellow, red	114.701	8	11	200-100.436
36	Lou Meyer	Ring Free	Lou Meyer	Miller	4	255	Stevens	red, white	117.938	4	12	200-100.256
15	Cliff Bergere	Victor Gasket	Phil Shafer	Buick	8	284	Rigling	green, white	114.162	16	13	196-out of gas
62	Harris Insinger	Cresco	Mikan & Carson	Studebaker	8	336	Mikan-Carson	slvr, orange, red	111.729	31	14	185-flagged
4	Al Miller	Boyle Products	H. C. Henning	Miller	4	260	Rigling	wht, red, blue	115.303	21	15	178-magneto
43	Ted Horn	Ford V8	Harry A. Miller	Ford V8*	8	220	Miller-Ford	black, white	113.213	26	16	145-steering
33	Rex Mays	Gilmore	Paul Weirick	Miller	4	269	Adams	blue, silver	120.736	1	17	123-spring shackle
7	Lou Moore	Foreman Axle	Lou Moore	Miller	4	255	Miller	red, silver	114.180	23	18	116-con. rod
37	George Connor	Marks-Miller	Joe Marks	Miller	8	248	Stevens	red, white	114.321	14	19	112-transmission
2	Mauri Rose	F.W.D.	Four Wheel Drive Auto Co.	Miller**	4	255	Miller	buff	116.470	10	20	103-mechanical failure
44	Tony Gulotta	Bowes Seal Fast	Leon Duray	Miller	4	220	Stevens	blk, wht, red	115.459	6	21	102-magneto
39	Jimmy Snyder	Blue Prelude	Joel Thorne	Studebaker	8	336	Snowberger	blue	112.249	30	22	97-spring
41	Frank Brisko	Art Rose	Kenneth Schroeder	Studebaker*	8	250	Rigling	black, silver	113.307	24	23	79-universal joint
42	Johnny Seymour	Ford V8	Harry A. Miller	Ford V8*	8	220	Miller-Ford	blue, silver	112.696	27	24	71-grease leak
17	Babe Stapp	Marks-Miller	Joe Marks	Miller	4	255	Adams	cream, red	116.736	12	25	70-radiator
35	George Bailey	Ford V8	Harry A. Miller	Ford V8*	8	220	Miller-Ford	silver, red	113.432	29	26	65-steering
3	Russ Snowberger	Boyle Products	H. C. Henning	Miller	8	270	Miller	wht, red, blue	114.209	11	27	59-exhaust pipe
26	Louis Tomei	Burd Piston Ring	Joe Lencki	Lencki	8	220	Miller	metal blue, red	110.794	32	28	47-valve
46	Bob Sall	Ford V8	Harry A. Miller	Ford V8*	8	220	Miller-Ford	gold, white	110.519	33	29	47-steering
6	Al Gordon	Cocktail Hour Cigar.	William S. White	Miller	4	220	Weil	cream, blue	119.481	2	30	17-wrecked T4
27	Freddy Winnai	Gyro-Duesenberg	Harry Hatz	Miller	4	234	Duesenberg	yellow	115.138	28	31	16-con. rod
45	Clay Weatherly	Bowes Seal Fast	Leon Duray	Miller	4	220	Stevens	blk, white, red	115.902	25	32	9-wrecked T4
66	Harry McQuinn	DeBaets	Michel DeBaets	Miller	4	220	Rigling	blue, red	111.111	18	33	4-con. rod

*Front drive **Four-wheel drive

Opposite page: Drivers and officials pose for the traditional pre-race snapshot (top). A typical cockpit had a simple gauge panel dominated by the tachometer (middle left). The Burd Piston Ring Special used a new Lencki eight (middle right), named after the car entrant. Wilbur Shaw's runner-up car is nearly lost in the post-race mob (bottom). *This page:* New green and yellow traffic lights (right) kept drivers informed around the track. The backstraight had low wooden guardrails. Firestone had its own garage (far right) from which it dispensed tires. Firestones were the winning tires for the 16th straight year.

Harry McQuinn

Al Miller

Frank Brisko

Johnny Seymour

Jimmy Snyder

Bob Sall

Chet Miller

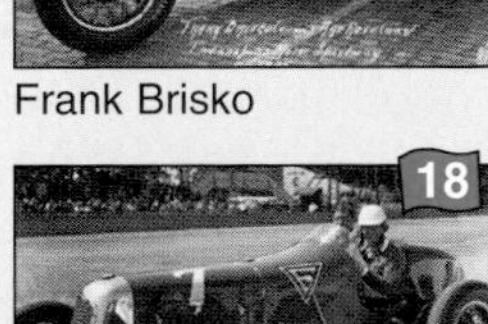
Wilbur Shaw

Lou Moore

Ted Horn

George Bailey

Louis Tomei

Cliff Bergere

Shorty Cantlon

Kelly Petillo

Clay Weatherly

Freddy Winnai

Harris Insinger

24th Race • May 30, 1936

Wider turns with safety aprons give the Speedway a new look this year. The inside walls of the turns are gone to give cars more runoff room, and stronger outside retaining walls tilt inward to make it harder for cars to vault over them.

For the first time, rookies must pass a driving test that includes running 10 laps in stages, starting at 80 mph and progressing to 110. A new 37.5-gallon limit on fuel heightens concerns about fuel economy.

Rex Mays wins his second straight pole at 119.644 mph with a four-cylinder Sparks engine. Mays leads the first 12 laps but has to stop to fix his throttle linkage. Wilbur Shaw's Offy is in front for 51 laps, but on lap 83 he has to pit to secure a loose hood and loses nearly 17 minutes.

Louis Meyer charges from the 28th starting spot to lead by the halfway mark in his four-cylinder Miller. When Meyer makes his last stop on lap 131, Ted Horn runs in front for the next 16 laps. Horn, driving the Miller that won in 1932, hands the lead back to Meyer when he stops on lap 146.

Meyer covers the last 125 miles at a record clip and pulls away to a two-minute, 17-second victory over Horn, becoming the first three-time winner in 500 history. His winning speed of 109.069 mph shatters the record for the fifth straight year. He ties Ray Harroun for winning from furthest back on the starting grid.

Meyer also drives home in the Packard One-Twenty pace car, starting a tradition that continues today. Two-time winner Tommy Milton, who drove the Packard on the pace lap, suggests the move.

The winner averages nearly 14.5 mpg to finish with fuel to spare. For others, low mileage is this year's grim reaper. Seven cars run out of fuel, including three running in the top 10 near the finish.

This is the first year for the Borg-Warner trophy, presented to the winner each year in victory lane. The face of every winning driver is engraved on the 51.5-inch sterling silver trophy.

A year after Kelly Petillo won the 500 with the first engine designated an Offenhauser, many people wondered why Louie Meyer called his winning four-cylinder a Miller. "At that time, I just couldn't bring myself to call that engine an 'Offy,'" Louie explained. "It had been designed in Harry Miller's shop, and I just felt it was still a Miller. . . . But I guess I was still a straight-eight man at heart," he said.

Eventually, Louie would gain respect for the four-banger. And when he and Dale Drake bought the engine concern from Fred Offenhauser, he changed the name to Meyer-Drake.

STARTING LINEUP

Average Field Qualifying Speed: 116.685

Numbers in flags indicate finish position

Chet Miller

Herb Ardinger

Wilbur Shaw

Freddy Winnai

Floyd Roberts

Babe Stapp

George Connor

Louis Tomei

Ted Horn

George Barringer

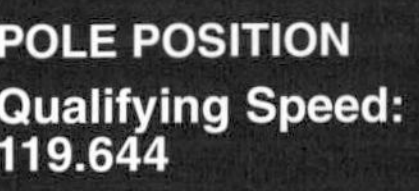
POLE POSITION
Qualifying Speed: 119.644

Rex Mays

Doc MacKenzie

Cliff Bergere

Shorty Cantlon

Bill Cummings

RESULTS

NO.	DRIVER	CAR	ENTRANT	ENGINE	CYL	DISP	CHASSIS	COLOR	QUAL SPD	START	FIN	LAPS / SPEED / REASON OUT
8	Lou Meyer	Ring Free	Lou Meyer	Miller	4	255	Stevens	red, white	114.171	28	1	200-109.069
22	Ted Horn	Miller-Hartz	Harry Hartz	Miller	8	183	Wetteroth	gray, blue	116.564	11	2	200-108.170
10	Doc MacKenzie	Gilmore Speedway	Kelly Petillo	Offy	4	262	Wetteroth	cream, red	116.961	4	3	200-107.460
36	Mauri Rose	F.W.D.	Four Wheel Drive Auto Co.	Miller**	4	255	Miller	white, red	113.890	30	4	200-107.272
18	Chet Miller	Boyle Products	Boyle Motor Products	Miller*	4	212	Summers	white, red	117.675	3	5	200-106.919
41	Ray Pixley	Fink Auto	Clarence Felker	Miller	4	203	Miller	blue, silver	116.703	25	6	200-105.253
3	Wilbur Shaw	Gilmore	W. Wilbur Shaw	Offy	4	255	Shaw	cream, red	117.503	9	7	200-104.233
17	George Barringer	Kennedy Tank	Phil Shafer	Offy	4	255	Rigling	red	112.700	14	8	200-102.630
53	Zeke Meyer	Boyle Products	Boyle Motor Products	Studebaker*	8	251	Cooper	white	111.476	32	9	200-101.331
38	George Connor	Marks Miller	Joe Marks	Miller	4	255	Adams	white, red	116.269	5	10	200-98.931
35	Freddy Winnai	Midwest Red Lion	Midwest Racing Team	Offy	4	255	Stevens	cream, red	116.221	12	11	199-flagged
9	Ralph Hepburn	Art Rose	Ralph Hepburn	Offy	4	255	Miller	white	112.673	24	12	196-flagged
28	Harry McQuinn	Sampson Radio	Alden Sampson II	Miller	4	247	Stevens	white	114.118	27	13	196-out of gas
7	Shorty Cantlon	Hamilton-Harris	William S. White	Miller	4	247	Weil	cream, blue	116.912	10	14	194-out of gas
33	Rex Mays	Gilmore	Paul Weirick	Sparks	4	239	Adams	blue, silver	119.644	1	15	192-out of gas
54	Doc Williams	Superior Trailer	Race Car Corp.	Miller*	4	246	Cooper	blue	112.837	23	16	192-out of gas
32	Lou Moore	Burd Piston Ring	Lou Moore	Offy	4	255	Miller	orange, black	113.996	29	17	185-out of gas
19	Emil Andres	Carew	J. Stewart Carew	Cragar	4	212	Whippet	blue, silver	111.455	33	18	184-flagged
4	Floyd Roberts	Burd Piston Ring	Joe Lencki	Offy	4	255	Stevens	orange, black	112.403	15	19	183-out of gas
14	Frank Brisko	Elgin Piston Pin	Elgin Piston Pin Co.	Brisko	4	255	Miller	orange, blue	114.213	20	20	180-out of gas
12	Al Miller	Boyle Products	Boyle Motor Products	Miller	4	258	Smith	white, red, blue	116.138	17	21	119-wrecked FS
42	Cliff Bergere	Bowes Seal Fast	Bowes Seal Fast Corp.	Miller	4	220	Stevens	blk, white, red	113.377	7	22	116-loose engine support
15	Deacon Litz	Deacon Litz	A. B. Litz	Miller	4	220	Miller	white	115.997	26	23	108-crankshaft
21	Babe Stapp	Pirrung	Gil Pirrung	Offy*	4	255	Shaw	blue, white	118.945	2	24	89-crankshaft
5	Billy Winn	Harry A. Miller	James M. Winn	Miller	4	255	Miller	white	114.648	19	25	78-crankshaft
52	Frank McGurk	Abels Auto Ford	Charles Worley	Cragar	4	214	Adams	cream, red, blk	113.102	22	26	51-crankshaft
27	Louis Tomei	Wheeler's	Babe Stapp	Miller	4	214	Wetteroth	yellow	111.078	8	27	44-engine support arm
44	Herb Ardinger	Bowes Seal Fast	Bowes Seal Fast Corp.	Miller	4	220	Stevens	blk, white, red	115.082	6	28	38-transmission
6	Chet Gardner	Gardner	Chester L. Gardner	Offy	4	255	Duesenberg	blue, red	116.000	18	29	38-clutch
43	Jimmy Snyder	Belanger Miller	Murrell Belanger	Miller	8	249	Stevens	white	111.291	16	30	21-oil leak
47	Johnny Seymour	Sullivan & O'Brien	William L. Cantlon	Miller	4	246	Stevens	cream, red, blk	113.169	21	31	13-clutch
46	Fred Frame	Burd Piston Ring	Moore & Fengler	Miller	4	255	Miller	orange, black	112.877	31	32	4-piston
2	Bill Cummings	Boyle Products	Boyle Motor Products	Offy*	4	255	Miller	wht, red, blue	115.939	13	33	0-clutch

*Front drive **Four-wheel drive

Crews make final preparations for the race in the pits (*opposite top*). An aerial view from south of the track (*opposite middle*) shows the immensity of the Speedway and the surrounding area that was still mostly undeveloped in 1936. Jimmy Snyder, with mechanic Jimmy Lowden (*opposite bottom*), was a crowd favorite with his aggressive style. At a Shrine lodge event at the track in June 1936 (*right*), future automaker Preston Tucker (in dark suit and bow tie) poses with Speedway official L. G. Epsteen and the Packard One Twenty pace car. Lou Meyer became the first three-time winner, and the first to drive home the pace car as a prize (*far right*).

Chet Gardner

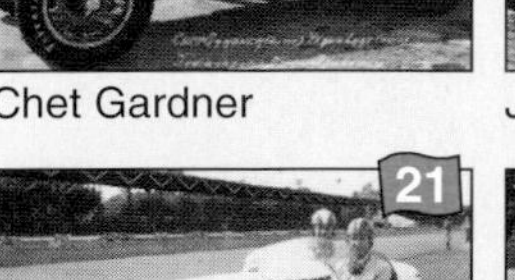

Johnny Seymour

Ralph Hepburn

Harry McQuinn

Mauri Rose

Emil Andres

Al Miller

Frank Brisko

Doc Williams

Deacon Litz

Lou Moore

Zeke Meyer

Jimmy Snyder

Billy Winn

Frank McGurk

Ray Pixley

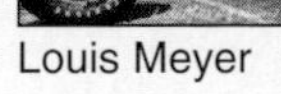
Louis Meyer

Fred Frame

1937

25th Race • May 31, 1937

Asphalt covers the bricks in the turns and short chutes for the 25th running of the 500, giving drivers a smoother, safer surface. Rule changes include a requirement for commercial fuel to circumvent the secret Gasoline Alley brews fortified with alcohol and other additives.

A tragic practice accident starts when the crankshaft breaks in Overton Phillips's Duesenberg. He crashes into another car in the pits, touching off a huge fire. George Warford, a firemen, and Otto Rhode, chief engineer for Champion Spark Plugs, die.

Four-cycle engines can again use superchargers, and nine qualify. Former winner Bill Cummings earns his second pole with an Offy in a front-drive Miller chassis. Cummings averages 123.343 mph for 10 laps to break Leon Duray's 1928 record of 122.391. On a later qualifying day, 1935 winner Kelly Petillo averages 124.129 in a rear-drive Offy.

Jimmy Snyder is fastest of all. He posts a lap of nearly 131 mph, but darkness halts his qualifying run. On his next try, Snyder's supercharged Sparks six-cylinder hits 127.155 on one lap and averages 125.287 for 10. He starts 19th, and Petillo is alongside in 20th.

In the race, the crowd-thrilling Snyder dashes into the lead by the fourth lap, but falls out on lap 27 with a broken transmission. After that, Wilbur Shaw is in front most of the way.

Shaw leads by more than a lap with 20 to go, but his Offy is almost out of oil. He slows to preserve his engine, allowing Ralph Hepburn to catch him on the last lap. Shaw wins a drag race to the checkered flag by 2.16 seconds, the closest finish in the race's 25-year history.

Shaw averages 113.58 mph, the sixth record speed in a row. Hepburn finishes second in an Offy-powered car that Louis Meyer drove to victory in 1936 and sold just days before this race. Ted Horn is third in a supercharged front-drive Miller, and Meyer is fourth in a rear-drive Miller.

Members of the 100 Mile an Hour Club, sponsored by Champion spark plugs, meet for their annual dinner before the 500 (*above*). Winning driver Wilbur Shaw and mechanic Jigger Johnson are surrounded by well-wishers in their garage (*below*). In a hint of the future, Lee Oldfield entered a rear-engine Marmon (*opposite, top left*) but couldn't get up to speed. Frank McGurk crashed the Belanger Special in practice (*opposite, top right*); riding mechanic Albert Opalko died in the wreck. GMC supplied the official trucks in 1937 (*opposite bottom*).

STARTING LINEUP

Average Field Qualifying Speed: 119.288

Numbers in flags indicate finish position

22 Herb Ardinger

2 Ralph Hepburn

11 Chet Gardner

9 George Connor

23 Frank Brisko

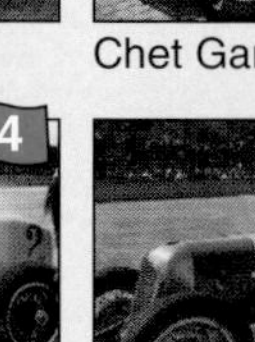
1 Wilbur Shaw

4 Lou Meyer

18 Mauri Rose

14 Deacon Litz

7 Billy DeVore

POLE POSITION
Qualifying Speed: 123.343

6 Bill Cummings

26 Billy Winn

8 Tony Gulotta

12 Ronney Householder

30 Chet Miller

When the AAA announced riding mechanics would be optional after the '37 race, Louie Meyer sold his winning car from '36 to Ralph Hepburn. Consequently, Louie came to Indy without a ride in '37. "Cotton Henning came to me about driving a car he'd rebuilt," Meyer said. "It was probably the fastest two-man car I ever drove." But it ran hot on race day. "We must've made four more stops than anybody else and we finished fourth. Hepburn drove my old car to second place and nearly beat Wilbur [Shaw]. You just never know."

Louis Tomei

Bob Swanson

Floyd Davis

Tony Willman

Russell Snowberger

Frank Wearne

Floyd Roberts

Kelly Petillo

Rex Mays

Al Miller

Ken Fowler

Ted Horn

Cliff Bergere

Jimmy Snyder

Harry McQuinn

Shorty Cantlon

George Bailey

Babe Stapp

Track owner Eddie Rickenbacker poses amid a group of AAA and Speedway officials (*top*). A LaSalle Series 50 driven by 1915 winner Ralph DePalma paced the field (*above*). The turns and short chutes were newly covered with asphalt (*below*). Racers line up in the pits prior to the race (*left*). Wilbur Shaw and mechanic Jigger Johnson acknowledge cheers after their victory (*opposite top*). They survived burns from an oil leak, low oil pressure, and a late challenge from Ralph Hepburn to win the 25th 500 in the Gilmore Special (*opposite bottom*).

RESULTS

NO.	DRIVER	CAR	ENTRANT	ENGINE	CYL	DISP	CHASSIS	COLOR	QUAL SPD	START	FIN	LAPS / SPEED / REASON OUT
6	Wilbur Shaw	Shaw-Gilmore	W. Wilbur Shaw	Offy	4	255	Shaw	cream, red	122.791	2	1	200-113.580
8	Ralph Hepburn	Hamilton-Harris	Louis Meyer	Offy	4	255	Stevens	red, white	118.809	6	2	200-113.565
3	Ted Horn	Miller-Hartz	Harry Hartz	Miller***	8	182	Wetteroth	gray, blue	118.608	32	3	200-113.434
2	Lou Meyer	Boyle	H. C. Henning	Miller	8	268	Miller	silver, red	119.619	5	4	200-110.730
45	Cliff Bergere	Midwest Red Lion	George H. Lyons	Offy	4	255	Stevens	cream, red	117.546	16	5	200-108.935
16	Bill Cummings	Boyle	H. C. Henning	Offy**	4	255	Miller	silver, red	123.343	1	6	200-107.124
28	Billy DeVore	Miller	H. E. Winn	Miller	4	255	Stevens	white, black	120.192	14	7	200-106.995
38	Tony Gulotta	Burd Piston Ring	Joe Lencki	Offy	4	255	Rigling	yellow, red	118.788	7	8	200-105.015
17	George Connor	Marks Miller	Joe Marks	Miller	4	265	Adams	maroon, silver	120.240	12	9	200-103.830
53	Louis Tomei	Sobonite Plastics	S.S. Engineering Co.	Studebaker	8	336	Rigling	maroon	116.437	18	10	200-101.825
31	Chet Gardner	Burd Piston Ring	Chester Gardner	Offy	4	255	Duesenberg	blue, red	117.342	9	11	199-flagged
23	Ronney Householder	Topping	Henry J. Topping, Jr.	Miller	4	234	Viglioni	white, red	116.464	10	12	194-flagged
62	Floyd Roberts	Thorne	Joel Thorne, Inc.	Miller	4	269	Miller	blue, white	116.996	17	13	194-flagged
35	Deacon Litz	Motorola	A. B. Litz	Miller	4	220	Miller	yellow, black	116.372	11	14	191-out of gas
32	Floyd Davis	Thorne	Joel Thorne, Inc.	Miller	4	255	Snowberger	blue, silver	118.942	24	15	190-wrecked T3
34	Shorty Cantlon	Bowes Seal Fast	Bill White Race Cars, Inc.	Miller	4	228	Weil	red, silver	118.555	25	16	182-flagged
42	Al Miller	Thorne	Joel Thorne, Inc.	Miller	4	255	Snowberger	blue, white	118.518	26	17	170-carburetor
1	Mauri Rose	Burd Piston Ring	Lou Moore	Offy	4	270	Miller	red, blk, silver	118.540	8	18	127-oil line
41	Ken Fowler	Lucky Teeter	E. M. "Lucky" Teeter	McDowell	4	233	Wetteroth	yellow	117.421	29	19	116-disqualified, pushed
25	Kelly Petillo	Petillo	Kelly Petillo	Offy	4	318	Wetteroth	blue, silver	124.129	20	20	109-out of oil
43	George Bailey	Duray-Sims	Sims & Duray	Miller*	4	220	Stevens	blue, gold	117.497	28	21	107-clutch
54	Herb Ardinger	Chicago Raw Hide	Lewis W. Welch	Offy*	4	255	Welch	copper	121.983	3	22	106-con. rod
24	Frank Brisko	Elgin Piston Pin	Frank Brisko	Brisko**	6	350	Stevens	maroon, silver	118.213	15	23	105-no oil pressure
44	Frank Wearne	Duray	Leon Duray	Miller*	4	220	Stevens	black, white	118.220	33	24	99-carburetor
26	Tony Wilman	F.W.D.	Peter DePaolo	Miller****	4	255	Miller	white, red	118.242	27	25	95-con. rod
10	Billy Winn	Miller	James M. Winn	Miller	4	255	Miller	white	119.922	4	26	85-oil line
12	Russ Snowberger	R.S.	Russ Snowberger	Packard***	8	282	Snowberger	blue, silver	117.354	30	27	66-clutch
33	Bob Swanson	Fink	Paul Weirick	Sparks	4	269	Adams	blue, silver	121.920	21	28	52-carburetor
47	Harry McQuinn	Sullivan-O'Brien	Thomas O'Brien	Miller*	4	247	Stevens	white, red	121.822	22	29	47-piston
7	Chet Miller	Boyle	H. C. Henning	Miller**	8	154	Summers	silver, red	119.213	13	30	36-ignition
15	Babe Stapp	Topping	Henry J. Topping, Jr.	Maserati*	8	305	Maserati	white, red	117.226	31	31	36-clutch
5	Jimmy Snyder	Sparks	Joel Thorne, Inc.	Sparks*	6	337	Adams	blue, white	125.287	19	32	27-transmission
14	Rex Mays	Bowes Seal Fast	Bill White Race Cars, Inc.	Alfa Romeo*	8	232	Alfa Romeo	red, silver	119.968	23	33	24-overheating

*Supercharged **Front drive ***Supercharged and front drive ****Four-wheel drive

Ronney Householder was one of the all-time great midget-car drivers. But in 1937, "House" realized that with some luck, he could earn more at Indy in one swipe than he could all year running midgets.

Landing a ride with the Henry J. Topping team, Householder was assigned a brute of a car. "It was a Miller," Householder said. "But the chassis was a joke. It wallowed me all over the track. It 'pushed' like mad. It skated like crazy." Every time Ronney tried to tell Topping about his problems with the car, the owner put him off.

"I told Topping his wife could probably do better with the car," Ronney grinned. "I don't think he thought it was funny. At the time, he was married to world figure skating champion Sonja Henie."

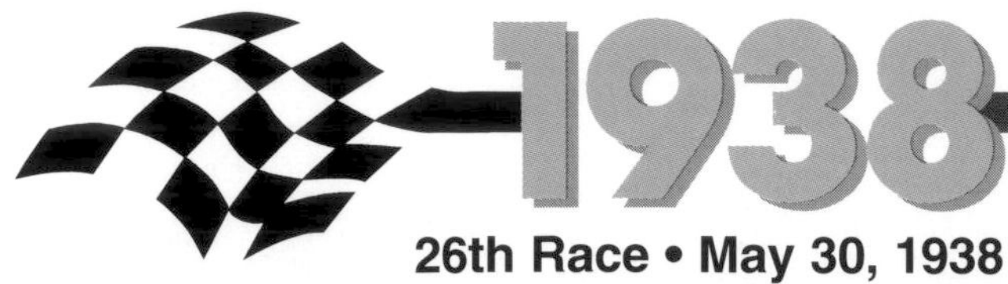

26th Race • May 30, 1938

Two-man cars with riding mechanics are history as the Speedway allows single-seaters for the first time since 1929 and adopts the same engine rules as the European Grand Prix circuit. Naturally aspirated engines can displace 275 cubic inches and supercharged engines 183.

Racing engines are again in vogue, and only a handful of stock-block production engines are among the 49 entries. For the first time since 1913, a Duesenberg is not in the race.

California sprint-car ace Floyd Roberts sits on the pole in a four-cylinder Miller, but a pair of formidable challengers line up behind.

Second-day qualifier Ronney Householder is slightly faster than Roberts with a record speed of 125.769 mph and starts 10th. His supercharged Sparks six-cylinder sits in a unique Adams chassis with the cockpit offset to the left and the driveshaft to the right, lowering the center of gravity. Teammate Jimmy Snyder is one row back with the same package.

Rex Mays starts on the outside of row one and jumps into the lead at the green flag in an Alfa Romeo Grand Prix car. He leads 16 laps, but exits on lap 45 with a frozen supercharger.

Snyder charges from 15th to grab the lead. Householder chases his teammate as Roberts hangs back in third. Snyder burns up his supercharger by lap 150, and Householder drops out with similar woes four laps later.

It is clear sailing for Roberts after that, who makes just one pit stop and leads the rest of the way. He builds a three-lap cushion while averaging 117.2 mph, 3.6 mph faster than the record set a year earlier.

Chet Miller runs second for more than 100 miles in a front-drive Offy, but pits just five laps from the finish, letting Wilbur Shaw slip by at the wire.

The most serious accident occurs on lap 45, when Emil Andres hits the Turn 2 wall and rolls three times. A loose wheel from his car kills a spectator in the infield.

"Electric eye" timing equipment provided precise lap times and speeds (*top*). Bill Cummings gets trackside tire service in practice (*above*). The scoring pagoda as it looked in the days leading up to the 1938 Indianapolis 500 (*opposite top*). Ralph Hepburn drew lots of attention with his unnumbered car (*opposite bottom*), which arrived late and failed to qualify. Innovator Harry Miller designed the rear-engine car around a supercharged flat six-cylinder engine and four-wheel drive. Mauri Rose finished 13th in the No. 27 Maserati (*opposite, far right*). The six-cylinder engine displaced just 91 cubic inches, but ran well until a supercharger failure after 165 laps.

STARTING LINEUP

Average Field Qualifying Speed: 120.032

Numbers in flags indicate finish position

Rex Mays

Ted Horn

Mauri Rose

Lou Meyer

Jimmy Snyder

Russell Snowberger

Chet Miller

Babe Stapp

Frank Brisko

Herb Ardinger

POLE POSITION
Qualifying Speed:
125.681

Floyd Roberts

Tony Gulotta

Wilbur Shaw

Ronney Householder

Joel Thorne

In 1937, when Wilbur Shaw took part in the Vanderbilt Cup race, he was astonished at the performance of the European Grand Prix cars. "If I had a car like that, I guarantee I'd win the Indianapolis 500," Shaw told Cotton Henning. Taking Wilbur at his word, Cotton—acting for car owner Mike Boyle—purchased a Maserati sight unseen. However, when the gleaming racer arrived, it was not the machine they'd expected. Instead of a powerful, supercharged straight-eight, the car was the small 6CM Model used in voiturette racing. The 91-cid, supercharged six-cylinder barely produced 155 horsepower. Disappointed with the car, Shaw bowed out of the deal.

In 1938, Henning signed Mauri Rose to drive the Maserati at Indy. Rose liked it immediately and qualified in the third row. Rose ran with the leaders, but his fine effort ended at 165 laps when the supercharger gave out.

Today, few people recall that Wilbur Shaw gave up on the original Boyle-sponsored Henning Maserati. They only recall his great wins at the wheel of the 8CTF Maserati that replaced it.

Chet Gardner

Kelly Petillo

Louis Tomei

Ira Hall

Billy DeVore

Duke Nalon

Frank Wearne

Shorty Cantlon

Al Putnam

Tony Willman

George Bailey

Cliff Bergere

Bill Cummings

George Connor

Al Miller

Harry McQuinn

Emil Andres

Henry Banks

The Hudson 112 pace car (*above*) was driven by Stuart Baits (*right*), the Hudson engineering vice president who designed it. Good fuel mileage enabled Floyd Roberts to win with just one pit stop in the No. 23 Burd Piston Ring Special (*below*), owned by retired driver Lou Moore. The infield is crowded with cars and spectators and the grandstands are packed as competitors dart down the front straight (*opposite top*). Although some female fans were daring to wear slacks to the race, dresses were still the most common attire for ladies; men generally continued to show up in jackets and neckties. The field heads into Turn 1 on a pace lap (*opposite, bottom left*). The scoreboard (*opposite, bottom right*) shows Jimmy Snyder in front after 20 laps, Rex Mays second, and Ronney Householder third. Snyder led for 92 laps, the same as winner Roberts, but was sidelined on lap 150 with supercharger trouble.

Recuperating from injuries suffered in a fiery crash at Pau, France, road racing legend Tazio Nuvolari visited Indianapolis. Nuvolari was so disgusted by his accident, he had announced his retirement from racing.

However, during practice for the 500, he began to take a renewed interest in the sport. It was even said that he tried out a couple of cars, but they suffered mechanical trouble before he could get up to speed.

On race day, a jubilant Nuvolari was perched on the flagman's stand with Seth Klein. Tazio acted as honorary starter, waving the green flag to start the race, one of the few times on record that anyone except the official starter ever flagged the 500 start.

It must have been what the doctor ordered. After fully recovering from his injuries, Nuvolari joined the German Auto Union team, winning two grands prix before season's end.

RESULTS

NO.	DRIVER	CAR	ENTRANT	ENGINE	CYL	DISP	CHASSIS	COLOR	QUAL SPD	START	FIN	LAPS / SPEED / REASON OUT
23	Floyd Roberts	Burd Piston Ring	Lou Moore	Miller	4	270	Wetteroth	red, blk, silver	125.681	1	1	200-117.200
1	Wilbur Shaw	Shaw	W. Wilbur Shaw	Offy	4	256	Shaw	cream, red	120.987	7	2	200-115.580
3	Chet Miller	I.B.E.W.	Boyle Racing Hdqtrs	Offy**	4	255	Summers	maroon	121.898	5	3	200-114.946
2	Ted Horn	Miller-Hartz	Harry Hartz	Miller***	8	182	Wetteroth	gray, blue	121.327	6	4	200-112.203
38	Chet Gardner	Burd Piston Ring	Joe Lencki	Offy	4	257	Rigling	yellow, red, slvr	120.435	18	5	200-110.311
54	Herb Ardinger	Offenhauser	Lewis W. Welch	Offy**	4	255	Miller-Ford	black, white	119.022	14	6	199-109.843
45	Harry McQuinn	Marchese	Carl Marchese	Miller	8	151	Marchese	white	119.492	25	7	197-108.694
58	Billy DeVore	P. R. & W.	Joel Thorne, Inc.	Offy	4	255	Stevens	cream, red	116.339	30	8	185-102.080
22	Joel Thorne	Thorne Engineering	Joel Thorne, Inc.	Offy**	4	256	Shaw	blue, silver	119.155	13	9	185-102.009
29	Frank Wearne	Indiana Fur	Paul Weirick	Offy	4	270	Adams	blue, silver	121.405	17	10	181-99.543
43	Duke Nalon	Kohlert-Miller	Henry Kohlert	Miller	8	154	Fengler	red, gold	113.828	33	11	178-flagged
12	George Bailey	Barbasol	Leon Duray	Duray*	4	182	Weil	red, blue, wht	116.393	29	12	166-clutch
27	Mauri Rose	I.B.E.W.	Boyle Racing Hdqtrs	Maserati*	6	91	Maserati	maroon	119.796	9	13	165-supercharger
16	Ronney Householder	Thorne-Sparks	Joel Thorne, Inc.	Sparks*	6	179	Adams	blue, white	125.769	10	14	154-supercharger hose
6	Jimmy Snyder	Sparks-Thorne	Joel Thorne, Inc.	Sparks*	6	179	Adams	blue, white	123.506	15	15	150-supercharger
5	Lou Meyer	Bowes Seal Fast	Bowes Racing, Inc.	Winfield*	8	179	Stevens	ivory, blk, red	120.525	12	16	149-oil pump
17	Tony Gulotta	Hamilton-Harris	Tony Gulotta	Offy	4	255	Stevens	red, white	122.499	4	17	130-con. rod
55	Al Miller	Domont's Pepsi-Cola	Jack Holly	Miller	4	255	Miller	blue gray, red	119.420	22	18	125-clutch
15	George Connor	Marks-Miller	Joseph Marks	Miller	4	272	Adams	maroon	120.326	19	19	119-engine trouble
9	Cliff Bergere	Kraft's Real Rye	George H. Lyons	Miller*	8	151	Stevens	yellow, red	114.464	32	20	111-piston
33	Henry Banks	Kimmel	Louis Kimmel	Voelker	12	273	Miller	blue	116.279	31	21	109-rod bearing
35	Kelly Petillo	Petillo	Kelly Petillo	Offy	4	271	Wetteroth	biue, silver	119.827	21	22	100-camshaft
21	Louis Tomei	P.O.B. Perfect Seal	H. E. Winn	Miller	4	255	Miller	white	121.599	24	23	88-con. rod
7	Bill Cummings	I.B.E.W.	Boyle Racing Hdqtrs	Miller**	8	268	Miller	maroon, silver	122.393	16	24	72-radiator tank leak
14	Russ Snowberger	D-X	Russel Snowberger	Miller**	4	255	Snowberger	tan	124.027	2	25	55-con. rod
34	Babe Stapp	McCoy Auto Service	Bill White Race Cars, Inc	Miller	4	228	Weil	red	120.595	8	26	54-valve
10	Tony Willman	Belanger	Murrell Belanger	Miller	8	247	Stevens	blue	118.458	26	27	47-valve
8	Rex Mays	Alfa-Romeo	Bill White Race Cars, Inc.	Alfa-Romeo*	8	182	A. R. Weil	red, silver	122.845	3	28	45-supercharger
42	Emil Andres	Piston Pin	Elgin Piston Pin Co.	Brisko	6	272	Adams	white, black	117.126	28	29	45-wrecked T2
37	Ira Hall	Greenfield Super Service	Nowiak & Magnee	Studebaker	8	250	Nowiak	white, blue	118.255	27	30	44-engine seized, hit wall T3
26	Frank Brisko	Shur-Stop Brake Equalizer	Frank Brisko	Brisko**	6	271	Stevens	red, white	121.921	11	31	39-oil line
36	Al Putnam	Troy Tydol	Arthur M. Sims	Miller	4	220	Stevens	orange, black	116.791	23	32	15-crankshaft
47	Shorty Cantlon	Kamm's	Thomas O'Brien	Miller*	4	247	Stevens	blk, white, red	120.906	20	33	13-supercharger loose

*Supercharged **Front drive ***Supercharged and front drive

1939

27th Race • May 30, 1939

Qualifying drops from 10 laps back to the traditional four, and speedy Jimmy Snyder wins his first pole at a record speed. His supercharged Sparks six-cylinder scorches the bricks at 130.138 mph, making him the first to qualify at 130.

George Bailey draws as much attention by qualifying sixth in the first rear-engine car to make the show. Built by Harry Miller, it boasts a supercharged six, four-wheel drive, and fully independent suspension. Bailey drops out on lap 47 with a broken valve.

Snyder bolts ahead at the start and leads until he makes his first stop and falls to fifth. Wilbur Shaw gets around Louis Meyer to claim first, but Snyder surges back into the lead when the others pit.

When Snyder makes his second stop on lap 103, three-time winner Meyer takes the lead and 1937 winner Shaw moves into second, starting a duel that continues the rest of the way.

On lap 107, defending 500 champ Floyd Roberts dies when he hits a spinning car and suffers a broken neck. The wreck seriously injures Chet Miller and Bob Swanson.

Meyer leads 79 laps until Shaw passes him on the front straight with 16 to go. On lap 192, Meyer spins in Turn 1 and blows a tire but stays off the wall. He limps all the way around to the pits for fresh rubber and resumes the chase, now a lap down to Shaw.

Meyer spins again on lap 198, hitting the inside guardrail on the backstretch. He is uninjured, but his car is finished. Meyer retires after the race, his third try at winning a fourth 500.

Shaw wins for the second time in three years. He leads a total of 51 laps in his supercharged Maserati, the first foreign car to win in 20 years. Firestone tires win for the 20th straight year. Snyder finishes second, one minute, 48 seconds back.

The Bear alignment crew (*above left*) balanced each tire before it hit the bricks. The AAA medical staff poses at the infield infirmary (*above right*). Popular Rex Mays (*opposite, top left*) led one lap in one of the Thorne Engineering entries. Veteran Johnny Seymour crashed a rear-engine Miller in practice (*opposite, top right*), but George Bailey made history by qualifying a similar car (*opposite, bottom row*) on the second row. Harry Miller, the engineer who created the car, is talking to Bailey in the photo at bottom left.

STARTING LINEUP

Average Field Qualifying Speed: 123.567

Numbers in flags indicate finish position

Wilbur Shaw

George Bailey

Herb Ardinger

George Connor

George Barringer

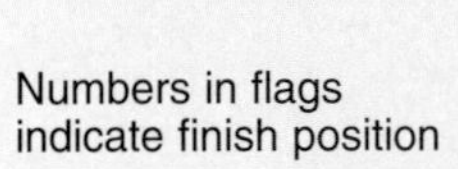

Lou Meyer

Chet Miller

Mauri Rose

Frank Brisko

Mel Hansen

POLE POSITION
Qualifying Speed: 130.138

Jimmy Snyder

Ted Horn

Shorty Cantlon

Cliff Bergere

Ralph Hepburn

In the closing stages of the 1939 race, Louie Meyer was trying to make up lost time following a blowout. With 10 laps remaining, he was within sight of leader Wilbur Shaw. "I had more top speed," Meyer recalled. "But in the turns, Wilbur and that wonderful Maserati chassis had us all beat." Nevertheless, it was obvious that Meyer was gaining ground on his friend and rival.

Coming out of the second turn on lap 198, Meyer went into a long skid. Just when he thought he had the car gathered up, it spun the rest of the way around, struck the wooden fence inside the backstretch, and leapt high into the air. Meyer was thrown out.

"When I got thrown out, I said to myself, 'That's it, I'm all done!' I'm probably the only guy who retired from racing in midair."

Ira Hall

30
Emil Andres

18
Kelly Petillo

11
Tony Gulotta

15
Louis Tomei

10
Billy DeVore

Frank Wearne

Joel Thorne

Floyd Roberts

Tony Willman

Floyd Davis

Harry McQuinn

Babe Stapp

Rex Mays

Bob Swanson

Russell Snowberger

Al Miller

Deacon Litz

The Buick Roadmaster pace car (*left*) was driven by Charlie Chayne, Buick's chief engineer. A special tonneau cover was stretched over the back seat of the four-door car. Other manufacturers continued to provide "official cars." Former race driver Charles Merz poses with the Chrysler Royal available to him for the month of May in his role as chief steward (*below left*). Wilbur Shaw outdueled Louis Meyer to earn a second spot on the Borg-Warner Trophy, which awaits him after he finishes post-race radio interviews (*below*). The smiling victor perches on the edge of his racer's cockpit, finally able to relax (*bottom*). Shaw leads 51 laps in his Maserati-powered eight-cylinder Boyle Special (*opposite top*), while Meyer leads 79 and second-place Jimmy Snyder leads 65. The fully restored No. 2 Maserati (*opposite bottom*) is in the Speedway's Hall of Fame Museum collection.

RESULTS

NO.	DRIVER	CAR	ENTRANT	ENGINE	CYL	DISP	CHASSIS	COLOR	QUAL SPD	START	FIN	LAPS / SPEED / REASON OUT
2	Wilbur Shaw	Boyle	Boyle Racing Hdqtrs	Maserati*	8	183	Maserati	maroon, cream	128.977	3	1	200-115.035
10	Jimmy Snyder	Thorne Engineering	Joel Thorne, Inc.	Sparks*	6	182	Adams	blue, white	130.138	1	2	200-114.245
54	Cliff Bergere	Offenhauser	Lewis W. Welch	Offy**	4	270	Miller- Ford	beige, red	123.835	10	3	200-113.698
4	Ted Horn	Boyle	Boyle Racing Hdqtrs	Miller**	8	268	Miller	maroon	127.723	4	4	200-111.879
31	Babe Stapp	Alfa Romeo	Bill White Race Cars, Inc.	Alfa Romeo*	8	181	A.R. Weil	red, silver	125.000	16	5	200-111.230
41	George Barringer	Bill White	Bill White Race Cars, Inc.	Offy	4	228	Weil	red	120.935	15	6	200-111.025
8	Joel Thorne	Thorne Engineering	Joel Thorne, Inc.	Sparks	6	272	Adams	blue, white	122.177	20	7	200-110.416
16	Mauri Rose	Wheeler's	W. Wilbur Shaw	Offy	4	256	Shaw	yellow, red	124.896	8	8	200-109.544
14	Frank Wearne	Burd Piston Ring	Moore & Roberts	Offy	4	270	Wetteroth	black, red	125.074	17	9	200-107.806
26	Billy DeVore	Leon Duray-Barbasol	Leon Duray	Duray*	4	182	Weil	wht, red, blue	116.527	33	10	200-104.267
62	Tony Gulotta	Burd Piston Ring	George Lyons	Offy	4	259	Stevens	yellow, red	121.749	27	11	200-103.938
45	Lou Meyer	Bowes Seal Fast	Bowes Racing, Inc.	Winfield*	8	179	Stevens	ivory, blk, red	130.067	2	12	197-wrecked BS
18	George Connor	Marks	Joseph Marks	Offy	4	255	Adams	white, red	123.208	12	13	195-stalled
51	Tony Willman	Burd Piston Ring	Joe Lencki	Lencki	6	270	Lencki	yellow, red, slvr	122.771	26	14	188-fuel pump
58	Louis Tomei	Alfa-Romeo	Frank T. Griswold	Alfa Romeo*	8	264	Alfa Romeo	red	118.426	30	15	186-flagged
15	Rex Mays	Thorne Engineering	Thorne Engineering Corp.	Sparks*	6	182	Adams	blue, white	126.413	19	16	145-rings
9	Herb Ardinger	Miller-Hartz	Harry Hartz	Miller***	8	182	Wetteroth	gray, blue	124.125	9	17	141-clutch
35	Kelly Petillo	Kay Jewelers	Kelly Petillo	Offy	4	270	Wetteroth	olive, silver	123.660	24	18	141-two broken pistons
49	Mel Hansen	Joel Thorne, Inc.	Joel Thorne, Inc.	Offy**	4	270	Shaw	blue, white	121.683	14	19	113-hit pit wall
38	Harry McQuinn	Elgin Piston Pin	F. Burren	Brisko	6	271	Blume	white	117.287	32	20	110-ignition
3	Chet Miller	Boyle	Boyle Racing Hdqtrs	Miller**	4	255	Summers	maroon	126.318	5	21	107-wrecked BS
25	Ralph Hepburn	Hamilton-Harris	Anthony Gulotta	Offy	4	270	Stevens	red, white	122.204	13	22	107-wrecked BS
1	Floyd Roberts	Burd Piston Ring	Lou Moore, Inc.	Offy	4	270	Wetteroth	red, blk, silver	128.968	23	23	106-wrecked BS
37	Ira Hall	Greenfield Super Service	Magnee & Nowiak	Studebaker	8	271	Nowiak	white, blue	121.188	18	24	89-head gasket
21	Russ Snowberger	D-X	Russell Snowberger	Miller**	4	258	Snowberger	brown	123.199	25	25	50-leaking radiator
17	George Bailey	Miller	Harry A. Miller	Miller****	6	180	Miller	silver, red	125.821	6	26	47-valve
56	Floyd Davis	W.B.W.	Ed Walsh	Offy	4	255	Miller	blue	119.375	29	27	43-shock absorber
42	Al Miller	Kennedy Tank	Paul Weirick	Offy	4	270	Adams	blue, silver	123.233	28	28	41-accel. pedal bracket
29	Frank Brisko	National Seal	Frank Brisko	Brisko**	6	272	Stevens	gray, gold	123.351	11	29	38-air pump
44	Emil Andres	Chicago Flash	Jimmy Snyder	Offy	4	255	Stevens	maroon, white	121.212	21	30	22-stripped plug threads
32	Bob Swanson	S.M.J.	Sampson Motors, Inc.	Sampson*	16	183	Stevens	cream, blue	129.431	22	31	19-rear axle
47	Shorty Cantlon	Automotive Service	Assoc. Enterprises, Ltd.	Offy	4	262	Stevens	silver	125.567	7	32	15-main bearing
53	Deacon Litz	Maserati	Richard T. Wharton	Maserati*	8	182	Maserati	silver, black	117.979	31	33	7-valve

*Supercharged **Front drive ***Supercharged and front drive ****Supercharged, rear engine, four-wheel drive

28th Race • May 30, 1940

The back straight is paved with asphalt for this year's race, leaving the front straight as the only part of the track that is still brick.

Driver George Bailey is the lone fatality this May. He dies when his rear-engine Miller crashes in Turn 2 during practice. Car owner Harry Miller withdraws after the accident.

Rex Mays wins his third pole at a non-record speed of 127.85 mph with a supercharged Winfield eight. Defending 500 champ Wilbur Shaw in last year's winning Maserati and Mauri Rose in an Offy share the front row.

Ten supercharged engines make the show and the naturally aspirated four-cylinder Offenhauser powers 15 starters. Just four cars use the Miller engine, the architecture of which inspired the Offy.

Gasoline Alley scuttlebutt says Argentine Raul Riganti has more horsepower than anyone with his new Maserati engine, but he qualifies well back in the pack and is not a factor in the race. His Maserati spins in Turn 1 on the 25th lap, hits the inside wall, and rolls twice. Riganti is thrown from the car, but suffers only minor injuries.

The front-row starters keep the lead to themselves. Mays leads 59 laps and Rose five, but Shaw takes command and pulls away to nearly a full lap advantage over both when rain starts to fall on the backstretch.

The yellow flag comes out and what promises to be an exciting finish turns into a slow-moving parade that lasts the final 50 laps. With the caution flag flying, all drivers must hold their position behind Shaw, who coasts to one of the easiest victories ever.

Shaw is the first to win two in a row and joins the recently retired Louis Meyer as the only three-time winners. Mays and Rose follow Shaw across the finish line, making this the first race in which the front row finishes 1-2-3. Ted Horn starts and finishes fourth.

Crew members gather around veteran Russell Snowberger's car on race day (*above*). Note the child's wagon used to tote starting batteries to and from the pits. Snowberger's car broke down early and finished a disappointing 31st in his 12th start. Rookie Joie Chitwood (*below*), later to be known for his daredevil auto thrill shows, lasted to the finish and placed 15th. One of the perks Ted Doescher enjoyed as the AAA's new chief steward was the use of this snappy 1940 Buick convertible (*opposite top*). The field gets ready to roll for the 28th running of the 500 (*opposite bottom*).

STARTING LINEUP

Average Field Qualifying Speed: 122.853

Numbers in flags indicate finish position

3 — Mauri Rose

27 — Cliff Bergere

32 — Tommy Hinnershitz

24 — Shorty Cantlon (for Stapp)

11 — Harry McQuinn

1 — Wilbur Shaw

8 — Mel Hansen

9 — Frank Brisko

31 — Russell Snowberger

13 — Sam Hanks

POLE POSITION
Qualifying Speed: 127.850

2 — Rex Mays

4 — Ted Horn

7 — Frank Wearne

5 — Joel Thorne

21 — Kelly Petillo

Louis Tomei

Ralph Hepburn

Raul Riganti

Chet Miller

Al Miller

Floyd Davis

George Connor

Bob Swanson

George Robson

Joie Chitwood

Paul Russo

Billy DeVore

George Barringer

Doc Williams

Emil Andres

Duke Nalon

Al Putnam

Rene LeBegue

1940

The Studebaker Champion pace car, the first enclosed auto to pace the 500, leads the field into Turn 1 (*above*). Land-speed record holder Ab Jenkins was the driver. First-time qualifier Rene LeBegue, in the No. 49 Maserati (*right, top*), leads Emil Andres en route to a 10th-place finish, the highest among this year's freshmen. Andres nailed down the 12th spot. Sam Hanks, also making his first start, runs in front of Louis Tomei (*right, bottom*). Hanks, driving a racer built and owned by Leon Duray, came home 13th; Tomei ended 16th. Wilbur Shaw chugs milk in victory lane for the third time in four years (*opposite top*) after winning under caution in his Maserati (*opposite bottom*). Polesitter Rex Mays was second and Mauri Rose finished third, his best placement since coming in second in 1934.

RESULTS

NO.	DRIVER	CAR	ENTRANT	ENGINE	CYL	DISP	CHASSIS	COLOR	QUAL SPD	START	FIN	LAPS / SPEED / REASON OUT
1	Wilbur Shaw	Boyle	Boyle Racing Headquarters	Maserati*	8	179	Maserati	maroon, crm	127.065	2	1	200-114.277
33	Rex Mays	Bowes Seal Fast	Bowes Racing, Inc.	Winfield*	8	180	Stevens	ivory, blk, red	127.850	1	2	200-113.742
7	Mauri Rose	Elgin Piston Pin	Lou Moore, Inc.	Offy	4	270	Wetteroth	orange, blue	125.624	3	3	200-113.572
3	Ted Horn	Boyle	Boyle Racing Headquarters	Miller**	8	268	Miller	maroon, crm	125.545	4	4	199-flagged
8	Joel Thorne	Thorne Donnelly	Joel Thorne, Inc.	Sparks	6	271	Adams	blue, white	122.434	10	5	197-flagged
32	Bob Swanson	Sampson	Sampson Motors, Inc.	Sampson*	16	183	Stevens	yellow, blue	124.882	20	6	196-flagged
9	Frank Wearne	Boyle	Boyle Racing Headquarters	Offy	4	257	Stevens	maroon, crm	123.216	7	7	195-flagged
31	Mel Hansen	Hartz	Harry Hartz	Miller***	8	182	Wetteroth	gray, blue	124.753	5	8	194-flagged
16	Frank Brisko	Elgin Piston Pin	Frank Brisko	Brisko**	6	271	Stevens	red, white	122.716	8	9	193-flagged
49	Rene LeBegue	Lucy O'Reilly Schell	Lucy O'Reilly Schell	Maserati*	8	183	Maserati	blue, silver	118.981	31	10	192-flagged
41	Harry McQuinn	Hollywood Pay Day	Bill White Race Cars, Inc.	Alfa Romeo*	8	181	A.R. Weil	silver	122.486	15	11	192-flagged
25	Emil Andres	Belanger-Folz	Murrell Belanger	Offy	4	255	Stevens	yellow, blue	122.963	22	12	192-flagged
28	Sam Hanks	Duray	Leon Duray	Duray*	4	182	Weil	black, white	123.064	14	13	192-flagged
6	George Barringer	Hollywood Pay Day	Bill White Race Cars, Inc.	Offy	4	255	Weil	gray, blue	121.889	16	14	191-flagged
42	Joie Chitwood	Kennedy Tank	Paul Weirick	Offy	4	270	Adams	blue, silver	121.757	26	15	190-flagged
26	Louis Tomei	Falstaff	Ed Walsh	Offy	4	270	Miller	blue, silver	119.980	18	16	190-exhaust pipe
34	Chet Miller	Alfa Romeo	Wharton-Dewart Racing	Alfa Romeo*	8	183	Alfa Romeo	blue, silver	121.392	27	17	189-flagged
14	Billy DeVore	Bill Holabird	W. Wilbur Shaw	Offy	4	256	Shaw	yellow	122.197	32	18	181-flagged
44	Al Putnam	Refinoil	Anthony Gulotta	Offy	4	255	Adams	green, white	120.818	28	19	179-flagged
61	Floyd Davis	Lencki	Joseph Lencki	Lencki	4	260	Lencki	blue, white	120.797	33	20	157-flagged
35	Kelly Petillo	Indiana Fur	Kelly Petillo	Offy	4	270	Wetteroth	brown, silver	125.331	13	21	128-rear main bearing
21	Duke Nalon	Marks	Joseph Marks	Offy	4	255	Silnes	maroon	121.790	25	22	120-con. rod
17	George Robson	Keller	Marty Keller	Offy**	4	255	Miller-Ford	black	122.562	23	23	67-shock absorber
24	Babe Stapp	Surber	Frederick K. Surber	Offy	4	262	Stevens	cream, red	123.367	12	24	64-oil line
36	Doc Williams	Quillen Bros. Refrig	Doc Williams	Miller**	4	255	Cooper	blue, white	122.963	19	25	61-oil line
10	George Connor	Lencki	Joseph Lencki	Lencki	6	265	Lencki	red, yellow	124.585	17	26	52-con. rod
5	Cliff Bergere	Noc-Out Hose Clamp	Lou Moore, Inc.	Offy	4	270	Wetteroth	red, blk, silver	123.673	6	27	51-oil line
38	Paul Russo	Elgin Piston Pin	Elgin Piston Pin Co.	Brisko	6	271	Blume	white	120.809	29	28	48-oil leak
54	Ralph Hepburn	Bowes Seal Fast	W. C. Winfield	Offy**	4	270	Miller-Ford	wht, blk, red	123.860	21	29	47-steering frozen, spun
58	Al Miller	Alfa Romeo	Frank T. Griswold, Jr.	Alfa Romeo*	8	177	Alfa Romeo	maroon	120.288	30	30	41-clutch
19	Russ Snowberger	Snowberger	Russell Snowberger	Miller**	4	255	Snowberger	dark blue	121.564	11	31	38-water pump
27	Tommy Hinnershitz	Marks Offenhauser	Joseph Marks	Offy	4	270	Adams	maroon	122.614	9	32	32-crankshaft, hit wall FS
29	Raul Riganti	Maserati	Raul Riganti	Maserati*	8	183	Maserati	blue, yellow	121.827	24	33	24-wrecked T2

* Supercharged ** Front drive *** Supercharged and front drive

1941

29th Race • May 30, 1941

World War II already engulfs Europe, and the last race before the U.S. joins the fight draws just 42 entries, the fewest since 1930.

The same three drivers fill the front row as in the previous year. Mauri Rose wins the pole at 128.691 mph in a supercharged Maserati. Rex Mays is next door in a supercharged Winfield, and three-time winner Wilbur Shaw is next to him in the Maserati that has won back-to-back races.

Thirty-three cars qualify, but Sam Hanks crashes in practice the day before the race and is seriously hurt. On race-day morning, fire sweeps through the garage area, damaging several cars and destroying George Barringer's rear-engine Miller that was supposed to start 15th. The fire delays the start two hours and only 31 cars take the green flag.

Though Rose starts from the pole, he initially falls behind Mays and Shaw. He surges into the lead by the 40th lap, only to be knocked out of the race by faulty spark plugs. He is not out of a ride long. Car owner Lou Moore orders Floyd Davis, who is running 14th, to pit on lap 72. Davis climbs out and Rose jumps into the No. 16 Offy.

Shaw appears to have a good shot at an unprecedented fourth win. He leads 107 laps, with Mays and Cliff Bergere chasing but unable to catch up.

On lap 152, a wheel collapses on Shaw's Maserati and he crashes in Turn 1, ending his day. After the race, Shaw claims the wheel should not have been used. Chalk markings identifying it as faulty were washed away when firefighters fought the garage fire, says Shaw, who decides to retire.

Rose is second when green-flag racing resumes. He picks off Bergere in 10 laps and streaks to a one-minute, 30-second victory margin over Mays. Rose and Davis share honors of driving the winning car.

Ted Horn is third with a Sparks six and Ralph Hepburn is fourth in the debut of the Novi V-8. Bergere, overcome by fumes and exhaustion, fades to fifth place, but earns recognition for driving a gasoline-powered car 500 miles without a stop for the first time.

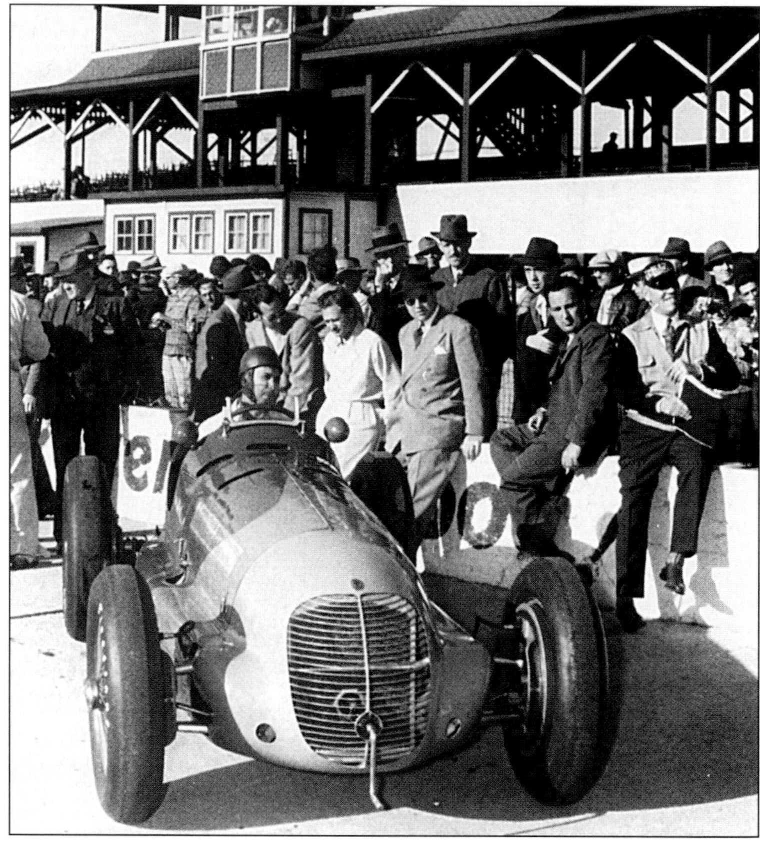

STARTING LINEUP

Average Field Qualifying Speed: 122.739

Numbers in flags indicate finish position

Wilbur Shaw

Frank Wearne

Chet Miller

Everett Saylor

Emil Andres

Rex Mays

Doc Williams

Billy DeVore

Russell Snowberger

Al Miller

POLE POSITION
Qualifying Speed: 128.691

Mauri Rose

Harry McQuinn

Cliff Bergere

Ralph Hepburn

George Connor

Cliff Bergere (*opposite top*) takes the checkered flag for his qualifying run, which placed him on the inside of row three with a speed just shy of 124 mph. However, he was more than four mph slower than Mauri Rose, who won the only pole of his career in a Lou Moore-owned Maserati (*opposite bottom*). On race day, Bergere managed a fifth-place finish by virtue of being able to run the entire 500 miles without a pit stop in his Offenhauser-powered Wetteroth. Drivers and others took time out for a round of golf on the Speedway course (*right*). Fire swept through the garage area on the morning of the race (*below*), damaging several cars. Miraculously, only one entry—George Barringer's rear-engine Miller—was destroyed in the blaze (*third from top, right*). Barringer had qualified the car in the 15th starting spot (*second from top, right*).

Paul Russo

Mel Hansen

Louis Tomei

Joie Chitwood

Duke Nalon

Floyd Davis/Mauri Rose

Tommy Hinnershitz

Joel Thorne

Overton Phillips

Deacon Litz

George Robson

Kelly Petillo

Frank Brisko

Tony Willman

Ted Horn

Al Putnam

Second-year driver Sam Hanks qualified the No. 28 Kurtis-Offy in 27th place (*top*), but crashed in practice the day before the race and failed to start. The stunning Chrysler Newport show car (*middle*) paced the field (*above*), a dramatic change from the staid Studebaker pace car of the previous year. Floyd Davis (*opposite top*) started the day in the No. 16 owned by Lou Moore, but co-winner Mauri Rose took over and drove it to victory. Ralph Hepburn (*opposite bottom*) brought the Novi V-8 power plant to a fourth-place finish in its first outing.

RESULTS

NO.	DRIVER	CAR	ENTRANT	ENGINE	CYL	DISP	CHASSIS	COLOR	QUAL SPD	START	FIN	LAPS / SPEED / REASON OUT
16	F. Davis-M. Rose	Noc-Out Hose Clamp	Lou Moore, Inc.	Offy	4	270	Wetteroth	red, blue	121.106	17	1	200-115.117
1	Rex Mays	Bowes Seal Fast	Bowes Racing, Inc.	Winfield*	8	180	Stevens	ivory, blk, red	128.301	2	2	200-114.459
4	Ted Horn	T.E.C.	Art Sparks	Sparks*	6	181	Adams	blue, white	124.297	28	3	200-113.864
54	Ralph Hepburn	Bowes Seal Fast	Bowes Racing, Inc.	Novi*	8	180	Miller-Ford	ivory, blk, red	120.653	10	4	200-113.631
34	Cliff Bergere	Noc-Out Hose Clamp	Cliff Bergere	Offy	4	270	Wetteroth	red, black	123.890	7	5	200-113.528
41	Chet Miller	Boyle	Boyle Racing Headquarters	Miller**	8	268	Miller	maroon	121.540	9	6	200-111.921
15	Harry McQuinn	Ziffrin	Bill White	Alfa Romeo*	8	181	A. R. Weil	blue, silver	125.449	4	7	200-111.795
7	Frank Wearne	Bill Holabird	Arthur M. Sims	Offy	4	255	Shaw	yellow, red	123.890	6	8	200-110.818
45	Paul Russo	Leader Card	Carl Marchese	Miller*	8	137	Marchese	white	125.217	18	9	200-105.628
27	Tommy Hinnershitz	Marks	Joe Marks	Offy	4	270	Adams	blue, silver	121.021	20	10	200-105.152
53	Louis Tomei	H-3	Hughes Bros.	Offy**	4	255	Miller-Ford	black	121.074	24	11	200-104.926
55	Al Putnam	Schoof	Val Johnson	Offy	4	255	Wetteroth	orange, black	121.951	31	12	200-101.381
26	Overton Phillips	Phillips	Overton A. Phillips	Miller	8	269	Bugatti	maroon, silver	116.298	26	13	187-flagged
25	Joie Chitwood	Blue Crown Spk Plug	Joe Lencki	Lencki	6	265	Lencki	blue, white	120.329	27	14	177-flagged
17	Duke Nalon	Elgin Piston Pin	Elgin Piston Pin Co.	Maserati*	8	183	Maserati	red, yellow	122.951	30	15	173-flagged
14	George Connor	Boyle	Boyle Racing Headquarters	Offy	4	257	Stevens	maroon	123.984	13	16	167-transmission
47	Everett Saylor	Bowles	Mark E. Bowles, M.D.	Offy	4	255	Weil	red, silver	119.860	12	17	155-wrecked T4
2	Wilbur Shaw	Boyle	Boyle Racing Headquarters	Maserati*	8	179	Maserati	maroon	127.836	3	18	151-wrecked T1
23	Billy DeVore	Pay Day Candy	Frederick K. Surber	Offy	4	272	Stevens	cream, red	121.770	8	19	121-con. rod
62	Tony Willman	Lyons	George Lyons	Offy	4	260	Stevens	yellow, red	123.920	25	20	117-con. rod
42	Russ Snowberger	Hussy's Sprtsmn Club	Russell Snowberger	Offy	4	255	Snowberger	dark blue	120.104	11	21	107-water pump
32	Deacon Litz	Sampson 16	Sampson Motors, Inc.	Sampson*	16	183	Stevens	cream, blue	123.440	29	22	89-oil trouble
8	Frank Brisko	Zollner Piston	Frank Brisko	Brisko**	6	271	Stevens	red, silver	123.381	22	23	70-valve spring
36	Doc Williams	Indiana Fur	Aero Marine Finishes Co.	Offy**	4	255	Cooper	gold, white	124.014	5	24	68-radiator leak
10	George Robson	Gilmore Red Lion	Leon Duray	Duray*	4	182	Weil	black, silver	121.576	16	25	66-oil leak
3	Mauri Rose	Elgin Piston Pin	Lou Moore, Inc.	Maserati*	8	183	Maserati	red, silver	128.691	1	26	60-spark plug problem
22	Kelly Petillo	Air Lines Sndwch Shp	Kelly Petillo	Offy	4	270	Wetteroth	wht, red, blue	124.417	19	27	48-con. rod
12	Al Miller	Miller	Eddie Offutt	Miller***	6	180	Miller	blue, white	123.478	14	28	22-transmission
9	Mel Hansen	Fageol	Lou Fageol	Offy**	4	270	Miller-Ford	white	124.599	21	29	11-con. rod
19	Emil Andres	Kennedy Tank	Joe Lencki	Lencki	6	265	Lencki	yellow, red	122.266	15	30	5-wrecked T3
5	Joel Thorne	Thorne Engineering	Joel Thorne, Inc.	Sparks	6	271	Adams	blue, white	121.163	23	31	5-wrecked T3
35	George Barringer	Miller	Eddie Offutt	Miller***	6	180	Miller	blue, white	122.299	—	—	Destroyed in garage fire
28	Sam Hanks	Tom Joyce 7-Up	Ed Walsh Corp.	Offy	4	270	Kurtis	red	118.211	—	—	Wrecked day before race

* Supercharged ** Front drive *** Supercharged and four-wheel drive

When Floyd Davis was told he was going to be relieved by Mauri Rose, he wasn't very happy. Films show him hesitantly getting out of the racer. But when Rose brought the car into Victory Lane, Davis couldn't have been happier. For years, the likable dirt track veteran had his own story. "I was ready to go into the lead when they called me in," Floyd said. In reality, when Rose took over the car, it was in 14th place.

But Davis joined an elite "group" that day. L. L. Corum was the only other driver designated as a co-winner of the Indianapolis 500-Mile Race. Davis and Corum also shared another distinction. Corum made six Indy starts and Davis took the green four times, yet while they are accorded every bit as much adulation as all the other race winners, neither driver ever led a lap of the 500.

30th Race • May 30, 1946

The Brickyard reopens after World War II with Tony Hulman as its new owner. Three-time winner Wilbur Shaw discovers how rundown the Speedway is when he conducts tire tests for the government in 1944. He persuades Hulman, a Terre Haute businessman, to buy the sagging facility from Eddie Rickenbacker. The deal is done on November 15, 1945, for a reported $750,000, and Shaw becomes president and general manager.

A record purse of $115,450 attracts 58 entries—nearly all pre-war cars—to the Speedway, which is refurbished in time for Memorial Day. Chassis and engine rules are the same as in 1941.

Cliff Bergere wins the pole with an Offy for his 15th start, and one of the most unusual cars to appear at the Speedway lines up second. Paul Russo's Fageol has two supercharged Offy engines, 91-cid four-cylinders built for midget racing. The engine in front powers the front wheels, and the engine in back powers the rear. Russo is first out of the race when he hits the Turn 3 wall on lap 17 and breaks a leg.

Bergere leads just two laps, and Rex Mays charges from 14th place to lead three before a cracked manifold sidelines him on lap 27. Mauri Rose leads eight laps, but spins on lap 41 and hits the wall.

Ralph Hepburn, also in his 15th race, qualifies after pole day at a record 133.944 mph with a supercharged Novi V-8, but starts 19th. The piercing scream of the Novi announces his surge to the front by lap 12. Hepburn leads 44 laps before a stop for brake repairs knocks him out of contention. His day ends on lap 122 when his engine quits.

George Robson starts 15th and moves to the front as the others falter. He leads 138 laps, including the last 108, to beat rookie Jimmy Jackson by 44 seconds. Only nine of 33 starters finish.

Though supercharged engines will compete at the Speedway for another 20 years, Robson's Sparks six-cylinder (basically an Offy with two more cylinders) is the last one to win.

After four years of neglect, much work was needed to get the Speedway ready for the resumption of racing. Jack Fortner mans the pavement roller (*above*). Henry Ford II bones up on his duties as driver of the Lincoln Continental pace car (*below*). Rookie Jimmy Wilburn made the show in the Alfa Romeo-powered Mobiloil Special (*opposite top*). Ralph Hepburn accepts congratulations after qualifying the Novi at a record 133.944 mph on the second day of time trials (*opposite middle*). It was Hepburn's 15th race. AAA officials confer around a 1947 Studebaker used as an official car (*opposite bottom*).

STARTING LINEUP

Average Field Qualifying Speed: 122.328

Numbers in flags indicate finish position

POLE POSITION
Qualifying Speed: 126.471

Sam Hanks

Louis Durant

Mauri Rose

Joie Chitwood

George Robson

Paul Russo

Jimmy Jackson

Duke Dinsmore

Emil Andres

Rex Mays

Cliff Bergere

Hal Cole

Ted Horn

Russell Snowberger

Al Putnam

Rudi Caracciola during practice, just moments before his car crashed.

New Speedway owner Tony Hulman and president Wilbur Shaw extended an invitation to grand prix ace Rudi Caracciola to come to Indy in 1946. The German champion's Mercedes-Benz didn't clear customs, but he decided to come anyway.

Upon arrival, Caracciola was hired by flamboyant owner/driver Joel Thorne to drive the potent "Big Six" Thorne-Sparks racer. Caracciola adapted to the car quickly and was soon up to qualifying speed. The only thing he didn't like was the AAA officials' insistence that he wear a hard crash helmet. Since Caracciola didn't own anything except cloth helmets, an artillery helmet was pressed into use.

During a practice run, Caracciola crashed coming off the second turn. Although it was said the driver was struck in the face by a bird, the cause of the accident was never resolved. Caracciola suffered a severely fractured skull, and it was several months before he knew anything about the first postwar 500, or even where he was living. Only when he began to recover did Rudi learn that Tony Hulman had taken him to his home in Terre Haute, Indiana, to recuperate. The act of kindness resulted in a lifelong friendship.

Harry McQuinn

Henry Banks

George Barringer

Mel Hansen

George Connor

Danny Kladis

Chet Miller

Shorty Cantlon

Hal Robson

Tony Bettenhausen

Frank Wearne

Duke Nalon

Jimmy Wilburn

Ralph Hepburn

Louis Tomei

Bill Sheffler

Luigi Villoresi

Billy DeVore

Since Joel Thorne seldom allowed his cars to race on dirt tracks, following his victory at Indy, George Robson needed another car to finish out the year. By mid-season, he'd settled into the cockpit of Cliff Bergere's car. This was the former Burd Piston Ring Special driven to victory by Floyd Roberts in 1938. (Unfortunately, Roberts lost his life in the 500 the following year.) It was also the same car Bergere drove to fifth place in 1941. Cliff had taken a liking to the machine, and when Lou Moore decided to sell it, Bergere closed the deal.

Robson had good success with the car, too. That is, until September 2, 1946, at Atlanta's Lakewood Speedway, where little George was involved in a multi-car accident which claimed his life and that of George Barringer (who was driving Wilbur Shaw's 500-winning car from 1937).

When the twisted racer was returned home, Bergere was very upset that his pal had been killed in the racer. "Two of my best friends have been killed in that thing," Cliff said. "And that's two too many." He went out to his shop, took an acetylene torch, and cut the car to pieces.

The pace car leads the field down the backstretch (*above*), and when the race gets under way, smoke pours from some of the front runners (*below*). Mechanical problems claimed a large chunk of the field, which was a patchwork of pre-war cars. Russ Snowberger's Maserati passes Hal Robson's Bugatti before the bleachers on the front straight (*opposite, top left*). A huge crowd attended the first race in five years and caused a major race-day traffic jam. Mauri Rose, gunning for a second straight win, led eight laps before smacking the Turn 3 wall hard in his Lencki (*opposite, top right*). British native George Robson, making his third start, avoided the early wrecks, worked his way to the front, and dominated the last half of the race to triumph in the supercharged six-cylinder No. 16 Adams-Sparks (*opposite bottom*). Robson never got a chance to defend his Indy title; he was killed on September 2, 1946, while racing in Atlanta.

RESULTS

NO.	DRIVER	CAR	ENTRANT	ENGINE	CYL	DISP	CHASSIS	COLOR	QUAL SPD	START	FIN	LAPS / SPEED / REASON OUT
16	George Robson	Thorne Engineering	Thorne Engineering Corp.	Sparks*	6	183	Adams	blue, white	125.541	15	1	200-114.820
61	Jimmy Jackson	Jackson	Jimmy Jackson	Offy**	4	255	Miller	green, gold	120.257	5	2	200-114.498
29	Ted Horn	Boyle Maserati	Boyle Racing Headquarters	Maserati*	8	179	Maserati	white, purple	123.980	7	3	200-109.819
18	Emil Andres	Elgin Piston Pin	Frank Brisko	Maserati*	8	183	Maserati	blk, wit, silver	121.139	11	4	200-108.902
24	Joie Chitwood	Noc-Out Hose Clamp	Fred A. Peters	Offy	4	270	Wetteroth	red, blue, silver	119.816	12	5	200-108.399
33	Louis Durant	Alfa Romeo	Milt Marion	Alfa Romeo*	8	182	Alfa Romeo	red, white	118.973	6	6	200-105.073
52	Gigi Villoresi	Maserati	Corvorado Filippini	Maserati*	8	181	Maserati	red, silver	121.249	28	7	200-100.783
7	Frank Wearne	Wolfe Motors, Tulsa	Ervin Wolfe	Offy	4	271	Shaw	cream, red	121.233	29	8	197-flagged
39	Bill Sheffler	Jack Maurer	Bill Sheffler	Offy	4	255	Bromme	red, cream	120.611	25	9	139-flagged
17	Billy DeVore	Schoof	William Schoof	Offy	4	255	Wetteroth	orange, black	119.876	31	10	167-spun T1
41	Mel Hansen	Offenhauser	Ross Page	Duray*	4	183	Kurtis	mrn, wht, slvr	121.431	27	11	143-crankshaft
25	Russ Snowberger	Jim Hussy's	R. A. Cott	Maserati*	8	183	Maserati	maroon, silver	121.593	10	12	134-differential
14	Harry McQuinn	Mobilgas	Robert J. Flavell	Sparks*	6	183	Adams	white, red	124.499	18	13	124-out of oil
2	Ralph Hepburn	Novi Governor	W. C. Winfield	Novi***	8	180	Kurtis	blue, red, yllow	133.944	19	14	121-stalled
12	Al Putnam	L.G.S. Spring Clutch	George L. Kuehn	Offy	4	255	Stevens	cream, blue	116.283	13	15	120-magneto, frame
3	Cliff Bergere	Noc-Out Hose Clamp	Shirley Bergere	Offy	4	270	Wetteroth	red, blk, silver	126.471	1	16	82-out of oil
45	Duke Dinsmore	Johnston	Fred W. Johnston	Offy	4	255	Adams	maroon, silver	123.279	8	17	82-con. rod
5	Chet Miller	Chet Miller	Chet Miller	Offy**	4	255	Cooper	blue, silver	124.649	17	18	64-oil line
63	Jimmy Wilburn	Mobiloil	Bill White	Alfa Romeo*	8	181	A.R. Weil	red, white	125.113	16	19	52-engine trouble
42	Tony Bettenhausen	Bristow-McManus	Robert J. McManus	Miller***	8	183	Wetteroth	cream, blue	123.094	26	20	47-con. rod
59	Danny Kladis	Grancor V8	Grancor	Ford V8**	8	274	Miller-Ford	blue, silver	118.890	33	21	46-towed, disqualified
54	Duke Nalon	Maserati	Corvorado Filippini	Maserati*	4	91	Maserati	red, silver	119.682	32	22	45-universal joint
8	Mauri Rose	Blue Crown Sprk Plg	Joe Lencki	Lencki	6	265	Lencki	red, blue, slvr	124.065	9	23	40-wrecked T3
38	George Connor	Walsh Offenhauser	Ed Walsh	Offy	4	270	Kurtis	red, yellow	120.006	30	24	38-piston
48	Hal Robson	Phillips Miller	Overton A. Phillips	Miller	8	269	Bugatti	maroon, silver	121.466	23	25	37-con. rod
15	Louis Tomei	Boxar Tool	Joseph Hosso	Brisko**	6	271	Stevens	maroon, white	119.193	22	26	34-oil line
31	Henry Banks	Automobile Shippers	Louis Rassey	Offy**	4	255	Snowberger	orange, black	120.220	21	27	32-stalled
64	Shorty Cantlon	H-3	Charles J. Hughes	Offy**	4	255	Miller-Ford	black	122.432	20	28	28-clutch
26	George Barringer	Tucker Torpedo	George Barringer	Miller*4R	6	180	Miller	blue, white	120.628	24	29	27-gear trouble
1	Rex Mays	Bowes Seal Fast	Bowes Racing, Inc.	Winfield*	8	180	Stevens	ivory, black	128.861	14	30	26-manifold
32	Sam Hanks	Spike Jones	Gordon Schroeder	Sampson*	16	183	Stevens	cream, blue	124.762	3	31	18-oil line
47	Hal Cole	Don Lee	Don Lee, Inc.	Alfa Romeo*	8	177	Alfa Romeo	maroon, silver	120.728	4	32	16-fuel leak
10	Paul Russo	Fageol Twin Coach	Lee Fageol	2 Offys****	8	180	Fageol	red, blue, wht	126.183	2	33	16-wrecked T3

* Supercharged ** Front drive *** Supercharged and front drive **** Supercharged, twin engines; front engine drove the rear wheels, rear engine drove the front wheels 4R = Supercharged, four-wheel drive, rear

1947

31st Race • May 30, 1947

A group of car owners and drivers forms the American Society for Professional Automobile Racing before the race and threatens to skip the 500 unless the prize money increases to 40 percent of the gate. ASPAR, which represents 16 entries, agrees to a settlement just days before the race, which has a record purse of $137,425. However, with little practice time, some of the ASPAR members fail to meet the 115-mph minimum qualifying speed, and only 30 cars start the race.

Ted Horn starts from the pole in the Maserati that won in 1939 and 1940 at the hands of Wilbur Shaw. Rookie Bill Holland qualifies on the second day in a front-drive Offy and sets fast time of 128.755 mph. Cliff Bergere, in his 16th and final 500, starts second in a Novi and leads 23 laps before a burned piston ends his day on lap 64.

Holland starts eighth and is leading on lap 41 when he spins in Turn 1. Veteran Shorty Cantlon loses control trying to avoid Holland and dies when he crashes hard into the outside wall.

Holland recovers from his spin to regain the lead and keeps his Blue Crown Special in front for 143 laps. He is well ahead of teammate Mauri Rose, who is running second, when owner Lou Moore displays an "EZY" sign for both of his drivers. Holland obediently slows down, but Rose keeps charging. On lap 193, Holland lets Rose pass, thinking that Rose is merely unlapping himself. Rose, however, is ignoring his owner's orders. He slips by Holland and pulls away to a 32-second victory, his second 500 win.

After the race, a stunned and angry Holland learns that he gave away the victory to his teammate. Rose defends his move by claiming he wanted to avoid a wheel-to-wheel duel at the finish that could have taken both cars out of the race and allow third-place finisher Horn to win.

STARTING LINEUP

Average Field Qualifying Speed: 121.039

Numbers in flags indicate finish position

POLE POSITION
Qualifying Speed: 126.564

Mauri Rose

Russell Snowberger

Ken Fowler

Roland Free

Frank Wearne

Cliff Bergere

Shorty Cantlon

Bill Holland

Milt Fankhouser

Walt Brown

Ted Horn

Herb Ardinger

Les Anderson

Jimmy Jackson

George Connor

Although the Nash name had been affixed to cars since 1917, it wasn't until 1947 that the pride of Kenosha, Wisconsin, paced the Indianapolis 500 (*opposite left*). Speedway President Wilbur Shaw poses at the wheel of the Nash Ambassador pacemaker (*opposite right*), but it was driven on race day by George Mason, president of the car company. A highly detailed badge (*above*) granted the bearer access to the pits for the 1947 event. Racers mass in the pits before being pushed onto the starting grid (*below*). The grandstands behind the pits were added by owner Tony Hulman the previous year to better serve the growing crowds drawn to the event.

Perhaps the longest shot in the 1947 race was the Miller-Ford entered by the Granatelli brothers, Andy, Vince, and Joe. After all, the car was 12 years old and driver Pete Romcevich had heretofore never risen much beyond the midget ranks. But by 20 laps, "Pistol Pete" had charged the flathead Ford V-8 from 17th to seventh.

On lap 30, Romcevich pitted with the granddaddy of all oil leaks and little or no oil pressure. Realizing the rule against adding oil once the race had started would disqualify the car, Andy Granatelli yelled for his brother Joe to bring the water bucket. In full view of officials and fans, Andy removed the radiator cap, placing it puposely onto the radiator shell. Leaning in, he blocked the official's view, while he quickly removed the oil breather cap and dumped two gallons of water into the crankcase. The water mixed with what oil was left in the engine. The nonplussed Pete and Joe watched the oil pressure return to normal.

Back in the race, Romcevich drove at a slightly reduced pace. The car lasted another 138 laps before the engine tore itself to bits. Nevertheless, the old racer finished 12th.

Duke Nalon

Paul Russo

Charles Van Acker

Duke Dinsmore

Emil Andres

Pete Romcevich

Rex Mays

Fred Agabashian

Henry Banks

Mel Hansen

Hal Robson

Al Miller

Joie Chitwood

Tony Bettenhausen

Cy Marshall

Photographers crowd around a pre-race favorite in the pit lane on the morning of the race (*above*). Still just forming up, the field stretches out behind the pace car prior to the start (*right*). After the green flag drops, Mauri Rose leads Russ Snowberger into Turn 1 while Rose's teammate, rookie Bill Holland, gives chase in an identical Blue Crown Spark Plug Special (*below*). Cliff Bergere, who started in the middle of the front row, already has pulled away from this trio into the lead with his Novi. The aggressive Rose (*opposite top*) won for the second time when he ignored orders from owner Lou Moore to slow down and blew by Holland. George Connor leads Duke Dinsmore's trim-looking No. 10 Wetteroth-Offy in the early going (*opposite bottom*). Dinsmore finished 10th, and Connor ended up 26th.

RESULTS

NO.	DRIVER	CAR	ENTRANT	ENGINE	CYL	DISP	CHASSIS	COLOR	QUAL SPD	START	FIN	LAPS / SPEED / REASON OUT
27	Mauri Rose	Blue Crown Sprk Plg	Lou Moore	Offy**	4	270	Deidt	blue, white	124.040	3	1	200-116.338
16	Bill Holland	Blue Crown Sprk Plg	Lou Moore	Offy**	4	270	Deidt	blue, white	128.755	8	2	200-116.097
1	Ted Horn	Bennett Bros.	H. C. Henning	Maserati*	8	179	Maserati	black, gold	126.564	1	3	200-114.997
54	Herb Ardinger	Novi Governor Mobil	W. C. Winfield	Novi***	8	180	Kurtis	red, cream	120.733	4	4	200-113.404
7	Jimmy Jackson	Jim Hussey	H. C. Henning	Offy**	4	258	Miller	green, gold	122.266	10	5	200-112.834
9	Rex Mays	Bowes Seal Fast	Bowes Racing, Inc.	Winfield*	8	180	Kurtis	blk, wht, red	124.412	20	6	200-111.056
33	Walt Brown	Permafuse	Milt Marion	Alfa Romeo*	8	182	Alfa Romeo	red, silver	118.355	14	7	200-101.744
34	Cy Marshall	Tattersfield	Bill White	Alfa Romeo*	8	183	A. R. Weil	red, white	115.644	28	8	197-flagged
41	Fred Agabashian	R. Page Offenhauser	Ross Page	Duray*	8	183	Kurtis	maroon, white	121.478	23	9	191-flagged
10	Duke Dinsmore	Schoof	Bill Schoof	Offy	4	270	Wetteroth	orange, black	119.840	27	10	167-flagged
58	Les Anderson	Kennedy Tank	Les Anderson	Offy	4	270	Maserati	red, white	118.425	7	11	131-flagged
59	Pete Romcevich	Camco Motors Ford	Anthony Granatelli	Ford V8**	8	256	Miller-Ford	blue, red	117.218	17	12	168-mechanical failure
3	Emil Andres	Preston Tucker Partner	Joe Lencki	Lencki	6	265	Lencki	blue, white	116.781	30	13	150-magneto
31	Frank Wearne	Superior Industries	Louis Rassey	Offy	4	263	Miller	orange, black	117.716	15	14	128-spun T3
47	Ken Fowler	Don Lee Alfa Romeo	Don Lee, Inc.	Alfa Romeo*	8	177	Alfa Romeo	red, silver	123.423	9	15	121-axle
46	Duke Nalon	Don Lee Mercedes	Don Lee, Inc.	Mercedes*	12	183	Mercedes	silver, red	128.082	18	16	119-piston
28	Roland Free	Bristow-McManus	Robert J. McManus	Miller***	8	183	Wetteroth	cream, blue	119.526	12	17	87-spun T1
29	Tony Bettenhausen	Belanger	Murrell Belanger	Offy	4	255	Stevens	blue, gold	120.980	25	18	79-timing gear
25	Russ Snowberger	Federal Engineering	R. A. Cott	Maserati*	8	183	Maserati	maroon, silver	121.331	6	19	74-oil pump
52	Hal Robson	Palmer	Richard L. Palmer	Offy	4	255	Adams	blue, silver	122.096	16	20	67-transmission
18	Cliff Bergere	Novi Governor Mobil	W. C. Winfield	Novi***	8	180	Kurtis	cream, red	124.957	2	21	63-piston
8	Joie Chitwood	Peters	Fred Peters	Offy	4	270	Wetteroth	red, blue	123.157	22	22	51-gears
24	Shorty Cantlon	Automobile Shippers	Louis Rassey	Miller**	16	272	Snowberger	orange, black	121.462	5	23	40-wrecked T1
43	Henry Banks	Federal Engineering	H. C. Henning	Offy**	4	255	Miller-Ford	black, red	120.923	26	24	36-oil line
66	Al Miller	Preston Tucker	Clay Ballinger	Miller*4R	6	180	Miller	blue, red	124.848	19	25	33-magneto
14	George Connor	Walsh	Ed Walsh	Offy	4	255	Kurtis	red, yellow	124.874	13	26	32-leaking fuel tank
38	Mel Hansen	Flavell-Duffy	Robert J. Flavell	Sparks*	6	183	Adams	blue, white	117.298	29	27	32-pushed, disqualified
15	Paul Russo	Wolfe Motors, Tulsa	Ervin Wolfe	Offy	4	271	Shaw	red, black	123.967	21	28	24-wrecked FS
44	Charles Van Acker	Preston Tucker Partner	Joe Lencki	Lencki	4	265	Stevens	blue, white	121.049	24	29	24-wrecked FS
53	Milt Fankhouser	Jack Maurer's Club	Milt Fankhouser	Offy	4	272	Stevens	maroon, silver	119.932	11	30	16-stalled T2

* Supercharged ** Front drive *** Supercharged and front drive 4 = Four-wheel drive R = Rear engined

32nd Race • May 31, 1948

The Novi V-8 proves too hot to handle for some. Cliff Bergere, driving the same Novi in which he led 23 laps in 1947, spins twice in practice and climbs out. Bergere, who is 52 and has 16 starts on his resume, calls the car unsafe and quits the Novi team. Ralph Hepburn, a veteran of 15 Indianapolis 500s, replaces Bergere and dies a few days later when he loses control in Turn 3 and crashes during practice.

Chet Miller bails out of a second Novi and accepts a ride in a Mercedes instead. Duke Nalon replaces Miller and sets the fast time of 131.603 mph, though he starts 11th because he misses pole-day qualifying.

Veteran Billy DeVore drives the most unique of the 80 entries. He qualifies well off the pace in 20th position, but still sets a record because his Kurtis chassis has three axles and six wheels. All four wheels mounted behind the cockpit are drive wheels, giving him four-wheel drive as well. DeVore finishes 12th.

Rex Mays, who wins a record fourth pole with a supercharged Winfield, leads 36 laps before a fuel leak forces him out.

Nalon is in the hunt all day with his Novi, but it consumes nearly a gallon of fuel per lap. To counter the Novi's poor economy, his car carries a 110-gallon tank, and his strategy is to make only one fuel stop. However, an air pocket in the massive tank gives an incorrect reading and he runs dry while leading with 16 laps to go. Nalon pits again and falls to third.

Teammates Mauri Rose and Bill Holland again finish 1-2 in front-drive Offys owned by Lou Moore, but this year there is no controversy between them. Rose beats Holland by 1 minute, 24 seconds and wins at a record 119.814 mph, joining Wilbur Shaw and Louis Meyer as a three-time winner.

Ted Horn leads 75 laps and finishes fourth, the ninth race in a row that he places fourth or higher. During this stretch, he completes 1799 out of a possible 1800 laps. Horn dies later that year at a race in DuQuoin, Ill.

Moments after the command to start engines, the pace car and front-row qualifiers begin to move down the track (*top*). A Chevrolet paced the field for the first time, and three-time winner and Speedway President Wilbur Shaw drove the gray Fleetmaster convertible (*above*). Billy DeVore set a new track record for most wheels on one car with the Pat Clancy Special (*opposite bottom*). The Offenhauser-powered Kurtis racer carried DeVore to a 12th-place finish. Both sets of rear wheels were drive wheels. The enormous number of cars parked in the infield on race day (*opposite top*) testifies to the phenomenal growth of fan interest in the 500 after World War II under new owner Tony Hulman.

STARTING LINEUP

Average Field Qualifying Speed: 125.505

Numbers in flags indicate finish position

POLE POSITION
Qualifying Speed: 130.577

Mauri Rose

Doc Williams

Les Anderson

Charles Van Acker

Sam Hanks

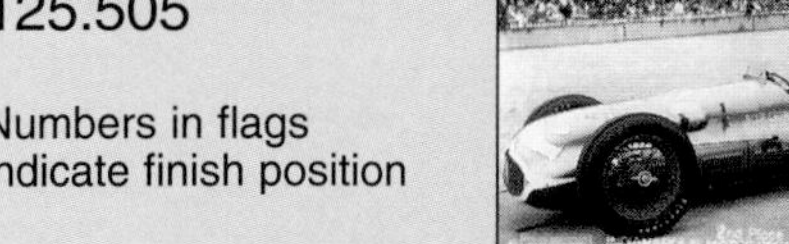

Bill Holland

Ted Horn

Johnny Mantz

Duke Nalon

Hal Cole

Rex Mays

Jimmy Jackson

Bill Cantrell

Joie Chitwood

Jack McGrath

National driving champion Ted Horn, was one of the favorites to win the '48 Indianapolis 500. And why not? Ted was wheeling Cotton Henning's famous Maserati, which had carried Wilbur Shaw to a pair of 500 victories. But after qualifying fifth fastest, people who knew Horn and Henning, noticed concern etched on their usually cheerful faces.

In the race, Horn took command and appeared headed for certain victory. But suddenly the Maserati slowed. Horn put up no fight at all as Mauri Rose, Bill Holland, and Duke Nalon relegated him to a fourth-place finish.

When Henning had torn down the engine in preparation for the race, he found that someone had dumped sand in the power plant. Try as he might, Cotton couldn't completely get it out of the smaller oil passages in the intricate lubrication system. Horn had detected the oil pressure dropping and backed off to save the engine and finish the race. Neither man said much about the incident publicly. Held in high regard by their peers, Horn and Henning seldom attracted enemies. But they must have had at least one.

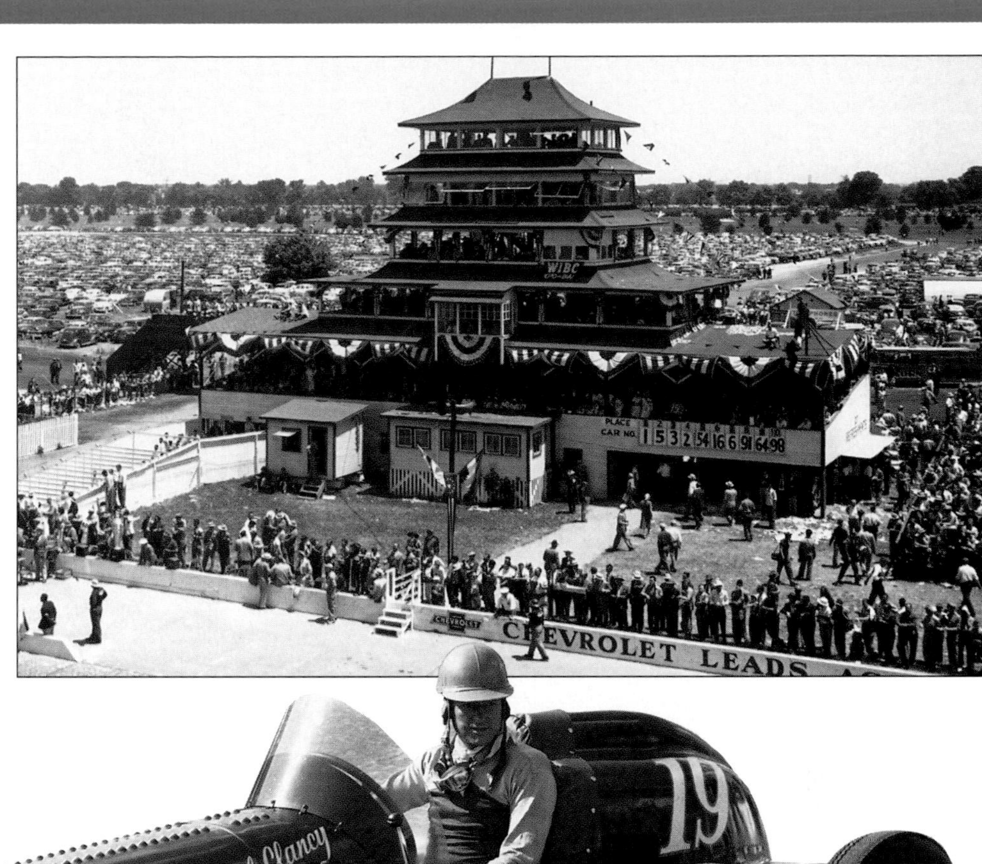

Hal Robson

Mack Hellings

Bill Sheffler

Johnny Mauro

Travis "Spider" Webb

Mel Hansen

George Connor

Billy DeVore

Tommy Hinnershitz

Harry McQuinn

Duane Carter

Fred Agabashian

Emil Andres

Chet Miller

Tony Bettenhausen

Paul Russo

Lee Wallard

Mike Salay

Doc Williams leads Les Anderson into Turn 1 early in the race (*top*). Mauri Rose comes to the pit wall to confer with his team while his car is serviced during a pit stop (*left*). Cars still pulled directly in and out of the pits on the front straight (*above*). Duane Carter loses a wheel and spins at the south end of the track (*below*). Rookie Lee Wallard in the No. 91 Meyer-Offy steered clear and finished seventh. A late fuel stop deprived Duke Nalon (*opposite top*) of victory in the No. 54 Novi. Mauri Rose won for the third time, the last two back-to-back for owner Lou Moore. Rose and Moore pose with the Borg-Warner Trophy (*opposite bottom*).

Running well up in the field with the Walsh-Kurtis entry, Eastern dirt-track ace Tommy Hinnershitz was enjoying his run toward the front. But just as Tommy was making his move, the magneto failed. After a pair of protracted stops, the difficulty with the ignition system was discovered. It took 24 minutes to replace the faulty magneto, destroying any chance for Tommy to win. But the "Flying Dutchman" charged after the leaders, passing cars wherever he encountered them. When the checkered flag flew, he was back to ninth place.

Had it not been for the ignition trouble, many felt that Hinnershitz had a real shot at winning the race. "That was nice of people to say that," Tommy said modestly. "Actually, there was only one guy I didn't pass all day—Mauri Rose."

RESULTS

NO.	DRIVER	CAR	ENTRANT	ENGINE	CYL	DISP	CHASSIS	COLOR	QUAL SPD	START	FIN	LAPS / SPEED / REASON OUT
3	Mauri Rose	Blue Crown Sprk Plg	Lou Moore	Offy**	4	270	Deidt	blue, white	129.129	3	1	200-119.814
2	Bill Holland	Blue Crown Sprk Plg	Lou Moore	Offy**	4	270	Deidt	blue, white	129.515	2	2	200-119.147
54	Duke Nalon	Novi Grooved Piston	W. C. Winfield	Novi***	8	180	Kurtis	cream, blk, red	131.603	11	3	200-118.034
1	Ted Horn	Bennett Bros.	H. C. Henning	Maserati*	8	179	Maserati	black, gold	126.565	5	4	200-117.844
35	Mack Hellings	Don Lee	Don Lee Division	Offy	4	270	KK2000	red	127.968	21	5	200-113.361
63	Hal Cole	City of Tacoma	Hal Cole	Offy	4	247	KK2000	cream, brown	124.391	14	6	200-111.587
91	Lee Wallard	Iddings	John Iddings	Offy	4	233	Meyer	blue	128.420	28	7	200-109.177
33	Johnny Mauro	Mauro Alfa Romeo	Johnny Mauro	Alfa Romeo*	8	182	Alfa Romeo	red	121.790	27	8	198-flagged
7	Tommy Hinnershitz	Kurtis-Kraft	Kurtis-Kraft, Inc.	Offy	4	270	Kurtis	red, silver	125.122	23	9	198-flagged
61	Jimmy Jackson	Howard Keck	Howard Keck Co.	Offy**	4	270	Deidt	maroon, gold	127.510	4	10	193-spindle, spun
4	Charles Van Acker	South Bend	Walter A. Redmer	Offy	4	270	Stevens	blue, red, slvr	125.440	12	11	192-flagged
19	Billy DeVore	Pat Clancy	Pat Clancy	Offy****	4	270	Kurtis	blue	123.967	20	12	190-flagged
98	Johnny Mantz	Agajanian	Smith & Jones Co.	Offy	4	270	KK2000	cream, red	122.791	8	13	185-flagged
6	Tony Bettenhausen	Belanger Motors	Murrell Belanger	Offy	4	270	Stevens	blue, gold	126.396	22	14	167-clutch
64	Hal Robson	Palmer Construction	Palmer Racing, Inc.	Offy	4	247	Adams	blue, white	122.796	18	15	164-valve
36	Bill Cantrell	Fageol Twin Coach	Lou Fageol	Fageol	6	273	Stevens	red, yellow	123.733	7	16	161-steering
55	Joie Chitwood	Nyquist	Ted Nyquist	Offy	4	268	Shaw	white, red	124.619	10	17	138-leaking fuel tank
53	Bill Sheffler	Sheffler Offy	Bayard T. Sheffler	Offy	4	270	Bromme	red, cream	124.529	24	18	132-spark plugs
5	Rex Mays	Bowes Seal Fast	Bowes Racing, Inc.	Winfield*	8	180	Kurtis	blk, wht, red	130.577	1	19	129-leaking fuel tank
31	Chet Miller	Don Lee Mercedes	Don Lee Division	Mercedes*	12	183	Mercedes	silver, red	127.249	19	20	108-oil trouble
52	Jack McGrath	Sheffler Offy	Bayard T. Sheffler	Offy	4	255	Bromme	red, white	124.580	13	21	70-stalled T2
16	Duane Carter	Belanger Motors	Murrell Belanger	Offy	4	270	Wetteroth	wht, gold, red	126.015	29	22	59-lost wheel, spun T2
26	Fred Agabashian	R. Page Offenhauser	Ross Page	Duray*	4	183	Kurtis	wht, mrn, gld	122.737	32	23	58-oil line
34	Les Anderson	Kennedy Tank	Les Anderson	Offy	4	270	Kurtis	cream, red	122.337	9	24	58-gears
17	Mel Hansen	Schafer Gear Works	Paul Weirick	Sparks	4	177	Adams	red, silver	122.117	33	25	42-too slow, disqualified
76	Sam Hanks	Flavell	Robert J. Flavell	Sparks*	6	181	Adams	white, red	124.266	15	26	34-clutch
51	Spider Webb	Fowle Bros.	Louis Bromme	Offy	4	270	Bromme	white, black	125.545	30	27	27-oil line
9	George Connor	Bennett Bros.	H. C. Henning	Miller	8	268	Stevens	black, gold	123.018	17	28	24-drive shaft
74	Doc Williams	Clarke Motors	Ford Moyer	Offy**	4	255	Cooper	blue	124.151	6	29	19-clutch
86	Mike Salay	Terman Marine	John Lorenz	Offy	4	255	Wetteroth	blue, crm, gld	123.393	31	30	13-stalled T3
8	Emil Andres	Tuffy's Offy	C. George Tuffanelli	Offy	4	270	KK2000	maroon, gold	123.550	16	31	11-steering
25	Paul Russo	Federal Engineering	R. A. Cott	Maserati*	8	179	Maserati	maroon, silver	122.595	25	32	7-oil leak
65	Harry McQuinn	Frank Lynch Motors	Gerald H. Brisko	Maserati*	8	183	Maserati	maroon, white	122.154	26	33	1-supercharger

* Supercharged ** Front drive *** Supercharged and front drive **** Six wheeler KK = Kurtis Kraft

33rd Race • May 30, 1949

Novi engines line up first and second in the hands of Duke Nalon and Rex Mays, and the supercharged V-8 looks like the one to beat this year. Nalon qualifies at a non-record 132.939 mph, more than three mph faster than everyone but Johnnie Parsons.

Eleven rookies are in the field when the green flag drops before a crowd of 175,000. A television audience of about 15,000 watches the first broadcast of the 500 by Indianapolis station WFBM.

Nalon sprints ahead from the start and builds a big lead as he runs at a record pace. On the 24th lap, his rear axle breaks in Turn 3, sending him into the wall in a flaming crash. Nalon suffers severe burns in the wreck.

Mays leads for 12 laps—the ninth time he leads the 500—but his Novi V-8 quits on lap 49 to end his day. Mays, who was national champion in 1940 and 1941, dies six months later in a racing accident in California. With the two Novis out, Lee Wallard takes over, but he breaks a drive gear and parks his Maserati.

Bill Holland takes command on the 55th lap in a front-drive Offy, and his only threat is teammate and nemesis Mauri Rose in an identical Blue Crown Special. With his team well in front, owner Lou Moore holds out the "EZY" sign for his drivers to slow down. In a replay of the 1947 race, Rose ignores the order and keeps charging as he guns for a possible record fourth win. This time, however, he falls short when a magneto strap breaks eight laps from the finish. Rose ends up 13th and is fired by Moore after the race.

Holland, runner-up the two previous years, cruises to an easy victory, finishing more than three minutes ahead of rookie Johnnie Parsons. Holland averages a record 121.327 mph, the first winner to top 120, and gives owner Moore his third win in a row. The Deidt chassis is the last front-drive car to win.

STARTING LINEUP

Average Field Qualifying Speed: 128.036

Numbers in flags indicate finish position

Jack McGrath

George Connor

Johnny Mantz

Johnnie Parsons

Duke Dinsmore

Rex Mays

Duane Carter

George Lynch

Hal Cole

Mack Hellings

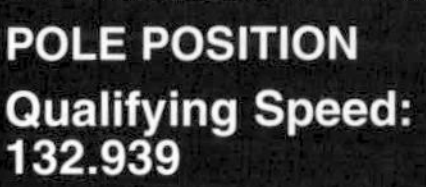
POLE POSITION
Qualifying Speed:
132.939

Duke Nalon

Bill Holland

Jimmy Jackson

Mauri Rose

Myron Fohr

RESULTS

NO.	DRIVER	CAR	ENTRANT	ENGINE	CYL	DISP	CHASSIS	COLOR	QUAL SPD	START	FIN	LAPS / SPEED / REASON OUT
7	Bill Holland	Blue Crown Sprk Plg	Lou Moore	Offy**	4	270	Deidt	blue, wht, red	128.673	4	1	200-121.327
12	Johnnie Parsons	Kurtis-Kraft	Kurtis-Kraft, Inc.	Offy	4	270	Kurtis	red, silver	132.900	12	2	200-119.785
22	George Connor	Blue Crown Sprk Plg	Lou Moore	Offy	4	270	Lesovsky	blue, white	128.228	6	3	200-119.595
2	Myron Fohr	Marchese	Carl Marchese	Offy	4	270	Marchese	wht, gold, blk	129.776	13	4	200-118.791
77	Joie Chitwood	Wolfe	Ervin Wolfe	Offy	4	270	KK2000	yellow, blk, red	126.863	16	5	200-118.757
61	Jimmy Jackson	Howard Keck	Howard Keck Co.	Offy**	4	268	Deidt	maroon, gold	128.023	7	6	200-117.870
98	Johnny Mantz	Agajanian	J. C. Agajanian	Offy	4	270	KK2000	cream, red	127.786	9	7	200-117.142
19	Paul Russo	Tuffy's Offy	Charles Pritchard	Offy	4	270	KK2000	maroon, gold	129.487	19	8	200-111.862
9	Emil Andres	Tuffy's Offy	Charles Pritchard	Offy	4	270	KK2000	maroon, gold	126.042	32	9	197-flagged
71	Norm Houser	Troy Oil Co.	Joe Langley	Offy	4	243	Langley	red, cream	127.756	24	10	181-flagged
68	Jim Rathmann	Pioneer Auto	John Lorenz	Offy	4	270	Wetteroth	red, black	126.516	21	11	175-flagged
64	Troy Ruttman	Carter	Ray W. Carter	Offy	4	270	Wetteroth	blue, white	125.945	18	12	151-flagged
3	Mauri Rose	Blue Crown Sprk Plg	Lou Moore	Offy**	4	270	Deidt	blue, wht, red	127.759	10	13	192-magneto strap
17	Duane Carter	Belanger	Murrell Belanger	Offy	4	270	Stevens	blue, gold	128.233	5	14	182-steering, spun T3
29	Duke Dinsmore	Norm Olson	Norm Olson	Offy	4	270	Olson	black, buff	127.750	15	15	174-radius rod
8	Mack Hellings	Don Lee	Don Lee Motors Corp.	Offy	4	270	KK2000	red, cream	128.260	14	16	172-valve
4	Bill Sheffler	Sheffler Offy	Bill Sheffler	Offy	4	270	Bromme	red, cream	128.521	22	17	160-con. rod
32	Johnny McDowell	Iddings	Henry Meyer	Offy	4	233	Meyer	red, silver	126.139	28	18	142-magneto
14	Hal Cole	Grancor	Grancor Auto Specialists	Offy	4	220	KK2000	blue, silver	127.168	11	19	117-rod bearing insert
38	George Fonder	Ray Brady	Ray T. Brady	Sparks*	6	183	Adams	blue, silver	127.289	25	20	116-valve
74	Bill Cantrell	Kennedy Tank	Leslie M. Anderson	Offy	4	274	Kurtis	maroon	127.191	30	21	95-drive shaft
57	Jackie Holmes	Pat Clancy	Pat Clancy	Offy****	4	270	Kurtis	blue, silver	128.087	17	22	65-drive shaft
6	Lee Wallard	Maserati	Indianapolis Race Cars	Maserati*	8	181	Maserati	black, white	128.912	20	23	55-gears
69	Bayliss Levrett	Wynn's Oil	Bayliss Levrett	Offy	4	270	KK2000	black, white	129.236	29	24	52-drain plug
5	Rex Mays	Novi Mobil	W. C. Winfield	Novi***	8	180	Kurtis	cream, red	129.552	2	25	48-engine trouble
33	Jack McGarth	City of Tacoma	Leo Dobry	Offy	4	247	KK2000	maroon, wht	128.884	3	26	39-oil pump
15	Fred Agabashian	Maserati	Indianapolis Race Cars	Maserati*	8	179	Maserati	black, white	127.007	31	27	38-overheating
52	Manuel Ayulo	Sheffler Offy	Bill Sheffler	Offy	4	255	Bromme	cream, red	125.799	33	28	24-con. rod
54	Duke Nalon	Novi Mobil	W. C. Winfield	Novi***	8	180	Kurtis	cream, red	132.939	1	29	23-rear axle, burned T3
18	Sam Hanks	Love Machine & Tool	Milt Marion	Offy	4	270	KK2000	blue, white	127.809	23	30	20-oil leak
10	Charley Van Acker	Redmer	Geneva Van Acker	Offy	4	270	Stevens	red, wht, silver	126.524	27	31	10-wrecked T4
26	George Lynch	Automobile Shippers	Louis Rassey	Offy	4	270	Snowberger	orange, black	127.823	8	32	1-wrecked T1
37	Spider Webb	Grancor	Lou & Bruce Bromme	Offy	4	270	Bromme	black, red	127.002	26	33	0-transmission

* Supercharged ** Front drive *** Supercharged and front drive **** Six wheeler KK = Kurtis Kraft

The powerful Novis entered by W. C. Winfield arrive at the Speedway (*opposite top*). The Rounds Rocket (*opposite middle*) was a Kurtis chassis with a rear-mounted Offy engine. Driver Bill Taylor failed to qualify this innovative car. The Purdue University band spells OLDS on the front straight (*opposite bottom*) in honor of the Olds 88 pace car (*above left*). Bill Cantrell survives a spin in the No. 74 Kurtis-Offy (*above middle*). Bill Holland (*above right*) finally beat teammate Mauri Rose to give car owner Lou Moore a third straight win.

Troy Ruttman | Jim Rathmann | Norm Houser | Charles Van Acker | Bill Cantrell | Manuel Ayulo

Jackie Holmes | Lee Wallard | Sam Hanks | Spider Webb | Bayliss Levrett | Emil Andres

Joie Chitwood | Paul Russo | Bill Sheffler | George Fonder | Johnny McDowell | Fred Agabashian

1950

34th Race • May 30, 1950

Rookie Walt Faulkner, a California midget-car racer, stuns the Indy establishment by winning the pole at a record 134.343 mph in an Offy powered Kurtis-Kraft, a dirt car that owner J. C. Agajanian converts to Speedway duty. Faulkner is the first rookie to earn the pole since 1914, when Frenchman Jean Chassagne drew the No. 1 starting position from a hat.

Only three front-drive cars make the field. Two belong to Lou Moore's Blue Crown Special team, and three-time winner Mauri Rose, now driving for Howard Keck, is in the other.

The powerful Novi V-8s suffer a series of mechanical woes and fail to qualify. Jimmy Jackson starts 32nd with a 401-cid Cummins six-cylinder diesel. Jackson's car is the only one of the 33 starters that doesn't have a four-cylinder Offy. He drops out on lap 52 with a broken supercharger.

Rose starts on the outside of row one, surges ahead of Faulkner on the backstretch, and leads the first nine laps.

California midget ace Johnnie Parsons starts fifth but doubts he can go the distance. His crew discovers a small crack in the block of his Offy on race-day morning, so he decides to hang it out and try to earn lap money before the engine fails. Still, Parsons passes Rose on lap 10 and sets a blistering pace. Behind him, old rivals Rose and Bill Holland duel for second.

Holland gets around Rose and challenges Parsons, but on lap 121, Holland overshoots his pit and has to go around again, losing valuable time. Parsons' engine survives until rain sends cars spinning on the track and halts the race at 345 miles. Parsons finishes 38 seconds ahead of Holland, and a naturally aspirated Offenhauser wins for the fourth year in a row. Rose survives a fire on a pit stop to place third.

This page: Above, from left, Chief Steward Tommy Milton and Speedway President Wilbur Shaw join Lincoln-Mercury General Manager Benson Ford and the Mercury pace car. Below, from left, Shaw and Tony Hulman pose with Clark Gable—a frequent visitor—and Jack Benny. *Opposite page:* Rookie Pat Flaherty finished 10th for the Granatelli brothers (top left). Screen idol Gable tries on a Ford Custom convertible for size near the garage area (top right). Walt Faulkner (bottom), driving J. C. Agajanian's Grant Piston Ring Special, was the first rookie on the pole since 1914.

STARTING LINEUP

Average Field Qualifying Speed: 131.033

Numbers in flags indicate finish position

3	14	5	4	21
Mauri Rose	Jack McGrath	Joie Chitwood	Cecil Green	Jerry Hoyt

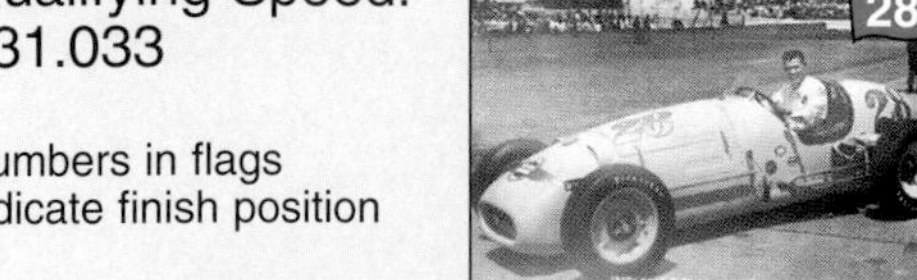

28	1	31	10	20
Fred Agabashian	Johnnie Parsons	Tony Bettenhausen	Pat Flaherty	Spider Webb

POLE POSITION
Qualifying Speed: 134.343

7	8	33	2	12
Walt Faulkner	George Connor	Duke Dinsmore	Bill Holland	Duane Carter

A midget-car driver came to Indy without a ride. Since it was late in the month and he was a virtual unknown, the rookie's friends tried to find him a car. The only one available was a tired old machine that had been a once-proud warrior. The rookie didn't really want to drive it, but his friends insisted. "No one expects you to make the race," they said. "But at least you'll have your rookie test behind you."

The rookie relented, and for the next couple of days, the graybeards in the crowd turned to watch wistfully as the four-wheeled veteran and the rookie made their rounds. The old car could barely muster up enough speed to complete the driver's test. But pass it they did, with flying colors.

It was an unceremonious end for one legend and the beginning for another. The veteran car was the famous Boyle Maserati, which carried Wilbur Shaw to a pair of Indy wins and Ted Horn to many high finishes. The rookie was future two-time 500 winner Bill Vukovich, Sr.

Dick Rathmann

Henry Banks

Troy Ruttman

Jimmy Davies

Jackie Holmes

Johnny McDowell

Bayliss Levrett

Walt Brown

Lee Wallard

Mack Hellings

Walt Ader

Jimmy Jackson

Myron Fohr

Paul Russo

Bill Schindler

Sam Hanks

Jim Rathmann

Gene Hartley

With Lincoln-Mercury boss Benson Ford at the wheel of the pace car, the field forms up into a tight pack (*above and right*). Once turned loose, however, polesitter Walt Faulkner leads Mauri Rose into Turn 2 on the opening lap (*below*). Rose passed him on the back straight and led the first nine laps. A pack of drivers battle for position as they streak down the back straight (*opposite top*), where only a low guardrail separates the cars from spectators. Defending national champ Johnnie Parsons (*opposite bottom*) feared his Offy engine wouldn't go the distance, but he led 115 laps and beat Bill Holland by 38 seconds in the rain-shortened race to break a three-year win streak by Lou Moore's Blue Crown team.

RESULTS

NO.	DRIVER	CAR	ENTRANT	ENGINE	CYL	DISP	CHASSIS	COLOR	QUAL SPD	START	FIN	LAPS / SPEED / REASON OUT
1	Johnnie Parsons	Wynn's Friction Proof	Kurtis-Kraft, Inc.	Offy	4	270	Kurtis	yellow, silver	132.044	5	1	138-124.002
3	Bill Holland	Blue Crown Sprk Plg	Lou Moore	Offy**	4	270	Deidt	blue, wht, red	130.482	10	2	137-122.638
31	Mauri Rose	Offenhauser	Howard Keck Co.	Offy**	4	270	Deidt	blue, gold	132.319	3	3	137-121.778
54	Cecil Green	John Zink	M. A. Walker	Offy	4	270	KK3000	blue, white	132.910	12	4	137-121.766
17	Joie Chitwood	Wolfe	Ervin Wolfe	Offy	4	270	KK2000	red, white	130.757	9	5	136-121.755
8	Lee Wallard	Blue Crown Sprk Plg	Lou Moore	Offy	4	270	Moore	blue, wht, red	132.436	23	6	136-121.009
98	Walt Faulkner	Grant Piston Ring	J. C. Agajanian	Offy	4	270	KK2000	cream, red	134.343	1	7	135-121.094
5	George Connor	Blue Crown Sprk Plg	Lou Moore	Offy	4	270	Lesovsky	blue, wht, red	132.163	4	8	135-121.086
7	Paul Russo	Russo-Nichels	Paul Russo & Ray Nichels	Offy	4	270	Nichels	black, silver	130.790	19	9	135-119.961
59	Pat Flaherty	Granatelli-Sabourin	Grancor Auto. Specialists	Offy	4	270	KK3000	blue	129.608	11	10	135-119.952
2	Myron Fohr	Bardahl	Carl Marchese	Offy	4	270	Marchese	wht, gold, blk	131.714	16	11	133-flagged
18	Duane Carter	Belanger	Murrell Belanger	Offy*	4	176	Stevens	blue, gold	131.666	13	12	133-flagged
15	Mack Hellings	Tuffy's Offy	Charles Pritchard	Offy	4	270	KK2000	maroon, gold	130.687	26	13	132-flagged
49	Jack McGrath	Hinkle	Jack B. Hinkle	Offy	4	270	KK3000	maroon, silver	131.868	6	14	131-spun in rain T3
55	Troy Ruttman	Bowes Seal Fast	Bowes Racing, Inc.	Offy	4	270	Lesovsky	blk, wht, red	131.912	24	15	130-flagged
75	Gene Hartley	Troy Oil	Joe Langley	Offy	4	240	Langley	blk, red, silver	129.213	31	16	128-flagged
22	Jim Davies	Pat Clancy	Pat Clancy	Offy	4	270	Ewing	blue, white	130.402	27	17	128-flagged
62	Johnny McDowell	Pete Wales	M. Pete Wales	Offy	4	235	KK2000	blue, silver	129.692	33	18	128-flagged
4	Walt Brown	Tuffy's Offy	Charles Pritchard	Offy	4	270	KK2000	maroon, gold	130.454	20	19	127-flagged
21	Spider Webb	Fadely-Anderson	R. A. Cott	Offy	4	270	Maserati	maroon	129.748	14	20	126-flagged
81	Jerry Hoyt	Morris	Ludson D. Morris, M.D.	Offy	4	270	KK2000	maroon, crm	129.520	15	21	125-flagged
27	Walt Ader	Sampson	Sampson Mfg. Co.	Offy*	4	177	Rae	white, black	129.940	29	22	123-flagged
77	Jackie Holmes	Norm Olson	Norm Olson	Offy	4	270	Olson	buff, black	129.697	30	23	123-spun in rain T3
76	Jack Rathmann	Pioneer Auto Repair	John Lorenz	Offy	4	270	Wetteroth	black, red	129.959	28	24	122-flagged
12	Henry Banks	I.R.C.	Indianapolis Race Cars, Inc.	Offy*	4	180	Maserati	yellow, black	129.646	21	25	112-flagged
67	Bill Schindler	Automobile Shippers	Louis Rassey	Offy	4	270	Snowberger	orange, black	132.690	22	26	111-universal joint
24	Bayliss Levrett	Palmer	Richard L. Palmer	Offy	4	270	Adams	red, silver	131.181	17	27	108-lost oil pressure
28	Fred Agabashian	Wynn's Frict Proof	Kurtis-Kraft, Inc.	Offy*	4	177	KK3000	yellow, silver	132.792	2	28	64-oil line
61	Jimmy Jackson	Cummins Diesel	Cummins Engine Co.	Cummins*	6	401	Kurtis	green, gold	129.208	32	29	52-supercharger
23	Sam Hanks	Merz Engineering	Milt Marion	Offy	4	270	KK2000	red	131.593	25	30	42-oil pressure
14	Tony Bettenhausen	Blue Crown Sprk Plg	Lou Moore	Offy**	4	270	Deidt	blue, wht, red	130.947	8	31	30-wheel bearing
45	Dick Rathmann	City of Glendale	A. J. Watson	Offy	4	264	Watson	white, blue	130.928	18	32	25-stalled
69	Duke Dinsmore	Brown Motor Co.	Verlin Brown	Offy	4	270	KK2000	brown, white	131.066	7	33	10-oil leak

* Supercharged ** Front drive

1951

35th Race • May 30, 1951

The distinctive scream of the Novi V-8 is back after missing the show in 1950. Duke Nalon wins his second pole position with a front-drive Novi, but third-day qualifier Walt Faulkner is quicker. Faulkner posts a record speed of 136.872 mph with a fuel-injected Offy.

Lee Wallard starts in the middle of row one in a trim, lightweight Kurtis dirt track car with Offy power, and Jack McGrath is on the outside in a Kurtis-Kraft Offy.

When the green flag drops, Wallard noses ahead of McGrath to lead the first two laps. McGrath forges in front on lap three as Nalon pits for emergency ignition repairs to his Novi, knocking him out of contention.

Wallard and McGrath battle for the lead as heat and mechanical failure claim several cars. By the halfway point, 14 cars are out and Wallard is firmly in command.

The attrition mounts: Faulkner charges from 14th starting position to run in the top five, but he goes out on the 124th lap with a broken crankshaft. On lap 127, a wheel collapses on Mauri Rose's front-drive Offy in Turn 3, and he spins and rolls into the infield mud. Though three-time winner Rose is unhurt, he retires after the race.

Wallard leads the last 120 laps and cruises to victory at a record 126.244 mph. He wins in 3 hours, 57 minutes to become the first to complete 500 miles in less than four hours. With practically no brakes left, Wallard coasts into victory lane sitting on top of his car. A few days later, he suffers severe burns in a sprint-car race and does not compete in another 500.

Rookie Mike Nazaruk finishes second in a Kurtis-Offy, 1 minute, 47 seconds back, and McGrath is third. Only eight cars finish.

In a sign of the changing times at the Speedway, Wallard wins with dual carburetors feeding his 241-cid Offy, but the next six finishers are fuel injected.

STARTING LINEUP

Average Field Qualifying Speed: 133.556

Numbers in flags indicate finish position

POLE POSITION
Qualifying Speed: 136.498

3 — Jack McGrath

23 — Troy Ruttman

9 — Tony Bettenhausen

12 — Sam Hanks

18 — Carl Scarborough

1 — Lee Wallard

14 — Mauri Rose

21 — Johnnie Parsons

17 — Fred Agabashian

15 — Walt Faulkner

10 — Duke Nalon

8 — Duane Carter

2 — Mike Nazaruk

22 — Cecil Green

26 — Walt Brown

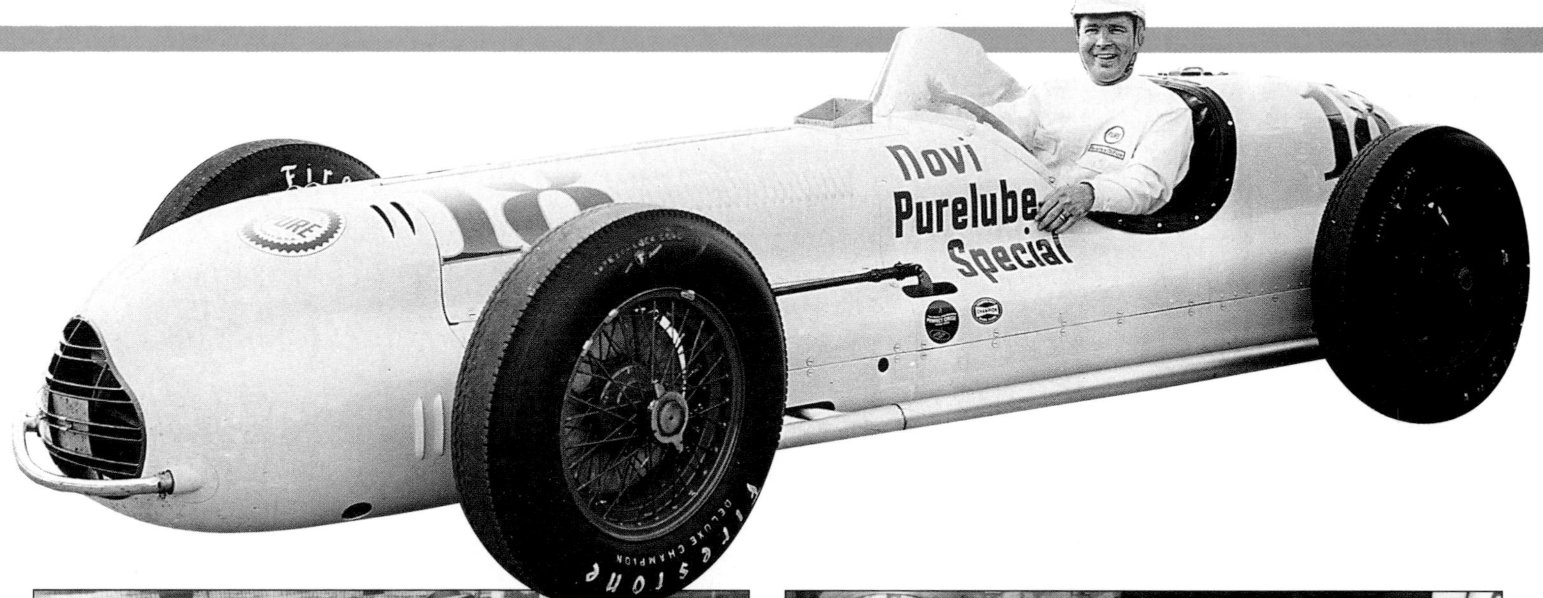

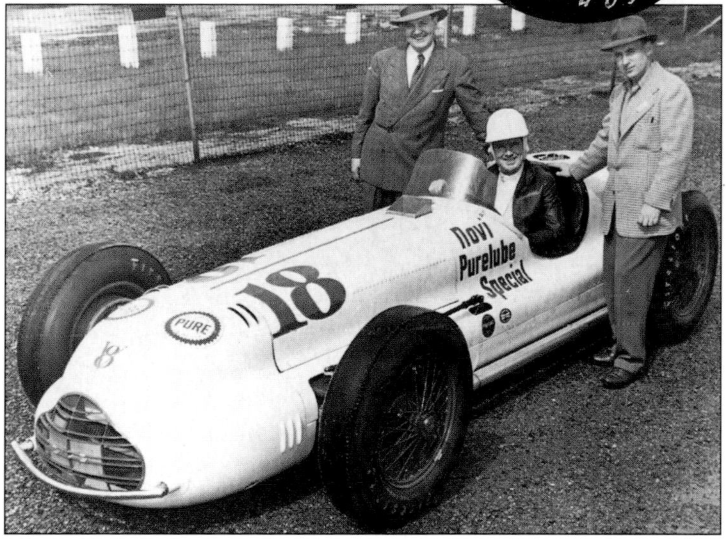

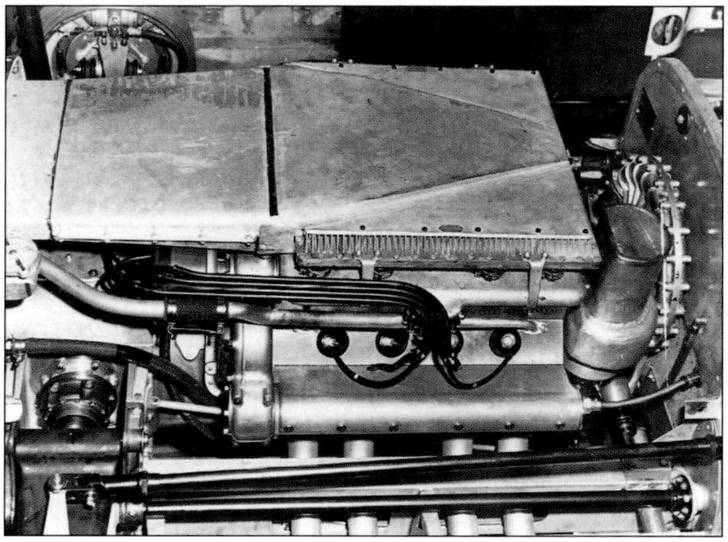

A pair of future Indy legends, Bill Vukovich (*opposite left*) and Rodger Ward (*opposite right*), finished 29th and 27th, respectively, in their first starts. Ward was the first to complete AAA's new rookie test requiring first-timers to demonstrate their skill by driving 10 consecutive laps at ascending speeds of 100, 110, 115, and 120 mph. After missing the '50 race, Duke Nalon put the No. 18 Novi Purelube Special (*top* and *above left*) on the pole, but fell back at the start and dropped out of contention when he had to pit for ignition repairs. He wound up 10th. The Novi V-8 engine (*above right*) displaced 181 cubic inches.

Cliff Griffith

George Connor

Carl Forberg

Jimmy Davies

Joe James

Bill Mackey

Henry Banks

Bill Vukovich

Mack Hellings

Johnny McDowell

Bobby Ball

Duke Dinsmore

Bill Schindler

Chuck Stevenson

Gene Force

Rodger Ward

Chet Miller

Andy Linden

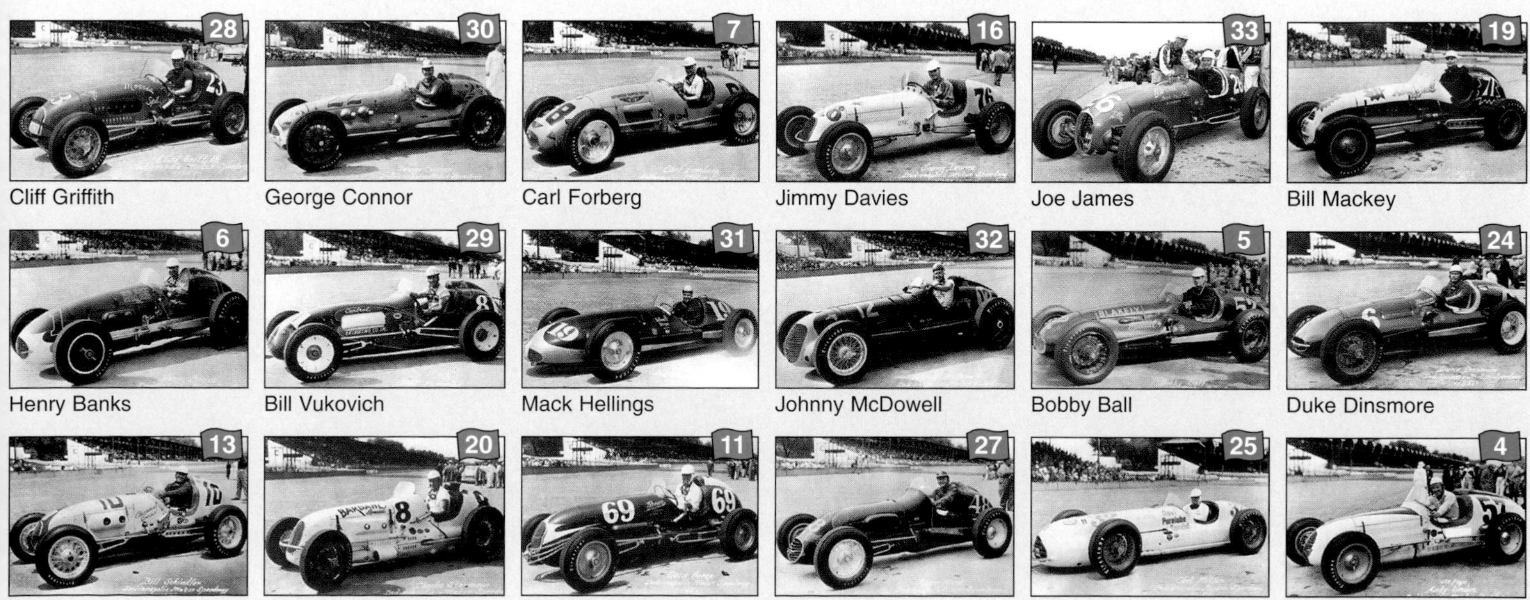

OFFICIAL PACE CAR
CHRYSLER
FirePower

OFFICIAL
PROGRAM
35th. 500 MILE RACE
May 30
1951
50¢ PAY NO MORE
INDIANAPOLIS MOTOR SPEEDWAY CORPORATION

MARQUETTE
AAA
FICIAL "500 Mile" WELDING SERVICE
IAL "500 Mile" Hi-Rate Battery Charging Service
Marquette Mfg. Co. Inc.
MINNEAPOLIS, MINNESOTA
MARQUETTE
A.C.Arc
Welders
Oxy-Acetylene
Welding & Cutting
Equipment
Electrodes
Rods
Morris
Spl.

BARDAHL
ADD IT TO YOUR MOTOR OIL

Opposite page: Actress Loretta Young with the Chrysler New Yorker pace car (top). Marquette Manufacturing provided on-site welding service (middle left). A Novi V-8 sat on the pole, but the four-cylinder Offenhauser (middle right) powered the winner for a fifth straight year. Offy-powered Jack McGrath (No. 9) and Lee Wallard (No. 99) shared the front row with Duke Nalon's Novi (bottom). *This page:* The '51 pace car (above) showcased Chrysler's new hemi-head V-8. Veteran George Connor (below) lasted just 29 laps in a Blue Crown car and finished 30th. Starters queue up for the annual pre-race driver's meeting (right).

Lee Wallard had paid his dues. The popular Easterner had learned to race driving an old jalopy in a circle around a neighbor's barn. "Every now and then, I had to go over and repair one or two places where I'd smashed into the barn," the personable Wallard would laugh. He spent several years honing his skills on the midget- and sprint-car circuits before making a try at Indianapolis.

But after 1951, Lee never again made the starting field for the 500. He came back for a year or two and tried. Oh, how he tried. But he finally came to the conclusion that he no longer had the stamina it took to go 500 grueling miles.

You see, just four days after his 500 win, Wallard took part in a sprint-car event at Reading, Pennsylvania. A carburetor float on Wallard's Mark Light Offy stuck, sending a gush of flaming fuel back into the cockpit. After driving past the pit area, Lee bailed out of the car. But he'd already received terrible burns.

In that day, skin grafts had not reached the level of development known today. Because of scar tissue, Wallard was never able to perspire as he should have. After only a few laps in a broiling cockpit, his strength was completely gone. So, too, was a great driving career.

Ray Harroun poses behind the wheel of the Chrysler New Yorker pace car. (*left*). Chrysler President David Wallace drove it on race day, however. Jack McGrath noses ahead of Lee Wallard as the tightly bunched field roars into Turn 1 at the start (*below*). Wallard takes the high groove around Duane Carter, who finished eighth (*bottom*). Wallard led the last 120 laps in his Belanger Special (*opposite top*) and was the first driver to complete the 500 miles in less than four hours. As Wallard celebrates in victory lane, Sid Collins, long the "Voice of the 500," extends a microphone to broadcast his comments (*opposite, bottom left*). Peter DePaolo holds the Borg-Warner trophy behind them. The modest rig used to transport the winning car (*opposite, bottom right*) exemplifies a simpler time in racing.

RESULTS

NO.	DRIVER	CAR	ENTRANT	ENGINE	CYL	DISP	CHASSIS	COLOR	QUAL SPD	START	FIN	LAPS / SPEED / REASON OUT
99	Lee Wallard	Belanger	Murrell Belanger	Offy	4	241	Kurtis	blue, gold	135.039	2	1	200-126.244
83	Mike Nazaruk	Jim Robbins	J. M. Robbins	Offy	4	270	Kurtis	yellow, slvr, red	132.183	7	2	200-125.302
9	Jack McGrath	Hinkle	Jack B. Hinkle	Offy	4	270	KK3000	maroon, silver	134.303	3	3	200-124.745
57	Andy Linden	Leitenberger	George H. Leitenberger	Offy	4	270	Sherman	wht, red, blk	132.226	31	4	200-123.812
52	Bob Ball	Blakely	John L. McDaniel	Offy	4	270	Schroeder	blue, white	134.098	29	5	200-123.709
1	Henry Banks	Blue Crown Sprk Plg	Lindsey Hopkins	Offy	4	270	Moore	blue, red, wht	133.899	17	6	200-123.304
68	Carl Forberg	Automobile Shippers	Louis Rassey	Offy	4	270	KK3000	orange, black	132.890	24	7	193-flagged
27	Duane Carter	Mobilgas	Rotary Engineering Corp.	Offy**	4	272	Deidt	blue, wht, red	133.749	4	8	180-flagged
5	Tony Bettenhausen	Mobiloil	Rotary Engineering Corp.	Offy**	4	270	Deidt	blue, wht, red	131.950	9	9	178-spun T4
18	Duke Nalon	Novi Purelube	Jean Marcenac	Novi***	8	181	Kurtis	white, blue	136.498	1	10	151-stalled BS
69	Gene Force	Brown Motor Co.	Brown Motor Co.	Offy	4	270	KK2000	brn, wht, gold	133.102	22	11	142-lost oil pressure
25	Sam Hanks	Schmidt	Peter Schmidt	Offy	4	270	KK3000	red, silver	132.998	12	12	135-spun T3
10	Bill Schindler	Chapman	H. A. Chapman	Offy	4	270	KK2000	yellow, blue	134.033	16	13	129-con. rod
16	Mauri Rose	Pennzoil	Howard Keck Co.	Offy**	4	270	Deidt	blk, yellow, red	133.422	5	14	126-wheel collap., wreck T3
2	Walt Faulkner	Agajanian Grant	J. C. Agajanian	Offy	4	270	Kuzma	cream, red	136.872	14	15	123-crankshaft
76	Jim Davies	Parks Offenhauser	L. E. Parks	Offy	4	270	Pawl	cream, red	133.516	27	16	110-rear end gears
59	Fred Agabashian	Granatelli-Bardahl	Grancor Auto. Specialists	Offy	4	270	KK3000	blue, silver	135.029	11	17	109-clutch
73	Carl Scarborough	McNamara	Lee Elkins	Offy	4	270	KK2000	red, crm, gold	135.614	15	18	100-axle
71	Bill Mackey	Karl Hall	Karl Hall	Offy	4	270	—	mrn, rd, wht, gld	131.473	33	19	97-clutch shaft
8	Chuck Stevenson	Bardahl	Carl Marchese	Offy	4	270	Marchese	white, black	133.764	19	20	93-caught fire
3	Johnnie Parsons	Wynn's Frict Proof	Ed Walsh	Offy	4	270	KK3000	yellow, slvr, red	132.154	8	21	87-magneto
4	Cecil Green	John Zink	M. A. Walker	Offy	4	270	KK3000	yellow, white	131.892	10	22	80-con. rod
98	Troy Ruttman	Agajanian	J. C. Agajanian	Offy	4	270	KK2000	cream, red	132.314	6	23	78-bearing
6	Duke Dinsmore	Brown Motors Co.	Brown Motors Co.	Offy	4	270	Schroeder	brown, gold	131.974	32	24	73-overheating
32	Chet Miller	Novi Purelube	Jean Marcenac	Novi***	8	181	Kurtis	white, blue	135.798	28	25	56-ignition
44	Walt Brown	Federal Eng	Federal Engineering Assoc.	Offy	4	270	KK3000	tan, silver	131.907	13	26	55-magneto
48	Rodger Ward	Deck Mfg.	Louis & Bruce Bromme	Offy	4	270	Bromme	red, black	134.867	25	27	34-oil line
23	Cliff Griffith	Morris	Ludson D. Morris, M.D.	Offy	4	270	KK2000	red, white	133.839	18	28	30-axle
81	Bill Vukovich	Central Excavating	Pete Salemi	Offy	4	270	Trevis	blue, wht, red	133.725	20	29	29-oil tank
22	George Connor	Blue Crown Sprk Plg	Lou Moore	Offy	4	270	Lesovsky	blue, wht, red	133.353	21	30	29-universal joint
19	Mack Hellings	Tuffanelli-Derrico	C. G. Tuffanelli & J. Derrico	Offy**	4	270	Deidt	maroon, gold	123.925	23	31	18-piston
12	Johnny McDowell	W. J.	Maserati Race Cars	Offy*	4	180	Maserati	tan, orange	132.475	26	32	15-gas tank
26	Joe James	Bob Estes Linc-Merc	Bob Estes	Offy	4	270	Watson	blue, white	134.098	30	33	8-drive shaft

* Supercharged ** Front drive *** Supercharged and front drive

1952

36th Race • May 30, 1952

The rules are the same, but this is a year of upheaval at the Brickyard as a diesel sits on the pole and a new chassis design makes a major impact.

Freddie Agabashian nabs the pole at a record 138 mph with the first turbocharged engine to make the race, a Cummins six-cylinder diesel, though his speed isn't due just to the 401-cid engine. Agabashian drives a radical cigar-shaped Kurtis-Kraft "lay-down" roadster in which the engine leans 90 degrees to the right to mount horizontally.

The driver sits on the floor and the driveshaft runs by his left hip, reducing the overall height for less air drag and lowering the center of gravity for more speed in the corners. Cummins reportedly spends an astronomical $500,000 to develop the car and engine.

Agabashian's qualifying record lasts only a week. Chet Miller sets a new mark of 139.034 the next weekend with a front-drive Novi and starts in the ninth row for his 16th race.

Neither Agabashian nor Miller leads a lap. Miller's Novi is out on lap 42 with supercharger problems and the diesel quits after 71 circuits with a clogged turbo inlet.

Ferrari is in the show for the first time with a V-12 Grand Prix car driven by Alberto Ascari, who wins the world driving championship later that year. Ascari starts 19th, but breaks a wheel on lap 41 to finish 31st.

The race is a battle between Californians Bill Vukovich and Troy Ruttman. Vukovich, driving a Kurtis roadster with a fuel-injected Offy engine tilted 37 degrees to the right, leads 150 laps until a steering pin breaks on lap 192 and he grinds to a halt along the Turn 3 wall.

Ruttman, with a Kuzma-Offy, inherits the lead and wins at a record speed of 128.922 mph. Though this is his fourth 500, he is just 22 years old, the youngest winner ever.

Jim Rathmann comes in second, more than four minutes behind Ruttman. Art Cross finishes fifth and wins a new award—Rookie of the Year.

Twenty cars are running at the finish, all rear-drive Offys, and it is the first time there are no relief drivers during the race. Ruttman's Kuzma chassis is the last dirt-track car to visit victory lane.

Studebaker provided the Commander convertible (*above*) that served as the 1952 pace car. The venerable South Bend, Indiana, company was celebrating its 100th year as a vehicle manufacturer. Freddie Agabashian won the pole at a record 138 mph with a turbocharged Cummins diesel engine and new "lay-down" Kurtis-Kraft roadster (*opposite*). Chet Miller (*below*) blew Agabashian's speed out of the record books the next weekend with his supercharged Novi and front-drive Kurtis. Neither was a factor in the race, however, as supercharger woes sidelined both cars well before the halfway point.

STARTING LINEUP

Average Field Qualifying Speed: 135.504

Numbers in flags indicate finish position

Jack McGrath

Duane Carter

Cliff Griffith

Henry Banks

Bill Schindler

Andy Linden

Sam Hanks

Bill Vukovich

Chuck Stevenson

George Connor

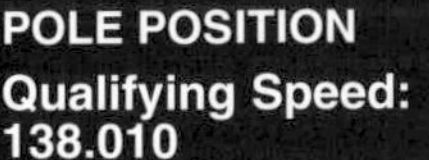

POLE POSITION
Qualifying Speed: 138.010

Freddie Agabashian

Duke Nalon

Troy Ruttman

Jim Rathmann

George Fonder

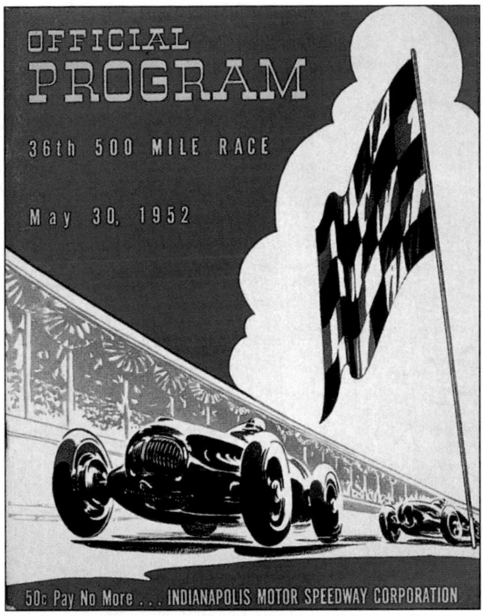
OFFICIAL
PROGRAM
36th 500 MILE RACE
May 30, 1952
50c Pay No More . . . INDIANAPOLIS MOTOR SPEEDWAY CORPORATION

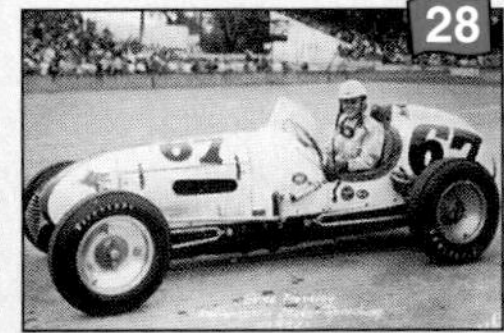

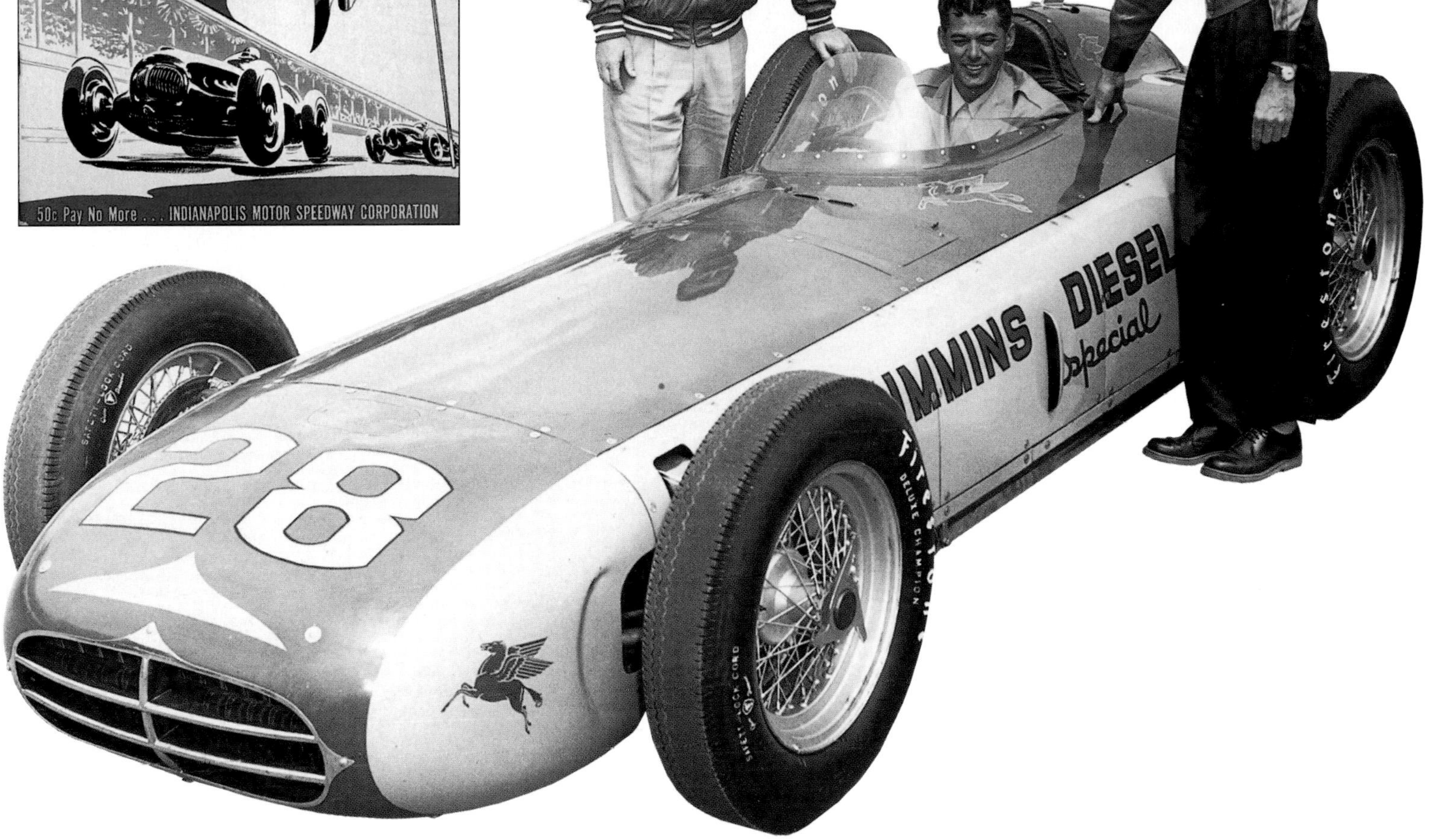
DIESEL
special
28

28
Gene Hartley

6
Jimmy Bryan

16
Eddie Johnson

30
Chet Miller

24
Tony Bettenhausen

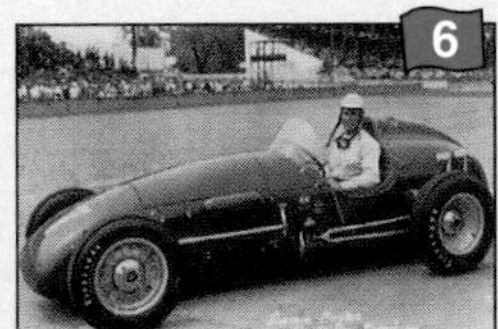

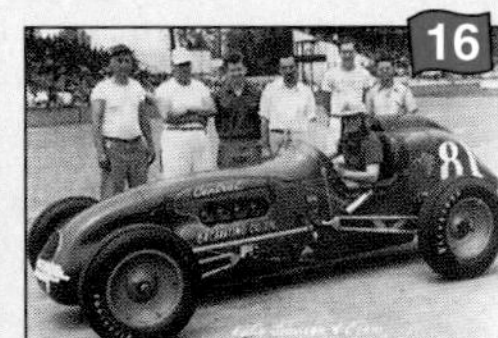

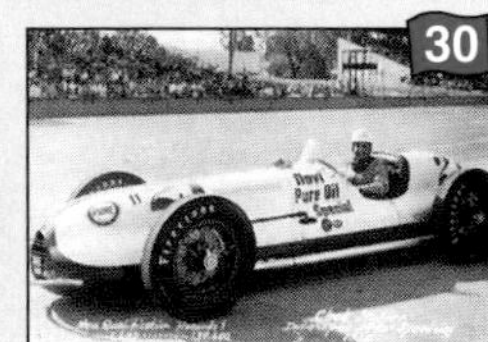

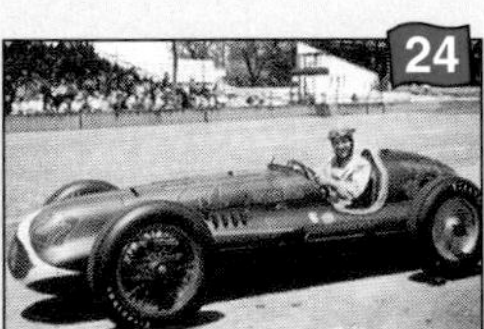

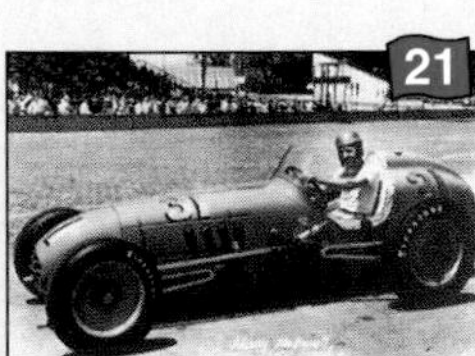

21
Johnny McDowell

32
Bobby Ball

5
Art Cross

7
Jimmy Reece

12
Jim Rigsby

22
Spider Webb

26
Bob Sweikert

13
Joe James

31
Alberto Ascari

23
Rodger Ward

29
Bob Scott

20
Manuel Ayulo

10
Johnnie Parsons

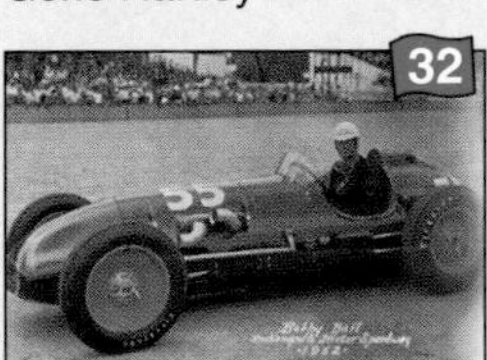

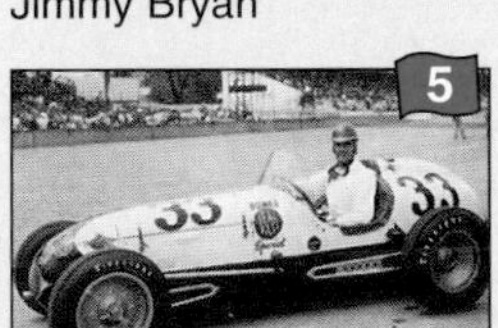

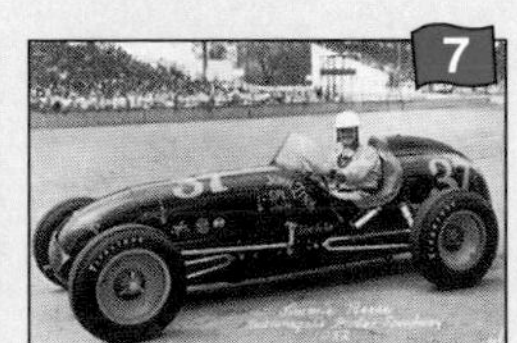

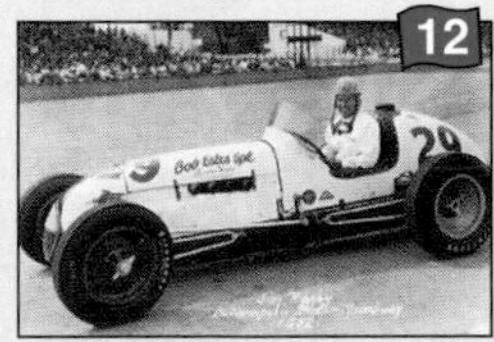

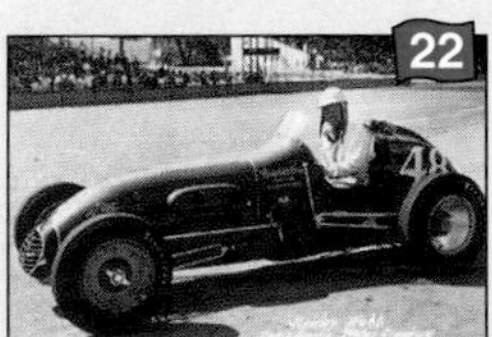

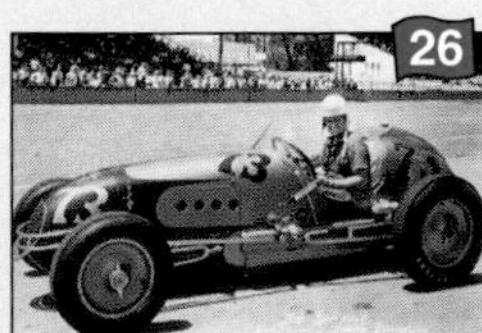

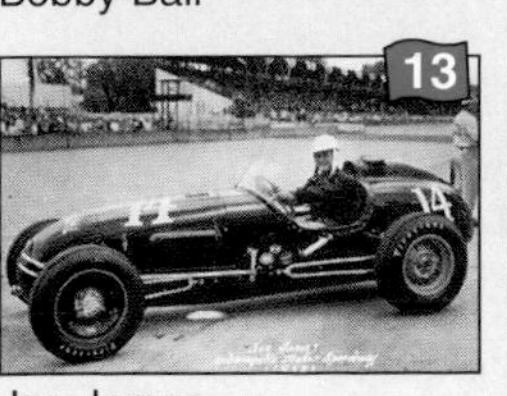

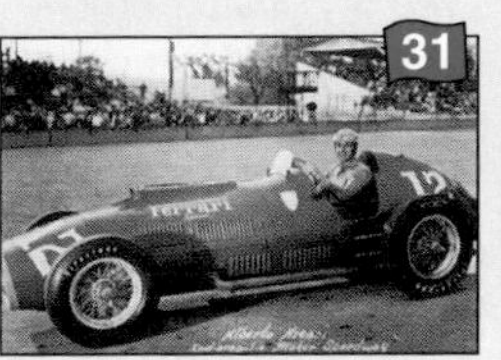

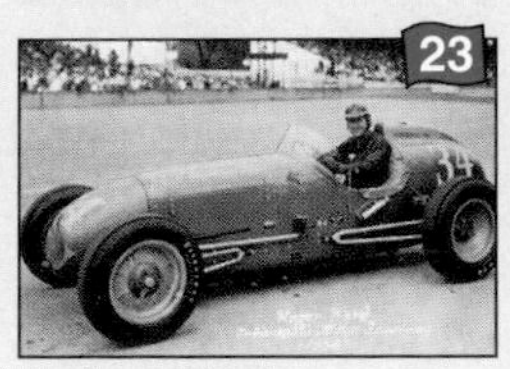

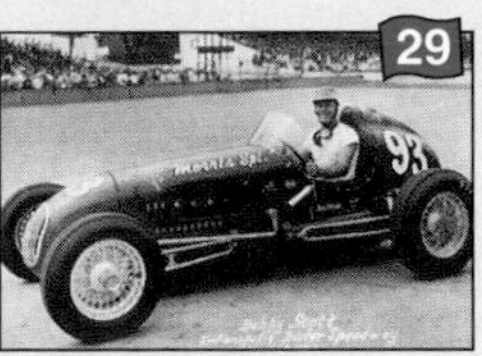

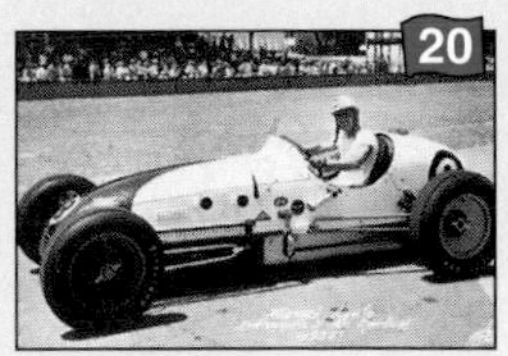

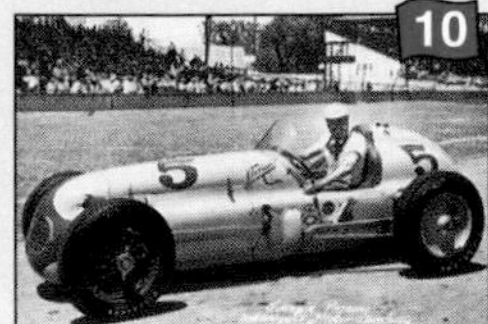

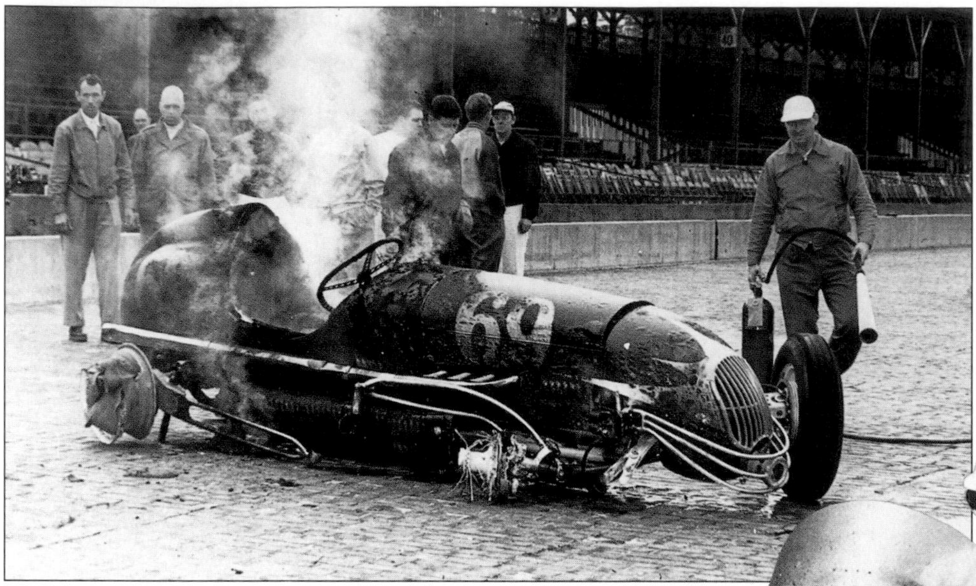

The remains of Bayliss Levrett's car (*left*) smolder on the front straight. Levrett somehow escaped serious injury when he was thrown from the Brown Motor Company entry after it hit the Turn 4 wall during practice and caught fire. Rookie Jimmy Reece gets a push as he leaves the pits (*below*) on his way to a seventh-place finish. Alberto Ascari's Ferrari spins into the infield after breaking a wheel in Turn 4 (*bottom*). For a time, the 500 counted toward the world driving championship, but lured few drivers from Formula 1.

During practice, hard-working Dick McGeorge, Champion Spark Plug's jack-of-all-trades, was leafing through the 1952 Indianapolis 500 program. McGeorge was scouting advertisements of other accessory firms. He was sure no one would match the huge advertisement Champion had purchased. Feeling self-assured, he continued to thumb through the program until he stopped in utter amazement. "Now how do you suppose that happened?" people heard McGeorge question aloud. He glanced away from the program, looking back a second time. "I don't believe it!" he exclaimed.

Over the next few hours, McGeorge showed the Champion advertisement to several associates and friends. "Tell me what's wrong with this ad," he said. Not a single person could detect what had McGeorge in such a state of dismay. "I don't know who did this, but they could have picked any other race car for this thing, other than the one they chose," he grumbled. Then he pointed it out: "They chose the Cummins Diesel," Dick explained. "It doesn't use spark plugs!"

Studebaker executive vice president P. O. Peterson wheels the pace car through the south short chute ahead of the field (*top*). More wider and lower chassis designs were finding their ways into the field, changing the look of the typical racing car. The look of the Speedway was changing, too; the double-deck grandstand in Turn 1 had been put up in 1949. A dejected Bill Vukovich contemplates what might have been behind the Turn 3 wall after crashing while leading with just nine laps to go (*above*). The steering broke on his Kurtis-Offy, sending him into the wall after he led 150 laps.

Following a serious crash during the 1951 Indy 500, three-time winner Mauri Rose announced his retirement from racing.

But Mauri's former car owner tried to lure him back for the '52 classic. The owner told Rose he had a car that would revolutionize racing. "Do you know how many times I've heard that?" Mauri replied. Besides, at well into his forties, Mauri felt his eyes were going. The owner called and begged Rose to just try the car. But the little champ could not be swayed. Not even when the owner assured him he could win an unprecedented fourth 500.

Finally, the owner gave up, hiring a West Coast midget-car driver to wheel the new machine. The car fit its driver like a glove. And the rest is history. The car owner was Howard Keck, the new racer was the Fuel-Injection Special, and the driver was Bill Vukovich, Sr. This combination nearly won in 1952, and came back to whip the field in '53 and '54.

Jack McGrath in the No. 4 Kurtis leads Jim Rathmann through the first turn (*above*). McGrath led for six laps, but slipped to 11th by the end of the race. Rathmann came home second. Drivers in the tightly bunched field head for the preferred line through the first turn (*below*) as they roar away to a safe, exciting start to the 36th race. *Opposite page:* Troy Ruttman (at left in top photo) became the youngest winner ever at age 22, giving car owner and fellow Californian J. C. Agajanian (in cowboy hat) his first visit to victory lane. The winner's Kuzma-Offy (bottom) was the last dirt-track car to win at Indy.

Obviously, drivers and mechanics must endure difficulties and sometimes hardships. And while a car owner goes through trials and tribulations, actual physical hardship is seldom a part of the month of May.

But during practice for the 1952 Indy classic, Bessie Lee Paoli, who with J. C. Agajanian's chief mechanic, Clay Smith, owned half interest in the Springfield Welding Special, became the exception. Seated in the stands behind her pit, she never missed a minute of track time. Paoli clocked every lap turned by her driver, Chuck Stevenson, and kept a log of everything done to the car. "She works as hard as the rest of us," Smith said of his partner.

While Stevenson only finished 18th at Indy, he went on to win the 1952 AAA championship. Perhaps it was poetic justice for all of Bessie Lee's suffering. Prior to May, she had broken her back in an equestrian accident and left the hospital, suffering with silent resolve, just to be at Indianapolis.

RESULTS

NO.	DRIVER	CAR	ENTRANT	ENGINE	CYL	DISP	CHASSIS	COLOR	QUAL SPD	START	FIN	LAPS / SPEED / REASON OUT
98	Troy Ruttman	Agajanian	J. C. Agajanian	Offy	4	263	Kuzma	cream, red	135.364	7	1	200-128.922
59	Jim Rathmann	Grancor-Wynn's Oil	Grancor Auto. Specialists	Offy	4	270	KK3000	yellow, slvr, red	136.343	10	2	200-126.723
18	Sam Hanks	Bardahl	Ed Walsh	Offy	4	263	KK3000	black, white	135.736	5	3	200-125.580
1	Duane Carter	Belanger Motors	Murrell Belanger	Offy	4	262	Lesovsky	blue, gold	135.522	6	4	200-125.259
33	Art Cross	Bowes Seal Fast	Ray T. Brady	Offy	4	270	KK4000	cream, blk, red	134.288	20	5	200-124.292
77	Jimmy Bryan	Schmidt	Peter Schmidt	Offy	4	270	KK3000	red, silver	134.142	21	6	200-123.914
37	Jimmy Reece	John Zink	John Zink	Offy	4	270	KK4000	black, orange	133.993	23	7	200-123.312
54	George Connor	Federal Eng	Federal Auto. Associates	Offy	4	270	KK3000	tan, cream	135.609	14	8	200-122.595
22	Cliff Griffith	Tom Sarafoff	Tom Sarafoff	Offy	4	263	KK2000	red, white	136.617	9	9	200-122.402
5	Johnnie Parsons	Jim Robbins	J. M. Robbins	Offy	4	270	Kurtis	yellow, red	135.328	31	10	200-121.789
4	Jack McGrath	Hinkle	Jack B. Hinkle	Offy	4	270	KK3000	maroon, silver	136.664	3	11	200-121.428
29	Jim Rigsby	Bob Estes	Bob Estes	Offy	4	270	Watson	blue, wht, red	133.904	26	12	200-120.587
14	Joe James	Bardahl	Ed Walsh	Offy	4	263	KK4400	black, white	134.953	16	13	200-120.108
7	Bill Schindler	Chapman	H. A. Chapman	Offy	4	270	Stevens	black, pink	134.988	15	14	200-119.280
65	George Fonder	Leitenberger	George H. Leitenberger	Offy	4	270	Sherman	red, wht, blue	135.947	13	15	197-flagged
81	Eddie Johnson	Central Excavating	Pete Salemi	Offy	4	270	Trevis	red, blue, wht	133.973	24	16	193-flagged
26	Bill Vukovich	Fuel Injection	Howard Keck Co.	Offy	4	270	KK500A	gray, red, yellow	138.212	8	17	191-steering, hit T3 wall
16	Chuck Stevenson	Springfield Welding	Bessie Lee Paoli	Offy	4	263	KK4000	red, white	136.142	11	18	187-flagged
2	Henry Banks	Blue Crown Sprk Plg	Lindsey Hopkins	Offy	4	263	Lesovsky	blue, wht, orng	135.962	12	19	184-flagged
8	Manuel Ayulo	Coast Grain Co.	Coast Grain Co.	Offy	4	270	Lesovsky	white, blue	135.982	28	20	184-flagged
31	Johnny McDowell	McDowell	Roger G. Wolcott	Offy	4	263	Kurtis	turq, gold	133.939	33	21	182-flagged
48	Spider Webb	Granatelli Rcng Enter.	Vincent Granatelli	Offy	4	270	Bromme	red, black	135.962	29	22	162-oil leak
34	Rodger Ward	Federal Eng	Federal Auto. Associates	Offy	4	270	KK4000	tan, cream	134.139	22	23	130-low oil pressure
27	Tony Bettenhausen	Blue Crown Sprk Plg	Earl F. Slick	Offy**	4	270	Deidt	blue, wht, red	135.384	30	24	93-starter
36	Duke Nalon	Novi Pure Oil	Lewis W. Welch	Novi***	8	181	Kurtis	white, blue	136.188	4	25	84-supercharger shaft
73	Bob Sweikert	McNamara	Lee Elkins	Offy	4	263	KK2000	red, gold	134.983	32	26	77-differential
28	Fred Agabashian	Cummins Diesel	Cummins Engine Co.	Cummins*	6	401	Kurtis	red, yellow	138.010	1	27	71-clogged supercharger
67	Gene Hartley	Mel-Rae	Mel B. Wiggers	Offy	4	270	KK4000	white, black	134.343	18	28	65-exhaust pipe
93	Bob Scott	Morris	Ludson D. Morris, M.D.	Offy	4	270	KK2000	red, white	133.953	25	29	49-drive shaft
21	Chet Miller	Novi Pure Oil	Lewis W. Welch	Novi***	8	181	Kurtis	blue, white	139.034	27	30	41-supercharger shaft
12	Alberto Ascari	Ferrari	Enzo Ferrari	Ferrari	12	271	Ferrari	red, white	134.308	19	31	40-hub flange, spun T4
55	Bob Ball	Ansted	Rotary Engineering Corp.	Offy	4	270	Stevens	blue, slvr, pink	134.725	17	32	34-gear case
9	Andy Linden	Miracle Power	Hart Fullerton	Offy*	4	183	KK4000	yelo, blue, red	137.002	2	33	20-oil leak

* Supercharged ** Front drive *** Supercharged and front drive

37th Race • May 30, 1953

A crash during practice kills 50-year-old Chet Miller, trying for his 17th start at the Brickyard. Miller, who set a qualifying record the previous year, dies when his car gets onto the dirt in Turn 1 during a hot lap and his Novi darts head-on into the south wall.

Novi teammate Duke Nalon, in his last race at the Speedway, qualifies 26th and finishes 11th. His car is the only one in the field that doesn't have an Offy engine. Though the Novi V-8 competes several more times, Nalon's Kurtis is the last front-drive car to appear in a 500.

Defending winner Troy Ruttman is a spectator this year because his right arm is in a sling from a racing accident. Bill Vukovich wins the pole at a non-record 138.392 but in dramatic fashion. He completes his four lap qualifying run in the rain with a "rooster tail" spraying behind his Kurtis roadster with its canted engine, the same car that led 150 laps the previous year.

Fred Agabashian lines up next to Vukovich with a Kurtis, and Jack McGrath is on the outside of row one with an upright Kurtis.

Air temperatures in the 90s and track temperatures of 130 degrees on race day threaten to take a heavy toll of cars and drivers. Andy Linden starts fifth but crashes in Turn 3 on the fourth lap, and he is first out of the race for the second year in a row.

Vukovich pulls away from the pack after a few laps and his fuel-injected Kurtis is clearly fastest. His low-slung roadster laps the field by the halfway mark, and the only time he gives up the lead is when he pits. In the most dominant performance since Billy Arnold led 198 laps in 1930, Vukovich leads 195 and wins by nearly three laps over Art Cross. Sam Hanks, with relief help from Duane Carter, is third.

Only 12 cars finish, and 10 drivers require relief from the heat. Carl Scarborough, making his second start, stops on the 70th lap and collapses in the pits. He dies in the infield hospital of heat prostration.

Ford marked its 50th anniversary with a pre-race banquet (*above*) and furnished the pace car, a Crestline Sunliner convertible. Mac Taggert of Champion Spark Plug welcomes 1952 winner Troy Ruttman to the 100 Mile an Hour Club (*opposite, top left*). Fellow members Sam Hanks and Henry Banks are with Ruttman. Speedway workers vacuum the bricks (*opposite, top right*), a chore performed annually before the race. The Ford pace car and a large crowd are on hand for Pole Day qualifying (*opposite bottom*). While the attention of the spectators is directed to a driver already on the track, Bob Scott awaits his chance to make a qualification attempt. Scott nailed down the 11th place on the grid.

STARTING LINEUP

Average Field Qualifying Speed: 136.429

Numbers in flags indicate finish position

Jack McGrath

Tony Bettenhausen

Sam Hanks

Art Cross

Don Freeland

Freddie Agabashian

Andy Linden

Johnnie Parsons

Bob Scott

Walt Faulkner

POLE POSITION
Qualifying Speed: 138.392

Bill Vukovich

Manuel Ayulo

Jerry Hoyt

Rodger Ward

Gene Hartley

Spider Webb

Jimmy Daywalt

Pat Flaherty

Duane Carter

Cal Niday

Johnny Thomson

Paul Russo

Ernie McCoy

Mike Nazaruk

Duke Nalon

Bob Sweikert

Jimmy Davies

Chuck Stevenson

Carl Scarborough

Marshall Teague

Jim Rathmann

Bill Holland

Jimmy Bryan

The stripped-down Kuzma chassis of Chuck Stevenson's ride (*above*), owned by J. C. Agajanian, was similar to the one Troy Ruttman drove to victory the year before. When kitted out with an Offenhauser engine and bodywork, Stevenson qualified the car in the 16th spot. On race day, though, a fuel leak waylaid him in 29th after just 42 laps. Meanwhile, a racing injury prevented Ruttman from taking a stab at defending his 500 crown. Workers perform the annual ritual of lettering the pit wall with the drivers' names, numbers, and sponsors (*right*). William Clay Ford became the fourth member of his family to drive a pace car at Indianapolis when he headed the '53 field (*below*). Brothers Henry II and Benson had piloted pacemakers in 1946 and 1950, respectively, and father Edsel drove the Lincoln that led the field in 1932.

Ford put 2000 replicas of the '53 pace car in dealerships to promote its connection to the 500. The replicas lacked the true pace-setter's spotlights and wire wheels (*left*). With engines fired, the 33 starters are ready to get under way (*above*). Polesitter Bill Vukovich pulls ahead of the field to lead going into the first turn at the start (*below*). Vukovich led 195 laps this year and won by more than three-and-a-half minutes in the same Kurtis roadster that nearly carried him to victory the year before.

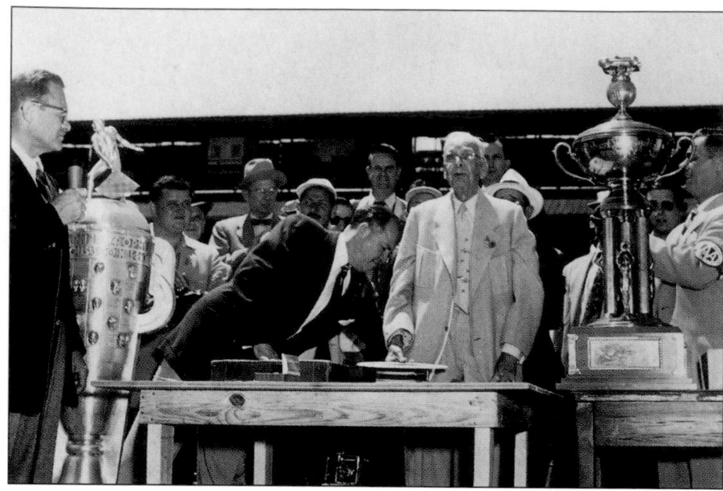

T. E. "Pop" Myers, who had worked for the Speedway since 1911, addresses the annual driver's meeting (*above*). Crews get ready in the pits for qualifications (*right*). Manuel Ayulo chases Bill Vukovich through Turn 1 on the opening lap (*below*). Sam Hanks, who finished third, leads 1950 winner Johnnie Parsons (*bottom left*). Chuck Stevenson pits (*bottom right*). He retired after 42 laps because of a fuel leak. Vukovich is all alone when he takes the checkers (*opposite, top left*), but is quite the popular fellow in victory lane (*opposite, top right*). Having secured the pole in the rain, Vukovich survived scorching race-day temperatures to make a winner of Howard Keck's Fuel-Injection Special (*opposite bottom*).

Following the 1952 Indy 500, the AAA announced that stock-block engine displacement would be raised to 335 cubic inches for the '53 event. With this information, many teams began work developing production passenger-car power plants for racing.

Among the earliest and best-developed programs was Roger Wolcott's stable of Chrysler-powered roadsters.

For years a story was told that a Wolcott Chrysler, driven either by Joe James or Joe Sostillio, took part in a "practice" 500, and averaged 134.5 mph. Since this was more than five mph faster than Troy Ruttman's record-setting time from '52, the Offy owners began to lobby for the AAA to reduce the limit on the stock-blockers. Sure enough, in January 1953, the governing body made the Detroit iron conform to the same rules as the race-bred Offenhauser.

For once, the AAA had been tricked; the "practice 500" had been nothing more than a rumor. "We never ran more than 10 or 20 laps at a time," veteran driver George Connor said. "That practice race business is a bunch of stuff," according to Herb Porter, Wolcott's chief mechanic. "The Offy guys just didn't want those cars to run."

RESULTS

NO.	DRIVER	CAR	ENTRANT	ENGINE	CYL	DISP	CHASSIS	COLOR	QUAL SPD	START	FIN	LAPS / SPEED / REASON OUT
14	Bill Vukovich	Fuel Injection	Howard Keck Co.	Offy	4	270	KK500A	gray, red, yelo	138.392	1	1	200-128.740
16	Art Cross	Springfield Welding	Bessie Lee Paoli	Offy	4	263	KK4000	red, white	137.310	12	2	200-126.827
3	Sam Hanks	Bardahl	Ed Walsh	Offy	4	270	KK4000	black, white	137.531	9	3	200-126.465
59	Fred Agabashian	Grancor-Elgin	Grancor Auto. Specialists	Offy	4	270	KK500B	blue, red, slvr	137.546	2	4	200-126.219
5	Jack McGrath	Hinkle	Jack B. Hinkle	Offy	4	270	KK4000	cream, black	136.602	3	5	200-124.556
48	Jimmy Daywalt	Sumar	Chapman S. Root	Offy	4	270	KK3000	blue, white	135.747	21	6	200-124.379
2	Jim Rathmann	Travelon Trailer	Ernest L. Ruiz	Offy	4	270	KK500B	orange, white	135.666	25	7	200-124.072
12	Ernie McCoy	Chapman	H. A. Chapman	Offy	4	270	Stevens	turquoise, red	135.926	20	8	200-123.404
98	Tony Bettenhausen	Agajanian	J. C. Agajanian	Offy	4	263	Kuzma	cream, red	136.024	6	9	196-axle, wreck T3 (Hartley)
53	Jim Davies	Pat Clancy	Pat Clancy	Offy	4	263	KK500B	gold, red	135.262	32	10	193-flagged
9	Duke Nalon	Novi Governor	Jean Marcenac	Novi*	8	181	Kurtis	cream, black	135.461	26	11	191-spun to avoid 98 T3
73	Carl Scarborough	McNamara	Lee Elkins	Offy	4	270	KK2000	tan, copper	135.936	19	12	190-flagged
88	Manuel Ayulo	Peter Schmidt	Peter Schmidt	Offy	4	270	Kuzma	red, silver	136.384	4	13	184-con. rod
8	Jimmy Bryan	Blakely Oil	John L. McDaniel	Offy	4	270	Schroeder	red, silver	135.506	31	14	183-flagged
49	Bill Holland	Crawford	Ray Crawford	Offy	4	270	KK500B	red, cream	137.868	28	15	177-cam gear
92	Rodger Ward	M. A. Walker Electric	M. A. Walker	Offy	4	270	Kurtis	blue, cream	137.468	10	16	177-stalled
23	Walt Faulkner	Automobile Shippers	Eugene A. Casaroll	Offy	4	270	KK500A	orange, black	137.117	14	17	176-flagged
22	Marshall Teague	Pure Oil	Hart Fullerton	Offy	4	270	KK4000	blue, wht, slvr	135.721	22	18	169-oil leak
62	Spider Webb	Lubri-Loy	3-L Racing Team	Offy	4	270	KK3000	wht, blue, orng	136.168	18	19	166-oil leak
51	Bob Sweikert	Dean Van Lines	A. E. Dean	Offy	4	270	Kuzma	white, black	136.872	29	20	151-radius rod
83	Mike Nazaruk	Kalamazoo	Lee Elkins	Offy	4	270	Turner	gold, maroon	135.706	23	21	146-stalled
77	Pat Flaherty	Peter Schmidt	Peter Schmidt	Offy	4	270	KK3000	red, silver	135.668	24	22	115-wrecked
55	Jerry Hoyt	John Zink	John Zink	Offy	4	270	KK4000	turq, orange	135.731	7	23	107-cockpit too hot
4	Duane Carter	Miracle Power	Murrell Belanger	Offy	4	270	Lesovsky	blue, yelo, red	135.267	27	24	94-ignition
7	Paul Russo	Federal Eng	Federal Auto. Associates	Offy	4	270	KK3000	yellow, blue	136.219	17	25	89-magneto
21	Johnnie Parsons	Belond Equa-Flow	J. S. Belond	Offy	4	270	KK500B	cream, red	137.667	8	26	86-crankshaft
38	Don Freeland	Bob Estes	Bob Estes	Offy	4	270	Watson	cream, red	136.867	15	27	76-wrecked T4
41	Gene Hartley	Federal Eng	Federal Auto. Associates	Offy	4	270	KK4000	yellow, blue	137.263	13	28	53-wrecked T3
97	Chuck Stevenson	Agajanian	J. C. Agajanian	Offy	4	270	Kuzma	red, wht, blk	136.560	16	29	42-fuel leak
99	Cal Niday	Miracle Power	Murrell Belanger	Offy	4	263	Kurtis	yelo, blue, red	136.096	30	30	30-magneto
29	Bob Scott	Belond Equa-Flow	Louis & Bruce Bromme	Offy	4	270	Bromme	cream, red	137.431	11	31	14-oil leak
56	Johnny Thomson	Dr. Sabourin	Dr. R. N. Sabourin, D.C.	Offy	4	270	Del Roy	blue, dark blue	135.262	33	32	6-ignition
32	Andy Linden	Cop-Sil-Loy	Rotary Engineering Corp.	Offy	4	270	Stevens	copper, blue	136.060	5	33	3-wrecked T3

* Supercharged and front drive

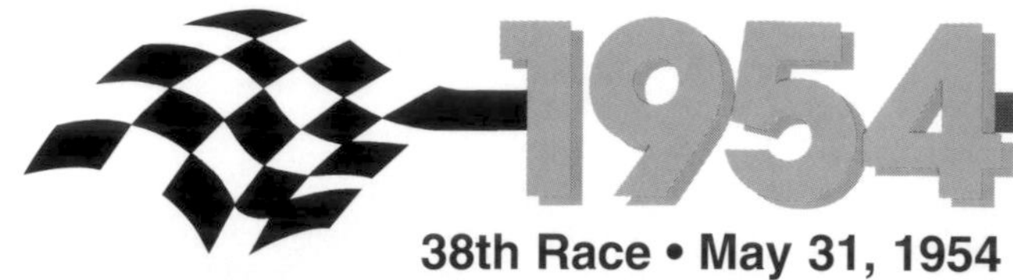

1954

38th Race • May 31, 1954

The entire field of 33 cars uses four-cylinder Offenhauser engines for the first time, and none is supercharged. The Novi V-8, a Ferrari V-12, and supercharged Offys fail to cut the mustard this year.

New nylon-cord Firestone tires provide more cornering grip to boost qualifying speeds. Jack McGrath sits on the pole at 141.033 mph, the first driver to average more than 140 for the four-lap run.

Defending winner Bill Vukovich can't get his Kurtis-Offenhauser roadster up to speed the first weekend, and he qualifies a disappointing 19th. The cars are tightly bunched, with only 3.36 mph separating McGrath and the slowest qualifier, Frank Armi.

McGrath jumps in front at the start, and Jimmy Bryan, who lines up on the outside of row one, gives chase. Troy Ruttman, the '52 winner, moves up from 11th to challenge Bryan for second, but shreds a tire and makes an unscheduled stop. Ruttman later blows a tire and spins but stays off the wall to finish fourth.

While McGrath and Bryan set a record pace, Vukovich starts from the seventh row and carefully works through the field. The race is nearly half over before "Vuky" leads for the first time.

Attrition is surprisingly low, and 19 cars finish. Bill Homeier is the first to go out when he hits the wall on lap 75 as he exits the pits. Relief drivers are in high demand, as 21 jump into 15 different cars.

Bryan takes the lead when Vukovich makes his second stop, but Bryan gives it back when he pits a third time. Though Vukovich slows with worn tires at the end, he elects not to make a third stop.

A broken front spring and rear shock absorber prevent Bryan from challenging Vukovich, and he finishes second, a lap down. McGrath places third, just 11 seconds behind Bryan. He also pits three times and loses about 45 seconds when he stalls on the second stop.

Vukovich leads 90 laps on his way to victory and averages 130.84 mph, the first to top 130. He joins Wilbur Shaw and Mauri Rose on the list of back-to-back winners.

Western film and television star Roy Rogers saddled up the Dodge Royal 500 pace car for a spin around the Brickyard (*top*), but Dodge division chief William C. Newberg drove it on race day (*above*). Speedway President Wilbur Shaw found this scooter (*opposite, top left*) handy for zipping around the 559-acre grounds. Aside from coming up with the pace car, Dodge furnished its new V-8-powered truck to provide emergency service at the track (*opposite, top right*). In his seventh start at Indy, Jack McGrath put his brightly trimmed Kurtis roadster (*opposite bottom*) on the pole when he became the first driver to qualify at more than 140 mph. McGrath led 47 laps and finished third.

STARTING LINEUP

Average Field Qualifying Speed: 138.632

Numbers in flags indicate finish position

Jimmy Bryan

Don Freeland

Bob Sweikert

Pat O'Connor

Johnnie Parsons

Jimmy Daywalt

Chuck Stevenson

Duane Carter

Troy Ruttman

Mike Nazaruk

POLE POSITION
Qualifying Speed: 141.033

Jack McGrath

Johnny Thomson

Jimmy Reece

Sam Hanks

Cal Niday

Long before Jim Nabors made the pre-race singing of Back Home Again in Indiana *his personal domain, many other well-known singers performed the refrain. For several years, James Melton was one of them.*

In 1954, Melton told of one of his earlier engagements at Indy. "It was one of my first years at the 500," Melton explained. "Of course, I was nervous. I had heard a fellow say that no one was interested in all that pomp and preliminaries. They just wanted to see the race get underway. So, I'm singing right along, doing my best not to make a mistake, with 2- or 300,000 people standing by. Just as I got to the last line, some mechanic jumped the gun, firing up one of the cars. Well, when that engine burst into its 'song,' I jumped straight up into the air. That's when I did it: I sang the last line from My Old Kentucky Home. *Do you suppose anyone noticed?"*

They sure did.

Bill Homeier

Tony Bettenhausen

Fred Agabashian

Art Cross

Jerry Hoyt

Frank Armi

Gene Hartley

Ernie McCoy

Andy Linden

Len Duncan

Spider Webb

Paul Russo

Rodger Ward

Bill Vukovich

Manuel Ayulo

Larry Crockett

Jim Rathmann

Ed Elisian

The annual drivers' meeting was held in the front straight stands (*right*). The Sumar team entered three cars (*bottom*), but only Jimmy Daywalt made the show, qualifying the No. 19 car second and leading eight laps before he crashed. To Daywalt's right are Jerry Hoyt, car-owner Chapman Root, and chief mechanic John Blough. Johnnie Parsons and Dean Martin, along with Speedway owner Tony Hulman, point out the short way around the Brickyard to comedian Jerry Lewis (*opposite, top left*). Stock-car ace Marshall Teague failed to qualify in the Fullerton Special (*opposite, second from top left*). Chief Starter Bill Vandewater gets ready to wave the checkers (*opposite, top right*). Jim Rathmann takes on fuel and fresh rubber (*opposite bottom*). Pat Flaherty later relieved Rathmann, but was involved in a crash with Daywalt.

The photo of Bill Vukovich taking the checkered flag while lapping Jimmy Bryan became a famous Indy image. It gave many the impression that "Vuky" had won an easy victory. But Bryan never made it easy for any-one to beat him.

At 350 miles, Bryan's old-fashioned dirt car had an advantage of more than a minute on Vukovich's roadster. But thereafter, things started to fall off Bryan's Dean Van Lines Special. The shocks broke, the brakes faded, and the differential began grinding its gears and vibrating. The accelerator return spring broke, making it necessary for Bryan to pull the throttle back with his toe. After the race, specks of blood showed through the back of Bryan's uniform. "Jimmy was black-and-blue all over," Clint Brawner, Bryan's mechanic, remembered. "I never saw a guy so beat up at Indy. Anyone else would have quit, but not Bryan."

In fact, Bryan was so battered from his second-place ordeal at Indy, he didn't race in the 100-miler at Milwaukee held six days after the 500.

Jimmy Bryan, in the hunt all day, chases eventual winner Bill Vukovich (*above*). However, a third pit stop for Bryan in the Dean Van Lines Special (*left*) relegated him to a second-place finish. A clear face shield affords the fueler some protection against possible spillage, but pit crewman otherwise lacked protective clothing. Vukovich takes the checkered flag (*below left*)—lapping Bryan in the process—and then tells the world what his day was like from victory lane for the second straight year (*below*). Towel-draped and grease-stained, Vukovich rehashes the race with fellow driver Ed Elisian (*opposite, bottom left*), who finished 18th, and then finds some solitude in a corner of his garage (*opposite, bottom right*). Vukovich piloted the 1954 iteration of the Offenhauser-powered Fuel Injection Special (*opposite top*) to 90 laps in the lead, raising his leadership total to a remarkable 435 in the last three races. At the time, that made him third on the all-time list.

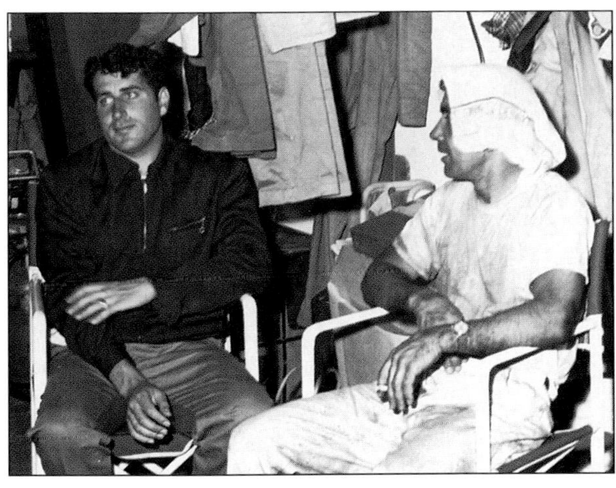

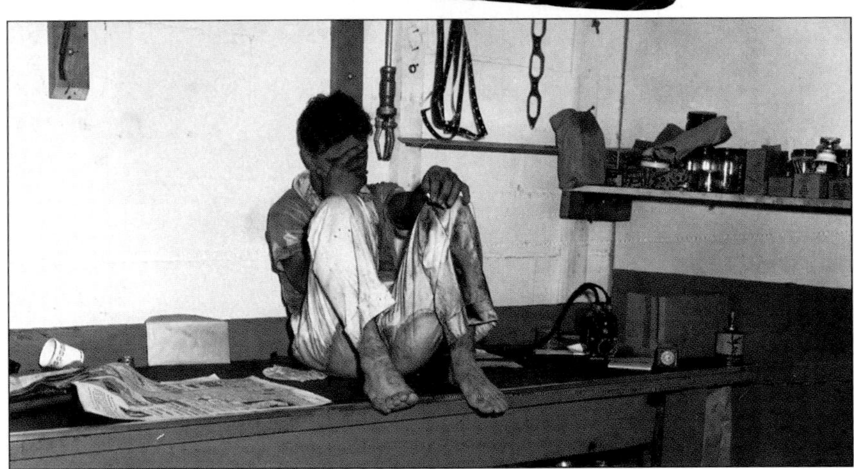

RESULTS

NO.	DRIVER	CAR	ENTRANT	ENGINE	CYL	DISP	CHASSIS	COLOR	QUAL SPD	START	FIN	LAPS / SPEED / REASON OUT
14	Bill Vukovich	Fuel Injection	Howard Keck Co.	Offy	4	270	KK500A	gray, red, yelo	138.478	19	1	200-130.840
9	Jimmy Bryan	Dean Van Lines	A. E. Dean	Offy	4	274	Kuzma	white, blue	139.665	3	2	200-130.178
2	Jack McGrath	Hinkle	Jack B. Hinkle	Offy	4	270	KK500C	cream, blk	141.033	1	3	200-130.086
34	Troy Ruttman	Automobile Shippers	Eugene A. Casaroll	Offy	4	270	KK500A	orange, blk	137.736	11	4	200-129.218
73	Mike Nazaruk	McNamara	Lee Elkins	Offy	4	270	KK500C	gold, red	139.589	14	5	200-128.923
77	Fred Agabashian	Merz Engineering	Miklos Sperling	Offy	4	271	KK500C	maroon, crm	137.746	24	6	200-128.711
7	Don Freeland	Bob Estes	Bob Estes	Offy	4	270	Phillips	cream, red	138.339	6	7	200-128.474
5	Paul Russo	Ansted Rotary	Hoosier Racing Team, Inc.	Offy	4	270	KK500A	blue, cream	137.678	32	8	200-128.037
28	Larry Crockett	Federal Eng	Federal Auto. Associates	Offy	4	270	KK3000	yellow, blue	139.557	25	9	200-126.899
24	Cal Niday	Jim Robbins	Jim Robbins Co.	Offy	4	270	Stevens	mrn, crm, red	139.828	13	10	200-126.895
45	Art Cross	Bardahl	Ed Walsh	Offy	4	270	KK4000	black, wht	138.675	27	11	200-126.232
98	Chuck Stevenson	Agajanian	J. C. Agajanian	Offy	4	270	Kuzma	cream, red	138.776	5	12	199-flagged
88	Manuel Ayulo	Schmidt	Peter Schmidt	Offy	4	270	Kuzma	red, silver	138.164	22	13	197-flagged
17	Bob Sweikert	Lutes	Francis Bardazon	Offy	4	270	KK4000	red, yellow	138.206	9	14	197-flagged
16	Duane Carter	Automobile Shippers	Eugene A. Casaroll	Offy	4	270	KK4000	orange, blk	138.238	8	15	196-flagged
32	Ernie McCoy	Crawford	Ray Crawford	Offy	4	270	KK500B	cream, red	138.419	20	16	194-flagged
25	Jimmy Reece	Malloy	Emmett J. Malloy	Offy	4	263	Pankratz	blk, red, wht	138.312	7	17	194-flagged
27	Ed Elisian	Chapman	H. A. Chapman	Offy	4	270	Stevens	turq, red	137.794	31	18	193-flagged
71	Frank Armi	Martin Bros.	T. W. & W. T. Martin	Offy	4	270	Curtis	salmon, wht	137.673	33	19	193-flagged
1	Sam Hanks	Bardahl	Ed Walsh	Offy	4	270	KK4000	black, wht	137.994	10	20	191-spun FS (J. Rathmann)
35	Pat O'Connor	Hopkins	Motor Racers, Inc.	Offy	4	270	KK500C	blue, orange	138.084	12	21	181-spun T2
12	Rodger Ward	Dr. Sabourin	Dr. R. N. Sabourin, D.C.	Offy	4	270	Pawl	white, blue	139.297	16	22	172-stalled BS
31	Gene Hartley	John Zink	John S. Zink	Offy	4	270	KK4000	red, white	139.061	17	23	168-engine trouble
43	Johnny Thomson	Chapman	H. A. Chapman	Offy	4	270	Nichels	red, turq	138.787	4	24	165-stalled
74	Andy Linden	Brown Motor Co.	Brown Motor Co.	Offy	4	270	Schroeder	brown, gold	137.820	23	25	165-torsion bar
99	Jerry Hoyt	Belanger	Murrell Belanger	Offy	4	270	Kurtis	blue, gold	137.825	30	26	130-engine trouble
19	Jimmy Daywalt	Sumar	Chapman S. Root	Offy	4	270	KK500C	blue, white	139.789	2	27	111-wrecked T4
38	Jim Rathmann	Bardahl	Ed Walsh	Offy	4	270	KK500C	black, white	138.228	28	28	110-wrecked T4 (Flaherty)
10	Tony Bettenhausen	Mel Wiggers	Mel B. Wiggers	Offy	4	270	KK500C	wht, red, gld	138.275	21	29	105-con. rod bearing
65	Spider Webb	Advance Muffler	Bruce Bromme	Offy	4	270	Bromme	red, yellow	137.979	29	30	104-oil leak
33	Len Duncan	Brady	Ray T. Brady	Offy	4	270	Schroeder	crm, blk, red	139.217	26	31	101-brakes
15	Johnnie Parsons	Belond Equa-Flow	So. Calif. Muffler Corp.	Offy	4	270	KK500C	yellow, red	139.578	15	32	79-stalled in pits
51	Bill Homeier	Jones & Maley	Cars, Inc.	Offy	4	270	KK500C	red, white	138.948	18	33	74-hit wall leaving pits

1955

39th Race • May 30, 1955

Speedway owner Tony Hulman takes on additional duties this year in the absence of Wilbur Shaw, the president and general manager, who died the previous October in a plane crash. For the first time in his 10 years as track owner, it is Hulman who gives the order to start engines on race day.

Only two cars qualify on pole day because high winds discourage most from trying. Jerry Hoyt wins the pole at a non-record 140.045 mph and Tony Bettenhausen lines up next to him.

The winds die down the next day, and Jack McGrath breaks his own qualifying record with a speed of 142.58 mph to start third. Naturally aspirated Offenhausers again power the entire field.

McGrath darts around Hoyt and Bettenhausen and leads the first three laps. Bill Vukovich, shooting for his third win in a row, charges from fifth starting spot and takes over on the fourth lap. He and McGrath stage a thrilling duel until McGrath retires on lap 54 with magneto trouble.

Vuky is in command on lap 57 when Rodger Ward breaks a front axle heading onto the back straight and hits the wall. As cars scramble to avoid Ward, Al Keller runs into Johnny Boyd, who hits Vukovich, sending his car end over end and out of the track. Vukovich dies of a massive skull fracture; Ward, Boyd, and two spectators are injured in the tragic accident. Vukovich's legacy includes leading 485 laps while dominating the last four races.

Defending national champion Jimmy Bryan leads the next 31 laps, but goes out with a broken fuel pump. That sets up a battle among Art Cross, Don Freeland, and Bob Sweikert.

With about 100 miles to go, Sweikert runs third. Cross blows an engine on lap 169, and Freeland's transmission breaks 10 laps later.

That clears the way for Sweikert, who coasts to victory more than two laps ahead of Bettenhausen's Kurtis. Bettenhausen fails to lead a lap but posts his best Speedway finish in nine tries with relief from Paul Russo.

Sweikert leads 86 laps in his rose and white roadster, the last Frank Kurtis designed car that wins.

Chevrolet's completely redesigned Bel Air, replete with a new "Super Turbo-Fire" V-8, paced this year's field and provided plenty of parade cars, too (*top*). Three-time 500 winner Mauri Rose gives driving tips to Chevy chief Tom Keating (*above*), who drove the pacemaker. Speedway owner Tony Hulman is the passenger. Sumar team owner Chapman Root (*opposite top*) created quite a stir with his head-turning streamlined racer, which looked like a car of the future. Under the swoopy skin was a conventional Kurtis chassis and four-cylinder Offy (*opposite, bottom left*). With the car's "fenders" and canopy removed (*opposite, bottom right*), Jimmy Daywalt qualified the car 17th and finished ninth.

STARTING LINEUP

Average Field Qualifying Speed: 138.796

Numbers in flags indicate finish position

Jack McGrath

Sam Hanks

Cal Niday

Pat Flaherty

33

Jimmy Reece

Tony Bettenhausen

Bill Vukovich

Andy Linden

Jimmy Bryan

Bob Sweikert

POLE POSITION
Qualifying Speed: 140.045

Jerry Hoyt

Fred Agabashian

Walt Faulkner

3

Jimmy Davies

Eddie Russo

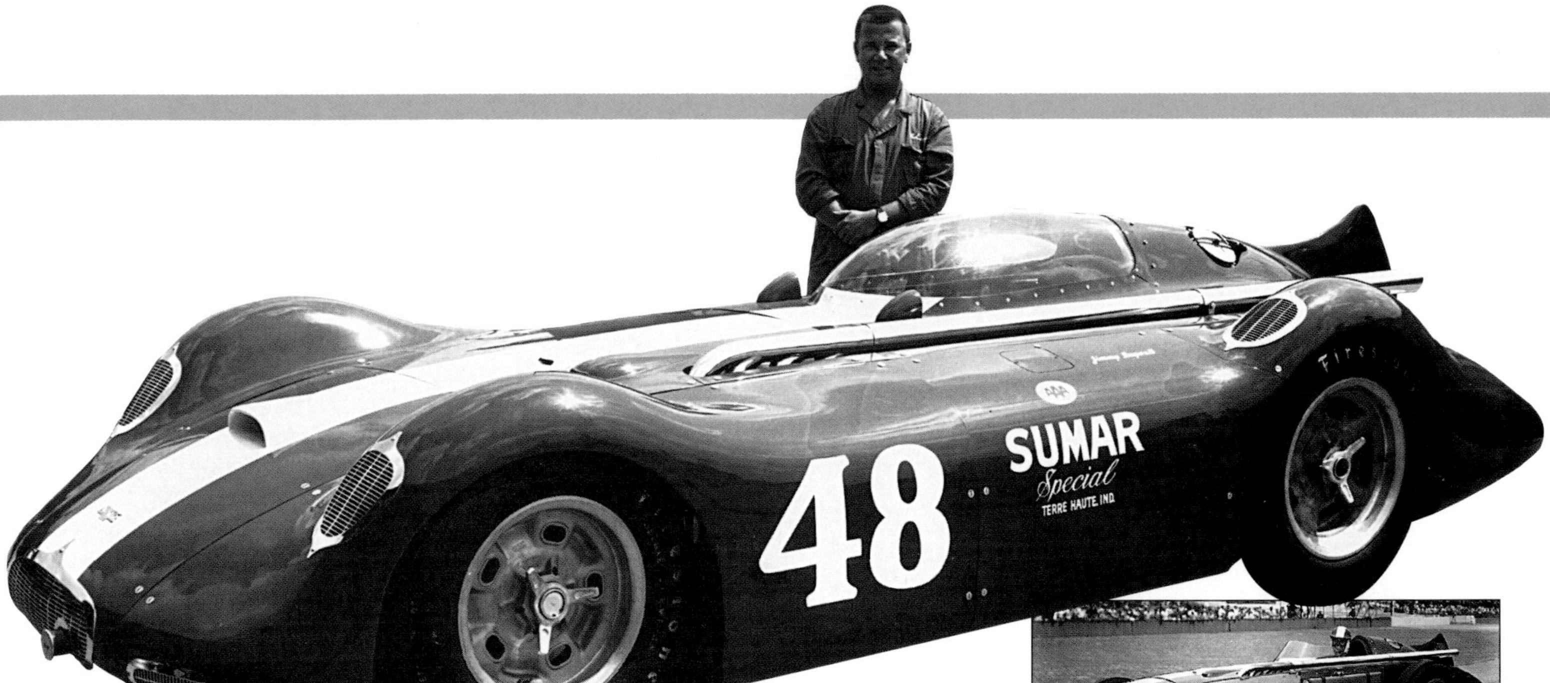

On the last day of qualifications in '55, just before the gun sounded to end all attempts at making the starting field, Ed Elisian took to the track. After turning two of three warmup laps alotted to every car, officials flagged Elisian off the course. To a chorus of boos from the crowd, chief steward Harry McQuinn stated that Elisian had taken his three warmup laps. Meanwhile, the 6 P.M. deadline had expired.

After a protest from Elisian and his Westwood Tool racing team, plus a lengthy recheck, it was found that someone had miscounted Ed's warmup laps. There was nothing to do, but give him another opportunity to qualify.

Darkness was descending and the grandstands were deserted as Elisian qualified at 135.333 mph, bumping Len Duncan from the lineup. The qualifying run came to be known as "Elisian's Midnight Ride."

Duane Carter

Don Freeland

Art Cross

Johnnie Parsons

Rodger Ward

Johnny Thomson

Jimmy Daywalt

Jim Rathmann

Ray Crawford

Johnny Boyd

Ed Elisian

Eddie Johnson

Al Herman

Pat O'Connor

Al Keller

Chuck Weyant

Keith Andrews

Shorty Templeman

Jim Rathmann finished 14th in the low-slung Belond Miracle Power Special (*top*). The chassis was designed by Quin Epperly and placed the racer's Offenhauser engine to the left, with the driver offset to the right. A cockpit canopy was available for the car (*above*). Jerry Hoyt sat on the pole, while Tony Bettenhausen and Jack McGrath also shared the front row (*below*). Bob Sweikert, in the No. 6 John Zink Special (*opposite, top left*), confers with his crew during practice. Dean Van Lines entered a car powered by a Dodge Hemi V-8 (*opposite, top right*), but Bob Christie failed to qualify with it. Eager spectators eyeball the race cars from just behind the pits (*opposite middle*). Tony Hulman poses with singer and television star Dinah Shore, who was the '55 race queen.

Red Ram
DODGE
PERFECT CIRCLE

JIM ROBBINS
SPECIAL
Firestone
PERFECT CIRCLE
MONROE

The field follows the pace car in tight formation prior to the green flag (*top*), and once the competition begins, Sam Hanks leads Duane Carter onto the front straight (*second from top, left*). Cal Niday suffered serious injuries when his D-A Lubricant Special crashed in Turn 4 on lap 171 (*second from top, right*). Earlier in the race, Niday leads a pack of cars running wheel-to-wheel into Turn 2 (*below*) as Pat Flaherty takes the high groove. Defending national champ Jimmy Bryan led 31 laps in the No. 1 Dean Van Lines Special (*below right*) before a broken fuel pump ended his race. His once immaculate racer slowly turned into an oily, smoky mess as the 500 wore on. Track workers remove Johnny Boyd's disabled No. 39 Sumar Special (*bottom left*), one of the cars involved in the wreck on the backstretch that claimed the life of two-time winner Bill Vukovich. Fred Agabashian's day ended early when his No. 14 Federal Engineering Special spun out in Turn 2 (*bottom right*). Bob Sweikert started in the middle of the fifth row and plugged away while other contenders suffered mechanical problems to earn the victory and valuable points that helped him win the national championship (*opposite top*). Sweikert's mount (*opposite bottom*) was the first of back-to-back winners sponsored by John Zink.

A few days before the race, A. J. Watson's wife was having a difficult childbirth. He was called to her bedside in California, leaving the John Zink roadster—for which Watson served as chief mechanic—in a thousand pieces. Watson left driver Bob Sweikert a note that read: "Have the crew put the chassis together. You build the engine." Sweikert shook his head. "Looks like the pitcher is going to have to hit a home run," Bob told the crew.

Watson returned to Indy just in time for the race. "I never turned a wrench on that engine," he says. "Sweikert put it together, and it won the 500."

Many feel—Watson included—that Sweikert never got enough credit for his abilities. Besides his obvious talent with a wrench, he is the only driver in history to win Indy, a national championship, and a major sprint-car title all in the same year.

RESULTS

NO.	DRIVER	CAR	ENTRANT	ENGINE	CYL	DISP	CHASSIS	COLOR	QUAL SPD	START	FIN	LAPS / SPEED / REASON OUT
6	Bob Sweikert	John Zink	John Zink Co.	Offy	4	270	KK500C	rose, wht, blk	139.996	14	1	200-128.209
10	Tony Bettenhausen	Chapman	H. A. Chapman	Offy	4	270	KK500C	turq, crm, red	139.985	2	2	200-126.733
15	Jim Davies	Bardahl	Pat Clancy	Offy	4	270	KK500B	black, white	140.274	10	3	200-126.299
44	Johnny Thomson	Schmidt	Peter Schmidt	Offy	4	270	Kuzma	red, silver	134.113	33	4	200-126.241
77	Walt Faulkner	Merz Engineering	Merz Engineering, Inc.	Offy	4	270	KK500C	bronze, crm	139.762	7	5	200-125.377
19	Andy Linden	Massaglia	Joseph Massaglia, Jr.	Offy	4	270	KK4000	rose, white	139.098	8	6	200-125.022
71	Al Herman	Martin Bros.	T. W. & W. T. Martin	Offy	4	270	Curtis	salmon, wht	139.811	16	7	200-124.794
29	Pat O'Connor	Ansted Rotary	Rotary Engineering Corp.	Offy	4	270	KK500D	cream, black	139.195	19	8	200-124.644
48	Jimmy Daywalt	Sumar	Chapman S. Root	Offy	4	270	Kurtis	blue, white	139.416	17	9	200-124.401
89	Pat Flaherty	Dunn Engineering	Harry Dunn	Offy	4	272	KK500B	white, black	140.149	12	10	200-124.086
98	Duane Carter	Agajanian	J. C. Agajanian	Offy	4	270	Kuzma	cream, red	139.330	18	11	197-flagged
41	Chuck Weyant	Federal Eng	Federal Auto. Associates	Offy	4	270	KK3000	yellow, blue	138.063	25	12	196-flagged
83	Eddie Johnson	McNamara	Kalamazoo Sports, Inc.	Offy	4	270	Trevis	maroon, gld	134.449	32	13	196-flagged
33	Jim Rathmann	Belond Miracle Power	So. Calif. Muffler Corp.	Offy	4	270	Epperly	yellow, blue	138.707	20	14	191-flagged
12	Don Freeland	Bob Estes	Bob Estes	Offy	4	270	Phillips	cream, red	139.866	21	15	178-transmission
22	Cal Niday	D-A Lubricants	Racing Associates	Offy	4	270	KK500B	yelo, blk, wht	140.302	9	16	170-wrecked T4
99	Art Cross	Belanger Motors	Murrell Belanger	Offy	4	270	KK500C	blue, gold	138.750	24	17	168-con. rod cap
81	Shorty Templeman	Central Excavating	Pete Salemi	Offy	4	270	Trevis	blue, white	135.014	31	18	142-stalled
8	Sam Hanks	Jones & Maley	Cars, Inc.	Offy	4	270	KK500C	red, wht, slvr	140.187	6	19	134-transmission
31	Keith Andrews	McDaniel	John L. McDaniel	Offy	4	270	Schroeder	blue, white	136.049	28	20	120-ignition
16	Johnnie Parsons	Trio Brass	Carl L. Anderson	Offy	4	270	KK500C	blue, white	136.809	27	21	119-magneto
37	Eddie Russo	Dr. Sabourin	Dr. R. N. Sabourin, D.C.	Offy	4	270	Pawl	white, blue	140.116	13	22	112-ignition
49	Ray Crawford	Crawford	Ray Crawford	Offy	4	270	KK500B	red, cream	139.206	23	23	111-valve
1	Jimmy Bryan	Dean Van Lines	A. E. Dean	Offy	4	270	Kuzma	white, blue	140.160	11	24	90-fuel pump
4	Bill Vukovich	Hopkins	Lindsey Hopkins	Offy	4	269	KK500C	blue, orng, wht	141.071	5	25	56-wrecked BS
3	Jack McGrath	Hinkle	Jack B. Hinkle	Offy	4	270	KK500C	cream, black	142.580	3	26	54-magneto
42	Al Keller	Sam Traylor Offy	Samuel W. Traylor, III	Offy	4	270	KK2000	black, gold	139.551	22	27	54-wrecked BS
27	Rodger Ward	Aristo Blue	E. R. Casale	Offy	4	270	Kuzma	white, blue	135.049	30	28	53-wrecked BS
39	Johnny Boyd	Sumar	Chapman S. Root	Offy	4	270	KK500D	blue, white	136.981	26	29	53-wrecked BS
68	Ed Elisian	Westwood Gge/Tool	M. Pete Wales	Offy	4	270	KK4000	blue, cream	135.333	29	30	53-stopped at wreck BS
23	Jerry Hoyt	Jim Robbins	Jim Robbins	Offy	4	270	Stevens	maroon, wht	140.045	1	31	40-oil leak
14	Fred Agabashian	Federal Eng	Federal Auto. Associates	Offy	4	270	KK500C	yellow, blue	141.933	4	32	39-spun T2
5	Jimmy Reece	Malloy	Emmett J. Malloy	Offy	4	269	Pankratz	blk, wht, red	139.991	15	33	10-con. rod, spun T1

1956

40th Race • May 30, 1956

The United States Auto Club sanctions the 500 for the first time. Speedway owner Tony Hulman organizes USAC after the American Automobile Association, which had sanctioned every previous race, withdraws from racing.

A new administration building and museum opens at the south end of the track, and a fresh layer of asphalt (except over the bricks that remain on the front straight) increases qualifying speeds.

Pat Flaherty breaks the record by three mph and sits on the pole at 145.596 mph. Flaherty drives a new roadster built by A. J. Watson that is taller than the Kurtis slant-engined roadsters because the engine mounts vertically. However, the power plant sits eight inches to the left of center, creating ideal weight distribution in Indy's left-hand turns. Light magnesium body panels and sleek styling give it more speed on the straights.

The hair-raising howl of the Novi is back after a two-year absence from the starting field. Paul Russo qualifies the supercharged V-8 eighth in a Kurtis, the first time the Novi makes the show in a rear-drive chassis.

Heavy rain washes out most of the second weekend of qualifying, and the track remains covered by water just three days before the race.

The race starts on schedule, as Flaherty and front-row starters Jim Rathmann and Pat O'Connor fight for the early lead. Russo blows by Flaherty and O'Connor on the front straight to grab the lead on lap 11.

The Novi jinx returns on lap 22 when Russo blows a tire and smacks the Turn 1 wall. This touches off a melee in which Sam Hanks and Keith Andrews collide, Troy Ruttman spins into the infield to avoid the others, and Johnny Thomson spins in the pits, breaking the leg of a mechanic working on another car. Russo, Ruttman, and Thomson are out, but Hanks and Andrews get back in the race.

Crashes claim several other cars, and the caution flag flies a record 11 times. Flaherty avoids trouble, takes the lead for keeps on the 77th lap, and holds off Hanks, who finishes second despite a bent frame from his early shunt.

The new Watson roadster finishes 21 seconds ahead of Hanks's Kurtis, the second-smallest victory margin to date.

DeSoto's only turn as the Indy pace car came in 1956 (*above*). Johnnie Parsons campaigned the No. 98 Kuzma-Offy for owner J. C. Agajanian (*below*). On race day he went from sixth on the grid to a fourth-place finish, his best since winning the '50 race. Having been picked for an early pre-race publicity photo may have been a good omen in '56 (*opposite*). Among the cars shown are Rodger Ward's eventual eighth-pace Filter Queen Special, left, and the John Zink Special, center, that Pat Flaherty drove to victory.

STARTING LINEUP

Average Field Qualifying Speed: 142.507

Numbers in flags indicate finish position

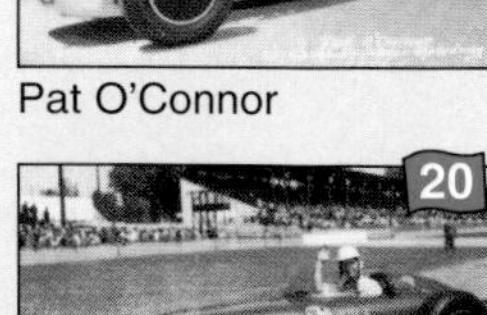
18 Pat O'Connor

4 Johnnie Parsons

27 Andy Linden

30 Johnny Boyd

8 Rodger Ward

20 Jim Rathmann

22 Tony Bettenhausen

33 Paul Russo

31 Troy Ruttman

23 Ed Elisian

POLE POSITION
Qualifying Speed: 145.596

1 Pat Flaherty

5 Dick Rathmann

12 Fred Agabashian

6 Bob Sweikert

2 Sam Hanks

When Pat Flaherty took the checkered flag in 1956, he had driven to one of the surest victories in Indy history. Starting from the pole position, he'd led almost at will. It wasn't until after he'd taken the checkered flag, that things started to go awry for him.

Most winners take two "insurance laps" just in case the scorers have miscounted the 200 circuits. But after taking the checkered flag, Flaherty slowed down to a crawl. He came coasting into victory lane, smiling and shaking his head. "I had just taken the flag when the engine went back to idle," Pat said. "I pushed on the gas, but nothing happened. The throttle shaft between the pedal and the injectors had broken. If that had happened a couple of minutes sooner, I'd never have made it to victory lane."

Johnny Thomson | Jimmy Reece | Jack Turner | Al Herman | Cliff Griffith | Duke Dinsmore

Ray Crawford | Keith Andrews | Bob Veith | Don Freeland | Billy Garrett | Eddie Johnson

Jimmy Daywalt | Jimmy Bryan | Gene Hartley | Bob Christie | Al Keller | Johnnie Tolan

Rookie Bill Boyd failed to qualify in the ground-hugging No. 33 Belond Miracle Power Special (*top left*). Popular Tony Bettenhausen started from the second row in the Belanger Motors entry (*top right*), but blew a tire in the race, hit the Turn 1 wall, and broke his collarbone. Racing machines roar to life on the grid (*above*) with the gold-and-white DeSoto pace car poised to lead them on a parade lap. Front-row qualifiers are dead even as they take the green flag (*opposite top*), but Jim Rathmann noses ahead of Pat O'Connor and Pat Flaherty as they clear the area in front of the pits and head for the first turn (*opposite bottom*). Rathmann maintained his lead for the first three laps, but fell back and later dropped out because of a burned piston. Meanwhile, O'Connor and Flaherty would have a longer and more eventful race.

GRAND STAND
C

In the opening laps of the race, Paul Russo and his famous Novi allowed the field to sort itself out. But at nine laps, Russo was a red blur, streaking into third place behind Pat O'Connor and Pat Flaherty. The crowd roared its approval as his racing machine made its move toward the front. Coming down the main straightaway on lap 11, Russo gave the thundering brute its head. Splitting the two leaders at 180 mph, Paul blazed into the lead before the trio entered the first turn. O'Connor managed to briefly retake the lead, but Russo surged past a second time. O'Connor and Flaherty gave chase, but until a blowout put the Novi into the wall some 10 laps later, they couldn't make a dent in Russo's advantage.

After the race, O'Connor was asked about the tremendous high-speed duel. "Flaherty and I were going at it pretty well foot to the floor," Pat said. "But when Russo went past us in that Novi, I took a quick look at my tachometer. He went by us so fast, I thought my engine had died!"

Early-race action has Jimmy Reece leading Jim Rathmann, Jimmy Bryan, and Andy Linden along the inside of the track through the first turn (*above*). Reece was the highest finisher of the bunch, coming in ninth. Fans eager to get a better view of the battle on the 2.5-mile track were not above erecting their own scaffolds (*left*). Paul Russo was leading when his tailfinned No. 29 Kurtis-Novi spun in Turn 1 (*below*) after he blew the right rear tire. Four other cars became involved in the accident that brought out one of a record 11 caution flags on the day. The supercharged Novi V-8 in Russo's car was the only non-Offenhauser power plant in the '56 field. Pat Flaherty led a total of 127 laps, including the last 124, to win in the first outing for A. J. Watson's new upright roadster (*opposite bottom*). It was owner John Zink's second straight win. For the first time, it is officials from the newly formed United States Automobile Club who greet the Indianapolis 500 winner (*opposite, top right*). Flaherty is the last winner to drive without fire-retardant clothing.

RESULTS

NO.	DRIVER	CAR	ENTRANT	ENGINE	CYL	DISP	CHASSIS	COLOR	QUAL SPD	START	FIN	LAPS / SPEED / REASON OUT
8	Pat Flaherty	John Zink	John Zink Co.	Offy	4	270	Watson	rose, white	145.596	1	1	200-128.490
4	Sam Hanks	Jones & Maley	Cars, Inc.	Offy	4	270	KK500C	red, wht, slvr	142.051	13	2	200-128.303
12	Don Freeland	Bob Estes	Bob Estes	Offy	4	270	Phillips	red, cream	141.699	26	3	200-127.668
98	Johnnie Parsons	Agajanian	J. C. Agajanian	Offy	4	270	Kuzma	cream, red	144.144	6	4	200-126.631
73	Dick Rathmann	McNamara	Kalamazoo Sports, Inc.	Offy	4	270	KK500C	red, gold	144.471	4	5	200-126.133 wrecked T1
1	Bob Sweikert	D-A Lubricant	Racing Associates	Offy	4	270	Kuzma	yellow, wht, blk	143.033	10	6	200-125.489
14	Bob Veith	Federal Eng	Federal Auto. Associates	Offy	4	270	KK500C	blue, yellow	142.535	23	7	200-125.048
19	Rodger Ward	Filter Queen	Ed Walsh	Offy	4	270	KK500C	red, mrn, gld	141.171	15	8	200-124.990
26	Jimmy Reece	Massaglia Hotels	Joseph Massaglia, Jr.	Offy	4	270	Lesovsky	wht, gold, blue	142.885	21	9	200-124.938
27	Cliff Griffith	Jim Robbins	Jim Robbins	Offy	4	270	Stevens	maroon, wht	141.471	30	10	199-flagged
82	Gene Hartley	Central Excavating	Pete Salemi	Offy	4	270	Kuzma	blue, silver	142.846	22	11	196-flagged
42	Fred Agabashian	Federal Engineering	Federal Auto. Associates	Offy	4	270	KK500C	blue, yellow	144.069	7	12	196-flagged
57	Bob Christie	Helse	H. H. Johnson	Offy	4	270	KK500D	mrn, gold	142.236	25	13	196-flagged
55	Al Keller	Sam Traylor	Samuel W. Traylor, III	Offy	4	270	KK4000	blue, gold	141.193	28	14	195-flagged
81	Eddie Johnson	Central Excavating	Pete Salemi	Offy	4	270	Kuzma	blue, silver	139.093	32	15	195-flagged
41	Billy Garrett	Greenman-Casale	E. R. Casale	Offy	4	263	Kuzma	white, blue	140.559	29	16	194-flagged
64	Duke Dinsmore	Shannon's	Shannon Bros.	Offy	4	270	KK500A	blue-green, wht	138.530	33	17	191-flagged
7	Pat O'Connor	Ansted Rotary	Ansted Rotary Corp.	Offy	4	270	KK500D	cream, black	144.980	3	18	187-flagged
2	Jimmy Bryan	Dean Van Lines	Dean Van Lines	Offy	4	270	Kuzma	white, blue	143.741	19	19	185-flagged
24	Jim Rathmann	Hopkins	Lindsey Hopkins	Offy	4	270	KK500C	blue, wht, orng	145.120	2	20	175-oil trouble
34	Johnnie Tolan	Trio Brass Foundry	Carl L. Anderson	Offy	4	270	KK500C	blue, white	140.061	31	21	173-flagged
99	Tony Bettenhausen	Belanger Motors	Murrell Belanger	Offy	4	270	KK500C	blue, gold	144.602	5	22	160-wrecked T1
10	Ed Elisian	Hoyt Machine	Fred Somers	Offy	4	270	KK500C	metal rose, wht	141.382	14	23	160-stalled
48	Jimmy Daywalt	Sumar	Chapman S. Root	Offy	4	270	KK500D	blue, white	140.977	16	24	134-wrecked T2
54	Jack Turner	Travelon Trailer	Ernest L. Ruiz	Offy	4	270	KK500B	turquoise, wht	142.394	24	25	131-engine trouble
89	Keith Andrews	Dunn Engineering	Harry Dunn	Offy	4	270	KK500B	white, black	142.976	20	26	94-spun NW
5	Andy Linden	Chapman	H. A. Chapman	Offy	4	270	KK500C	cream, blue	143.056	9	27	90-oil leak
12	Al Herman	Bardahl	Pat Clancy	Offy	4	270	KK500B	black, white	141.610	27	28	74-wrecked FS
49	Ray Crawford	Crawford	Ray Crawford	Offy	4	270	KK500B	red, cream	140.884	17	29	49-wrecked NW
15	Johnny Boyd	Bowes Seal Fast	George Bignotti	Offy	4	270	KK500E	wht, blk, red	142.337	12	30	35-engine trouble
53	Troy Ruttman	John Zink	John S. Zink	Offy	4	270	KK500C	rose, wht, blk	142.484	11	31	22-spun FS
88	Johnny Thomson	Schmidt	Peter Schmidt	Offy	4	270	Kuzma	red, silver	145.549	18	32	22-spun FS
29	Paul Russo	Novi Vespa	Novi Racing Corp., Inc.	Novi*	8	183	Kurtis	red, cream	143.546	8	33	21-blew tire, wrecked T1

* Supercharged

1957

41st Race • May 30, 1957

A new five-story steel and glass control tower replaces the 31-year-old pagoda that was a Speedway landmark. The entire inside of the main straight has a new look with a wider pit apron, new concrete wall separating the pits from the track, and new tower terrace grandstands.

Maximum displacement drops to 256 cubic inches for unblown engines and 171 cid for supercharged engines in an effort to slow the cars.

Before a crowd of about 130,000, Pat O'Connor wins the pole at a non-record 143.948 mph in a Kurtis. Rookie Eddie Sachs, a blink of an eye slower, starts second in a Kuzma.

Second-day qualifier Paul Russo is faster, pushing his supercharged Novi to 144.817 to start 10th. Tony Bettenhausen qualifies 22nd in another Novi, and he and Russo are the only ones without Offy power.

The cars line up in single file on the new pit apron, and as they assemble into rows of three on the back stretch during the parade lap, rookie Elmer George runs into the back of Eddie Russo, knocking both cars out.

After the green flag falls, O'Connor, Paul Russo, and 1952 winner Troy Ruttman fight over first. Ruttman leads four laps, but burns a piston and parks his Watson roadster on the 14th lap. O'Connor and Russo also lead, but both make extra pit stops and fall out of contention.

Veteran Sam Hanks starts from the fifth row, grabs the lead from Russo on lap 37, and runs at a record clip in a new George Salih-designed roadster, which features a more radical "lay-down" design than the Kurtis roadster. The engine tilts 72 degrees to the right, giving the Salih a profile that is just 21 inches high. Salih builds the car next to his California home, then goes out on a financial limb to enter it himself.

The most serious threat to Hanks in the last half of the race comes from Jim Rathmann, who starts 32nd in an Epperly, works his way to the front, and takes the lead when Hanks pits.

Hanks is too fast, however. He regains the lead and beats Rathmann by 22 seconds. He averages 135.6 mph, and the first 11 finishers top the old record of 130.84 set by Bill Vukovich three years earlier.

Hanks, 42, wins in his 12th try at the Brickyard, collects $103,844 of a $300,252 purse—both record amounts—and announces his retirement in victory lane.

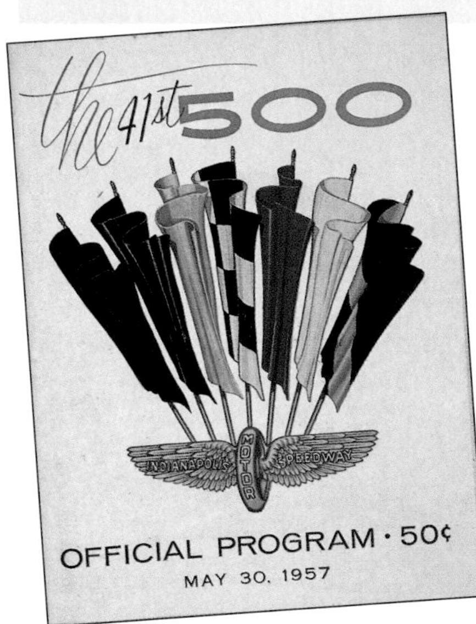

STARTING LINEUP

Average Field Qualifying Speed: 141.444

Numbers in flags indicate finish position

Troy Ruttman

Jimmy Reece

Elmer George

Andy Linden

Jimmy Bryan

Eddie Sachs

Johnny Boyd

Al Keller

Johnny Thomson

Gene Hartley

POLE POSITION
Qualifying Speed: 143.948

Pat O'Connor

Fred Agabashian

Ed Elisian

Paul Russo

Sam Hanks

One of the most flamboyant cars of the Fifties, the Mercury Convertible Cruiser (*opposite*), led the starters to the green flag in '57. The infield is packed with cars (*above*) that bore an eager crowd to qualifications. Pat O'Connor won the pole, but second-day qualifier Paul Russo (*below*) was faster, cranking his Novi V-8 up to 144.817 mph.

Jim Rathmann may have had trouble getting qualified, but running in the '57 race was another story. Starting in 32nd position, Jim came up through the field like he'd been shot out of a cannon. Car after car got the wave from the blue Chiropractic Special. At 111 laps, Rathmann took the lead. He led 23 circuits, before being overhauled by eventual winner Sam Hanks. Rathmann ended up second.

This great finish was due to some magnificent driving, and equally fine pit work. Rathmann made three stops: one on lap 44 took 33 seconds, the second on lap 100 was 32, and the third ate up just 31 ticks of the clock. They were the fastest pit stops in the race. The left front tire wasn't changed on the last two stops, which meant the tire covered 300 competitive miles. And there's a good reason for the great tire wear. Jim was driving the turns so hard, the left front was in the air most of the time.

24 Mike Magill

17 Don Freeland

30 Rodger Ward

19 Don Edmunds

21 Al Herman

13 Bob Christie

16 Dick Rathmann (for Parsons)

25 Eddie Johnson

26 Bill Cheesbourg

32 Eddie Russo

28 Jimmy Daywalt

2 Jim Rathmann

9 Bob Veith

11 Jack Turner

15 Tony Bettenhausen

14 Chuck Weyant

7 Marshall Teague

20 Johnnie Tolan

Mechanic Jack Beckley inspects valves destined to go into one of the famed four-cylinder Offenhauser engines that powered numerous Indy cars for decades (*left*). Do-it-yourselfers arrived early to build a colony of infield "skyscrapers" (*above*). Dancer Cyd Charisse takes part in the pre-race pageantry (*below*). Paul Russo was the fastest qualifier in the No. 54 Novi (*opposite top*) and finished fourth. Teammate Tony Bettenhausen finished 15th in the No. 27 car. The front stretch of the venerable old Brickyard had a new look for the '57 event. A widened and paved pit apron (*opposite bottom*) was separated from the track by a concrete wall, and a new glass-and-steel control tower replaced the Twenties-vintage pagoda.

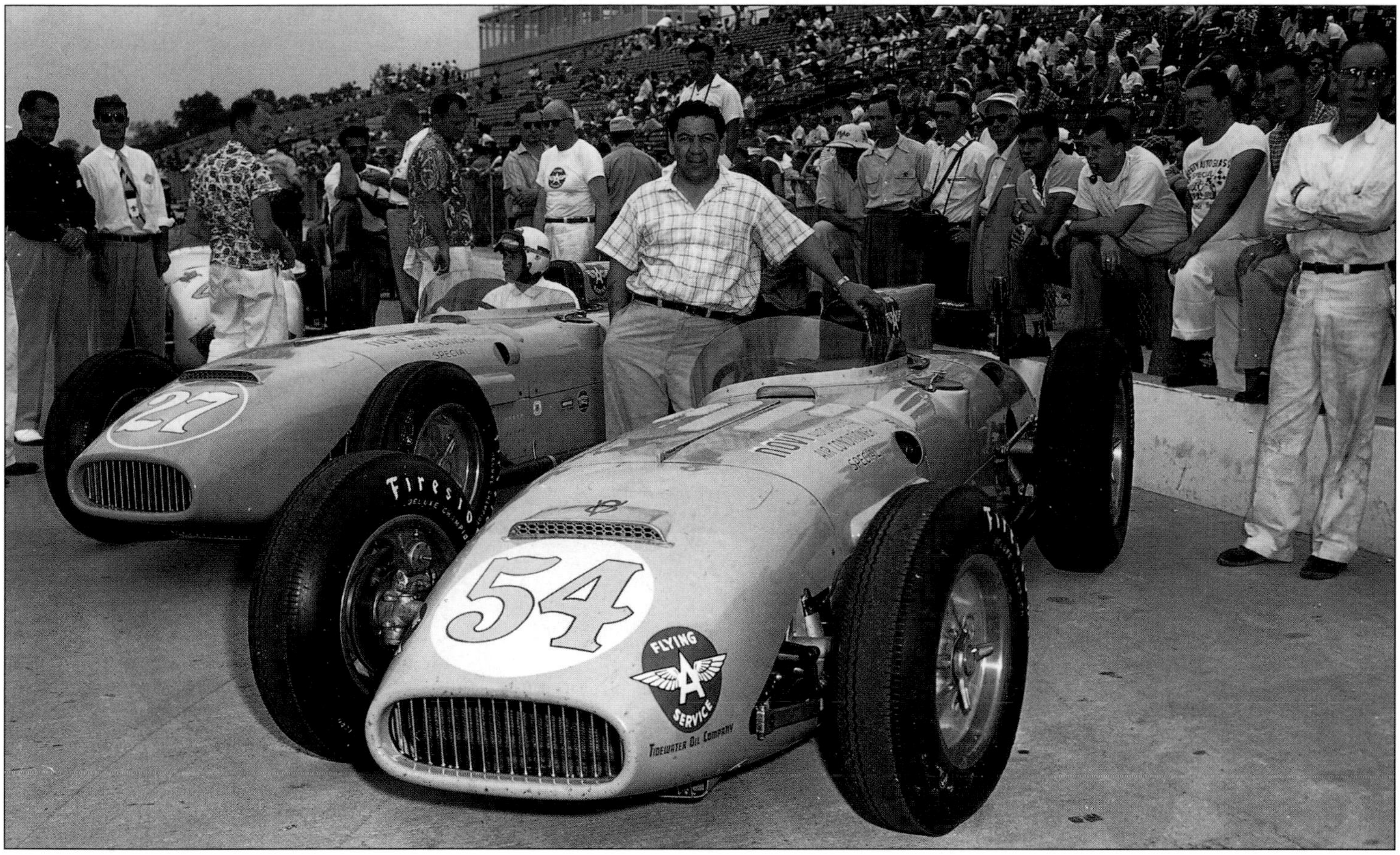
27
54
FLYING
SERVICE
TIDEWATER OIL COMPANY

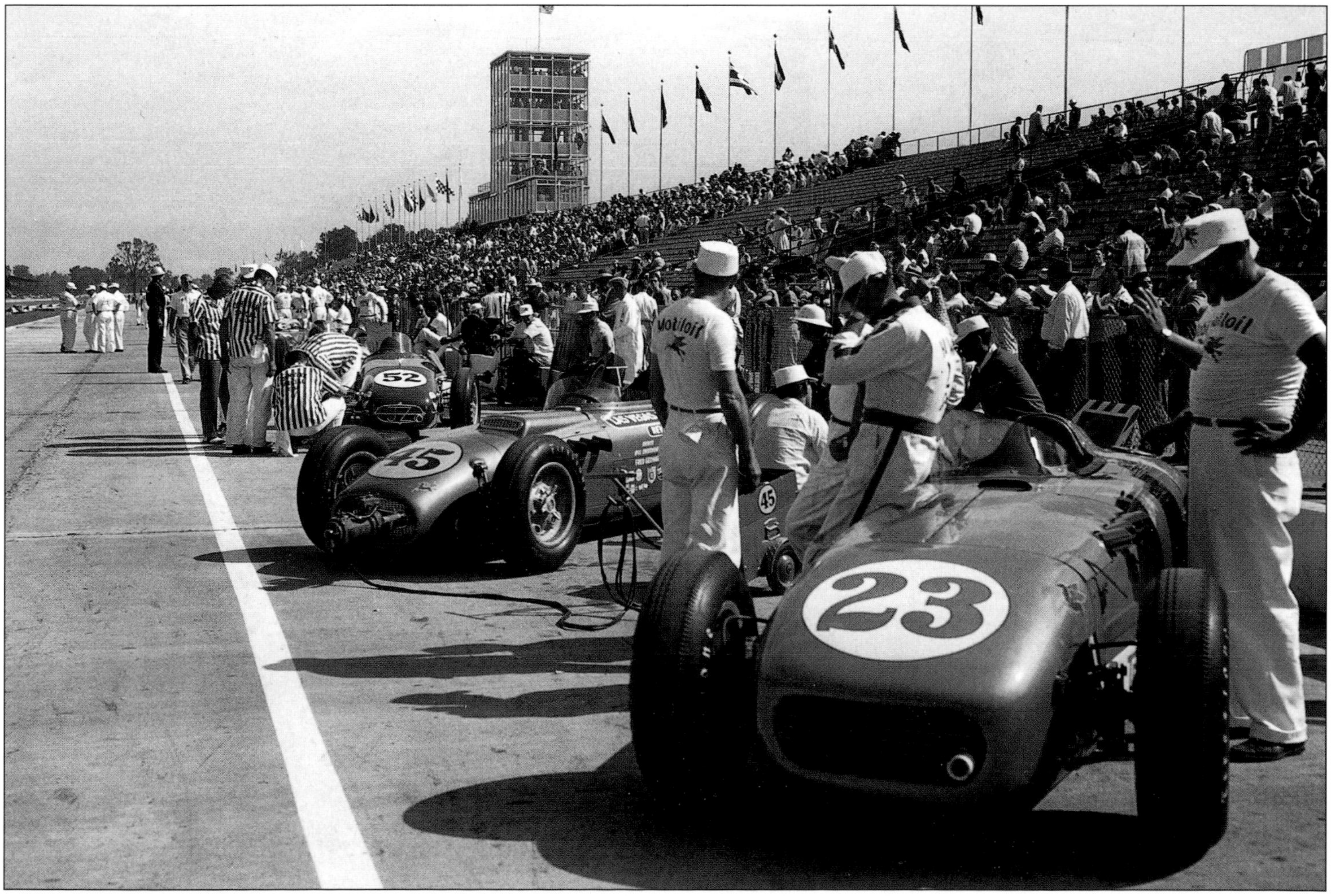
52
45
23

Tony Bettenhausen, in a Kurtis-Novi, holds a slim advantage over Eddie Sachs in a Kuzma-Offy (*top*). Bettenhausen was already an established crowd favorite and Sachs, a rookie in '57, would go on to become one, too. Nineteen fifty-two winner Troy Ruttman leads Paul Russo during some close racing (*above*). Ruttman led for four laps and Russo for 24. Fred Agabashian, who started from the inside of the second row, tucks in behind polesitter Pat O'Connor as the field chases them into Turn 1 (*above right*). After outrunning Jim Rathmann, a triumphant Sam Hanks pulls into victory lane (*right*), where he announced his retirement. A veteran of 12 500s, Hanks (*opposite top*) had been an Indy fixture since 1940. His first-place prize money topped $103,000. Hanks drove the new Salih roadster (*opposite bottom*), which gave rise to the term "lay down." Its Offenhauser engine was nearly horizontal, allowing a track-hugging design with a low nose. The Salih design copied the prominent dorsal fin used on the Novi-powered Kurtis chassis.

It was truly a shock when both Dan LeVine's Federal Engineering Specials, driven by Billy Garrett and George Amick, were bumped from the starting lineup. But just in case, LeVine had chief mechanic Russ Snowberger prepare the immaculate roadsters for race day. After all, as the 34th and 35th fastest cars, they were designated as first and second alternate starters. If something should happen to any of the 33 starters, they would—or so the rules always stated—be inserted into the lineup.

On race day, during the parade lap, Elmer George and Eddie Russo collided. The damage their cars absorbed prevented both from taking the starter's flag. When an extra pace lap was necessary to clear the track of debris, LeVine thought his cars would be sent for. But while he argued the point with USAC officials, the race got under way. Neither of LeVine's cars were allowed to start.

Since LeVine was the president of the Car Owners Association, he was in a position to argue the point. With several owners on his side, he filed a protest of the race. Ultimately, this was disallowed. And although alternate starters were designated for many years, no additional car, unnamed as a starter before the morning of the race, has ever taken the starting flag.

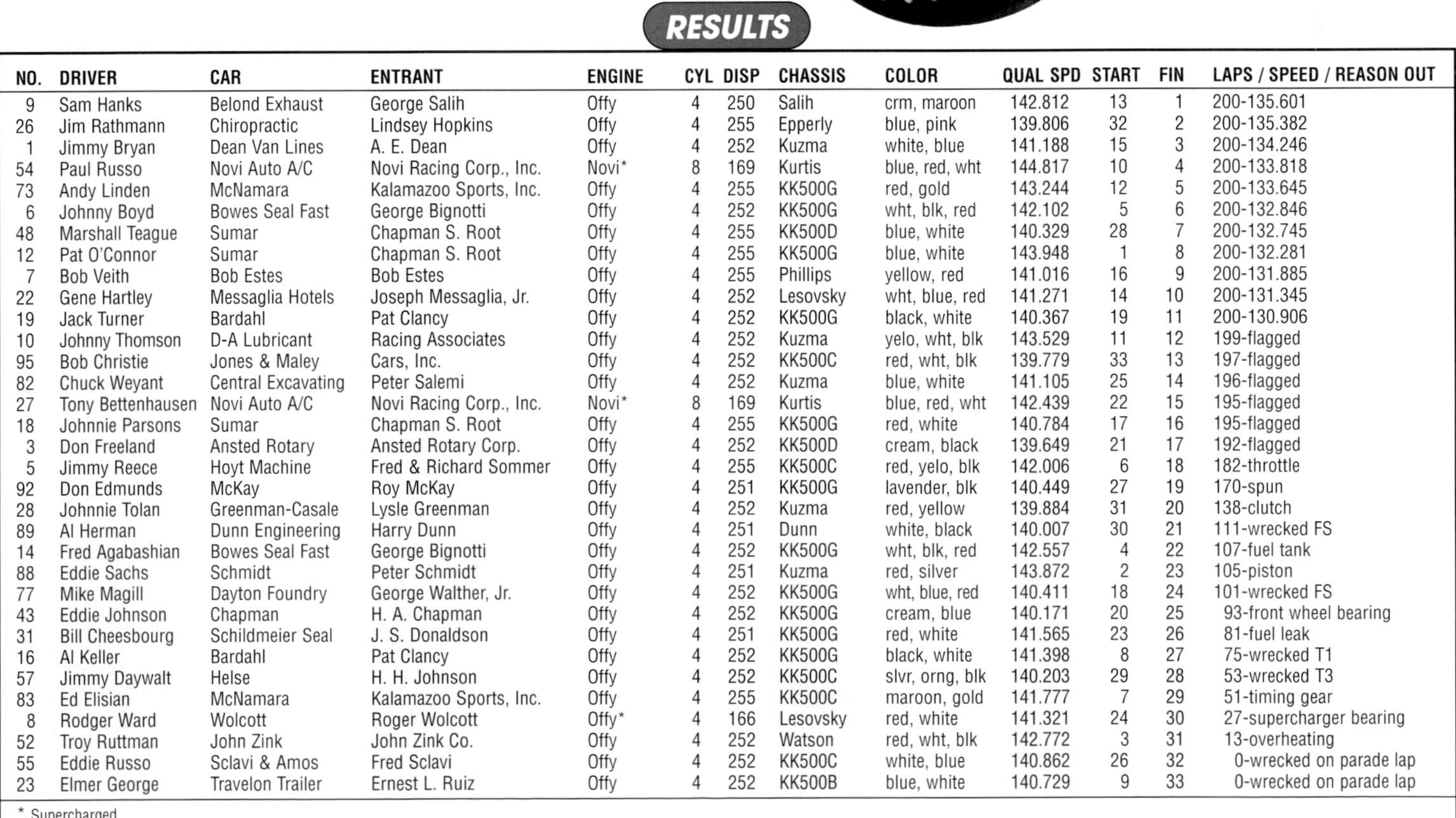

RESULTS

NO.	DRIVER	CAR	ENTRANT	ENGINE	CYL	DISP	CHASSIS	COLOR	QUAL SPD	START	FIN	LAPS / SPEED / REASON OUT
9	Sam Hanks	Belond Exhaust	George Salih	Offy	4	250	Salih	crm, maroon	142.812	13	1	200-135.601
26	Jim Rathmann	Chiropractic	Lindsey Hopkins	Offy	4	255	Epperly	blue, pink	139.806	32	2	200-135.382
1	Jimmy Bryan	Dean Van Lines	A. E. Dean	Offy	4	252	Kuzma	white, blue	141.188	15	3	200-134.246
54	Paul Russo	Novi Auto A/C	Novi Racing Corp., Inc.	Novi*	8	169	Kurtis	blue, red, wht	144.817	10	4	200-133.818
73	Andy Linden	McNamara	Kalamazoo Sports, Inc.	Offy	4	255	KK500G	red, gold	143.244	12	5	200-133.645
6	Johnny Boyd	Bowes Seal Fast	George Bignotti	Offy	4	252	KK500G	wht, blk, red	142.102	5	6	200-132.846
48	Marshall Teague	Sumar	Chapman S. Root	Offy	4	255	KK500D	blue, white	140.329	28	7	200-132.745
12	Pat O'Connor	Sumar	Chapman S. Root	Offy	4	255	KK500G	blue, white	143.948	1	8	200-132.281
7	Bob Veith	Bob Estes	Bob Estes	Offy	4	255	Phillips	yellow, red	141.016	16	9	200-131.885
22	Gene Hartley	Messaglia Hotels	Joseph Messaglia, Jr.	Offy	4	252	Lesovsky	wht, blue, red	141.271	14	10	200-131.345
19	Jack Turner	Bardahl	Pat Clancy	Offy	4	252	KK500G	black, white	140.367	19	11	200-130.906
10	Johnny Thomson	D-A Lubricant	Racing Associates	Offy	4	252	Kuzma	yelo, wht, blk	143.529	11	12	199-flagged
95	Bob Christie	Jones & Maley	Cars, Inc.	Offy	4	252	KK500C	red, wht, blk	139.779	33	13	197-flagged
82	Chuck Weyant	Central Excavating	Peter Salemi	Offy	4	252	Kuzma	blue, white	141.105	25	14	196-flagged
27	Tony Bettenhausen	Novi Auto A/C	Novi Racing Corp., Inc.	Novi*	8	169	Kurtis	blue, red, wht	142.439	22	15	195-flagged
18	Johnnie Parsons	Sumar	Chapman S. Root	Offy	4	255	KK500G	red, white	140.784	17	16	195-flagged
3	Don Freeland	Ansted Rotary	Ansted Rotary Corp.	Offy	4	252	KK500D	cream, black	139.649	21	17	192-flagged
5	Jimmy Reece	Hoyt Machine	Fred & Richard Sommer	Offy	4	255	KK500C	red, yelo, blk	142.006	6	18	182-throttle
92	Don Edmunds	McKay	Roy McKay	Offy	4	251	KK500G	lavender, blk	140.449	27	19	170-spun
28	Johnnie Tolan	Greenman-Casale	Lysle Greenman	Offy	4	252	Kuzma	red, yellow	139.884	31	20	138-clutch
89	Al Herman	Dunn Engineering	Harry Dunn	Offy	4	251	Dunn	white, black	140.007	30	21	111-wrecked FS
14	Fred Agabashian	Bowes Seal Fast	George Bignotti	Offy	4	252	KK500G	wht, blk, red	142.557	4	22	107-fuel tank
88	Eddie Sachs	Schmidt	Peter Schmidt	Offy	4	251	Kuzma	red, silver	143.872	2	23	105-piston
77	Mike Magill	Dayton Foundry	George Walther, Jr.	Offy	4	252	KK500G	wht, blue, red	140.411	18	24	101-wrecked FS
43	Eddie Johnson	Chapman	H. A. Chapman	Offy	4	252	KK500G	cream, blue	140.171	20	25	93-front wheel bearing
31	Bill Cheesbourg	Schildmeier Seal	J. S. Donaldson	Offy	4	251	KK500G	red, white	141.565	23	26	81-fuel leak
16	Al Keller	Bardahl	Pat Clancy	Offy	4	252	KK500G	black, white	141.398	8	27	75-wrecked T1
57	Jimmy Daywalt	Helse	H. H. Johnson	Offy	4	252	KK500C	slvr, orng, blk	140.203	29	28	53-wrecked T3
83	Ed Elisian	McNamara	Kalamazoo Sports, Inc.	Offy	4	255	KK500C	maroon, gold	141.777	7	29	51-timing gear
8	Rodger Ward	Wolcott	Roger Wolcott	Offy*	4	166	Lesovsky	red, white	141.321	24	30	27-supercharger bearing
52	Troy Ruttman	John Zink	John Zink Co.	Offy	4	252	Watson	red, wht, blk	142.772	3	31	13-overheating
55	Eddie Russo	Sclavi & Amos	Fred Sclavi	Offy	4	252	KK500C	white, blue	140.862	26	32	0-wrecked on parade lap
23	Elmer George	Travelon Trailer	Ernest L. Ruiz	Offy	4	252	KK500B	blue, white	140.729	9	33	0-wrecked on parade lap

* Supercharged

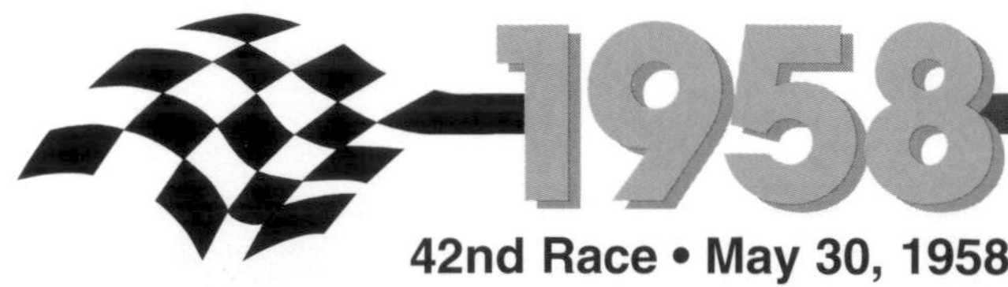

1958

42nd Race • May 30, 1958

George Salih's low-slung leader from '57 spurs a number of imitators for the 42nd running of the May classic, which has eight rookies in the field.

On pole day, Ed Elisian sets a one-lap record of 146.508 mph in a Watson-Offy. A short time later, Dick Rathmann, also in a Watson-Offy, posts a four-lap average of 145.974 to narrowly win the pole.

Five-time world driving champion Juan Manual Fangio can't find enough speed to qualify a Kurtis-Offy, but second-year driver Mike Magill gets it into the last row on the final day of qualifying.

Rathmann and Elisian take the green flag and go wheel to wheel around the track. Neither driver backs off as they go into Turn 3, and Elisian spins, collects Rathmann, and sends them both into the wall, starting a 15-car pileup.

Pat O'Connor, who starts fifth and is chasing the leaders, dies when his car flips and lands upside down on the track. Rookie Jerry Unser runs over the top of another car and rolls over the outside wall, dislocating a shoulder. The accident knocks eight cars out of the race before a lap is complete, including four cars from the first two rows.

After the restart, Tony Bettenhausen has one of his best days at the Speedway, leading 24 laps and finishing fourth. The day, however, belongs to Jimmy Bryan, a three-time national champion who starts seventh and wins his only 500. Bryan fights off Bettenhausen and the other challengers to lead 139 laps in the Salih roadster Sam Hanks drove to victory in 1957.

Rookie George Amick comes from 25th starting position to lead 18 laps and finish 28 seconds behind Bryan. His second-place finish earns Amick Rookie-of-the-Year honors.

Another rookie, Texan A. J. Foyt, Jr., is less impressive. Foyt spins in the south short chute on lap 149 and ends up 16th.

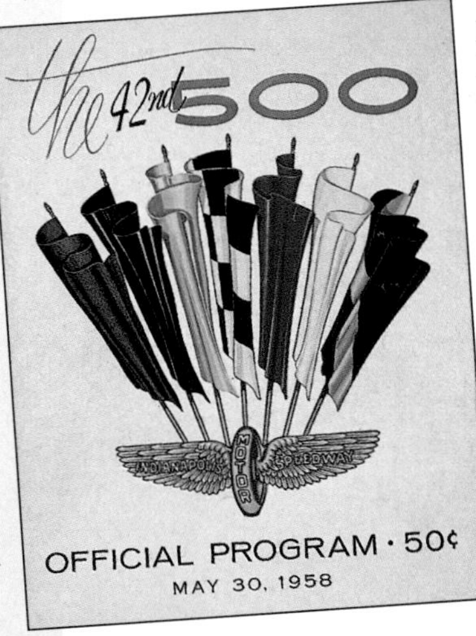

Five-time Formula 1 champion Juan Manuel Fangio took a crack at the 500 in 1958 (*above*), but failed to qualify. The Argentine ace complained it was the Dayton Steel Foundry Special that was to blame and he was proven correct before Mike Magill put the car in the field. Johnnie Parsons and car owner J. C. Agajanian give visitor Nino Farina some seat time in Agajanian's racer (*opposite top*), which didn't make the show despite the best efforts of Troy Ruttman to qualify it. Fuel management is almost as important as speed in the course of a race, so it's little wonder three-time national champion Jimmy Bryan, known for his speed, took an interest in this new "Gas Miser" Mercury Medalist (*opposite bottom*).

STARTING LINEUP

Average Field Qualifying Speed: 143.445

Numbers in flags indicate finish position

6 Jimmy Reece

12 Johnnie Parsons

4 Tony Bettenhausen

16 A. J. Foyt

21 Billy Garrett

28 Ed Elisian

29 Pat O'Connor

3 Johnny Boyd

20 Rodger Ward

18 Paul Russo

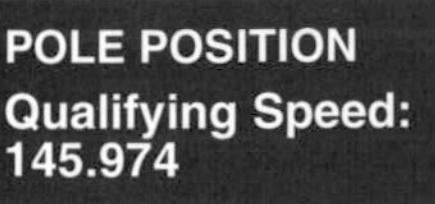
POLE POSITION
Qualifying Speed: 145.974

27 Dick Rathmann

26 Bob Veith

1 Jimmy Bryan

25 Jack Turner

7 Don Freeland

When five-time World Driving Champion Juan Manuel Fangio decided to take a shot at Indy in 1958, he was assigned to the Dayton Steel Foundry Special. Although he reportedly turned a lap at 142 mph in practice, it's doubtful he ever topped 139 or 140. Fangio was mystified by the roadster's handling. He complained that, in a given situation, the Offy-powered car never did the same thing twice. He claimed the car would understeer in one turn, then oversteer in the next corner. He would make a sliding gesture while uttering "eeeeeeee, eeeeeeee," his best impression of the tires howling in the turns.

Revered veteran though he may have been, critics figured "the old man" was a fish out of water in an Indy car. After a few laps in one of the Novis, Fangio said the cars drove nothing alike. After a huge spin with his original ride, which nearly involved several other cars, Fangio finally gave up, and went back to the grand prix circuit. The consensus was that the F1 star didn't have what it took to drive at Indy.

But when Mike Magill took over the Dayton Steel Foundry entry, he encountered the same problems Fangio had described. Magill insisted the car be torn down and inspected. Sure enough, a crack that allowed the chassis to flex was found. Therefter, Magill qualified the car at 142.276.

Fangio had been right all along.

Eddie Sachs

Al Keller

Jerry Unser

Len Sutton

Johnnie Tolan

Bill Cheesbourg

Bob Christie

Jim Rathmann

Shorty Templeman

Eddie Johnson

Chuck Weyant

Dempsey Wilson

Paul Goldsmith

Jud Larson

Johnny Thomson

George Amick

Art Bisch

Mike Magill

This page: The front row, from left, included Jimmy Reece, Ed Elisian, and pole winner Dick Rathmann (above). All three drove roadsters built by A. J. Watson, who stands at the left. Jack Turner (left) heads out of the pits in the No. 25 for his qualifying run in a Lesovsky-chassised, Offy-powered car. Sam Hanks, who retired after winning the 1957 race, drove the Pontiac Bonneville pace car (below). *Opposite page:* Speedway owner Tony Hulman and Hanks clown for the cameras with actress Shirley MacLaine (top left). Television's interest in the Speedway's activities during the month of May was growing in the Fifties (top right). The pace car leads the field down the front straight and into Turn 1 before the usual packed house (bottom).

WFBM-TV CHANNEL 6
WFBM-TV

An opening-lap pileup in Turn 3 (*above left*) involved 15 cars and claimed the life of Pat O'Connor. Rookie Jerry Unser rode over the top of another car and went flying over the outside wall (*above*), dislocating his shoulder. Eight cars were knocked out of the race, but Bill Cheesbourg in the No. 54 Novi was able to continue and finished 10th (*opposite, top left*). After the smoke cleared, clean-up took some time (*opposite, top right*). The Watson-Offys of polesitter Dick Rathmann and Ed Elisian—who started second—were among the casualties (*left*). Once racing resumed, Tony Bettenhausen in the No. 33 car dueled with Jimmy Bryan in the No. 1 entry (*below left*) in a battle of lay-down roadsters. Bettenhausen finished fourth, but Bryan ultimately prevailed. In the wake of his victory, he enjoys a victory stogie in his garage (*below*). Bryan drove the same George Salih-built car that Sam Hanks took to victory lane the year before (*opposite bottom*). Runner-up George Amick was the top rookie of 1958.

RESULTS

NO.	DRIVER	CAR	ENTRANT	ENGINE	CYL	DISP	CHASSIS	COLOR	QUAL SPD	START	FIN	LAPS / SPEED / REASON OUT
1	Jimmy Bryan	Belond A P	George Salih	Offy	4	252	Salih	yellow, red	144.185	7	1	200-133.791
99	George Amick	Demler	Norman C. Demler	Offy	4	255	Epperly	yellow, red	142.710	25	2	200-133.517
9	Johnny Boyd	Bowes Seal Fast	Robert M. Bowes, II	Offy	4	252	KK500G	wht, blk, red	144.023	8	3	200-133.099
33	Tony Bettenhausen	Jones & Maley	Cars, Inc.	Offy	4	252	Epperly	red, white	143.919	9	4	200-132.855
2	Jim Rathmann	Leader Card 500 Rdstr	Lindsey Hopkins	Offy	4	252	Epperly	blue, pink, wht	143.147	20	5	200-132.857
16	Jimmy Reece	John Zink	John Zink	Offy	4	252	Watson	maroon, wht	145.513	3	6	200-132.443
26	Don Freeland	Bob Estes	Bob Estes	Offy	4	252	Phillips	yellow, red	143.033	13	7	200-132.403
44	Jud Larson	John Zink	John Zink Co.	Offy	4	252	Watson	red, white	143.512	19	8	200-130.550
61	Eddie Johnson	Bryant Heat/Cool	J. S. "Duke" Donaldson	Offy	4	251	KK500G	red, white	142.670	26	9	200-130.156
54	Bill Cheesbourg	Novi Auto A/C	Novi Racing Corp., Inc.	Novi*	8	169	Kurtis	silver, red	142.546	33	10	200-129.149
52	Al Keller	Bardahl	Pat Clancy	Offy	4	252	KK500G-2	black,white	142.931	21	11	200-128.498
45	Johnnie Parsons	Gerhardt	Fred Gerhardt	Offy	4	252	Kurtis	white, red	144.683	6	12	200-128.254
19	Johnnie Tolan	Greenman-Casale	Lysle Greenman	Offy	4	252	Kuzma	red, yellow	142.309	30	13	200-128.150
65	Bob Christie	Federal Eng	Federal Auto. Associates	Offy	4	251	KK500C	blue, yellow	142.253	17	14	189-spun NE
59	Dempsey Wilson	Sorenson	Bob Sorenson	Offy	4	252	Kuzma	yellow, black	134.272	32	15	151-clutch pedal, fire
29	A. J. Foyt	Dean Van Lines	Dean Van Lines	Offy	4	252	Kuzma	white, blue	143.130	12	16	148-spun T2
77	Mike Magill	Dayton Foundry	George Walther, Jr.	Offy	4	255	KK500G	wht, blue, red	142.276	31	17	136-black flagged
15	Paul Russo	Novi Auto. A/C	Novi Racing Corp., Inc.	Novi*	8	169	Kurtis	blue-gray, red	142.959	14	18	122-radiator
83	Shorty Templeman	McNamara	Kalamazoo Sports, Inc.	Offy	4	255	KK500D	maroon, gold	142.817	23	19	116-brakes
8	Rodger Ward	Wolcott Fuel Inject	Roger Wolcott	Offy	4	252	Lesovsky	red, white	143.266	11	20	93-fuel pump
43	Billy Garrett	Chapman	H. A. Chapman	Offy	4	252	KK500G	blue, cream	142.778	15	21	80-cam gear
88	Eddie Sachs	Schmidt	Peter Schmidt	Offy	4	255	Kuzma	red, silver	144.660	18	22	68-universal joint
7	Johnny Thomson	D-A Lubricant	Racing Associates	Offy	4	251	Kurtis	yelo, wht, blk	142.908	22	23	52-steering damaged
89	Chuck Weyant	Dunn Engineering	Harry Dunn	Offy	4	251	Dunn	white, black	142.608	29	24	38-brakes locked, wrecked
25	Jack Turner	Massaglia Hotels	Joseph Massaglia, Jr.	Offy	4	252	Lesovsky	wht, red, blue	143.438	10	25	21-fuel pump
14	Bob Veith	Bowes Seal Fast	Robert M. Bowes, II	Offy	4	252	KK500G	wht, blk, red	144.881	4	26	1-wrecked T3
97	Dick Rathmann	McNamara	Kalamazoo Sports, Inc.	Offy	4	255	Watson	slvr, wht, red	145.974	1	27	0-wrecked T3
5	Ed Elisian	John Zink	Ellen McKinney Zink	Offy	4	252	Watson	wht, red, blk	145.926	2	28	0-wrecked T3
4	Pat O'Connor	Sumar	Chapman S. Root	Offy	4	255	KK500G	blue, white	144.823	5	29	0-wrecked T3
31	Paul Goldsmith	City of Daytona	Henry "Smokey" Yunick	Offy	4	255	KK500G	black, gold	142.744	16	30	0-wrecked T3
92	Jerry Unser	McKay	Roy McKay	Offy	4	251	KK500G	lavndr, maroon	142.755	24	31	0-wrecked T3
68	Len Sutton	Jim Robbins	Jim Robbins	Offy	4	255	KK500G	maroon, crm	142.653	27	32	0-wrecked T3
57	Art Bisch	Helse	H. H. Johnson	Offy	4	251	Kuzma	blue-gray, wht	142.631	28	33	0-wrecked T3

* Supercharged

1959

43rd Race • May 30, 1959

Jerry Unser, who was hurt on the first lap of the previous race, crashes in Turn 4 during practice and dies of burns two weeks later. After Unser's accident, fire-resistant driving suits, already used by most drivers, become mandatory.

Two days after Unser dies, rookie Bob Cortner's car gets caught by a gust of wind and crashes in Turn 3. Cortner dies of head injuries.

Veteran Tony Bettenhausen destroys his car when he flips in Turn 2 on pole day but escapes with a bloody nose. Officials credit the newly mandatory rollbar with preventing serious injury. Bettenhausen qualifies in a different car and finishes fourth for the second year in a row.

Johnny Thomson's pole-wining speed of 145.908 mph is shy of the record, but he posts a new one-lap mark of 146.532. Offenhauser engines again power all 33 starters.

Jimmy Bryan, first across the finish line in 1958, is first out of the race this year. He parks with a broken camshaft after one lap. A multi-car accident on lap 45 eliminates four cars, but there are no serious injuries.

Thomson, front-row starter Jim Rathmann, and second-row starter Rodger Ward engage in a heated struggle for the lead. Pat Flaherty, making his first appearance since he won in 1956, displays his old form. He starts 18th and charges into the lead on lap 28 to make it a four-way battle.

Flaherty leads 11 laps before he spins on the front straight and hits the pit wall on lap 163. Flaherty skids to a stop at the pit entrance, leaving just enough room for Ward to squeeze by and make his final stop. Thomson leads 40 laps, but makes an extra stop to replace worn rear tires and drops to third.

Ward, competing in his ninth straight 500, dominates the second half. His upright Watson roadster wins by 23 seconds and averages a record 135.857 mph. Rathmann, also in a Watson, finishes second for the third time.

Integral air jacks installed on Ward's car and some others shorten pit stops by about 10 seconds. Ward pits three times for fuel and three fresh tires, and the times range from 22 to 25 seconds.

Despite going out on lap 86 with ignition trouble, Bobby Grim is Rookie of the Year. He starts fifth, finishes 26th, and suffers a dislocated shoulder while signaling other drivers to slow down during a caution period.

STARTING LINEUP

Average Field Qualifying Speed: 143.004

Numbers in flags indicate finish position

Jim Rathmann

Rodger Ward

11
Gene Hartley

7
Duane Carter

Tony Bettenhausen

Eddie Sachs

Bobby Grim

Eddie Johnson

Johnny Boyd

Jack Turner

POLE POSITION
Qualifying Speed: 145.908

3
Johnny Thomson

Dick Rathmann

Bob Veith

Don Branson

Jimmy Daywalt

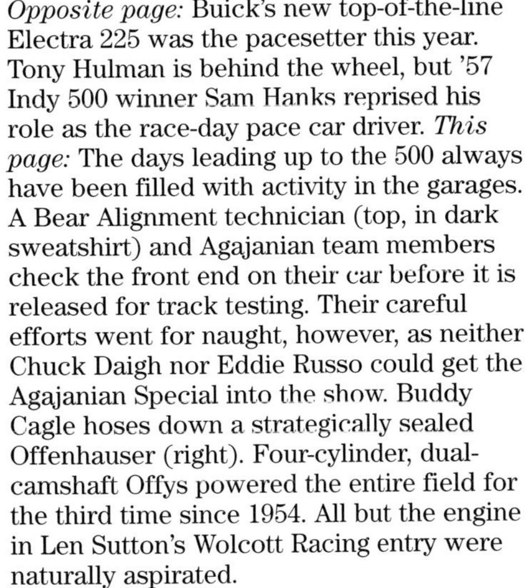

Opposite page: Buick's new top-of-the-line Electra 225 was the pacesetter this year. Tony Hulman is behind the wheel, but '57 Indy 500 winner Sam Hanks reprised his role as the race-day pace car driver. *This page:* The days leading up to the 500 always have been filled with activity in the garages. A Bear Alignment technician (top, in dark sweatshirt) and Agajanian team members check the front end on their car before it is released for track testing. Their careful efforts went for naught, however, as neither Chuck Daigh nor Eddie Russo could get the Agajanian Special into the show. Buddy Cagle hoses down a strategically sealed Offenhauser (right). Four-cylinder, dual-camshaft Offys powered the entire field for the third time since 1954. All but the engine in Len Sutton's Wolcott Racing entry were naturally aspirated.

Pat Flaherty

Chuck Arnold

Bob Christie

Paul Russo

Bill Cheesbourg

Jim McWhithey

10

A.J. Foyt

33

Jimmy Bryan

Al Herman

Red Amick

Chuck Weyant

Ray Crawford

5

Paul Goldsmith

Jud Larson

Len Sutton

Don Freeland

Al Keller

Mike Magill

As seen from paving-brick level, Jim Rathmann started from the outside of row one, Eddie Sachs from the middle, and Johnny Thomson from the pole (*top*). Rathmann drove an upright Watson chassis, while Sachs had a Kuzma and Thomson a Lesovsky chassis, both with lay-down designs. The queen of the annual 500 Festival and her court are accorded prime seats in front of the control tower (*above*). Polesitter Thomson, with Speedway owner Tony Hulman (*above right*), hoped to see his likeness on the Borg-Warner trophy. Young Texan A. J. Foyt, Jr., talks with gesticulating car owner Al Dean (*right*). Foyt finished 10th in his second start at Indianapolis. As the Buick pace car dashes through the pits, the field approaches the start/finish line in tight formation before packed grandstands on the front straight (*opposite bottom*).

On lap 45, Chuck Weyant blew a tire, collecting Mike Magill on the way to the wall. Magill's roadster flipped over. A rear tire contacted the pavement, sending the car down the track upside down at tremendous speed. Jud Larson and Red Amick tangled trying to miss the capsized machine.

With fuel from the overturned car running everywhere and the unconscious Magill trapped in the cockpit, rescue workers were reluctant to go near the smoking racer. Over the confused shouting of the moment, one voice drowned out the rest. "If'n you ain't gonna do nothin', get outta the way!" Larson's Texas drawl boomed. Jud started to shoulder the rescue crew aside, but a guard tried to stop him. Larson decked the guard with a right hook, then proceeded to lift the tail of the racer off Magill by himself. By then, Weyant and Amick were on the scene. They helped Larson right the car and pull Magill out of the wreckage.

"I'm sure glad Jud was there," Magill says today. "He yanked that thing right up off me."

Throughout the first half of the race, fans were treated to a three-way duel between Rodger Ward, Jim Rathmann, and Johnny Thomson. And after 1956 winner Pat Flaherty charged through the field to join the fray, no one could say who would go to victory lane. But in the last third of the race, the outcome gained a sharper perspective.

On lap 162, Flaherty crashed without serious injury. Thomson began experiencing handling problems, which caused him to make an extra pit stop for tires. The hard-charging Rathmann was still in contention. But his pit crew couldn't match the precision pit stops of Ward's team. Ward took the checkered flag 23.27 seconds ahead of Rathmann.

But as easy as the victory appeared, Ward's chief mechanic, A. J. Watson, was astonished at what he found when he tore down the winning engine. The piston pin plug, which held the piston in proper clearance, had worked loose in the second cylinder. It had gone through the oil ring and one of two compression rings on the piston. It was only a matter of a few miles before the remaining ring would have let go too. And Ward would have missed his biggest payday to date.

The field organizes itself on the pace lap (*opposite top*). Len Sutton was the second driver out of the race when he spun the Wolcott Special in Turn 2 and hit the wall (*opposite middle*). Jim Rathmann chases down Pat Flaherty on the front straight (*opposite bottom*). Former winner Flaherty charged into the lead, but spun and crashed at the pit entrance. Rathmann led 19 laps and finished second. Rodger Ward, who led 130 laps, won by 23 seconds for the Leader Card team and mechanic/car designer A. J. Watson (*below*). He earned $106,850, the pace car (*above*), and a smooch from his wife (*left*).

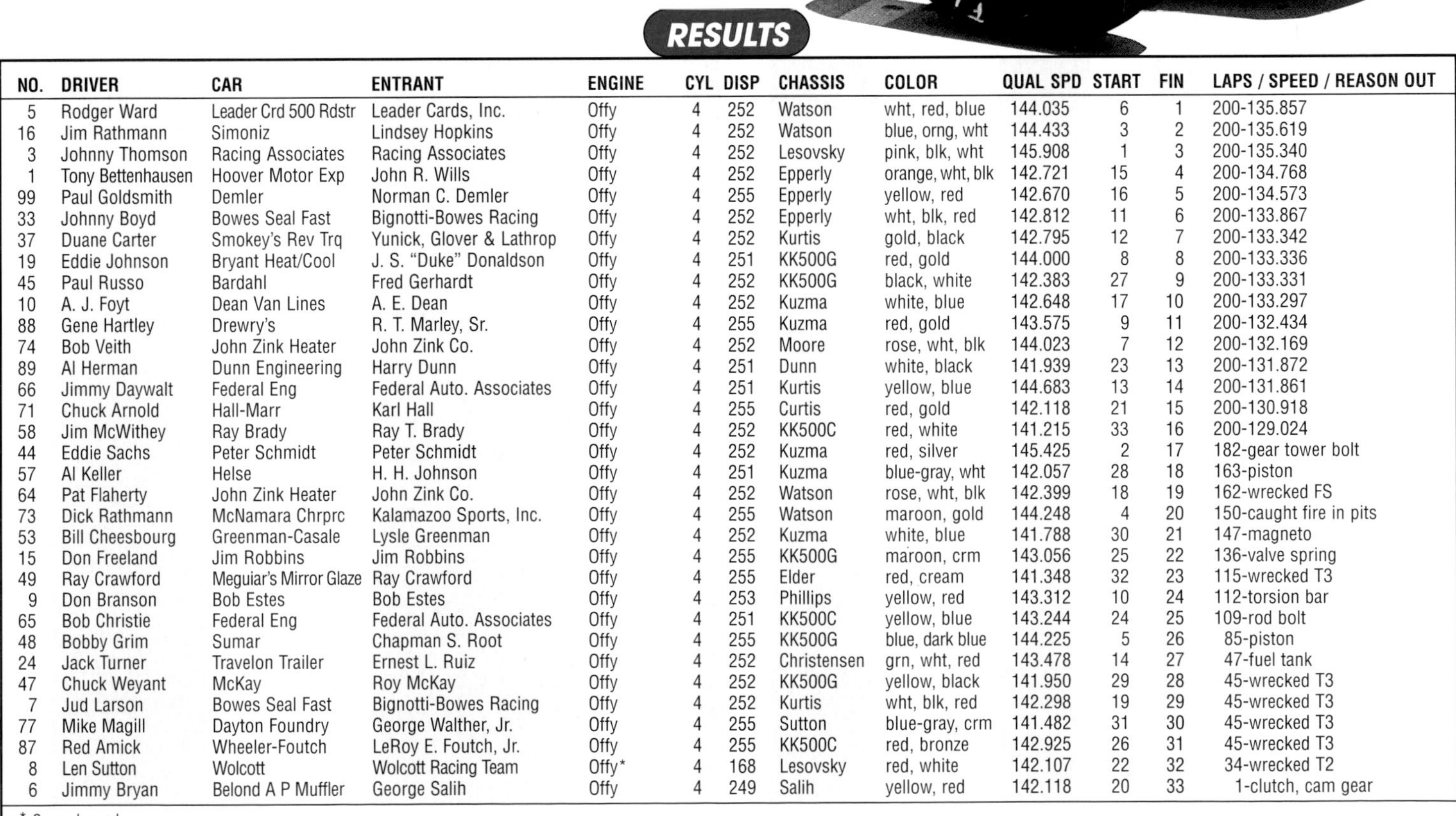

RESULTS

NO.	DRIVER	CAR	ENTRANT	ENGINE	CYL	DISP	CHASSIS	COLOR	QUAL SPD	START	FIN	LAPS / SPEED / REASON OUT
5	Rodger Ward	Leader Crd 500 Rdstr	Leader Cards, Inc.	Offy	4	252	Watson	wht, red, blue	144.035	6	1	200-135.857
16	Jim Rathmann	Simoniz	Lindsey Hopkins	Offy	4	252	Watson	blue, orng, wht	144.433	3	2	200-135.619
3	Johnny Thomson	Racing Associates	Racing Associates	Offy	4	252	Lesovsky	pink, blk, wht	145.908	1	3	200-135.340
1	Tony Bettenhausen	Hoover Motor Exp	John R. Wills	Offy	4	252	Epperly	orange, wht, blk	142.721	15	4	200-134.768
99	Paul Goldsmith	Demler	Norman C. Demler	Offy	4	255	Epperly	yellow, red	142.670	16	5	200-134.573
33	Johnny Boyd	Bowes Seal Fast	Bignotti-Bowes Racing	Offy	4	252	Epperly	wht, blk, red	142.812	11	6	200-133.867
37	Duane Carter	Smokey's Rev Trq	Yunick, Glover & Lathrop	Offy	4	252	Kurtis	gold, black	142.795	12	7	200-133.342
19	Eddie Johnson	Bryant Heat/Cool	J. S. "Duke" Donaldson	Offy	4	251	KK500G	red, gold	144.000	8	8	200-133.336
45	Paul Russo	Bardahl	Fred Gerhardt	Offy	4	252	KK500G	black, white	142.383	27	9	200-133.331
10	A. J. Foyt	Dean Van Lines	A. E. Dean	Offy	4	252	Kuzma	white, blue	142.648	17	10	200-133.297
88	Gene Hartley	Drewry's	R. T. Marley, Sr.	Offy	4	255	Kuzma	red, gold	143.575	9	11	200-132.434
74	Bob Veith	John Zink Heater	John Zink Co.	Offy	4	252	Moore	rose, wht, blk	144.023	7	12	200-132.169
89	Al Herman	Dunn Engineering	Harry Dunn	Offy	4	251	Dunn	white, black	141.939	23	13	200-131.872
66	Jimmy Daywalt	Federal Eng	Federal Auto. Associates	Offy	4	251	Kurtis	yellow, blue	144.683	13	14	200-131.861
71	Chuck Arnold	Hall-Marr	Karl Hall	Offy	4	255	Curtis	red, gold	142.118	21	15	200-130.918
58	Jim McWithey	Ray Brady	Ray T. Brady	Offy	4	252	KK500C	red, white	141.215	33	16	200-129.024
44	Eddie Sachs	Peter Schmidt	Peter Schmidt	Offy	4	252	Kuzma	red, silver	145.425	2	17	182-gear tower bolt
57	Al Keller	Helse	H. H. Johnson	Offy	4	251	Kuzma	blue-gray, wht	142.057	28	18	163-piston
64	Pat Flaherty	John Zink Heater	John Zink Co.	Offy	4	252	Watson	rose, wht, blk	142.399	18	19	162-wrecked FS
73	Dick Rathmann	McNamara Chrprc	Kalamazoo Sports, Inc.	Offy	4	255	Watson	maroon, gold	144.248	4	20	150-caught fire in pits
53	Bill Cheesbourg	Greenman-Casale	Lysle Greenman	Offy	4	252	Kuzma	white, blue	141.788	30	21	147-magneto
15	Don Freeland	Jim Robbins	Jim Robbins	Offy	4	255	KK500G	maroon, crm	143.056	25	22	136-valve spring
49	Ray Crawford	Meguiar's Mirror Glaze	Ray Crawford	Offy	4	255	Elder	red, cream	141.348	32	23	115-wrecked T3
9	Don Branson	Bob Estes	Bob Estes	Offy	4	253	Phillips	yellow, red	143.312	10	24	112-torsion bar
65	Bob Christie	Federal Eng	Federal Auto. Associates	Offy	4	251	KK500C	yellow, blue	143.244	24	25	109-rod bolt
48	Bobby Grim	Sumar	Chapman S. Root	Offy	4	255	KK500G	blue, dark blue	144.225	5	26	85-piston
24	Jack Turner	Travelon Trailer	Ernest L. Ruiz	Offy	4	252	Christensen	grn, wht, red	143.478	14	27	47-fuel tank
47	Chuck Weyant	McKay	Roy McKay	Offy	4	252	KK500G	yellow, black	141.950	29	28	45-wrecked T3
7	Jud Larson	Bowes Seal Fast	Bignotti-Bowes Racing	Offy	4	252	Kurtis	wht, blk, red	142.298	19	29	45-wrecked T3
77	Mike Magill	Dayton Foundry	George Walther, Jr.	Offy	4	255	Sutton	blue-gray, crm	141.482	31	30	45-wrecked T3
87	Red Amick	Wheeler-Foutch	LeRoy E. Foutch, Jr.	Offy	4	255	KK500C	red, bronze	142.925	26	31	45-wrecked T3
8	Len Sutton	Wolcott	Wolcott Racing Team	Offy*	4	168	Lesovsky	red, white	142.107	22	32	34-wrecked T2
6	Jimmy Bryan	Belond A P Muffler	George Salih	Offy	4	249	Salih	yellow, red	142.118	20	33	1-clutch, cam gear

* Supercharged

44th Race • May 30, 1960

Eddie Sachs leads Pole Day qualifiers at a record 146.592 mph, and Watson roadsters fill the entire front row. Jim Rathmann lines up second and 1959 winner Rodger Ward is third.

Rookie Jim Hurtubise steals the show on Bump Day by averaging a stunning 149.056 mph in his Offy-powered Christensen to start 23rd.

Race day starts on a tragic note when a homemade grandstand collapses in the Turn 3 infield on the parade lap, killing two spectators and injuring several others.

When the green flag drops, Ward leads the first lap, but Sachs surges in front on lap 2. Ward takes over again on lap 4, setting a pattern of lead-swapping that continues the rest of the way. Troy Ruttman comes from the fourth row to lead, and when he pits on lap 25, Rathmann goes in front. Ward loses ground when he kills his engine twice on his first pit stop.

Sachs works back to the front and engages in a three-way battle with Ruttman and Rathmann until he pits on lap 83 with steering problems, knocking him out of contention. Sachs drops out on lap 133 with ignition trouble, and Ruttmann parks two laps later with a broken drive gear.

That sets up a thrilling second-half duel between Rathmann and Ward, and the lead changes hands eight times in the last 31 laps alone. Ward has the stronger car at the end and passes Rathmann with six laps to go, but then slows with a badly worn right front tire.

Rathmann takes the lead for good on lap 197 when he turns 146.128 mph, the fastest lap of the race, and pulls away to beat Ward by nearly 13 seconds. After finishing second three times, Rathmann finally pulls into victory circle, his own right front tire worn down to the cord.

Rathmann leads 100 laps and averages a record 138.767 mph. The lead changes hands a record 29 times, and runner-up Ward holds it on 10 occasions. Paul Goldsmith starts 26th and finishes third. Hurtubise runs as high as fifth before blowing his engine late in the race and earns Rookie of the Year honors.

STARTING LINEUP

Average Field Qualifying Speed: 144.070

Numbers in flags indicate finish position

POLE POSITION
Qualifying Speed: 146.592

Rodger Ward

Troy Ruttman

Chuck Stevenson

Lloyd Ruby

Wayne Weiler

Jim Rathmann

Len Sutton

Don Branson

Don Freeland

Bob Christie

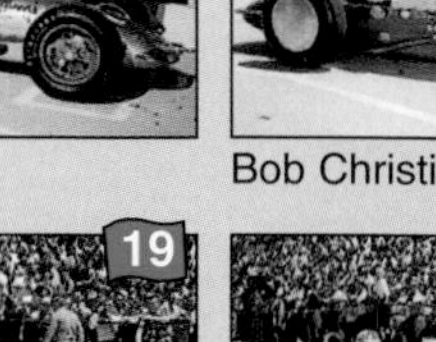

Eddie Sachs

Dick Rathmann

Eddie Johnson

Jimmy Bryan

Johnny Boyd

Speedway owner Tony Hulman is behind the wheel of the Olds Ninety-Eight pace car (*opposite*), but past winner Sam Hanks drove it on race day for the third straight year. The Ninety-Eight was Oldsmobile's first pace car since 1949. The competition that would reach its peak on Memorial Day hummed throughout the month of May. A stream of cars is lined up to be rolled out for the third day of qualifying (*below*). Identifiable cars include Eddie Russo's 46, Russ Congdon's 79, and Dempsey Wilson's 23.

While Eddie Sachs was a tenacious driver, he understood very little about the mechanical side of racing. Having put the Dean Van Lines Special on the pole, Eddie decided to help out his mechanic, Clint Brawner. In order to obtain a clean spark plug reading a few days prior to the 500, Brawner told Sachs to cut some fast laps, then blip the throttle to clear the Offy's plugs. After turning some rapid circuits, Eddie kicked the racer out of gear at top speed and floored the throttle. "I cleaned her out good, Boss," Sachs told Brawner. Actually, he'd bent every valve in the engine. Brawner and his crew had to work nonstop to rebuild the engine before race day.

Just minutes before the start, Eddie informed Clint that the steering felt loose. Making a last-minute adjustment went against Clint's grain, but Eddie insisted. With the steering snugged down, Sachs went out to do battle.

After leading some of the early laps, Sachs began to drop back. On one pit stop, he complained that he could hardly turn the wheel. But by then, the bearings and gears had galled. After lap 132, Sachs parked the racer. The official reason was listed as magneto trouble. "I didn't have the heart to tell them the real cause," Brawner lamented. "The steering had gone out."

Tony Bettenhausen

Bobby Grim

Gene Hartley

Duane Carter

Al Herman

Jimmy Daywalt (for Wilson)

Johnny Thomson

Gene Force

Jim Hurtubise

Paul Goldsmith

Eddie Russo

Jim McWithey

A. J. Foyt

Shorty Templeman

Red Amick

Bob Veith

Bud Tingelstad

Bill Homeier

In the latter stages of this beautifully driven race—many contend it was the greatest Indy 500 of them all—Jim Rathmann and Rodger Ward began receiving startling pit signals. Daring sprint car ace Johnny Thomson, who had been as much as 39 seconds behind the leaders, was cutting into their advantage. "I kept getting signs: 'Thomson 20, 18, 15 seconds back,'" Jim Rathmann says. Thomson's tires were in better shape than the leaders', and he was set to charge the finish. On some laps, he made up as much as 1.8 seconds on the furiously dueling duo. "We were going as hard as we could, Ward and me," Jim says. "I kept wondering, what are we going to do if he catches us?" With a little more than 20 laps remaining, Thomson had cut the margin to 11 seconds. A couple of circuits more, and he had the leaders in sight. But at 190 laps, Johnny's engine suddenly went sour. Running on three cylinders, he began dropping back to finish a distant fifth.

Johnny Thomson had made his final bid to win Indy an indelible memory. Four months later, he would die in a sprint-car accident. But those who witnessed that incredible race must echo Jim Rathmann's contemplation. What would they have done?

Red Amick's No. 27 Salih-Offy is on the hook after a spin during practice (*opposite top*). He was not hurt in the incident. Rookie Jim Hurtubise receives the *Motor Age* trophy (*opposite bottom*) at the driver's meeting for being fastest qualifier. Radio announcer Sid Collins, the "Voice of the 500," enjoys a great vantage point from the timing and scoring tower (*top left*). Pole winner Eddie Sachs congratulates Hurtubise (*top right*) after "Herk" qualified at a record 149.056 mph on the last day. Al Keller could not get his stock-block Chevy V-8 (*second from top left*) fast enough to make the field. *Above:* The front row trio, from left, of Rodger Ward, Jim Rathmann, and Sachs all drove Watson roadsters. Every car in the race was powered by a naturally aspirated Offy engine. The Oldsmobile pace car brings the field into Turn 1 before the huge crowd (*left*).

GASOLINE ALLEY

A. J. Foyt's No. 5 Kurtis (*opposite top*) leads Wayne Weiler and Lloyd Ruby into Turn 1 in the early going. Ruby and Don Branson duel for position as they pursue Paul Goldsmith's No. 99 Demler Special (*opposite, middle*). Though none led a lap, all three finished in the top seven. Racers are towed to pit row (*opposite, bottom left*). Eddie Sachs makes a pit stop in the No. 6 Dean Van Lines Special (*opposite bottom right*). Polesitter Sachs led 21 laps before succumbing to ignition failure. Weiler's No. 32 (*right*) gets fuel and fresh rubber. He later crashed in Turn 2 while running ninth. Despite a badly worn front tire on his Ken-Paul Special (*below*), Jim Rathmann outlasted Rodger Ward in a grueling battle to finally make it into victory lane. The lead changed hands a record 29 times in what many regard as one of the best 500s ever.

RESULTS

NO.	DRIVER	CAR	ENTRANT	ENGINE	CYL	DISP	CHASSIS	COLOR	QUAL SPD	START	FIN	LAPS / SPEED / REASON OUT
4	Jim Rathmann	Ken-Paul	Ken-Paul, Inc.	Offy	4	252	Watson	blue, wht, red	146.371	2	1	200-138.767
1	Rodger Ward	Leader Card 500	Leader Cards, Inc.	Offy	4	252	Watson	wht, red, blue	145.560	3	2	200-138.631
99	Paul Goldsmith	Demler	Norman C. Demler	Offy	4	255	Epperly	yellow, red	142.783	26	3	200-136.792
7	Don Branson	Bob Estes	Bob Estes	Offy	4	252	Phillips	yellow, red	144.753	8	4	200-136.785
3	Johnny Thomson	Adams Qtr Horse	Racing Associates	Offy	4	252	Lesovsky	pink, blk, wht	146.443	17	5	200-136.750
22	Eddie Johnson	Jim Robbins	Jim Robbins Co.	Offy	4	252	Trevis	maroon, wht	145.003	7	6	200-136.137
98	Lloyd Ruby	Agajanian	J. C. Agajanian	Offy	4	252	Watson	maroon, silver	144.208	12	7	200-135.983
44	Bob Veith	Schmidt	Peter Schmidt	Offy	4	252	Meskowski	red, silver	143.363	25	8	200-135.452
18	Bud Tingelstad	Jim Robbins	Jim Robbins Co.	Offy	4	252	Trevis	maroon, wht	142.354	28	9	200-133.717
38	Bob Christie	Federal Engineering	Federal Auto. Associates	Offy	4	255	KK500C	yellow, blue	143.638	14	10	200-133.416
27	Red Amick	King O' Lawn	Leonard A. Fass, Sr.	Offy	4	252	Salih	blue, wht, red	143.084	22	11	200-131.946
17	Duane Carter	Thompson Ind	J. Ensley & S. Murphy	Offy	4	252	Kuzma	red, silver, wht	142.631	27	12	200-131.882
39	Bill Homeier	Ridgewood Builders	Norman Hall	Offy	4	252	Kuzma	slvr, blk, orng	141.248	31	13	200-131.367
48	Gene Hartley	Sumar	Chapman S. Root	Offy	4	252	KK500G	blue, dark blue	143.896	24	14	196-flagged
65	Chuck Stevenson	Leader Card 500	Leader Cards, Inc.	Offy	4	252	Watson	white, blue	144.665	9	15	196-flagged
14	Bobby Grim	Bill Forbes	William P. Forbes	Offy	4	252	Meskowski	pearl, red, orng	143.158	21	16	194-flagged
26	Shorty Templeman	Federal Engineering	Federal Auto. Associates	Offy	4	255	KK500C	yelo, blue, blk	143.856	19	17	191-flagged
56	Jim Hurtubise	Travelon Trailer	Ernest L. Ruiz	Offy	4	252	Christensen	pink pearl, prpl	149.056	23	18	185-con. rod
10	Jimmy Bryan	Metal-Cal	George Salih	Offy	4	252	Epperly	yellow, black	144.532	10	19	152-fuel pump drive
28	Troy Ruttman	John Zink Heater	John Zink Co.	Offy	4	252	Watson	red, wht, blk	145.366	6	20	134-rear end gear
6	Eddie Sachs	Dean Van Lines	Dean Van Lines Racing Div.	Offy	4	252	Ewing	white, blue	146.592	1	21	132-magneto
73	Don Freeland	Ross-Babcock Trvlr	Racing Associates	Offy	4	252	Kurtis	lavndr, red, yelo	144.352	11	22	129-magneto
2	Tony Bettenhausen	Dowgard	Lindsey Hopkins	Offy	4	252	Watson	blue, orng, wht	145.214	18	23	125-con. rod
32	Wayne Weiler	Ansted Rotary	Ansted Rotary Corp.	Offy	4	252	Epperly	cream, black	143.512	15	24	103-wrecked T2
5	A. J. Foyt	Bowes Seal Fast	Bignotti-Bowes Racing	Offy	4	252	Kurtis	pearl, red, blk	143.466	16	25	90-clutch
46	Eddie Russo	Go-Kart	C. O. Prather	Offy	4	255	KK500G	yelo, red, blue	142.203	29	26	84-wrecked T2
8	Johnny Boyd	Bowes Seal Fast	Bignotti-Bowes Racing	Offy	4	252	Epperly	wht, blk, red	143.770	13	27	77-piston
37	Gene Force	McKay	Roy McKay	Offy	4	255	KK500G	lavndr, wht, red	143.472	20	28	74-brakes
16	Jim McWithey	Hoover Motor Exp	Hoover Motor Express, Inc.	Offy	4	252	Epperly	orng, silver, blk	140.378	32	29	60-brakes
9	Len Sutton	S-R Racing Enter	Peter Salemi & Nick Rini	Offy	4	252	Watson	tan, yelo, blk	145.443	5	30	47-engine trouble
97	Dick Rathmann	Jim Robbins	Jim Robbins Co.	Offy	4	255	Watson	maroon, white	145.543	4	31	42-brake line
76	Al Herman	Joe Hunt Magneto	Joe Hunt	Offy	4	252	Ewing	blk, wht, red	141.838	30	32	34-clutch
23	Dempsey Wilson	Bryant Heat & Cool	J. S. "Duke" Donaldson	Offy	4	251	KK500G	red, white	143.215	33	33	11-magneto

1961

45th Race • May 30, 1961

A double-deck steel-and-concrete paddock grandstand gives the Speedway a new look for the Golden Anniversary of the 500, total prize money grows to $400,000, and a rear-engine car makes the field for the first time since 1947.

The day before qualifying starts, popular two-time national champion Tony Bettenhausen is sorting out a Watson for Paul Russo when a steering bolt breaks. The car veers to the right on the front straight, flips several times along the outside wall, and bursts into flames, killing Bettenhausen.

World driving champ Jack Brabham, an Australian, qualifies a revolutionary rear-engine Cooper-Climax at a respectable 145.144 mph to start 13th. Though Brabham's 168-cid Climax four-cylinder is clearly down on power to the larger Offys, the low-slung, British-built Cooper is quicker through the turns than the bulkier front-engine roadsters.

Eddie Sachs wins his second pole in a row at a non-record 147.481, but the 33-car field averages 145.302, the fastest ever.

Jim Hurtubise starts on the outside of row one, jumps in front on the first lap, and leads until he pits for fuel and tires. Rookie Parnelli Jones becomes a crowd favorite when he charges past Sachs and former winners Jim Rathmann and Rodger Ward on the same lap to grab the lead.

By the 80th lap, A. J. Foyt catches and passes Jones, who pits with a sick engine. Troy Ruttman challenges Foyt while Sachs and Ward stay in the hunt. Hurtubise survives an engine fire in the pits, but his engine blows on lap 103. Three laps later, Ruttman goes out with clutch problems, setting up a three-way fight involving Foyt, Sachs, and Ward.

Foyt's fueling rig breaks during his third and last scheduled stop on lap 160. With his car low on fuel, Foyt is faster and pulls ahead of Sachs and Ward. Meanwhile, his crew borrows a fueling rig from another team.

Foyt skids into his pit on lap 184 for a splash-and-go, giving Sachs what looks to be an insurmountable 25-second lead. However, Sachs makes an emergency stop on lap 197 for a fresh right rear tire, and Foyt snatches the lead before Sachs gets back up to speed. Texan Foyt wins by 8.28 seconds, the second closest finish to date. He leads 71 laps in his Offy-powered Trevis roadster, prepared by George Bignotti.

Brabham's underpowered rear-engine Cooper goes the distance, carrying him to ninth place. The car's lighter weight helps fuel economy and the better weight distribution proves easier on tires.

Above: Among the celebrities who visited the Brickyard on the 50th anniversary of the first 500 were Dan Blocker, second from left, and Lorne Greene, far right, stars of the hit television western *Bonanza.* The Ford Thunderbird was the year's pace car, and Ford provided a full field of 33 golden T-birds for a media event (*opposite top*). The backdrop for the trail of Thunderbirds is the new double-deck paddock grandstand built to replace the series of wooden seating areas that had served many a Speedway spectator since the track's earliest days. A dapper Eddie Sachs proudly welcomes visitors to his garage (*opposite bottom*), home of the pole-winning car for the second consecutive year.

STARTING LINEUP

Average Field Qualifying Speed: 145.302

Numbers in flags indicate finish position

Jim Hurtubise

Dick Rathmann

Bill Cheesbourg

Wayne Weiler

Gene Hartley

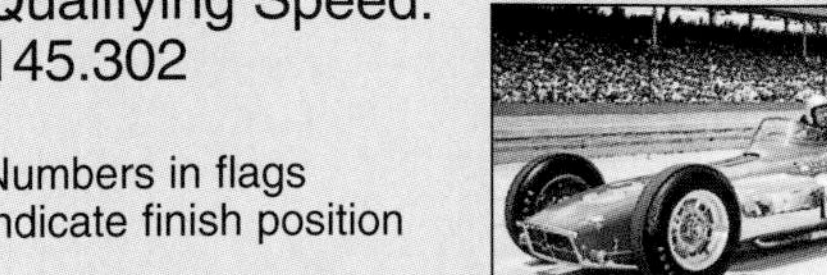

Don Branson

Parnelli Jones

Len Sutton

Jim Rathmann

A. J. Shepherd

POLE POSITION
Qualifying Speed: 147.481

Eddie Sachs

Rodger Ward

A. J. Foyt

Eddie Johnson

Jack Brabham

Former Eastern Sprint Car Champion Bill Randall was having problems coming to terms with the Safety Auto Glass Special during practice. The big Offy roadster didn't feel right to the rookie, but Bill chalked it up to his inexperience with Indy cars.

On Sunday, May 21, with the field full, Randall went out to try and bump his way into the field. After cutting some pretty decent warm-up laps, Bill lost control of the ancient machine in the north turn's short chute. The roadster darted left and right, then made a big arc toward the infield. Randall fought the car through the slide. But just when he seemed to have regained control, he found the fourth wall leading into the front stretch looming. The racer struck with a mighty bang, sliding several hundred feet before it stopped. Randall was shaken and stunned. The racer was a loss, but the Safety Auto Glass people didn't see it that way.

After gutting the car of its engine and running gear, they affixed it to the top of the sign on their glass shop, where it resides to this day.

Shorty Templeman

Jack Turner

Bobby Grim

Don Davis

Cliff Griffith

Bobby Marshman

Paul Goldsmith

Johnny Boyd

Jimmy Daywalt

Al Keller

Roger McCluskey

Norm Hall

Bob Christie

Ebb Rose

Troy Ruttman

Lloyd Ruby

Chuck Stevenson

Dempsey Wilson

Much has been said about the performance of Jack Brabham's Cooper-Climax in the "Golden Anniversary 500." Except for one brief moment, Brabham thoroughly enjoyed his drive at Indy. Very few realize how near he came to being involved in a terrific accident.

For several laps, Brabham and veteran Eddie Johnson had been running in tandem, swapping positions, while racing through the traffic. On lap 128, Johnson held a slight advantage over the little Cooper, when his Jim Robbins Special went out of control coming into the front stretch. The big roadster did a billiard-ball act from one retaining wall to the other. Reducing his speed, Brabham had a split second to go inside or outside of the careening racer.

"I quickly decided that I would have to squeeze between the car and the outer wall," Jack explained. "I just got through. In fact I very much doubt whether, if I had been driving an Indy special, I would have been able to get through. But my Cooper steered as well to the right as to the left and its maneuverability saved the day."

Len Sutton qualified the No. 8 Bryant Heating & Cooling Special (*opposite top*) eighth. For race fans, the 500 long has been equal parts day-long picnic and sporting event. Having staked out their place in the infield, these fans (*above left*) show that the trunk of the 1959 Cadillac has room enough to hold the essentials for a barbecue or seat two adults. Tony Bettenhausen gives visiting Boy Scouts the scoop on Firestone's Deluxe Champion racing tires (*above right*). Eddie Sachs put his Ewing chassis on the pole and was joined on the front row by the trim Epperlys of Don Branson and Jim Hurtubise (*below*).

Paul Russo took some practice laps in Tony Bettenhausen's No. 5 Autolite Special (*top left*). Ironically, Bettenhausen was killed a few days later testing Russo's car. Gene Hartley (*top right*) finished 11th in John Chalik's Trevis-Offy. The field follows the Thunderbird pace car in tight formation (*above*). Dick Rathmann gets routine service in the No. 97 Jim Robbins Special (*left*). Rathmann started sixth and ran in the top 10 until a broken fuel pump ended his day. Cars charge wheel-to-wheel into Turn 1 on the opening lap (*opposite top*). Defending national champion A. J. Foyt (*opposite bottom*) grabbed the lead for keeps with just three laps to go to beat Eddie Sachs by just 8.28 seconds, the second closest finish to date.

RESULTS

NO.	DRIVER	CAR	ENTRANT	ENGINE	CYL	DISP	CHASSIS	COLOR	QUAL SPD	START	FIN	LAPS / SPEED / REASON OUT
1	A. J. Foyt	Bowes Seal Fast	Bignotti-Bowes Racing	Offy	4	252	Trevis	pearl, blk, red	145.903	7	1	200-139.130
12	Eddie Sachs	Dean Van Lines	Dean Van Lines; Racing Div.	Offy	4	252	Ewing	white, blue	147.481	1	2	200-139.041
2	Rodger Ward	Del Webb's Sun City	Leader Cards, Inc.	Offy	4	252	Watson	wht, red, blue	146.187	4	3	200-138.539
7	Shorty Templeman	Bill Forbes Racing	William P. Forbes	Offy	4	252	Watson	wht, maroon	144.341	18	4	200-136.873
19	Al Keller	Konstant Hot	Bruce Homeyer	Offy	4	253	Phillips	black, yellow	146.157	26	5	200-136.034
18	Chuck Stevenson	Metal-Cal	C & H Supply Co.	Offy	4	252	Epperly	yelo, maroon	145.191	28	6	200-135.742
31	Bobby Marshman	Hoover Motor Exp	Hoover Motor Express	Offy	4	252	Epperly	orange, silver	144.293	33	7	200-135.534
5	Lloyd Ruby	Autolite	Lindsey Hopkins	Offy	4	254	Epperly	white, rose	146.909	25	8	200-134.860
17	Jack Brabham	Cooper-Climax	Cooper Car Co., Ltd.	Climax R	4	168	Cooper	green, white	145.144	13	9	200-134.116
34	Norm Hall	Federal Engineering	Federal Automotive Assoc.	Offy	4	255	KK500C	blue, yellow	144.555	32	10	200-134.104
28	Gene Hartley	John Chalik	John Chalik	Offy	4	252	Trevis	blue, white	144.817	15	11	198-flagged
98	Parnelli Jones	Agajanian Willard Batt	J. C. Agajanian	Offy	4	252	Watson	pearl, blue, red	146.080	5	12	192-flagged
97	Dick Rathmann	Jim Robbins	Jim Robbins Co.	Offy	4	252	Trevis	mroon, wht, gld	146.033	6	13	164-fuel pump
10	Paul Goldsmith	Racing Associates	Racing Associates	Offy	4	252	Lesovsky	black, gold	144.741	17	14	160-con. rod
15	Wayne Weiler	Hopkins	Lindsey Hopkins	Offy	4	252	Watson	blue, orange	145.349	12	15	147-wheel bearing
35	Dempsey Wilson	Lysle Greenman	Lysle Greenman	Offy	4	252	Kuzma	blue, white	144.202	31	16	145-fuel pump
32	Bob Christie	North Electric	William Tucker, Inc.	Offy	4	252	Kurtis	white, blue	144.782	16	17	132-burned piston
33	Eddie Johnson	Jim Robbins	Jim Robbins Co.	Offy	4	252	Kuzma	blue, white	145.843	10	18	127-wrecked T4
8	Len Sutton	Bryant Heat & Cool	Pete Salemi & Nick Rini	Offy	4	252	Watson	blue, white	145.897	8	19	110-clutch
52	Troy Ruttman	J. Zink Trackburner	John S. Zink	Offy	4	252	Moore	red, white	144.799	22	20	105-clutch
41	Johnny Boyd	Leader Card 500	Leader Cards, Inc.	Offy	4	252	Watson	orange, white	144.092	20	21	105-clutch
99	Jim Hurtubise	Demler	Norm Demler, Inc.	Offy	4	256	Epperly	yellow, red	146.306	3	22	102-piston
86	Ebb Rose	Meyer Speedway	Racing Associates	Offy	4	252	Porter	black, pink	144.338	19	23	93-con. rod
26	Cliff Griffith	McCullough	Edgar R. Elder	Offy	4	252	Elder	yellow, black	145.038	30	24	55-piston
45	Jack Turner	Bardahl	Fred Gerhardt	Offy	4	252	Kurtis	black, white	144.904	21	25	52-wrecked FS
73	A. J. Shepherd	Travelon Trailer	Ernest L. Ruiz	Offy	4	252	Watson	slvr, gld, blue	144.954	14	26	51-wrecked FS
22	Roger McCluskey	Racing Associates	Racing Associates	Offy	4	252	Watson	black, red	145.068	29	27	51-wrecked FS
14	Bill Cheesbourg	Dean Van Lines	Dean Van Lines; Racing Div.	Offy	4	252	Kuzma	white, blue	145.873	9	28	50-wrecked FS
83	Don Davis	Dart-Kart	Trevis & Morcroft	Offy	4	252	Trevis	blue, white	145.349	27	29	49-wreck FS
4	Jim Rathmann	Simoniz	Ken-Paul, Inc.	Offy	4	252	Watson	black, gold	145.413	11	30	48-magneto
55	Jimmy Daywalt	Schulz Fueling Equip	C. O. Prather	Offy	4	251	KK500G	red, gold	144.219	23	31	27-brake line
16	Bobby Grim	Thompson Ind	Ansted-Thompson Racing	Offy	4	252	Watson	red, gold	144.029	24	32	26-piston
3	Don Branson	Hoover Motor Exp	Hoover Motor Express	Offy	4	252	Epperly	orange, silver	146.843	2	33	2-bent valves

R = rear engine

1962

46th Race • May 30, 1962

Asphalt now covers the front straight, completing a paving process started in 1935. A yard of exposed bricks at the start-finish line is the only visible reminder of the Speedway's heritage as "the Brickyard."

Parnelli Jones, co-Rookie of the Year in 1961, shows his first-year performance is no fluke by winning the pole at 150.370 mph. Jones, driving a two-year-old Watson, is the first to top 150 in qualifying and average less than one minute per lap.

Rodger Ward qualifies on Pole Day at a disappointing 147 mph in a new upright Watson, thinks he can do better, and withdraws his time. Ward qualifies again late in the day at 149.371, second fastest. Bobby Marshman, the other 1961 co-Rookie of the Year, starts third.

One rear-engine car makes the show. Rookie Dan Gurney starts eighth in a ground-hugging car built by innovator Mickey Thompson. A production-based aluminum Buick V-8 powers Thompson's car, which is just 31 inches tall and weighs 1470 pounds with a full load of fuel and Gurney aboard.

Jones bolts into the lead from the pole and dominates the first half of the race. Defending winner A. J. Foyt starts fifth, leads a couple of laps while other leaders pit, and runs third when his engine dies in the pits and won't restart. Foyt's crew is pushing him to the garage when he finally fires it up and gets back in the race. However, he loses a wheel on lap 70 to end his day.

Jones is in front 120 of the first 125 circuits and appears on his way to victory until a worn brake line forces him to pit. Jones continues with virtually no brakes, and his crew sets up a tire barrier in the pits to help him stop for fuel. Jones still manages to place seventh.

Ward moves into command the rest of the way, leading 66 of the last 75 laps. Roger McCluskey challenges Ward, but spins on lap 169 while running second and drops out.

Ward cruises to an 11.5-second victory over Leader Card teammate Len Sutton for his second win. Eddie Sachs comes from the 27th starting spot to finish third.

Speed records fall as the top three finishers average better than 140 mph, and for the first time the top four finishers are on the lead lap when the checkered flag flies.

STARTING LINEUP

Average Field Qualifying Speed: 147.330

Numbers in flags indicate finish position

5 — Bobby Marshman

11 — Shorty Templeman

16 — Roger McCluskey

4 — Don Davis

19 — Bobby Grim

1 — Rodger Ward

23 — A. J. Foyt

20 — Dan Gurney

12 — Don Branson

28 — Paul Russo

POLE POSITION
Qualifying Speed: 150.370

7 — Parnelli Jones

2 — Len Sutton

6 — Jim McElreath

15 — Bud Tingelstad

24 — Dick Rathmann

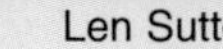

Dan Gurney is always associated with early rear-engine efforts at Indy. In 1962, the Grand Prix ace drove Mickey Thompson's rear-engine Buick-powered Harvey Aluminum Special. Later, he and Jim Clark drove Colin Chapman's Lotus entries. By the late Sixties, Gurney was producing his own Eagle racers.

But in '62, in order to compete on the F1 circuit, Dan was busy flying back and forth between America and Europe. Also absent was the car he was assigned to drive, John Zink's rear-engine turbine-powered "TrackBurner Special," hadn't arrived when the Speedway opened on April 28.

However, there was a good reason for the turbine's late arrival. John Zink decided to test the racer on a quarter-mile track located on his Skiatook, Oklahoma, ranch. A diverter used to control the turbine's output stuck in the open position. The machine careened off the track, struck a drainage ditch, and flipped over. Zink was unhurt, but it took several days to iron the dents and bumps out of the new racer prior to its being shipped to Indy.

The car failed to qualify.

Tony Hulman is joined by Studebaker President Sherwood Egbert in the Lark pace car (*opposite*). But the new product Studebaker wanted to promote was its fiberglass-bodied Avanti sports coupe (*left*). Instead of the Lark, Studebaker presented one of the new cars to race-winner Rodger Ward when they became available later in the year. He reportedly became the first private owner of an Avanti. Super fan Larry Bisceglia (*top*) drove from California to be the first spectator in line for the 14th straight year.

Eddie Johnson

Chuck Rodee

Lloyd Ruby

Eddie Sachs

Troy Ruttman

Jimmy Daywalt

Elmer George

Gene Hartley

Jim Rathmann

Paul Goldsmith

Jim Hurtubise

Ebb Rose

Chuck Hulse

Bob Veith

Allen Crowe

Jack Turner

Johnny Boyd

Bob Christie

Car owner Norm Demler had the utmost faith in Jim Hurtubise. And after "Herk's" showing in Demler's roadster in the '61 Indy 500, it was a justifiable faith.

That's why in 1962, Demler turned his famous Indy car over to Hurtubise to make any modifications he felt necessary. Since the machine was four years old, Jim decided the chassis needed to go on a diet. He simply cut some of the cross bracing out of the front of the chassis, and the Demler car instantly became one of the lightest racers entered that year.

But when the builder of the Demler Special, Quin Epperly, realized what Hurtubise had done, he tried to warn Norm. "Jim will never be able to keep that car pointed in the right direction," Epperly said.

"Oh, it'll be okay," Demler replied. "I'm saving the pieces he cut out. If it doesn't handle, we'll weld them back in. Besides, Hurtubise is a good enough driver; if it doesn't handle, he'll make up for it."

On May 11, Hurtubise was practicing at high speed, when the car suddenly jumped sideways, striking the wall in the south turn. Fortunately, except for a cut on his leg and bruised pride, Jim was okay. The venerable race car wasn't so lucky.

A new Offenhauser engine is installed in A. J. Foyt's Trevis roadster (*opposite top*). As the defending winner and reigning national open-wheel racing champ, Foyt was in demand by Speedway visitors (*opposite middle*). The Agajanian racing team proudly poses with the first car to qualify at more than 150 mph (*opposite bottom*). Owner J. C. Agajanian holds the pit board signifying the milestone achievement. Driver Parnelli Jones, who averaged 150.370 mph for four laps in the Watson-Offy, is third from the right. Dan Gurney removes the rookie stripes from the tail of the front-engine car he used to pass the mandatory USAC tests (*bottom left*). To earn his first start, however, he qualified Mickey Thompson's innovative Buick-powered rear-engine car (*left*). Gurney started from the third row and dropped out with gear problems. Other rear-engine cars failed to qualify, including the No. 33 Kimberly Special (*bottom right*) and a turbine-powered car entered by John Zink that Gurney unsuccessfully tried to put in the field.

The crowd rises to its feet as the field starts out after the Studebaker Lark pace car prior to the start of the 46th Indy 500 (*above*). In the distance, crewmen are still scampering away after having gotten cars in the back rows started. Over the years, tickets to first-turn seats have become some of the most coveted in sports. The grandstand visible in Turn 4 was a new addition to the Speedway for '62. Bud Tingelstad's crew is over the wall to service the Konstant Hot Special (*left*). In the foreground, pit workers from another team signal to their driver. Tingelstad finished 15th, the last car still running at the end. Rodger Ward takes the checkered flag for his second win in four years (*opposite bottom*). In just his second Indy start, Parnelli Jones dominated the first 300 miles at a record pace, but slowed with brake problems, allowing Ward and the Leader Card roadster (*opposite top*) to take command over the last 150 miles. Ward collected $125,015 of the $426,152 purse (both record amounts) and went on to win the USAC national championship.

RESULTS

NO.	DRIVER	CAR	ENTRANT	ENGINE	CYL	DISP	CHASSIS	COLOR	QUAL SPD	START	FIN	LAPS / SPEED / REASON OUT
3	Rodger Ward	Leader Card 500	Leader Cards, Inc.	Offy	4	252	Watson	wht, red, blue	149.371	2	1	200-140.293
7	Len Sutton	Leader Card 500	Leader Cards, Inc.	Offy	4	252	Watson	blue, red, wht	149.328	4	2	200-140.167
2	Eddie Sachs	Dean-Autolite	Dean Van Lines; Racing Div.	Offy	4	252	Ewing	white, blue	146.431	27	3	200-140.075
27	Don Davis	J.H. Rose Truck Line	Bob Philipp	Offy	4	252	Lesovsky	black, rose	147.209	12	4	200-139.768
54	Bobby Marshman	Bryant Heat & Cool	Your Bryant Dealer	Offy	4	252	Epperly	black, silver	149.347	3	5	200-138.790
15	Jim McElreath	Schulz Fueling Equip	C. O. Prather	Offy	4	252	Kurtis	red, white	149.025	7	6	200-138.653
98	Parnelli Jones	Agajanian Willard Batt	J. C. Agajanian	Offy	4	252	Watson	pearl, blue, red	150.370	1	7	200-138.534
12	Lloyd Ruby	Thompson Ind	Ansted-Thompson Racing	Offy	4	253	Watson	cream, blue	146.520	24	8	200-138.182
44	Jim Rathmann	Simoniz Vista	Smokey Yunick	Offy	4	252	Watson	black, gold	146.610	23	9	200-136.913
38	Johnny Boyd	Metal-Cal	C & H Supply Co.	Offy	4	252	Epperly	yelo, maroon	147.047	28	10	200-136.600
4	Shorty Templeman	Bill Forbes Racing	William P. Forbes	Offy	4	252	Watson	wht, maroon	149.050	6	11	200-135.844
14	Don Branson	Mid-Continent Sec	Lindsey Hopkins	Offy	4	252	Epperly	blue, orange	147.312	11	12	200-135.836
91	Jim Hurtubise	Jim Robbins	John Marco Pusilo	Offy	4	252	Trevis	maroon, wht	146.963	29	13	200-135.655
86	Ebb Rose	J. H. Rose Truck Line	Herb Porter	Offy	4	252	Porter	black, pink	146.336	32	14	200-134.001
5	Bud Tingelstad	Konstant Hot	Bruce Homeyer	Offy	4	252	Phillips	black, gold	147.753	10	15	200-133.170
17	Roger McCluskey	Bell Lines Trucking	Sclavi, Inc.	Offy	4	252	Watson	yellow, white	147.759	9	16	168-spun SE
21	Elmer George	Sarkes Tarzian	Mari George	Offy	4	252	Lesovsky	blue, maroon	146.092	17	17	146-engine seized
26	Troy Ruttman	Jim Robbins	Jim Robbins Co.	Offy	4	252	Kuzma	ivory, blue	146.765	30	18	140-burned piston
18	Bobby Grim	Morcroft	Gilbert E. Morcroft	Offy	4	252	Trevis	white, red	146.604	15	19	96-oil leak
34	Dan Gurney	Thompson Ent	Mickey Thompson	Buick R	8	256	Thompson	white, blue	147.886	8	20	92-rear end gear
19	Chuck Hulse	Federal Engineering	Federal Automotive Assoc.	Offy	4	252	KK500C	blue, yellow	146.377	16	21	91-fuel pump
79	Jimmy Daywalt	Albany, N.Y.	Tassi Vatis	Offy	4	252	Kurtis	blue, orange	146.318	33	22	74-transmission
1	A. J. Foyt	Bowes Seal Fast	Bignotti-Bowes Racing	Offy	4	252	Trevis	pearl, red, blk	149.074	5	23	69-lost wheel, spun T2
9	Dick Rathmann	Chapman	H. A. Chapman	Offy	4	252	Watson	ivory, gold	147.161	13	24	51-magneto
32	Eddie Johnson	Polyaire Foam	Peter G. Torosian	Offy	4	252	Trevis	blue, red, wht	146.592	18	25	38-magneto
53	Paul Goldsmith	Bowes Seal Fast	Bignotti-Bowes Racing	Offy	4	252	Epperly	pearl, maroon	146.437	26	26	26-magneto
88	Gene Hartley	Drewry's	M & W Racing Associates	Offy	4	252	Watson	maroon, gold	146.969	20	27	23-steering
62	Paul Russo	Denver-Chicago Trkng	Myron E. Osborn	Offy	4	252	Watson	wht, blue, red	146.687	14	28	20-engine trouble
45	Jack Turner	Bardahl	Fred Gerhardt	Offy	4	252	Kurtis	blk, wht, orng	146.496	25	29	17-wrecked FS
29	Bob Christie	North Electric	William Tucker, Inc.	Offy	4	252	Kurtis	blue, white	146.341	31	30	17-wrecked FS
83	Allen Crowe	S-R Racing Ent	Pete Salemi & Nick Rini	Offy	4	252	Watson	blue, white	146.831	22	31	17-wrecked FS
67	Chuck Rodee	Travelon Trailer	Ernest L. Ruiz	Offy	4	252	Watson	pink, purple	146.969	21	32	17-wrecked FS
96	Bob Veith	Meguiar's Mirror Glze	Ray Crawford	Offy	4	252	Elder	red, yellow	146.157	19	33	12-engine trouble

R = rear engine

1963

47th Race • May 30, 1963

Fresh competition threatens the dominance of the Offenhauser engine and front-engine roadsters. After a four-year absence from the race, the whine of the supercharged Novi is back, and a new breed of rear-engine cars challenges the Indy establishment.

Three cars qualify with the Novi V-8, all owned by colorful Chicago businessman Andy Granatelli. Two Mickey Thompson-built rear-engine cars make the show with aluminum-block Chevrolet V-8s.

British race-car builder Colin Chapman, lured to the Brickyard by American driver Dan Gurney, is the biggest threat to the traditional roadsters with his rear-engine Lotus, powered by a Ford V-8.

Chapman stretches the Lotus Grand Prix car five inches to meet USAC rules and hold the Ford engine, an aluminum 256-cid version of the Fairlane small-block V-8. The pushrod engine has four Weber carburetors instead of fuel injection and runs on gasoline instead of methanol. Ford pegs horsepower at 375, about 75 less than the Offy, but this is offset by the car's lower weight and faster speeds in the turns.

Change looms on the tire front as well. One of Thompson's cars has a lightweight chassis and 12-inch diameter, low-profile tires. The Lotus cars use wide 15-inch diameter tires, while most front-engine roadsters run 16-inchers in front and 18s in back.

A. J. Foyt creates a stir during practice when he runs on Goodyear stock-car tires, the first time Goodyear has been at the Brickyard since 1922. Gusty winds hold Foyt's speed to 146 mph. He switches back to Firestones for qualifying and the race, but Goodyear vows to return in 1964.

PRACTICE AND QUALIFYING

WEDNESDAY, MAY 1: World driving champion Graham Hill of Britain survives a spin in a new rear-engine Thompson to be the year's first to pass the rookie test.

SATURDAY, MAY 4: Hill gets too high in Turn 3, hits the wall, and spins down the short chute. The car suffers heavy right-side damage. Hill is unhurt, but has to go back to Europe for Grand Prix testing. He returns to Indy later in May, but decides not to attempt to qualify because of lack of practice time. ➔

The Chrysler 300 was the '63 official pace car, but the white one that Tony Hulman is getting into (*above*) must be "unofficial." The 300 that paced the field on race day was turquoise (*opposite, top right*). Sam Hanks did the driving for the sixth and final time. Two of Mickey Thompson's rear-engine Harvey Aluminum Specials made the show. Duane Carter drove the new No. 83 with its 12-inch diameter wheels and Al Miller finished ninth in the No. 84, which had debuted the previous year. The 255-cubic-inch Chevrolet engine in Carter's car blew just after the 250-mile mark and he went out in the 23rd spot.

STARTING LINEUP

Average Field Qualifying Speed: 149.028

Numbers in flags indicate finish position

POLE POSITION
Qualifying Speed: 151.153

5 — Don Branson

6 — Jim McElreath

18 — Paul Goldsmith

7 — Dan Gurney

23 — Duane Carter

22 — Jim Hurtubise

2 — Jim Clark

3 — A. J. Foyt

8 — Chuck Hulse

15 — Roger McCluskey

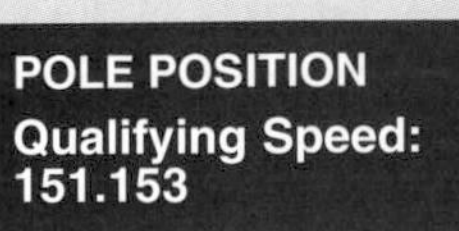
1 — Parnelli Jones

4 — Rodger Ward

16 — Bobby Marshman

17 — Eddie Sachs

27 — Allen Crowe

At half-distance, following his terrific duel with Parnelli Jones, Jim Hurtubise brought the Novi to a screeching halt in the pits. Due to the sudden stop, oil gushed out a breather. A USAC official took a closer look while Andy Granatelli and the crew wiped oil from the car. Long after the racer was refueled and the tires changed, the official was still holding the car. After long contemplation, Hurtubise was sent back out. But when he charged down the front straight the next lap, the dreaded black flag fluttered over the Novi. Following a long consultation, the Novi was ruled out of the race due to an oil leak.

After the race was over, the deep moan of the Novi could be heard coming from the garage area. Granatelli had called a news conference to express his side of the Novi's disqualification. Seated in the cockpit, Andy wound the big brute up to 8000 rpm, holding it there for several minutes. There was no oil leak.

It seems ironic that one car with an admitted oil leak should go on to victory, while its main competitor was eliminated by a superficial pit incident.

Bob Christie

Eddie Johnson

Bob Veith

Johnny Boyd

Dempsey Wilson

Troy Ruttman

Dick Rathmann

Bobby Grim

Art Malone

Johnny Rutherford

Jim Rathmann

Ebb Rose

Bobby Unser

Lloyd Ruby

Chuck Stevenson

Bud Tingelstad

Elmer George

Al Miller

SUNDAY, MAY 5: Dan Gurney posts fast time for the day at 149.975 mph in a Lotus-Ford, and his teammate, Scottish Formula 1 ace Jimmy Clark, is close behind at 149.303.

THURSDAY, MAY 16: Running on 15-inch Firestone Wide Ovals, Parnelli Jones sets fast practice time for the month at 153.557 mph in the same Offy-powered Watson roadster in which he led the race with the past two years. More teams switch to the 15-inch tires, and nine others top 150 mph in practice.

SATURDAY, MAY 18: A crowd of more than 200,000 watches Parnelli Jones win the pole at a record 151.153 mph in windy conditions. Jim Hurtubise averages 150.257 with a Novi to sit on the middle of the front row, and Don Branson clocks 150.188 in a Watson-Offy to sit on the outside.

Jim Clark qualifies his rear-engine Lotus-Ford at 149.75, good for the middle of the second row.

SUNDAY, MAY 19: A. J. Foyt qualifies at 150.6 mph, second fastest, and lines up ninth. Jack Turner flips on the front straight for the third year in a row (the first two were during the race) and announces his retirement from his hospital bed.

THE RACE

Start: Novi muscle enables Hurtubise to pull ahead of Jones and lead the first lap.

Lap 2: Jones snatches the lead away from Hurtubise as rookie Bobby Unser spins and crashes in Turn 1 in another Novi. Art Malone pits the third Novi with clutch problems and drops out 16 laps later.

Lap 39: Roger McCluskey passes Hurtubise for second as Jones stretches his lead to nearly 20 seconds.

Lap 67: After Jones and McCluskey pit, Jim Clark takes over first place and Dan Gurney moves into second, putting the Lotus-Ford team 1-2.

Lap 96: Clark makes his only pit stop, giving the lead back to Jones. Clark runs second, Hurtubise clings to third, and A. J. Foyt runs fourth.

Lap 102: The last Novi is out of the race when Hurtubise, now running sixth, gets black-flagged for leaking oil.

Lap 170: Jones is turning laps at more than 150 mph despite a smoking engine, but Clark is less than 10 seconds behind and closing.

Lap 182: Eddie Sachs, having survived a spin a few laps earlier, loses a wheel and crashes in the north short chute, bringing out the yellow flag.

Lap 193: When green-flag racing resumes, Clark is 21 seconds behind Jones, whose engine is still smoking.

Lap 198: McCluskey spins in Turn 3 while running third and later blames it on oil from Jones's car. In a post-race controversy, McCluskey and Sachs claim Jones should have been black-flagged.

Finish: Jones's front-engine roadster wins by nearly 34 seconds ahead of Clark's rear-engine Lotus, and Foyt is third. Jones leads 167 laps and averages a record 143.137 mph to give owner J. C. Agajanian his second win and Firestone its 40th in a row.

Mickey Thompson's "wide track" No. 83 (*below*) had the more radical design, but Colin Chapman's Lotus (*above*) had greater success. Scotsman Jim Clark finished second in the No. 92 car (*opposite, top left*), and American teammate Dan Gurney came in seventh in another of the Lotus-Fords. Jim Hurtubise started second in the No. 56 Novi (*bottom*) but was flagged out with an oil leak. Parnelli Jones ruled the Brickyard with his reliable front-engine Watson roadster (*opposite bottom*). Jones qualified at a record speed, won at a record clip, and earned a record $148,513 for himself and owner J. C. Agajanian (*opposite, top right*).

In the wake of the great oil controversy, opinions flew left and right. Some of the Team Lotus contingent chalked it up to Yankee favoritism. Others, especially the vociferous Eddie Sachs, claimed to have spun or been put off by Jones's oil leak. And while Parnelli Jones may not have put an end to the talk, he at least stopped it for awhile.

The day after the race, Jones and other top finishers were to be honored at a luncheon. Sachs began jawing with Jones. "I spun and crashed in your oil," Sachs complained. "Your 500 win will always be tainted!" With that, Parnelli delivered a right hook to Eddie's jaw, which sprawled the accuser flat on his back. For some time, no one said much to Jones about oil. To Eddie's credit, he posed for photographers, flat on his back, waving a small white flag.

Lost in all the uproar, were the words of Jim Clark. "Parnelli Jones drove a great race," Clark said. "I would have been sorry to have seen him black-flagged."

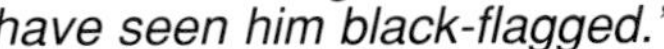

RESULTS

NO.	DRIVER	CAR	ENTRANT	ENGINE	CYL	DISP	CHASSIS	COLOR	QUAL SPD	START	FIN	LAPS / SPEED / REASON OUT
98	Parnelli Jones	Agajanian Willard Batt	J. C. Agajanian	Offy F	4	252	Watson	pearl, blue, red	151.153	1	1	200-143.137
92	Jim Clark	Lotus/Ford	Lotus Indianapolis Project	Ford R	8	256	Lotus	green, yellow	149.750	5	2	200-142.752
2	A. J. Foyt	Sheraton-Thompson	Ansted-Thompson Racing	Offy F	4	252	Trevis	pearl, red, blue	150.615	8	3	200-142.210
1	Rodger Ward	Kaiser Aluminum	Leader Cards, Inc.	Offy F	4	252	Watson	wht, red, blue	149.800	4	4	200-141.090
4	Don Branson	Leader Card 500	Leader Cards, Inc.	Offy F	4	252	Watson	white, blue	150.188	3	5	200-140.866
8	Jim McElreath	Bill Forbes Racing	William P. Forbes	Offy F	4	252	Watson	white, maroon	149.744	6	6	200-140.862
93	Dan Gurney	Lotus/Ford	Lotus Indianapolis Project	Ford R	8	256	Lotus	white, blue	149.019	12	7	200-140.071
10	Chuck Hulse	Dean Van Lines	Dean Van Lines	Offy R	4	252	Ewing	white, blue	149.340	11	8	200-140.064
84	Al Miller	Thompson Harvey	Mickey Thompson	Chevy R	8	255	Thompson	orange, cream	149.613	31	9	200-139.524
22	Dick Rathmann	Chapman	Harry Allen Chapman	Offy F	4	252	Watson	red, white	149.130	17	10	200-138.845
29	Dempsey Wilson	Vita Fresh OJ	Gordon Van Liew	Offy F	4	252	Kuzma	white, orange	147.832	30	11	200-138.574
17	Troy Ruttman	Robbins Autocrat	Jim Robbins Co.	Offy F	4	252	Kuzma	ivory, blue	148.374	33	12	200-138.244
65	Bob Christie	Travelon Trailer	Ernest L. Ruiz	Offy F	4	252	Watson	pink pearl, prpl	149.123	18	13	200-136.104
32	Ebb Rose	Sheraton-Thompson	Ansted-Thompson Racing	Offy F	4	252	Watson	wht, red, blue	148.545	32	14	200-132.347
14	Roger McCluskey	Konstant Hot	Bruce Homeyer	Offy F	4	252	Watson	black, gold	148.680	14	15	198-spun T3
5	Bobby Marshman	Econo-Car Rental	Lindsey Hopkins	Offy F	4	252	Epperly	white, pink	149.458	7	16	196-rear end
9	Eddie Sachs	Bryant Heat & Cool	D.V.S., Inc.	Offy F	4	252	Watson	yelo, red, slvr	149.570	10	17	181-lost wheel T3
99	Paul Goldsmith	Demler	Norm Demler, Inc.	Offy F	4	252	Watson	yellow, red	150.163	9	18	149-crankshaft bearing
52	Lloyd Ruby	J. Zink Trackburner	John S. Zink	Offy F	4	252	Moore	red, white	149.123	19	19	126-hit wall T4
88	Eddie Johnson	Drewry's	M & M Racing Assn.	Offy F	4	252	Watson	maroon, gold	148.509	21	20	112-hit wall BS
45	Chuck Stevenson	Bardahl	Fred Gerhardt	Offy F	4	252	Watson	blk, orng, wht	148.386	22	21	110-valve
56	Jim Hurtubise	Hotel Tropicana	Novi, Inc.	Novi *F	8	166	Kurtis	rose, wht, gld	150.257	2	22	102-oil leak
83	Duane Carter	Thompson Harvey	Mickey Thompson	Chevy R	8	255	Thompson	red, white	148.002	15	23	100-threw rod
16	Jim Rathmann	Coral Harbour	Lindsey Hopkins	Offy F	4	252	Watson	blue, pink	147.838	29	24	99-magneto
26	Bobby Grim	Morcroft	Gilbert E. Morcroft	Offy F	4	252	Trevis	purple, gold	148.717	20	25	79-oil leak
86	Bob Veith	Racing Associates	Racing Associates	Offy F	4	252	Porter	rose, black	148.289	24	26	74-valve
35	Allen Crowe	Gabriel Shocker	Pete Salemi & Nick Rini	Offy F	4	252	Trevis	white, orange	148.877	13	27	47-lost wheel T1
54	Bud Tingelstad	Hoover, Inc.	Tidewater Associates, Inc.	Offy F	4	252	Epperly	orng, chrome	148.227	25	28	46-hit wall, T2
37	Johnny Rutherford	U.S. Equipment Co.	Ed Kostenuk	Offy F	4	252	Watson	white, red	148.063	26	29	43-transmission
21	Elmer George	Sarkes Tarzian	Mari George	Offy F	4	252	Lesovsky	blue, ivry, mroon	147.893	28	30	21-handling
75	Art Malone	STP	Novi, Inc.	Novi *F	8	166	Kurtis	white, red	148.343	23	31	18-clutch
23	Johnny Boyd	Bowes Seal Fast	Salih-Paddock Corp.	Offy F	4	252	Epperly	pearl, red, blk	148.038	27	32	12-oil leak
6	Bobby Unser	Hotel Tropicana	Novi, Inc.	Novi *F	8	166	Kurtis	yellow, black	149.421	16	33	2-hit wall T1

* = supercharged F = front engine R = rear engine

48th Race • May 30, 1964

The rear-engine revolution picks up steam as A. J. Watson, designer of the front-engine roadsters that won the five previous 500s, joins the advance to the rear.

Though 12 front-engine Watsons are in the field, the Leader Card team enters new rear-engine Watsons for two-time winner Rodger Ward and Don Branson. Ward's has a Ford engine and Branson's has the venerable four-cylinder Offy.

Ford transforms its pushrod small-block V-8, which debuted with the Lotus team in 1963, into a true racing engine: dual overhead camshafts, four valves per cylinder, fuel injection, and 420 bhp, 45 more than the pushrod version. Seven of the 12 rear-engine starters use the dual-cam Ford V-8; the other five are Offy-powered.

Andy Granatelli installs the supercharged Novi V-8 at the front of a new British-built, four-wheel-drive Ferguson chassis. Second-year driver Bobby Unser qualifies the car 22nd, and two other Novis make the show.

The most unusual entry is the Hurst Floor Shift Special, a rear-engine car built by Smokey Yunick. The car is so compact there's no room for a driver. Yunick's solution is to attach a sidecar to the left side, motorcycle-style. Stock-car racer Bobby Johns, trying to make the field on Bump Day as an Indy rookie, wrecks the car before his first qualifying lap.

Best car name goes to Norm Hall's Watson-Offy: the Nothing Special.

PRACTICE AND QUALIFYING

WEDNESDAY, MAY 4: Wider tires developed for the Speedway provide higher cornering speeds. Rodger Ward sets fast time for the day, 151.1 mph in a rear-engine Watson, but the buzz in Gasoline Alley is over Mickey Thompson's Sears-Allstate Specials, which pass tech inspection.

Thompson revamps his 1963 rear-engine cars with the dual-cam Ford V-8, aero fiberglass bodywork that covers the wheels, and Allstate tires (15-inch as mandated by USAC). The most controversial feature is that the right rear wheel steers with the front wheels, and the cars prove tricky to handle.

FRIDAY, MAY 6: A. J. Foyt decides against running a rear-engine car and clocks a hot lap of 154.189 mph in a front-engine Watson-Offy with Goodyear tires—an unofficial record speed. Goodyear later withdraws and releases its drivers from their contracts. Foyt runs on Firestone tires for qualifying and the race.

SATURDAY, MAY 7: Parnelli Jones, who also rejects a rear-engine car, ups the ante to 156.223 in practice with "Calhoun," the previous year's winning car.

THURSDAY, MAY 12: Bobby Marshman sets fast time of the month at 157.178 in a rear-engine Lotus-Ford, increasing expectations of record speeds on Pole Day.

FRIDAY, MAY 15: Running in the cool early morning, Marshman gets up to 158.758—more than seven mph →

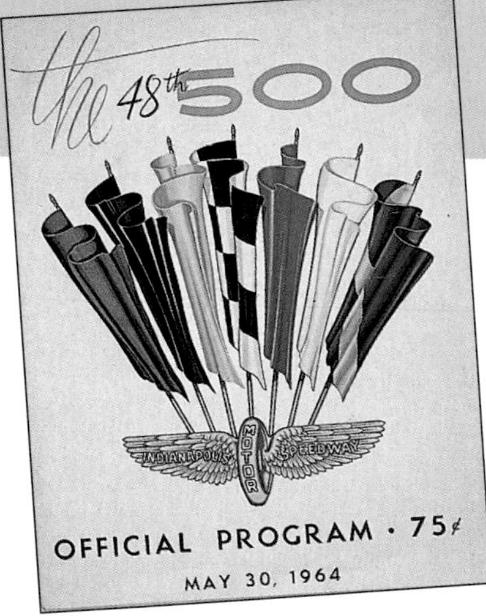

STARTING LINEUP

Average Field Qualifying Speed: 152.540

Numbers in flags indicate finish position

Rodger Ward

Dan Gurney

Don Branson

Dick Rathmann

Johnny Rutherford

Bobby Marshman

A. J. Foyt

Len Sutton

Jim Hurtubise

Dave MacDonald

POLE POSITION
Qualifying Speed: 158.828

Jim Clark

Parnelli Jones

Lloyd Ruby

Walt Hansgen

Johnny Boyd

Though technically a 1965 model, Ford's new Mustang was a runaway success in the marketplace and the pace car in '64 (*top*). Andy Granatelli's STP team was hard on the eyes when in uniform (*row above*) but easy to pick out from the crowd. Bobby Unser (*right*) qualified an STP four-wheel-drive Ferguson chassis 22nd, but crashed on the second lap. A group from Wheel Horse tractors made up its own grid during an outing at the Speedway (*opposite*).

Troy Ruttman

Johnny White

Eddie Johnson

Bob Harkey

Art Malone

Bill Cheesbourg

Eddie Sachs

Bobby Grim

Bob Veith

Jim McElreath

Chuck Stevenson

Bob Wente

Ronnie Duman

Bud Tingelstad

Bobby Unser

Jack Brabham

Bob Mathouser

Norm Hall

Talk about revolutionary: Legendary mechanic Smokey Yunick (*top right*) made Mickey Thompson look downright conventional with the Hurst Floor Shift Special, a rear-engine car so compact that the driver had to sit in a motorcycle sidecar on the left (*top left*). Veteran Duane Carter tried the Offy-powered creation (*right*) but bailed out. Rookie Bobby Johns also gave it a shot (*above*); after he crashed in practice (*above right*), Yunick withdrew the car. Twelve rear-engine cars made the field, including Mickey Thompson's Ford-powered Thompson-Sears Allstate Special (*opposite top*). Rookie Dave MacDonald spun the No. 83 car and crashed on the second lap, the gasoline-laden racer erupting in flames. Popular Eddie Sachs (*opposite, middle* and *bottom*), in another rear-engine car, rammed into MacDonald. Sachs's car also burst into flames, and both drivers were killed. Five other cars were damaged and the race was stopped for nearly two hours. Among the young drivers sidelined as a result of the incident were future 500 legends Johnny Rutherford and Bobby Unser, both of whom were making just their second starts at the Brickyard.

faster than the qualifying record.

This touches off two mad dashes: Teams scramble to be first in line to qualify the next morning, and as tempers flare, Andy Granatelli and his tow tractor tip over. Meanwhile, a much longer line forms outside the Speedway as an anticipated crowd of 200,000 assembles for Pole Day.

SATURDAY, MAY 16: Marshman electrifies the crowd with a practice lap over 160. Foyt is first to attempt to qualify, but waves off when gusty winds slow him down. Jones is next and burns a piston on his first lap.

Jim Clark, running on Dunlop tires, is the surprise pole winner, averaging 158.828 in his Lotus-Ford to break Jones's qualifying record by 7.6 mph. Marshman is second fastest at 157.867, and Ward third at 156.406, giving the entire front row to rear-engine cars.

THE RACE

Start: Jim Clark gets a good jump and pulls away from the pack with Bobby Marshman in pursuit.

Lap 2: Rookie Dave MacDonald skids coming out of Turn 4, hits the inside wall, and his gasoline-powered Thompson-Ford bursts into flames. A huge plume of black smoke fills the sky as the rear of the field spins and scatters to avoid the wreck. Johnny Rutherford rides up and over MacDonald's car, but Eddie Sachs hits it broadside and his car erupts in flames.

For the first time in 500 history, an accident halts the race. Sachs and MacDonald die in the fiery wreck, which knocks seven cars out of the race.

Restart: After a delay of one hour, 42 minutes, 26 cars restart in single file and Clark pulls away again.

Lap 7: As Clark slows to lap backmarkers, Marshman slips by into first. Dan Gurney, Clark's Lotus teammate is third, and Rodger Ward is fourth—all in rear-engine cars.

Lap 39: Marshman builds a big lead, but first place becomes a hot potato. Marshman scrapes an oil plug loose by running too low in the turns, slows down, and retires, giving the lead back to Clark.

Lap 47: Clark's left rear tire shreds, damaging his suspension, and he parks his Lotus in the Turn 1 infield, handing the lead to Parnelli Jones.

Lap 55: When Jones stops for fuel, static electricity causes his fuel tank to explode in the pits, ending his day and giving the lead to A. J. Foyt. Jones suffers minor burns.

Lap 112: Foyt holds a comfortable lead over Ward as Gurney in the second Lotus team car calls it quits. As with Clark, the Dunlop tires on Gurney's car are overheating and shredding.

Lap 140: The leaders pit for fuel, but for Foyt it is his second and final stop, while Ward makes his third. A balky fueling valve prevents Ward from getting a full tank, and he has to stop again late in the race.

Finish: Foyt leads the last 146 laps to win for the second time at a record speed of 147.350 mph, four mph faster than 1963. He earns $153,650 of a $506,625 purse. Ward is second, a lap down, and Lloyd Ruby, third.

Ward's is the only rear-engine car among the top 10, all of which are Ford-powered. Art Malone is 11th with a Novi. The top 12 finishers go the distance on a single set of Firestone tires made from a new synthetic rubber.

When Eddie Sachs was no more than a child, he accompanied his travelling salesman father on long trips. Eddie would pile cushions and pillows in the driver's seat, and take the wheel while his father slept. Invariably, Papa Sachs awoke to find Eddie happily flying down the road at better than 90 mph.

Sachs came up through the ranks. His great dream, which became an obsession, was to win Indianapolis. "Just wait until I win the 500," he'd tell anyone who'd listen. "All I've got to do is get there!"

Eddie tried to make the field in 1953 and '54, but he was sent back to the sprinters for more experience. One year, he was taken bodily to the Speedway gate and thrown out. "You can throw me out, but I'll be back," Eddie said. He took jobs driving a taxi, even washing dishes to stay near the Speedway.

In '57, he qualified second fastest. But mechanical trouble sidelined him. In 1960 and '61, Sachs became the first driver since Rex Mays in 1935 and '36, to win the pole two years straight. And he came so close to winning in '61.

Indy had an emotional hold on Eddie. Fans would see him wiping his eyes on the parade lap. "I start crying when they play Back Home Again in Indiana, *and I can't stop until the pace lap," he'd say. Those who knew him best still wonder if his tears had dried when he was caught up in the tremendous second-lap crash that claimed his life.*

The front row (*left*) was made up of all rear-engine cars for the first time. Jim Clark sat on the pole and Bobby Marshman in the middle in Lotuses, and two-time winner Rodger Ward was on the outside in a Watson. All three cars had Ford V-8 power. Mustangs, the queen and her court, and the Borg-Warner trophy parade before the race (*opposite middle*). The cars are lined up on the track during the posting of the colors (*opposite bottom*). Seasoned front-row drivers form a straight line on the pace lap (*below*). As smoke rises in the distance from the deadly multi-car accident near Turn 4 on lap two, police and safety officials keep the curious with access to pit lane at a distance while the race is halted (*bottom left*). When racing resumes, battles rage between the new and the traditional: Don Branson's rear-engine Watson leads Johnny White's front-engine Watson (*bottom right*). Branson dropped out after 187 laps; White went the distance to finish fourth.

1964

In preparation for the 1964 race, A. J. Watson decided to use alcohol fuel in his rear-engine Ford-powered racer. The rest of the Fords were all using gasoline. Watson knew the engine would run cooler on alcohol, but that fuel mileage would suffer. He decided to install a cockpit mounted metering valve to "lean" the mixture. In this way, when driver Rodger Ward was cruising, he could conserve fuel for a time when performance would really matter. During practice, with the valve installed, complete with a label on the dash, the car got great mileage. Watson figured Ward could go through on two pit stops.

But on the morning of the race, Ward told Watson the valve stuck out so far under the dash, it would cut off circulation in his leg. He wanted the valve changed. Watson simply inverted the mechanism, giving Ward the clearance he desired.

During the race, Ward's car guzzled fuel at an enormous rate. Every time Rodger seemed to be reeling in A. J. Foyt, he'd have to make another stop. They kept telling Ward to "lean it down." But the switch had no effect. He made five visits to the pits, four for fuel. Foyt went through on three stops. Ward could never challenge Foyt, and had to settle for second place.

After the race, it was discovered that flipping the valve changed the lean setting to the rich mixture. But in the heat of competition, no one considered that possibility.

Don Branson's Wynn's Friction Proofing Special leads Bobby Grim's front-engine roadster and Bob Veith's rear-engine Huffaker (*opposite top*). Walt Hansgen closes on Branson (*opposite middle*). Hansgen and Veith drove MG Liquid Suspension Specials that used the MG sedan's water-filled rubber springs instead of conventional springs and shocks. Lloyd Ruby's roadster chases Hansgen's rear-engine car (*opposite bottom*). A. J. Foyt dominated to reach victory lane for the second time (*left*), his Watson roadster (*below*) beating the rear-engine car of Rodger Ward by a lap. It would be the last hurrah for race engineering's old guard.

RESULTS

NO.	DRIVER	CAR	ENTRANT	ENGINE	CYL	DISP	CHASSIS	COLOR	QUAL SPD	START	FIN	LAPS / SPEED / REASON OUT
1	A. J. Foyt	Sheraton-Thompson	Ansted-Thompson Racing	Offy F	4	252	Watson	pearl, red, blue	154.672	5	1	200-147.350
2	Rodger Ward	Kaiser Aluminum	Leader Cards, Inc.	Ford R	8	255	Watson	wht, red, blue	156.406	3	2	200-146.339
18	Lloyd Ruby	Bill Forbes Racing	William P. Forbes	Offy F	4	252	Watson	white, maroon	153.932	7	3	200-144.320
99	Johnny White	Demler	Norm Demler, Inc.	Offy F	4	252	Watson	yellow, red	150.893	21	4	200-143.206
88	Johnny Boyd	Vita Fresh OJ	Gordon Van Liew	Offy F	4	252	Kuzma	orange, gold	151.835	13	5	200-142.345
15	Bud Tingelstad	Federal Engineering	Federal Automotive Assoc.	Offy F	4	252	Trevis	cream, blue	151.210	19	6	198-flagged
23	Dick Rathmann	Chapman	Harry Allen Chapman	Offy F	4	252	Watson	maroon, wht	151.860	12	7	197-flagged
4	Bob Harkey	Wally Weir Mobilgas	Walter Weir, Jr.	Offy F	4	252	Watson	blue	151.573	27	8	197-flagged
68	Bob Wente	Morcroft-Taylor	G. E. Morcroft-R. Taylor	Offy F	4	252	Trevis	yellow, red	149.869	32	9	197-flagged
16	Bobby Grim	Konstant Hot	Vatis Enterprises, Inc.	Offy F	4	252	Kurtis	yellow, blk	151.038	20	10	196-flagged
3	Art Malone	Studebaker-STP	STP Division, Studebaker	Novi *F	8	168	Kurtis	blue, pink	151.222	30	11	194-flagged
5	Don Branson	Wynn's Friction Proof	Leader Cards, Inc.	Offy R	4	252	Watson	yellow, red	152.672	9	12	187-clutch
53	Walt Hansgen	MG Liquid Susp	Kjell H. Qvale	Offy R	4	252	Huffaker	blue, white	152.581	10	13	176-flagged
56	Jim Hurtubise	Tombstone Life	D.V.S., Inc.	Offy F	4	252	Hurtubise	red, gold, blk	152.542	11	14	141-oil pressure
66	Len Sutton	Bryant Heat & Cool	Vollstedt Enterprises, Inc.	Offy R	4	252	Vollstedt	silver, red	153.813	8	15	140-fuel pump
62	Bill Cheesbourg	Arizona Apache Air	Myron E. Osborn	Offy F	4	252	Epperly	red, silver	148.711	33	16	131-engine trouble
12	Dan Gurney	Lotus Ford	Team Lotus, Ltd.	Ford R	8	255	Lotus	white, blue	154.487	6	17	110-tire wear
14	Troy Ruttman	Dayton Steel Wheel	George Walther, Jr.	Offy F	4	252	Watson	white, blue	151.292	18	18	99-spun T3
54	Bob Veith	MG Liquid Susp	Kjell H. Qvale	Offy R	4	252	Huffaker	wht, blue, red	153.381	23	19	88-burned piston
52	Jack Brabham	Zink-Urschel Trckbrnr	Zink, Urschel, Slick, Inc.	Offy R	4	252	Brabham	red, white	152.504	25	20	77-split fuel tank
28	Jim McElreath	Studebaker-STP	STP Division, Studebaker	Novi F	8	168	Kurtis	white, red	152.381	26	21	77-engine trouble
77	Bob Mathouser	Dayton Disc Brake	George Walther, Jr.	Offy F	4	252	Walther	blue, white	151.451	28	22	77-brakes
98	Parnelli Jones	Agajanian Bowes Seal Fast	J. C. Agajanian	Offy F	4	252	Watson	pearl, blue, red	155.099	4	23	55-pit fire
6	Jim Clark	Lotus Ford	Team Lotus, Ltd.	Ford R	8	255	Lotus	green, yellow	158.828	1	24	47-rear suspension
51	Bobby Marshman	Pure Oil Firebird	Lindsey Hopkins	Ford R	8	255	Lotus	white, blue	157.867	2	25	39-oil plug
84	Eddie Johnson	Thompson-Sears Allstate	Mickey Thompson	Ford R	8	255	Thompson	white, blue	152.905	24	26	6-fuel pump
86	Johnny Rutherford	Bardahl	Racing Associates	Offy F	4	252	Watson	yellow, black	151.400	15	27	2-wrecked FS
95	Chuck Stevenson	Diet Rite Cola	Leader Cards, Inc.	Offy F	4	252	Watson	white, blue	150.830	29	28	2-wrecked FS
83	Dave MacDonald	Thompson-Sears Allstate	Mickey Thompson	Ford R	8	255	Thompson	red, white	151.464	14	29	1-exploded FS
25	Eddie Sachs	American Red Ball	D.V.S., Inc.	Ford R	8	255	Halibrand	wht, red, gld	151.439	17	30	1-hit No. 83, exploded
64	Ronnie Duman	Clean Wear Serv Co.	Nicholas E. Fulbright	Offy F	4	252	Trevis	pink, black	149.744	16	31	1-wrecked FS
9	Bobby Unser	Studebaker-STP	STP Division, Studebaker	Novi *4F	8	268	Ferguson	red, chrome	154.865	22	32	1-wrecked FS
26	Norm Hall	Hurst	Pope-Hall Enterprises	Offy F	4	252	Watson	blue, red	150.094	31	33	1-spun, hit wall T4

* = supercharged R = rear engine F = front engine 4 = four-wheel drive

49th Race • May 31, 1965

USAC announces sweeping safety changes in the wake of the fiery crash that killed two drivers the previous year. The new rules require methanol fuel, banning the highly volatile gasoline most Ford engines used in 1964.

Rubber bladders are required inside fuel tanks, which are restricted to a maximum capacity of 75 gallons. No fuel tanks or crossover tubes are allowed ahead of the driver. A minimum two pit stops are mandatory and gravity-feed 400-gallon fuel tanks replace the pressurized rigs in the pits to reduce the chances of fueling accidents.

With weight-saving magnesium and titanium in wide use, a new minimum weight of 1250 pounds promotes stronger chassis designs.

Despite A. J. Foyt's win the year before in a front-engine Watson roadster, the swing to rear-engine cars continues. Foyt, Parnelli Jones, and other holdouts from 1964 jump into rear-engine cars, which earn 27 of the 33 starting spots.

Ford massages its dual-cam V-8 to boost horsepower to 495, more than the reliable Offenhauser. There are 17 Ford V-8s on the starting grid, 14 Offys, and two Novis (with an estimated 775 bhp). Ford spends a bundle trying to win, signaling a new era at the Speedway. Ford delivers sealed engines to its teams and then ships them back to Dearborn for rebuilds.

Bobby Unser qualifies eighth in a four-wheel-drive Ferguson-Novi, the fastest car that has neither a Ford V-8 nor a rear-engine chassis.

A rookie class of 11 starts the race, the most since 1951, and includes future stars Mario Andretti, who qualifies fourth, Gordon Johncock, and Al Unser, the younger brother of Bobby.

PRACTICE AND QUALIFYING

TUESDAY, MAY 4: On the first day of open practice without speed limits, defending winner A. J. Foyt is fastest at 155 mph in a rear-engine Lotus-Ford with Goodyear tires.

WEDNESDAY, MAY 5: Foyt spins and crashes on the backstretch when a wheel-hub carrier breaks. The next day, USAC officials ground six rear-engine Lotus and Lola cars until the hub carriers are strengthened.

THURSDAY, MAY 13: Foyt posts an unofficial record lap of 161.146, and Jim Clark, also in a Lotus-Ford, hits 160.142.

SATURDAY, MAY 15: Foyt's Lotus is hooked up on Pole Day. He qualifies on Goodyear tires at a record 161.233, nipping Clark, who is close behind at 160.729. Dan Gurney is third fastest, giving Lotus-Ford the entire front row. Rear-engine cars also fill the next four spots.

Two-time winner Rodger Ward continues to have problems. After blowing two Ford V-8s in the past week, he fails to get up to speed on two qualifying attempts in his rear-engine Watson.

THURSDAY, MAY 20: Parnelli Jones, already set to start fifth in the race, slams the wall in Turn 4, heavily damaging his Lotus-Ford. His crew says it can fix the car for the race.

SATURDAY, MAY 22: Ward crashes coming out of Turn 2 on the warmup lap for a qualification run. Despite heavy damage, chief mechanic A. J. Watson says the car will be ready for another qualifying run on Sunday. ➔

Goodyear brought its 15-inch diameter stock-car racing tire to the Speedway to challenge Firestone. Goodyear's claim to fame was a pioneering safety liner inside the tire (*opposite bottom*) that gave drivers a second layer of rubber to run on if the outer tread was damaged. The battle with entrenched Firestone intensified when A. J. Foyt won the pole on Goodyears at a record speed of 161.233 mph. A 1965 Sport Fury (*opposite top*) marked Plymouth's first foray into Indy's pace car realm.

STARTING LINEUP

Average Field Qualifying Speed: 156.058

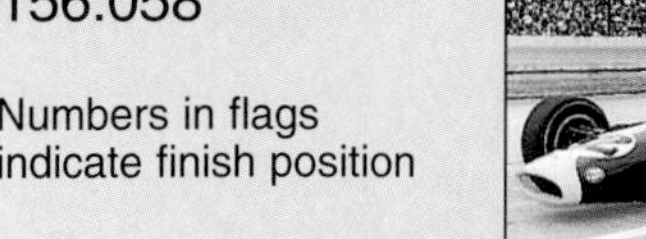

Numbers in flags indicate finish position

Dan Gurney

Billy Foster

Lloyd Ruby

Len Sutton

Mickey Rupp

Jim Clark

Parnelli Jones

Bobby Unser

Johnny Rutherford

Gordon Johncock

POLE POSITION
Qualifying Speed: 161.233

A. J. Foyt

Mario Andretti

Al Miller

Bob Veith

Jim McElreath

Don Branson

Walt Hansgen

Bud Tingelstad

Joe Leonard

Chuck Rodee

Bill Cheesbourg

Jerry Grant

Jim Hurtubise

Roger McCluskey

Chuck Stevenson

Johnny Boyd

Al Unser

George Snider

Arnie Knepper

Bobby Johns

Ronnie Duman

Eddie Johnson

Masten Gregory

SUNDAY, MAY 23: Ward completes a four-lap qualifying run, but his speed of 153.623 is too slow to bump Bill Cheesbourg. Ward falls .151 mph short of making his 15th straight race.

THE RACE

Start: Jim Clark challenges A. J. Foyt at the green flag and noses ahead to lead the first lap. Foyt comes back to lead lap two, but Clark regains the upper hand on the third pass and eventually builds a quarter-lap cushion. Jim Hurtubise's Novi drops out after one lap with transmission woes.

Lap 66: Clark pits for fuel, and his Wood Brothers crew of NASCAR fame gets him out in just 19.8 seconds. Foyt leads until he stops eight laps later for 44 seconds, giving the lead back to Clark.

Lap 70: Bobby Unser, who is running in the top 10, drops out with a broken oil fitting. The Novi V-8 has run its last race lap at the Speedway.

Lap 115: With Clark still well ahead, Foyt pulls into the pits with a damaged gearbox, his race over. Parnelli Jones moves into second place.

Finish: Clark breezes to a two-lap victory at a record clip of 150.686 mph, averaging less than one minute per lap. It is the seventh year in a row a record speed is set.

Clark's race speed, including pit stops, nearly matches the four-lap qualifying record set just three years earlier by Jones, the first driver to top 150.

Tradition takes a holiday this year. Clark, who leads 190 laps, is the first foreign driver to win since Dario Resta in 1916. His Lotus is the first rear-engine car to win, he gives Ford its first 500 victory, and he ends a string of Offenhauser victories that dates to 1946.

One tradition that endures is that Firestone wins for the 42nd straight time. Several cars run on Goodyears, with Don Branson the highest finisher in eighth.

Mario Andretti finishes third, just six seconds back of Jones, to win Rookie of the Year. Newcomer Gordon Johncock is fifth in a three-year-old Watson-Offy, the only front-engine roadster among the top nine finishers.

Cars are impounded after the race (*below*) to go through USAC's final inspection. Three-time starter Johnny Rutherford made the switch to a rear-engine car (*bottom*) and qualified 11th in the No. 24 Racing Associates Halibrand-Offenhauser. However, he dropped out early when his transmission broke. A. J. Foyt proved a quick study when he jumped to a rear-engine chassis. He put his Lotus-Ford Sheraton-Thompson Special (*opposite top*) on the pole. Foyt is flanked by car owners Shirley Murphy, left, and Bill Ansted, right. The starting field strings out loosely behind the Plymouth pace car (*opposite bottom*).

Whenever Mickey Thompson filed an entry at Indy, one thing was always a certainty: His machine would be a radical design.

Long before most people thought a rear-engine car would work at Indy, Thompson entered one powered by a hopped-up aluminum Buick V-8. But his M/T Challenger went even further against established trends.

During practice, driver Bob Mathouser had his hands full controlling the thundering monster. Powered by a naturally aspirated small-block Chevy V-8, the car thad a tendency to hop sideways in the turns.

But on the final day of qualifications, Mathouser endeavored to put the beast in the show. After two or three harrowing laps, the engine threw a rod.

What made the car so unique? The fact that Thompson, one of the first proponents of rear-engine Indy cars, had pinned his hopes on a front-engine car, after nearly everyone else had gone to "funny cars," was one. But perhaps the strangest thing of all was the use of a concept that allowed Mathouser and the strange car to establish a record speed of 153.374. This was the fastest lap ever attained by a racer with front-wheel drive, something that hadn't been seen at Indy since the last "puller" Novi failed to make the race in 1955.

1965

When rookie Gordon Johncock drove to an outstanding fifth-place finish, no one gave much thought to the well broken-in roadster he was wheeling. However, his Weinberger Homes Special had a long, successful past.

Built in 1962 by A. J. Watson for the Bill Forbes Racing Team, the roadster survived a spin and contact with the wall. Despite seven minutes to repair the damage, and slowed by a broken front sway bar, Shorty Templeman soldiered the racer home in 11th place. In '63, Jim McElreath and the now familiar white and red machine finished sixth. In '64, Dave Laycock rebuilt the Forbes beauty, and Lloyd Ruby drove it to third place. And when Johncock brought home the venerable racer in fifth in '65, it was against a field containing 27 rear-engine cars.

When Johncock qualified the racer at 155.012, the four-time Indy veteran went into the books as the fastest unblown roadster in 500 history. Its '65 finish made it the last roadster to go the distance at Indy. It was arguably Indy's most successful roadster: In four straight years, it completed the entire 2000 miles, a feat unequaled by any car of its type.

The field goes through the short chute between turns one and two on the pace lap (*opposite top*). When the green flag comes out, pole winner A. J. Foyt pulls ahead of Jim Clark and Dan Gurney (*opposite middle*). Eddie Johnson is about to be overtaken by Parnelli Jones and Clark (*opposite bottom*). Clark tastes the fruits of victory (*left* and *above*) won in his green Lotus-Ford (*below*).

RESULTS

NO.	DRIVER	CAR	ENTRANT	ENGINE	CYL	DISP	CHASSIS	COLOR	QUAL SPD	START	FIN	LAPS / SPEED / REASON OUT
82	Jim Clark	Lotus/Ford	Team Lotus (Overseas) Ltd.	Ford R	8	255	Lotus	green, yellow	160.729	2	1	200-150.686
98	Parnelli Jones	Agajanian Hurst	J. C. Agajanian	Ford R	8	255	Kuzma-Lotus	gold, ivory	158.625	5	2	200-149.200
12	Mario Andretti	Dean Van Lines	Auto Techs, Inc.	Ford R	8	255	Brawner	white, blue	158.849	4	3	200-149.121
74	Al Miller	Alderman Ford-Lotus	Jerry Alderman Ford Sales	Ford R	8	255	Lotus	white, blue	157.805	7	4	200-146.581
76	Gordon Johncock	Weinberger Homes	Weinberger & Wilseck Ent.	Offy F	4	251	Watson	white, blue	155.012	14	5	200-146.417
81	Mickey Rupp	G. C. Murphy	Pete Salemi	Offy R	4	251	Gerhardt	white, blue	154.839	15	6	198-flagged
83	Bobby Johns	Lotus/Ford	Team Lotus (Overseas) Ltd.	Ford R	8	255	Lotus	green, yellow	155.481	22	7	197-flagged
4	Don Branson	Wynn	Leader Cards, Inc.	Ford R	8	255	Watson	yellow, red	155.501	18	8	197-flagged
45	Al Unser	Sheraton-Thompson	Ansted-Thompson Racing	Ford R	8	255	Lola	pearl, red, blue	154.440	32	9	196-flagged
23	Eddie Johnson	Chapman	H. Allen Chapman	Offy F	4	251	Watson	maroon, white	153.998	28	10	195-flagged
7	Lloyd Ruby	Dupont Golden 7	David R. McManus	Ford R	8	255	Halibrand	gld, red, wht	157.246	9	11	184-blown engine
16	Len Sutton	Bryant Heat & Cool	Jim Robbins & Vollstedt	Ford R	8	255	Vollstedt	gold, maroon	156.121	12	12	177-flagged
14	Johnny Boyd	Geo. Bryant Proj	Geo. Bryant Racing Projects	Ford R	8	255	BRP	blue, white	155.172	29	13	140-gear box
53	Walt Hansgen	MG-Liquid Susp	Kjell H. Qvale	Offy R	4	251	Huffaker	orange, black	155.662	21	14	117-fuel line
1	A. J. Foyt	Sheraton-Thompson	Ansted-Thompson Racing	Ford R	8	255	Lotus	pearl, red, blue	161.233	1	15	115-rear end gears
5	Bud Tingelstad	American Red Ball	Lindsey Hopkins	Ford R	8	255	Lola	wht, gold, red	154.672	24	16	115-hit wall T3
66	Billy Foster	Jim Robbins	Jim Robbins & Vollstedt	Offy R	4	251	Vollstedt	maroon, gold	158.416	6	17	85-water manifold
18	Arnie Knepper	Konstant Hot	Vatis Enterprises, Inc.	Offy F	4	251	Kurtis	black, yellow	154.513	19	18	80-cylinder wall
9	Bobby Unser	STP Gas Treatment	STP Division Studebaker	Novi *4F	8	167	Ferguson	red, chrome	157.467	8	19	69-oil connection
52	Jim McElreath	Zink-Urschel Trckbrnr	Zink, Urschel, Slick, Inc.	Offy R	4	251	Brabham	red, white	155.878	13	20	66-rear end gears
94	George Snider	Gerhardt Offy	Fred Gerhardt	Offy R	4	251	Gerhardt	lavender, yelo	154.825	16	21	64-rear end gears
65	Ronnie Duman	Travelon Trailer	Ernest L. Ruiz	Offy R	4	251	Gerhardt	purple, gold	154.533	25	22	62-rear end gears
41	Masten Gregory	Geo. Bryant & Staff	Geo. Bryant Racing Projects	Ford R	8	255	BRP	blue, white	154.540	31	23	59-lost oil pressure
54	Bob Veith	MG-Liquid Susp	Kjell H. Qvale	Offy R	4	251	Huffaker	red, white	156.427	10	24	58-burned piston
88	Chuck Stevenson	Vita Fresh OJ	Gordon Van Liew	Offy F	4	251	Kuzma	pearl, orng, gld	154.725	26	25	50-burned piston
17	Dan Gurney	Yamaha	All American Racers, Inc.	Ford R	8	255	Lotus	white, blue	158.898	3	26	42-timing gears
48	Jerry Grant	Bardahl MG	Kjell H. Qvale	Offy R	4	251	Huffaker	yellow, black	154.606	17	27	30-magneto
19	Chuck Rodee	W. Weir's Mobilgas	Walter Weir, Jr.	Offy R	4	251	Halibrand	white, orange	154.546	30	28	28-rear end gears
29	Joe Leonard	All American Racers	All American Racers, Inc.	Ford R	8	255	Halibrand	wht, blue, red	154.268	27	29	27-oil leak
25	Roger McCluskey	All American Racers	All American Racers, Inc	Ford R	8	255	Halibrand	white, blue	155.186	23	30	18-clutch
24	Johnny Rutherford	Racing Associates	Racing Associates	Ford R	8	255	Halibrand	wht, blue, slvr	156.291	11	31	15-transmission
47	Bill Cheesbourg	WIFE Good Guy	Lane-Fulbright Racing Team	Offy R	4	251	Gerhardt	white, black	153.774	33	32	14-magneto
59	Jim Hurtubise	STP-Tombstone Life	Chemical Compounds Div.	Novi *F	8	168	Kurtis	red, gold, blk	156.863	20	33	1-transmission

* = supercharged R = rear engine F = front engine 4 = four-wheel drive

50th Race • May 30, 1966

Front-engine roadsters are nearly extinct for the 50th running of the 500, but the venerable Offenhauser engine stays alive with the help of artificial aspiration.

Veteran Bobby Grim drives the only roadster in the race, a Watson-turbocharged Offy that starts 31st and is the slowest car in the field. Nine more Offys start, one other with a turbo, four with superchargers, and three naturally aspirated.

USAC rules allow 256-cid naturally aspirated engines and 171-cid engines with a turbo or supercharger. The Offy proves competitive in its new "blown" configuration, which includes a smaller block and shorter stroke, and Parnelli Jones qualifies fourth in a supercharged Offy.

Dual-cam Ford V-8s rule the Brickyard, however, with 24 on the grid.

Car owner Al Stein enters a Huffaker chassis powered by two Porsche flat six-cylinder engines, the first twin-engine car at the Speedway since 1946. Bill Cheesbourg practices in the Valvoline-sponsored car but fails to make a qualifying run.

PRACTICE AND QUALIFYING

WEDNESDAY, MAY 4: Grand Prix driver Jackie Stewart of Scotland passes his rookie test in a Lola-Ford. He joins two Formula 1 champions in Gasoline Alley: Graham Hill and 1965 winner Jim Clark.

MONDAY, MAY 9: National champion Mario Andretti turns a lap at 164.926 mph in a year-old Brawner-Ford, nearly three mph faster than A. J. Foyt's qualifying record. Foyt, in a Coyote-Ford, and George Snider, in a Lotus-Ford, reach 162.1 as they draft with each other. Three others top 160 in practice.

WEDNESDAY, MAY 11: Andretti and friends push the speed envelope further. Andretti runs 167.5 mph, Clark 165.7, and Dan Gurney 164.8.

SATURDAY, MAY 14: Records fall on Pole Day. Snider qualifies at a record 162.521 mph, but it lasts a short time as Andretti roars to a four-lap average of 165.899.

➔

Mercury's new Comet Cyclone GT was the pace car for the 50th running of the 500, and it shows the evolution of the automobile when lined up next to the Stoddard-Dayton tourer that paced the 1911 field (*above*). Chief Steward Harlan Fengler, himself an Indy competitor in the Twenties, shook down the pace car (*opposite bottom*), but Benson Ford drove it on race day, his second stint as the pacemaker in three years. Long-time team owner J. C. Agajanian entered a pair of rear-engine, Offy-powered Shrike chassis in '66 (*opposite top*). Agajanian is seen with team drivers Parnelli Jones, in car No. 98, and rookie Dick Atkins, in No. 97. Only 1963 winner Jones made the field, starting from the fourth position.

STARTING LINEUP

Average Field Qualifying Speed: 160.251

Numbers in flags indicate finish position

George Snider

Gordon Johncock

Don Branson

Billy Foster

Graham Hill

Jim Clark

Lloyd Ruby

Chuck Hulse

Jackie Stewart

Johnny Boyd

POLE POSITION
Qualifying Speed: 165.899

Mario Andretti

Parnelli Jones

Jim McElreath

Jerry Grant

Rodger Ward

A. J. Foyt

Roger McCluskey

Cale Yarborough

Bud Tingelstad

Al Miller

Ronnie Duman

Mel Kenyon

Joe Leonard

Al Unser

Arnie Knepper

Eddie Johnson

Larry Dickson

Gary Congdon

Dan Gurney

Jim Hurtubise

Carl Williams

Bobby Unser

Bobby Grim

Clark waves off a run of more than 164 mph in a daring attempt to top Andretti. Clark settles for 164.144 late in the day to line up second and push Snider to the outside of row one. Ford V-8s power all three.

The death of Chuck Rodee in a Turn 1 crash tempers the euphoria over the record speeds. Rodee becomes the third driver to die during a qualifying attempt when he crashes on a warmup lap.

SUNDAY, MAY 15: Foyt, back after a Pole Day crash, and Gurney are fastest of five second-day qualifiers to line up 18th and 19th.

THE RACE

Start: Billy Foster, who starts on the outside of row four, gets squeezed up into the wall as the field takes the green flag, triggering a huge pileup on the front straight that brings out the red flag. Though there are no serious injuries, the wreck eliminates 11 cars, including those of A. J. Foyt, Dan Gurney, and the entire sixth and 11th rows.

Restart: Following a delay of one hour, 24 minutes, the field lines up in single file according to qualifying speed. After only 10 seconds of green-flag racing, Johnny Boyd hits the Turn 1 wall, bringing out the yellow flag.

Lap 17: Leader Mario Andretti slows as his engine starts to smoke. Jim Clark passes Andretti for the lead.

Lap 22: George Snider, running fourth, spins in Turn 2 and is hit by Chuck Hulse, who is sixth, eliminating both.

Lap 27: Andretti, his car still trailing smoke, gets black-flagged and becomes the 16th car out of the race.

Lap 35: Lloyd Ruby slips underneath Parnelli Jones in Turn 1 to take over second place behind Clark.

Lap 64: Clark spins in Turn 4 but keeps it off the wall and ducks into the pits, giving the lead to Ruby.

Lap 82: Clark, back in front after Ruby pits, spins again, this time in Turn 3. He does three complete spins, miraculously avoids contact, and pits for fresh tires. Ruby regains the lead; Clark and Jackie Stewart pursue.

Lap 147: Ruby leads by nearly a lap when smoke starts pouring from his engine. Ruby pits and his crew spends eight minutes stopping an oil leak, giving the lead to Stewart and putting Clark second.

Lap 161: Al Unser, running third, spins and hits the Turn 4 wall.

Lap 192: Stewart leads by more than a lap and has victory in sight when his Ford V-8 suddenly loses oil pressure. Stewart immediately shuts down the engine and coasts to a halt on the grass in Turn 4.

Surprised Lola teammate Graham Hill flashes by and takes the lead.

Finish: Hill faces no challenges in the final laps and wins by 41 seconds over Clark's Lotus-Ford. Jim McElreath is third and Gordon Johncock fourth. The first three ride on Firestones and Johncock on Goodyears. All four have Ford V-8s.

Vince Granatelli claims Clark's STP Lotus is ahead at the finish, but the protest is thrown out. Hill is the first rookie winner since George Souders in 1927 and the second straight from the United Kingdom. Only seven cars finish, the fewest ever, and the winning speed of 144.317 is some six mph below the record because of six caution flags.

Graham Hill's American Red Ball Special (*opposite top*) was one of three Lolas entered by owner John Mecom, Jr. Englishman Hill and fellow Formula 1 driver Jackie Stewart drove Ford-powered versions, and American teammate Rodger Ward used a supercharged Offy. Parnelli Jones's No. 98 Shrike goes back to the garage after a practice run (*opposite middle*). Jones dropped out of the race in 14th place with wheel-bearing failure. Rookie Greg Weld had one of those days on May 22, the last qualifying day. First, he crashed the No. 15 STP Novi (*opposite bottom*), and then crashed again in a different car later that afternoon. Weld's Novi was the last of the venerable V-8s to show up at the Speedway. *Right:* Joe Leonard discusses qualifying strategy with All American racers owner Dan Gurney, who had a four-car team—including one for himself—that used his new Eagle chassis. The aluminum tub of Rodger Ward's No 26 Lola *sans* engine and running gear rests in the garage area (*below*). Entertainers Tom and Dick Smothers (*bottom*) were among the celebrities in the 500 Festival parade.

When Art Malone crashed his car, Speedway Medical Director Dr. Thomas Hanna noticed someting odd. When Malone hopped out of the car, he wasn't wearing any shoes. Art had trouble getting down into the cramped rear-engine cars, and had removed his shoes in order to make a more comfortable fit.

When confronted about the missing footwear, Malone quickly pointed out to Hanna that there was no rule that said a driver must wear shoes. A quick look at the USAC rule book confirmed Art's position.

"That's something you just didn't consider," Hanna said. "I guess everyone assumed the drivers would all be wearing shoes. We had something similar once before. The rules stated exactly how a helmet should be constructed, but didn't say a word about the wearing of one being mandatory."

To be sure, at the next USAC rules meeting, the wearing of shoes in a racing car was made compulsory.

Front-row starters closely follow the pace car as it leads the field away from the starting grid before another full-house crowd (*right*). Just as the green flag flies, chaos breaks out on the front straightaway, sending crewmen rushing to the track to check on their drivers (*below*). Billy Foster hit the outside wall, touching off a multi-car pileup that brought out the red flag. No one was seriously hurt, but 11 cars were knocked out in the mishap and the race was halted nearly an hour and a half. Among the casualties were the cars of two-time winner A. J. Foyt and three rookies who failed to complete a lap: Gary Congdon, Larry Dickson, and Cale Yarborough. Jim McElreath roars out of the pits in the No. 3 Brabham after a routine stop, while Gordon Johncock's No. 72 Gerhardt gets service (*bottom*). Graham Hill, the first rookie to win in 39 years (*opposite top*), celebrates in victory lane (*opposite, bottom left*) and later accepts a $12,500 check from STP President Andy Granatelli (*opposite, bottom right*). Hill collected a total of $156,297.

Many people wondered why Colin Chapman constructed Jim Clark's new Lotus with an extended wheelbase. The car didn't handle nearly as well as its predecessors, and Clark spun the machine twice during the race. The reason for the longer wheelbase was simple. Chapman had expected to use a 16-cylinder BRM engine, which was nearly twice as long as the Ford V-8. During tests at their Folkingham, England, facility, BRM claimed the 4.2-liter power plant had topped 200 mph. This was an advantage Chapman looked forward to enjoying.

With expectations of Clark qualifying on May 14, Team Lotus was anxiously awaiting the engine's arrival in Indy. However, when employees arrived at the BRM works in early May, they found the engine shop in disarray. Burglars had broken in and stolen most of the major engine parts for the 16-cylinder engine. There was no way they could replace the components in time for Clark to qualify.

Chapman installed an Indy-Ford V-8. And even with the two spins, Clark very nearly won the 500.

RESULTS

NO.	DRIVER	CAR	ENTRANT	ENGINE	CYL	DISP	CHASSIS	COLOR	QUAL SPD	START	FIN	LAPS / SPEED / REASON OUT
24	Graham Hill	American Red Ball	John Mecom, Jr.	Ford R	8	255	Lola	wht, red, gold	159.243	15	1	200-144.317
19	Jim Clark	STP Gas Treatment	STP Division Studebaker	Ford R	8	255	Lotus	red, white	164.144	2	2	200-143.843
3	Jim McElreath	Zink-Urschel-Slick	Zink-Urschel-Slick	Ford R	8	255	Brabham	red, white	160.908	7	3	200-143.742
72	Gordon Johncock	Weinberger Homes	W. & W. Enterprises	Ford R	8	255	Gerhardt	blue, wht, orng	161.059	6	4	200-143.084
94	Mel Kenyon	Gerhardt Offy	Fred Gerhardt	Offy R	4	251	Gerhardt	lavender, wht	158.555	17	5	198-flagged
43	Jackie Stewart	Bowes Seal Fast	John Mecom, Jr.	Ford R	8	255	Lola	white, blk, red	159.972	11	6	190-oil pressure
54	Eddie Johnson	Valvoline II	Vatis Enterprises, Inc.	Offy R	4	251	Huffaker	mroon, wht, gld	158.898	29	7	175-stalled
11	Bobby Unser	Vita Fresh	Gordon Van Liew	Offy T R	4	168	Huffaker	orng, pearl, gld	159.109	28	8	171-flagged
6	Joe Leonard	Yamaha Eagle	All American Racers	Ford R	8	255	Eagle	blue, white	159.560	20	9	170-engine trouble
88	Jerry Grant	Bardahl-Pacesetter Homes	All American Racers	Ford R	8	255	Eagle	blue, slvr, grn	160.335	10	10	167-flagged
14	Lloyd Ruby	Bardahl Eagle	All American Racers	Ford R	8	255	Eagle	pearl, maroon	162.433	5	11	166-cam stud
18	Al Unser	STP Oil Treatment	STP Division Studebaker	Ford R	8	255	Lotus	red, white	162.372	23	12	161-hit wall T4
8	Roger McCluskey	G.C. Murphy	Lindsey Hopkins	Ford R	8	255	Eagle	blue, white	159.271	21	13	129-oil line
98	Parnelli Jones	Agajanian's Rev 500	J. C. Agajanian	Offy *R	4	168	Shrike	blue, white	162.484	4	14	87-wheel bearing
26	Rodger Ward	Bryant Heat & Cool	John Mecom, Jr.	Offy *R	4	168	Lola	white, blue	159.468	13	15	74-handling
77	Carl Williams	Dayton Steel Wheel	George Walther, Jr.	Ford R	8	255	Gerhardt	blue	159.645	25	16	38-oil line
56	Jim Hurtubise	Gerhardt Offy	Fred Gerhardt	Offy T R	4	168	Gerhardt	orange, ivory	159.208	22	17	29-oil line
1	Mario Andretti	Dean Van Lines	Dean Racing Enterprises	Ford R	8	255	Brawner	white, blue	165.899	1	18	27-valve
82	George Snider	Sheraton-Thompson	Ansted-Thompson Racing	Ford R	8	255	Coyote	wht, red, blue	162.521	3	19	22-wreck T1
12	Chuck Hulse	Wynn's	Leader Cards, Inc.	Ford R	8	255	Watson	yelo, red, wht	160.844	8	20	22-hit No. 82
22	Bud Tingelstad	Federal Engineering	Federal Automotive Assoc.	Offy *R	4	168	Gerhardt	blue, white	159.144	27	21	16-radiator
28	Johnny Boyd	Prestone	George R. Bryant	Ford R	8	255	B.R.P	yelo, red, gld	159.384	14	22	5-hit wall T1
4	Don Branson	Leader Card Racer 4	Leader Cards, Inc.	Ford R	8	255	Gerhardt	blue, white	160.385	9	23	0-wreck FS
27	Billy Foster	Jim Robbins	J. M. Robbins	Ford R	8	255	Vollstedt	red, yellow	149.490	12	24	0-wreck FS
53	George Congdon	Valvoline	Vatis Enterprises, Inc.	Offy R	4	251	Huffaker	wht, blue, gld	158.688	16	25	0-wreck FS
2	A. J. Foyt	Sheraton-Thompson	Ansted-Thompson Racing	Ford R	8	255	Lotus	wht, blue, red	161.355	18	26	0-wreck FS
31	Dan Gurney	All American Racers Eagle	All American Racers	Ford R	8	255	Eagle	blue, white	160.499	19	27	0-wreck FS
66	Cale Yarborough	Jim Robbins	J. M. Robbins	Ford R	8	255	Vollstedt	red, yellow	159.794	24	28	0-wreck FS
37	Arnie Knepper	Sam Liosi	D.V.S., Inc.	Ford R	8	255	Cecil	blue, white	159.440	26	29	0-wreck FS
75	Al Miller	Alderman Ford Lotus	Jerry Alderman Ford Sales	Ford R	8	255	Lotus	white, blue	158.681	30	30	0-wreck FS
39	Bobby Grim	Racing Associates	Herb Porter	Offy TF	4	168	Watson	maroon, blk	158.367	31	31	0-wreck FS
34	Larry Dickson	Michner Petroleum	Michner Petroleum, Inc.	Ford R	8	255	Lola	black, gold	159.144	32	32	0-wreck FS
96	Ronnie Duman	Harrison	J. Frank Harrison	Ford R	8	255	Eisert	gold, wht, blk	158.646	33	33	0-wreck FS

* = supercharged T = turbocharged R = rear engine F = front engine

1967

51st Race • May 30-31, 1967

Andy Granatelli ditches the ill-fated Novi V-8 and focuses on a new engine that makes a stronger statement despite being nearly silent.

Granatelli installs a Pratt & Whitney turbine engine on the left side of a new four-wheel-drive chassis, slaps STP logos all over the car and its crew, hires Parnelli Jones to do the driving, and creates even greater controversy than the now dominant rear-engine cars.

Despite the bulky appearance of the turbine car and the added burden of 4WD, it weighs 1400 pounds, just 50 over the minimum. The turbine weighs 260 pounds and makes about 550 bhp.

Jones dubs the quiet-running turbine "Silent Sam," while the press calls it the "Whooshmobile." Among a record 90 entries, the red No. 40 STP turbine seems to get more attention during the month of May than the rest combined. Nervous competitors warn that the revolutionary entry threatens to render their piston engines obsolete.

When qualifying ends, the field has 23 Ford dual-cam V-8s, one stock-block pushrod Ford V-8, eight blown Offys, one turbine, and 14 different kinds of chassis. For the first time, a front-engine car fails to make the field; Jim Hurtubise's Mallard roadster gets bumped the last day.

PRACTICE AND QUALIFYING

SATURDAY, MAY 13: Dan Gurney emerges as the driver to beat on Pole Day when he qualifies at a record 167.224 mph in a Ford-powered Eagle. Gurney's record and claim to the pole last just three minutes, however. Mario Andretti, next on the track in a Hawk-Ford, averages 168.982 mph and just misses 170 on his best lap to grab the pole. Gordon Johncock is third fastest at 166.559.

Parnelli Jones, one of the favorites to win the pole, is sixth fastest in the side-engine STP turbine car at 166.075. All five cars ahead of him are rear-engine Fords.

SUNDAY, May 14: Rain washes out second-day qualifying.

SUNDAY, MAY 21: Two of the biggest names in racing struggle to make the field on Bump Day. Jackie Stewart, 1966 Rookie of the Year, qualifies 29th in a Lola-Ford, and defending winner Graham Hill bumps his way into the last row in an STP-sponsored Lotus-Ford.

THE RACE

Start: Polesitter Mario Andretti leads through the first two turns, but Parnelli Jones blows by everyone on the backstretch in the STP turbine to take charge on the opening lap.

→

Above: Texan Johnny Rutherford, "Lone Star J.R." to his fans, qualified for his fourth 500, but spun and crashed halfway through the race. *Opposite:* Chevrolet had a big presence in '67, with its new Camaro serving as the pace car (top) and a fleet of pickups (middle) available for a variety of duties at the Speedway. These nurses (bottom left) were part of the infield hospital's staff. Pole winner Mario Andretti and wife Dee Ann are with their sons, future Indy 500 competitors Michael and Jeff (bottom right).

STARTING LINEUP

Average Field Qualifying Speed: 164.173

Numbers in flags indicate finish position

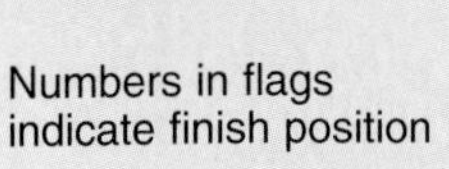

POLE POSITION
Qualifying Speed: 168.982

Gordon Johncock

Parnelli Jones

Al Unser

Bobby Grim

Wally Dallenbach

Dan Gurney

Joe Leonard

Bobby Unser

Jim McElreath

Mel Kenyon

Mario Andretti

A. J. Foyt

Lloyd Ruby

George Snider

Art Pollard

Every driver worth his salt dreams of winning the 500. But if anybody could have dreamt exactly how *they'd win the race, A. J. Foyt could.*

A night or two before the 1967 race, A. J. had a dream that he was coming around the final turn to take the checkered flag, when he found the track blocked. He had to gear down and weave his way through a maze of twisted, wrecked racing machinery.

On race day, after Parnelli Jones and the STP turbine fell out of the lead with four laps to go, Foyt concentrated on avoiding trouble. "I had taken the white flag, gone down the back stretch, and was entering the north turn, when that dream suddenly came back to me," Foyt recalled. "I thought maybe I'd better slow it down and take a good look coming out the fourth turn."

What Foyt saw was the end of an accident that involved five cars. The track was all but blocked. Bobby Grim, Chuck Hulse, and Carl Williams had bounced off one another and the wall. Bud Tingelstad and Larry Dickson were still spinning as Foyt began to thread his way past the first three cars. "I dropped her down to low gear," A. J. said. "I'd made up my mind if any of them spun back into my way, I was going to push them clear across the finish line."

Thankfully, that wasn't necessary. But if he hadn't remembered his dream, Foyt might not have taken his third checkered flag at Indy.

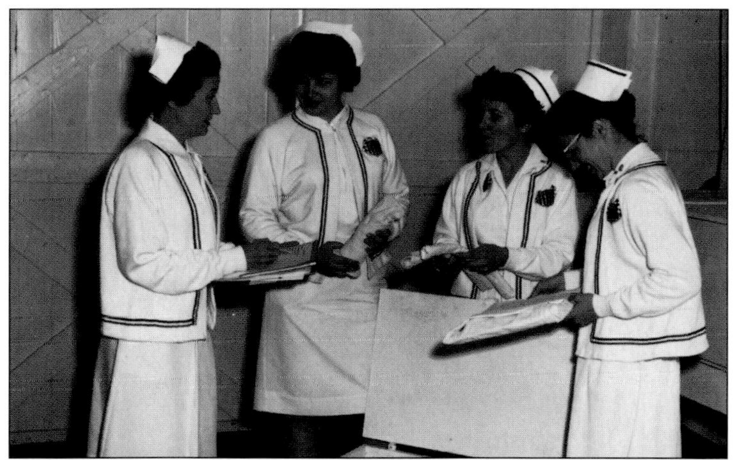

Arnie Knepper

Larry Dickson

Denis Hulme

Chuck Hulse

Jerry Grant

Al Miller

Ronnie Duman

Cale Yarborough

Carl Williams

Lee Roy Yarbrough

Jackie Stewart

Jochen Rindt

Jim Clark

Johnny Rutherford

Roger McCluskey

Bud Tingelstad

Bob Veith

Graham Hill

Lap 6: Carrying a nearly full fuel load, Jones turns the fastest lap of the race, 164.926 mph, just over one mph slower than his qualifying speed.

Lap 14: Andretti pits with a blown clutch as rain starts to fall, bringing out the caution flag.

Lap 18: USAC halts the race because of the rain and ultimately postpones it to the next day. The delay gives Andretti's crew ample time to change his clutch on pit road, but he lines up at the rear of the field.

Restart: Jones sprints away from the field on the single-file restart and sets the pattern for the day. The turbine furnishes abundant power on the straightaways, and the four-wheel-drive chassis lets Jones run a lower line through the turns.

Lap 23: Defending winner Graham Hill, in an STP-sponsored Lotus-Ford, retires with a burned piston.

Lap 35: Hill's teammate, 1965 winner Jim Clark, exits with a burned piston.

Lap 52: NASCAR star Lee Roy Yarbrough spins in Turn 4 for the second time and almost collects Jones, who narrowly avoids a collision and hangs on to the lead. Rookie Yarbrough recovers and stays in the race.

Lap 58: Andretti loses a wheel in Turn 1 and spins into the infield, out of the race. Jones still leads.

Lap 99: Cale Yarborough, another NASCAR regular, spins at the north end of the track. Lee Roy Yarbrough and Lloyd Ruby (in relief of George Snider) hit the wall trying to avoid the spinning car and are out. Cale Yarborough restarts, but crashes later in the race.

Lap 131: Jones makes his second pit stop, allowing A. J. Foyt to move into first.

Lap 150: When Foyt makes his second stop, Jones resumes command and builds a half-lap cushion.

Lap 193: Gordon Johncock loses a wheel in Turn 3, spins, and stops on the track, bringing out the caution flag. Jones leads Foyt by 43 seconds.

Lap 197: A resounding roar from the fans in Turn 4 announces trouble for Jones, who rolls slowly toward the pit entrance on the inside of the track. After leading 171 laps, a $6 transmission bearing fails in the turbine car, just three laps short of giving Jones his second win.

Foyt, having chased Jones all day, is in command for a third victory.

Lap 200: As Foyt comes around on his final lap, Bobby Grim hits the wall on the north end of the main straight, causing Chuck Hulse and Carl Williams to collide. Bud Tingelstad and Larry Dickson spin to avoid the others, and the front straight is strewn with wrecked cars and obscured by smoke.

Foyt slows, drops to the inside, and carefully steers his way through the wreckage to become the fourth three-time champion in 500 history.

The red flag flies to end the race as Foyt, who leads 27 laps, crosses the finish line. Al Unser is second two laps down, Foyt's teammate, Joe Leonard, is third, and New Zealander Denis Hulme—destined to win the '67 Formula 1 championship—comes home fourth to be Rookie of the Year.

Jones winds up sixth. Owner Andy Granatelli suffers a crushing defeat, but the turbine car makes his STP oil additive a household name.

Despite 10 caution flags, Foyt averages a record 151.207 mph. Goodyear tires win for the first time since 1919, snapping Firestone's 43-race streak. Ford sweeps the first five spots with its 255-cid, dual-cam V-8, the third straight win for this engine.

When A. J. Foyt won the Indy 500 for the third time, he entered a very elite band of outstanding drivers. At the time, Louie Meyer, Wilbur Shaw, and Mauri Rose were the only other drivers to win the 500 three times. But Foyt entered another, possibly even more exclusive group that day.

Just as Foyt had done with his bright orange Coyotes, Ray Harroun, Meyer, and Shaw had all designed and/or built their winning cars. Harroun did it in 1911. Meyer—with some help from Myron Stevens—accomplished it in 1936, a year before Shaw attained the same plateau.

Opposite page: Andy Granatelli and his STP turbine (top row) were the talk of the Brickyard. Granatelli let television host Johnny Carson try the car on for size (bottom left). Parnelli Jones qualified the side-engine No. 40 (bottom row, middle and right) sixth, though some rivals thought he was sandbagging on speed. *This page:* NASCAR star Lee Roy Yarbrough wrecked in practice (top), but qualified for his first Indy start in a different car. Mario Andretti, the reigning national champion, emerged as a favorite at Indy when he placed his Hawk-Ford (middle) on the pole. A portrait of the front-row drivers (left) includes, from left, up-and-comer Gordon Johncock, Dan Gurney, and Andretti.

The Camaro pace car provides an ideal vantage point to capture the field on film (*right*) and is the best seat in the house for the parade lap (*below*) before the green flag drops. The broad-shouldered, offset turbine car on the outside of the second row offers a marked contrast to the narrower racers that make up the rest of the field. A. J. Foyt led just 27 laps on his Coyote-Ford but was in the right place at the right time when a transmission bearing failed on Parnelli Jones's STP turbine four laps from the finish. Foyt's dogged pursuit of the faster turbine-powered car and skillful avoidance of a last-lap wreck paid off with his third victory in seven years (*opposite top*). Foyt takes a victory lap with his wife, Lucy, and the Borg-Warner trophy (*opposite, bottom left*) and accepts congratulations from Speedway owner Tony Hulman at the annual victory banquet (*opposite, bottom right*).

RESULTS

NO.	DRIVER	CAR	ENTRANT	ENGINE	CYL	DISP	CHASSIS	COLOR	QUAL SPD	START	FIN	LAPS / SPEED / REASON OUT
14	A. J. Foyt	Sheraton-Thompson	Ansted-Thompson Racing	Ford R	8	255	Coyote	orange, white	166.289	4	1	200-151.207
5	Al Unser	Retzloff Chemical	Mecom Racing Enterprises	Ford R	8	255	Lola	wht, blue, blk	164.594	9	2	198-flagged
4	Joe Leonard	Sheraton-Thompson	A. J. Foyt, Jr.	Ford R	8	255	Coyote	orange, black	166.098	5	3	197-flagged
69	Denis Hulme	City of Daytona Beach	Smokey Yunick	Ford R	8	255	Eagle	gold, black	163.376	24	4	197-flagged
2	Jim McElreath	J. Zink Trackburner	John S. Zink	Ford R	8	255	Moore	red, white	164.241	11	5	197-flagged
40	Parnelli Jones	STP Oil Treatment	STP Div. of Studebaker Corp.	Turbine 4	0	AIA 23.9	Granatelli	red, black	166.075	6	6	196-gear box
8	Chuck Hulse	Hopkins	Interstate Racer Team	Offy T R	4	168	Lola	pearl, red, prpl	162.925	27	7	195-wrecked FS
16	Art Pollard	Thermo King A/C	D. Gerhardt & P. Casey	Offy T R	4	168	Gerhardt	wht, blue, pink	163.897	13	8	195-flagged
6	Bobby Unser	Rislone	Leader Cards, Inc.	Ford R	8	255	Eagle	blk, wht, yelo, red	164.752	8	9	193-flagged
41	Carl Williams	George R. Bryant	Geo. R. Bryant Racing Team	Ford R	8	255	B.R.P.	brown, gold	163.696	23	10	189-wrecked FS
46	Bob Veith	Thermo King A/C	Fred Gerhardt	Offy TR	4	168	Gerhardt	brown, silver	162.580	28	11	189-flagged
3	Gordon Johncock	Gilmore Broadcasting	Johncock Racing Team	Ford R	8	255	Gerhardt	blue, wht, red	166.559	3	12	188-spun T3
39	Bobby Grim	Racing Associates	Racing Associates	Offy TR	4	168	Gerhardt	pearl maroon	164.084	12	13	187-wrecked FS
10	Bud Tingelstad	Federal Engineering	Federal Automotive Assoc.	Ford R	8	255	Gerhardt	wht, blue, gld	163.228	25	14	182-spun FS
22	Larry Dickson	Vita Fresh OJ	Gordon Van Liew	Ford R	8	255	Lotus	pearl, orng, gld	162.543	21	15	180-spun FS
15	Mel Kenyon	Thermo King A/C	Fred Gerhardt	Offy TR	4	168	Gerhardt	blue, white	163.778	14	16	177-wrecked T3
21	Cale Yarborough	Byant Heat & Cool	Vollstedt Enterprises, Inc.	Ford R	8	255	Vollstedt	yellow, red	162.830	20	17	176-wrecked T3
24	Jackie Stewart	Bowes "Seal Fast"	Mecom Racing Ent., Inc.	Ford R	8	255	Lola	wht, red, blk	164.099	29	18	168-blown engine
12	Roger McCluskey	G. C. Murphy	Lindsey Hopkins	Ford R	8	255	Eagle	blue, pearl, red	165.563	22	19	165-blown engine
42	Jerry Grant	All American Racers Eagle	All American Racers, Inc.	Ford R	8	255	Eagle	blue, white	163.808	30	20	162-rings
74	Dan Gurney	Wagner Lockheed Brk. Fld.	All American Racers, Inc.	Ford R	8	255	Eagle	blue, white	167.224	2	21	160-burned piston
19	Arnie Kneeper	M.V.S. Racers	M.V.S., Inc.	Ford R	8	255	Cecil	wht, red, yelo	162.900	18	22	158-blown engine
98	Ronnie Duman	Agajanian's Rev 500	J. C. Agajanian	Offy *R	4	168	Shrike	white, blue	162.903	17	23	153-fuel trouble
48	Jochen Rindt	Wagner Lockheed Brk. Fld.	All American Racers, Inc.	OHV Ford	8	303	Eagle	blue, white	163.051	32	24	108-valve
45	Johnny Rutherford	Weinberger Homes	W. & W. Enterprises	Ford R	8	255	Eagle	pearl, blk, gld	162.859	19	25	103-wrecked BS
26	George Snider/L. Ruby	Wagner Lockheed Brk. Fld.	Vel's Racing Team	Ford R	8	255	Mongoose	pearl, blue	164.256	10	26	99-wrecked T4
67	Lee Roy Yarbrough	J. Robbins Seat Belt	Jim Robbins Co.	Ford R	8	255	Vollstedt	pearl, blue, gld	163.066	26	27	87-wrecked T4
32	Al Miller	Cleaver-Brooks	Walter-Weir, Inc.	Ford R	8	255	Gerhardt	red, white	162.602	33	28	74-oil leak
53	Wally Dallenbach	Valvoline	Vatis Enterprises, Inc.	Offy TR	4	168	Huffaker	mroon, prl, blue	163.540	15	29	73-wrecked FS
1	Mario Andretti	Dean Van Lines	Dean Racing Ent., Inc.	Ford R	8	255	Hawk	white, blue	168.982	1	30	58-lost wheel T1
31	Jim Clark	STP Oil Treatment	STP Div. of Studebaker Corp.	Ford R	8	255	Lotus	red, white	163.213	16	31	35-burned piston
81	Graham Hill	STP Oil Treatment	STP Div. of Studebaker Corp.	Ford R	8	255	Lotus	red, white	163.317	31	32	23-burned piston
25	Lloyd Ruby	American Red Ball	Gene White Co. of Indy	Offy TR	4	168	Mongoose	wht, red, gld	165.229	7	33	3-valve

* = supercharged   T = turbocharged   R = rear engine   4 = four-wheel drive   AIA = anulus inlet area

1968

52nd Race • May 30, 1968

USAC puts the squeeze on Andy Granatelli's turbines, but the Whooshmobiles are faster than ever. The month of May, however, becomes another roller-coaster ride for the STP team.

New rules restrict the turbines to a 16-inch air inlet (down from 24 inches in 1967) to reduce their power. Granatelli counters by hiring Colin Chapman to build new wedge-shaped, four-wheel-drive Lotus chassis that carry the Pratt & Whitney turbine engine in the rear.

Granatelli enters five turbine cars and signs former winners Parnelli Jones and Graham Hill, and Grand Prix ace Jackie Stewart. At least one seat is open when practice opens at the Brickyard because of the death in April of 1965 winner Jim Clark, who was set to drive one of the new "flying doorstops."

Driver/builder Carroll Shelby also gets caught up in the turbine spin. He enters cars with General Electric turbines for New Zealanders Denis Hulme and Bruce McLaren. The side-engine, 4WD Shelbys are similar to Jones's '67 turbine car.

Turbines dominate the news, but turbochargers dominate the grid on race day. All 14 Offy four-cylinders are turbocharged. Four cars use Ford's new 168-cid turbo V-8. The Ford turbo is a short-stroke version of the 255-cid naturally aspirated V-8, and there are 10 of those in the field.

PRACTICE AND QUALIFYING

FRIDAY, MAY 3: Parnelli Jones stuns Gasoline Alley when he announces he is withdrawing from the race. Jones feels the No. 40 STP turbine, the same car that dominated the race last year, is incapable of winning with the new inlet restrictions.

TUESDAY, MAY 7: In a morning run, rookie Mike Spence, a Grand Prix driver, clocks the fastest lap so far at 169.555 mph in the wedge-shaped No. 60 STP turbine. Late in the afternoon, Spence goes out in the No. 30 STP turbine to shake down the handling. Spence gets too high entering Turn 1, loses control, and hits the wall. Spence dies of severe head injuries. After Spence's accident, Carroll Shelby withdraws his two turbine-powered cars because of safety concerns.

SUNDAY, MAY 12: Joe Leonard, driving the No. 40 STP turbine car vacated by Jones, spins in Turn 1 and backs into the wall. Leonard is okay, but the badly damaged car is withdrawn.

MONDAY, MAY 13: Granatelli and the STP team suffer another blow. Jackie Stewart announces he can't compete because of a wrist fracture suffered in a Formula 1 accident. Granatelli now has three cars and just one driver—Hill—only five days before qualifying starts.

THURSDAY, MAY 16: Leonard hits 170.422 in the No. 60 turbine and signs on as driver.

SATURDAY, MAY 18: The qualifying record falls quickly on Pole Day. Hill, the first to complete a four-lap run, averages 171.208 mph in the No. 70 STP turbine. It is the seventh straight year for a record qualifying speed.

About four hours later, Leonard tops teammate Hill with a speed of 171.559. Leonard shaves .43 seconds off Hill's time to put turbine cars in the first two starting spots. Bobby Unser is third fastest.

SUNDAY, MAY 26: Eight spots are still open on Bump Day, but rain keeps cars off the track until practice starts at 6:55 p.m. It is 7:32 and nearly dark when Bill Cheesbourg qualifies at 157.274 mph.

Bill Puterbaugh rejects an option to qualify the next morning and averages 157.301 mph to make the field. →

STARTING LINEUP

Average Field Qualifying Speed: 164.958

Numbers in flags indicate finish position

Bobby Unser [1] | Al Unser [26] | Gordon Johncock [27] | Wally Dallenbach [17] | Jerry Grant [23]

Graham Hill [19] | Lloyd Ruby [5] | A. J. Foyt [20] | Art Pollard [13] | Jim Malloy [22]

POLE POSITION
Qualifying Speed: 171.559

Joe Leonard [12] | Mario Andretti [33] | Roger McCluskey [29] | Dan Gurney [2] | Jim McElreath [14]

The Ford Torino GT pacesetter (*opposite*) was driven by William Clay Ford. *Top left:* Ford's participation didn't prevent a "Chevy guy," Corvette chief engineer Zora Arkus-Duntov (right), from visiting at the Speedway. He's with Chief Steward Harlan Fengler (left) and Tony Hulman. Actor Jim Garner (*top right*) was an avid race fan and future pace-car driver. Veteran Chuck Stevenson retired after damaging the No. 94 Valvoline car in practice (*above left*). Rookie Sam Sessions got it into the show. Bob Hurt suffered a career-ending spinal injury when he crashed on the final day of qualifying (*above right*).

When the STP-Lotus turbines of Joe Leonard and Art Pollard flamed out within seconds of each other, it seemed more than coincidental. First reports from the STP garages claimed that an alternative fuel caused fuel pump shaft trouble that sidelined the two provocative racing machines. Later reports had this statement in error. However, other sources explained the problem.

While it's true that turbine engines will run on most any combustible liquid, experts at Pratt & Whitney said the recommended J-4 aircraft-quality kerosene helped to lubricate the fuel system. This was especially true of the fuel pump. But when it was discovered that gasoline gave the cars additional accleration off turns, the team decided to use it in the race. (The team also had an additional sponsorship from the American Oil Company, which wanted to advertise its new unleaded gasoline.)

However, the loss of the kerosene's lubricating properties contributed to the seizure of the phosphor-bronze shaft used in the pump. The situation was aggravated at low speed, such as a yellow-light condition, the exact scenario in which Leonard and Pollard found themselves when their cars gave out.

The "flying doorstop" Lotuses created by Colin Chapman made the STP turbines a serious threat again despite inlet restrictions. Graham Hill qualified the No. 70 (*top left*) second, and teammate Joe Leonard sat on the pole. However, Mike Spence died in a Turn 1 crash in the No. 30 car (*top right* and *above*) on May 7. Hill ran in the top five until he wrecked on lap 111 (*below*). While the STP team was the focus of attention, Bobby Unser quietly dialed in the No. 3 Eagle-Offy (*opposite, top left*) and qualified on the outside of row one. Unser's younger brother, Al, escaped injury when he crashed the Retzloff Chemical Special in practice (*opposite, top right*) and then qualified another car on the second row. The Torino pace car runs a comfortable distance ahead of the field as the starters get up to speed (*opposite bottom*).

RISLONE
RACING
BOBBY UNSER
RISLONE
RACING
3
RISLONE
RACING

the 52nd 500
INDIANAPOLIS MOTOR SPEEDWAY
OFFICIAL PROGRAM
INDIANAPOLIS MOTOR SPEEDWAY
MAY 30, 1968
ONE DOLLAR

1968

MONDAY, MAY 27: Twenty-one cars are eligible to qualify for the six remaining spots on this extra day of qualifying. The day gets off to a bad start when rookie Bob Hurt hits the Turn 1 wall and is paralyzed with a spinal injury.

Cheesbourg and Puterbaugh, who qualified in the dark the night before, are bumped. Among those who make the field is Jim Hurtubise in an Offy-powered Mallard roadster.

THE RACE

Start: Joe Leonard beats Bobby Unser to the line to lead the first lap as Graham Hill drops back.

Lap 2: Mario Andretti, who starts fourth, pulls into the pits with smoke pouring from his Ford turbo. He goes back out after losing several laps, only to come in for good with a burned piston.

Lap 8: As Leonard backs off while lapping slower cars, Unser shoots by into the lead.

Lap 9: Jim Hurtubise quits with a burned piston. His Mallard is the last front-engine car to compete in a 500.

Lap 41: Al Unser loses a wheel and crashes in the south short chute; the errant wheel knocks the nose off Arnie Knepper's car. Gary Bettenhausen runs over a wheel hub on the track, which tears up the bottom of his car and injures his foot.

Lap 56: Green-flag racing resumes after a long caution, and Bobby Unser easily pulls away from second-place Leonard. Neither driver pits under yellow, but Leonard comes in under green on Lap 57. One lap later, Unser comes in as Leonard leaves. Lloyd Ruby, who stops during the yellow, takes the lead. Unser and Leonard fall in right behind, and Hill is a close fourth.

Lap 90: Unser snatches the lead from Ruby.

Lap 94: Ruby turns the fastest lap of the race, 168.666 mph, but slows on the next lap and loses second place to Leonard.

Lap 109: Leonard, still running second, pits under green, while leader Unser stays out. One lap later, Hill's turbine crashes in Turn 2 when his suspension breaks. This allows Unser to stop under yellow and gain track position, though his transmission sticks in top gear as he exits the pits.

Lap 120: When the green flag comes out, Unser slips inside of Leonard on the front straight and takes the lead.

Lap 166: Unser is the last of the three leaders to make his final stop, and with his damaged transmission, he accelerates slowly out of the pits and falls to third behind Ruby and Leonard.

Lap 174: Ruby's engine misfires as he slows on the front straight, allowing Leonard's turbine to flash by into the lead. Ruby pits and falls out of contention.

Lap 183: Carl Williams crashes hard into the outside wall coming out of Turn 2 and his car bursts into flames. Williams is unhurt.

As the field slowly circles in single file under yellow, there are five lapped cars between leader Leonard and second-place Unser.

Lap 190: As starter Pat Vidan waves the green flag for the restart, Leonard's engine stalls—a turbine "flameout"—and he slows on the front straight. As the huge crowd roars, Unser zooms by into first place.

A speechless Andy Granatelli stares in disbelief as Leonard rolls to a stop on the infield grass near victory lane. For the second year in a row, almost certain victory turns into crushing defeat.

Finish: With second-place driver Dan Gurney just ahead of him on the track, Unser cruises the final 10 laps and wins by nearly 54 seconds. Taking no chances, he runs two extra laps to make sure.

Unser leads 127 laps and averages a record 152.882 mph. A turbocharged engine wins for the first time, and an Offy wins for the first time in four years. Nine of the first 11 finishers use turbo Offys. Goodyear wins for the second straight year.

None of the three STP turbines finishes. Leonard places 12th, and teammate Art Pollard, whose engine also stalls, is 13th. After the race, USAC restricts the air inlet for turbines to just 12 inches, choking off enough horsepower to render them uncompetitive.

RESULTS

NO.	DRIVER	CAR	ENTRANT	ENGINE	CYL	DISP	CHASSIS	COLOR	QUAL SPD	START	FIN	LAPS / SPEED / REASON OUT
3	Bobby Unser	Rislone	Leader Cards, Inc.	Offy T R	4	168	Eagle	blk, wht, red, yelo	169.507	3	1	200-152.882
48	Dan Gurney	Olsonite Eagle	All American Racers, Inc.	Ford-Weslake R	8	305	Eagle	blue, white	166.512	10	2	200-152.187
15	Mel Kenyon	City of Lebanon	Fred Gerhardt	Offy T R	4	168	Gerhardt	white,blue	165.191	17	3	200-149.224
42	Denis Hulme	Olsonite Eagle	All American Racers, Inc.	Ford R	8	255	Eagle	blue, white	164.189	20	4	200-149.140
25	Lloyd Ruby	Gene White Co.	Gene White Co.	Offy T R	4	168	Mongoose	red, white	167.613	5	5	200-148.529
59	Ronnie Duman	Cleaver-Brooks	Hayone Racing Enterprises	Offy T R	4	168	Brabham	blue, yellow	162.338	26	6	200-flagged
98	Bill Vukovich, Jr.	Wagner Lockheed	J. C. Agajanian	Offy T R	4	168	Shrike	blue, white	163.510	23	7	198-flagged
90	Mike Mosley	Zecol-Lubaid	Leader Cards, Inc.	Offy T R	4	168	Finley	wht, blue, red	162.499	27	8	197-flagged
94	Sam Sessions	Valvoline	Vatis Enterprises, Inc.	Offy T R	4	168	Finley	wht, blue, red	162.118	31	9	197-flagged
6	Bobby Grim	Gene White Co.	Gene White Co.	Offy T R	4	168	Mongoose	white, red	162.866	25	10	196-flagged
16	Bob Veith	Thermo-King	Don Gerhardt	Offy T R	4	168	Gerhardt	slvr, red, gld	163.495	24	11	196-flagged
60	Joe Leonard	STP Oil Treatment	STP Corporation	Turbine 4	0	AIA15.9	Lotus	fluorescent red	171.559	1	12	191-broken fuelshaft
20	Art Pollard	STP Oil Treatment	STP Corporation	Turbine 4	0	AIA15.9	Lotus	fluorescent red	166.297	11	13	188-broken fuelshaft
82	Jim McElreath	Jim Greer	James H. Greer	Ford R	8	255	Coyote	orange	165.327	13	14	179-stalled
84	Carl Williams	Sheraton-Thompson	Ansted-Thompson Racing	Ford R	8	255	Coyote	orange	162.323	28	15	163-wrecked T2
10	Bud Tingelstad	Federal Engineering	Federal Automotive Associates	Ford R	8	255	Gerhardt	blue, wht, gld	164.444	18	16	158-lost oil pressure
54	Wally Dallenbach	Vavoline	Vatis Enterprises, Inc.	Offy T R	4	168	Finley	wht, blue, red	165.548	12	17	148-engine failure
18	Johnny Rutherford	City of Seattle	Alan Green	Ford R	8	255	Eagle	yelo, blk, wht	163.830	21	18	125-wrecked, split oil tank
70	Graham Hill	STP Oil Treatment	STP Corporation	Turbine 4	0	AIA15.9	Lotus	fluorescent red	171.208	2	19	110-wrecked T2
1	A. J. Foyt	Sheraton-Thompson	Ansted-Thompson Racing	Ford R	8	255	Coyote	orange	166.821	8	20	86-rear end failure
45	Ronnie Bucknum	Weinberger Homes	W. & W. Enterprises	Ford R	8	255	Eagle	wht, red, blk	164.211	19	21	76-fuel leak
27	Jim Malloy	Jim Robbins Co.	Jim Robbins Co.	Ford R	8	255	Vollstedt	white, gold	165.032	14	22	64-rear end failure
78	Jerry Grant	Bardahl Eagle	Friedkin Enterprises	Ford T R	8	168	Eagle	blk, wht, gld	164.782	15	23	50-oil leak
11	Gary Bettenhausen	Thermo-King	Don Gerhardt	Offy T R	4	168	Gerhardt	pearl, red, slvr	163.562	22	24	43-hit Unser's debris, injured
21	Arnie Knepper	Bryant Heating	Volstedt Enterprises, Inc.	Ford T R	8	168	Vellstedt	yellow, red	161.900	32	25	42-hit Unser's whl, broken rad.
24	Al Unser	Retzloff Chemical	Retzloff Racing Team	Ford T R	8	168	Lola	red, pearl	167.069	6	26	40-wrecked T1
4	Gordon Johncock	Gilmore Broadcasting	Johncock Racing Team	Offy T R	4	168	Gerhardt	blue, orng, wht	166.775	9	27	37-rear engine failure
64	Larry Dickson	Overseas Nat. Airways	Andretti Racing Enterprises	Ford R	8	255	Hawk II	white, blue	161.124	33	28	24-broken piston
8	Roger McCluskey	G. C. Murphy	Lindsey Hopkins	Offy T R	4	168	Eagle	blue, pink	166.976	7	29	16-broken oil filter
56	Jim Hurtubise	Pepsi-Frito Lay	Jim Hurtubise	Offy T F	4	168	Mallard	wht, blue, red	162.191	30	30	9-broken piston
29	George Snider	Vel's Parnelli Jones	Vel's Racing Team	Ford R	8	255	Mongoose	orange, white	162.264	29	31	9-oil leak
35	Jochen Rindt	Repco-Brabham	Motor Racing Deve. Ltd.	Repco R	8	254	Brabham	blue	164.144	16	32	5-broken piston
2	Mario Andretti	Overseas Nat. Airways	Andretti Racing Enterprises	Ford T R	8	168	Hawk III	white, blue	167.691	4	33	2-broken piston

T = turbocharged F = front engine R = rear engine 4 = four-wheel drive AIA = anulus inlet area

Ralph Liguori made his first trip to Indy as a driver in 1959. Ten years later, "Ralphie the Racer" was still trying to complete a successful qualifying run.

Ligouri was highly successful at other venues, especially on dirt. For many years, he held the 50-lap sprint-car record at Langhorne, Pennsylvania. But he remained snakebit at Indy.

Either his cars lacked speed or mechanical gremlins caused him to miss racing's biggest show. One year, a Novi blew up in his face. In '67, driving Walt Flynn's entry, he had a good qualifying run in the works, when he tested the south wall.

When he came back in '68, Ralph was still a rookie. USAC made him take the full four-phase test for a record 10th time.

"Actually, I don't care about taking the full test again," Ralph said. "I think it's a good thing and that everyone who has missed a race should take all four phases just to get the feel of things."

At age 41, Ralph had high hopes for his ride in the Dayton Steel Wheel Special. But the engine didn't respond to treatment. Liguori missed making the field again.

Although he still occasionally drives a midget car, Liguori finally gave up on his dream of racing in the 500. Even so, he is still known as Indy's oldest rookie.

Joe Leonard streaks off well ahead of Bobby Unser (*opposite top*) on the way to leading the first lap. Roger McCluskey and Lloyd Ruby pursue Unser, while Graham Hill lags behind at the front of the main pack. Art Pollard, in the No. 20 STP Lotus, takes a low line to pass Sam Sessions, in the Valvoline entry (*opposite middle*), in close wheel-to-wheel racing. Pollard dropped out late in the race when his turbine stalled; Sessions finished ninth in this, his first appearance in the 500. Unser inherited the lead when Leonard's turbine stalled on a restart with 10 laps to go, dealing Andy Granatelli and his STP team another crushing defeat. The Borg-Warner trophy and a $175,139 payoff await Unser as he pulls into victory lane (*opposite bottom*). His Rislone-sponsored, Offy-powered entry (*above*) was the first turbocharged car to win, and he gave the Leader Cards team its first victory since 1962. The Eagle chassis was created by Dan Gurney, who finished second.

53rd Race • May 30, 1969

With the turbine engine obsolete, resilient Andy Granatelli renews his 20-year quest for victory with a multi-pronged attack.

He enters new wedge-shaped Lotus four-wheel-drive cars, hires two-time national champion Mario Andretti to drive one of them, and, always the innovator, talks Chrysler Corporation into building a stock-block V-8 for his STP team.

Art Pollard shakes down the pushrod Plymouth V-8 in one of last year's wedge-shaped Lotus cars that wears new aero features, including wide front wings, NACA-style air ducts, and rear fairings that flow into an integral spoiler. A variety of mechanical and aerodynamic problems leave the Plymouth-powered car uncompetitive, and Pollard switches to a new Lotus-Offy.

Other cars grow wings as teams start to tinker with the benefits of downforce, and the "flying doorstop" shape becomes more popular. Turbochargers are really in vogue, and 30 starters (20 Offys, 10 Fords) have them. Dan Gurney's stock-block Ford and the Repco V-8s of Jack Brabham and Peter Revson are the only naturally aspirated engines.

PRACTICE AND QUALIFYING

WEDNESDAY, MAY 7: Three-time winner A. J. Foyt posts the fastest practice lap, 169.237 mph, in one of his own Coyote chassis with a turbocharged Ford V-8.

MONDAY, MAY 12: Mario Andretti gets his new four-wheel-drive Lotus hooked up and clocks a lap of 170.179 mph, fastest for the month.

FRIDAY, MAY 16: Andretti runs 171.789, Foyt hits 170.908, and Roger McCluskey, Foyt's teammate, does 170.283, setting up a three-way battle for the pole.

SATURDAY, MAY 17: Rain curtails track activity on Pole Day, and only one driver attempts to qualify in the afternoon.

Rookie Jigger Sirois runs three laps in the 160-162 mph range, but his crew fears it is too slow and waves off his attempt.

Rain resumes before anyone else can qualify and continues through Sunday, delaying the run for the pole until the next weekend. Considering that he could have been the lone qualifier this day, Sirois blows a chance to win the pole and secure a place in history. (Sirois will make six more attempts at making the race, but never starts an Indy 500.)

➔

Chevrolet's Camaro SS paced the field again. Chevy built 3675 pace car replicas, most of which seemed to be at the Speedway for a pre-race publicity event (*above*). Chief Steward Harlan Fengler sorted out the pacemaker (*below*) before turning it over to 1960 winner Jim Rathmann on race day. Former racer Rathmann owned a Florida Chevrolet dealership. Though listed as having a 396-cubic-inch engine, the pace car allegedly had a 427.

STARTING LINEUP

Average Field Qualifying Speed: 166.295

Numbers in flags indicate finish position

Bobby Unser

Roger McCluskey

Gary Bettenhausen

Art Pollard

George Snider

Mario Andretti

Gordon Johncock

Lee Roy Yarbrough

Joe Leonard

Sonny Ates

POLE POSITION
Qualifying Speed: 170.568

A. J. Foyt

Mark Donohue

Jim McElreath

Dan Gurney

Jim Malloy

Full-Steam Ahead: The Proposed Lear "Vapordyne" Racer

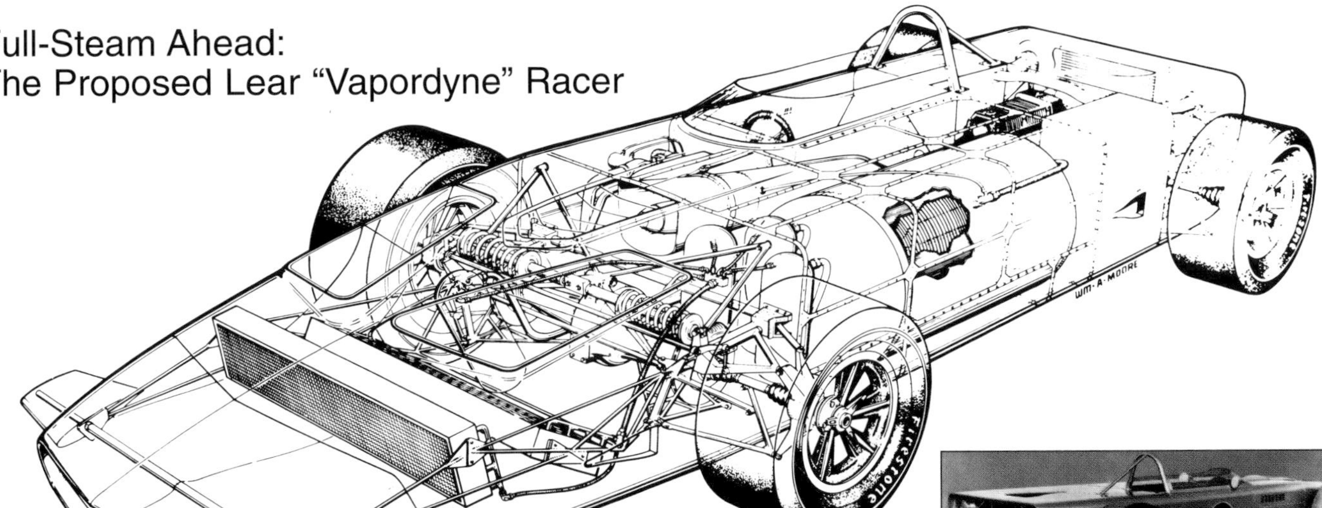

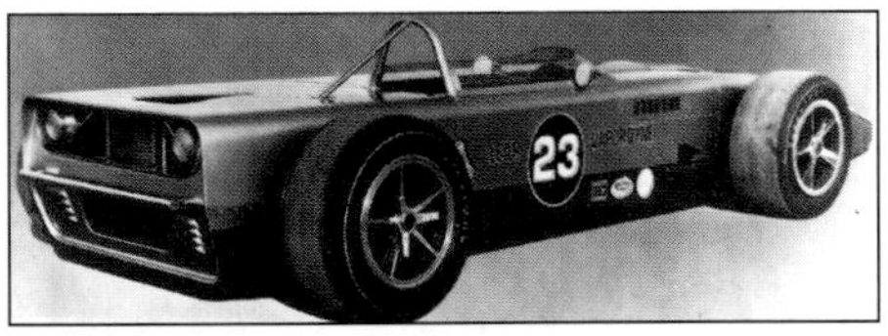

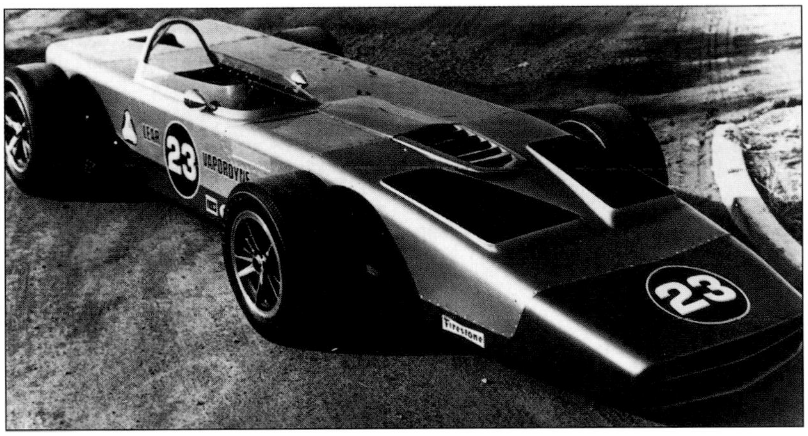

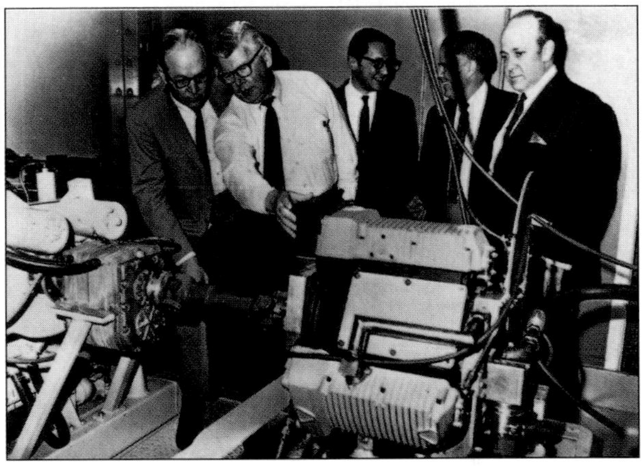

Lear Motors Corporation intrigued the racing world when it showed the "Vapordyne" steam-powered racer at auto shows. Seen in cutaway (*top left*), its engine sat next to the cockpit. Its apparearance (*top right* and *above left*) was not unlike the '68 turbine cars. *Above:* William Lear (second from left) and board members inspect an engine prototype.

Bud Tingelstad

Arnie Knepper

Mel Kenyon

George Follmer

Carl Williams

Peter Revson

Johnny Rutherford

Lloyd Ruby

Sam Sessions

Bill Vukovich, Jr.

Jack Brabham

Bobby Johns

Ronnie Bucknum

Wally Dallenbach

Mike Mosley

Denis Hulme

Bruce Walkup

Larry Dickson

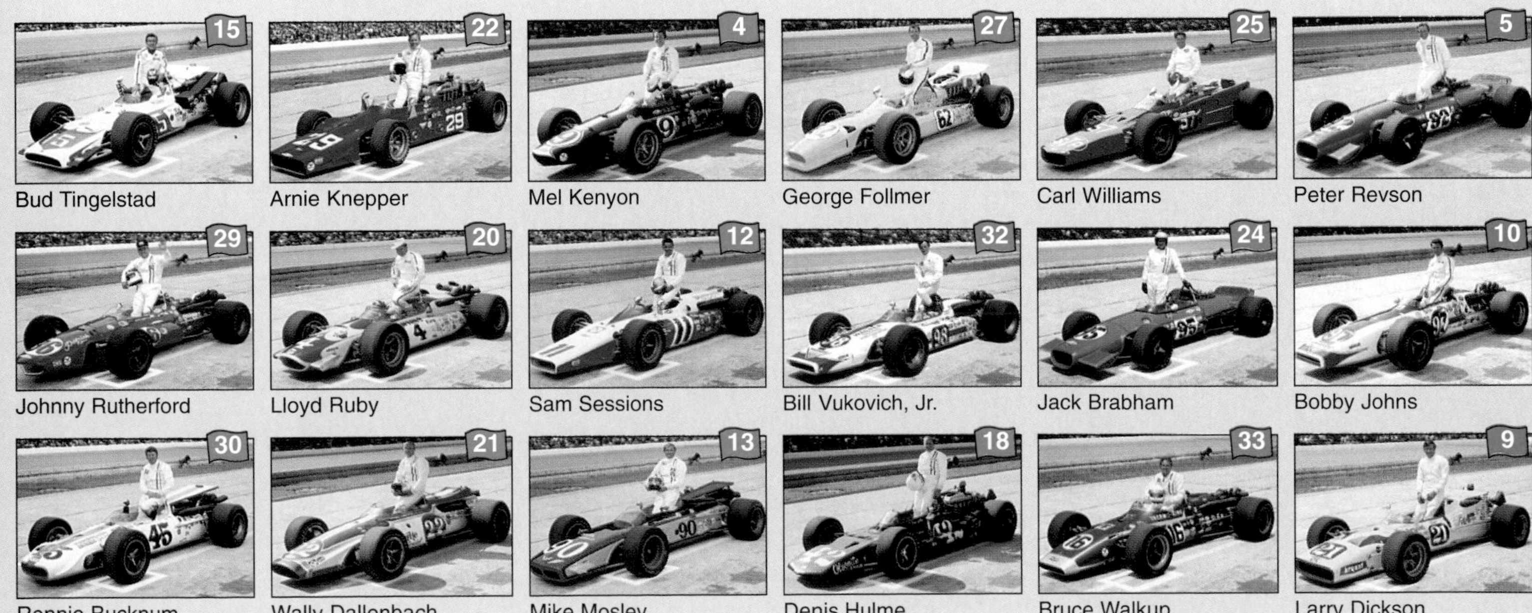

1969

Few people took William Lear's entry seriously. But following two years of near misses by the exotic turbine-powered cars, others felt anything could happen. What Lear, of aircraft fame, proposed was using space-age technology to harness one of man's oldest sources of power. Lear's "Vapordyne" Indy car was to be powered by steam. It sounded farfetched, until one realized the simplicity of the idea.

The racer was to carry a small tank of kerosene or propane to operate the boiler, with pit stops made to replenish water as the primary fuel source. Lear's Delta Motor design was a six-cylinder with 12 driving pistons operating three crankshafts in a triangular arrangement. The four-wheel-drive chassis was super light, and the horsepower output was said to be higher than that generated by the conventional Ford or Offy. Calculations had the car going the distance on two pit stops.

However, even though the sleek racer made the rounds of the auto shows, time ran out on the project before May '69. And after the fallout from the new rules governing the turbines, USAC never did arrive at a definite way to measure the Lear Delta's horsepower.

Eventually, Bill Lear dropped the project. But the concept behind the Vapordyne still gives pause to those who understand the power of steam.

WEDNESDAY, MAY 21: Foyt unofficially breaks Joe Leonard's qualifying record with a practice lap of 172.315. A few minutes later, Andretti loses a wheel in Turn 4 and the left rear of his Lotus whacks the wall. The car sustains heavy damage and Andretti suffers minor facial burns.

FRIDAY, MAY 23: Andretti nearly reaches 170 mph in his backup car, a two-year-old Hawk updated with front and rear wings and a Ford turbo. Foyt hits 172.315 and McCluskey 170.5.

SATURDAY, MAY 24: Foyt fails to break the record, but 170.568 mph is fast enough to win his second pole. Andretti qualifies second fastest at 169.851. Defending winner Bobby Unser, in an Offy-powered four-wheel-drive Lola, starts third for the second year in a row.

Rookie Mark Donohue, in a rear-drive Lola-Offy owned by Roger Penske, lines up fourth.

SUNDAY, MAY 25: Rookie Peter Revson bumps his way into the 33rd spot at 160.851 mph, slower than the speed that could have put Sirois on the pole. Sirois makes another qualifying attempt but pulls in after one lap with mechanical trouble.

THE RACE

The Start: Andretti zips in front of Foyt to grab the lead from the polesitter.

Lap 5: Urged on by the crowd hoping to see him win a fourth time, Foyt surges past Andretti on the front straight for the lead.

Lap 25: Jim McElreath's engine blows in Turn 1 and bursts into flames. He stops along the outside wall and emergency crews put out the fire before there are any injuries.

Lap 51: Foyt and Andretti, still 1-2, pit on the same lap, but A. J. gets out in 28 seconds while Mario languishes for 43.

Lap 79: Foyt still leads when his Ford engine loses power, and Andretti and Lloyd Ruby streak past him. Foyt stops a few laps later and cools his tires for 23 minutes while he gets a new turbocharger. He gets back in and finishes eighth.

Lap 105: Ruby, after passing Andretti for the lead, meets disaster on his second pit stop. He starts to leave before his crew disconnects the fuel hose, ripping a hole in his tank. Andretti goes back in front.

Lap 150: Joe Leonard runs second when debris punches a hole in his radiator. He loses 14 minutes in the pits getting a new one but still finishes sixth.

Finish: Andretti goes the rest of the way without challenge to win for Andy Granatelli and his STP team. A jubilant Granatelli appears to plant a big wet one on Mario's cheek in victory lane.

Andretti, who goes the distance on one set of Firestones, leads 116 laps and pockets $206,727 of the $805,128 purse (both record amounts). With only two caution flags, he averages a record 156.867 mph, 21 mph faster than Rodger Ward's winning speed 10 years earlier.

Dan Gurney is runner-up for the second year in a row, two laps down with his stock-block Ford. Defending winner Bobby Unser wrestles with an ill-handling car and stops five times for tires, yet still finishes third.

Rookie Peter Revson starts 33rd and finishes fifth, but Mark Donohue is Rookie of the Year. Donohue runs in the top 10 all day, gets as high as third, and places seventh after spending 12 minutes getting a new magneto late in the race.

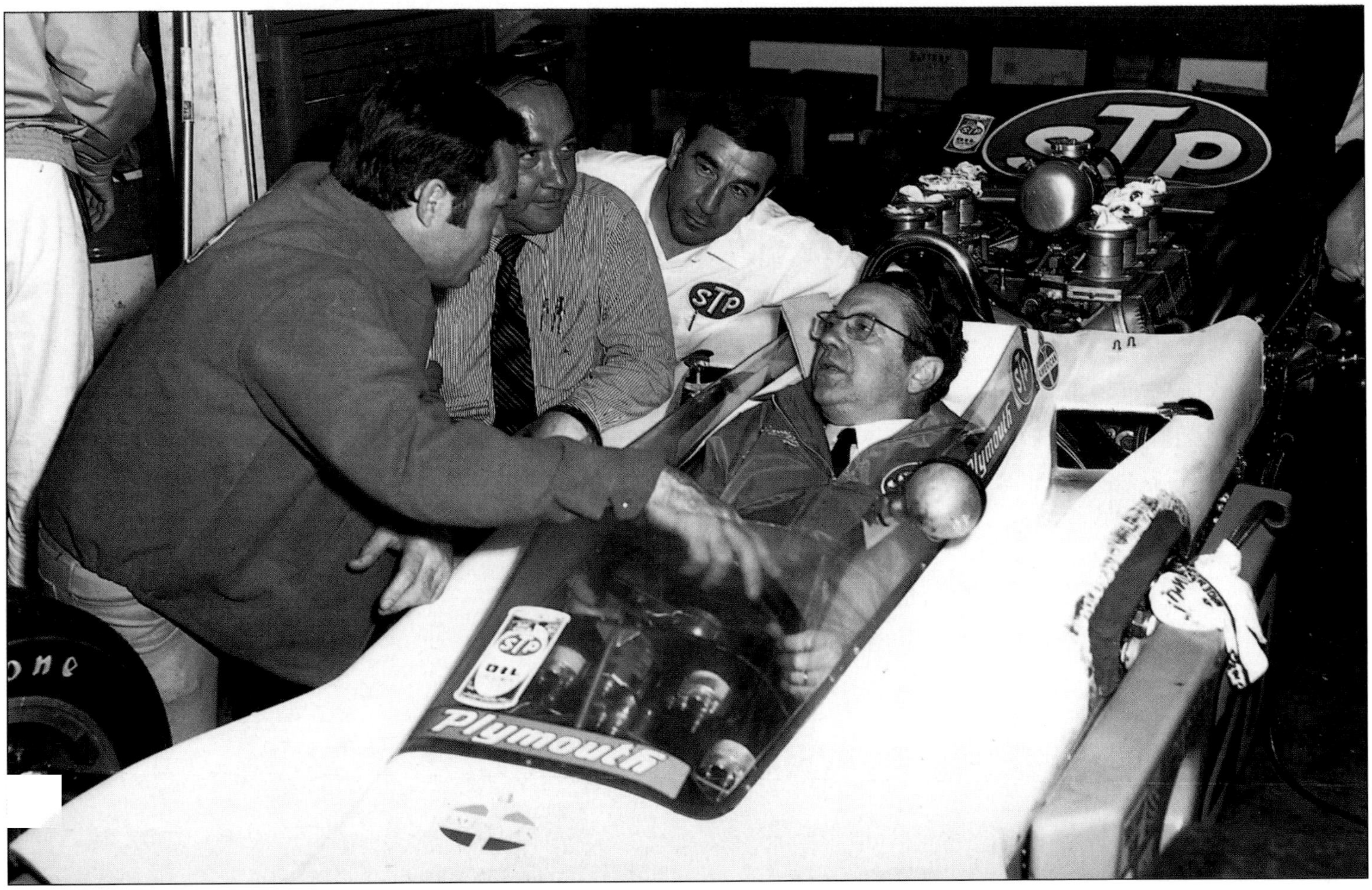

Mario Andretti was assigned to Andy Granatelli's new wedge-shaped, four-wheel-drive Lotus (*opposite*). However, Andretti damaged the Lotus when he hit the wall in practice and switched to a two-year-old Hawk—the same car he put on the pole in 1967. *Above:* Driver Art Pollard and Andy and Joe Granatelli give Indiana Senator Vance Hartke, who is in the driver's seat, the inside story on the Plymouth-powered Lotus. The car failed to make the grade, however. When rain halted Pole Day qualifying, former driver Sam Hanks (*right*) staged a paper airplane race. Gary Bettenhausen qualified for his second start in as many years in the Thermo-King air conditioning-sponsored entry (*below left*). A. J. Foyt received $6000 from Coca-Cola's Lindsey Hopkins (*below right*) as a reward for winning the pole, his second at Indianapolis.

1969

In 1969, the turbocharged Ford V-8 was in its infancy. While the downsized engine created plenty of power, it tended to overheat at high speed.

"That thing was like a rolling furnace," said Clint Brawner, Mario Andretti's mechanic. "I never saw an engine carry a temperature anywhere near that high. The engine literally boiled in its own oil." After Andretti qualified, Brawner installed an extra radiator behind the roll bar. Chief steward Harlan Fengler decreed the new cooler violated the configuration rule, changing the outside bodywork of the car. Grudgingly, Clint removed the cooler.

On the eve of the race, the cagy Brawner worked alone in his locked garage. "I put a radiator under the driver's seat," Clint said. "This didn't violate the rules. And no one—not even Mario—knew it was there."

When Andretti charged away from the field, everyone expected his engine to blow. It never missed a beat. According to Clint, Mario said it was the hottest ride he'd ever had. "He didn't know he was sitting on top of a radiator with 240-degree coolant running through it," Clint smiled.

One of the Camaro SS pace car replicas provides livery for participants in the annual 500 Festival as they are paraded around the track on race day (*opposite top*). In 1997, when Chevrolet marked the Camaro's 30th anniversary, it issued a special edition in the '69 pace car color scheme. The Gasoline Alley garages in the infield are packed on race day as the press and fans try to get a glimpse of the cars and drivers before they take their places on the track (*opposite bottom*). Mario Andretti's veteran Hawk-Ford (*below*) outclassed a diverse group of newer chassis to finally give Andy Granatelli the prize he had been chasing for more than 20 years (*right*). Andretti validated the promise inherent in his 1965 Rookie of the Year award by winning in his fifth start, and at the age of 29, he appeared a cinch to add his name to the list of repeat winners at the Speedway. Among the top five finishers, there were four kinds of engines and five different chassis.

RESULTS

NO.	DRIVER	CAR	ENTRANT	ENGINE	CYL	DISP	CHASSIS	COLOR	QUAL SPD	START	FIN	LAPS / SPEED / REASON OUT
2	Mario Andretti	STP Oil Treatment	STP Corporation	Ford T	8	159	Hawk III	flrscnt red, blk	169.851	2	1	200-156.867
48	Dan Gurney	Olsonite Eagle	All American Racers	Ford-Weslake	8	319	Eagle	blue, slvr, wht	167.341	10	2	200-155.337
1	Bobby Unser	Bardahl	Leader Cards, Inc.	Offy T	4	159	Lola	yellow, black	169.683	3	3	200-154.090
9	Mel Kenyon	Krohne Grain Trans	3-K Racing Enterprises	Offy T	4	159	Gerhardt	blk, wht, yelo	165.426	24	4	200-152.177
92	Peter Revson	Repco-Brabham	Motor Racing Dvp.	Repco	8	254	Brabham	blue	160.851	33	5	197-flagged
44	Joe Leonard	City of Daytona Beach	Smokey Yunic, Inc.	Ford T	8	159	Eagle	gold, black	167.240	11	6	193-flagged
66	Mark Donohue	Sunoco-Simoniz	U.S. Racing, Inc.	Offy T	4	159	Lola	blue, wht, yelo, red	168.903	4	7	190-flagged
6	A. J. Foyt	Sheraton-Thompson	Ansted-Thompson Racing	Ford T	8	159	Coyote	orange, white	170.568	1	8	181-flagged
21	Larry Dickson	Bryant Heat & Cool	Vollstedt Enterprises, Inc.	Ford T	8	159	Vollstedt	yellow, red	163.014	31	9	180-flagged
97	Bobby Johns	Wagner-Lockheed	J. C. Agajanian	Offy T	4	159	Shrike	white, maroon	160.901	32	10	171-flagged
10	Jim Malloy	Jim Robbins Co.	Jim Robbins Co.	Offy T	4	159	Vollstedt	wht, mroon, gld	167.092	13	11	165-flagged
11	Sam Sessions	Valvoline	Vatis Enterprises, Inc.	Offy T	4	159	Finley	pearl, red, blue	165.434	23	12	163-flagged
90	Mike Mosley	Zecol-Lubaid	Leader Cards, Inc.	Offy T	4	159	Eagle	blk, red, yelo	166.113	22	13	162-broken piston
82	Roger McCluskey	G. C. Murphy	Foyt & Greer	Ford T	8	159	Coyote	orange, white	168.350	6	14	157-broken header
15	Bud Tingelstad	Vel's Parnelli Jones	Vel's Parnelli Jones Ford	Offy T	8	159	Lola	pearl, blue, red	166.597	18	15	155-engine trouble
84	George Snider	Sheraton-Thompson	Ansted-Thompson Racing	Ford T	8	159	Coyote	orange, white	166.914	15	16	152-flagged
59	Sonny Ates	Krohne Transport	3-K Racing Enterprises	Offy T	4	159	Brabham	blue, yellow	166.968	14	17	146-magneto trouble
42	Denis Hulme	Olsonite Eagle	All American Racers	Ford T	8	159	Eagle	blue, slvr, wht	165.092	25	18	145-clutch trouble
12	Gordon Johncock	Gilmore Broadcasting	Johncock Racing Team	Offy T	4	159	Gerhardt	blue, wht, red	168.626	5	19	137-broken piston
4	Lloyd Ruby	Wynn's Spitfire	Gene White Co.	Offy T	4	159	Mongoose	yellow, red	166.428	20	20	105-fuel hose connection
22	Wally Dallenbach	Sprite	Lindsey Hopkins	Offy T	4	159	Eagle	wht, grn, orng	166.497	19	21	82-broken clutch
29	Arnie Knepper	M.V.S	M.V.S., Inc.	Ford T	8	159	Cecil	red, white	166.220	21	22	82-wrecked T4
67	Lee Roy Yarbrough	Jim Robbins Co.	Jim Robbins Co.	Ford T	8	159	Vollstedt	wht, mroon, gld	168.075	8	23	65-broken header
95	Jack Brabham	Repco-Brabham	Motor Racing Dvp.	Repco	8	254	Brabham	blue, flrscnt grn	163.875	29	24	58-ignition trouble
57	Carl Williams	STP Gas Treatment	STP Corporation	Offy	4	159	Gerhardt	fluorescent red	163.265	30	25	50-clutch trouble
8	Gary Bettenhausen	Thermo King A/C	Don Gerhardt	Offy T	4	159	Gerhardt	blue, silver	167.777	9	26	35-broken piston
62	George Follmer	Retzloff/Follmer	Retzloff Follmer Enterprises	Ford T	8	159	Gilbert	yellow	164.286	27	27	26-engine trouble
38	Jim McElreath	Jack Adams Airplanes	Two Jacks, Inc.	Offy T	4	159	Hawk II	wht, orng, gld, blk	168.224	7	28	24-engine caught fire
36	Johnny Rutherford	Patrick Petrol Eagle	Michner Petroleum, Inc.	Offy T	4	159	Eagle	red, silver	166.628	17	29	24-split oil tank
45	Ronnie Bucknum	Weinberger Homes	W. & W. Enterprises	Offy T	4	159	Eagle	white, orange	166.636	16	30	16-broken piston
40	Art Pollard	STP Oil Treatment	STP Corporation	Offy T 4	4	159	Lotus	fluorescent red	167.123	12	31	7-broken drive line
98	Bill Vukovich	Wagner Lockheed	J. C. Agajanian	Offy T	4	159	Mongoose	white, maroon	165.843	26	32	1-broken con. rod
16	Bruce Walkup	Thermo King A/C	Don Gerhardt	Offy T	4	159	Gerhardt	blue, silver	163.942	28	33	0-broken transmission

T = turbocharged   4 = four-wheel drive

54th Race • May 30, 1970

The announced purse reaches an all-time high of $1,000,002, illustrating the remarkable growth of the race since 1960, when drivers competed for $400,000 in prize money.

A handful of stock-block engines, including an AMC six-cylinder, and one turbine-powered car are among the 84 entries, but none makes the final cut. For the first time, the entire field is turbocharged, 17 of them Ford V-8s and 16 Offy four-cylinders.

The chassis menu has much greater variety, with 14 different brands of rear-engine cars lining up on race day. The wedge shape started by Lotus two years earlier gains more followers, as does Goodyear, which outnumbers Firestone two-to-one on the grid.

Bruce Walkup's Mongoose is unique among the 33 starters for of its roll cage, borrowing a safety feature popular among sprint and midget drivers. Walkup's mirrors are mounted on a horizontal bar above the cockpit.

PRACTICE AND QUALIFYING

THURSDAY, MAY 7: After a few days of sorting out their cars, drivers start to post impressive speeds. Mark Donohue is fastest at 168.9 mph, and Al Unser, Dan Gurney, and A. J. Foyt are close behind with speeds between 168.2 and 168.8.

All use a turbocharged Ford V-8 except Gurney, who has a turbocharged Offy. Each rides a different chassis. Donohue is in a Lola, Unser is in a Parnelli Jones-designed Colt, Gurney has one of his own Eagles, and Foyt is in one of his Coyotes.

SUNDAY, MAY 10: Unser is fastest for the third time and the first to crack 170 in practice, turning a lap at 170.973 in his Colt-Ford. Art Pollard is second fastest at 169.1 in a new Kingfish-Offy.

MONDAY, MAY 11: Defending winner Mario Andretti spins in Turn 4 and bangs the inside wall. Andretti damages the left side of his new British-built McNamara chassis but escapes injury.

Unser ups his speed to 171.233 mph, close to Joe Leonard's 1968 qualifying record of 171.559, set with a turbine engine.

TUESDAY, MAY 12: New Zealander Denis Hulme suffers ➔

Two-time winner Rodger Ward drove the Oldsmobile 4-4-2 in his only appearance as a pace-car driver (*above*). The usual fleet of pace car lookalikes was created for parade duty (*opposite top*). As for the Vista Cruiser wagon (*below*), despite the sign on the door, it was just an "official car." Jim Hurtubise got his front-engine Mallard roadster (*opposite bottom*) on to the track but not into the field.

STARTING LINEUP

Average Field Qualifying Speed: 167.139

Numbers in flags indicate finish position

POLE POSITION
Qualifying Speed: 170.221

A. J. Foyt

Art Pollard

Jim Malloy

Mike Mosley

Rick Muther

Johnny Rutherford

Mark Donohue

Mario Andretti

Dan Gurney

Bruce Walkup

Al Unser

Roger McCluskey

Bobby Unser

George Snider

Lee Roy Yarbrough

Overheating was a problem that beset the turbocharged Ford engines that ran at the Speedway in the late Sixties and early Seventies. No one was more aware of this than master mechanic George Bignotti, who was building Al Unser's Johnny Lightning Special. Bignotti took his problem to a radiator shop owner in downtown Indianapolis.

Ira Hicks was hardly your run-of-the-mill radiator repairman. He routinely sorted out all sorts of overheating puzzles. Hicks mulled over Bignotti's problem for a few days, then set to work fashioning the radiator. The completed unit looked too small and frail to keep the screaming Ford cool. There were no big vents, just little slots that daylight couldn't even penetrate. But on race day, unlike most of his competitors, Unser could use as much of the Ford's power as he wished. His engine temperature was never anywhere near the red line.

And what was Hicks's trick? "I just used the same type cooler that we use in an ordinary heater core found under the dash of any passenger car," Ira explained. "It's made to dissipate heat faster on a frosty morning."

Or on a hot afternoon in May.

Joe Leonard

George Follmer

Wally Dallenbach

Ronnie Bucknum

Bill Vukovich, Jr.

Jim McElreath

Gordon Johncock

Gary Bettenhausen

Donnie Allison

Jack Brabham

Jerry Grant

Sam Sessions

Peter Revson

Carl Williams

Mel Kenyon

Lloyd Ruby

Greg Weld

Dick Simon

Right: The front row had, from right, Al Unser's Colt on the pole, Johnny Rutherford in the middle in a three-year-old Eagle, and three-time champ A. J. Foyt on the outside in a Coyote. Bruce Walkup's Mongoose chassis (*bottom*) gets repairs. One of the Leader Cards Eagles (*opposite, second from top*) gets fuel at the Ashland Oil garage before practice. McLaren entered a sleek new Offy-powered design (*opposite, third from top*). Peter Revson finished 22nd in the No. 73 and Carl Williams placed ninth in the No. 75 (*opposite bottom*).

Al Unser's birthday party in 1970 may have been a day late, but the delay certainly wasn't due to lack of funds. Al stood to collect around $271,000 for his slightly more than three hours of work on Memorial Day at Indianapolis. Back in the garage area, another cake was waiting. Its blue, yellow, and white icing—the colors of his winning Johnny Lightning Special—was beginning to melt. But Al was about to receive another "gift."

Henry Orenstein, of Topper Toys, producers of the Johnny Lightning line of miniature cars, handed Unser a check for $30,000 as a bonus for his first-place finish. Later, Al admitted that he could have doubled the amount of the payment. The morning of the race, Orenstein told Unser he'd pay him $30,000 if he won the race.

"Gee, I don't know whether I can do that," Al replied.

"Then I'll make it $60,000," Orenstein countered.

But Al settled for the original offer.

second- and third-degree burns on his hands and feet when his car catches fire in Turn 3. Hulme withdraws from the race.

SATURDAY, MAY 16: Foyt is the first serious contender on Pole Day, averaging 170.004 mph, but Unser later tops his speed with a non-record 170.221.

Johnny Rutherford, in a three-year-old Eagle-Offy, stirs up the huge crowd with a first lap of 171.135 mph. Rutherford gets slightly loose in Turn 3 on his third lap, just enough to make him .003 seconds too slow to win the pole.

Unser, who missed the 1969 race because he broke a leg in a motorcycle accident in the Speedway infield, captures the only pole position of his career at Indy.

SUNDAY, MAY 24: Veteran Jim McElreath, bumped the day before, bumps his way back into the field in a Coyote-Ford to start 33rd.

THE RACE

The Start: An early morning rain delays the race half an hour, and then a mishap on the pace lap delays it further. The rear suspension breaks on Jim Malloy's Gerhardt, which is on the outside of row three, sending him into the Turn 4 wall. Malloy spins across the track but everyone manages to avoid a collision.

When the green flag finally falls, Johnny Rutherford surges into the lead from the middle of the front row. Al Unser catches Rutherford on the backstretch and pulls away on the front stretch.

Lap 49: Unser pits for the first time, giving the lead to A. J. Foyt. Foyt pits a lap later, and crowd favorite Lloyd Ruby, charging to the front from 25th starting position, takes over.

Lap 52: Ruby gets a black flag for leaking fluid and pits. He gets back into the race, but his car catches fire three laps later and he quits with a broken drive gear.

Lap 53: With Ruby in the pits, Mark Donohue leads one lap until he makes his first stop. Unser resumes command of the race.

Lap 101: Unser, running at a record clip, makes his second stop for fuel. Donohue leads until he pits a few laps later.

Lap 151: Unser makes a 22-second stop for fuel, his third and final stop, but is far enough ahead that he keeps the lead. Foyt runs second and Donohue, third.

Lap 160: Roger McCluskey, in relief of Mel Kenyon, breaks a wheel and bangs the Turn 3 wall. Ronnie Bucknum spins to avoid McCluskey and also hits the wall.

Sammy Sessions grazes the wall as he squeezes through, and Jerry Grant, Jack Brabham, and Bobby Unser spin to avoid the melee. All except McCluskey and Bucknum are able to continue. Neither is seriously hurt.

Finish: With the race in hand, Al Unser backs off and cruises to a 32-second victory at a non-record 155.749 mph. Unser dominates by leading 190 laps and goes the distance on a single set of Firestones. Al and Bobby Unser become the first siblings to win the Indianapolis 500.

Donohue finishes second as Foyt experiences transmission problems and drops to 10th. Despite two extra pit stops, Dan Gurney takes third and NASCAR star Donnie Allison comes in fourth to win Rookie of the Year. Jim McElreath starts 33rd and finishes fifth.

12

OFFICIAL PACE CAR

Lloyd Ruby (*opposite, top left*) struggled in qualifying but finally found enough speed in a different car to make his 11th straight start. Television personality Edie Adams greeted the crowd in the pre-race parade (*opposite, second from top left*). The field lines up behind the pace car under hazy skies (*opposite, top right*). Early in the race, Dick Simon in the No. 44 Bryant Heating Special tries to get around Carl Williams (*opposite bottom*). A. J. Foyt, Wally Dallenbach, and Johnny Rutherford are closing in. Al Unser dominated the race in his Colt-Ford (*above*), leading 190 laps, to duplicate the winning ways of older brother Bobby, who won in 1968. The Unsers were the first family to produce winners among brothers; an approving "Mom" Unser greets her son in victory lane (*right*).

RESULTS

NO.	DRIVER	CAR	ENTRANT	ENGINE	CYL	DISP	CHASSIS	COLOR	QUAL SPD	START	FIN	LAPS / SPEED / REASON OUT
2	Al Unser	Johnny Lightning 500	Vel's Parnelli Jones Ford	Ford T	8	159	'70 P. J. Colt	blue, yelo, red	170.221	1	1	200-155.749
66	Mark Donohue	Sunoco	U.S. Racing, Inc.	Ford T	8	159	'70 Lola	blu, yelo, red, wht	169.911	5	2	200-155.317
48	Dan Gurney	Olsonite Eagle	Olsonite Division	Offy T	4	159	Eagle	blue, slvr, yelo	166.860	11	3	200-153.201
83	Donnie Allison	Greer	Foyt & Greer	Ford T	8	159	Eagle	orange, white	165.662	23	4	200-152.777
14	Jim McElreath	Sheraton-Thompson	Ansted-Thompson Racing	Ford T	8	159	Coyote	orange, white	166.821	33	5	200-152.182
1	Mario Andretti	STP Oil Treatment	STP Corporation	Ford T	8	159	McNamara	fluorescent red	168.209	8	6	199-flagged
89	Jerry Grant	Nelson Iron Works	Jerry Grant Racing Ent.	Offy T	4	159	Eagle	prl, red, orng	165.983	29	7	198-flagged
38	Rick Muther	The Tony Express	Two Jacks, Inc.	Offy T	4	159	Hawk II	wht, blk, gld, orng	165.654	15	8	197-flagged
75	Carl Williams	McLaren	Bruce McLaren Mo. Rac.	Offy T	4	159	'70 McLaren	orange, blue	166.590	19	9	197-flagged
7	A. J. Foyt	Sheraton-Thompson	Ansted-Thompson Racing	Ford T	8	159	Coyote	orange, white	170.004	3	10	195-flagged
3	Bobby Unser	Wagner-Lockheed	Leader Cards, Inc.	Ford T	8	159	Eagle	red, wht, blue	168.508	7	11	192-flagged
67	Sam Sessions	Jim Robbins Co.	Jim Robbins Co.	Ford T	8	159	Vollstedt	wht, red, blk, gld	165.373	32	12	190-flagged
32	Jack Brabham	Brabham-Gilmore Brocst.	Motor Racing Dvp.	Repco T	4	158	Brabham	blue-green	166.397	26	13	175-broken piston
44	Dick Simon	Bryant Heating	Racing International	Ford T	8	159	Vollstedt	purple, gold	165.548	31	14	168-flagged
19	Ronnie Bucknum	M.V.S.	M.V.S. Inc.	Ford T	8	159	Morris	dark red, wht	166.136	27	15	162-wrecked T3
23	Mel Kenyon	Sprite	Lindsey Hopkins	Offy T	4	159	Coyote	wht, orng, grn	165.906	22	16	160-wrecked T3 (McCluskey)
22	Wally Dallenbach	Sprite	Lindsey Hopkins	Ford T	8	159	Eagle	wht, orng, grn	165.601	24	17	143-coil trouble
18	Johnny Rutherford	Patrick Petroleum	Michner Petroleum, Inc.	Offy T	4	159	'67 Eagle	yellow, maroon	170.213	2	18	135-broken header
27	LeeRoy Yarbrough	Jim Robbins Co.	Jim Robbins Co.	Ford T	8	159	Vollstedt	wht, red, blk, gld	166.559	13	19	107-broken turbo gear
84	George Snider	Greer	Foyt & Greer	Ford T	8	159	Coyote	orange, white	167.660	10	20	105-broken suspension
9	Mike Mosley	G. C. Murphy	Leader Cards, Inc.	Offy T	4	159	'68 Eagle	blue, wht, red	166.651	12	21	96-leaking radiator
73	Peter Revson	McLaren	Bruce McLaren	Offy T	4	159	'70 McLaren	orange, blue	167.942	16	22	87-magneto trouble
58	Bill Vukovich	Sugaripe Prune	Jerry O'Connell	Offy T	4	159	Brabham	gold, blk, prple	165.753	30	23	78-clutch trouble
15	Joe Leonard	Johnny Lightning 500	Vel's Parnelli Jones Ford	Ford T	8	159	'70 P. J. Colt	blue, yelo, red	166.898	18	24	73-broken switch
11	Roger McCluskey	Quickick	Hayhoe Racing Enterprises	Ford T	8	159	Scorpion	wht, blue, red	169.213	4	25	62-broken suspension
16	Gary Bettenhausen	Thermo King Auto A/C	Don Gerhardt	Offy T	4	159	Gerhardt	blue, silver	166.451	20	26	55-broken valve
25	Lloyd Ruby	Daniels Cablevision	Gene White Co.	Offy T	4	159	Mongoose	blue, wht, red	168.895	25	27	54-broken drive gear
5	Gordon Johncock	Gilmore Brdcstng	Johncock Racing Team	Ford T	8	159	Gerhardt	blue, orng, wht	167.015	17	28	45-broken piston
97	Bruce Walkup	Wynn's Spit Fire	Agajanian-Faas Racers	Offy T	4	159	Mongoose	yelo, red, blk	166.459	14	29	44-broken timing gear
10	Art Pollard	Art Pollard Car Wash	Race-Go Corp.	Offy T	4	159	Kingfish	red, pearl, blue	168.595	6	30	28-broken piston
20	George Follmer	STP Oil Treatment	STP Corporation	Ford T	8	159	Hawk III	fluorescent red	166.052	21	31	18-oil gasket
93	Greg Weld	Art Pollard Car Wash	Race-Go Corporation	Offy T	4	159	Gerhardt	red, pearl, blue	166.121	28	32	12-broken piston
31	Jim Malloy	Stearns Mfg	Federal Auto Assoc	Offy T	4	159	Gerhardt	wht, blue, blk	167.895	9	33	0-wrecked FS

T = turbocharged

1971

55th Race • May 29, 1971

Congress designates the last Monday of May as the official observance of Memorial Day, but the Speedway schedules the 500 for Saturday, May 29 instead. It is the first time since 1915 that the scheduled date is not May 30 or 31. A new victory circle near the scoring tower awaits the winner.

ABC provides same-day television coverage of the race on a tape-delay basis, bringing the 500 to millions of viewers in their homes for the first time.

McLaren, a British firm successful on the Grand Prix and Can Am circuits, introduces a new wedge-shaped car, the M16, for its second season at the Brickyard. The M16 wears prominent front wings and a large rear wing, and it rides a longer wheelbase that allows mounting the engine in front of the rear axle instead of over it.

PRACTICE AND QUALIFYING

WEDNESDAY, MAY 5: Mark Donohue is fastest of the day at 174.757 mph in a McLaren-Offy, unofficially shattering the track record. Denis Hulme, also in a new McLaren, is second fastest at 172.944.

THURSDAY, MAY 6: Donohue becomes the early favorite to win the pole by averaging 176.3 mph for four laps, hitting a high of 177.901.

SUNDAY, MAY 9: Stock-car ace Lee Roy Yarbrough loses control of his Gurney Eagle in Turn 1 and clips the wall. Yarbrough is okay, but the car sustains too much damage to be ready for qualifying. Teammate Bobby Unser runs 174.6 mph in a similar car.

THURSDAY, MAY 13: Donohue tops 181 mph in his McLaren, cementing his standing as pole favorite. Peter Revson, also in a McLaren, is second fastest, about six mph off Donohue's pace.

SATURDAY, MAY 15: A. J. Foyt, the fourth driver to attempt to qualify and the first to succeed, averages 174.317 mph to break the record by nearly three mph.

Donohue is next in line, and he blows Foyt off the pole with a run of 177.087, reaching 178.6 on his best lap.

An hour or so later, Donohue gets the same treatment from Team McLaren's Peter Revson, who hits 179.354 and averages 178.696 to snatch the pole.

Before the day ends, Bobby Unser, Denis Hulme, and Al Unser all post faster times than Foyt. Despite being the first to break the 1968 qualifying record, Foyt winds up sixth fastest.

SATURDAY, MAY 22: Rookie John Mahler qualifies at a solid 170 mph to nail down the 27th starting spot. Two days later, after qualifying ends, car owner Dick Simon supplants Mahler in the car. Simon, bumped from the field on the final day, replaces Mahler to "fulfill sponsorship obligations" and lines up 33rd.

➔

Convertibles left the Dodge Challenger lineup after 1971, but before they did, one was selected to serve as the pace car at Indy (*right* and *opposite bottom*). Another 50 or so replicas were painted the same "Hemi Orange." Speedway owner Tony Hulman is with car-owner Roger Penske (*opposite, top left*), whose versatile driver, Mark Donohue, qualified second. Driver nameplates are stacked up in preparation for their use on pit message boards (*opposite, top right*).

STARTING LINEUP

Average Field Qualifying Speed: 171.665

Numbers in flags indicate finish position

POLE POSITION
Qualifying Speed: 178.696

Bobby Unser

A. J. Foyt

Mario Andretti

Gordon Johncock

Bentley Warren

Mark Donohue

Al Unser

Joe Leonard

Bill Vukovich, Jr.

Cale Yarborough

Peter Revson

Denis Hulme

Lloyd Ruby

Jim Malloy

Gary Bettenhausen

Rick Muther

George Snider

Johnny Rutherford

Steve Krisiloff

Mel Kenyon

Dick Simon

Bud Tingelstad

Donnie Allison

Wally Dallenbach

Larry Dickson

George Follmer

Bob Harkey

David Hobbs

Mike Mosley

Roger McCluskey

Sam Sessions

Denny Zimmerman

Art Pollard

A group of dealers was behind the '71 pace car program, not the factory, and the local businessmen were happy to be seen with the pacesetter and Tony Hulman (*top left*) *Today Show* host Joe Garagiola (*top right*) was among the celebrities in the pre-race activities, and he brought his own camera to record the occasion. The field heads into a pace lap just before the start of the 55th running of the 500 (*above*). Turn 1 action (*left*) has Bill Vukovich, Jr., leading Wally Dallenbach and Bud Tingelstad. Teammates Vukovich and Tingelstad finished fifth and seventh, respectively, and Dallenbach dropped out with a broken valve. Further back, Johnny Rutherford runs his yellow Eagle-Offenhauser on the apron as he dices with A. J. Foyt, who came in third. Rutherford struggled to an 18th-place finish.

On the first day of qualifications, Cale Yarborough's Mongoose-Ford suddenly emitted a puff of white smoke as it exited the fourth turn. Flagged into the pits, Yarborough and his crew thought the engine was about to let go.

Cale's teammate, Lloyd Ruby, was of the opinion that the Ford V-8 had burned a piston in the number three cylinder. He even offered to bet a crew member that he was correct in his observation.

Back in the garage area, the crew was about to pull the engine when one of them decided to take up Ruby's challenge. When the number three spark plug was removed, there was no indication of any mechanical trouble. Another mechanic decided to check the fuel tanks. Sure enough, they were little more than damp. Yarborough had simply run out of fuel.

Left: New Zealand's Denis Hulme, in a orange McLaren, and stock-car veteran Donnie Allison, in a red Coyote, pursue Mike Mosley's Eagle into Turn 1. Allison, Rookie of the Year in 1970, was the highest finisher of the three, coming in sixth. Despite two strong finishes, he never raced at Indy again after '71. *Below:* Jim Malloy stays a step ahead of Bill Vukovich, Jr., as Gary Bettenhausen pursues them both. Malloy finished fourth and Vukovich fifth.

Al Unser makes one of his four pit stops in the Johnny Lightning Special (*left*) on his way to winning a second straight 500, making him the first driver to win back-to-back races since Bill Vukovich in the Fifties. A. J. Foyt's Coyote is in front of polesitter Peter Revson's orange McLaren as they follow the groove into Turn 1 (*above*). Revson got by Foyt later in the race to finish second, one spot ahead of the three-time Indy champion. Winner Unser (*opposite bottom*) is the center of attention in the Dodge pace car, barely visible amid a sea of well-wishers on the front straight (*opposite, top left*). Unser's smiling chief mechanic, George Bignotti, stays close to his car and the Borg-Warner trophy in the new victory circle (*opposite, top right*).

THE RACE

Start: The field gets away cleanly, but the Dodge Challenger pace car, driven by local dealer Eldon Palmer, carries too much speed through the pits. Palmer hits the brakes, locks up the wheels, and the car skids into a photographer's stand at the south end of the pits.

The photo stand collapses, and 29 people are hurt, two seriously. Among the slightly injured is Speedway President Tony Hulman, a passenger in the pace car, who sprains an ankle.

On the track, Mark Donohue streaks ahead of polesitter Peter Revson to grab the lead on the first lap as Bobby Unser moves into second.

Lap 4: Denis Hulme's McLaren spins in Turn 3, but he avoids contact and continues to the pits.

Lap 12: Donohue still leads when Steve Krisiloff's Ford V-8 blows in Turn 3, spewing oil onto the track. Mel Kenyon spins in the oil and hits the wall, and Gordon Johncock plows into Kenyon and flies over the disabled car. Mario Andretti also spins and bangs into Johncock. All four cars are out of the race, but none of the drivers is seriously hurt.

Lap 51: When first-place Donohue and second-place Al Unser pit, the lead shuffles first to Joe Leonard and then to Bobby Unser.

Lap 65: Donohue blows by Bobby Unser to regain the lead and his next lap is the fastest of the race, a record 174.961 mph.

Lap 67: Donohue suddenly slows on the north end of the track and parks on the grass on the inside of Turn 4. After leading 52 laps, a broken transmission ends his day. Al Unser inherits the lead, the first time two brothers lead the same race.

Lap 98: Al Unser stops for fuel, giving the lead to Lloyd Ruby. When Ruby pits a few laps later, Bobby Unser takes over.

Lap 113: As Al Unser regains the lead from brother Bobby, David Hobbs's transmission breaks on the front straight, and Rick Muther loses control trying to dodge Hobbs. The two collide and Muther's car momentarily gets up on two wheels.

Both Unsers escape harm, but Al later reports a piece of debris bounced off his helmet.

Lap 159: Al Unser makes his fourth and final stop for fuel without losing the lead. Ruby runs second and Peter Revson third.

Lap 167: Mike Mosley loses a wheel in Turn 4 and crashes into the abandoned cars of Mark Donohue and Steve Krisiloff, which are parked along the inside retaining wall, flips over and catches fire.

Bobby Unser, who is running fourth, misses Mosley's burning wreck but hits the wall and is out of the race. Bill Vukovich, Jr., son of the late two-time winner, spins, avoids contact, and continues on to finish fifth.

Gary Bettenhausen stops his car in Turn 4, jumps out and tries to rescue Mosley, who suffers serious burns and a broken leg and elbow. Bettenhausen rejoins the race and finishes 10th.

Lap 174: As the cars slowly circle the track under yellow, Ruby pulls into the pits and retires with gear problems. Al Unser still holds first, with Revson and A. J. Foyt behind.

Lap 189: When green-flag racing resumes, Al Unser pulls away from Revson and Foyt.

Finish: Despite the lengthy caution period, Al Unser averages a record 157.735 mph and becomes the fourth driver to win two in a row. Unser leads 103 laps and finishes 23 seconds ahead of Revson. The Unser family celebrates in victory circle for the third time in four years.

It also is two in a row for Parnelli Jones's Colt chassis and three straight for Ford's turbocharged V-8 and Firestone tires.

Second-place Revson fails to lead a lap but runs in the top five most of the race. Foyt, who makes five pit stops to Revson's three, comes in third.

RESULTS

NO.	DRIVER	CAR	ENTRANT	ENGINE	CYL	DISP	CHASSIS	COLOR	QUAL SPD	START	FIN	LAPS / SPEED / REASON OUT
1	Al Unser	Johnny Lightning	Vel's Parnelli Jones Ford	Ford T	8	158	'71 P.J. Colt	blue, yelo, red	174.522	5	1	200-157.735
86	Peter Revson	McLaren	McLaren Cars, Inc.	Offy T	4	159	'71 McLaren	orng, blue, wht	178.696	1	2	200-157.419
9	A. J. Foyt	ITT Thompson	Thompson Industries	Ford T	8	159	'71 Coyote	orange, white	174.317	6	3	200-156.069
42	Jim Malloy	Olsonite Eagle	Dan Gurney	Offy T	4	158	'70 Eagle	blue, wht, gld	171.838	10	4	200-154.577
32	Bill Vukovich, Jr.	Sugaripe Prune	Jerry O'Connell	Offy T	4	158	'68 Brabham	yellow, maroon	171.674	11	5	200-154.563
84	Donnie Allison	Purolator	Foyt & Greer	Ford T	8	159	'71 Coyote	orange, white	171.903	20	6	199-flagged
58	Bud Tingelstad	Sugaripe Prune	Jerry O'Connell	Offy T	4	158	'68 Brabham	yellow, maroon	170.156	17	7	198-flagged
43	Denny Zimmerman	Fiore Racing	Frank J. Fiore	Offy T	4	159	'66 Vollstedt	wht, red, black	169.755	28	8	189-flagged
6	Roger McCluskey	Sprite	Lindsey Hopkins	Ford T	8	159	'70 Kuzma	green, orng, wht	171.241	22	9	188-flagged
16	Gary Bettenhausen	Thermo King	Don Gerhardt	Offy T	4	159	'70 Gerhardt	blue, silver	171.233	13	10	178-flagged
12	Lloyd Ruby	Utah Stars	Gene White Racing	Ford T	8	159	'70 Mongoose	blue, red, wht	173.821	7	11	174-gear failure
2	Bobby Unser	Olsonite Eagle	Dan Gurney	Offy T	4	158	'71 Eagle	wht, blue, orng	175.816	3	12	164-wrecked T4
4	Mike Mosley	G. C. Murphy	Leader Cards, Inc.	Ford T	8	159	'68 Eagle	wht, blue, orng	169.579	19	13	159-wrecked T4
44	Dick Simon	TraveLodge Sleeper	Dick Simon, Ltd.	Ford T	8	159	'67 Vollstedt	red, black	170.164	33	14	151-flagged
41	George Follmer	Grant King Racers	Grant King Racers	Offy T	4	158	'70 Kingfish	white, red	169.205	29	15	147-broken piston
21	Cale Yarborough	Gene White Firestone	Gene White Racing	Ford T	8	159	'70 Mongoose	red, wht, blue, gld	170.156	14	16	140-oil leak
85	Denis Hulme	McLaren	McLaren Cars, Ltd.	Offy T	4	159	'71 McLaren	orng, blue, wht	174.910	4	17	137-broken valve
18	Johnny Rutherford	Patrick Petroleum	Michner Petroleum, Inc.	Offy T	4	159	'67 Eagle	yellow, maroon	171.151	24	18	128-flagged
15	Joe Leonard	Samsonite	Vel's Parnelli Jones Ford	Ford T	8	158	'71 P. J. Colt	yelo, blue, red	172.761	8	19	123-broken fuel pump
68	David Hobbs	Penske Products	U.S. Racing, Inc.	Ford T	8	160	'70 Lola	blue, yelo, red, wht	169.571	16	20	107-gearbox failure
38	Rick Muther	Arkansas Aviation	Two Jacks, Inc.	Offy T	4	159	'65 Hawk II	white, orange	169.972	18	21	85-wrecked FS
99	Bob Harkey	Joe Hunt Magneto	Joe Hunt	Offy T	4	159	'69 Gerhardt	blue, gold, red	169.197	32	22	77-rear end failure
95	Bentley Warren	Classic Wax	Vatis Enterprises, Inc.	Offy T	4	159	'66 Eagle	wht, red, black	169.627	15	23	76-gearbox failure
22	Wally Dallenbach	Sprite	Lindsey Hopkins	Offy T	4	159	'70 Kuzma	grn, orng, wht	171.160	23	24	69-broken valve
66	Mark Donohue	Sunoco	U.S. Racing, Inc.	Offy T	4	159	'71 McLaren	blue, yelo, red, wht	177.087	2	25	66-transmission failure
64	Art Pollard	Gilmore Broadcasting	Gilmore Champion Racing	Ford T	8	159	'70 Scorpion	wht, red, blue	169.500	31	26	45-broken valve
98	Sam Sessions	Wynn's Kwik-Kool	Agajanian Faas Racers	Ford T	8	159	'68 Lola	blue, wht, red	170.358	25	27	43-engine failure
45	Larry Dickson	Grant King Racers	Grant King Racers	Offy T	4	159	'71 Kingfish	white, red	170.285	26	28	33-engine failure
7	Gordon Johncock	Norris Industries	Vollstedt Enterprises	Ford T	8	159	'70 McLaren	orange	171.388	12	29	11-wrecked T3
5	Mario Andretti	STP Oil Treatment	STP Corporation	Ford T	8	159	'71 McNamara	fluorescent red	172.612	9	30	11-wrecked T3
20	Steve Krisiloff	STP Gas Treatment	STP Corporation	Ford T	8	159	'71 McNamara	fluorescent red	169.835	27	31	10-oil leak, spun T3
23	Mel Kenyon	Sprite	Lindsey Hopkins	Ford T	8	159	'71 Kuzma	grn, wht, orng	170.205	30	32	10-wrecked T3
80	George Snider	G. C. Murphy	Leader Cards, Inc.	Offy T	4	159	'68 Eagle	white, blue	171.600	21	33	6-stalled

T = turbocharged

1972

56th Race • May 27, 1972

USAC rules allow larger rear wings this year, and speeds soar as a result. (Several cars top 190 mph in tire tests at the Speedway before practice opens on April 29.) The larger rear wings create more downforce, making the cars much faster in the turns.

Speed in the pits becomes more important this year because four pit stops are mandatory instead of three.

Ford is officially out of racing, but the company's turbocharged V-8 survives with a new name on the cam covers: Foyt. The three-time winner has taken over Ford's engine program for Indy and the USAC championship.

Parnelli Jones, co-owner of the last two winning cars, arrives with a new chassis that wears a wide, shovel-shaped nose and unusual diagonal side wings. Driving the new Parnelli is a "super team" that consists of Al Unser, gunning for his third straight win, 1969 winner Mario Andretti, and defending national champion Joe Leonard. All three qualify after the controversial side wings are removed.

Dan Gurney, now retired from driving, introduces a new Eagle chassis patterned after the McLaren M16 that debuted the previous year. Veteran Roger McCluskey qualifies in a sharp-nosed Antares chassis designed on a computer.

PRACTICE AND QUALIFYING

MONDAY, MAY 1: On the first practice day without speed limits, Jim Malloy runs a lap at 181.415 in an Eagle-Offy, unofficially topping Peter Revson's single-lap qualifying record by more than two mph.

FRIDAY, MAY 5: Speeds continue to climb. Bill Vukovich, Jr., hits 186.335 mph in his backup after blowing the Offy engine in his primary car. Malloy is fastest again, posting a lap of 188.048 late in the day.

SUNDAY, MAY 7: Gary Bettenhausen is the first to top 190 mph in practice, and he does it on two laps. His best is 190.315. Peter Revson is second fastest of the day at 188.3. Both are in McLaren-Offys.

WEDNESDAY, MAY 10: The Eagle flies early this week as 1968 winner Bobby Unser runs 194.721 mph during a "happy hour" practice lap. Unser's Eagle-Offy is now the favorite to win the pole on Saturday.

SATURDAY, MAY 13: Rain delays the run for the pole until 4:30 P.M. Denny Zimmerman and Roger McCluskey make attempts, but both abort their runs when they fail to get up to speed.

As closing time approaches, A. J. Foyt does 188.5 mph on his second warmup lap. His shot at the pole ends when he blows an engine after taking the green flag, leaving the field wide open for the next day.

SUNDAY, MAY 14: Pole favorite Bobby Unser lives up to expectations by averaging 195.940 mph in his Eagle, topping the old record by more than 17 mph, the biggest jump in qualifying speed in Speedway history.

Rain limits qualifying, and only 12 drivers make the field today, but 11 shatter the old record. When the day ends, five drivers are still eligible for the pole, including last year's polesitter Peter Revson.

During morning practice, Jim Malloy loses control of his Eagle and slams the wall coming out of Turn 3, suffering broken arms and legs and serious burns. He dies four days later.

SATURDAY, MAY 20: The pole is still up for grabs, but nobody catches Bobby Unser's Eagle. Peter Revson earns the second starting spot at 192.885 mph and Mark Donohue lines up third at 191.408. Revson and Donohue are in McLarens, and the entire front row has Offy power and Goodyear tires.

SUNDAY, MAY 21: Cale Yarborough bumps his way in with a four-lap average of 178.864 mph, nearly 10 mph faster than last year's slowest car and slightly quicker than last year's fastest car.

THE RACE

Start: Bobby Unser surges into the lead and pulls away from the pack with Peter Revson in pursuit.

Lap 23: Revson drops out with a →

STARTING LINEUP

Average Field Qualifying Speed: 183.655

Numbers in flags indicate finish position

Mark Donohue

Joe Leonard

Swede Savage

Mel Kenyon

Jerry Grant

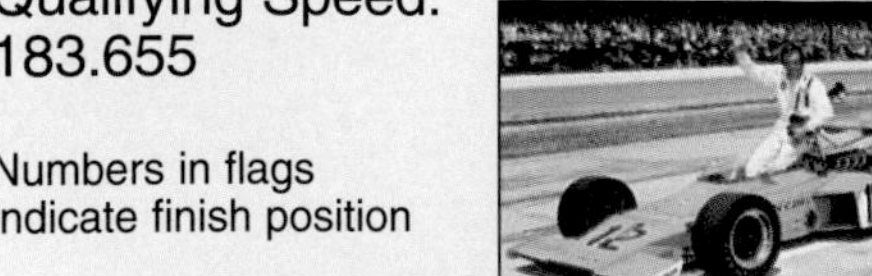

Peter Revson

Mario Andretti

Johnny Rutherford

Lloyd Ruby

John Martin

POLE POSITION
Qualifying Speed:
195.940

Bobby Unser

Gary Bettenhausen

Sam Posey

Steve Krisiloff

Jim Hurtubise

In 1972, there seemed to be an unusual spate of engine trouble, mechanical problems, and accidents during practice and qualifications. Veteran car builder Frank Kurtis, whose Kurtis-Kraft roadsters, sprint cars, and midgets had been the scourge of America's speedways in years gone by, was at the Indianapolis Motor Speedway observing the happenings. Although Kurtis had retired several years before, he still had a keen interest in racing. Watching his old friends fight through one problem after another, Frank confided his views to a friend.

"I had a new car on the drawing board," Kurtis said. "But after seeing all the problems everyone is having, it's going to stay there."

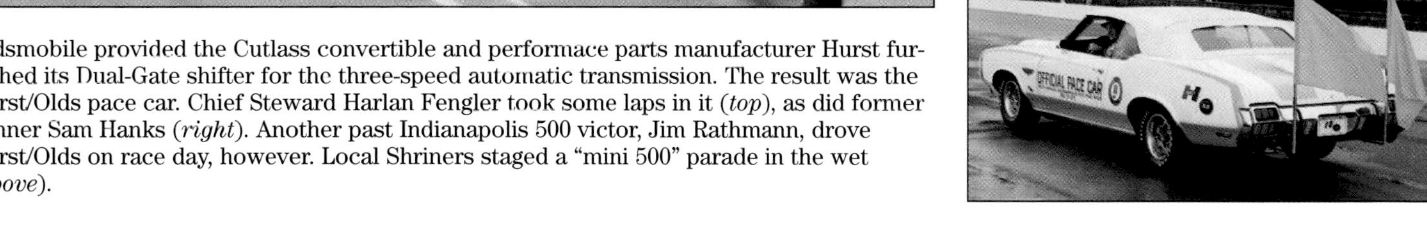

Oldsmobile provided the Cutlass convertible and performace parts manufacturer Hurst furnished its Dual-Gate shifter for the three-speed automatic transmission. The result was the Hurst/Olds pace car. Chief Steward Harlan Fengler took some laps in it (*top*), as did former winner Sam Hanks (*right*). Another past Indianapolis 500 victor, Jim Rathmann, drove Hurst/Olds on race day, however. Local Shriners staged a "mini 500" parade in the wet (*above*).

Bill Vukovich, Jr.

George Snider

Sam Sessions

Salt Walther

Lee Kunzman

Wally Dallenbach

A. J. Foyt

Roger McCluskey

Dick Simon

Gordon Johncock

John Mahler

Cale Yarborough

Mike Mosley

Al Unser

Carl Williams

Mike Hiss

Denny Zimmerman

Jimmy Caruthers

Roger McCluskey drove the computer-designed Antares (*left*). Cars that didn't qualify: Larry Dickson's No. 19 (*below*), Wally Dallenbach's No. 10 (*second from top, left*), and George Snider's No. 35 (*second from top, right*). Art Pollard broke his leg when he crashed the STP Lola (*opposite top*). Linda Vaughn, Miss Hurst Golden Shifter, waves to the crowd (*opposite middle*). *Bottom:* The front row, from left, of Donohue, Revson, and Bobby Unser. The field takes its pace lap (*opposite bottom*).

With only a few hours left before qualifications closed, Vince Granatelli and the STP crew began a thrash to replace the car Art Pollard had crashed after making the field. From parts off the wrecked racer and another tub, they made one car out of two and were granted 33rd spot for this "backup" car. Pollard was injured in the crash, so Wally Dallenbach was hired to drive.

In the race, Dallenbach clawed his way toward the front in spite of the car. The rear end was loose and part of the windshield broke off after 100 miles, allowing the wind to buffet his head. But Wally kept on gunning it. While he was running, few on the track could stay with him. But his pit stops were horrendous. On three of his stops, the fuel refilling nozzle stuck, sending gallons of methanol all over the car and into the cockpit. On all three occasions, the car caught fire. Dallenbach had to bail out of the cockpit once, but he scrambled back into the singed racer. He finally took the flag in 14th place.

After the outstanding run, Dallenbach counted his injuries. Fortunately, he'd only lost a few eyelashes and his hands were a little warm. "It sure was a good feeling to take that old checkered flag," Wally related. "In six starts, that's the first time I've taken the flag at Indy."

He certainly had earned it the hard way.

broken transmission, giving second place to Gary Bettenhausen. Mark Donohue is third.

Lap 31: Bobby Unser coasts into the pits without power. His Offy engine quits with ignition failure, knocking him out of the race. Bettenhausen moves into first place and Mike Mosley is second.

Lap 42: A faulty fuel valve causes Wally Dallenbach's car to catch fire in the pits, but he gets back into the race.

Lap 56: Mosley zips around Bettenhausen to grab the lead, but the next time around he loses a wheel and crashes in Turn 4. The car catches fire and Mosley escapes with burns to his feet, hands, and face. Bettenhausen slips by to regain the lead.

Lap 81: Dallenbach's car catches fire again while refueling, but his crew puts it out and he gets back into the race.

Lap 150: Third-place Donohue—in pursuit of Bettenhausen and second-place Jerry Grant—runs the fastest lap of the race, 187.539 mph.

Lap 151: Bettenhausen runs 186.838 mph, fastest lead lap of the race. Meanwhile, Dallenbach's car is on fire in the pits a third time. He again manages to get back out and finishes 15th, 18 laps down.

Lap 176: Bettenhausen leads 138 laps and appears on his way to victory when he develops engine problems and slows. Grant grabs the lead, with Donohue chasing. Six laps later, Bettenhausen coasts to a halt, the victim of ignition failure.

Lap 188: Leader Grant makes an emergency stop for fresh front tires but overshoots his pit stall. He gets a splash of fuel from teammate Bobby Unser's pit and goes back out running second behind Donohue.

Grant closes in on Donohue but runs out of time to catch him. In any event, USAC stops counting Grant's laps for taking on fuel from another pit, and he ends up in 12th place.

Finish: Donohue leads only 13 laps, but with Grant out of the picture, he wins by more than three laps over Al Unser. Donohue averages 162.962 to beat the old record by more than five mph and give owner Roger Penske his first 500 win.

Runner-up Unser misses a chance to win an unprecedented three in a row. Teammates Joe Leonard and Mario Andretti finish third and eighth, respectively.

Offys sweep the top three spots, and Goodyear wins for the first time since 1968.

Opposite page: Relaxed was the dress code for the Seventies infield crowd (top). Wally Dallenbach leads Roger McCluskey and Mike Hiss (bottom right). Lee Kunzman limps in (bottom left). *This page:* Gary Bettenhausen's crew goes to work (above). Winner Mark Donohue (below) celebrates with owner Roger Penske (above right).

RESULTS

NO.	DRIVER	CAR	ENTRANT	ENGINE	CYL	DISP	CHASSIS	COLOR	QUAL SPD	START	FIN	LAPS / SPEED / REASON OUT
66	Mark Donohue	Sunoco McLaren	Roger Penske Enterprises	Offy T	4	159	McLaren	blu, yelo, rd, wht	191.408	3	1	200-162.962
4	Al Unser	Viceroy	Vel's Parnelli Jones Racing	Offy T	4	158	Parnelli	red, wht, blue	183.617	19	2	200-160.192
1	Joe Leonard	Samsonite	Vel's Parnelli Jones Racing	Offy T	4	158	Parnelli	yelo, blue, wht	185.223	6	3	200-159.327
52	Sam Sessions	Gene White Firestone	Gene White Racing	Ford T	8	159	Lola	white, black	180.415	24	4	200-158.411
34	Sam Posey	Norris Eagle	Champ Carr, Inc.	Offy T	4	158	Eagle	red, white	184.379	7	5	198-flagged
5	Lloyd Ruby	Wynn's	Gene White Racing	Foyt T	8	159	Atlanta	wht, lavndr, orng	181.415	11	6	196-flagged
60	Mike Hiss	STP Pylon Wip. Blade	Page Racing Enterprises	Offy T	4	158	Eagle	yelo, red, blue	179.015	25	7	196-flagged
9	Mario Andretti	Viceroy	Vel's Parnelli Jones Racing	Offy T	4	158	Parnelli	red, wht, blue	187.617	5	8	194-flagged
11	Jimmy Caruthers	U.S.A.F./Steed	Quality Racing, Inc.	Foyt T	8	159	Scorpion	yellow, blue	178.909	31	9	194-flagged
21	Cale Yarborough	Bill Daniels GOP	Gene White Racing	Foyt T	8	159	Atlanta	wht, red, blue	178.864	32	10	193-flagged
84	George Snider	ITT Thompson	A.J. Foyt, Jr. Enterprises	Foyt T	8	159	Coyote	orng, blk, wht	181.855	21	11	190-flagged
48	Jerry Grant	Mystery Eagle	All American Racers	Offy T	4	158	Eagle	purple, white	189.294	15	12	188-illegal fuel stop
44	Dick Simon	TraveLodge Sleeper	Dick Simon, Ltd.	Foyt T	8	159	Lola	orng, blk, wht	180.424	23	13	186-flagged
7	Gary Bettenhausen	Sunoco McLaren	Roger Penske Enterprises	Offy T	4	158	McLaren	blu, yelo, rd, wht	188.877	4	14	182-ignition failure
40	Wally Dallenbach	STP Oil Treatment	STP Corporation	Foyt T	8	159	Lola	red, blk, slvr	181.626	33	15	182-flagged
89	John Martin	Unsponsored	Automotive Technology	Offy T	4	158	Brabham	red, wht, blk	179.614	14	16	161-fuel leak
37	Lee Kunzman	Caves Buick Co.	Caves Buick Co.	Offy T	4	158	Gerhardt	blue	179.265	30	17	131-lost tire spun
23	Mel Kenyon	Gilmore Racing Team	Lindsey Hopkins	Foyt T	8	159	Coyote	red, wht, blk	181.388	12	18	126-injector failure
17	Denny Zimmerman	Bryant Hea & Cool	Vollstedt Enterprises	Offy T	4	159	Coyote	orange, black	180.027	28	19	116-broken distributor
24	Gordon Johncock	Gulf McLaren	McLaren Cars, Ltd.	Offy T	4	162	McLaren	orng, wht, blue	188.511	26	20	113-broken exhaust valve
15	Steve Krisiloff	Lloyds Ayr-Way	Grant King Racers	Offy T	4	158	Kingfish	brown, gold	181.433	10	21	102-turbocharger failure
31	John Mahler	Harbor Fuel Oil	Vanguard Racing	Offy T	4	158	McLaren	orng, blue, wht	179.497	29	22	99-broken piston
56	Jim Hurtubise	Miller High Life	M.V.S., Inc.	Foyt T	8	158	Coyote	wht, red, gold	181.050	13	23	94-off course, disqualified
14	Roger McCluskey	Am. Mar. Undrwrtrs	Lindsey Hopkins	Offy T	4	158	Antares	blue, white	182.676	20	24	92-burned valve
2	A. J. Foyt	ITT Thompson	A. J. Foyt Enterprises	Foyt T	8	159	Coyote	orange, silver	188.996	17	25	60-engine failure
98	Mike Mosley	Vivitar	Leader Cards, Inc.	Offy T	4	159	Eagle	wht, blue, red	189.145	16	26	56-wrecked T4
18	Johnny Rutherford	Patrick Petroleum	Michner-Patrick Racing	Offy T	4	158	Brabham	yelo, red, black	183.234	8	27	55-broken con. rod
3	Bill Vukovich, Jr.	Sugaripe Prune	Jerry O'Connell	Offy T	4	158	Eagle	yelo, maroon	184.814	18	28	54-rear end failure
95	Carl Williams	Vatis	Vatis Enterprises, Inc.	Offy T	4	158	Eagle	blue, yelo, red	180.469	22	29	52-broken oil cooler
6	Bobby Unser	Olsonite Eagle	Olsonite Division	Offy T	4	158	Eagle	wht, blue, orng	195.940	1	30	31-broken dis. rotor
12	Peter Revson	Gulf McLaren	McLaren Cars, Ltd.	Offy T	4	162	McLaren	orng, wht, blue	192.885	2	31	23-broken gearbox
42	Swede Savage	Michner Industries	Michner-Patrick Racing	Offy T	4	158	Eagle	brown, yellow	181.726	9	32	5-broken con. rod
33	Salt Walther	Dayton Disc Brake	Walmotor, Inc.	Foyt T	8	159	P.J. Colt	blue, orng, wht	180.542	27	33	0-magneto failure

T = turbocharged

1973

57th Race • May 28-30, 1973

The landscape around 16th Street and Georgetown Road changes with new hospitality suites towering over Turn 2 as an addition to the Speedway Motel.

A new main entrance at the south end of the Speedway includes a four-lane tunnel under the south chute, greatly improving ingress and egress to the track. The new entrance proves invaluable because the race crowd goes home twice before seeing a lap of competition. The race finally starts and ends on the third day.

The Offenhauser four-cylinder, whose roots date to the Miller straight-eight of the Twenties, dominates. Turbocharged Offys power 26 starters, including the first six rows. Only six Ford-based Foyt V-8s qualify.

Only three rookies make the race, the fewest since 1941: stock-car star Bobby Allison, New Zealander Graham McRae, and Jerry Karl, who qualifies a stock-block Chevrolet V-8 entered by Smokey Yunick.

Dan Gurney's Eagle is the chassis of choice this year, used by 20 starters. Seven drivers use McLarens.

PRACTICE AND QUALIFYING

FRIDAY, MAY 4: Gordon Johncock hits 194.636 mph in practice with his STP-sponsored Eagle-Offy. Johncock is one of the favorites to win the pole because he topped 199 in March during a Goodyear tire test.

SATURDAY, MAY 5: Practice speeds take a big jump as second-year driver Swede Savage posts 197.8 mph during "happy hour." Three others top 195: Gordon Johncock (Savage's teammate), Gary Bettenhausen, and Johnny Rutherford.

SATURDAY, MAY 12: Pole Day starts on a tragic note when veteran Art Pollard loses control of his Eagle-Offy in Turn 1 during practice and crashes into the outside wall. Pollard dies from the impact, which rips the right-side wheels off his car.

Once qualifying starts, Texan Rutherford electrifies the crowd, estimated at 250,000 by the Speedway, with a run of 198.413 mph to top the record set a year earlier by nearly three mph. His best lap is 199.071.

Twenty-three other drivers qualify, and 1968 winner Bobby Unser comes closest to knocking Rutherford off the pole. Unser falls just .21 seconds short with a speed of 198.183. Defending winner Mark Donohue takes the outside of row one at 197.412.

SUNDAY, MAY 20: Jim McElreath, driving his fourth different car of the month, bumps his way in to earn his 10th start. McElreath is the slowest of the 33 qualifiers at 188.64 mph. The second-slowest is three-time winner A. J. Foyt, who lines up 23rd with a speed of 188.927.

The field averages a record 192.329 mph, nearly nine mph faster than the 1972 starters.

THE RACE

MONDAY, MAY 28

Start: Rain delays the start nearly four hours. As the field heads for the green flag, second-time starter Salt Walther crashes into the outside wall on the front straight, and his McLaren flips over and erupts in flames.

Walther suffers severe burns and internal injuries, 11 spectators are hurt, and 11 other cars are caught in the fiery melee. The red flag halts the race before it starts.

Rain returns a short time after the wreck, and the race is postponed until 9 A.M. Tuesday.

TUESDAY, MAY 29

Start: Rain delays the start until about 10:15 A.M. With the pace car about to pull into the pits and 32 cars ready to take the green flag, it starts to rain again.

At 2 P.M., USAC officials postpone the race to Wednesday, the first time the race is postponed two days in a row.

WEDNESDAY, MAY 30

Start: More rain delays the start a third time, but when the green flag finally flies shortly after 2 P.M., Bobby Unser surges in front of polesitter Johnny Rutherford to grab the lead.

Lap 4: Peter Revson spins in Turn 4 and hits the inside wall, knocking his McLaren out of the race. Bobby Unser stays in front. Rutherford falls back as Mark Donohue and Swede Savage pursue Unser. ➔

STARTING LINEUP

Average Field Qualifying Speed: 192.329

Numbers in flags indicate finish position

POLE POSITION
Qualifying Speed: 198.413

Mark Donohue · Mario Andretti · Jimmy Caruthers · Bobby Allison · Lloyd Ruby

Bobby Unser · Gary Bettenhausen · Al Unser · Gordon Johncock · Roger McCluskey

Johnny Rutherford · Swede Savage · Steve Krisiloff · Peter Revson · Graham McRae

Cadillac's massive Eldorado was the first front-drive pace car since the 1930 Cord L-29. Cadillac removed the air conditioner and pollution controls, and fortified the 500-cubic-inch V-8 to produce more than 500 horsepower, enough to prepare the 5000-pound convertible for race-day duty at the Speedway.

Jerry Grant

Mike Mosley

John Martin

Dick Simon

George Snider

Jim McElreath

Salt Walther

Wally Dallenbach

A. J. Foyt

Mike Hiss

Joe Leonard

Sam Sessions

Bill Vukovich, Jr.

Mel Kenyon

David Hobbs

Lee Kunzman

Jerry Karl

Bob Harkey

GOODYEAR
SUNOCO
66
OLSONITE EAGLE
8
GOODYEAR
DAN GURNEY RACING

GOODYEAR

20
GOODYEAR
20
Ashland
STP

Left: Johnny Rutherford put his No. 7 McLaren on the pole and was joined on the front row by the Eagles of former winners Bobby Unser (center) and Mark Donohue (far left). Mario Andretti (*opposite, middle left*) jokes with David Hobbs, who qualified for his second start. Gordon Johncock has a word in the pits with Chief Steward Harlan Fengler (*opposite, middle right*). Johncock and chief mechanic George Bignotti (*opposite bottom*) made the STP Eagle a strong contender. Actor Chad Everett tours the Brickyard on race day (*below left*). Defending winner Mark Donohue again was a threat in Roger Penske's Sunoco entry (*below*). The pack heads out under ominous skies (*bottom*).

Lap 40: Bobby Unser pits, giving the lead to Gordon Johncock, who moves up from 11th starting position.

Lap 43: Savage grabs the lead from Johncock.

Lap 54: Al Unser bolts inside of Savage on the front straight to take the lead.

Lap 58: Savage grazes the wall in Turn 4, slides sideways across the track and slams into the inside wall, his Eagle bursting into flames and spreading burning fuel on the track.

As a fire truck speeds through the pits to reach Savage, it strikes and kills Armando Teran, a member of Graham McRae's crew.

Savage suffers severe burns and other injuries, and officials stop the race.

Lap 59: The race restarts more than an hour after Savage's crash, and leader Al Unser pulls away from the pack.

Lap 73: Al Unser slows with mechanical problems, giving the lead to Johncock. Unser drops out two laps later with a broken piston. Bill Vukovich, Jr., moves into second, and Bobby Unser runs third, a lap down.

Lap 100: As other cars fall off the pace, Johncock turns the fastest lead lap of the race, 184.805 mph. Vukovich remains the only other car on the lead lap, some 20 seconds behind.

Lap 129: The yellow flag comes out as rain starts to fall.

Finish: It is raining harder as Johncock takes the checkered flag on the 133rd lap, ending one of the grimmest 500s in history. Johncock leads 64 laps in his Eagle-Offy, including the last 61. He gives chief mechanic George Bignotti his sixth victory and Andy Granatelli his second. This time, however, Granatelli is a sponsor (Pat Patrick is the owner).

Only 10 cars are running at the end. Vukovich finishes second. Roger McCluskey, who turns the fastest lap of the race at 186.916 mph, comes in third, two laps down. Polesitter Rutherford fails to lead a lap and struggles to a ninth place finish.

Savage, Johncock's STP teammate, dies July 2 from his injuries.

RESULTS

NO.	DRIVER	CAR	ENTRANT	ENGINE	CYL	DISP	CHASSIS	COLOR	QUAL SPD	START	FIN	LAPS / SPEED / REASON OUT
20	Gordon Johncock	STP Double Oil Filter	Patrick Racing Team	Offy T	4	157	'73 Eagle	red, black	192.555	11	1	133-159.036
2	Bill Vukovich, Jr.	Sugaripe Prune	Jerry O'Connell	Offy T	4	161	Eagle	yellow, maroon	191.103	16	2	133-flagged
3	Roger McCluskey	Lindsey Hopkins Buick	Lindsey Hopkins	Offy T	4	159	McLaren	blue, white	191.928	14	3	131-flagged
19	Mel Kenyon	Atlanta Falcons	Lindsey Hopkins	Foyt T	8	159	Eagle	red, white	190.225	19	4	131-flagged
5	Gary Bettenhausen	Sunoco DX	Roger S. Penske	Offy T	4	159	McLaren	blue, yelo, wht, red	195.599	5	5	130-flagged
24	Steve Krisiloff	Elliott-Norton Spirit	Grant King Racers	Offy T	4	158	Kingfish	blue, yellow	194.932	7	6	129-flagged
16	Lee Kunzman	Ayr-Way/Lloyd's	Lindsey Hopkins	Offy T	4	159	Eagle	blue, rose	193.092	25	7	127-flagged
89	John Martin	Unsponsored	Automotive Technology	Offy T	4	156	McLaren	red, white	194.384	24	8	124-flagged
7	Johnny Rutherford	Gulf McLaren	McLaren Cars, Ltd.	Offy T	4	159	McLaren	orng, blue, wht	198.413	1	9	124-flagged
98	Mike Mosley	Lodestar	Leader Cards, Inc.	Offy T	4	161	Eagle	wht, blue, red	189.753	21	10	120-broken con. rod bolt
73	David Hobbs	Carling Black Label	Roy Woods Racing	Offy T	4	158	Eagle	black, red, wht	189.454	22	11	107-flagged
84	George Snider	Gilmore Racing	A. J. Foyt, Sr.	Foyt T	8	159	Coyote	orng, wht, blue	190.355	30	12	101-gearbox failure
8	Bobby Unser	Olsonite	Olsonite Division	Offy T	4	159	Eagle	wht, blue, orng	198.183	2	13	100-broken con. rod bolt
44	Dick Simon	TraveLodge	Dick Simon, Ltd.	Foyt T	8	160	Eagle	wht, red, orng	191.276	27	14	100-broken piston
66	Mark Donohue	Sunoco DX	Roger S. Penske	Offy T	4	159	Eagle	blue, yelo, rd, wht	197.412	3	15	92-burned piston
60	Graham McRae	STP Gas Treatment	STP Corporation	Offy T	4	159	Eagle	red, black	192.031	13	16	91-broken header
6	Mike Hiss	Thermo King	Don Gerhardt	Offy T	4	159	Eagle	blue, yelo	191.939	26	17	91-broken valve
1	Joe Leonard	Samsonite	Vel's Parnelli Jones Racing	Offy T	4	159	Parnelli	yellow, black	189.954	29	18	91-broken hub
48	Jerry Grant	Olsonite	All American Racer's, Inc.	Offy T	4	159	Eagle	wht, prpl, blk, orng	190.235	18	19	77-broken con. rod bolt
4	Al Unser	Viceroy	Vel's Parnelli Jones Racing	Offy T	4	159	Parnelli	red, wht, blue	194.879	8	20	75-broken piston
21	Jimmy Caruthers	Cobre	Robert L. Fletcher	Offy T	4	159	Eagle	turq, wht, gld, blk	194.217	9	21	73-broken suspension
40	Swede Savage	STP Oil Treatment	Patrick Racing Team	Offy T	4	157	Eagle	red, black	196.582	4	22	57-wrecked T4-died
35	Jim McElreath	Norris Eagle	Champ Car Enterprises	Offy T	4	159	Eagle	red, white	188.640	33	23	54-broken con. rod bolt
62	Wally Dallenbach	Olsonite Eagle	All American Racers, Inc.	Offy T	4	159	Eagle	wht, blue, orng	190.194	20	24	48-broken con. rod bolt
14	A. J. Foyt	Gilmore Racing	A. J. Foyt, Sr.	Foyt T	8	159	Coyote	orng, wht, blue	188.927	23	25	37-broken con. rod bolt
30	Jerry Karl	Oriente Express	Smokey Yunick	Chevy T	8	208	Eagle	blk, gld, red	190.799	28	26	22-flagged
18	Lloyd Ruby	Comndr Mtr Homes	Milce Slater	Offy T	4	159	Eagle	wht, orng, brn	191.622	15	27	21-broken piston
9	Sam Sessions	M.V.S.	M.V.S., Inc.	Foyt T	8	159	Eagle	rd, wht, blue, yelo	188.986	32	28	17-oil leak
28	Bob Harkey	Bryant Heat & Cool	Lindsey Hopkins	Foyt T	8	159	Kenyon-Eagle	red, white	189.733	31	29	12-engine seized
11	Mario Andretti	Viceroy	Vel's Parnelli Jones Racing	Offy T	4	159	Parnelli	wht, red, gld, blue	159.059	6	30	4-burned piston
15	Peter Revson	Gulf McLaren	McLaren Cars, Ltd.	Offy T	4	159	McLaren	orng, blue, wht	192.606	10	31	3-wrecked T4
12	Bobby Allison	Sunoco DX	Roger S. Penske	Offy T	4	159	McLaren	blue, red, yelo, wht	192.308	12	32	1-broken con. rod bolt
77	Salt Walther	Dayton-Walther	Walmotor, Inc.	Offy T	4	159	McLaren	blue, orng, wht	190.739	17	33	0-wrecked FS

T = turbocharged

Opposite page: Steve Krisiloff stalks Wally Dallenbach (top). Mark Donohue gets service in the pits (middle left) and seeks a way past Lee Kunzman on the track (middle right). Kunzman and Roger McCluskey harry Swede Savage (bottom left). Gordon Johncock pits (bottom right). *This page:* Johncock roars by Joe Leonard (above). Johncock (right) led when rain ended the race.

58th Race • May 26, 1974

Safety and fuel economy concerns generate major changes to the cars, the schedule for the month of May, and the race itself.

In the aftermath of Swede Savage's fiery crash the year before, maximum fuel capacity drops from 75 gallons to 40. USAC also mandates that the tanks be on the left side of the cars to reduce the chances of fire if a car hits an outside wall. The smaller tanks promise to alter race strategy because the cars will now require fuel stops every 25 laps or so.

Johnny Rutherford came within a whisker of 200 mph in his record-setting 1973 qualifying run, but speeds are lower this year. Maximum rear wing width drops from 64 inches 55 to slow the cars in the turns, and new rules limit turbocharged engines to 80 inches of manifold boost pressure. To keep mechanics honest, USAC requires new "popoff" valves that open when turbo boost exceeds 80 inches.

Safety measures at the track include higher outside and inside retaining walls at a uniform 32 inches tall. Several rows of trackside seats are removed along the front straight and a second safety fence is added.

The pit lane extends further north so drivers exit the track from Turn 4 instead of negotiating a tight left-hand kink off the front straight.

In a bow to fuel economy issues arising from the OPEC oil embargo, the Speedway cuts practice from three weeks to two and reduces qualifying from two weekends to successive Saturdays. Though politically correct, the latter move leads to a court fight.

The Speedway finally rescinds its never-on-a-Sunday policy, changing a tradition that dates to 1911. For the first time, the schedule calls for the race to run on the last Sunday of May, the day before the national observance of Memorial Day.

PRACTICE AND QUALIFYING

MONDAY, MAY 6: The first casualty of the month occurs before the first car gets on the track. During the traditional race to be the first car out, eager crew members start pushing their cars toward pit road before 71-year-old track steward Walt Myers gets out of the way. Myers trips and breaks a hip and a wrist.

New Chief Steward Tom Binford fines the Penske →

Hurst and Oldsmobile teamed up again to customize a Cutlass S coupe with a removable roof panel, a 455-cubic-inch V-8, and Hurst's Dual-Gate shifter for pace car use (*below*). New Chief Steward Tom Binford (*opposite bottom*) put his seal of approval on the Hurst/Olds. Oldsmobile also decked out Delta 88 convertibles (*opposite top*) and Cutlass sedans (*opposite middle*) in pace car trim. The official-vehicles fleet gets a soggy sendoff (*above*).

STARTING LINEUP

Average Field Qualifying Speed: 182.787

Numbers in flags indicate finish position

Mike Hiss

Mike Mosley

David Hobbs

Jimmy Caruthers

Steve Krisiloff

Wally Dallenbach

Mario Andretti

Tom Sneva

Gary Bettenhausen

Salt Walther

POLE POSITION
Qualifying Speed:
191.632

A. J. Foyt

Gordon Johncock

Bobby Unser

Dick Simon

George Snider

From his very first laps on the track in May 1974, A. J. Foyt had been a marked man. And following his sensational pole winning qualifying run of 191.632 mph, many sportswriters and fans tabbed him to win his fourth Indy 500.

A. J. didn't like all the fuss and talk about such a possibility. It put a great deal of pressure on him to perform—but no more than the talented Texan put on himself. Two days prior to the 500, Foyt decided to blow off some steam.

The tension reliever came in the form of wheeling his own sprint car around the one-mile dirt track at the Indiana State Fairgrounds. The "Hoosier Sprints," a night program comprised of two 50-lap feature events, attracted some of the finest sprint drivers around. Most Indy drivers hardly would have chosen such a diversion so close to the big race, even if they had experience with the man-eating, 500-horsepower, 1300-pound thunderbolts. But here was Foyt, not just running through the clouds of arc-lit dust, but handily winning both feature events on the card.

"I just wanted to see if I could keep up with these kids," Foyt drawled. "They're really tough."

"I wanted to get some of the tension off before Sunday."

Lloyd Ruby

Pancho Carter

Rick Muther

Roger McCluskey

Jim McElreath

Larry Cannon

Jerry Grant

Bill Simpson

Tom Bigelow

Al Unser

Johnny Parsons

Jan Opperman

Bill Vukovich, Jr.

Jerry Karl

John Martin

Johnny Rutherford

Jim Hurtubise

Bob Harkey

and Vollstedt teams $100 each for jumping the green.

TUESDAY, MAY 7: Three-time winner A. J. Foyt shows he's ready to claim another space on the Borg-Warner trophy by running 192.349 mph in his Coyote. Foyt uses a Ford-based V-8 with his own name on the valve covers. Offenhauser pilot Johnny Rutherford and 1968 winner Bobby Unser top 190.

A two-car crash in Turn 1 severely damages the cars of Tom Bigelow and Lee Brayton, but both drivers escape injuries.

FRIDAY, MAY 10: In the final practice before Pole Day, Bobby Unser sets the fast time of 192.513 mph, and both Foyt and Rutherford are over 190.

SATURDAY, MAY 11: Foyt is the first to run for the pole, and he qualifies at 191.632 mph. The expected challenge from Bobby Unser fizzles when Unser runs a disappointing 185.176.

Wally Dallenbach, his Offy engine benefiting from a larger and controversial turbocharger, posts the second fastest time at 189.683 before rain suspends qualifying for three hours.

When qualifying resumes, no one challenges Foyt's speed before the 6 P.M. quitting time. Ten drivers are still in line to run for the pole, including defending winner Gordon Johncock and 1969 champ Mario Andretti. However, this year's abbreviated schedule requires they wait until next Saturday.

SATURDAY, MAY 18: None of the 10 eligible drivers comes close to knocking Foyt off the pole. He wins his third pole and is joined on the front row by Dallenbach's Eagle-Offy and Mike Hiss's McLaren-Offy.

Rain halts qualifying from 12:45 to 4:20 P.M., and a long line of cars is ready when the track finally dries. Johnny Rutherford is fastest of the second-day qualifiers at 190.446 mph and second only to Foyt overall.

Just before the 6 P.M. gun sounds, rookie Jan Opperman bumps his way into the last row, officially ending qualifying. Six cars that have yet to make a qualifying run remain in line, and the owners immediately file a protest with USAC.

TUESDAY, MAY 21: Denied a chance to make the field, the car owners file for a court injunction to reopen qualifying or delay the race.

THURSDAY, MAY 23: A couple of hours after drivers complete their final Carburetion Day tests, Superior Court Judge Frank Symmes, Jr., denies the request for an injunction. The race will run on Sunday.

THE RACE

Start: Wally Dallenbach surges ahead of A. J. Foyt at the green flag and leads the first lap.

Lap 2: Leader Dallenbach runs the race's fastest lap, a record 191.408.

Lap 3: Dallenbach pulls into the pits with a burned piston, giving the lead to Foyt.

Lap 25: Bobby Unser takes the lead when Foyt makes his first pit stop. Foyt regains the lead two laps later.

Lap 49: Foyt makes his second stop, and Bobby Unser takes the lead for three laps. When Foyt goes back in front, Johnny Rutherford is on his tail. →

The freshman class of '74 included (*opposite*), from left, Tom Sneva, Pancho Carter, Bill Simpson, Jan Opperman, Tom Bigelow, Larry Cannon, and Johnny Parsons, Jr. A clear tube showing the fuel-tank level (*far left*) allowed crews to track mileage during the race. Long-time entrant Lindsey Hopkins (*left*) owned Roger McCluskey's car. After Jim Nabors sang *Back Home Again in Indiana* (*below*) and Speedway owner Tony Hulman commanded, "Gentlemen, start your engines" (*below left*), Wally Dallenbach jumped ahead of A. J. Foyt to lead at the start (*bottom*).

Lap 64: Leader Foyt and second-place Rutherford pit at the same time. Rutherford takes on fuel only while Foyt lingers for fresh rubber. Rutherford gets out first and grabs the lead.

Lap 125: Foyt regains the lead when Rutherford makes the fifth of his eight pit stops.

Lap 135: Foyt pits, and Rutherford goes back into first place.

Lap 138: With the crowd on its feet, Foyt catches Rutherford on the front straight and slips underneath him in Turn 1, grabbing the lead.

Lap 139: The black flag waves at Foyt as his Coyote starts to drop oil on the track.

Lap 141: Foyt pulls into the pits but stays long enough only for a splash of fuel before roaring back onto the track. Rutherford inherits the lead.

Lap 142: The black flag flies again for Foyt, and this time he makes the hard left turn off pit road into the garage area. A broken scavenger pump ends his bid for a fourth victory.

Finish: Rutherford leads the rest of the way, except for his final stop on Lap 176, and finishes 22 seconds ahead of Bobby Unser. Rutherford, who didn't lead a lap in his 10 previous races, leads 122 this day while averaging 158.589 mph.

Unser's Eagle is the only other car to finish on the lead lap. Bill Vukovich, Jr., second the year before, finishes third, a lap down.

It is the third win in a row for the Offy engine and Goodyear tires, and the first for McLaren Cars, Ltd. Offys power 28 of the 33 starters (the other five use Foyt V-8s) and the top seven finishers.

In a welcome contrast to recent previous years, there are no serious injuries during the race.

Pole-sitter A. J. Foyt and his front-row mates loosen up their cars on a pre-race parade lap (*top*). Jerry Karl leads Gordon Johncock and Bill Vukovich, Jr (*second from top*). Gary Bettenhausen (*right*) lasted just two laps. Jerry Grant has Lloyd Ruby, Vukovich, and Bill Simpson in his mirrors (*below*). Johnny Rutherford takes a victory lap with his family (*opposite top*) after cruising to victory over Bobby Unser in his McLaren (*opposite bottom*).

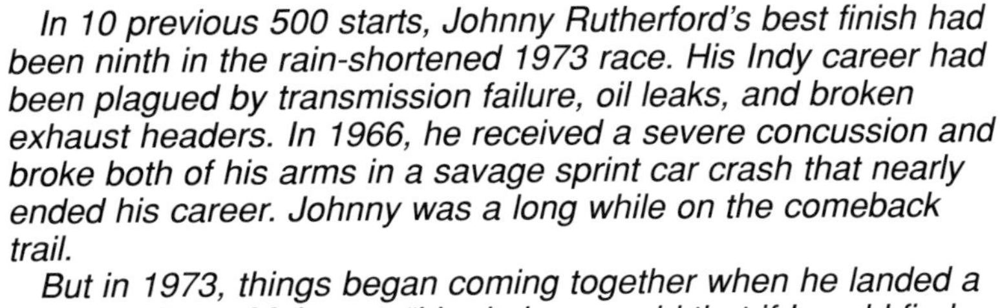

In 10 previous 500 starts, Johnny Rutherford's best finish had been ninth in the rain-shortened 1973 race. His Indy career had been plagued by transmission failure, oil leaks, and broken exhaust headers. In 1966, he received a severe concussion and broke both of his arms in a savage sprint car crash that nearly ended his career. Johnny was a long while on the comeback trail.

But in 1973, things began coming together when he landed a ride with Team McLaren. "I had always said that if I could find a team that wanted to go racing as badly as I did—and to work as hard at trying to accomplish—that I would be a winner," Rutherford said.

Because Johnny was forced to qualify the second weekend in '74, he was consigned to 25th spot on the starting grid despite a speed of 190.446. But Rutherford didn't let that stop him. His brilliant charge and resultant duel with A. J. Foyt rewarded the popular pilot with a well-deserved victory. Only Ray Harroun in 1911, Fred Frame in '32, and Louie Meyer in '36 had won from further back in the field.

Apparently, all Rutherford had to do to win Indy was finish. The 1974 race marked the first time he'd gone the entire 500 miles.

RESULTS

NO.	DRIVER	CAR	ENTRANT	ENGINE	CYL	DISP	CHASSIS	COLOR	QUAL SPD	START	FIN	LAPS / SPEED / REASON OUT
3	Johnny Rutherford	McLaren	McLaren Cars, Ltd.	Offy T	4	159	McLaren	orange, blue	190.446	25	1	200-158.589
48	Bobby Unser	Olsonite Eagle	All American Racers	Offy T	4	159	Eagle	white, blue	185.176	7	2	200-158.278
4	Bill Vukovich, Jr.	Sugaripe Prune	Jerry O'Connell	Offy T	4	159	Eagle	yellow, maroon	182.500	16	3	199-flagged
20	Gordon Johncock	STP Double Oil Filter	Patrick Racing Team	Offy T	4	157	Eagle	Day-glo red	186.287	4	4	198-flagged
73	David Hobbs	Carling Black Label	McLaren Cars, Ltd.	Offy T	4	159	McLaren	black, red	184.833	9	5	196-flagged
45	Jim McElreath	Thermo King	Fred Gerhardt	Offy T	4	159	Eagle	white, blue	177.279	30	6	194-flagged
11	Pancho Carter	Cobre Firestone	R. L. Fletcher	Offy T	4	159	Eagle	copper, turq	180.605	21	7	191-flagged
79	Bob Harkey	Peru Circus	Lindsey Hopkins Racing	Foyt T	8	158	Kenyon	red, white	176.687	31	8	189-flagged
9	Lloyd Ruby	Unlimited Racing	Unlimited Racing Team	Offy T	4	159	Eagle	brown, gold	181.699	18	9	187-out of fuel
55	Jerry Grant	Cobre Firestone	R. L. Fletcher	Offy T	4	159	Eagle	turq, copper	181.781	17	10	175-flagged
89	John Martin	Sea Snack Shrmp Cktl	Automotive Technology	Offy T	4	159	McLaren	dark red, wht	180.406	22	11	169-flagged
27	Tom Bigelow	Bryant Heat & Cool	Vollstedt Enterprises	Offy T	4	159	Vollstedt	blue, yellow	180.144	23	12	166-flagged
18	Bill Simpson	American Kids Racer	Richard Beith	Offy T	4	159	Eagle	silvr, blu, mroon	181.041	20	13	163-broken gears
68	Mike Hiss	Norton Spirit	Penske Racing, Inc.	Offy T	4	159	McLaren	blue, yellow	187.490	3	14	158-flagged
14	A. J. Foyt	Gilmore Racing Team	A. J. Foyt, Sr.	Foyt T	8	160	Coyote	orange	191.632	1	15	142-turbo scavenger pump
1	Roger McCluskey	English Leather	Lindsey Hopkins Racing	Offy T	4	159	Riley	blue, white	181.005	27	16	141-gearbox
77	Salt Walther	Dayton-Walther	Walmotor, Inc.	Offy T	4	159	McLaren	blu, orng, wht	183.927	14	17	141-broken piston
15	Al Unser	Viceroy	Vel's Parnelli Jones Racing	Offy T	4	160	Eagle	red, white	183.889	26	18	131-gears
42	Jerry Karl	Ayr-Way/Lloyd's	Lindsey Hopkins Racing	Offy T	4	159	Eagle	blue, white	181.452	19	19	115-wrecked T3
24	Tom Sneva	Raymond Companies	Grant King Racing	Offy T	4	159	Kingfish	red, white	185.149	8	20	94-rear end gears
51	Jan Opperman	Viceroy Parnelli	Vel's Parnelli Jones Racing	Offy T	4	159	Parnelli	red, white	176.186	32	21	85-spun T2
60	Steve Krisiloff	STP Gas Treatment	Patrick Racing Team	Offy T	4	157	Eagle	Day-glo red	182.519	15	22	72-clutch
21	Jimmy Caruthers	Cobre Firestone	R. L. Fletcher	Offy T	4	159	Eagle	turq, copper	184.049	12	23	64-gearbox
59	Larry Cannon	American Financial	Richard Hoffman	Offy T	4	159	Eagle	yellow, red	173.963	33	24	49-blown engine
56	Jim Hurtubise	Miller High Life	Gohr Distributing	Offy T	4	159	Eagle	white, red	180.288	28	25	31-broken piston
94	Johnny Parsons	Vatis	Vatis Enterprises	Offy T	4	159	Finley	yellow, black	180.252	29	26	18-engine failure
61	Rick Muther	Eisenhour	Eisenhour-Brayton Racing	Foyt T	8	161	Coyote	yellow, red	179.991	24	27	11-broken piston
82	George Snider	Gilmore Racing Team	J. H. Greer	Foyt T	8	160	Atlanta	orange	183.993	13	28	7-broken valve
98	Mike Mosley	Lodestar	Agajanian-Leader Cards	Offy T	4	159	Eagle	wht, blu, orng	185.319	6	29	6-blown engine
40	Wally Dallenbach	STP Oil Treatment	Patrick Racing Team	Offy T	4	157	Eagle	Day-glo red	189.683	2	30	3-burned piston
5	Mario Andretti	Viceroy	Vel's Parnelli Jones Racing	Offy T	4	160	Eagle	red, white	186.027	5	31	2-broken piston
8	Gary Bettenhausen	Score	Penske Racing, Inc.	Offy T	4	159	McLaren	red, black	184.492	11	32	2-broken valve
44	Dick Simon	TraveLodge	Dick Simon	Foyt T	8	160	Eagle	wht, orng, blk	184.502	10	33	1-cracked valve

T = turbocharged

59th Race • May 25, 1975

The ruffled feathers from last year are smoothed and the Speedway returns to the traditional four days of qualifying over two weekends.

While the number of qualifying days doubles, the number of tire suppliers is cut in half. Firestone, which won 43 races in a row at the Brickyard from 1920 through 1966, withdraws from racing. That leaves Goodyear, winner in the last three races, as the lone tire supplier.

Former winner Parnelli Jones, now an owner, enters a new chassis-engine combination that fails to make the show but generates considerable interest.

Jones alters a Formula 1 chassis to meet USAC specs and installs a turbocharged Cosworth-Ford V-8, also based on F1 hardware. The Cosworth DFX shows ample power on the straights and good fuel economy, but the VPJ6 chassis suffers handling problems that even lead driver Mario Andretti can't sort out. Andretti and teammate Al Unser qualify instead with proven Eagle chassis and Offenhauser engines.

Offy again dominates the grid, powering 29 starters. Two of them are Drake-Goossen-Sparks engines, an offshoot of the turbocharged Offenhauser. A. J. Foyt and two others use the trusty Ford-based Foyt V-8, and Jerry Karl qualifies 20th in Smokey Yunick's turbocharged Chevrolet V-8.

PRACTICE AND QUALIFYING

TUESDAY, MAY 6: 1973 winner Gordon Johncock is the first driver to top 190 mph in practice, hitting 190.88 in a George Bignotti-tuned Wildcat with a DGS engine. Bobby Unser, the 1968 winner, is second fastest at 187.852 in a new Eagle-Offy.

WEDNESDAY, MAY 7: A. J. Foyt gets his Coyote howling and sets fast time of the month, 193.924 mph. Johncock is second quickest at 192.184, and Bobby Unser clocks a lap over 190.

THURSDAY, MAY 8: Johncock regains bragging rights to fast time of the month with a lap at 195.228. Foyt runs second at 192.431.

FRIDAY, MAY 9: About 60,000 fans show up to see Johncock win the final pre-pole skirmish with Foyt. Johncock does 193.543 and Foyt 192.431. ➔

This year's Buick pace car (*above*) wasn't an off-the-shelf Century Custom. It had a 455-cubic-inch V-8 with 325 bhp, 2.5-inch diameter dual exhaust, special Goodyear GR70×15 steel-belted radials, and Hurst removable T-tops. Tamer replicas, 1800 of them, were available through Buick dealers. The division also provided the requisite official cars (*opposite top*), including a brace of LeSabre convertibles for 500 Festival parade use. Chief Steward Tom Binford (*opposite bottom*) turned the pacesetter over to actor James Garner, an accomplished amateur race driver, on race day. While the winning driver drove off in the Century pace car, a GMC Sierra Classic pickup (*above*) awaited the chief mechanic for the first-place car.

STARTING LINEUP

Average Field Qualifying Speed: 185.057

Numbers in flags indicate finish position

POLE POSITION
Qualifying Speed: 193.976

Bobby Unser

Lloyd Ruby

Salt Walther

Johnny Parsons

Bill Puterbaugh

Gordon Johncock

Mike Mosley

Bill Vukovich, Jr.

Al Unser

Jerry Grant

A. J. Foyt

Tom Sneva

Johnny Rutherford

Jimmy Caruthers

Bobby Allison

Pancho Carter

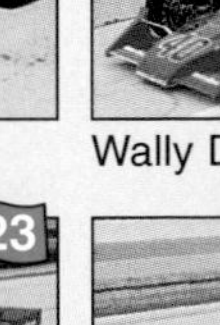

Wally Dallenbach

George Snider

Mario Andretti

Dick Simon

Tom Bigelow

Bentley Warren

Jerry Karl

Bob Harkey

Sheldon Kinser

Steve Krisiloff

Eldon Rasmussen

John Martin

Gary Bettenhausen

Roger McCluskey

Sammy Sessions

Larry McCoy

Mike Hiss

SATURDAY, MAY 10: A. J. Foyt aborts a qualification run after a first lap of 189.185 mph. Tom Sneva later averages 190.094 to stake an early claim to the pole. Bobby Unser knocks Sneva off the pole by running 191.073, but Gordon Johncock, the next driver out, does the same by averaging 191.652.

Shortly after 4 P.M., Foyt takes his Coyote out for a second attempt, and this time he is dialed in. Foyt's first lap is 195.213, and he slows down the next three to average 193.976 and capture his fourth pole position (tying Rex Mays's record) and second in a row. With Unser and Johncock alongside Foyt, former winners make up the entire front row.

THURSDAY, MAY 22: Just two minutes before the end of Carburetion Day practice, Pancho Carter smacks the outside wall in Turn 1 and slides into the infield, where he hits a parked fire truck. Carter pulls a back muscle and extensively damages his Eagle, but his crew vows to fix it in time for the race.

THE RACE
Start: Gordon Johncock gets the jump on A. J. Foyt as they head into Turn 1 and takes the lead.

Lap 2: Johncock runs 187.11 mph, fastest lap of the race.

Lap 9: Foyt catches and passes Johncock for the lead while Bobby Unser follows in third place and Johnny Rutherford runs fourth. Johncock parks two laps later with a broken gear.

Lap 40: Mike Hiss breaks a U-joint in Turn 3 and spins in front of Roger McCluskey before hitting the outside wall. ➔

Jim Hurtubise continued to hold out hope for front-engine cars (*below*). Three former winners occupied the front row (*bottom*): from left, Bobby Unser, Gordon Johncock, and polesitter A. J. Foyt. Popular Lloyd Ruby (*opposite top*) qualified a McLaren in the second row. Tony Hulman observes preparations to start one of the Buick Bugs that ran at the Speedway in its pre-500 years (*opposite, middle left*). Jerry Grant's Spirit of Orange County (*opposite, middle right*) was decorated in honor of its sponsor.

If you ask any veteran fan who they'd have liked to have seen win racing's most coveted prize, Lloyd Ruby would be on most any short list. From his very first year at the Speedway, "Rube" was always a contender. He'd successfully driven sprints, midgets, sports cars, and stocks. He'd dominated Indy-car races at Milwaukee and Trenton. But something always transpired to keep him out of Indy's victory lane.

He'd led nearly every 500 in which he'd taken part. In 1966, he was well on his way to victory when his Ford sprang an oil leak. In 1969, he'd lapped the field, but a freak pit-stop accident jerked the neck out of his fuel tank.

But in 1975, Ruby looked like he really had the combination. Paired with Johnny Rutherford, wasn't he driving one of Team McLaren's track-eating racers? Just look what "Lone Star J. R." had done with one the year before. Friends and fans thought Ruby had a bulletproof chance, especially after he qualified sixth at 186.984 mph.

But after seven laps, Ruby blew a piston. He bowed out in 32nd.

"I thought we could run all day," Lloyd said as he munched a sandwich in his garage. "I can't really say what it is here at Indy. This year was like the rest of them. It seems like it's always something."

Foyt continues in front, but second-place Rutherford is challenged by Wally Dallenbach, moving up from 21st starting spot.

Lap 59: Dallenbach, having gotten past Rutherford, storms by Foyt into first place and opens up a two-second lead.

Lap 69: Mario Andretti spins on the back straight and crashes into the inside retaining wall.

Lap 126: Tom Sneva makes contact with Eldon Rasmussen's car in Turn 2 while running fifth. Sneva's McLaren flips over Rasmussen, hits the outside wall and bursts into flames. Sneva suffers burns on face, hands, and legs. Rasmussen is not hurt.

Dallenbach remains the leader, building a comfortable margin over Rutherford and Bobby Unser. Foyt falls to fourth with tire problems.

Lap 162: Dallenbach, who holds a 20-second lead and appears on his way to victory, slows and pulls into the pits with a burned piston after leading 96 laps. Defending winner Rutherford inherits the lead, and Unser moves up to second.

Lap 164: Rutherford loses the lead to Unser when he makes a regular pit stop.

Lap 171: When a light rain brings out the yellow flag, both leader Unser and second-place Rutherford duck into the pits for splash-and-go stops to have enough fuel for a dash to the finish.

Finish: A sudden downpour on Lap 174 brings out the red flag to halt the race just as Unser comes down the front straight and receives the checkered flag. Rutherford follows in second and Foyt is third, nearly a lap down.

As the race ends, cars slide out of control on the wet track. Bill Puterbaugh loops on the front straight and is hit by Bentley Warren and Jimmy Caruthers. Bill Vukovich, Jr., spins in Turn 4 and hits the wall. Teammate Pancho Carter spins in the same vicinity, Steve Krisiloff does a doughnut at the start-finish line, and Sheldon Kinser gets sideways in Turn 1. There are no injuries from all the race-end mishaps.

A few minutes later, the rain stops and Unser enjoys his victory lap in an open-top Buick Century. Unser leads just 10 laps to earn his second victory, the first for owner Dan Gurney, and the fourth for the Unser family.

The third-place Foyt V-8 is the only non-Offy engine among the first 12 finishers.

It really looked like Wally Dallenbach's year. The veteran driver and his brilliant red Wildcat-DGS racer seemed to have the field covered. Wally led for 96 laps, and was enjoying a 41-second cushion over second place when Eldon Rasmussen and Tom Sneva tangled on lap 126. The tremendous accident scattered debris all over Turn 2, and Dallenbach had to dive into the grass to avoid the shrapnel. But he didn't quite make it.

Something punctured his left rear tire, causing a very slow leak. All Wally knew was the rear end started to get loose.

"I had been running 184 [mph]," Wally explained. "I had dropped all the way back to 179 and it killed me."

"Wally had to run part throttle," chief mechanic George Bignotti said. "That leaned the engine out. It's [the engine] already red hot and it just fried the piston."

Dallenbach limped around on three cylinders. By the time the heavy rain came on lap 174, washing out the remaining 26 laps, his engine had already expired. Even through five cars behind him were still running, Wally had been so far ahead he still finished ninth.

RESULTS

NO.	DRIVER	CAR	ENTRANT	ENGINE	CYL	DISP	CHASSIS	COLOR	QUAL SPD	START	FIN	LAPS / SPEED / REASON OUT
8	Bobby Unser	Jorgensen Eagle	All American Racers	Offy T	4	159	Eagle	blue	191.073	3	1	174-149.213
2	Johnny Rutherford	Gatorade	McLaren Cars, Ltd.	Offy T	8	161	McLaren	grn, wht, orng	185.998	7	2	174-148.308
14	A. J. Foyt	Gilmore Racing	A.J. Foyt Enterprise	Foyt T	8	161	Coyote	orng, wht, blue	193.976	1	3	174-147.684
11	Pancho Carter	Cobre Tire	Fletcher Racing Team	Offy T	4	159	Eagle	wht, cppr, turq	183.449	18	4	169-flagged
15	Roger McCluskey	Silver Floss Sauerkraut	Lindsey Hopkins Racing	Offy T	4	159	Riley	dk. grey, silver	183.964	22	5	167-flagged
6	Bill Vukovich, Jr.	Cobre Tire	Fletcher Racing Team	Offy T	4	159	Eagle	turq, cppr, wht	185.845	8	6	166-flagged
83	Bill Puterbaugh	McNamara-D.I.A.	McNamara Motor Express	Offy T	4	159	Eagle	gold, red	183.833	15	7	165-flagged
97	George Snider	Leader Card Lodestar	Leader Cards, Inc.	Offy T	4	159	Eagle	wht, blu, red	182.918	24	8	165-flagged
40	Wally Dallenbach	Sinmast Wildcat	Patrick Racing Team	SGD T	4	159	Wildcat	red, blk, wht	190.648	21	9	162-blown piston
33	Bob Harkey, Walther	Dayton-Walther	Walmotor, Inc.	Offy T	4	159	McLaren	blue, red, wht	183.786	23	10	162-flagged
98	Steve Krisiloff	Leader Card Lodestar	Leader Cards, Inc.	Offy T	4	159	Eagle	wht, blue, red	182.408	29	11	162-flagged
19	Sheldon Kinser	Spirit of Indiana	Grant King Racing	Offy T	4	159	Kingfish	wht, blue, yelo	182.389	26	12	161-flagged
30	Jerry Karl	Jose Johnson	Smokey Yunick	Chevy T	8	207	Eagle	black, gold	182.537	20	13	161-flagged
78	Jimmy Caruthers	Alex Foods	Alex Morales	Offy T	4	159	Eagle	wht, orng, brn	185.615	10	14	161-flagged
45	Gary Bettenhausen	Thermo King	Fred Gerhardt	Offy T	4	159	Eagle	red, wht, blu	182.611	19	15	158-lost wheel, FS
4	Al Unser	Viceroy	Vel's Parnelli Jones	Offy T	4	159	Eagle	wht, red, blue	185.452	11	16	157-broken con. rod
36	Sammy Sessions	Cmndr Mtr. Homes	Unlimited Racing Team	Offy T	4	159	Eagle	white, black	182.750	25	17	155-engine failure
17	Tom Bigelow	Bryant Heat & Coo	Vollstedt Enterprises, Inc.	Offy T	4	159	Vollstedt	black, white	181.864	33	18	151-burnt piston
93	Johnny Parsons	Ayr-Way WNAP Bzrd	Vatis Enterprises, Inc.	Offy T	4	159	Eagle	wht, blck, pink	184.521	12	19	140-transmission shaft
73	Jerry Grant	Spirit of Orange Co.	Fred W. Carrillo	Offy T	4	159	Eagle	wht, orng, grn	184.266	14	20	137-burnt piston
44	Dick Simone	Bruce Cogle Ford	Dick Simon, Ltd.	Foyt T	8	161	Eagle	wht, blue, mrn	181.892	30	21	133-flagged
68	Tom Sneva	Norton Spirit	Penske Racing, Inc.	Offy T	4	159	McLaren	blu, wht, yelo	190.094	4	22	125-accident T2
24	Bentley Warren	The Bottomhalf	Grant King Racing	Offy T	4	159	Kingfish	red, white	183.589	17	23	120-flagged
58	Eldon Rasmussen	Anacomp-Wild Rose	Eldon Rasmussen	Foyt T	8	161	Rascar	yellow, black	181.910	32	24	119-leaking fuel valve
16	Bobby Allison	CAM2 Motor Oil	Penske Racing, Inc.	Offy T	4	159	McLaren	red, white	184.398	13	25	112-broken gearbox
12	Mike Mosley	Sugaripe Prune	Jerry O'Connell	Offy T	4	159	Eagle	yelo, maroon	187.822	5	26	94-engine failure
89	John Martin	Unsponsored	Automotive Technology, Inc.	Offy T	4	159	McLaren	red, white	183.655	16	27	61-broken radiator
21	Mario Andretti	Viceroy	Vel's Parnelli Jones	Offy T	4	159	Eagle	red, wht, blue	186.480	27	28	49-accident, T3
94	Mike Hiss	Ayr-Way WNAP Bzrd	Vatis Enterprises, Inc.	Offy T	4	159	Finley	wht, blk, pink	181.754	31	29	39-accident, T4
63	Larry McCoy	Shurfine Foods	Bidwell & McCoy, Sr.	Offy T	4	159	Rascar	red, wht, blue	182.760	28	30	24-burnt piston
20	Gordon Johncock	Sinmast Wildcat	Patrick Racing Team	DGS T	4	159	Wildcat	red, wht, blk	191.652	2	31	11-ignition
7	Lloyd Ruby	Allied Polymer	McLaren Cars, Ltd.	Offy T	4	159	McLaren	wht, blue, red	186.984	6	32	7-burnt piston
77	Salt Walther	Dayton-Walther	Walmotor, Inc.	Offy T	4	159	McLaren	blue, wht, red	185.701	9	33	2-ignition

T = turbocharged

Pancho Carter runs in front of Roger McCluskey (*opposite top*). Wally Dallenbach took the No. 40 Wildcat (*opposite, bottom left*) into the lead before his engine blew. Bobby Allison's CAM2 Special McLaren is pushed to its pit stall (*opposite, bottom right*) after the gearbox broke. Bill Vukovich, Jr., finished sixth in the Cobre Tire Eagle (*left*). Bobby Unser (*below*) grabbed the lead 10 laps before a downpour stopped the race, notching his second win and fourth for the Unser family.

1976

60th Race • May 30, 1976

Among the 71 entries this year is one for Janet Guthrie, a 38-year-old sports-car racer from New York City. Guthrie, the first woman to seek a starting position at Indy, passes her rookie test but does not try to qualify because her Vollstedt-Offy has more mechanical problems than speed.

A new Hall of Fame Museum opens in April inside the main entrance at the south end of the Speedway, providing larger quarters for the growing collection of winning cars, pace cars, and other memorabilia.

The track gains red lights around the perimeter as a safety measure so drivers will see that the race has been stopped before they reach the flag stand on the front straight.

The Cosworth-Ford V-8, which Parnelli Jones entered the year before, makes the show this year in a Parnelli chassis driven by two-time winner Al Unser. A. J. Foyt has the only Foyt V-8 in the field, and there is one other new engine. Jerry Grant qualifies 20th with a turbocharged AMC stock-block V-8.

The other 30 cars have four-cylinder Offys, including the Patrick Racing team of Gordon Johncock and Wally Dallenbach, which uses the Drake-Goossen-Sparks version of the Offy.

PRACTICE AND QUALIFYING
SUNDAY, MAY 9: Former winner Johnny Rutherford laps the track at 187.698 in his McLaren-Offy to set fast practice time on Mother's Day.

MONDAY, MAY 10: Rutherford has fast time again—188.363—but Al Unser is close behind at 188.048 in his Parnelli-Cosworth.

TUESDAY, MAY 11: Rookie Eddie Miller destroys his car when he loses control in Turn 1, slides into a drainage ditch, and flips before stopping upside down in the infield. Miller fractures two vertebrae.

WEDNESDAY, MAY 12: Rutherford, Al Unser, and A. J. Foyt have the hot setup today and are the best bets to win the pole. Each driver does better than 189 mph, with "J. R." on top at 189.833.

SATURDAY, MAY 15: Rain delays the start of qualifying until after 3 P.M. Gordon Johncock is the first serious pole contender, and he qualifies at 188.531. That speed holds until Rutherford qualifies at 188.957, just .43 seconds quicker over four laps.

Foyt battles an ill-handling car and qualifies at a disappointing 185.261, still good for fifth starting position. The only others with a shot are Tom Sneva and Unser, and neither comes close to Rutherford's speed. Rutherford wins his second pole in four years.

SUNDAY, MAY 16: Mike Mosley and two-time winner Bobby Unser both qualify at more than 187.5 mph, but they wind up on row 4 because they do it on the second day of time trials.

MONDAY, MAY 17: Janet Guthrie passes her rookie test, the first woman to achieve that feat.

SATURDAY, MAY 22: Mario Andretti, who misses the first weekend of qualifying to compete in a Grand Prix event, qualifies faster than polesitter Rutherford. Andretti averages 189.404 mph in a two-year-old McLaren-Offy owned by Roger Penske to line up 19th.

SUNDAY, MAY 23: Guthrie, whose Vollstedt entry appears too slow to make the field, finds a potential guardian angel from an unlikely source—A. J. Foyt. Foyt offers Guthrie a chance to qualify his backup Coyote, which he runs at 190 mph in practice. Guthrie gets it up to nearly 181 mph in practice, giving her a shot at making the field.

In the end, Foyt decides not to run the car. He says he lacks the crew to run a second car without hurting his own chances at winning a fourth time.

Guthrie vows to try again in 1977.

THE RACE
Start: Johnny Rutherford leads from the pole into Turn 1 and stays in front for the first three laps.

Lap 4: A. J. Foyt passes Rutherford for the lead, while Mario Andretti charges from the seventh row up to seventh place. →

STARTING LINEUP

Average Field Qualifying Speed: 183.785

Numbers in flags indicate finish position

Tom Sneva

Pancho Carter

Bill Vukovich, Jr.

Bobby Unser

John Martin

Gordon Johncock

A. J. Foyt

Gary Bettenhausen

Mike Mosley

Johnny Parsons

POLE POSITION
Qualifying Speed: 188.957

Johnny Rutherford

Al Unser

Wally Dallenbach

Larry Cannon

Roger McCluskey

In 1976, when Janet Guthrie came to Indy, she had no trouble at all passing her driver's test. After all, she had a great deal of experience racing with the Sports Car Club of America at venues like Daytona, Sebring, and Watkins Glen. The eyes of the entire world were upon the friendly, outgoing lady.

However, her car didn't have the speed to qualify. While many people simply wrote her off, a knight in Coyote orange came to her rescue. A. J. Foyt loaned Guthrie his car.

"It was all very melodramatic," Janet recalls. "It was the final day of time trials." In only a few laps, she was running fast enough to make the field. "I had about nine laps in when Jim Hurtubise spun and brought out the yellow," Guthrie continued. "I heard later that someone said 'It's "Herk"' when the yellow went on. A. J. must have thought they said 'It's her.'"

In the end, Foyt chose not to run a second car. And while no other car owners came forward, Indy hadn't seen the last of Janet Guthrie.

She was the first woman to file an entry for the 500, but many sportswriters erroneously claimed she was the first woman to drive an Indy car at the Speedway. In reality, that was accomplished on November 7, 1963, during a tire testing session, when Paula Murphy—"Miss STP"—drove five laps in a Novi.

Janet Guthrie (*left*) became the first woman to pass the rookie test, and A. J. Foyt (*above*) offered her one of his backup cars. A Buick Century made history as the first V-6 pace car (*below*). Its turbocharged engine design led to a 500 racing engine.

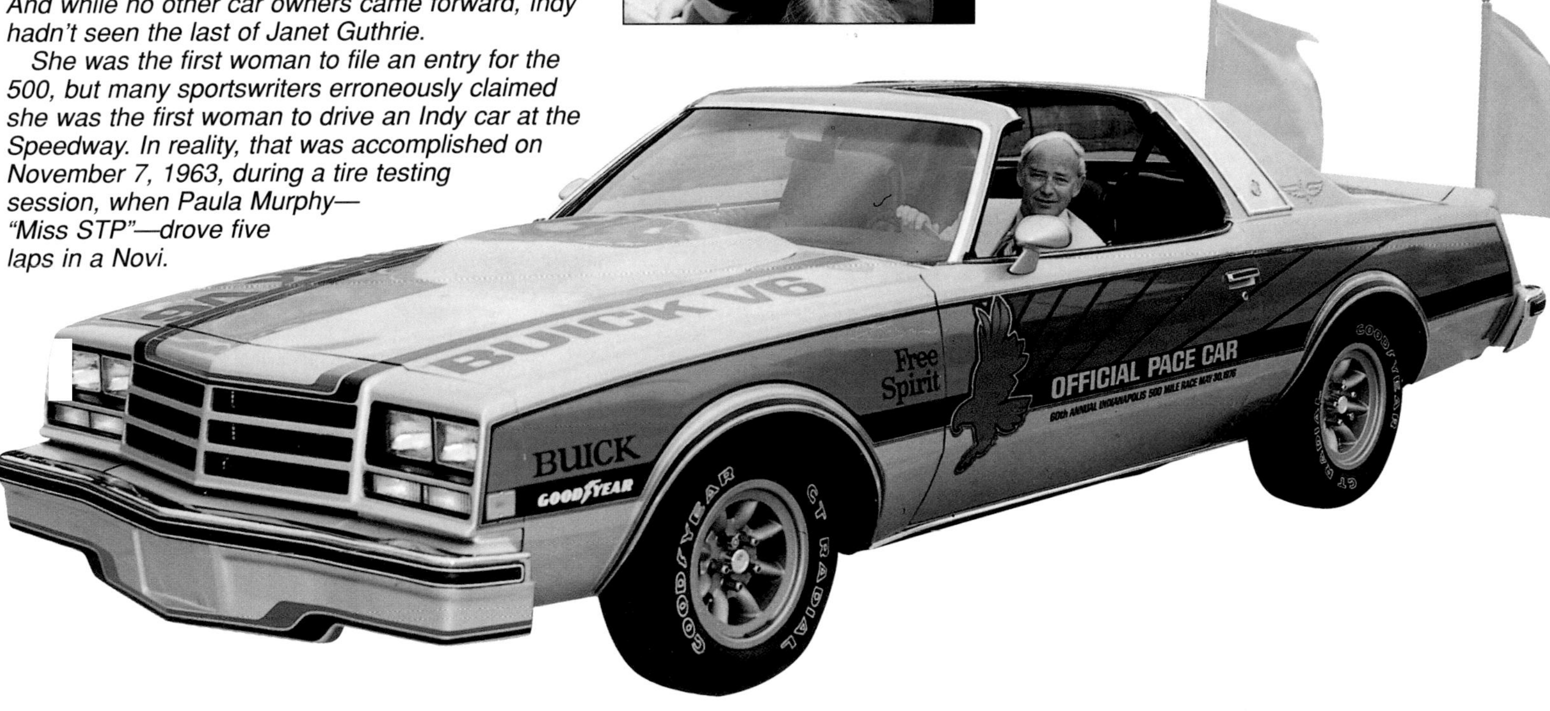

Bill Puterbaugh

Billy Scott

Al Loquasto

George Snider

Lloyd Ruby

Jan Opperman

Vern Schuppan

Jerry Grant

Steve Krisiloff

Larry McCoy

Sheldon Kinser

Tom Bigelow

Dick Simon

Mario Andretti

Salt Walther

Spike Gehlhausen

Bob Harkey

David Hobbs

Janet Guthrie wasn't able to get the No. 17 Bryant Heating and Cooling entry (*right*) fast enough to qualify, but she vowed to return to Indianapolis. The slope-nose No. 56 Moran Electric-sponsored Mallard roadster of Jim Hurtubise, with its front-mounted Offenhauser engine, had some track time (*middle*) but not enough speed. "Herk" quixotically trotted out Indy's last roadster as late as 1980. Sheldon Kinser made the show with the No. 97 Dragon-Offy owned by Grant King (*bottom*). Starting 29th, Kinser lasted 97 laps for a 19th-place finish.

Jim McElreath was bumped, but he didn't go home empty-handed. He got the $2000 Almost-Made-It consolation prize (*left*). *Below* and *middle:* Two cars; three drivers; no luck: Neither of the City of Syracuse entries wound up in the field. McElreath and Lee Kunzman struck out trying to get the No. 64 car into the race. Kunzman and Larry Dickson tried in vain in the No. 65 entry. Ronald Reagan (*bottom left*)—then campaigning for the Republican presidential nomination—dropped in at the Speedway early in the spring. Comedian Bob Hope visited, too (*bottom right*).

Lap 9: Roger McCluskey spins in someone else's oil and backs into the Turn 3 wall.

Lap 12: The leaders pit under yellow, and Pancho Carter goes in front. As Foyt leaves the pits, a six-foot-long wrench used to adjust his rear wing from behind the pit wall sticks to the back of his Coyote. The wrench falls off after Foyt gets back on the track, and a worker retrieves it before it does damage.
Andretti loses valuable track position in the pits while his crew wrestles with a balky air hose and wheel nut.

Lap 17: Wally Dallenbach blows by Carter on the back straight to take the lead.

Lap 20: Gordon Johncock passes teammate Dallenbach on the front straight to become the new leader.

Lap 38: After a second round of pit stops, Rutherford leads Foyt by a couple of seconds, and Johncock is third.

Lap 60: Johnny Parsons loses his right front wheel as he leaves the pits, and he limps around the track to get back to pit road.
The leaders pit under the ensuing yellow, and Foyt beats Rutherford back onto the track to grab the lead.

Lap 80: Foyt slows with handling problems, and Rutherford slips by in Turn 3 to regain the lead.

Lap 100: With Rutherford still leading and Foyt second, the yellow flag comes out when it starts to rain. Johncock sits in third, the only other car on the lead lap.

Lap 103: As the rain intensifies, the red flag comes out to stop the race. It is not yet 1 P.M., so USAC officials hold off on declaring the race officially over in hopes the weather will clear.
While the 27 cars still in the race sit on pit road, Foyt discovers the cause of his handling problems: a broken front sway bar. USAC rules allow repairs in the pits, so his crew replaces the sway bar.
Nearly two hours later, the rain returns and the race becomes official. At just 255 miles, it is the shortest "500" in history, and the third in the last four that doesn't go the distance.
Rutherford wins for the second time in three years, while Foyt leads for the third year in a row but fails again to post a fourth victory.
The venerable Offenhauser engine wins for the fifth straight—and final—time. The new Cosworth V-8 comes in seventh, a lap down in the hands of Al Unser.

The Buick Century pace car pulls out to a safe lead ahead of the almost perfectly aligned field on the pace lap (*top*). Mike Mosley's No. 12 Sugaripe Prune Special gets attention in the pits (*middle*). Mosley drove the Eagle-Offenhauser to 15th place in his ninth consecutive start in the Indianapolis 500. A. J. Foyt accepts fuel and new rubber (*right*) en route to a second-place finish in the Gilmore Racing Coyote. Foyt led 29 laps of the rain-shortened race, stirring visions of a possible fourth victory, but was slowed by a broken front sway bar that kept him from catching fellow Texan Johnny Rutherford.

Winner Johnny Rutherford and his family are reunited with the Borg-Warner trophy at the 1976 edition of the victory dinner held the day after each race (*left*). As he did in 1974, Rutherford piloted a McLaren with Drake-Offenhauser power to victory in '76 (*below*). Unlike his earlier triumph, when he had to outlast Bobby Unser to win, Rutherford had to outwait the weatherman to prevail this year. Rain prompted a red flag, halting the field with 102 laps and 255 miles in the books. When the skies failed to clear, the race was declared over with leader Rutherford named the winner.

RESULTS

NO.	DRIVER	CAR	ENTRANT	ENGINE	CYL	DISP	CHASSIS	COLOR	QUAL SPD	START	FIN	LAPS / SPEED / REASON OUT
2	Johnny Rutherford	Hy-Gain	Team McLaren, Inc.	Offy	4	159	McLaren	orange, blue	188.957	1	1	102-148.725
14	A. J. Foyt	Gilmore Racing Team	A. J. Foyt Enterprises	Foyt	8	161	Coyote	orange	185.261	5	2	102-148.355
20	Gordon Johncock	Sinmast	Patrick Racing Team	DGS	4	159	Wildcat	Day-Glo red	188.531	2	3	102-146.238
40	Wally Dallenbach	Sinmast	Patrick Racing Team	DGS	4	159	Wildcat	Day-Glo red	184.455	7	4	101-running
48	Pancho Carter	Jorgensen	E. M. Jorgensen	Offy	4	159	Eagle	blue	184.824	6	5	101-running
68	Tom Sneva	Norton Spirit	Penske Racing, Inc.	Offy	4	159	McLaren	blue, wht, red	186.355	3	6	101-running
21	Al Unser	Amer. Racing Wheels	Vel's Parnelli Jones Racing	Cosworth	8	161	Parnelli	blue, white	186.258	4	7	101-running
6	Mario Andretti	CAM 2 Motor Oil	Penske Racing, Inc.	Offy	4	159	McLaren	red, white, blk	189.404	19	8	101-running
77	Salt Walther	Dayton-Walther	Walmotor, Inc.	Offy	4	159	McLaren	blue, wht, red	182.797	22	9	100-running
3	Bobby Unser	Cobre Tire	Robert L. Fletcher	Offy	4	159	Eagle	cpper, turq, wht	187.520	12	10	100-running
51	Lloyd Ruby	Fairco Drugs	Michael Devin	Offy	4	159	Eagle	yelo, wht, red, blk	186.480	30	11	100-running
93	Johnny Parsons	Ayr-Way/WIRE	Vatis Enterprises	Offy	4	159	Eagle	wht, blk, pink	182.843	14	12	98-running
23	George Snider	Hubler Chevrolet Co.	Leader Cards, Inc.	Offy	4	159	Eagle	yellow, blue	181.141	27	13	98-running
24	Tom Bigelow	Leader Card Racers	Leader Cards, Inc.	Offy	4	159	Eagle	yellow, black	181.965	32	14	98-running
12	Mike Mosley	Sugaripe Prune	Jerry O'Connell	Offy	4	159	Eagle	yellow red	187.888	11	15	98-running
8	Jan Opperman	Routh Meat Packing	Richard Routh	Offy	4	159	Eagle	white, blk, red	181.717	33	16	97-running
69	Larry Cannon	Amer. Finan. Corp.	Hoffman Auto Racing	Offy	4	159	Eagle	blk, white, red	181.388	10	17	97-running
9	Vern Schuppan	Jorgensen	E. M. Jorgensen	Offy	4	159	Eagle	blue, black	182.011	17	18	97-running
97	Sheldon Kinser	The Bottom Half	Agajanian/King	Offy	4	159	Dragon	red, white	181.114	29	19	97-running
96	Bob Harkey	Dave McIntire Ford	Agajanian/King	Offy	4	159	Kingfish	red, white	181.141	28	20	97-running
98	John Martin	Genesee Beer	Agajanian/King/Hammond	Offy	4	159	Dragon	red, white	182.417	15	21	96-running
83	Bill Puterbaugh	McNamara Mtr Exp.	McNamara Motor Exp.	Offy	4	159	Eagle	maroon, white	182.002	18	22	96-running
28	Billy Scott	Spirit of Public Ent.	Warner Hodgdon	Offy	4	159	Eagle	wht, blue, red	183.383	21	23	96-running
92	Steve Krisiloff	1st Natl. City Trvlrs. Cks.	Vatis Enterprises	Offy	4	159	Eagle	wht, blk, yelo	182.131	23	24	95-running
86	Al Loquasto	Frostie Root Beer	Al Loquasto, Sr.	Offy	4	159	McLaren	wht, yelo, blue	182.002	24	25	95-running
63	Larry McCoy	Shurfine Foods	Spirit of America Racers	Offy	4	159	Ras-Car	red, wht, blk	181.388	26	26	91-running
73	Jerry Grant	California-Oklahoma	Fred W. Carrillo	AMC	8	208	Eagle	wht, orng, blu	183.617	20	27	91-running
45	Gary Bettenhausen	Thermo-King	Gerhardt Racers, Inc.	Offy	4	159	Eagle	blk, red, wht	181.791	8	28	52-waste gate
33	David Hobbs	Dayton Walther	Walmotor, Inc.	Offy	4	159	McLaren	blue, wht, red	183.580	31	29	10-water leak
7	Robert McCluskey	Hopkins	Lindsey Hopkins	Offy	4	159	Lightning	blue, wht, red	186.500	13	30	8-accident
5	Bill Vukovich, Jr.	Alex Foods	Alex Morales	Offy	4	159	Eagle	wht, orng, blk	181.433	9	31	2-rod
17	Dick Simon	Bryant Heat & Cool	Vollstedt Enterprises	Offy	4	159	Vollstedt	silver, black	182.343	16	32	1-rod
19	Spike Gehlhausen	Spirit of Indiana	Carl Gehlhausen	Offy	4	159	McLaren	yelo, blue, wht	181.717	25	33	0-oil pressure

61st Race • May 29, 1977

Anticipation builds that this is the year someone will finally top 200 mph—45 seconds a lap—in qualifying when 1973 winner Gordon Johncock does it unofficially during tire testing in March.

The Speedway repaves the track after the 1976 race, and the new asphalt gives the cars better grip and higher speeds. This is the first time since bricks were laid in 1909 that the entire 2.5 miles gets a new surface at the same time.

USAC takes steps to control qualifying speeds by limiting turbo boost to 80 inches of manifold pressure for qualifying, the same limit that has been in effect since 1976 for the race.

Janet Guthrie returns for a second crack at becoming the first woman to qualify. Young sprint-car driver James McElreath joins his father, veteran Jim McElreath, on the entry list in a bid to be the first father-son combination in the race. Dad qualifies for his 12th appearance, while son is too slow to make the field.

More teams sign on to the Cosworth-Ford engine that powered Al Unser to a second-row start and seventh-place finish the year before, including Team McLaren with defending winner Johnny Rutherford.

PRACTICE AND QUALIFYING

TUESDAY, MAY 10: Four former winners get close to 200 mph in practice. A. J. Foyt, aiming for a 20th straight start and a fourth win, is slowest of the group at 196.979. Johnny Rutherford is fastest at 198.6, and Mario Andretti and Al Unser are in between.

Running at about 191 mph, Janet Guthrie loses control of her Lightning-Offy in Turn 2 and hits the wall. The car suffers minor damage to the right front and Guthrie walks away with a bruised shin.

WEDNESDAY, MAY 11: Andretti is the first to top 200 mph in practice, running 200.311 during "happy hour" in his McLaren-Offy. Minutes later, Foyt pushes his Coyote-Foyt to 200.117.

THURSDAY, MAY 12: Rutherford pushes the envelope to 200.624 mph in his McLaren Cosworth. ➔

General Motors downsized its largest family cars for 1977; one of them, an Oldsmobile Delta 88 Royale coupe, was selected as the Indianapolis pace car. Though the actual pacemaker had a removable roof panel (*opposite, top right*), a power sunroof was available on the replicas (*above*). It was the fourth time an Olds was chosen since 1970. Janet Guthrie (*opposite, top left*) made the big show this time, becoming the first woman to qualify for the 500. She started 26th in the Bryant Heating and Cooling Special (*opposite bottom*) and finished 29th. A broken timing gear ended her groundbreaking run.

STARTING LINEUP

Average Field Qualifying Speed: 189.488

Numbers in flags indicate finish position

Al Unser

Mario Andretti

Mike Mosley

Sheldon Kinser

Al Loquasto

Bobby Unser

Gordon Johncock

Pancho Carter

Johnny Parsons

Bobby Olivero

POLE POSITION
Qualifying Speed: 198.884

Tom Sneva

A. J. Foyt

Danny Ongais

Wally Dallenbach

George Snider

Roger McCluskey

Gary Bettenhausen

Lee Kunzman

Cliff Hucul

Dick Simon

Bubby Jones

Johnny Rutherford

Jim McElreath

Bill Vukovich, Jr.

Janet Guthrie

Clay Regazzoni

Eldon Rasmussen

Jerry Sneva

Lloyd Ruby

Tom Bigelow

Steve Krisiloff

Bill Puterbaugh

John Mahler

1977

SATURDAY, MAY 14: A. J. Foyt is first in line to qualify on Pole Day, and his average of 193.465 mph disappoints both driver and fans, who were expecting close to 200. Shortly after Foyt's run, Al Unser's Cosworth temporarily has the pole with a speed of 195.95.

Tom Sneva, driving a McLaren-Cosworth for Penske Racing, shocks the crowd of more than 250,000 with a first lap of 44.91 seconds—200.401 mph—the first official 200-mph lap and faster than his practice speeds. His second lap is 200.535. He slows on his third and fourth laps to average a record 198.884.

USAC Chief Steward Tom Binford rules that a faulty popoff valve hampered Foyt's earlier run, and he gets a second chance. Foyt averages 194.563 this time. Two-time winner Bobby Unser is the last threat to Sneva, and Unser's Offy is second fastest at 197.618.

When the gun sounds at 6 P.M., Sneva owns the pole, and the brothers Unser share the front row.

SUNDAY, MAY 15: Johnny Rutherford is the first to qualify on the second day, and his speed of 197.325 mph is third fastest overall, but the defending winner will start from the 17th position. Six former winners are in the field, and all except Rutherford start from the first two rows.

SUNDAY, MAY 22: On the last qualifying day, Janet Guthrie averages a solid 188.403 mph to become the first woman to earn a spot in the 500.

THE RACE
Start: Al Unser gets ahead of Tom Sneva and brother Bobby at the start and leads the first 17 laps.

Lap 12: Johnny Rutherford, last year's winner, is first out of the race with bent valves.

Lap 15: Janet Guthrie pits for nearly two minutes with engine problems. She goes back out for one lap, and comes back in for a 23-minute stay. She later parks for the day with a broken timing gear after completing 27 laps, good for 29th place.

Lap 18: Gordon Johncock, who starts fifth in his Wildcat, catches and passes Al Unser for the lead.

Lap 21: When Johncock pits, A. J. Foyt inherits the lead for three laps until he makes his first stop. After all the leaders pit, Foyt emerges as the leader.

Lap 35: The suspension breaks on Lloyd Ruby's car, sending him hard into the Turn 2 wall and ending his 18th and final race.

Lap 42: Trying to make up for a long pit stop, rookie Danny Ongais runs the fastest lap of the race, 192.678 mph, in a Parnelli-Cosworth.

Lap 52: On the first green lap after a caution period, Johncock dives underneath Foyt in Turn 3 and grabs the lead. Foyt clings to the back of Johncock's car another 20 laps before Johncock can open some space between them.

Lap 92: Foyt coasts into the pits out of fuel as Johncock stretches his lead to more than half a lap.

Lap 180: Johncock makes his final pit stop for a splash of fuel, giving the lead to Foyt, who has to make one more stop.

➔

A. J. Foyt (*above*) got a second chance to qualify his No. 14 Coyote (*below*), putting it on the second row. Tom Bigelow spun in qualifying (*bottom*), but kept his car off the wall and qualified the second weekend. Two-time winner Al Unser (*opposite, top left*) was a contender this year. Wally Dallenbach finished fourth in the STP-sponsored Wildcat (*opposite, top right*), the best result for the three-car Patrick team. Tom Sneva whoops it up (*opposite middle*) after his record pole run, which included the first official 200-mph lap. The field gets up to speed (*opposite bottom*).

From the outset, Jerry Sneva had a difficult run in the 500. At the start, the younger brother of second-place driver Tom Sneva, couldn't get his McLaren-Offy into third gear. The first lap was nearly complete by the time Jerry got into gear. Thereafter, he lost a couple of the face shields he had taped to his helmet.

"We had a real bad problem with wind," Jerry said. "We raised the windshield some and that helped a little. But when someone would get in front of me, I'd have to back off. The air was coming right in on top of me."

But with all the problems, the car kept on running and never missed a beat until the end.

After A. J. Foyt took the checkered flag, Jerry made another lap—his 187th—and ended up in 10th place. A few seconds later, the engine went dead. Jerry coasted into the garage area, his Offy having lasted just long enough.

Lap 183: Foyt pits, taking on fuel and right-side tires, giving the lead back to Johncock.

Lap 184: Johncock suddenly slows with mechanical problems, steers out of the racing groove and parks on the grass. A broken crankshaft ends his bid for a second victory just 16 laps from the finish. As Foyt zips by into the lead, Johncock waves to the apparent winner.

Finish: A triumphant Foyt goes the rest of the way without challenge and wins his fourth 500 by 29 seconds over Sneva, the only other driver on the lead lap. Al Unser is third, a lap down, giving the Cosworth engine a 2-3 finish. Johncock, who leads 129 laps, places 11th. As eager fans stream onto the track to congratulate Foyt, starter Pat Vidan waves the red flag to stop race cars still circling the oval.

Foyt averages 161.331 mph, a non-record speed for a historic race marked by records. It is the last win for the four-cam Foyt-Ford V-8 that debuted in 1968.

Speedway owner Tony Hulman joins the four-time winner in a victory lap around the track. It is the last race for Hulman, who resurrected the Speedway after World War II. He dies later in the year at the age of 76.

Opposite page: Defending winner Johnny Rutherford (top) was the first to drop out. A. J. Foyt (second from top) remained in contention all day. Pancho Carter dodges Eldon Rasmussen's spin (third from top). Bobby Unser led briefly before parking his Lightning-Offy (bottom left). Al Unser, in car 21, duels with Lloyd Ruby (bottom right) on his way to third place. *This page:* After taking the checkered flag for a record fourth win, Foyt is surrounded by the checkered shirts of his jubilant team (left). A broken crankshaft on Gordon Johncock's car put Foyt (below) in first.

RESULTS

NO.	DRIVER	CAR	ENTRANT	ENGINE	CYL	DISP	CHASSIS	COLOR	QUAL SPD	START	FIN	LAPS / SPEED / REASON OUT
14	A. J. Foyt	Gilmore Racing Team	A. J. Foyt Enterprises	Coyote	8	161	Coyote	orng, wht	194.563	4	1	200-161.331
8	Tom Sneva	Norton Spirit	Penske Racing, Inc.	Cosworth	8	158	McLaren	blue, wht, yelo	198.884	1	2	200-160.918
21	Al Unser	American Racing	Vel's Parnelli Jones Racing	Cosworth	8	159	Parnelli	white, blue	195.950	3	3	199-running
40	Wally Dallenbach	STP Oil Treatment	Patrick Racing	DGS	4	159	Wildcat	red, black	189.563	10	4	199-running
60	Johnny Parsons	STP Wildcat	Patrick Racing	DGS	4	159	Wildcat	red, black	189.255	11	5	193-running
24	Tom Bigelow	Thermo King	Leader Cards, Inc.	Offy	4	159	Watson	wht, red, blu, blk	186.471	22	6	192-running
65	Lee Kunzman	City of Syracuse	Patrick Santello	Offy	4	159	Eagle	blue, red, yelo	186.384	24	7	191-running
11	Roger McCluskey	1st Natl. City Trvlrs. Cks.	Lindsey Hopkins	Offy	4	159	Lightning	blue, wht, red	190.992	18	8	191-running
92	Steve Krisiloff	Dave McIntire Chev.	Vatis Enterprises, Inc.	Offy	4	159	Eagle	red, white, blk	184.691	25	9	191-running
36	Jerry Sneva	21st Amendment	James C. Bidwell	Offy	4	159	McLaren	white, red, blk	186.616	16	10	187-running
20	Gordon Johncock	STP Double Oil Filter	Patrick Racing	DGS	4	159	Wildcat	red, black	193.517	5	11	184-engine
16	Bill Puterbaugh	Dayton-Walther	Lee Elkins	Offy	4	159	Eagle	blue, wht, red	186.800	28	12	170-oil leak
58	Eldon Rasmussen	Rent-A-Racer, Inc.	Eldon Rasmussen	Foyt	8	161	Ras-Car	yelo, blk, blue	185.119	32	13	168-rear end
42	John Mahler	Mergard 20th Cen.	Donald Mergard	Offy	4	159	Eagle	orange, white	185.242	31	14	157-running
48	Pancho Carter	Jorgensen	Dan Gurney	Offy	4	159	Eagle	blue, dk. blue	192.452	8	15	156-engine
98	Gary Bettenhausen	Agajanian/Evel Knievel	Agajanian/King	Offy	4	159	Kingfish	wht, red, blu, gld	186.596	21	16	138-stalled
84	Bill Vukovich, Jr.	Gilmore Racing Team	A. J. Foyt Enterprises	Foyt	8	161	Coyote	orange, white	186.393	23	17	110-broken rod
6	Bobby Unser	Cobre Tire Clayton Dyno	Fletcher Racing	Offy	4	159	Lightning	turq, white	197.618	2	18	94-oil line
5	Mike Mosley	Sugaripe Prune	Jerry O'Connell	Offy	4	159	Lightning	yellow, red	190.069	9	19	91-engine
25	Danny Ongais	Interscope Racing	Interscope/T. Fields	Cosworth	8	158	Parnelli	blk, wht, pink	193.040	7	20	90-lost power
72	Bubby Jones	Bruce Cogle Ford	Hillin's Longhorn Racing	Offy	4	159	Eagle	brown, white	184.938	33	21	78-valve
29	Cliff Hucul	Team Canada	Hucul, Hunter & Arndt	Offy	4	159	McLaren	red, wht, yelo	187.198	27	22	72-rear end
73	Jim McElreath	Carrillo Rods	Fred W. Carrillo	AMC	8	208	Eagle	yellow, blue	187.715	20	23	71-waste gate
18	George Snider	Mel Simon	Grwd. Ctr.	DGS	4	159	Wildcat	wht, orng, blk	188.976	13	24	65-valve
78	Bobby Olivero	Alex Foods	Alex Morales	Offy	4	159	Lightning	wht, brn, orng	188.452	14	25	57-blower pressure
9	Mario Andretti	CAM 2 Motor Oil	Penske Racing, Inc.	Offy	4	159	McLaren	white, red, blk	193.351	6	26	47-broken header
10	Lloyd Ruby	1st Natl. City Trvlrs. Cks.	Lindsey Hopkins	Offy	4	159	Lightning	red, blue, wht	190.840	19	27	34-accident
86	Al Loquasto	Frostie Root Beer	Al Loquasto, Sr.	Offy	4	159	McLaren	yelo, blk, wht	187.647	15	28	28-engine
27	Janet Guthrie	Bryant Heat & Cool	Rolla Volstedt	Offy	4	159	Lightning	wht, grn, red, blk	188.403	26	29	27-engine
38	Clay Regazzoni	Theo. Racing Hong Kong	E. J. Simpson	Offy	4	159	McLaren	red, wht, yelo	186.047	29	30	25-fuel tank
17	Dick Simon	Bryant Heat & Cool	Rolla Volstedt	Offy	4	159	Vollstedt	black, white	185.615	30	31	24-engine
97	Sheldon Kinser	Genesee Beer	Agajanian/King	Offy	4	159	Kingfish	red, white	189.076	12	32	14-engine
2	Johnny Rutherford	1st Natl. City Trvlrs. Cks.	Team McLaren, Ltd.	Cosworth	8	158	McLaren	wht, blue, red	197.325	17	33	12-gear box

1978

62nd Race • May 28, 1978

Following the death of owner Tony Hulman the previous October, his widow, Mary Fendrich Hulman, becomes chairman of the board. She delivers the traditional command for drivers to start their engines on race day. Long-time treasurer Joe Cloutier becomes the new president.

The Lola chassis, absent since 1972, returns with a new team at Indy, Jim Hall's Chaparral Racing. Hall signs two-time winner Al Unser to drive the Cosworth-powered car.

Rain is a problem all month, and when it washes out the entire first weekend of qualifying, 1969 winner Mario Andretti and car owner Roger Penske face a conundrum: How does Andretti get into the 500 when he is supposed to be at a Formula 1 race in Belgium?

The solution is to hire unemployed driver Mike Hiss to qualify the car (while Andretti wins the Belgian Grand Prix) and turn it over to Mario on race day. Hiss qualifies on the third row, but Andretti starts 33rd because of the driver switch. Hiss, who has four 500s on his resume, never makes the field again.

PRACTICE AND QUALIFYING

SATURDAY, MAY 6: Second-year driver Danny Ongais is fast right out of the box, clocking a lap over 196 mph on opening day in a Parnelli-Cosworth.

WEDNESDAY, MAY 10: On a clear day, you can see cars go faster. The rain stays away and Mario Andretti hits 201.838 mph in his new Penske-Cosworth. Later, Ongais tops him at 201.974.

FRIDAY, MAY 12: Andretti is fastest the day before the run for the pole, running 203.482 mph during "happy hour." Rookie teammate Rick Mears is close behind at 201.703. Four-time winner A. J. Foyt cranks his Coyote-Foyt over 200, and two-time champ Johnny Rutherford does the same with his McLaren-Cosworth.

SATURDAY, MAY 13: Rain washes out Pole Day and the next day as well. It is the first time since 1969 that no cars qualify on the first weekend.

➔

STARTING LINEUP

Average Field Qualifying Speed: 192.584

Numbers in flags indicate finish position

23 — Rick Mears

3 — Gordon Johncock

22 — Larry Dickson

32 — Sheldon Kinser

9 — Janet Guthrie

18 — Danny Ongais

1 — Al Unser

10 — Johnny Parsons

25 — Roger McCluskey

27 — Tom Bagley

POLE POSITION
Qualifying Speed: 202.156

2 — Tom Sneva

13 — Johnny Rutherford

5 — Wally Dallenbach

19 — Dick Simon

4 — Steve Krisiloff

Jim McGee is congratulated at the annual driver's meeting for being chief mechanic of the pole-winning car driven by Tom Sneva (*opposite top*). Steve Krisiloff's No. 40 Wildcat sports an unusual front wing (*opposite bottom*), but it apparently served the Patrick team well. Krisiloff shot up from 13th on the grid to finish fourth and teammate Gordon Johncock jumped three places to third by the time the checkered flag flew. Sheldon Kinser, who made his name as a successful sprint-car driver before coming to Indy, started 12th in the No. 24 Watson-Offy (*right*), but it overheated after just 15 laps. Chief Steward Tom Binford tries out the Corvette pace car (*below*), the first time Chevrolet's sports car got the call to lead the field. Street replicas went on to become highly sought collector cars.

Tom Bigelow

Pancho Carter

Joe Saldana

Cliff Hucul

Larry Rice

Mario Andretti

John Mahler

A. J. Foyt

George Snider

Jim McElreath

Phil Threshie

Jerry Sneva

Spike Gehlhausen

Bobby Unser

Salt Walther

Mike Mosley

Jerry Karl

Gary Bettenhausen

SATURDAY, MAY 20: Qualifying finally gets underway, and none of the early attempts break 200 mph until Tom Sneva goes out.

Sneva, driving a Penske-Cosworth, gets the crowd on its feet with a first lap of 203.620. His next three laps are slower, but he still averages 202.156, the first driver to qualify at more than 200 mph.

Rick Mears is next and does 200.078, fast enough to put the rookie on the outside of row one. Danny Ongais squeezes between Sneva and Mears with a speed of 200.122.

A. J. Foyt is the last driver with a chance at the pole, but he waves off his run. Foyt mistakenly thinks he has a faulty popoff valve, and the day ends before he can make another attempt, losing his shot for the pole.

Janet Guthrie, a late arrival this year with her own team and Texaco sponsorship, qualifies on the outside of row five at 190.325, insuring her second straight start. She finishes ninth in the race.

SUNDAY, MAY 21: Foyt atones for Saturday's mistake by matching Ongais's speed of 200.122 mph, second fastest overall. Foyt, however, starts 20th.

The 33 starters average a record 192.584 mph.

THE RACE

Start: Polesitter Tom Sneva and Danny Ongais jump in front at the start, and Ongais gets to Turn 1 first to grab the lead.

Lap 2: Sheldon Kinser stalls on the back straight, bringing out the yellow. Ongais maintains first place after the restart.

Lap 9: Kinser stalls again on the back straight, bringing out the second yellow.

Lap 12: Sneva gets the jump on Ongais when the green flag comes out and takes the lead, while Foyt moves up to eighth.

Lap 13: Ongais barges back into the lead. Sneva drops to second and Al Unser moves into third.

Lap 20: Mario Andretti, after charging from last place to 11th, loses more than six minutes in the pits getting a new ignition coil.

Lap 23: Sneva pits for fuel, giving second place to Al Unser.

Lap 24: Spike Gehlhausen crashes in Turn 2, and leader Ongais pits under yellow. However, his crew struggles with the right rear tire, and Ongais comes back out in third place behind new leader Steve Krisiloff and Sneva.

Lap 31: When the green flag returns, Krisiloff loses a lap for exceeding the 80-mph speed limit during the caution period. Sneva regains the lead, but a lap later Ongais dusts Sneva and goes back in front. →

After Janet Guthrie made the starting field in 1977, finishing 29th, she returned in '78 with a much better ride. Qualifying her Wildcat-DGS solidly on the outside of row five at 190.325 mph, she turned in a fine performance, finishing ninth.

But the shock of the entire month occured the following evening at the Victory Banquet. Janet walked on stage to join the other drivers with her right arm in a sling. At the podium, Janet revealed that a few days before the 500, she'd fallen at a charity tennis match and fractured her right wrist.

"I don't play tennis to begin with," Janet says. "But the drivers' wives asked me to show up anyway. I went and tripped over my own feet and cracked my wrist. Now, other drivers have driven with a broken something or other. But under the circumstances, I thought I had a little more to worry about.

"I was shooting for a top-five finish," Janet continued. "But I'll settle for ninth. The biggest trouble was shifting gears. The lever was on the right and I nearly got eaten alive on one restart. So I started reaching across and shifting left-handed."

Guthrie doesn't make a big thing about her finest run at Indy. But her courage can't be doubted. It's not easy handling a 700-horsepower racer while being buffeted by "dirty air" from other cars with just your left hand—especially, as in Janet's case, when you're right-handed.

Fans who arrived early enough for the pre-race pageantry got to see actor Norman Fell (*opposite, top left*), star of the television comedy *Three's Company*, and the comely Hurst Girls (*opposite, top right*). A loosely bunched race field follows the pace car prior to the start (*opposite bottom*). With the caution flag displayed (*left*), Bobby Unser runs in fifth place, ahead of Johnny Parsons, Steve Krisiloff, and Wally Dallenbach. All were top-10 finishers. *Below:* Dallenbach (No. 6) cruises ahead of Parsons (No. 16), Dick Simon (No. 17), and Larry Dickson (No. 80) on the parade lap.

Lap 48: A yellow flag for debris on the track results in a flurry of pit stops, and Ongais remains in front, followed by Sneva, Gordon Johncock, Al Unser, and Bobby Unser, all on the lead lap.

Lap 66: Al Unser passes Sneva for second place, with Ongais in front by about eight seconds.

Lap 75: Ongais is the last of the leaders to pit for fuel and, despite a stop of only 14 seconds, he loses the lead to Al Unser. Sneva and Johncock are third and fourth, respectively, still on the lead lap.

Lap 84: The yellow comes on again for debris, bringing the leaders back into the pits. When the green flag comes out on Lap 86, Sneva is still on pit road and falls to fourth.

Lap 135: Al Unser still leads when he and Ongais pit together. Unser wins the sprint back onto the track.

Lap 145: Smoke trailing behind his ailing Parnelli-Cosworth, Ongais slowly pulls into the pits with a blown engine. Al Unser cruises by, 28 seconds ahead of Sneva, the only other driver still racing on the lead lap.

Lap 155: The leaders stop for fuel, and Unser gets out in 14.9 seconds. Sneva, however, stalls and requires 20.5 seconds.

Lap 180: Unser makes his final stop but overshoots his pit and hits a tire, bending his right front wing. As Unser exits the pits, Sneva comes in and crosses the start-finish line first, getting credit for leading the lap. Back on the track, Unser has a 30-second cushion.

Lap 192: Unser slows because of his bent wing while Sneva charges to within 18.5 seconds of the lead.

Finish: Sneva runs out of laps to catch Unser's wounded Lola, and he falls eight seconds short—the second closest finish yet. Johncock is third, one lap in arrears.

Al Unser becomes the fifth driver to win three races, and the Unser family chalks up its fifth victory. The Cosworth engine and car owner Jim Hall visit victory lane for the first time. Unser leads 121 laps while averaging 161.363 mph. He makes nine pit stops to Sneva's eight, and the last one almost costs him the race.

Danny Ongais (*top left*) started second, led 71 laps, and was among the leaders when his engine blew. With the Goodyear blimp overhead, the scoring pylon shows Ongais in front after 50 laps (*left*). Jerry Karl leads a pack (*above*) that includes rookie Rick Mears, Mike Mosley, Mario Andretti, and John Mahler. Al Unser led 121 laps and joined the list of three-time winners despite a bent front wing on his Lola that slowed him late in the race. *Opposite:* The victor (propped in the cockpit of his racer), Jim Hall—who won in his first year as the owner of a car in the 500—and their spouses pose for pictures the day after the race.

RESULTS

NO.	DRIVER	CAR	ENTRANT	ENGINE	CYL	DISP	CHASSIS	COLOR	QUAL SPD	START	FIN	LAPS / SPEED / REASON OUT
2	Al Unser	1st Natl. City Tvrls. Cks.	Chaparral Racing Ltd.	Cosworth	8	161	Lola	red, wht, blue	196.474	5	1	200-161.363
1	Tom Sneva	Norton Spirit	Penske Racing, Inc.	Cosworth	8	161	Penske	red, wht, blue	202.156	1	2	200-161.244
20	Gordon Johncock	North Amer. Van Lines	Patrick Racing Team	DGS	4	159	Wildcat	blue, wht, red	195.833	6	3	199-running
40	Steve Krisiloff	Foreman Industries	Patrick Racing Team	DGS	4	159	Wildcat	blue, white	191.255	13	4	198-running
6	Wally Dallenbach	Sugaripe Prune	Jerry O'Connell	Cosworth	8	161	McLaren	yellow, red	195.228	7	5	195-out of fuel
48	Bobby Unser	ARCO Graphite	Dan Gurney	Cosworth	8	161	Eagle	blk, red, yelo	194.658	19	6	195-running
14	A. J. Foyt	Gilmore Racing/Citicorp	A. J. Foyt Enterprises	Foyt	8	161	Coyote	orange, white	200.122	20	7	191-running
84	George Snider	Gilmore Racing/Citicorp	A. J. Foyt Enterprises	Foyt	8	161	Coyote	orange, white	192.627	23	8	191-running
51	Janet Guthrie	Texaco Star	Janet Guthrie Racing	DGS	4	159	Wildcat	wht, pink, red	190.325	15	9	190-running
16	Johnny Parsons	1st Natl. City Tvrls. Cks.	Lindsey Hopkins	Offy	4	159	Lightning	red, white, blk	194.280	8	10	186-running
35	Larry Rice	Bryant Heating/WIBC	Headback Corp.	Offy	4	159	Lightning	wht, blue, blk	187.393	30	11	186-engine
7	Mario Andretti	The Gould Charge	Penske Racing, Inc.	Cosworth	8	161	Penske	blue, wht, red	194.647	33	12	185-running
4	Johnny Rutherford	1st Natl. City Trvlrs Cks.	Team McLaren, Ltd.	Cosworth	8	161	McLaren	wht, blue, red	197.098	4	13	180-running
88	Jerry Karl	Machinists Union	Frank Fiore	Offy	4	159	McLaren	red, wht, blue	187.549	28	14	176-running
69	Joe Saldana	Mr. Wize Buys Carpet	Hoffman Auto Racing	Offy	4	159	Eagle	blk, red, wht	190.809	24	15	173-running
98	Gary Bettenhausen	Oberdorfer	Agajanian/King/Purcell	Offy	4	159	Kingfish	wht, blk, yelo	187.324	31	16	147-piston
78	Mike Mosley	Alex XLNT Foods	Alex Morales	Offy	4	159	Lightning	wht, orng, yelo	188.719	25	17	146-broken gear
25	Danny Ongais	Interscope Racing	Interscope Racing	Cosworth	8	161	Parnelli	blk, wht, pink	200.122	2	18	145-piston
17	Dick Simon	La Machine	Volstedt Enterprises	Offy	4	159	Vollstedt	black, white	192.967	10	19	138-wheel bearing
26	Jim McElreath	Circle City Coal	Jim McElreath	Offy	4	159	Eagle	wht, blue, yelo	188.058	26	20	132-engine
43	Tom Bigelow	Armstrong Mould	Sherman E. Armstrong	DGS	4	159	Wildcat	blk, wht, orng	189.115	18	21	107-connecting rod
80	Larry Dickson	Polak/Stay-On-Car Glaze	Russel Polak	Cosworth	8	159	McLaren	blue, yelo, red	193.434	9	22	104-oil pressure
71	Rick Mears	CAM 2 Motor Oil	Penske Racing, Inc.	Cosworth	8	161	Penske	red, wht, blue	200.078	3	23	103-engine
8	Pancho Carter	Budweiser	Fletcher Racing Team	Cosworth	8	161	Lightning	red, wht, blk	196.829	21	24	92-exhaust header
11	Roger McCluskey	National Engineering Co.	Warner Hodgdon	AMC	8	207	Eagle	blk, wht, rd, blu	192.256	11	25	82-clutch
39	John Mahler•	Tibon	Carl Gelhausen	Offy	4	159	Eagle	blue, yelo, red	189.773	17	26	58-timing gear
22	Tom Bagley	Kent Oil	Leader Cards, Inc.	Offy	4	159	Watson	blue, yellow	190.941	14	27	25-overheating
77	Salt Walther	Dayton-Walther	Walmotor, Inc.	Cosworth	8	161	McLaren	blue, wht, red	193.226	22	28	24-transmission
19	Spike Gehlhausen	Hubler Chev./WIRE Radio	Carl Gelhausen	Offy	4	159	Eagle	blue, yellow	190.325	16	29	23-accident
47	Phil Threshie	Circle Chev/Tutwiler Cad	Phil Threshie	Offy	4	159	Lighting	wht, blu, prpl	187.520	29	30	22-oil pressure
30	Jerry Sneva	Smock Mtrl. Handling	Bill Freeman Racing	Offy	4	159	McLaren	silver, white	187.266	32	31	18-rear end
24	Sheldon Kinser	Thermo-King	Lead Cards, Inc.	Offy	4	159	Watson	wht, red, blue	192.051	12	32	15-overheating
29	Cliff Hucul	Wendy's Hamburgers	Cliff Hucul	Offy	4	159	McLaren	yellow, red	187.803	27	33	4-oil line

1979

63rd Race • May 27, 1979

New rules reduce turbo boost from 80 inches of manifold pressure to 50 during qualifying and 70 during the race as USAC tries to slow the cars and make stock-block engines more competitive.

To control speeds and prevent cars from moving up during caution periods, the pace car will come on to the track and, indeed, set the pace under yellow. The race cars will line up behind in their track position.

Even before qualifying starts, there is plenty of action, mostly in the courtroom. Six owners affiliated with the recently formed Championship Auto Racing Teams sue in federal court when USAC denies their entries. The court rules in favor of the owners, who are allowed to compete.

During qualifying, accusations fly that several teams exceeded the 50-inch boost limit, and that ends up in court, too. This results in an extra qualifying session that enables two more drivers to make the field.

Not all the news involves lawyers. Team owners Roger Penske, whose car won in 1972, and Jim Hall, who won last year with a Lola chassis in his first try, enter new chassis with "ground effects" designs copied from Formula 1 cars.

The bottoms of Penske's PC-7 and Hall's Chaparral 2K are shaped to create a low-pressure area that literally pulls the car closer to the pavement and allows faster cornering speeds. The driver sits well forward in these new cars, and the fuel tank is behind the driver.

A record 103 entries overwhelm the Speedway's garage area, and some teams start the month of May in open areas around the infield. Nearly half the entries and 20 starters use the Cosworth V-8 that finished 1-2 in 1978, and the trusty Offenhauser engine appears on its way out.

PRACTICE AND QUALIFYING

TUESDAY, MAY 8: Second-year driver Rick Mears sets fast time for the month in the new Penske-Cosworth: 193.5 mph. Al Unser is second fastest at 189.2 in the new Chaparral-Cosworth.

WEDNESDAY, MAY 9: Four-time winner A. J. Foyt tries out a new package—a Parnelli chassis and Cosworth engine—and needs only seven laps to set fast time of the day, ➔

The redesigned Ford Mustang (*opposite bottom*) was the pace car. A fleet of mini Mustangs (*top*) gave Speedway wannabes some track time. The Cosworth engine (*above*) powered 20 of the 33 starters. As the official fuel supplier, Valvoline had a big presence at the track (*opposite top*).

STARTING LINEUP

Average Field Qualifying Speed: 186.737

Pole Position Qualifying Speed: 193.736

Al Unser

A. J. Foyt

Johnny Parsons

Mike Mosley

Tom Bagley

Cliff Hucul

Tom Sneva

Gordon Johncock

Johnny Rutherford

Lee Kunzman

Janet Guthrie

Pancho Carter

Rick Mears

Bobby Unser

Wally Dallenbach

Sheldon Kinser

Howdy Holmes

Salt Walther

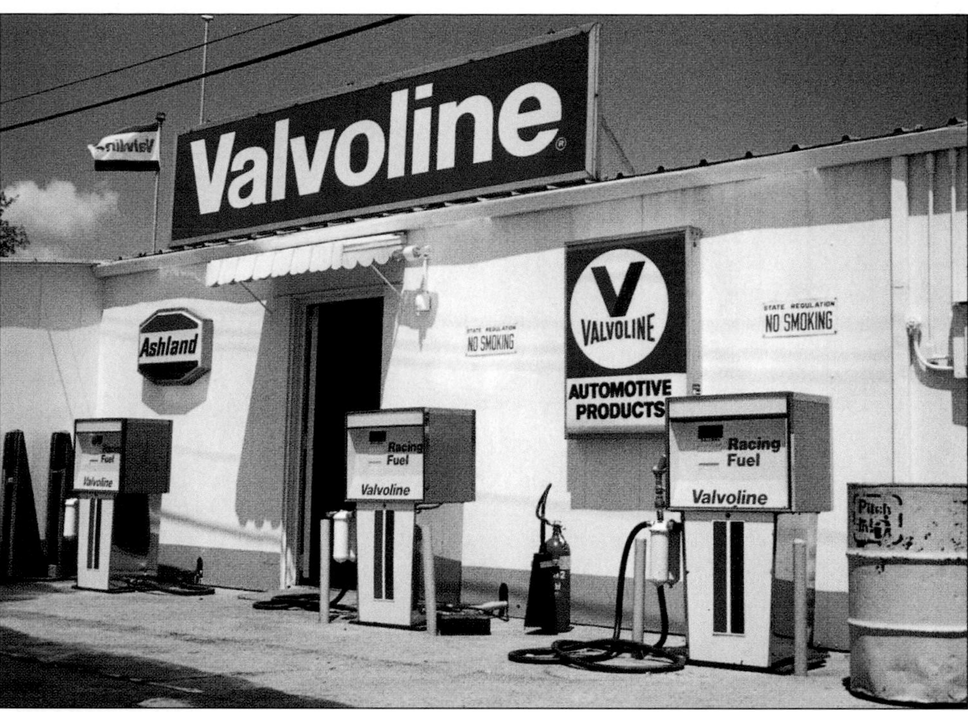

Spike Gehlhausen and teammate Al Loquasto were bumped from the lineup in 1979, a year when many teams were accused of cheating on the turbo boost. Spike believed he and Loquasto were the victims of such shenanigans. They weren't about to trying bucking the trend in the same cars.

Although Spike quickly found a great ride in a George Bignotti-prepared Wildcat-Cosworth that he proceeded to put into the lineup, he really wasn't happy. The owner of Spike's original car was his father, Carl Gehlhausen. Spike wanted to live up to the faith his father had in his abilities.

"I've had opportunities before to move to other teams," Spike said. "Dad said he didn't mind so long as it was a first-class team. The offers I've had were good. All of them made the show here. Maybe I let my personal feelings get ahead."

Whatever the case, the Bignotti entry proved to be Spike's shining moment at Indy. Starting 31st, he brought the car home in 10th place, his best Indy finish ever.

And since Carl Gehlhausen had recently suffered a stroke, Spike's effort meant even more to the veteran car owner.

194 mph. Unser is again second fastest at 193.4.

THURSDAY, MAY 10: Foyt is quickest again at 194.89 mph, and Danny Ongais moves into contention for the pole with a lap over 193 in a Penske-Cosworth. Mears and two-time winner Johnny Rutherford also top 190.

SATURDAY, MAY 12: Rain delays the run for the pole, but the track dries in time for late-afternoon practice. Danny Ongais spins coming out of Turn 4 and hits the inside wall twice. Ongais is badly bruised and may miss qualifying.

SUNDAY, MAY 13: Unser stakes an early claim to the pole with a speed of 192.503 mph in his Chaparral. Tom Sneva, gunning for his third straight pole, moves Unser aside by averaging 192.998 in a McLaren-Cosworth.

Foyt starts his run with a first lap of 191.775 and climbs to 192 the second time around, but then falls off to 188 and 186 the next two laps to lower his average to 189.613.

Mears, the last driver in line, hits 194.847 on his first lap and averages 193.736 to win the pole in just his second race. Sneva and Al Unser share the front row, and though each has a different chassis, all run with Cosworth power.

SATURDAY, MAY 19: USAC throws out the qualifying run of Dick Ferguson after finding his engine exceeds 50 inches of turbo boost and fines owner Wayne Woodward $5000.

SUNDAY, MAY 20: USAC throws out two more qualifiers, Tom Bigelow and Steve Krisiloff, for exceeding the boost limit and fines their owners $5000 each. Both drivers qualify again. Danny Ongais, cleared by his doctors to drive, qualifies at 188 mph to earn a spot on the ninth row.

Late in the day, USAC throws out the qualifying run of Bill Alsup in one of the Team Penske cars because he uses the same engine with which teammate Bobby Unser had already made the show. John Mahler bumps Bill Vukovich, Jr., as the 6 P.M. gun sounds, but the shooting is far from over.

SATURDAY, MAY 26: Faced with lawsuits and an uproar among owners and drivers, USAC schedules a special 9 A.M. qualifying session for eight cars bumped from the field. To make the race, these cars have to qualify at 183.9 mph (Roger McCluskey's speed in 25th starting position) or faster, and no one already in can be bumped.

Vukovich tops 187 mph and George Snider does 185.3 to line up 34th and 35th, the first time since 1933 there are more than 33 starters.

THE RACE

Start: When the green flag drops, the legal bickering finally stops. Al Unser shoots around Rick Mears and Tom Sneva into the first turn and pulls away to take the lead.

Lap 3: Unser stretches his lead over Mears and Sneva with a lap of 192.143 mph, fastest lead lap of the race. Meanwhile, Janet Guthrie pulls into the pits. Her third and final appearance ends with a burned piston.

Lap 8: Leader Unser, aiming for his fourth win and second straight, already starts to lap slower cars as Mears falls six seconds back.

Lap 25: Unser pits, giving the lead to Mears. When Mears stops two laps later, A. J. Foyt leads for a lap before he pits. After everyone stops, Unser is back in front, Mears is second, and Sneva third; only nine cars are still on the lead lap.

➔

Janet Guthrie (*opposite top*) qualified for her third—and last—race. Two-time 500 champ Bobby Unser (*opposite middle*) joined the Penske stable. Owner Roger Penske confers with endurance racer Hurley Haywood (*opposite bottom*), who didn't make the field. Rick Mears put the new Penske chassis (*top left*) on the pole. Pancho Carter has a pitside talk (*top right*) with veteran driver Bob Harkey, who is in the cockpit. Danny Ongais (*above*) charged to a fourth-place finish. The starters roll out on a parade lap (*second from top, right*). Joining Mears on the front row (*third from top*) were Tom Sneva and Al Unser. Lee Kunzman went out early in 30th place in the No. 89 Parnelli (*below*).

Lap 45: After a second round of pit stops, Al Unser is still setting a blistering pace, with Johnny Rutherford second and Bobby Unser third. Mears falls to sixth from a long pit stop.

Lap 70: Bobby Unser takes over the lead for four laps when brother Al pits. When Bobby pits, it goes to Mears, who leads for three laps before stopping for fuel. Once everyone is back on track, Al leads Bobby, and Rutherford and Mears run third and fourth.

Lap 83: Foyt passes Mears for fourth place and 10 laps later gets by Rutherford for third.

Lap 94: All the leaders pit under yellow. Foyt stalls after taking on fuel and needs a push start from his crew. He falls a lap down to sixth place.

Lap 96: Al Unser comes back in with smoke coming from under his Chaparral. After a quick inspection, his crew sends him back out in third place behind Bobby Unser—who regains the lead—and Mears.

Rutherford, who was third, comes in again. He makes an extended stay for transmission repairs.

Lap 104: Al Unser is shown the black flag as smoke pours from the back of his car. He pulls into the pits with a small fire at the rear. After leading 85 of the first 96 laps, Unser's hopes for a fourth victory die with a broken transmission seal.

Lap 108: Foyt, running fourth, passes Bobby Unser to get back on the lead lap. Mears is about a second behind teammate Unser, and third-place Sneva is about four seconds back.

Lap 127: Sneva runs out of fuel and coasts into the pits, falling a lap down to sixth. Unser puts Foyt a lap down again.

Lap 156: The two Penske cars are the last of the leaders to pit, and they come in together under yellow. Unser gets out first to maintain the lead.

Lap 181: Foyt, still a lap down to leader Unser and second-place Mears, passes Mears. While Foyt and Mears come roaring out of the fourth turn, Unser slows on the main straight.

Lap 182: Mears takes over the lead as Unser, the top gear gone in his transmission, stays on the track at reduced speed. Third-place Foyt, having passed Mears, is now on the lead lap.

Lap 187: The leaders make their final stops for fuel, and they come out in the same order: Mears, Unser, Foyt.

Lap 190: Foyt passes Unser for second place, but then Foyt slows in Turn 1 as smoke comes from under his car.

Before Mears can lap Foyt, the yellow light comes on: Sneva crashes in Turn 4 when the rear wing flies off his McLaren. As the cars bunch up behind the pace car under yellow, there are 15 between Mears and Foyt. Unser lines up behind Mears but is a lap down in third.

Finish: When the green flag flies on Lap 196, Mears has a clear track ahead while Foyt fights through traffic.

As Mears takes the checkered flag, Foyt is nowhere in sight. He finally rolls slowly onto the front straight, his engine having failed. He coasts across the finish line in second, just two seconds ahead of Mike Mosley. Danny Ongais is fourth and Bobby Unser limps into fifth.

Mears, who started in off-road racing, leads 25 laps while the Unser brothers lead a combined 174 laps. He averages 158.9 mph, and for the seventh straight year, it is not a record.

Cosworth engines sweep the first seven spots.

Third-row qualifiers (*opposite, top left*) Wally Dallenbach (No. 6), Johnny Rutherford (No. 4), and Johnny Parsons (No. 15) anticipate the green flag. The yellow No. 1 of Tom Sneva leads Rick Mears and A. J. Foyt past slower cars (*opposite, bottom left*). Dick Simon's No. 17 Vollstedt-Offy is in front of a tight pack of cars on the front straight. Johnny Rutherford's McLaren (*top left*), Pancho Carter's Lightning (*top right*), and Mears's Penske (*middle*) get pit service. Mears (*below*) sped to victory when Bobby Unser and Foyt faltered near the finish.

RESULTS

NO.	DRIVER	CAR	ENTRANT	ENGINE	CYL	DISP	CHASSIS	COLOR	QUAL SPD	START	FIN	LAPS / SPEED / REASON OUT
9	Rick Mears	The Gould Change	Penske Racing, Inc.	Cosworth	8	161	Penske	red, wht, blue	193.736	1	1	200-158.899
14	A. J. Foyt	Gilmore Racing Team	A. J. Foyt Vel's P.J.	Cosworth	8	161	Parnelli	orange, white	189.613	6	2	200-158.260
36	Mike Mosley	Theodore Racing	Daniel S. Gurney	Cosworth	8	161	Eagle	white, red	186.278	12	3	200-158.228
25	Danny Ongais	Interscope/Panasonic	Interscope Racing Corp.	Cosworth	8	161	Penske	blk, wht, pink	188.009	27	4	199-running
12	Bobby Unser	The Norton Spirit	Penske Racing, Inc.	Cosworth	8	161	Penske	blue, white	189.913	4	5	199-running
3	Gordon Johncock	North Amer. Van Lines	Patrick Racing Team	Cosworth	8	161	Penske	blue, wht, red	189.753	5	6	197-running
46	Howdy Holmes	Armstrong Mold/Jiffy Mix	Sherman Armstrong	Cosworth	4	159	Wildcat	blk, wht, orng	185.864	13	7	195-running
22	Bill Vukovich, Jr.	Hubler/WNDE/Thermo-King	Leader Cards, Inc.	Offy	4	160	Watson	red, wht, blue	187.042	34	8	194-running
11	Tom Bagley	Dairy Queen/Kent Oil	Bobby Hillin	Cosworth	8	160	Penske	wht, blue, red	185.514	15	9	193-running
19	Spike Gehlhausen	Sta-On Glaze	Patrick Racing Team	Cosworth	8	160	Wildcat	wht, red, blue	185.061	31	10	192-running
7	Steve Krisiloff	Frosty Acres/Winston	Fletcher Racing Team	Offy	4	159	Lightning	red, white	186.287	28	11	192-running
77	Salt Walther	Dayton-Walther	Walmotor, Inc.	Cosworth	8	161	Penske	blue, wht, gld	184.162	16	12	191-running
72	Roger McCluskey	Natl. Engineering Co.	Natl. Engineering Co.	Cosworth	8	161	McLaren	wht, blue, red	183.908	25	13	191-running
44	Tom Bigelow	Armstrong Mould	Sherman Armstrong	Cosworth	8	161	Lola	blk, orng, wht	185.147	30	14	190-running
1	Tom Sneva	Sugaripe Prune	Jerry O'Connell	Cosworth	8	161	McLaren	yellow, red	192.998	2	15	188-accident
69	Joe Saldana	KBHL/Spirit of Nebraska	Hoffman Auto Racing	Offy	4	159	Eagle	blk, red, wht	188.778	26	16	185-running
97	Phil Threshie	Guiffre Bros. Crane	Agajanian/King	Chevy	8	347	King	blue, white	185.854	29	17	172-running
4	John Rutherford	Budweiser	Team McLaren Ltd.	Cosworth	8	161	McLaren	wht, red, blue	188.137	8	18	168-running
31	Larry Rice	S & M Electric	S & M Electric Co.	Offy	4	159	Lightning	blue, wht, blk	184.219	23	19	142-accident
10	Pancho Carter	Alex XLNT foods	Alex Moroles	Offy	4	159	Lightning	wht, orng, blk	185.806	17	20	129-wheel bearing
34	Vern Schuppan	Wysard Motor Co.	Herb and Rose Wysard	DGS	4	159	Wildcat	white, yellow	184.341	22	21	111-transmission
2	Al Unser	Pennzoil	Chaparral Racing Ltd.	Cosworth	8	161	Chaparral	yelo, blk, red	192.503	3	22	104-transmission seal
50	Eldon Rasmussen	Vans by Bivouac/WFMS	B.F.M. Enterprises, Ltd.	Offy	4	159	Antares	blue, black	183.927	33	23	89-exhaust header
80	Larry Dickson	Russ Polak	Russel Polak	Cosworth	8	161	Penske	blue, yelo, red	184.181	24	24	86-fuel pump belt
92	John Mahler	Intercomp/Sports Mag.	Intercomp	Offy	8	161	Eagle	white, black	184.322	32	25	66-fuel pump
17	Dick Simon	Sanyo	Vollstedt Enterprises	Offy	4	159	Vollstedt	black, white	185.071	20	26	57-clutch
6	Wally Dallenbach	Foreman Industries	Patrick Racing Team	Cosworth	8	161	Penske	red, wht, blk	188.285	7	27	43-lost rear wheel
24	Sheldon Kinser	Genesee Beer	Leader Cards, Inc.	Offy	4	159	Watson	maroon, gold	186.674	10	28	40-piston
29	Cliff Hucul	Hucul Racing	Hucul, Hunter & Arndt	Offy	4	159	McLaren	wht, red, yelo	186.200	18	29	22-engine
89	Lee Kunzman	Vetter Windjammer	Conqueste Racing Team	Cosworth	8	161	Parnelli	blk, slvr, red	186.403	11	30	18-oil pump
73	Jerry Sneva	Natl Engineering AMC	Natl Engineering	AMC	8	208	Spirit	blk, red, wht, blue	184.379	21	31	16-turbocharger
15	Johnny Parsons	Hopkins	Lindsey Hopkins	Offy	4	159	Lightning	red, wht, blue	187.813	9	32	16-piston
59	George Snider	KBHL/Spirit of Nebraska	Hoffman Auto Racing	Offy	4	159	Lightning	black, white	185.319	35	33	7-valve
45	Janet Guthrie	Texaco Star	Sherman Armstrong	Cosworth	8	161	Lola	wht, blk, rd, pink	185.720	14	34	3-piston
23	Jim McElreath	Amax Coal Co.	Shirley McElreath	Cosworth	8	161	Penske	blue, red, wht	185.883	19	35	0-valve

1980

64th Race • May 25, 1980

In a welcome change from last year's name-calling and legal struggles, 1980 is more peaceful and harmonious. John Cooper, after years in various roles with USAC, takes over as Speedway president.

After the stunning success of the Chaparral and Penske "ground effects" cars in 1979, virtually every chassis maker rushes to improve the aerodynamics underneath their cars. That includes Chaparral owner Jim Hall, who updates the 2K for his new driver, Johnny Rutherford. Roger Penske has a new PC-9 chassis for his three drivers: defending champ Rick Mears, two-time winner Bobby Unser, and 1969 winner Mario Andretti, back at the Brickyard after focusing on Formula 1.

Twelve different brands of chassis take the green flag on race day, but 24 starters use the now dominant Cosworth engine. There are just five Offys on the starting grid, three of them the latest Drake-Goossen-Sparks variety. Four Chevrolet stock-block engines make the field, a turbocharged V-6 driven by rookie Hurley Haywood, and three naturally-aspirated V-8s.

In contrast to last year, when Howdy Holmes was the lone rookie (the fewest since 1939), 10 make the field this year. The biggest freshman class since 1965 includes brothers Bill and Don Whittington. Seven former winners are in the field, too.

PRACTICE AND QUALIFYING

MONDAY, MAY 5: Johnny Rutherford's screaming yellow Chaparral has the fastest practice speed so far, 192.472 mph. Spike Gehlhausen is close behind in a year-old Penske chassis.

THURSDAY, MAY 8: Rutherford is fastest again at 191.9 mph, but Mario Andretti does 190.9 to put himself among the contenders for Saturday's pole. Gordon Johncock loses control of his Penske-Cosworth in Turn 1 and bangs the outside wall, fracturing his left ankle.

FRIDAY, MAY 9: Rookie Tim Richmond, who has been fast all week, is fastest of all today. He runs 193.5 mph, beating Rutherford's best lap of 193.0. A. J. Foyt does an impressive 192.5 and Gehlhausen hits 191.9. Team Penske gets ready to run for the pole with speeds over 191 from Rick Mears and Andretti and 190.9 from Bobby Unser.

→

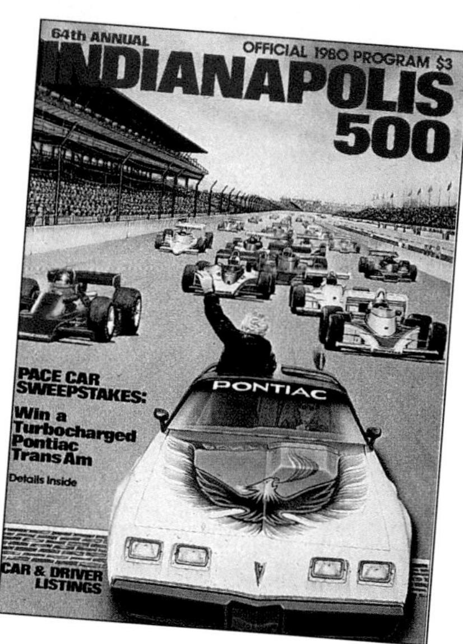

The Pontiac Turbo-Trans Am pace car (*above*) was driven by Johnnie Parsons, who was reunited with the Wynn's Friction Proofing Kurtis-Offy that carried him to victory in 1950 (*opposite top*). Prior to the start of the '80 race, he lapped the Speedway in his trusty old mount. Parsons's son, Johnny, made his seventh start this year and finished 26th. The high-performance Firebird was the first Pontiac pace car since 1958. Speedway Chairman Mary Fendrich Hulman (*opposite bottom*) makes her annual race day appearance to give the field the command to start engines.

STARTING LINEUP

Average Field Qualifying Speed: 185.570

Numbers in flags indicate finish position

POLE POSITION
Qualifying Speed: 192.256

Bobby Unser

Rick Mears

Al Unser

A. J. Foyt

Dick Ferguson

Mario Andretti

Jerry Sneva

Pancho Carter

Jim McElreath

Larry Cannon

Johnny Rutherford

Spike Gehlhausen

Johnny Parsons

Roger Rager

Tom Bagley

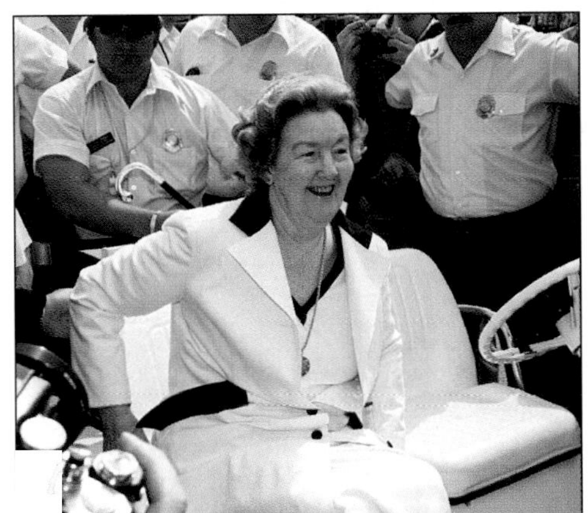

When Gary Bettenhausen qualified Sherman Armstrong's five-year-old Wildcat-Offy, no one considered the entry a threat to win. This included Gary, who told his wife on race day, "When this thing blows up, I want everybody to head straight for the car. We're getting out of here and beat the traffic."

Bettenhausen had good cause to feel that way. For one thing, he'd barely made the field. And if it hadn't rained, he would probably have been bumped from the lineup. On carburetion day, the old machine would hardly run. Bettenhausen and his sprint-car owner, Willie Davis, borrowed parts from other teams, threw the rest of the crew out of the garage, and went to work. Among other things, they rebuilt the entire fuel system and trusted the rest to luck.

Once the green flag flew, however, Bettenhausen charged all the way from 32nd starting position to chase the leaders. At one point it looked as if Gary might even have a shot at winning. It didn't shake out that way, but his torrid, stirring run from the last row to third place stunned and excited those who witnessed the race.

The only traffic Gary beat that day was at the Brickyard.

Don Whittington

George Snider

Dennis Firestone

Bill Whittington

Bill Vukovich, Jr.

Tom Sneva

Gordon Johncock

Gordon Smiley

Greg Leffler

Mike Mosley

Dick Simon

Gary Bettenhausen

Danny Ongais

Tim Richmond

Bill Engelhart

Hurley Haywood

Jerry Karl

Tom Bigelow

SATURDAY, MAY 10: In morning practice on Pole Day, Tim Richmond spins in Turn 1 and clips the outside wall. He escapes injury, but his car receives heavy damage.

Mario Andretti rouses the crowd with a run of 191.012 and becomes the driver to beat. Johnny Rutherford meets the challenge, guiding his Chaparral to 192.256 to win his third pole. Bobby Unser manages 189.994 to earn the outside of the front row.

Janet Guthrie, trying to make her fourth straight race, waves off a qualifying run in the 184-mph range, which ultimately proves fast enough to make the race. Her engine blows the next weekend in practice, and she fails to make another qualifying attempt.

SUNDAY, MAY 11: Danny Ongais qualifies 16th at 186.6 mph and Gordon Johncock lines up next to him as the biggest names to make the field on the second day.

WEDNESDAY, MAY 14: Tom Sneva, whose McLaren is already qualified, cuts a tire when he runs over debris and whacks the Turn 1 wall. Sneva has minor injuries, but the car sustains heavy damage. He moves to a backup and starts 33rd as a result.

SUNDAY, MAY 18: Tim Richmond finally gets his car back together and posts a creditable 188.334 mph, fastest qualifier on the final day.

THE RACE

Start: Bobby Unser forges ahead from the outside of row one into the first turn, but Johnny Rutherford passes him on the back straight for the lead.

Lap 10: Bill Whittington spins in Turn 2 and hits the wall. Dick Ferguson is hit by Whittington and goes up on his left-side wheels, lands on all four and slides into the wall. Whittington suffers a broken leg and Ferguson a broken toe. After the leaders pit, George Snider emerges as the leader.

Lap 19: With the green flag back out, Gordon Johncock passes Snider for the lead, and one lap later Bobby Unser moves ahead of Snider into second.

Lap 25: Following a yellow flag for Spike Gehlhausen's single-car crash in Turn 1, Bobby Unser gets around Johncock to grab first place. Rutherford, who falls back after an earlier pit stop, charges up to third place.

Lap 31: When the yellow flag comes out again for a stalled car, most of the leaders pit. Johncock regains the lead and Pancho Carter is second.

Lap 36: Carter snatches the lead from Johncock.

Lap 40: Rutherford gets around Carter for the lead, and Tim Richmond moves into third.

→

This page: Johnny Rutherford climbs out of his Chaparral after winning the pole (above) and confers with owner Jim Hall (right). Rival Roger Penske gets the lowdown from Mario Andretti (far right), who started second. *Opposite page:* Penske clocks one of his drivers (top left). Gordon Johncock's Wildcat suffered extensive damage in a crash during practice (top right). Gary Bettenhausen (middle left) was the slowest qualifier, but charged to a third-place finish. Mike Mosley's crew works on his Eagle (middle right). The field makes a sun-drenched parade lap (bottom).

Race drivers are a superstitious lot. Given their sometimes precarious circumstances, few can blame them.

Johnny Rutherford's personal talisman has always been the ladybug. "I had always been told as a youngster that if a ladybug landed on you, it was a good-luck omen," Johnny says. "One time I had a sign painter put a ladybug on my race car. From that point on, I always had a ladybug on my car."

But on the morning of the 1980 Indy 500, a ladybug decided it was time to get up close and personal with Johnny Rutherford.

"Just before the start, something flew into my hair," Johnny explained. "When I reached up and took it out, it was the biggest, orangest ladybug you've ever seen. I told Jim Hall and my crew chief, Steve Roby, to tell the rest of these guys to load up and go home; we just won this thing."

Sure enough, Rutherford dominated the entire race. Everyone else was running for second.

"After that, people started sending us all kinds of ladybug stuff," Johnny continued. "[Wife] Betty has ladybug broaches, earrings, pins, rings, all kinds of things."

But you couldn't say they're bugged by the attention.

Lap 47: During the fifth caution period of the race, another flurry of pit stops shuffles the lead to Mario Andretti.

Lap 57: Under yellow again, leader Andretti stops for fresh right-side tires, giving the lead to Carter. One lap later, Carter pits and Rutherford moves back into first, with Rick Mears and Bobby Unser in pursuit.

Lap 72: Andretti, running fourth, blows his engine to bring out the seventh yellow of the day. When the leaders pit, Tom Sneva, who starts last, moves into first and brother Jerry runs second.

Lap 76: Rutherford gets by Jerry Sneva and chases leader Tom Sneva.

Lap 85: The yellow flag is out again, and Bobby Unser takes the lead when Tom Sneva, Rutherford, and Mears pit. Richmond takes over second.

Lap 103: Unser pits for fuel, giving the lead to Rutherford. Mears and Tom Sneva move up to second and third, and Unser falls to fourth.

Lap 114: Rutherford stops for fuel and right-side tires, giving the lead to Mears for three laps. Rutherford regains first when Mears and then Unser make their stops, and Rutherford opens up a comfortable lead.

Lap 122: Unser is back in the pits, and a few minutes later he climbs out of the car. A bad ignition coil ends his day.

Lap 131: Rutherford and Mears pit under yellow, and Tom Sneva's three-year-old McLaren goes back into first.

Lap 148: Rutherford blows by Sneva into first place and next time around he runs the fastest lap of the day, 190.074 mph.

Lap 159: Rutherford is still in command when Sneva and Mears pit, falling to third and fourth. Gary Bettenhausen, in a four-year-old Wildcat, passes Johncock for second, continuing a dog fight that starts around the halfway mark and lasts to the end.

Lap 172: Rutherford makes his final stop for fuel under green, giving the lead to Mears. Sneva runs second.

Lap 177: Mears and Sneva catch a break when A. J. Foyt stops in Turn 3 with a broken valve, bringing out the 13th caution flag. Mears and Sneva pit under yellow, and Sneva beats Mears back onto the track to take over second. Bettenhausen and Johncock run fourth and fifth on the lead lap.

Lap 179: Rutherford pulls away from Sneva on the restart. Four laps later, Mears pits again for right-side tires and falls to fifth, a lap down.

Finish: No one can keep pace with Rutherford, who builds a 30-second lead to win easily for the third time in the last seven races. Sneva finishes second for the third time in four years. About three seconds behind Sneva, Bettenhausen edges Johncock for third place.

Rutherford leads 119 laps. His average of 142.862 mph is the eighth straight non-record speed.

Bettenhausen's third-place finish is the last hurrah for the famed Offy engine. The Offy, an offspring of the Miller straight-eight that won the 1932 race, finally fades away as teams switch to the Cosworth V-8.

Mike Mosley's No. 48 (*opposite, top left*) retired early with a blown gasket. Danny Ongais slips by a spinning Spike Gehlhausen in Turn 1 (*opposite, top right*). Gordon Smiley's Valvoline car (*opposite, bottom left*) succumbed to a blown turbocharger. Jim McElreath slides backwards into the wall (*opposite, bottom right*) after spinning upon exiting Turn 1. Johnny Rutherford enjoys the view from victory lane for the third time (*left*). Rutherford earned $318,819 in owner Jim Hall's year-old "ground effects" Chaparral (*below*), which started from the pole and led 119 laps.

RESULTS

NO.	DRIVER	CAR	ENTRANT	ENGINE	CYL	DISP	CHASSIS	COLOR	QUAL SPD	START	FIN	LAPS / SPEED / REASON OUT
4	Johnny Rutherford	Pennzoil	Chaparral Racing Ltd.	Cosworth	8	161	Chaparral	yellow, red, blk	192.256	1	1	200-142.862
9	Tom Sneva	Bon Jour Action Jeans	Jerry O'Connell	Cosworth	8	161	McLaren	yellow, black	185.290	33	2	200-142.524
46	Gary Bettenhausen	Armstrong Mould	Sherman Armstrong	DGS	4	160	Wildcat II	blk, wht, orng	182.463	32	3	200-142.485
20	Gordon Johncock	North Amer. Van Lines	Patrick Racing Team	Cosworth	8	160	Penske PC-6	blue, white	186.075	17	4	200-142.482
1	Rick Mears	The Gould Charge	Penske Racing, Inc.	Cosworth	8	158	Penske PC-9	blue, white	187.490	6	5	199-running
10	Pancho Carter	Alex XLNT Foods	Alex Morales Co.	Cosworth	8	161	Penske PC-7	orange, white	186.480	8	6	199-running
25	Danny Ongais	Interscope/Panasonic	Interscope	Cosworth	8	161	Parnelli	blk, wht, pink	186.606	16	7	199-running
43	Tom Bigelow	Armstrng Mld/Jiffy Mix	Sherman Armstrong	Cosworth	8	161	Lola	blk, orng, wht	182.547	31	8	198-running
21	Tim Richmond	UNO/Q95 Starcruiser	MACH 1 Racing	Cosworth	8	161	Penske PC-7	wht, red, yelo	188.334	19	9	197-out of fuel
44	Greg Leffler	Starcraft R.V.	Sherman Armstrong	Cosworth	8	161	Lola	blk, orng, wht	183.748	23	10	197-running
29	Bill Engelhart	Master Lock	Beaudoin Racing	Cosworth	8	161	McLaren	yelo, blue, wht	184.237	22	11	193-running
2	Bill Vukovich, Jr.	Hubler Chevy/WFMS	Leader Cards, Inc.	Offy	4	160	Watson	blue, wht, red	182.741	30	12	192-running
96	Don Whittington	Sun System	Whittington Bros.	Cosworth	8	161	Penske PC-7	yelo, brn, red	183.927	18	13	178-running
14	A. J. Foyt	Gilmore Racing Team	A. J. Foyt Enterprises	Cosworth	8	161	Parnelli	orange, white	185.500	12	14	173-valve
16	George Snider	Gilmore Racing Team	A. J. Foyt Enterprises	Cosworth	8	161	Parnelli	orange, white	185.385	21	15	169-engine
18	Dennis Firestone	Scientific Drilling Cont.	Jack L. Rhodes	Cosworth	8	161	Penske PC-6	maroon, red, wht	183.702	24	16	137-transmission
7	Jerry Sneva	Hugger Bev. Holders	AMI Racing Division	Cosworth	8	161	Lola	blue, white	187.852	5	17	130-accident
99	Hurley Haywood	Sta-On/Guarantee/KISS 99	Lindsey Hopkins	Chevy V-6	6	207	Lightning	wht, red, blue	183.561	25	18	127-turbocharger
11	Bobby Unser	The Norton Spirit	Penske Racing, Inc.	Cosworth	8	161	Penske PC-9	blue, wht, yelo	189.994	3	19	126-ignition coil
12	Mario Andretti	Essex	Penske Racing, Inc.	Cosworth	8	161	Penske PC-9	blue, red, slvr, wht	191.012	2	20	71-engine
38	Jerry Karl	Tonco Trailer Co.	Willie Compton	Chevy	8	351	McLaren	wht, blue, yelo	183.011	28	21	64-clutch
8	Dick Simon	Vt. Am../Silhtte Sps/Rgl Inns	Dick Simon Racing	Offy	4	160	Vollstedt	yellow, blk, red	182.788	29	22	58-lost wheel
66	Roger Rager	Adv. Clean Sweep/Carp. Bus	Gail & Roger Rager	Chevy	8	357	Wildcat	white, red	186.374	10	23	55-accident
23	Jim McElreath	McElreath	Shirley McElreath	Cosworth	8	161	Penske PC-6	wht, blue, red	186.249	11	24	54-accident
70	Gordon Smiley	Valvoline/Dia. Hd. Ranch	Patrick Racing Team	Cosworth	8	161	Phoenix	blue, yelo, wht	186.948	20	25	47-turbocharger
15	Johnny Parsons	Wynn's	Lindsey Hopkins	Offy	4	160	Lightning	white, red	187.412	7	26	44-piston
5	Al Unser	Longhorn Racing	Bobby Hillin	Cosworth	8	161	Longhorn	white, blk, red	186.442	9	27	33-cylinder
40	Tom Bagley	Kent Oil	Patrick Racing Team	Cosworth	8	161	Wildcat	blue, yelo, wht	185.405	13	28	29-pump drive
35	Spike Gehlhausen	Winston Sales	Fletcher Racing Team	Cosworth	8	161	Penske PC-7	red, white, blk	188.344	4	29	20-accident
94	Bill Whittington	Sun Systems	Whittington Bros.	Cosworth	8	161	Parnelli	yellow, brn, red	183.262	27	30	9-accident
26	Dick Ferguson	AMS/Oil	Steve & Richard Sanett	Cosworth	8	161	Penske PC-6	red, white, blk	182.880	15	31	9-accident
48	Mike Mosley	Theodore Racing	Daniel S. Gurney	Chevy	8	355	Eagle	white, red	183.449	26	32	5-gasket
95	Larry Cannon	Kraco Car Stereos	Kraco Enterprises	DGS	4	160	Wildcat	blue, yellow	183.253	14	33	2-camshaft

1981

65th Race • May 24, 1981

A record 105 entries includes 23 rookies, and USAC competition director Roger McCluskey, a veteran of 18 Indy 500s, institutes a new program to accommodate first-timers. A week-long Rookie Orientation Program in April gives new drivers time to hone their skills and take rookie driving tests before veterans arrive for practice. For the second year in a row, 10 rookies start the race.

Turbocharged Cosworth engines rule, powering 29 starters. The other four are stock-block Chevrolet V-8s, three of them naturally-aspirated.

There is far more variety on the chassis side with 14 different brands in the field. A. J. Foyt fields a new Coyote for himself, Dan Gurney has a new Eagle for Mike Mosley, and perennial challenger Tom Sneva is in a new British-built March, as are brothers Bill and Don Whittington.

Mario Andretti, who still divides his time between USAC Championship cars and Formula 1, again finds himself out of luck when rain limits qualifying the first weekend. Wally Dallenbach qualifies the No. 40 STP Wildcat on the third row, but vacates the seat when Andretti returns from Monaco. He starts 32nd because of the driver change.

After just three practice laps, George Snider qualifies a year-old Parnelli that Foyt owns. Tim Richmond, the 1980 Rookie of the Year, gets bumped from the field and starts 33rd when he replaces Snider.

PRACTICE AND QUALIFYING

MONDAY, MAY 4: On the third day of practice, Bobby Unser blasts around the Brickyard at 197.715 mph in his Penske-Cosworth. Teammate Rick Mears is second quickest at 195.993.

FRIDAY, MAY 8: Team Penske drivers Unser and Mears are fastest the day before pole qualifying, both hitting about 199.5 mph. Mario Andretti is close behind at 198.4 in a Wildcat-Cosworth.

SATURDAY, MAY 9: Rain delays the start of qualifying until mid-afternoon, and A. J. Foyt, the first to complete a four-lap run, averages 196.078 mph, giving him an outside chance for a record fifth pole. Defending winner Johnny Rutherford is second fastest at 195.387 before the 6 P.M. gun ends qualifying with pole contenders still in line.

SUNDAY, MAY 10: Rain postpones the completion of pole qualifying until the next weekend.

TUESDAY, MAY 12: Danny Ongais is the first to reach 200 mph in three years in his new Interscope-Cosworth. Andretti and Bobby Unser top 199.

FRIDAY, MAY 15: Unser tunes up for the resumption of Pole Day with a hot lap of 201.387 mph.

SATURDAY, MAY 16: It doesn't take long on Pole Day II before Bobby Unser knocks off Foyt. Unser runs a fast lap of 201.342

➔

STARTING LINEUP

Average Field Qualifying Speed: 191.244

Numbers in flags indicate finish position

13
A. J. Foyt

23
Josele Garza

17
Al Unser

4
Kevin Cogan

5
Geoff Brabham

33
Mike Mosley

32
Johnny Rutherford

22
Gordon Smiley

26
Gary Bettenhausen

20
Tom Bigelow

POLE POSITION
Qualifying Speed:
200.546

1
Bobby Unser

9
Gordon Johncock

11
Bill Alsup

28
Pancho Carter

19
Bob Lazier

If it took the rest of sprint-car ace Sheldon Kinser's life, he wanted at least one good finish at Indianapolis. In 1981, Sheldon landed a sponsorship from Sergio Valente jeans and hooked up with car owner Bobby Hillin, Sr., for the 500. But the team had a couple of strikes against it. For one, sprint car drivers were no longer in vogue at Indy. And this particular race car, which had been built for a former Indy winner, had been written off as less than competitive. Few experts even thought it would make the race.

But they hadn't counted on Sheldon's tenacity.

Kinser's qualifying speed of 189.454—good for 23rd starting position—was three mph faster than the car had gone in 1980. In the race, Kinser's steady pace moved him into the top 10. When the checkered flag fell, he was running an outstanding sixth. It was a stunning display of determination.

But Sheldon was no surprise to Bobby Hillin. "The surprise was the car lasted," Hillin says. "If he'd had a better ride, he would have won in Indy cars. He was real smooth. I'll always remember that he never complained about the equipment."

And the name of the 500 winner who had given up on Hillin's racer? Al Unser, Sr.

A Buick Regal powered by a 4.1-liter V-6 was the pace car (*opposite*). The engine's compression and horsepower were bumped up to 12.5:1 and 281, respectively. Retired racer Duke Nalon (*top*) did the driving on race day. Sheldon Kinser not only made a fashion statement in the No. 81 Sergio Valente entry (*above left*), he also finished sixth in his last 500 start.

Vern Schuppan

Danny Ongais

Pete Halsmer

Bill Whittington

Tom Klausler

Tim Richmond

Steve Krisiloff

Tom Sneva

Sheldon Kinser

Don Whittington

Scott Brayton

Mario Andretti

Tony Bettenhausen

Larry Dickson

Rick Mears

Michael Chandler

Dennis Firestone

Jerry Karl

and averages 200.546 en route to winning his second pole (nine years after his first).

Rick Mears makes a serious run with two laps around 200, but pulls in early with an engine vibration. Mears returns later in the day as a second-day qualifier and runs 194 in his backup car to start 22nd.

The surprise of the day is Mike Mosley, who averages 197.141 in a new Gurney Eagle with a 351-cid stock-block Chevy to claim the middle of the front row, moving Foyt to the outside.

Two other second-day qualifiers make statements. Tom Sneva is fastest qualifier at 200.691 in a George Bignotti March, but starts 20th. Next to him is Danny Ongais, who is quick enough to be on the front row.

THE RACE

Start: Bobby Unser grabs the lead from the pole. Johnny Rutherford charges up from row two into second as A. J. Foyt moves into third.

Lap 2: As Bobby Unser stretches his lead, brother Al moves from the ninth starting position into fourth. Faster cars in the back of the field are on the move as well. Tom Sneva advances six positions to 14th, and Mario Andretti moves up 10 to 22nd.

Lap 13: Sneva is flying. He darts inside to pass Gordon Johncock and Al Unser, and a lap later he sweeps by Foyt into third place.

Lap 16: Mosley steers onto the grass in Turn 1, his Chevy engine overheating, to be the first out of the race.

Lap 24: Rutherford coasts to a stop on the backstretch, apparently out of fuel, and requires a tow back to the pits. It turns out to be a broken fuel pump that ends his bid for a fourth win.

After a round of pit stops during the ensuing caution period, Bobby Unser regains the lead with Sneva second. Andretti and STP teammates Johncock and Gordon Smiley occupy third through fifth.

Lap 32: Don Whittington loses control coming out of Turn 2, slams the outside wall, and slides across the track into the infield. Whittington's disabled car catches fire as it is being hoisted by a tow truck. Moments later, Gary Bettenhausen pulls up with his car on fire. Neither driver is hurt, and Bettenhausen gets back in the race.

Bobby Unser pits under yellow, while Sneva stays on the track and inherits the lead. Smiley moves into second and Rick Mears into third. Al Unser starts a lengthy pit stop for a new CV joint, killing his chances for a fourth win.

Lap 51: After several laps of green-flag racing, Sneva maintains the lead, but Mears passes Smiley for second. Bobby Unser runs fourth.

Lap 57: Sneva stops for fuel, but stalls and loses time while his crew restarts the engine. A small fire breaks out but is quickly doused.

Lap 58: Leader Mears comes in for fuel, but his car catches fire when fuel sloshes on to the hot engine. Mears and several crew members suffer burns as fire and smoke engulf his car.

Lap 63: After leading four laps, Danny Ongais pulls into the pits for fuel, giving the lead to Johncock. Ongais stalls, and his pit stop stretches to 46 seconds before he gets back on track.

Lap 64: Ongais slams into the Turn 3 wall. His car bursts into flames as wheels and body panels fly off, and he suffers internal injuries and a leg fracture. →

In 1981, when Mexico's Josele Garza came to Indy, he had an ongoing battle with the barrier. It wasn't the driver's test; he had no trouble running fast enough. It was the language barrier. Garza asked a lot of questions and the veteran drivers were always obliging, but he didn't always understand the answers. It was the racing terminology that really threw him a curve.

"I was working with American mechanics and I didn't know how to say the car was pushing or didn't have enough downforce," Josele said. "I had a problem with all the technical words and American slang."

Apparently he mastered it all pretty well. He started in sixth place with a four-lap qualifying run of 195.101 mph. And despite being caught up in an accident, he was honored as Rookie of the Year. But one thing never changed.

"It was still hard to understand some of the jokes at the drivers' meetings," Garza said.

Gordon Johncock qualified the No. 20 STP Wildcat (*above*) on the second row, led 52 laps, and was still battling for a second victory when his Cosworth engine expired near the end. A. J. Foyt (*opposite, top left*) started on the front row but failed to lead a lap and finished 13th. Roger Penske has a face-to-face meeting with Bobby Unser (*opposite, top right*). Unser won the second pole of his 19-year Indy career. Mario Andretti, who drove the No. 40 Wildcat (*opposite, middle right*) for Patrick Racing, missed qualifying because of Formula 1 commitments. Wally Dallenbach qualified the car in Andretti's absence, then vacated the seat for Mario, who started 32nd. Racers order themselves in neat rows in anticipation of the start of the race (*opposite bottom*).

Valvoline
A.J. Foyt Jr.
Ingersoll-Rand
PROTO
14

Valvoline
GOODYEAR
STP
40
Valvoline

Lap: 82: When green-flag racing returns, Johncock leads Andretti and Unser. Three laps later, Unser takes second from Andretti.

Lap 92: Unser surges by Johncock for the lead, but pits three laps later. First place remains a hot potato as Johncock, Andretti, and rookie Josele Garza take turns in front for the next 50 laps.

Lap 139: Garza, running fourth on the lead lap, breaks a suspension component in Turn 3 and slides to a halt along the outside wall. All the leaders pit, and Andretti emerges in front.

Lap 149: Stopping under yellow for another incident, Unser and Andretti leave the pits at the same time. Instead of merging with traffic as they return to the track, leader Unser passes several cars before getting into line, and second-place Andretti passes two.

Lap 182: In the 24th lead change of the day (second only to the 1960 race), Unser takes back first place from Johncock, who stays within two seconds of the lead. Andretti is third.

Lap 193: Johncock slows on the back straight when his engine expires, and Andretti flashes by into second, some 14 seconds behind Unser.

Finish: Bobby Unser eases up the last few laps, allowing Andretti to close to within five seconds for the second-closest finish to date. Unser captures his third 500 victory, matching brother Al.

The race may be over, but it is far from settled. The next morning, USAC penalizes Unser one lap for passing cars under yellow on Lap 150 and announces Andretti as the new winner. Unser's car owner, Roger Penske, files an appeal with USAC. Hearings drag on through the summer, and the USAC Appeals Board finally announces a split decision on October 8. Two of the three board members vote to rescind the one-lap penalty and instead fine Unser $40,000.

Unser's third victory becomes official months after the 47-year-old veteran of 19 consecutive 500s runs his final race at the Brickyard.

Eventual winner Bobby Unser, in the No. 3 Norton Spirit, runs ahead of Mario Andretti and A. J. Foyt (*top*). Unser and Andretti, the latter of whom started from the last row, stayed in the hunt throughout the race, but Foyt fell off the pace after opening the race on the outside of the front row. Defending winner Johnny Rutherford (*middle*) led three circuits in his Pennzoil Chaparral before a broken fuel pump knocked him out after just 25 laps. Foyt gets routine pit service (*right*) in what proved to be a long day for the four-time winner. Scott Brayton's first start lasted 174 laps before a blown engine in the No. 37 Penske-Cosworth ended his day (*opposite, top left*). Unser keeps pace with brother Al when he celebrates his third 500 victory (*opposite, top right*). However, first place was awarded to Andretti the next day after USAC penalized Bobby Unser for passing under yellow. Owner Roger Penske appealed, and the victory was officially handed to Unser nearly four months later. Unser earned $299,124 in prize money and called it a career.

RESULTS

NO.	DRIVER	CAR	ENTRANT	ENGINE	CYL	DISP	CHASSIS	COLOR	QUAL SPD	START	FIN	LAPS / SPEED / REASON OUT
3	Bobby Unser	The Norton Spirit	Penske Racing, Inc.	Cosworth	8	161	Penske PC-9B	blue, wht, yelo	200.546	1	1	200-139.084
40	Mario Andretti	STP Oil Treatment	Patrick Racing Team	Cosworth	8	160	Wildcat VIII	blue, red, wht	193.040	32	2	200-139.029
33	Vern Schuppan	Red Roof Inns/Theo. Racing	Theodore Racing	Cosworth	8	161	McLaren	wht, red, blk	186.548	18	3	199-running
32	Kevin Cogan	Jerry O'Connell Racing	Jerry O'Connell	Cosworth	8	161	Phoenix	wht, red, yelo	189.444	12	4	197-running
50	Geoff Brabham	Psachie-Garza	Esso	Cosworth	8	161	Penske PC-9	wht, red, green	187.990	15	5	197-running
81	Sheldon Kinser	Sergio Valente Jeans	Bobby Hillin	Cosworth	8	161	Longhorn	wht, maroon, gld	189.454	23	6	195-running
16	Tony Bettenhausen	Provimi Veal	H & R Racing	Cosworth	8	161	McLaren	blue, wht, red	187.013	16	7	195-running
53	Steve Krisiloff	Psachie-Garza Esso	Psachie-Garza	Cosworth	8	161	Penske PC-7	wht, blk, red	186.722	17	8	194-running
20	Gordon Johncock	STP Oil Treatment	Patrick Racing Team	Cosworth	8	160	Wildcat VIII	blue, red, wht	195.429	4	9	194-engine
4	Dennis Firestone	Rhoades Aircraft Sales	Jack Rhoades	Cosworth	8	160	Patrick VIII	blue, red	187.784	28	10	193-engine
7	Bill Alsup	AB Dick Pacemaker	Wm. Alsup	Cosworth	8	161	Penske PC-9B	brn, wht, red	193.154	7	11	193-running
74	Michael Chandler	Natl. Engineering Co.	Warner-Hodgdon	Cosworth	8	161	Penske PC-7	red, wht, blue	187.568	25	12	192-running
14	A. J. Foyt	Valvoline-Gilmore	A. J. Foyt Enterprises	Cosworth	8	161	Coyote	orange, white	196.078	3	13	191-running
84	Tim Richmond	UNO/WTTV/Guarantee Auto	MACH 1 Racing	Cosworth	8	161	Parnelli	orange, white	189.255	33	14	191-running
38	Jerry Karl	Tonco Trailer	Jerry Karl	Chevy	8	351	McLaren-Karl	red, wht, blk	186.008	31	15	189-running
37	Scott Brayton	Forsythe Industries	Forsythe Racing	Cosworth	8	161	Penske PC-6	wht, red, yelo, blue	187.774	29	16	174-engine
88	Al Unser	Valvoline-Longhorn	Bobby Hillin	Cosworth	8	161	Longhorn	white, blue	192.719	9	17	166-running
31	Larry Dickson	Machinist Union	I.A.M.A.W.	Cosworth	8	161	Penske PC-7	cream, blue, red	186.278	19	18	165-piston
35	Bob Lazier	Monty Ward Auto Club	Robert L. Fletcher	Cosworth	8	161	Penske PC-7	yelo, blue, wht	189.424	13	19	154-engine
56	Tom Bigelow	Genesee Beer	Gohr Distributing Co.	Chevy	8	351	Penske PC-7	blue, wht, slvr	188.294	14	20	152-engine
90	Bill Whittington	Kraco Car Stereo	Whittington Bros.	Cosworth	8	161	March	yellow, black	197.098	27	21	146-stalled
60	Gordon Smiley	Intermedics	Patrick Racing Team	Cosworth	8	161	Wildcat VIII	blue, red, wht	192.988	8	22	141-accident
55	Josele Garza	Psachie-Garza	Psachie-Garza Esso	Cosworth	8	161	Penske PC-9	wht, grn, red, blk	195.101	6	23	138-accident
79	Pete Halsmer	Hubler Chev/KISS 99/Colonial	Frank Arciero	Cosworth	8	161	Penske PC-7	yelo, red, blk, wht	181.919	24	24	123-accident
2	Tom Sneva	Blue Poly	Bignotti-Cotter, Inc.	Cosworth	8	161	March	blue, wht, red	200.691	20	25	96-clutch
8	Gary Bettenhausen	Hopkins	Lindsey Hopkins	Cosworth	8	161	Lightning	blue, wht, chrome	190.870	11	26	69-broken rod
25	Danny Ongais	Interscope Racing	Interscope	Cosworth	8	161	Interscope	blk, wht, pink	197.694	21	27	64-accident
5	Pancho Carter	Alex Foods	Alex Morales	Cosworth	8	161	Penske PC-7	orange, white	191.022	10	28	62-compression
51	Tom Klausler	IDS Idea	Douglas Schulz	Chevy	8	208	Schkee	wht, red, blk	186.732	30	29	60-gear box
6	Rick Mears	The Gould Charge	Penske Racing, Inc.	Cosworth	8	161	Penske PC-9B	blue, wht, red	194.018	22	30	58-pit fire
91	Don Whittington	Whittington Bros.	Whittington Bros.	Cosworth	8	161	March	red, white	187.237	26	31	32-accident
1	Johnny Rutherford	Pennzoil	Chaparral Racing Ltd.	Cosworth	8	161	Chaparral	yelo, blk, red	195.387	5	32	25-fuel pump
48	Mike Mosley	Pepsi Challenger	All-American Racers	Chevy	8	351	Eagle	yelo, red, wht	197.141	2	33	16-radiator

1982

66th Race • May 30, 1982

USAC adopts stringent new pit rules in response to growing concerns over fires during fuel stops. Among the new requirements are positive shutoff valves to reduce fuel spills and a drain tube on the cars to prevent fuel overflows from running onto the engine or driver.

All pit personnel must wear fire-retardant clothing, and the fuel tanks that hold a team's supply of methanol are bolted to the concrete to keep them from tipping over. The Speedway installs a water line behind the pit wall to wash down methanol spills.

Shortly before practice opens, John Cooper resigns as Speedway president after two years at the helm. Joe Cloutier returns for a second tour of duty.

A $2 million purse, up more than $400,000 over the previous year, draws a record 109 entries. Several teams switch to the British-made March chassis, which had Tom Sneva in front for 25 laps in its 1981 debut. Among the converts is four-time winner A. J. Foyt, who makes a record 25th consecutive start.

There also are more Whittingtons on the track this year, as rookie Dale joins siblings Don and Bill in the starting lineup, the only time three brothers are in the same race. This year is quite the family affair, with Bettenhausen, Mears, and Sneva brothers also in the show.

South African Desire Wilson, a Formula 1 veteran, attempts to be the second woman to qualify, but five blown engines keep her sidelined.

PRACTICE AND QUALIFYING

SUNDAY, MAY 9: Rick Mears does 203.6 mph on the second day of practice in a Penske-Cosworth, and Mario Andretti is runner-up for the day at 200.1 in a Patrick Racing Wildcat-Cosworth.

MONDAY, MAY 10: Mears sets an unofficial speed record of 205 mph in practice, and teammate Kevin Cogan clocks a lap at 202.2.

WEDNESDAY, MAY 12: Practice speeds continue to climb. Cogan zips around the Brickyard at 206.3 mph, and Mears is right behind at 205.8. →

STARTING LINEUP

Average Field Qualifying Speed: 197.740

Numbers in flags indicate finish position

A. J. Foyt

Bill Whittington

Danny Ongais

Johnny Rutherford

Hector Rebaque

Kevin Cogan

Gordon Johncock

Don Whittington

Chip Ganassi

Herm Johnson

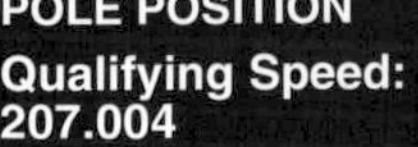
POLE POSITION
Qualifying Speed: 207.004

Rick Mears

Mario Andretti

Tom Sneva

Pancho Carter

Danny Sullivan

Chevrolet's redesigned muscle car, the Camaro Z28 (*opposite, top*), paced the field this year. Former winner Jim Rathmann carried out the driving duties for the sixth time. *Opposite bottom:* Two other former winners, Johnny Rutherford, left, and Mario Andretti, swap war stories along pit road during a break in practice. Ken Hamilton created and drove the decidedly "cab-forward" Eagle Aircraft Flyer (*top*), but withdrew the Chevy-powered racer when it proved a handful to control. Desire Wilson (*above*), a South African with Formula 1 experience, tried to become the second woman to qualify. A series of blown Cosworth engines in her Theodore Racing entry kept her from getting up to speed. Wilson had no better luck at the Speedway in 1983 and '84, either.

Seldom does anyone hear a driver sing the praises of a rule. But on the third day of qualifications in 1982, Jerry Sneva was doing just that.

Assigned to the Hoffman Family's March-Cosworth, Jerry made only three laps during morning practice. Then, when Jerry was ready for his timed qualification attempt, an official reminded him of the new two warm-up lap rule. (In prior years, qualifiers had been allowed three laps prior to the green flag.) Thereafter, the starter broke and the crew had to push-start the racer—not an easy proposition with a turbocharged engine. Once under way, Jerry took his two warm-up laps, then got down to business.

His first circuit was 195.908 mph, the second 196.937, and the third 195.101.

"I came off turn four," Jerry recalled. "The crew's got the green flag out, the starter's showing me the checkered, and I'm smiling, thinking everything is fine."

But about 300 yards from the finish line, the engine blew in a cloud of smoke. Sneva kicked the car out of gear and coasted over the wire at 193.175. His average of 195.270 earned the 28th slot on the grid.

"I guess we practiced just the right amount of laps," Jerry said with a grin.

Howdy Holmes

Dennis Firestone

Jim Hickman

Tony Bettenhausen

Gary Bettenhausen

Josele Garza

Bobby Rahal

Geoff Brabham

Dale Whittington

George Snider

Chet Fillip

Pete Halsmer

Al Unser

Roger Mears

Michael Chandler

Johnny Parsons

Jerry Sneva

Tom Bigelow

FRIDAY, MAY 14: The day before the run for the pole, Team Penske has the hot setup. Mears runs 208.7 mph and Cogan 207.8. Patrick Racing drivers Mario Andretti and Gordon Johncock post identical speeds of 203.2.

SATURDAY, MAY 15: Cogan is first to qualify and shatters both the single- and four-lap records. His fastest circuit is 204.638 mph and he averages 204.082.

While Cogan accepts congratulations over the public-address system, Rick Mears boosts the single-lap record to 207.612 and averages 207.004. Several cars are still in line, but Mears appears to have his second pole in the bag.

About an hour later, two-time starter Gordon Smiley gets loose on his second warmup lap and slams head-on into the outside wall of Turn 3. His car disintegrates and Smiley dies instantly. His is the first fatality at the Speedway since 1973.

The track reopens about two hours later, and no one matches Cogan's speed, let alone Mears's. A. J. Foyt comes closest at 203.3 to join the Penske drivers on the front row. Patrick teammates Mario Andretti and Gordon Johncock are fourth and fifth fastest.

THE RACE

Start: As the field approaches the green flag, Kevin Cogan suddenly veers right and runs into A. J. Foyt's car. Cogan bounces off Foyt, swings around to the left and gets hit by Mario Andretti. Further back in the field, Dale Whittington rear ends Roger Mears. The red flag comes out.

Cogan and Andretti are out of the race, as are rookies Whittington and Roger Mears (the older brother of Rick). Foyt's car has a bent steering rod that the driver "fixes" with a hammer.

Restart: Foyt bolts ahead of Rick Mears on the front straight and pulls away to lead lap one for the first time. He runs the first lap at a record speed, 194.342 mph, and continues to set records on subsequent laps. Mears runs second ahead of Gordon Johncock.

Lap 22: Mears is the first of the leaders to pit, followed by Foyt and then Johncock. When everyone gets back on track, Foyt leads, Mears is second, and Johncock third.

Lap 36: As they lap slower traffic, Mears slips by Foyt into the lead.

Lap 39: Tony Bettenhausen breaks a halfshaft on the front straight and spins into the outside wall nose first. Bettenhausen is unhurt.

After a flurry of pit stops, Tom Sneva comes out in front of Mears, Johncock, and Foyt.

Lap 58: Mears, who had fallen to third, gets around Johncock to reclaim second place. Two laps later, Mears passes Sneva for the lead.

Lap 63: Danny Ongais, running fifth, spins in Turn 2, bangs the outside wall and slides to the inside of the track. Rookie Chet Fillip slows to avoid Ongais, and Jerry Sneva runs into Fillip. All three cars are out of the race, but none of the drivers is hurt.

Lap 65: When Foyt pits under yellow, fuel spills into the cockpit of his car. He comes back in the next lap, and his crew douses him and the car with water to flush the methanol, but he falls a lap down.

→

Opposite page: Front-row drivers (top) included, from left, A. J. Foyt, pole winner Rick Mears, and Kevin Cogan. Michael Chandler drove the No. 68 Eagle-Chevy (second from top). Danny Ongais talks things over with Interscope Racing's "head wrench," Phil Casey (third from top). Mears's crew won the annual pit-stop competition (bottom). *This page:* Photographers mob the cars on the grid (top row). Four cars were knocked out before the start (middle right, left, and above), beginning when Cogan's car veered into Foyt's. Mario Andretti's ride is facing the wrong way on the inside wall and Cogan's is on the outside wall (middle left).

Lap 94: Leader Mears pits under green while Johncock passes Sneva for second. Johncock comes in a lap later, and when the yellow flag comes out to slow the field, he moves into first place. Mears, Sneva, and Pancho Carter follow on the lead lap.

Foyt, meanwhile, pits a third straight lap with balky shift linkage. He finally gets out of the car, locates his favorite hammer and tries in vain to correct it himself. He gives up and calls it a race after leading 32 laps—the last time he leads a 500.

Lap 109: Mears bursts by Johncock to grab the lead. Two laps later, Johncock loses second to Sneva, and a lap after that he falls to fourth behind Carter.

Lap 142: Mears still leads after two caution periods, but when the green flag comes out, Sneva darts around him on the front straight to move back into first. Carter is back on the lead lap in third, and Johncock is fourth.

Lap 153: Rookie Danny Sullivan, running ninth, hits the outside wall in Turn 4 and skids to a halt on the front straight. The leaders pit under yellow, and Mears regains first with a 14-second stop while a balky fuel hose keeps Sneva in for 54 seconds. Sneva falls to third behind Johncock, and Carter runs fourth on the lead lap.

Lap 160: Back under green, Johncock blows by Mears into first, but Mears keeps the No. 40 Wildcat in sight.

Lap 184: When Mears and Sneva, running second and third, come barreling into the pits together, Mears locks up his brakes trying to avoid Herm Johnson but still bumps Johnson's right rear tire with his left front wing. Mears continues to his pit, takes on fuel, and gets away in 18 seconds.

Lap 186: Johncock makes his last stop, stays just 13 seconds, and leads Mears by 11 seconds once he gets back up to speed.

Lap 193: Mears, running at 197 mph, closes to within 6.4 seconds.

Lap 196: Mears, running at 199 mph, is just three seconds back.

Lap 197: As Mears continues closing on Johncock, Sneva's engine blows, and he limps to the pits with smoke pouring from his car.

Finish: With a lap to go, Mears darts inside and pulls even with Johncock on the front straight, but Johncock shuts the door going into Turn 1. When Mears catches up at the end of the back straight, Johncock holds him off again in Turn 3.

Mears tries to pass on the outside as they come out of Turn 4, then moves inside for a drag race to the finish. Johncock gets there .16 seconds ahead of Mears—less than a car length—for the closest finish to date.

Johncock, 45, wins for the second time in 18 starts and nine years after his victory in the grim 1973 race. In a year in which many speed records fall, his average of 162.029 mph falls just short of Mark Donohue's 1972 record pace.

Carter finishes third, a lap down. Sneva settles for fourth place after leading for the third year in a row and sixth of the last seven.

What kind of luck do you expect from a driver who starts in 13th position? Rookie Danny Sullivan hits the wall coming out of Turn 4 and slides sideways down the front straight late in the race (*above*). Sullivan finished in 14th place. Seven cars battle for position before the packed grandstands (*above right*). Rookie Hector Rebaque (*right*) was running in the top 10 when his car caught fire in the pits, ending his only run at the Brickyard. Gordon Johncock is hounded by Tom Sneva's No. 7 Texaco Star entry (*opposite left*). Johncock (*opposite right*) survived a thrilling challenge in the late laps from Rick Mears—including a drag race to the finish line—to earn his second win.

There's no doubt about it: The finish of the 1982 Indianapolis 500 was one of the most thrilling moments in Speedway history. Dodging and weaving through lapped traffic, Rick Mears tried desperately to find a way around cagy Gordon Johncock. And, in turn, Gordy pulled out all the stops during his all-or-nothing charge to the finish.

Since then, Mears has admitted to having watched a VCR tape of the race—especially the last few laps—over and over again. Rick seems amazed that they were able to stay on the track. But when asked why he often watches the finish, Mears breaks into a broad grin.

"I just have to see it again," he chuckles. "I think, 'Maybe this time I'll get around Gordy.'"

RESULTS

NO.	DRIVER	CAR	ENTRANT	ENGINE	CYL	DISP	CHASSIS	COLOR	QUAL SPD	START	FIN	LAPS / SPEED / REASON OUT
20	Gordon Johncock	STP Oil Treatment	STP Patrick Racing Team	Cosworth	8	161	Wildcat VIII	red, blk, blue	201.884	5	1	200-162.029
1	Rick Mears	The Gould Charge	Penske Cars Ltd.	Cosworth	8	160	Penske PC-10	blue, white	207.004	1	2	200-162.026
3	Pancho Carter	Alex Foods	Alex Morales Co., Inc.	Cosworth	8	161	March	red, white	198.950	10	3	199-running
7	Tom Sneva	Texaco Star	Bignotti-Cotter, Inc.	Cosworth	8	161	March 82C	white, red, blk	201.027	7	4	197-engine
10	Al Unser	Longhorn Racing	Longhorn Racing, Inc.	Cosworth	8	161	Longhorn	wht, blue, yelo	195.567	16	5	197-running
91	Don Whittington	The Simoniz Finish	Whittington Bros., Inc.	Cosworth	8	161	March	yellow, black	200.725	8	6	196-running
42	Jim Hickman	Stroh's March	Harry H. Schwartz	Cosworth	8	161	March 82C	red, yellow	196.217	24	7	189-running
5	Johnny Rutherford	Pennzoil Chaparral	Chaparral Racing, Ltd.	Cosworth	8	161	Chaparral	yelo, red, blk	197.066	12	8	187-engine
28	Herm Johnson	Menard Cashway Lumber	Menard Champ. Racing	Chevy	8	355	Eagle	wht, yellow, blk	195.929	14	9	186-running
30	Howdy Holmes	Domino's Pizza	Douglas Shierson Racing	Cosworth	8	161	March 82C	red, wht, blue	194.468	18	10	186-running
19	Bobby Rahal	Red Roof Inns	Truesports Co.	Cosworth	8	161	March 82C	red, white, blk	194.700	17	11	174-engine
8	Gary Bettenhausen	Kraco Car Stereo	Lindsey-Hopkins	Cosworth	8	161	Lightning	blue, orange	195.673	30	12	158-engine
52	Hector Rebaque	Carta Blanca	Forsythe Racing, Inc.	Cosworth	8	161	March 82C	wht, orng, blk	195.684	15	13	150-pit fire
53	Danny Sullivan	Forsythe-Bown Racing	Forsythe Racing, Inc.	Cosworth	8	161	March 82C	wht, blk, orng	196.292	13	14	148-accident
12	Chip Ganassi	First Comm. Corp.	Rhoades Racing, Inc.	Cosworth	8	161	Wildcat	red, blk, wht	197.704	11	15	147-engine
94	Bill Whittington	Whittington/Hodgdon	Whittington Bros., Inc.	Cosworth	8	161	March	yellow, black	201.658	6	16	121-engine
68	Michael Chandler	Freeman/Gurney Eagle	Bill Freeman Racing, Inc.	Chevy	8	355	Eagle	red, wht, yelo	198.042	22	17	104-gear box
27	Tom Bigelow	H.B.K. Racing	Hall Bros.	Chevy	8	355	Eagle	white, black	194.784	31	18	96-engine
14	A. J. Foyt	Valvoline/Gilmore	A. J. Foyt Enterprise	Cosworth	8	161	March	orange, pearl	203.332	3	19	95-transmission
34	Johnny Parsons	Silhtte Spas/WIFE Tmbstne	Wysard Motor Co., Inc.	Cosworth	8	161	March	white, red, blk	195.929	25	20	92-accident
35	George Snider	Cobre Tire	Robert L. Fletcher	Cosworth	8	161	March	red, white, blk	195.493	26	21	87-transmission
25	Danny Ongais	Interscope Racing	Interscope Racing Corp.	Cosworth	8	161	Interscope	blk, wht, pink	199.948	9	22	62-accident
69	Jerry Sneva	Great Amer. Spirit	Hoffman Auto Racing	Cosworth	8	161	March	white, blue, red	195.270	28	23	61-accident
39	Chet Fillip	Circle Bar Truck Corral	Circle Bar Auto Racing	Cosworth	8	161	Eagle	turquoise, orng	194.879	29	24	60-body damage
66	Pete Halsmer	Col. Bread Pay Less St.	Arciero Racing	Chevy	8	208	Eagle	yelo, red, blue	194.295	32	25	38-transmission
16	Tony Bettenhausen	Provimi Veal	H & R Racing	Cosworth	8	161	March	blue, yellow	195.429	27	26	37-accident
75	Dennis Firestone	B.C.V. Racing	B.C.V. Racing, Inc.	Cosworth	8	355	Eagle	red, yellow	197.217	21	27	37-rear end
21	Geoff Brabham	Pentax Super	Bignotti-Cotter, Inc.	Cosworth	8	161	March 82C	wht, blk, yellow	198.906	20	28	12-engine
55	Josele Garza	Schlitz Gusto	Garza Racing	Cosworth	8	161	March	brown, white	194.500	33	29	1-engine
4	Kevin Cogan	The Norton Spirit	Penske Cars, Ltd.	Cosworth	8	161	Penske PC-10	wht, blue, yelo	204.082	2	30	0-accident
40	Mario Andretti	STP Oil Treatment	STP Patrick Racing Team	Cosworth	8	161	Wildcat VIII B	red, blue, wht	203.172	4	31	0-accident
31	Roger Mears	Machinist's Union	I.A.M.A.W.	Cosworth	8	161	Penske PC-98	crm, blue, red	194.154	19	32	0-accident
95	Dale Whittington	Whittington/Hodgdon	Whittington Bros., Inc.	Cosworth	8	161	March	yellow, black	197.694	23	33	0-accident

67th Race • May 29, 1983

After last year's record speeds, USAC tries to slow the cars down by eliminating ground-hugging side skirts, moving the rear wings forward, and reducing turbo boost by one inch of manifold pressure. Popoff valves are now set for 47 inches on the Cosworth racing V-8s and 57 on stock-block engines.

The Unsers, winners six times already, send a new competitor to the Speedway this year, 21-year-old Al, Jr., in a bid to have the first father-son combination in the starting lineup.

Galles Racing enters "Little Al" for its first year at the Brickyard, while three-time winner "Big Al" moves to Team Penske. The seat opens for Al, Sr., when Penske drops Kevin Cogan, a front-row starter last year who crashed before the race started.

Other veterans find new rides this year. Mario Andretti, the 1969 winner, switches from Patrick Racing to the new Paul Newman-Carl Haas team and Lola chassis, while three-time winner Johnny Rutherford signs on with Patrick.

PRACTICE AND QUALIFYING

SUNDAY, MAY 8: Rick Mears blasts around the oval at 202.565 mph to be fastest so far. Before Johnny Rutherford gets up to speed, he wrecks his No. 40 Wildcat-Cosworth in Turn 1, suffering a puncture wound to his right leg and assorted bruises.

MONDAY, MAY 9: Mears is fastest again at 203.85 mph, but four others top 200. Al Unser, Jr., runs 199.866, more than two mph faster than his dad.

WEDNESDAY, MAY 11: Don Whittington runs 205.2 mph as someone finally goes faster than Mears, who does 203.8. Several others top 200, including rookie Teo Fabi, Unsers senior and junior, and A. J. Foyt.

THURSDAY, MAY 12: The first serious injury of the month occurs when 52-year-old Bob Harkey bumps Mike Mosley and ricochets into the Turn 4 wall. Harkey suffers fractures to the neck and ribs, a broken wrist, and a bruised lung. Mosley escapes injury.

FRIDAY, MAY 13: Rookie John Paul, Jr., fractures his left ankle in a morning crash in Turn 1. Two-time starter Geoff Brabham replaces Paul.

SATURDAY, MAY 14: Intermittent rain on Pole Day keeps cars off the track until 4:13 P.M., leaving time for practice but not for qualifying. More rain Sunday delays qualifying until the following weekend.

→

STARTING LINEUP

Average Field Qualifying Speed: 198.406

Numbers in flags indicate finish position

Rick Mears

Bobby Rahal

Tony Bettenhausen

Howdy Holmes

Bill Whittington

Mike Mosley

Al Unser, Jr.

Roger Mears

Mario Andretti

Pancho Carter

POLE POSITION
Qualifying Speed: 207.395

Teo Fabi

Tom Sneva

Al Unser, Sr.

Gordon Johncock

George Snider

During the first week of practice, a troop of Boy Scouts wandered along behind the pit area. One of the Scouts spotted a well-known driver. "Let's get his autograph," he suggested.

As the Scouts queued up, the star driver tried to appear busy. He finally brushed the lads aside and disappeared down pit row. Another "name" saw the Scouts coming. And although he was in serious conversation with his mechanics, the "name" crossed to the other side of the pit lane. Standing there looking aloofly up the track, he pretended not to hear their pleas for his signature.

However, one driver took note of the situation. Placing his sandwich down on a paper bag, he walked over to the boys. In broken English, the driver asked them if they wanted his autograph. They accepted the driver's offer. And when the last signature was signed, some 15 or 20 minutes later, the driver went back to his lunch.

"Who is that guy?" one Scout asked.

"I don't know," the other replied. "But at least he paid attention to us."

A few days later, those Scouts would have had to stand in a much longer line to get that same autograph. The rookie driver was Teo Fabi of Italy, and his record-smashing qualifying average of 207.395 mph took the pole.

Twenty years after Buick introduced its personal-luxury Riviera, it fortified its topless Riv for pace-car duty in 1983 (*opposite*). The front-drive Riviera was powered by a 4.1-liter V-6 with twin turbochargers that helped it generate 450 horsepower. The actual pace car was painted cream over golden brown, but the parade and official cars (*left*) were all white and came with a turbocharged 3.8-liter V-6. White street replicas available through Buick dealers could also be had in coupe form. Former 500 competitor Duke Nalon returned for his second stint as driver of a pace car. To accompany the Buick pacesetter, corporate cousin GMC furnished the official trucks for a variety of duties at the Speedway (*above*).

Josele Garza

Danny Ongais

A. J. Foyt

Don Whittington

Mike Chandler

Dennis Firestone

Patrick Bedard

Dick Simon

Johnny Parsons

Geoff Brabham

Scott Brayton

Chet Fillip

Chip Ganassi

Steve Chassey

Kevin Cogan

Chris Kneifel

Derek Daly

Steve Krisiloff

WEDNESDAY, MAY 18: Rutherford crashes in a Wildcat for the second time in 10 days, this time in Turn 3. Fractures to his left foot and right ankle end a string of 16 straight starts for Rutherford.

FRIDAY, MAY 20: Danny Ongais posts the fastest lap of the month, 205.996, in a March-Cosworth. Unfortunately for Ongais, his car arrives too late to be eligible for the pole.

SATURDAY, MAY 21: Pole Day finally happens, and Mike Mosley, the second car to qualify, sets the early standard at 205.372 mph. Al Unser, Jr., is slower at 202.1, but solidly in the field for his first start.

Rick Mears, one of the favorites, brushes the wall in Turn 4 while posting a four-lap average of 204.3. Teammate Al Unser, Sr., runs 201.954, slightly slower than "Junior" but fast enough to insure the first father-son duo on race day. "Little Al" lines up fifth and "Big Al" seventh.

Tom Sneva, who has two poles on his resume, falls short of a third with a run of 203.7, good enough for the second row. Rookie Teo Fabi goes out next, whips up the crowd with a first lap of 207.273, and then breaks Mears' record with a second lap of 208.049. The veteran of Can-Am and Formula 1 racing finishes with a four-lap record of 207.395. Fabi is the first rookie since Walt Faulkner in 1950 to win the pole. Mosley and Mears share the front row.

A record 33 drivers qualify this day, including A. J. Foyt for the 26th year in a row. Immediately after making the field, Foyt rushes to Houston, where later that night his father dies of cancer.

SUNDAY, May 22: On the final day, Dennis Firestone is the only driver to bump his way into the field, which averages a record 198.406 mph. This is despite a qualifying speed of 183.146 for Chet Fillip on the last row, some 24 mph slower than polesitter Fabi.

THE RACE

Start: Teo Fabi pulls ahead from the pole to lead the first lap as Mike Mosley drops in behind Rick Mears.

Lap 3: Fabi holds a three-second advantage as he posts the fastest lap of the race, 197.5 mph. Tom Sneva gets around Al Unser, Jr., for fifth place.

Lap 11: A black flag summons Dennis Firestone and Chet Fillip, the first drivers that Fabi laps, to the pits. Fillip quits for the day, and Firestone changes tires and goes back out.

Lap 24: Fabi pits for fuel and four fresh tires, giving the lead to Mosley for one lap. When Mosley pits, Mears leads until he pits, giving first to teammate to Al Unser, Sr. A. J. Foyt comes in a second time, and his day ends with broken shift linkage, placing him 31st.

Lap 28: Rookie Pat Bedard hits the outside wall coming out of Turn 4, causing the first caution period. Unser, Sr., pits under yellow and comes out still in front. Sneva is second, Bobby Rahal third, and Mears fourth.

Lap 36: Sneva passes Unser, Sr., in the south chute, but Unser takes it back on the back straight. As they approach a slower car on the front straight, Sneva shoots by into first to lead his fourth straight race.

Lap 44: Roger Mears spins into the south chute wall, bringing out the second yellow flag and the leaders into the pits. Fabi, running third, is about to complete his stop when fuel gushes onto the side pods of his car. An O-ring that closes the fuel valve comes loose, and Fabi's storybook rookie year ends. He wins Rookie of the Year honors.

After everyone pits, Unser regains the lead, Rahal is second, Mears is third, and Howdy Holmes, fourth.

➔

Rain kept the cars in Gasoline Alley for two straight days (*above*), postponing Pole Day until the third weekend of May. Race day was warm and sunny (*right*), and the front straight was abuzz with activity before the start (*opposite*).

Lap 53: One lap after the green flag comes out, Unser gets caught in traffic and Rahal slips by into first place. Sneva gains three spots in two laps, passing Mears for third.

Lap 57: Sneva bursts by Unser for second, while Geoff Brabham charges into fourth past Mears, who struggles with handling problems.

Lap 67: As Brabham moves ahead of Unser for third, Sneva is on leader Rahal's tail. As they approach a slower car, Sneva dives low into Turn 3 to pass both and snatch the lead.

Lap 81: Johnny Parsons passes Mario Andretti on the inside in Turn 1, but when his rear tires start to slide, Parsons hits Andretti and both crash into the outside wall. Neither driver is hurt.

Lap 90: When green-flag racing resumes, Unser leads, Mears is second, Holmes third, and Sneva fourth. Three laps later, Sneva passes Holmes and runs just behind Unser and Mears. Brabham moves up to fourth.

Lap 104: Sneva gets by Mears for second place.

Lap 109: Sneva blasts by Unser at the start-finish line for the lead, and a lap later Brabham passes Mears for third. Rahal, after running in the top 10 all day, retires with a hole in his radiator.

Lap 147: After another round of pit stops under green, Sneva leads Unser by 28 seconds. Brabham is third, Holmes fourth, and Mears fifth, all on the lead lap.

Lap 163: A car stalls on the track, bringing out the yellow. Sneva stays out and maintains the lead, while Unser and Mears pit and line up close behind. Brabham and Holmes fall a lap down from lengthy pit stops.

Lap 171: Mosley spins in Turn 1 and smacks the outside wall right in front of Sneva, who slips underneath the spinning car unscathed. When the yellow comes out, Sneva and Unser pit together. Unser beats Sneva back onto the track to grab the lead. Mears remains third on the same lap.

Lap 177: As the pace car pulls into the pits, Al Unser, Jr., who is several laps behind, darts around several cars ahead of him and is the first car across the start-finish line when the green flag comes out. Unser, Jr., slows to let his father pass, and then runs interference for Unser, Sr. Young Unser ignores a "move over" flag and remains in front of second-place Sneva, who clearly is faster but can't get around the rookie.

Lap 190: Leader Al Unser, Sr., encounters traffic as he heads into Turn 3. A daring Sneva darts underneath both Unsers, grabs the lead and pulls away.

Finish: After settling for second place three times, Sneva sprints away to an 11-second win over Al Unser, Sr. Mears comes in third.

Sneva's March-Cosworth dominates, leading 98 laps. He gives famed chief mechanic and co-owner George Bignotti his seventh Indy win. Sneva's average speed of 162.117 mph is slightly faster than the previous year, but not fast enough to break Mark Donohue's 1972 record.

Al Unser, Jr., runs out of fuel and receives a two-lap penalty for passing under the yellow, but still places 10th.

Mike Mosley's March-Cosworth gets service (*top*). Steve Krisiloff slips under Dennis Firestone (*above*). Johnny Parsons collects Lola-Cosworth pilot Mario Andretti (*below*) when he spins in Turn 1. Tom Sneva (*bottom*) gets fuel and tires. Gordon Johncock blows by Kevin Cogan on the front straight (*opposite, top left*). After three second-places, Sneva was finally the star (*opposite, top right*). In the team photo (*opposite bottom*), co-owners Dan Cotter and George Bignotti are directly right of Sneva.

RESULTS

NO.	DRIVER	CAR	ENTRANT	ENGINE	CYL	DISP	CHASSIS	COLOR	QUAL SPD	START	FIN	LAPS / SPEED / REASON OUT
5	Tom Sneva	Texaco Star	Bignotti-Cotter, Inc.	Cosworth	8	161	March	wht, blue, red	203.687	4	1	200-162.117
7	Al Unser, Sr.	Hertz Penske	Penske Cars, Ltd.	Cosworth	8	161	Penske PC-7	yellow, blue	201.954	7	2	200-161.954
2	Rick Mears	Pennzoil Penske	Penske Cars, Ltd.	Cosworth	8	161	Penske PC-7	red, yellow, blk	204.301	3	3	200-161.799
12	Geoff Brabham	UNO/British Sterling	VDS Associates, Inc.	Cosworth	8	161	Penske PC-10	red, white	198.613	26	4	199-running
16	Kevin Cogan	Caesar's Pl./Mast. Mech.	Bignotti-Cotter, Inc.	Cosworth	8	161	March	white, blue	201.528	22	5	198-running
30	Howdy Holmes	Domino Pizza	Shierson Racing Inc.	Cosworth	8	161	March	red, wht, blue	199.295	12	6	198-running
21	Pancho Carter	Alex Foods Pinata	Alex Morales Co.	Cosworth	8	161	March	blk, orng, yelo	198.207	14	7	197-running
60	Chip Ganassi	Sea Ray Boats	Patrick Racing Team	Cosworth	8	161	Wildcat	blue	197.608	16	8	195-running
37	Scott Brayton	SME Cement	Brayton Engineering	Cosworth	8	161	March	red, white	196.713	29	9	195-running
19	Al Unser, Jr.	Coors Light Silver Bullet	Gallas/Roman Wheels	Cosworth	8	161	Eagle	wht, silver, red	202.146	5	10	192-running
56	Steve Chassey	Genesee Beer/Sizzler/WLNM	Gohr Distributing Co.	Chevy	8	355	Eagle	wht, blue, slvr	195.108	19	11	191-running
72	Chris Kneifel	Primus/C.F.I.	Primus Racing, Inc.	Cosworth	8	161	Primus	white, black	198.625	25	12	191-running
18	Mike Mosley	Kraco Car Stereo	Kraco Enterprises, Inc.	Cosworth	8	161	March	blue, yelo, red	205.372	2	13	169-hit wall T1
20	Gordon Johncock	STP Oil Treatment	Patrick Racing Team	Cosworth	8	161	Wildcat	blue, red	199.748	10	14	163-gear box
22	Dick Simon	Vermont American	Dick Simon Racing, Inc.	Cosworth	8	161	Rattlesnake	red, wht, blk	192.993	20	15	161-running
29	Mike Chandler	Agajanian/Mike Curb	Rattlesnake Racing, Inc.	Cosworth	8	161	Rattlesnake	blk, red, prple	194.934	30	16	153-transmission
10	Tony Bettenhausen	Provimi Veal	Provimi Racing, Inc.	Cosworth	8	161	March	blue, yellow	199.893	9	17	152-half shaft
94	Bill Whittington	Whittington Bros.	Whittington Bros.	Cosworth	8	161	March	yellow, black	197.755	15	18	146-gear box
34	Derek Daly	Wysard Motor Co.	Herb & Ross Wysard	Cosworth	8	161	March	red, wht, blue	197.658	28	19	126-blown engine
4	Bobby Rahal	Red Roof Inns	Truesports Co.	Cosworth	8	161	March	red, wht, brn	202.005	6	20	110-radiator hole
25	Danny Ongais	Interscope Racing	Interscope Racing Corp.	Cosworth	8	161	March	blk, pink, wht	202.320	21	21	101-vibration
66	Johnny Parsons	Colonial Brad/Arciero	Arciero Racing	Cosworth	8	161	Penske PC-10	yellow, red	199.984	23	22	80-spun, hit by No. 3
3	Mario Andretti	Newman/Haas/Budweiser	Newman/Haas Racing	Cosworth	8	161	Lola	red, white	199.404	11	23	80-hit No. 66, hit wall
90	Dennis Firestone	Simpson Sports	Simpson, Jones, Hackman	Cosworth	8	161	March	blue,yellow	190.888	33	24	77-engine
55	Josele Garza	Mach. Union/Silhouette	I.A.M.A.W.	Cosworth	8	161	March	pearl, blue, red	195.671	18	25	64-burned piston
33	Teo Fabi	Skoal Bandit	Forsythe Racing	Cosworth	8	161	March	green, white	207.395	1	26	47-fuel gasket
91	Don Whittington	Simoniz Finish	Whittington Bros.	Cosworth	8	161	March	yellow, black	198.597	27	27	44-electrical
9	Roger Mears	Machinists Union	I.A.M.A.W.	Cosworth	8	161	March	pearl, blue, red	200.108	8	28	43-hit wall T1
43	Steve Krisiloff	Armstrong Mould, Inc.	AMI Racing Division	Cosworth	8	161	Lola	blk, red, yelo	191.192	31	29	42-universal
35	Patrick Bedard	Escort Radar Warning	Brayton Engineering	Cosworth	8	161	March	black, white	195.941	17	30	25-hit wall T4
14	A. J. Foyt	Valvoline-Gilmore	A. J. Foyt Enterprises, Inc.	Cosworth	8	161	March	orange, pearl	199.557	24	31	24-gear shift
1	George Snider	Calumet Farms	A. J. Foyt Enterprises, Inc.	Cosworth	8	161	March	orange, blue	198.544	13	32	22-ignition
38	Chet Fillip	Circle Bar Truck Corral	Circle Bar Auto Racing	Cosworth	8	161	Eagle	blue, orange	183.146	32	33	11-flagged

68th Race • May 27, 1984

The 67th running of the 500 draws a record 117 entries, and 87 cars actually roll into Gasoline Alley, also an all-time high.

While the number of entries grows, there is less variety on race day. The Cosworth V-8, winner of the last six races, powers 30 starters. The March chassis, which won in 1983, is the choice of 29. Roger Penske shelves his own chassis this year, and Pat Patrick does the same with his American-made Wildcat, which won in 1982.

Some teams dare to be different. Brayton Racing introduces the Buick V-6, a turbocharged stock-block engine. Dan Gurney continues his interest in stock-block engines with a 355-cubic-inch Pontiac V-8. The naturally aspirated Pontiac V-8 fits into a new Gurney Eagle chassis.

French Formula 1 team Ligier enters a car of its own design for Kevin Cogan, and Doug Shierson enters new DSRs for three-time winner Johnny Rutherford and Danny Sullivan. Neither new chassis makes the show, but all three drivers qualify in other cars.

With corporate sponsorship becoming increasingly important in racing, a new two-level C Stand on the front straight opens with 27 hospitality suites at the top that provide a commanding view.

PRACTICE AND QUALIFYING

SATURDAY, MAY 5: Practice gets off to a flying start as Bobby Rahal tops 205 mph. Herm Johnson is second quickest at 203.85, and rookie Michael Andretti, 21-year-old son of Mario, comes in third at 203.

SUNDAY, MAY 6: A total of 44 cars crowd the track today, and Rahal is again fastest, this time a whisker below 206 mph. Mario Andretti finds the groove with a lap of 205.373 in his Lola-Cosworth, and Rick Mears is right behind at 205.151.

MONDAY, MAY 7: Mario Andretti's Lola is tops for the day at 207.66, and Danny Ongais is a close second at 207.4 in a March. A herd of 18 others tops 200 mph in practice, and what was a magical number just a few years ago is now routine.

WEDNESDAY, MAY 9: Mario Andretti posts the first unofficial lap over 210 mph. He runs 210.575, and Mears is →

Pontiac's brand-new mid-engine Fiero (*above* and *opposite bottom*) was the pace car. General Motors bored its four-cylinder engine to 165 cubic inches and tweaked it to 232 bhp, good for 136 mph on the track. GMC again provided the official trucks (*top*). Michael Andretti (*opposite, top left*) qualified for his first start; Dick Simon (*opposite, top right*) made his 13th. Pit signalmen work in a tight space, literally, at trackside (*opposite middle*).

STARTING LINEUP

Average Field Qualifying Speed: 203.686

Numbers in flags indicate finish position

Rick Mears

Mario Andretti

Herm Johnson

A. J. Foyt

Al Unser, Jr.

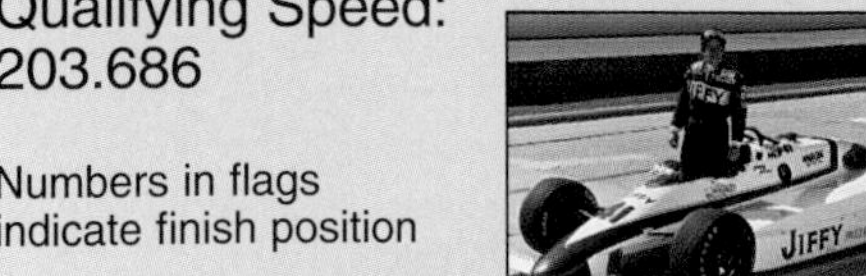

Howdy Holmes

Gordon Johncock

Geoff Brabham

Danny Ongais

Teo Fabi

POLE POSITION
Qualifying Speed: 210.029

Tom Sneva

Michael Andretti

Roberto Guerrero

Al Unser, Sr.

Tom Gloy

When Dick Simon endeavored to make his 13th start in the 500, much ado was made about his effort, especially, after his qualifying run of 201.834 mph. For his part, Simon couldn't understand what all the fuss was about.

"I feel like I'm at my physical prime," Dick remarked. "I'm more worried about my equipment than myself. There may be a big difference in my age and other drivers, but not in physical conditioning."

And with that insight, Simon answered at least part of what had people all excited. At 50, Dick Simon was at the time the oldest qualifier in Indy history to exceed 200 mph.

Bobby Rahal | Pancho Carter | Josele Garza | Kevin Cogan | Johnny Rutherford | Chris Kneifel

Tony Bettenhausen | Dick Simon | Emerson Fittipaldi | Scott Brayton | Derek Daly | Dennis Firestone

Al Holbert | Patrick Bedard | Chip Ganassi | Spike Gehlhausen | Danny Sullivan | George Snider

nearly as quick at 209.937. Others above 205 include last year's polesitter, Teo Fabi, and rookies Michael Andretti and Roberto Guerrero, a Formula 1 vet from Colombia.

FRIDAY, MAY 11: The day before the pole run, 200 mph makes you an also-ran. Mario Andretti hits 212.4, and Gordon Johncock does 211-plus. Of 56 cars on the track today, 29 top 200.

Mike Chandler, driving Dan Gurney's Eagle-Pontiac, slams the wall in Turn 3 and suffers head injuries that prevent him from qualifying.

SATURDAY, MAY 12: On a warm, sunny Pole Day, speeds are slower than expected. Even so, Rick Mears, the first to qualify, sets a one-lap record of 208.5 mph and a four-lap mark of 207.847. Michael Andretti earns his first 500 start just .016 second slower than Mears.

Mario Andretti's first lap is a record 209.687, and he appears on his way to knocking Mears off the pole when an electrical glitch on his last lap slows his average to 207.467, slightly slower than son Michael. Both Andrettis wind up on the second row.

Defending winner Tom Sneva runs his first two laps at more than 209, and then increases to 210.423 on the third. His final lap is fastest of all, 210.689, for an average of 210.029. Sneva wins his third pole, and the first man to top 200 mph is also the first to top 210.

Sneva's Mayer Racing teammate, Howdy Holmes, later qualifies at 207.977, fast enough to bump Mears over to the outside of row one. At the end of the day, 28 cars qualify at an average speed of 203.5 mph.

SATURDAY, MAY 19: The second weekend of qualifying has teams scrambling. Kevin Cogan, replacing the injured Mike Chandler, gets Dan Gurney's Eagle-Pontiac in at 203.6 mph.

Owner Doug Shierson withdraws the DSR-Cosworth Danny Sullivan qualified the previous weekend at just 196 mph. Sullivan jumps into a Lola-Cosworth and averages a safe 203.567.

Johnny Rutherford, who earlier in the week quit the Shierson team, fails to qualify a Chevy V-6 A. J. Foyt owns. That afternoon, Foyt and partner Jim Gilmore buy a March chassis from Galles Racing, change the numbers, and send Rutherford out on the track 10 minutes before the final gun. Rutherford averages 202 mph to bump Chris Kneifel.

With one day of qualifying to go, all 33 cars in the field average more than 200 mph.

SUNDAY, MAY 20: Rain washes out the final day of qualifying.

WEDNESDAY, MAY 23: Dr. Henry Bock, head of the Speedway medical staff, rules that rookie Jacques Villeneuve cannot compete in the race because of a concussion he suffers in a post-qualifying crash. Villeneuve's team withdraws his car. Chris Kneifel, bumped last Saturday, moves into the 33rd starting spot with the slowest qualifying speed, 199.831 mph. →

When Dennis Firestone qualified for the 33rd starting position, you would have thought he'd won the pole. Not only was Dennis all smiles, but his mechanic, Dave Thomas, was overjoyed. After all, it's hard to hold your breath for four laps, even when your driver is flying along at an average of 201.217 mph.

Firestone was probably the darkest dark horse to make the field in many a moon. Not only was his two-year-old March C-15 outdated, but everything that could go wrong did for the likable veteran. First, the engine blew, then a transmission failed, a blockage developed in a fuel tank, the engine caught fire, and—a few days prior to final qualifying—he lost a wheel.

And so, during what appeared to be a successful qualifying run (completed just as a downpour hit), Firestone's fourth lap dropped off to 198.217. It was nail-gnawing time until the average speed was announced. But Thomas couldn't leave well enough alone. Like any good crew chief, he had to know what caused the drop in speed.

"I contacted the wall coming out of Turn 2," Firestone replied. "I started picking up a wobble. I was a little concerned about putting too much on it those last two turns."

Opposite page: Scott Brayton (top left) put a Buick V-6 in the race for the first time. An electrical glitch slowed the qualifying run made by Mario Andretti (top middle). Son Michael's crew won the pit-stop competition (top right). Roger Penske draws for qualifying position as USAC official Art Meyers looks on (bottom left). Penske driver Rick Mears qualified third, Howdy Holmes was second, and defending winner Tom Sneva won his third pole (bottom right, from left). *This page:* Al Unser, Sr., drove the No. 2 Penske car (below left) to a third. "The Captain" inspects Mears's March (below). Balloons are released before the start (bottom left). The pace car leads the field into Turn 1 (bottom right).

THE RACE

Start: Rick Mears pulls in front when the green comes out to lead for a record sixth race in a row. Polesitter Tom Sneva tucks in behind Mears and Michael Andretti moves up to third from the second row.

Lap 10: With Mears still in front by about a second, Michael Andretti gets by Sneva for second on the front straight. Mario Andretti is fourth.

Lap 18: Michael Andretti slows while lapping traffic, and Sneva surges by to reclaim second.

Lap 25: Mears pits for fuel and fresh tires, giving the lead to archrival Sneva, who is in front for the fifth race in a row. Mario Andretti assumes second and moves up to first when Sneva pits the next lap.

Lap 40: Mario Andretti leads at 100 miles at a record speed of 192.724. Sneva grabs second place from Mears. One lap later, Al Unser, Jr., takes third from Mears.

Lap 48: Just after Sneva passes Andretti for the lead, the yellow comes out for a spin in Turn 1. Andretti takes on only fuel during the ensuing pit stops and comes out first, ahead of Mears, Sneva, and Unser, Jr.

Lap 53: Back under green, Sneva charges past Mears for second. On the next lap, Mears passes Sneva, who gets a tow. Both cars shoot by Andretti, who drops to third. Two laps later, he drops to fourth as Unser, Jr., blows by.

Lap 58: Second-year driver Pat Bedard spins into the Turn 3 earthen barrier and flips as his car disintegrates from the impact. He lands upside down and suffers a broken jaw and concussion.

As drivers swerve to avoid the debris, Danny Sullivan rides over Roberto Guerrero's left rear tire and breaks his right front wheel and suspension. Sullivan is out, but Guerrero suffers no damage and continues.

The front-runners pit, giving the lead to Teo Fabi and second place to Danny Ongais.

Lap 71: After two laps under green, Ongais smokes Fabi for first place.

Lap 74: Fabi takes the lead back from Ongais, and a lap later Ongais drops to fourth when Al Unser, Jr., and Sneva sweep past.

Lap 81: Out of sequence with the other leaders, Fabi stops for fuel and tires. Sneva bolts past Unser, Jr., for the lead, but two laps later, Unser retaliates and reclaims first. After they make their regular stops, Sneva goes back in front and Unser falls to second.

Lap 104: Fabi, running fourth, pulls into the pits with engine problems and gets out of his car. Moments later, two-time winner Gordon Johncock clips the outside wall in Turn 4 and slides across the pit entrance. Johncock smacks the inside pit wall, spins around and hits the outer wall, breaking an ankle and narrowly missing nearby crew members.

After the leaders pit under yellow, Mears runs first, Sneva second, and Al Unser, Jr., third.

Lap 131: Unser, Jr., running second, loses his water pump →

There is one lap to go before the start as the field circles in formation (*opposite top*). After the start, Michael Andretti, in the No. 99 Kraco March-Cosworth, closes on Scott Brayton's Buick-powered No. 37 March (*opposite bottom*). Twenty-one-year-old Andretti started fourth, finished fifth, and shared Rookie of the Year honors with Roberto Guerrero, a native of Colombia who qualified seventh and finished in second place. Brayton retired after 150 laps with transmission problems in his third 500. As the race starts (*top*), Rick Mears noses ahead of Tom Sneva, while Howdy Holmes drops back and Michael Andretti moves up on the inside from the second row. Brayton leads a herd of pursuers through a corner in the early going (*above left*). Derek Daly in the No. 61 March-Cosworth is first in line among the group pursuing Brayton. The field spreads out on the front straight after the clean start (*above*). Mears's pit crew sends the No. 6 Pennzoil car back into the fray following a routine stop (*left*). Note that the left-side mirror appears to have fallen off Mears's machine.

and retires after leading four laps in his second 500. Sneva goes back into second, the only car still on the lead lap with Mears, who is about 10 seconds ahead. Guerrero runs third, a lap down.

Lap 153: Guerrero spins entering the back straight, comes to a stop on the track without hitting anything or killing his engine, and continues on to the pits for fresh rubber.

With the yellow out, heavy traffic on pit road results in Mario Andretti rear-ending Josele Garza. Andretti retires with a crumpled nose cone, but Garza gets back in the race.

Lap 163: The transmission on Scott Brayton's Buick V-6 gives out, and he coasts to a stop on the track, bringing out another yellow. Mears still leads and lines up directly behind the pace car. Sneva lies second, with only three cars between him and Mears.

Lap 168: As the field gets ready to go green, sparks start to fly off the back of Sneva's March. As Mears and the rest of the field take off, Sneva pulls into the pits with a broken left CV joint, ending his bid for a second straight victory. Mears holds a two-lap advantage over Al Unser, Sr., who moves up to second.

Finish: Mears makes one more stop for fuel and covers the remaining distance without drama to post his second victory at the Speedway. He leads 119 laps and averages 163.612 mph, breaking Mark Donohue's 11-year-old record. Mears collects a record $434,061 for his efforts. For the 10th straight year, the winner starts from the first two rows.

Rookie Guerrero runs laps at more than 200 mph near the end to edge 19-year veteran Unser, Sr., for second place, two laps back. Two more rookies, Al Holbert and Michael Andretti, finish fourth and fifth, the first time in years that three rookies place in the top five. Guerrero and Andretti are co-Rookies of the Year.

Sign language, Brickyard style (*opposite top*). The black No. 25 Interscope March-Cosworth of Danny Ongais tries to hold off Al Holbert in No. 21 and Derek Daly in No. 61 (*opposite middle*). Pancho Carter, Bobby Rahal, and Josele Garza are also in pursuit. Rick Mears's bright yellow March (*opposite bottom*) reunited him with the Borg-Warner trophy (*left*), with which he first became acquainted in '79. He and owner Roger Penske shared $434,061 in long green. After the shouting, the debris left behind (*above*) is clear proof a crowd of nearly 400,000 was on hand on race day.

RESULTS

NO.	DRIVER	CAR	ENTRANT	ENGINE	CYL	DISP	CHASSIS	COLOR	QUAL SPD	START	FIN	LAPS / SPEED / REASON OUT
6	Rick Mears	Pennzoil Z-7	Penske Cars, Ltd.	Cosworth	8	161	'84 March	yellow, red	207.847	3	1	200-163.612
9	Roberto Guerrero	Master Mechanic	Bignotti-Cotter, Inc.	Cosworth	8	161	'84 March	blue, white	205.707	7	2	198-running
2	Al Unser, Sr.	Miller High Life	Penske Cars, Ltd.	Cosworth	8	161	'84 March	red, white	204.441	10	3	198-running
21	Al Holbert	C.R.C. Chemical	Alex Morales Co.	Cosworth	8	161	'84 March	red, wht, blk	203.016	16	4	198-running
99	Michael Andretti	Electrolux/Kraco	Kraco Enterprises	Cosworth	8	161	'84 March	blue, yelo, red	207.805	4	5	198-running
14	A. J. Foyt	Gilmore-Foyt	A. J. Foyt Enterprises	Cosworth	8	161	'84 March	orange, white	203.860	12	6	197-running
5	Bobby Rahal	7 Eleven/Red Roof Inns	Truesports Co.	Cosworth	8	161	'84 March	wht, blue, red	202.203	18	7	197-running
28	Herm Johnson	3M/Menard Cashway	Menard, Inc.	Cosworth	8	161	'84 March	blk, white, red	204.618	9	8	194-running
25	Danny Ongais	Interscope Racing	Interscope Racing Corp.	Cosworth	8	161	'84 March	blk, wht, red	203.978	11	9	193-running
55	Josele Garza	Schaefer/Mach. U.	I.A.M.A.W.	Cosworth	8	161	'84 March	tan, blue, red	200.615	24	10	193-running
4	George Snider	Calumet Farms	A. J. Foyt Enterprises	Cosworth	8	161	'84 March	orng, blue, wht	201.860	31	11	193-running
50	Dennis Firestone	Hoosier Transp.	Purcell Racing	Cosworth	8	161	'82 March	red, wht, blk	201.217	32	12	186-running
41	Howdy Holmes	"Jiffy" Mixes	Mayer Motor Racing	Cosworth	8	161	'84 March	wht, blue, red	207.977	2	13	185-running
77	Tom Gloy	"The Simoniz Finish"	Rick Galles	Cosworth	8	161	'84 March	yelo, blk, red	200.758	13	14	179-engine
73	Chris Kneifel	Spa Erobics/Living Well	Primus Racing	Cosworth	8	161	'84 Primus	black, white	199.831	33	15	175-transmission
1	Tom Sneva	Texaco Star	Mayer Motor Racing	Cosworth	8	161	'84 March	wht, red, blue	210.029	1	16	168-left CV joint
3	Mario Andretti	Budweiser Lola	Newman/Haas	Cosworth	8	161	'84 Lola	red, wht, blue	207.467	6	17	153-nose cone
37	Scott Brayton	Buick Dealers of Amer.	Brayton Engineering	Buick	6	208	'84 March	brown, cream	203.637	26	18	150-transmission
10	Pancho Carter	American Dream	American Dream R.T.	Cosworth	8	161	'84 March	red, wht, blue	201.820	21	19	141-engine
98	Kevin Cogan	Dubonnet/Curb Records	Dan Gurney	Pontiac	8	356	'84 March	red, white	203.622	27	20	137-wheel froze
7	Al Unser, Jr.	Coors Light Silver Bullet	Rick Galles	Cosworth	8	161	'84 March	blk, silver, wht	203.404	15	21	131-water pump
84	Johnny Rutherford	Gilmore/Greer/Foyt	A. J. Foyt Enterprises	Cosworth	8	161	'84 March	orange, white	202.062	30	22	116-engine
22	Dick Simon	Break Free	Dick Simon Racing	Cosworth	8	161	'84 March	grn, red, wht	201.834	20	23	112-running
33	Teo Fabi	Skoal Bandit	Forsythe Racing	Cosworth	8	161	'84 March	green, white	203.600	14	24	104-fuel system
20	Gordon Johncock	STP Oil Treatment	Patrick Racing	Cosworth	8	161	'84 March	blue, red, wht	207.545	5	25	103-crash
16	Tony Bettenhausen	Provimi Veal	Provimi Racing	Cosworth	8	161	'84 March	yellow, blue	202.813	17	26	86-piston
61	Derek Daly	Provimi Veal	Provimi Racing	Cosworth	8	161	'84 March	yellow, blue	202.443	29	27	76-handling
40	Chip Ganassi	Old Milwaukee	Patrick Racing	Cosworth	8	161	'84 March	red, white	201.612	22	28	61-engine
30	Danny Sullivan	Domino's Pizza	Shireson Racing	Cosworth	8	161	'84 March	blk, wht, blue, red	203.567	28	29	57-broken wheel
35	Patrick Bedard	Escort Radar	Brayton Engineering	Cosworth	8	208	'84 March	black, white	201.915	19	30	56-crash
57	Spike Gehlhausen	Little Kings	Indy Auto Racing	Cosworth	8	161	'83 March	wht, blue, red	200.478	25	31	45-spun out
47	Emerson Fittipaldi	W.I.T. Promotions	W.I.T. Promotions	Cosworth	8	161	'84 March	prple, lavender	201.078	23	32	37-oil pressure
18	Geoff Brabham	Kraco Car Stereo	Kraco Enterprises	Cosworth	8	161	'84 March	yelo, blue, red	204.931	8	33	1-fuel line

69th Race • May 26, 1985

The Speedway has a history of promoting stock-block engines to increase fan interest and lower costs, but racing engines dominate the 500 for decades. A handful of owners, particularly Dan Gurney, have some success with stock blocks, though there is no sustained effort.

Current USAC rules allow naturally aspirated stock-block engines up to 355 cubic inches and turbocharged stock-blocks up to 209 cubic inches, with 57 inches of manifold boost pressure. The limits on multi-cam racing engines like the Cosworth are 161 cubic inches and 47 inches of boost, but they rev much higher and are designed for sustained high speeds.

Buick is the first to make a serious stab at ending the domination of purpose-built racing engines with its turbocharged Indy V-6, a pushrod engine derived from a passenger-car V-6 that dates to 1962. Buick arrives at Indy in 1984, when two of its V-6s make the show. Scott Brayton drops out when his transmission packs up, and teammate Pat Bedard crashes out. Neither has much impact.

This year, Buick returns with a three-team effort. Forsythe Racing driver Howdy Holmes fails to get up to speed with the Buick, and his team switches to Cosworth. Brayton and Galles Racing's Pancho Carter, however, give the Cosworth a run for the money in qualifying.

Vital statistics for 1985 include 79 entries (down sharply from a record 117 the year before), a total purse of $3.2 million (more than double the $1.5 million paid in 1980), and a 40th year behind the microphone for track announcer Tom Carnegie.

PRACTICE AND QUALIFYING

MONDAY, MAY 6: On the third day of practice, Bobby Rahal runs 210.97 mph to unofficially break Tom Sneva's qualifying record.

TUESDAY, MAY 7: Mario Andretti's unofficial lap record of 212.4 mph set last year is history. Roberto Guerrero clocks one at 212.8.

WEDNESDAY, MAY 8: Defending winner Rick Mears, still recovering from serious foot injuries he suffers the previous fall, runs 213.4 mph in a March-Cosworth. Pancho Carter →

STARTING LINEUP

Average Field Qualifying Speed: 208.138

Numbers in flags indicate finish position

Bobby Rahal

Don Whittington

Geoff Brabham

Bill Whittington

Michael Andretti

Scott Brayton

Emerson Fittipaldi

Danny Sullivan

Al Unser, Jr.

Dick Simon

POLE POSITION
Qualifying Speed: 212.583

Pancho Carter

Mario Andretti

Al Unser, Sr.

Rick Mears

Tom Sneva

Thirty-five-year-old Danny Sullivan (*opposite top*) became a member of the Penske team for his third attempt at winning the Indianapolis 500. Oldsmobile pulled out all the stops to transform its new front-wheel-drive compact Calais into a pace car. First, it converted a coupe into a ragtop (*below*). Then, it took a 151-cubic-inch engine, bored it to 167 cubes, and bumped horsepower up to 215, more than double the ouput of the stock version. The engine teamed with a three-speed automatic transmission. The interior (*left*) was dressed up with silver leather seats with red trim. The safety of pace-car passengers was enhanced through the addition of competition-style safety belts anchored to the floor behind the front seats. A Calais convertible was never built for sale, so pace-car replicas for the street all were coupes. While the Calais was tuned for speed, heavy-duty work was left to the GMC official trucks (*opposite bottom*).

Josele Garza | A. J. Foyt | John Paul, Jr. | Jim Crawford | Johnny Rutherford | Rich Vogler

Danny Ongais | Arie Luyendyk | Raul Boesel | Johnny Parsons | Tony Bettenhausen | Kevin Cogan

Roberto Guerrero | Howdy Holmes | Ed Pimm | Chip Ganassi | George Snider | Derek Daly

cranks his Buick to 212.5.

Canadian Jacques Villeneuve, who couldn't start last year after suffering a concussion in practice, hits the wall for the second time in four days when a CV joint breaks. Villeneuve is okay, but the following week Johnny Parsons replaces him behind the wheel.

THURSDAY, MAY 9: Rahal moves practice speeds up another notch to 214.183 mph, and he does it at 1:15 P.M., in full sun instead of the cool of late-afternoon "happy hour," when shadows cover much of the track.

Danny Sullivan, now with the Penske team, goes 212.6 before blowing an engine, and Scott Brayton does 212.5, matching yesterday's speed by fellow Buick driver Carter.

FRIDAY, MAY 10: Two-time winner Gordon Johncock announces his retirement, and Patrick Racing immediately hires Don Whittington to replace him.

Mario Andretti runs the fastest lap of the month, 214.3 mph, in his Lola-Cosworth in morning practice. Guerrero hits 213.7 in "happy hour," and Sullivan is right behind at 213.3.

SATURDAY, MAY 11: Brayton is the first to qualify on Pole Day, and his Buick V-6 produces a one-lap record of 214.199 the third time around. On the last lap, his transmission starts to go, but he averages a record 212.354 to stake a strong claim to the pole.

Carter is the fourth one out, and his Buick V-6 falls short of Brayton's one-lap record, but Carter is more consistent and averages 212.583 to move onto the pole, though about 25 cars are still in line.

As the day goes on, the sun gets hotter and the wind picks up, slowing qualifying speeds. Mario Andretti develops a push on his run and also falls one mph short. Bobby Rahal is the last threat to the Buicks, and he comes in third fastest at 211.8. Perennial pole contender Rick Mears has an off day at 209.8 to start 10th.

When the 6 P.M. gun sounds, Carter wins the pole in record fashion, giving a big boost to stock-block engines and Buick.

SATURDAY, MAY 18: After just one hot practice lap, George Snider makes the show for the 21st consecutive year in a March-Chevy V-6 that buddy A. J. Foyt owns. John Paul, Jr., qualifies for the first time.

SUNDAY, MAY 19: Johnny Rutherford gets bumped at 5 P.M., but a few minutes later he roars back with a speed over 208 mph, nailing down his 21st start. →

When Pancho Carter won the pole position with a new track record of 212.583 mph, many thought the second-generation driver stood a chance of winning all the marbles. Certainly, Pancho's turbocharged stock-block Buick V-6 was putting out enough horses to get the job done.

But on race day, even on the parade and pace laps, the engine didn't have the same throaty exhaust note it had bellowed all month long. When the green flag flew, Carter went straight to the rear of the field. Sadly, he never led a lap. And after only six circuits, a plume of blue smoke began trailing the sleek machine. The engine had blown, relegating Carter to 33rd place.

Most people felt the rumbling pushrod Buick V-6 engine had given up. But the problem wasn't with the engine or anything else that carried a Buick trademark. The "slim-iron" oil pump had failed, and it was made by Cosworth, the same folks who made the engine Danny Sullivan drove to victory.

The Buick V-6, bulked up with additional turbo boost, flexed its muscles this year. Pancho Carter (*above*) won the pole at a record speed in the No. 6 Galles Racing entry, and Scott Brayton (*opposite top*) was second fastest in the No. 37 car belonging to Brayton Engineering. Just .229 mph separated the two stock-block-powered cars during the run for the pole. Team Penske's formidable lineup of drivers relaxes during practice (*middle left*): three-time winner Al Unser, Sr., two-time winner Rick Mears, and new recruit Danny Sullivan. Crowd favorite Mario Andretti (*middle right*), who turned the fastest lap in practice, qualified his Lola-Cosworth on the second row. The pace car was driven by actor James Garner (*opposite bottom*).

PPG Buick
35
37
Dreisbach & Sons
BUICK
PRO TECTA LINER

PENNZOIL
PPG
BOSCH
Marlboro
PENNZOIL
PPG
Miller
AMERICAN RACING

Beatrice
VALVOLINE

OFFICIAL PACE CAR

THE RACE

Start: Bobby Rahal pulls ahead of Pancho Carter and Scott Brayton, sweeping down through Turn 1 to take the lead. Mario Andretti moves from fourth to second on the back straight, and Scott Brayton falls to third as Pancho Carter drops back.

Lap 7: Polesitter Carter pulls into the pits with smoke pouring from his Buick V-6. He drops out with a broken oil pump. Rahal still leads, with Mario Andretti second and Brayton third.

Lap 14: George Snider coasts to a stop near the pit entrance after his Chevy V-6 engine expires. A lap later, 10th-place Josele Garza's Cosworth blows. When most front runners pit, Brayton stays out to lead a lap.

Andretti moves into the lead when Brayton pits. Al Unser, Sr., gets a one-lap penalty for running over an air hose in the pits and drops to 18th.

Lap 20: Smoke belches from Brayton's Buick as he drops oil on the track before he stops in Turn 3. All three stock-block engines are out.

Lap 29: Back under green, leader Andretti pulls away from Rahal and third-place Emerson Fittipaldi.

Lap 49: Andretti pits under green, handing the lead to Fittipaldi. When Fittipaldi stops three laps later, Danny Sullivan moves into first. Rahal comes in a second time, and his crew removes the engine cover, signalling a lengthy stop.

Lap 57: Sullivan makes a routine pit stop, and Andretti regains the lead. Fittipaldi comes up to second, and Al Unser, Jr., is third.

→

When Danny Sullivan made his famous spin in front of Mario Andretti on lap 120, he was the victim of a mistake. The tire-smoking loop was the result of Sullivan mistaking what he heard on his radio.

"For some reason, I thought there were only 12 laps left," Danny said. "That's why I was anxious to get by Mario. I thought that's all she wrote, but it spun around and I didn't hit anything. And all of a sudden the smoke cleared and I was facing Turn 2. So I just stuck it down and took off."

Only 20 laps later, Sullivan passed Andretti in the same spot in which he'd spun earlier. This time, the young charger put his foot to the floor and never looked back.

Perhaps it was a stroke of luck that Danny never hit anything in his so-called "spin and win" effort. Or perhaps it was his training. Although a native of Louisville, Kentucky, Sullivan lived for some time in New York City—where he drove a taxi.

The first in line—Pancho Carter's pole-winning March-Buick—was the first one out. Carter fell back at the start and fell out on lap seven with a busted oil pump (*opposite top*). A. J. Foyt's March-Cosworth was sidelined by a damaged front wing, and then a minor fire broke out in his pit. With Foyt already out of the car, firefighters come over the wall to quell the blaze (*opposite middle*). Mario Andretti hunkers down in the Beatrice Foods-sponsored car (*above*), and battles Danny Sullivan for the lead (*left*). The defining moment in the race came on lap 120 (*row below*). Just after Sullivan passed Andretti in the south short chute, the rear wheels on Sullivan's March lost grip, sending him into a 360-degree spin a few feet in front of Andretti. Sullivan remarkably never hit the wall and recovered to point the car in the right direction.

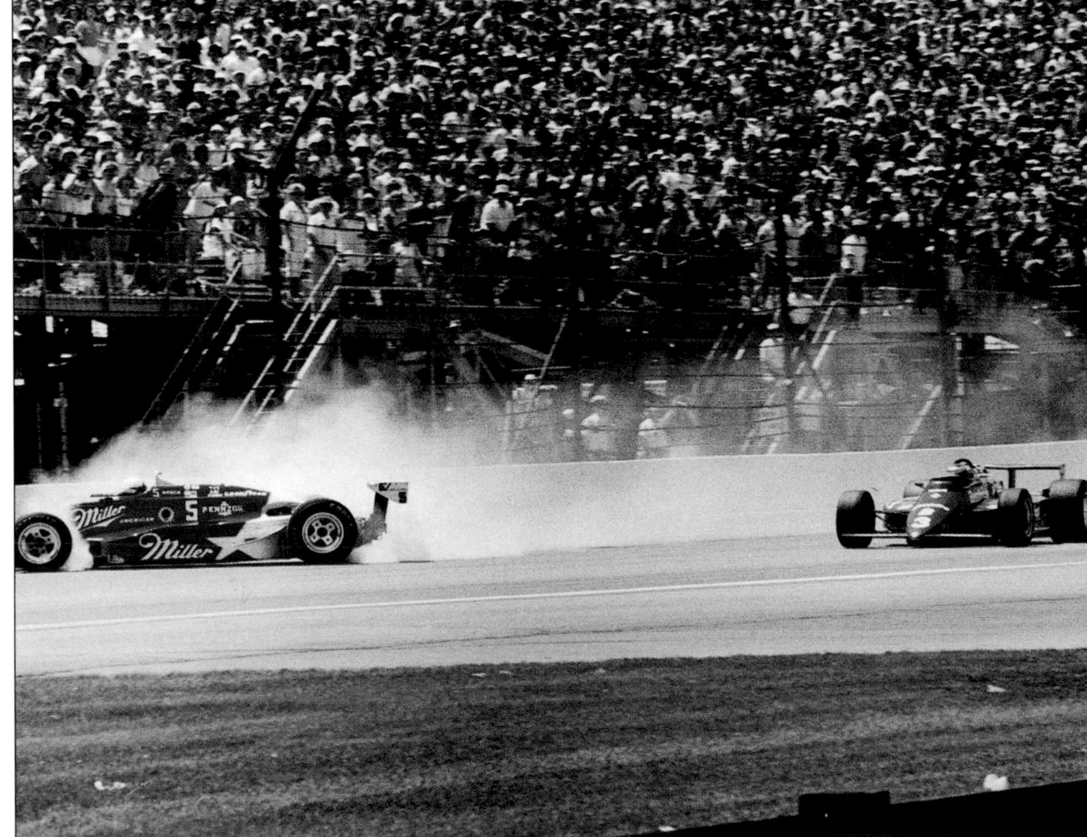

Lap 91: Second-place Fittipaldi closes to within three seconds of Andretti. Third-place Unser falls out of the race when he loses oil pressure. Tom Sneva moves up to third and Geoff Brabham to fourth.

Lap 100: Andretti leads by 2.5 seconds at a record pace. Four others are still on the lead lap: Fittipaldi, Sneva, Brabham, and Sullivan.

Lap 110: After a round of pit stops, Sullivan is second, about four seconds behind Andretti, and closing.

Lap 120: Sullivan catches Andretti and they go side-by-side into Turn 1. Just as Sullivan pulls ahead on the short chute, the back end of his March comes around and he does a complete spin right in front of Andretti.

Their cars are inches apart when Andretti darts to the left and slips by. Sullivan completes a full loop, miraculously stays off the outside wall, and ends up pointed toward Turn 2. Sullivan makes an incredible save, and when the yellow comes out, both drivers pit.

Andretti gets fuel only and retains the lead, while Sullivan stays longer for four new tires and drops to third behind Sneva.

Lap 124: Back under green, Andretti dodges another bullet. Two lapped cars make contact in Turn 1, and Rich Vogler spins across the track in front of the leaders into the outside wall. This happens as Sneva tries to pass Andretti on the inside, and Sneva locks his brakes and spins into the wall.

Lap 134: When the green comes out, Sullivan resumes his chase of first-place Andretti.

Lap 139: Sullivan pulls even with Andretti near the start-finish line and again goes low into Turn 1 for a pass. This time he finishes it cleanly to grab the lead. Sullivan consistently runs laps over 200 mph to pull away from Andretti.

Lap 159: Fittipaldi gets inside of Andretti in Turn 1 and moves into second. Robert Guerrero follows in fourth on the lead lap.

Lap 176: The field bunches up behind the pace car during a caution period. Sullivan is first, Andretti is back in second, and Guerrero is third. Fittipaldi falls to fourth from an untimely pit stop. After the green comes out, Sullivan pulls away to a five-second advantage, and Fittipaldi soon retires with fuel problems.

Finish: Sullivan is cruising when another accident brings out the caution flag on lap 193. When racing resumes on Lap 197, Andretti closes to within 2.5 seconds but can't catch Sullivan, who wins in his third outing at the Brickyard.

Sullivan leads 67 laps to give owner Roger Penske his fifth 500 win and second in a row. Sullivan pockets a record $517,662 for his Sunday spin.

For Andretti, it is his best finish since 1981, when he also placed second. He leads 107 laps, his best day's work since his 1969 victory. Guerrero comes home third, about 12 seconds behind Sullivan, giving him top three finishes his first two years. Al Unser, Sr., is fourth, a lap down from the pit-stop penalty he incurs early in the race.

The Turn 3 wall bit Bill Whittington (*opposite top*). One more look at Danny Sullivan's spin shows how close Mario Andretti came to the out-of-control racer (*opposite bottom*). Sullivan demonstrates his appreciation for his sponsor as he whoops it up in victory lane (*left*). Even with his wild ride, Sullivan's winning March-Cosworth (*below*) fared far better than one infield spectator's car (*above*).

RESULTS

NO.	DRIVER	CAR	ENTRANT	ENGINE	CYL	DISP	CHASSIS	COLOR	QUAL SPD	START	FIN	LAPS / SPEED / REASON OUT
5	Danny Sullivan	Miller American	Penske Cars, Ltd.	Cosworth	8	161	'85 March	red, white	210.298	8	1	200-152.982
3	Mario Andretti	Beatrice Foods	Newman/Haas Racing	Cosworth	8	161	'85 Lola	red, blue, wht	211.576	4	2	200-152.950
9	Roberto Guerrero	Master Mechanic/Emerson	Bignotti-Cotter Racing	Cosworth	8	161	'85 March	wht, blk, red	208.062	16	3	200-152.832
11	Al Unser, Sr.	Hertz Special	Penske Cars, Ltd.	Cosworth	8	161	'85 March	yellow	210.523	7	4	199-flagged
76	Johnny Parsons	Canadian Tire	Canadian Tire Corporation	Cosworth	8	161	'85 March	red, blue	205.778	26	5	198-flagged
21	Johnny Rutherford	Vermont Am./Alex Foods	Alex Morales Company, Inc.	Cosworth	8	161	'85 March	wht, red, blk	208.254	30	6	198-flagged
61	Arie Luyendyk	Dutch Treat/Sports/Provimi	Provimi Racing, Inc.	Cosworth	8	161	'85 Lola	black, white	206.004	20	7	198-flagged
99	Michael Andretti	Electrolux/Kraco	Kraco Enterprises, Inc.	Cosworth	8	161	'85 March	blue, red, yelo	208.185	15	8	196-flagged
98	Ed Pimm	Skoal Bandit	Gurney-Curb All Am. Racers, Inc.	Cosworth	8	161	'85 Eagle	green, white	205.724	22	9	195-flagged
33	Howdy Holmes	Jiffy Mix	Forsythe Racing, Inc.	Cosworth	8	161	'85 Lola	blue, wht, red	206.372	19	10	194-flagged
18	Kevin Cogan	Kraco/Wolf Sun	Kraco Enterprises, Inc.	Cosworth	8	161	'85 March	yelo, blue, red	206.368	32	11	191-flagged
29	Derek Daly	Kapsreiter Bier	Tom Hess Racing	Cosworth	8	161	'85 Lola	red, yellow	207.548	31	12	189-flagged
40	Emerson Fittipaldi	7-Eleven	STP-Patrick Racing Team, Inc.	Cosworth	8	161	'85 March	blue, wht, red	211.322	5	13	188-fuel line
12	Bill Whittington	B&B Properties	Arciero Racing Teams	Cosworth	8	161	'85 March	white	209.006	12	14	183-accident T3
43	John Paul, Jr.	Satellite Technology	AMI Racing Division	Cosworth	8	161	'85 March	wht, blue, red	206.340	24	15	164-accident T2
34	Jim Crawford	Canadian Tire	Wysard Motor Co., Inc.	Cosworth	8	161	'85 Lola	wht, blue, red	205.525	27	16	142-electrical
25	Danny Ongais	Panavision	Interscope Racing	Cosworth	8	161	'85 March	black	207.220	17	17	141-engine
23	Raul Boesel	Break Free	Dick Simon Racing, Inc.	Cosworth	8	161	'85 March	blue, red	206.498	23	18	134-radiator
7	Geoff Brabham	Coors Light Silver Bullet	Galles Racing	Cosworth	8	161	'85 March	blk, red, sliver	210.074	9	19	130-engine
2	Tom Sneva	Skoal Bandit	Gurney-Curb All Am. Racers, Inc.	Cosworth	8	161	'85 Eagle	green, white	208.927	13	20	123-accident T1
1	Rick Mears	Pennzoil Z-7 Special	Penske Cars, Ltd.	Cosworth	8	161	'85 March	yelo, red, blk	209.796	10	21	122-shift linkage
84	Chip Ganassi	Calumet Farm	A. J. Foyt Enterprises, Inc.	Cosworth	8	161	'85 March	orange	206.104	25	22	121-fuel line
60	Rich Vogler	Kentucky Fried Chicken	Patrick Racing Team, Inc.	Cosworth	8	161	'85 March	blue, red	205.653	33	23	119-accident T1
20	Don Whittington	STP Oil Treatment	STP-Patrick Racing Team, Inc.	Cosworth	8	161	'85 March	blue, red, wht	210.991	6	24	97-engine
30	Al Unser, Jr.	Domino's Pizza	Team Shierson	Cosworth	8	161	'85 Lola	red, wht, blue	209.215	11	25	91-engine
22	Dick Simon	Break Free	Dick Simon Racing, Inc.	Cosworth	8	161	'85 March	blk, red, wht	208.536	14	26	86-oil pressure
10	Bobby Rahal	Budweiser	Truesports Company	Cosworth	8	161	'85 March	red	211.818	3	27	84-waste gate
14	A. J. Foyt	Copenhagen-Gilmore	A. J. Foyt Enterprises, Inc.	Cosworth	8	161	'85 March	orange	205.782	21	28	62-front wing
97	Tony Bettenhausen	Skoal Bandit	Gurney-Curb All Am. Racers, Inc.	Cosworth	8	161	'85 Lola	green, wht	204.824	29	29	31-wheel bearing
37	Scott Brayton	Hardee's	Brayton Engineering	Buick V-6	6	208	'85 March	red, orng, wht	212.354	2	30	19-cylinder wall
55	Josele Garza	Schaefer/Machinist	Machinist Racing Team	Cosworth	8	161	'85 March	wht, blue, red	206.677	18	31	15-engine
44	George Snider	A. J. Foyt Chevrolet	A. J. Foyt Enterprises, Inc.	Chevy V-6	6	205	'85 March	orange	205.455	28	32	13-engine
6	Pancho Carter	Valvoline Buick Hawk	Galles Racing	Buick V-6	6	161	'85 March	blue, wht, red	212.583	1	33	6-oil pump

1986

70th Race • May 25-26; 31, 1986

Revised chassis rules call for larger cockpits and more foot room in response to serious leg and foot injuries to drivers in recent seasons. Ground effects tunnels underneath the cars are smaller as USAC tries again to slow the cars. A $4 million purse, however, entices drivers to go faster than ever.

The 1986 race is the first for the Chevrolet-Indy V-8, a dual-overhead-camshaft engine developed specifically for Indy-car racing. Though Chevy's name is on the engine, a British engineering firm, Ilmor, does most of the engineering. Team Penske is the first to get the Chevy-Ilmor engine, installing it in a new Penske PC-15 chassis driven by three-time winner Al Unser, Sr.

The other Penske drivers, defending winner Danny Sullivan and two-time victor Rick Mears, return in March chassis with Cosworth power.

Unser qualifies the Chevy on the second row, but struggles during the race, fails to lead a lap, and retires on Lap 149 due to engine vibrations.

Three Buick V-6s make the show. Unlike last year, when two were on the front row, the Buicks start from well back in the pack. Like last year, none goes the distance.

Gasoline Alley has a new look with 96 concrete garages, more than enough to accommodate this year's 68 entries.

For a while, it looks like the 1986 race will never run. Rain postpones the race two days in a row on Memorial Day weekend. When the race finally runs on Saturday, May 31, the weather is sunny and warm.

Rain not only postpones the race but the advent of live television coverage. The previous fall, ABC and the Speedway agree to a three-year deal to broadcast the race live instead of on the tape-delay basis that dates to 1971.

PRACTICE AND QUALIFYING

SATURDAY MAY 3: Mario Andretti is quickest in opening day practice at 210.329 mph in his Lola-Cosworth. Son Michael is a close second at 210.133 in a March-Cosworth.

MONDAY, MAY 5: Rick Mears's lap of 211.118 mph is best for the day. Al Unser, Sr., is next at just 208 with the new Penske-Chevy package.

➔

STARTING LINEUP

Average Field Qualifying Speed: 210.280

Numbers in flags indicate finish position

POLE POSITION
Qualifying Speed: 216.828

Michael Andretti

Kevin Cogan

Al Unser, Jr.

Johnny Rutherford

Jacques Villeneuve

Danny Sullivan

Al Unser, Sr.

Roberto Guerrero

Emerson Fittipaldi

Pancho Carter

Rick Mears

Bobby Rahal

Tom Sneva

Ed Pimm

Randy Lanier

Because both the Indianapolis 500 and Chevrolet were celebrating the 75th anniversaries of their foundings in 1986, a Corvette was a natural selection to be the pace car. Chevy revived the Corvette convertible this year after an 11-year absence, and the yellow ragtop that led the field to the green flag required no mechanical modifications, as did the 1978 Corvette, the last pace car to serve in street-legal tune (*opposite top*). This year's pace car came with a 230-horsepower 350-cubic-inch V-8 (*opposite bottom*), the same small-block engine that had been raced in some Indy cars in modified form. The only modifications to the pace car were safety lights, five-point harnesses instead of regular seatbelts, and an on-board fire extinguisher. Retired Air Force General Chuck Yeager (*above*), a World War II fighter ace who knew a thing or two about going fast considering he was the first pilot to break the sound barrier, drove the pace car (*top left*). Chevrolet also provided the official track service and safety trucks for the race (*bottom left*).

Tony Bettenhausen

A. J. Foyt

Phil Krueger

Rich Vogler

Mario Andretti

Dick Simon

Josele Garza

Geoff Brabham

Scott Brayton

Jim Crawford

Gary Bettenhausen

Roberto Moreno

Danny Ongais

Arie Luyendyk

Raul Boesel

Chip Ganassi

Johnny Parsons

George Snider

TUESDAY, MAY 6: Herm Johnson is hurt for the second year in a row in practice. A piece of his car comes loose in Turn 1, and he spins and hits the wall. He fractures both feet and the lumbar area of the spine. Danny Ongais and Johnny Parsons also hit the wall, but neither is hurt.

WEDNESDAY, MAY 7: Teammates Rick Mears and Danny Sullivan raise the stakes as Pole Day nears. Mears goes 214.7 mph and Sullivan 214.1. Michael Andretti and Bobby Rahal top 213, and Unser, Sr., reaches 212 with the Penske-Chevy.

FRIDAY, MAY 9: Five drivers top 214 mph the day before the run for the pole. Mario Andretti leads the way at 214.643. Mears, Rahal, Michael Andretti, and Tom Sneva are in the hunt for the pole as well.

SATURDAY, MAY 10: Mario Andretti is first to qualify, and his speed of 212.3 mph, barely below the record, looks precarious for the front row.

Sullivan is the second to qualify and sets a single-lap record of 215.729 and four-lap record of 215.382 to blow Andretti off the pole.

Not much later, Mears rewrites both records with a first lap of 217.581 and an average of 216.828, but a couple of other contenders have yet to show.

Michael Andretti's speed of 214.522 knocks his father off the front row. Bobby Rahal manages 213.55, which squeezes him into the fourth position ahead of Mario. After that, no one else comes close.

Mears adds a third pole position to his growing list of Speedway achievements.

SUNDAY, MAY 11: A. J. Foyt has some spark left at the age of 51. Foyt leads second-day qualifiers at 213.2 mph, fifth fastest overall, to make his 29th consecutive 500.

WEDNESDAY, MAY 14: Mario Andretti, who qualifies fifth on Pole Day, spins in Turn 3 when his suspension breaks and hits the wall head on. He suffers bruises and the team withdraws the badly damaged car, forcing Andretti to start at the rear of the field in his backup Lola T86.

→

From the late Forties into the Fifties, Jack McGrath proved time and again that the pole position wasn't the most advantageous place from which to start the Indy 500. McGrath's favorite starting spot—and he usually shot for and won it—was the outside of the front row.

In the Eighties, this was still a trend. Most every start was dominated by the car starting third on the grid. But it wasn't until 1986, when young Michael Andretti and his March 86C17-Cosworth led the opening circuit, that the outside front-row spot really became known as "the short way around." On that initial lap, Michael established a new record of 202.940 mph, the first time anyone had turned the opening lap at over 200 mph.

Al Unser, Jr., greets young fans (*opposite top*). Actor/racer Paul Newman (*opposite middle*), co-owner of Mario Andretti's car, spent a lot of time at the Speedway, as did actor and frequent pace-car driver James Garner (*above*). Team Penske's No. 11 entry (*top*) used the new Chevrolet Indy V-8. Rick Mears is at the wheel, but Al Unser, Sr., far left, drove it. Official vehicles loop the track early in the period leading up to the race (*opposite bottom*). *Right:* Chuck Sprague, chief mechanic for 1985 winner Danny Sullivan, is honored by Snap-on Tools. Sullivan and boss Roger Penske are on the right.

THURSDAY, MAY 22: A bizarre Carburetion Day accident starts in Turn 4 with a spin by Dennis Firestone and eventually involves George Snider, Roberto Moreno, and Josele Garza, who is on pit road getting fresh tires.

Snider and Moreno start 31st and 32nd, respectively, in backup cars. Firestone, who lacks a backup, withdraws from the race. First alternate Dick Simon starts for the 15th time instead and lines up 33rd. At 52, Simon is the oldest driver to start a 500. The starting field averages a record 210.280 mph.

THE RACE
Start: On the parade lap, former winner Tom Sneva suddenly turns left and hits the inside wall of Turn 2 when a suspension part breaks.

Lap 1: Michael Andretti gets to Turn 1 ahead of Rick Mears to take the lead as Danny Sullivan falls back.

Lap 15: Andretti still leads when the yellow flag comes out for his father, who stalls in Turn 3 with electrical problems. Mario Andretti gets a tow to the pits, goes back out after losing nine laps, and retires with a total of 19 laps to his credit, the second former winner to depart early.

The leaders pit under yellow, and Michael Andretti takes on fuel and fresh rubber without giving up first place. Josele Garza, who starts 17th, stays on the track and moves up to second.

Lap 28: Garza, running third behind Michael and Mears, makes his first stop. Kevin Cogan moves up to third, but two laps later Bobby Rahal takes it away. The four-way battle involving Andretti, Mears, Rahal, and Cogan continues the rest of the way.

Lap 42: Andretti, Mears, and Rahal pit under green, giving the lead to Cogan for a lap. When Cogan stops, Al Unser, Jr., moves into first.

Lap 49: After all the leaders make their stops, Mears emerges as the new leader. Andretti and Rahal are in pursuit.

Lap 75: Rahal is less than a second behind leader Mears as the front runners start a round of pit stops.

Lap 82: Rahal passes Mears for the lead, and Cogan is less than three seconds away in third.

→

Two straight days of rain prevented Speedway Chairman Mary Fendrich Hulman (*opposite, top left*) from ordering the cars to be started on the scheduled date. Driver Ed Pimm heads for shelter (*opposite right*) as a steady rain drenches the track (*opposite, bottom left*), forcing a postponement to the next weekend. When the race was finally run, the weather was warm and sunny, and the grandstands were full (*above*). A broken suspension sent the March of former winner Tom Sneva into the wall on the parade lap (*left*). A. J. Foyt's race ended on lap 135 when his brakes locked as came into his pit stall. A.J.'s car spun backwards into the pit wall (*below left*), breaking the rear wing on his March-Cosworth (*below*). Foyt reported losing the front brakes on his car early on.

Lap 97: Al Unser, Jr., catches up to Cogan in traffic and slips by into third, but Cogan soon reclaims the position. Leader Rahal runs about five seconds ahead of Mears.

Lap 119: Cogan and Mears are waging a terrific battle for second, and they swap positions again on successive laps.

Lap 123: Mears slows when he encounters traffic, and Cogan passes him for second. Andretti soon catches up and puts Mears in fourth. Mears pits a few laps later and falls to fifth.

Lap 135: The yellow comes out when Rich Vogler hits the Turn 3 wall. The leaders pit except for Mears, who moves back up to first. Cogan lines up second, Andretti third, and Rahal fourth. Mears opens up a 10-second lead after the green flag comes out.

Lap 170: After a yellow flag and pit stops, Mears still leads, and Rahal is now second ahead of Cogan. Mears is able to hold on to first when racing resumes, but can't shake his pursuers.

Lap 186: Rahal passes Mears for first on the back straight, and a lap later Cogan dives under Rahal in Turn 1 for the lead and builds a cushion of about three seconds.

Lap 194: Arie Luyendyk cuts a tire and spins coming out of Turn 4, hitting the inside wall. During the ensuing caution, none of the leaders pits. Cogan is first in line behind the pace car and appears to have the race in hand. Rahal and Mears line up right behind.

Lap 198: On the restart, Rahal gets on the throttle quicker and shoots inside of Cogan on the front straight for the 19th lead change of the day. Rahal is able to pull away a little on the backstretch.

Finish: Rahal posts the fastest race lap in 500 history at 209.152 in his March-Cosworth to beat Cogan by 1.441 seconds. A Cosworth engine wins for the ninth year in a row in what turns out to be a real nail-biter.

Mears is third, just 1.881 seconds behind, for the closest 1-2-3 finish so far. Roberto Guerrero's fourth-place finish is the lowest of his impressive three-year career.

Rahal is the first driver to complete the 500 in less than three hours, and his speed of 170.722 beats the 1984 record by more than seven mph. He drives into a new victory lane with a platform that elevates him and the winning car to give the crowd a better view.

One sad note to this victory is that Jim Trueman, Rahal's car owner, dies of cancer just 11 days after the race at the age of 52.

Rick Mears roars out of the pits in the No. 4 Penske-Cosworth (*right*) on his way to a third-place finish. Mears led 78 laps, more than anyone else, but was passed by Bobby Rahal and Kevin Cogan late in the race. Winner Rahal signals he is No. 1 in victory lane (*below right*), a claim he backed up by winning the national championship in 1986. Rahal zoomed into the lead in his March-Cosworth (*opposite bottom*) on the final restart when Cogan was too slow on the draw as the green flag came out. Rahal accepts the keys to the pace car from Speedway photography director Ron McQueeney (*opposite top*). Sadly, car owner Jim Trueman, died of cancer within days after the race at the age of 52.

When Bobby Rahal roared under the checkered flag to win the 1986 Indianapolis 500, he smashed the long-standing average speed record for the race. Rahal's mark of 170.722, eclipsed the record of 162.962 held by the late Mark Donohue since 1972. (As a matter of fact, the first four finishers in the '86 race shattered Donohue's standard.) But this wasn't the only record destroyed by "Rapid Robert" Rahal.

The old all-time record had stood an incredible 29 years, established in 1957 during the so-called "Race of Two Worlds" at Monza, Italy. Won by Jim Rathmann in an A. J. Watson-built roadster, the race was held in a three-heat format pitting American open-wheel racers against the cream of Europe's Formula 1 crop. The combined time stood as a world mark for 500 miles in an Indy-type car. Rathmann's astonishing average for the distance was 166.73 mph.

RESULTS

NO.	DRIVER	CAR	ENTRANT	ENGINE	CYL	DISP	CHASSIS	COLOR	QUAL SPD	START	FIN	LAPS / SPEED / REASON OUT
3	Bobby Rahal	Budweiser/Truesports	Truesports Company	Cosworth	8	161	'86 March	red	213.550	4	1	200-170.722
7	Kevin Cogan	7-Eleven	Patrick Racing, Inc.	Cosworth	8	161	'86 March	blue, wht, red	211.922	6	2	200-170.698
4	Rick Mears	Pennzoil Z-7 Special	Penske Cars, Ltd.	Cosworth	8	161	'86 March	yellow	216.828	1	3	200-170.691
5	Roberto Guerrero	True Value	Team Cotter Racing	Cosworth	8	161	'86 March	wht, blue, red	211.576	8	4	200-170.551
30	Al Unser, Jr.	Domino's Pizza/Shierson	Douglas Shierson Racing, Inc.	Cosworth	8	161	'86 Lola	red, wht, blue	211.533	9	5	199-flagged
18	Michael Andretti	STP-Lean Machine	Kraco Enterprises, Inc.	Cosworth	8	161	'86 March	yellow, blue	214.522	3	6	199-flagged
20	Emerson Fittipaldi	Marlboro	Patrick Racing, Inc.	Cosworth	8	161	'86 March	white, red	210.237	11	7	199-flagged
21	Johnny Rutherford	Vermont Am./Morales	Alex Morales Co., Inc.	Cosworth	8	161	'86 March	red, white	210.220	12	8	198-flagged
1	Danny Sullivan	Miller American	Penske Cars, Ltd.	Cosworth	8	161	'86 March	red, white	215.382	2	9	197-flagged
12	Randy Lanier	Mola/Franco's	Arciero Racing Teams	Cosworth	8	161	'86 March	red	209.964	13	10	195-flagged
25	Gary Bettenhausen	Vita Fresh-Timex	Leader Cards, Inc.	Cosworth	8	161	'86 March	white	209.756	29	11	193-flagged
8	Geoff Brabham	Valvoline Spirit	Rick Galles-Galles Racing	Cosworth	8	161	'86 Lola	blue, wht, red	207.082	20	12	193-flagged
22	Raul Boesel	Duracell Copper Top	Dick Simon Racing, Inc.	Cosworth	8	161	'86 Lola	blk, copper, red	211.202	22	13	192-flagged
23	Dick Simon	Duracell Copper Top	Dick Simon Racing, Inc.	Cosworth	8	161	'86 Lola	blk, copper, red	204.978	33	14	189-flagged
61	Arie Luyendyk	MCI-Race For Life	Hasselhoff-Groenvelt Racing, Inc.	Cosworth	8	161	'86 Lola	black	207.811	19	15	188-accident T4
15	Pancho Carter	Coors Light Silver Bullet	Rick Galles-Galles Racing	Cosworth	8	161	'86 Lola	blk, silver, red	209.635	14	16	179-wheel bearing
66	Ed Pimm	Skoal-Pace	Mike Curb Motorsports	Cosworth	8	161	'86 March	green	210.874	10	17	168-electrical
55	Josele Garza	Schaefer/Machinist Union	Int. Assoc. Mach. & Aerospace Workers	Cosworth	8	161	'86 March	wht, blue, red	208.939	17	18	167-flagged
9	Roberto Moreno	Valvoline/Five Star	Rick Galles-Galles Racing	Cosworth	8	161	'86 Lola	wht, blue, red, yelo	209.469	32	19	158-stalled
81	Jacques Villeneuve	Living Well	Hemelgarn Racing, Inc.	Cosworth	8	161	'86 March	white, red	209.397	15	20	154-main bearing
59	Chip Ganassi	Bryant/Machinist Union	Int. Assoc. Mach. & Aerospace Workers	Cosworth	8	161	'86 March	wht, blu, red	207.590	25	21	151-engine
11	Al Unser, Sr.	Hertz	Penske Cars, Ltd.	Chevy Indy	8	161	'86 Penske	yellow	212.295	5	22	149-vibration
25	Danny Ongais	GM Goodwrench	Panavision	Buick V-6	6	208	'86 March	black, white	209.158	16	23	136-ignition
14	A. J. Foyt, Jr.	Gilmore-Copenhagen	A. J. Foyt Enterprises	Cosworth	8	161	'86 March	red, blk, gold	213.212	21	24	135-spun in pits
6	Rich Vogler	Byrd's KFC Chicken	Alex Morales Co., Inc.	Cosworth	8	161	'86 March	red, white	209.089	27	25	132-accident T3
84	George Snider	Calumet Farm	A. J. Foyt Enterprises	Cosworth	8	161	'86 March	red, blk, gold	209.025	31	26	110-ignition
95	Johnny Parsons	Pizza Hut	Int. Assoc. Mach. & Aerospace Workers	Cosworth	8	161	'86 March	white	207.894	28	27	100-CV joint
16	Tony Bettenhausen	Stuart-Skillman Olds	Bettenhausen Racing	Cosworth	8	161	'86 March	yellow, white	208.933	18	28	77-valve spring
31	Jim Crawford	Team ASC	ASC Incorporated	Buick V-6	6	208	'86 March	black, red	208.911	26	29	70-head gasket
71	Scott Brayton	Hardee's-Living Well	Hemelgarn Racing, Inc.	Buick V-6	6	208	'86 March	wht, red, blue	208.079	23	30	69-engine
42	Phil Kruger	Squirt-Moran	Leader Cards, Inc.	Cosworth	8	161	'85 March	white	207.948	24	31	67-engine
2	Mario Andretti	Beatrice Lola	Newman-Haas Racing	Cosworth	8	161	'86 Lola	red, blue, wht	212.300	30	32	19-ignition
33	Tom Sneva	Skoal Bandit	Mike Curb Motorsports	Cosworth	8	161	'86 March	green	211.878	7	33	0-DNS-accident T2

1987

71st Race • May 24, 1987

More teams use the Chevrolet-Ilmor V-8 this year, and a car owner involves a Japanese manufacturer in the 500 for the first time.

Team owner Rick Galles takes Honda's Formula 3000 V-8, hires engine builder John Judd to trim it to Indy car specs, and enlists Honda to provide technical support. The result is the Brabham-Honda engine, which drivers Geoff Brabham and rookie Jeff MacPherson qualify.

Team Penske had exclusive use of the Chevy V-8 in 1986, but this year Newman-Haas gets one for Mario Andretti and Patrick Racing gets two for its duo of Kevin Cogan and Emerson Fittipaldi, a two-time Formula 1 champ.

When the green flag falls on race day, however, the roar of 21 Cosworth engines still drowns out the others.

On the chassis front, it is March versus Lola. Twenty-eight starters go with March, which has won the last four races. Two notables who switch to Lola are defending winner Bobby Rahal and four-time winner A. J. Foyt, who shoots for a 30th straight start at the age of 52.

In the never-ending quest to control speeds, USAC fine tunes chassis rules instead of mandating sweeping changes, and the field averages 207 mph, three mph less than last year.

Two-time winner Gordon Johncock returns to action after two years of retirement. Popular driver Danny Ongais moves to the Penske team, putting three-time champ Al Unser, Sr., out of a job. Roberto Guerrero, with top-four finishes in his first three races, works for new management; Vince Granatelli, son of Andy, buys the team from hardware magnate Dan Cotter.

Six rookies make the field and share the grid with nine former winners, the most in any race to date.

PRACTICE AND QUALIFYING

SUNDAY, MAY 3: Pancho Carter survives a wild ride without injury when his March spins in Turn 3, flips as it gets airborne, and lands upside down in Turn 4.

Mario Andretti's Lola-Chevy is fastest for the day at 213.4 mph despite recurring electrical gremlins. Bobby Rahal is second at 212.5 in a Lola-Cosworth, and Michael Andretti reaches 211.7 in a March-Cosworth.

TUESDAY, MAY 5: Mario Andretti makes history at 218.2 ➔

STARTING LINEUP

Average Field Qualifying Speed: 207.194

Numbers in flags indicate finish position

POLE POSITION
Qualifying Speed: 215.390

Rick Mears

Dick Simon

Michael Andretti

Jeff MacPherson

Gary Bettenhausen

Bobby Rahal

Roberto Guerrero

Johnny Rutherford

Rich Vogler

Geoff Brabham

Mario Andretti

A. J. Foyt

Arie Luyendyk

Ludwig Heimrath, Jr.

Scott Brayton

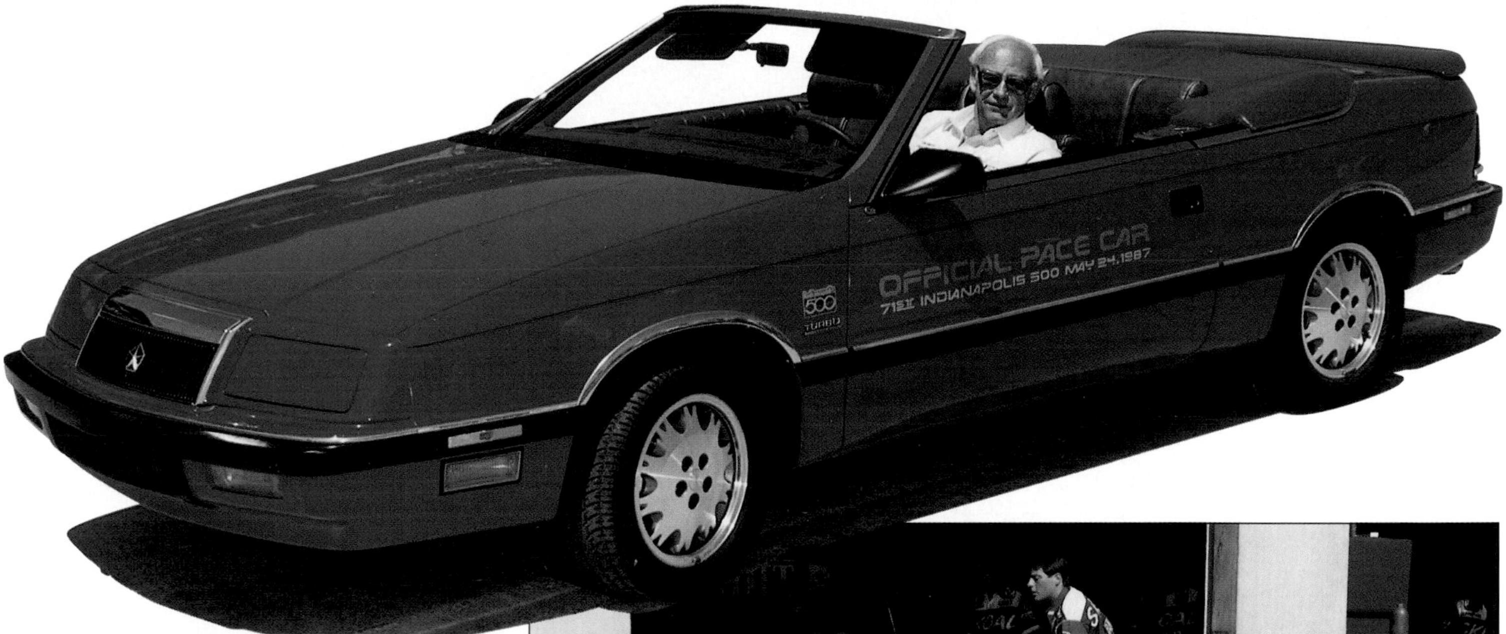

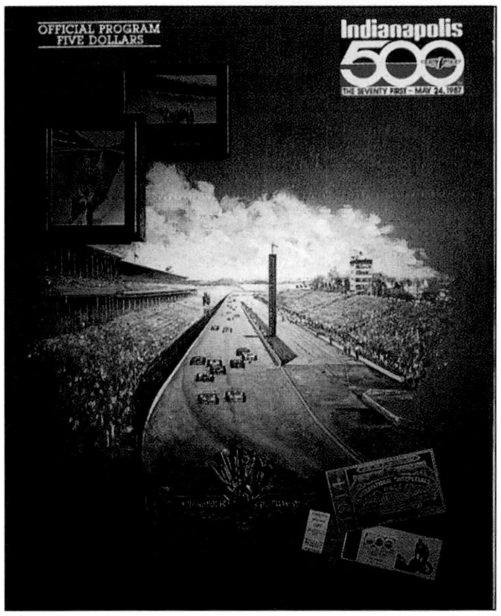

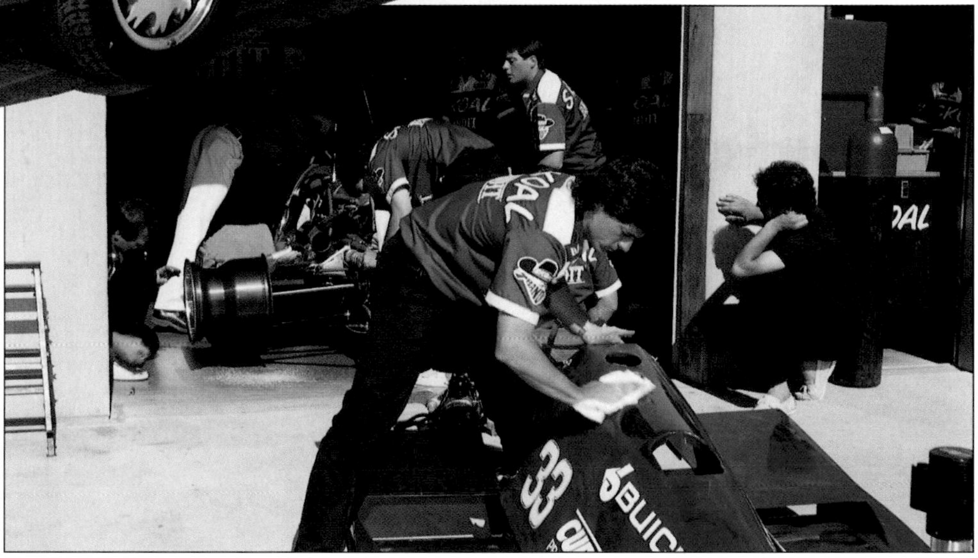

Chrysler's redesigned LeBaron convertible paced this year's field. USAC Chief Steward Tom Binford had his picture taken behind the wheel (*top*), but Carroll Shelby, famed sports car racer and builder turned performance consultant for Chrysler, drove it during the race. Safety lights were integrated into the rear spoiler (*opposite bottom*). Chrysler's corporate cousin, Dodge, provided the official trucks to the Speedway, including some of the new Dakota line (*opposite top*). Tom Sneva's crew prepares the Skoal Bandit (*above*).

Gordon Johncock

Tom Sneva

Kevin Cogan

Tony Bettenhausen

Ed Pimm

Emerson Fittipaldi

Fabrizio Barbazza

Al Unser, Sr.

Randy Lewis

Stan Fox

Pancho Carter

Steve Chassey

Danny Sullivan

Derek Daly

Al Unser, Jr.

Josele Garza

Davy Jones

George Snider

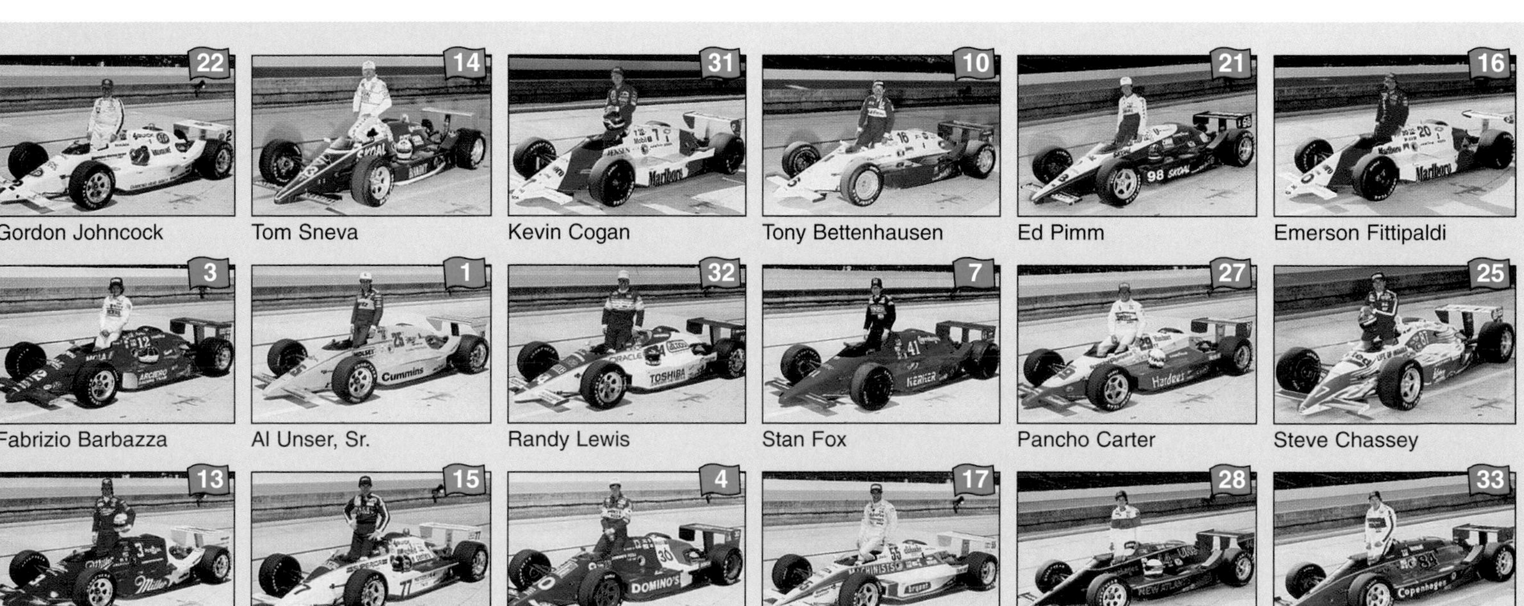

mph, the fastest unofficial lap ever. Rahal is second fastest at 213.

THURSDAY, MAY 7: As the Penske team struggles to get speed from its new chassis, Danny Ongais crashes hard into the Turn 4 wall with his PC-16. Ongais suffers a concussion that may keep him from qualifying. Later in the day, when Rick Mears only wrings 206 mph out of his PC-16, owner Roger Penske decides to switch to last year's March chassis.

SATURDAY, MAY 9: Strong winds and a hot sun make records unlikely on Pole Day. Rick Mears goes out early in a 1986 March-Chevy that arrives at the Speedway the previous afternoon and averages 211.467, five mph slower than his record speed last year.

Bobby Rahal, next in line, ups the ante to 213.316. When other drivers either pass or encounter problems, pole favorite Mario Andretti is the next to qualify. Andretti clicks off four laps at an average 215.39 to win his first pole in 20 years and the first for the Chevy-Ilmor engine. Remarkably, the first three who attempt to qualifiy end up on the front row.

A. J. Foyt makes his 30th race at 210.9, giving him the inside of row two, his best starting position in five years.

Jim Crawford's attempt with a Buick V-6 ends in disaster for the Scot. He loses it in Turn 1 and crashes into the outside wall, breaking both ankles. Gordon Johncock later fills Crawford's seat and qualifies.

SUNDAY, MAY 10: Seven drivers qualify, but 1983 winner Tom Sneva crashes for the second time in three days.

TUESDAY, MAY 12: Speedway medical director Dr. Henry Bock announces that Ongais has not recovered enough from last week's concussion to get back on the track. Roger Penske hires Al Unser, Sr., to replace Ongais.

→

A. J. Foyt (*above*) qualified for a record 30th straight start. He started fourth. Phil Krueger's bid for a second start ended when he spun in Turn 1 and crashed during qualifying (*below*). Gordon Johncock came out of retirement to drive March-Buick for old sponsor STP (*opposite top*). Randy Lewis lets off some steam from a blown radiator during practice (*opposite, bottom left*). Famed mechanic/builder A. J. Watson (in white shirt) calmly stands clear. Rick Mears (*opposite, bottom right*) put the bright yellow Pennzoil colors on the front row for a second straight year.

STP
JOHNCOCK
VALVOLINE
BUICK DEALERS
STP
VALVOLINE
GOODYEAR
GOODYEAR
2
GOODYEAR
GOODYEAR
ORACLE
COMPUTERWORLD
PENNZOIL
GOODYEAR

SATURDAY, MAY 16: Team Penske pulls the PC-16 Danny Sullivan qualified at 205 mph a week earlier, and Sullivan justifies the move by qualifying a 1986 March-Chevy at 210. Unser, Sr., earns his 22nd start with a run over 207 in a year-old March with a Cosworth engine because Penske runs out of Chevy V-8s. Sneva qualifies a Buick V-6 next to Unser.

THURSDAY, MAY 21: Two Carburetion Day wrecks affect race-day expectations. Foyt loses control in Turn 1 and hits the outside wall, inflicting heavy damage to his Lola. Foyt decides to repair it instead of going to a backup car to keep the fourth starting position.

Emerson Fittipaldi slams the Turn 3 wall, destroying his March. The team switches to a backup, and Fittipaldi moves from the inside of row four to 33rd.

THE RACE

Start: George Snider pulls into the pits on the second parade lap with his Chevy V-6 on fire. Next time around, the green comes out, and Mario Andretti holds off Rick Mears going into Turn 1 to take the lead.

As the front of the field heads into Turn 2, Josele Garza spins in Turn 1. Garza just misses Al Unser, Sr., and bangs into teammate Pancho Carter. The yellow comes out, and both Garza and Carter continue on to the pits.

Mario Andretti leads Mears and Rahal, and Foyt falls to seventh on the opening lap.

Lap 6: Andretti takes off when racing resumes and next time around goes 204.885 mph, fastest lead lap of the race.

Lap 28: Roberto Guerrero leads for one lap when Mario Andretti pits during a caution, but Andretti resumes command when Guerrero makes his stop. Michael Andretti slowly comes into the pits, and then his car catches fire, putting him out of the race.

Lap 50: No one can keep up with Mario Andretti, who 

When Danny Ongais crashed his Roger Penske entry, suffering injuries that would keep him out of the race, "The Captain" needed a new "shoe." Al Unser, Sr., who had arrived at the Speedway without a ride, was signed to drive a year-old backup car.

This particular March 86C-22-Cosworth had been making the rounds of car shows and hotel lobbies. When the crew went to pick it up, the racer was sitting on a stage-type platform. Before the men realized what was happening, the car got away from them and was headed for a long drop off the stage. Stopping it at the very last moment, the frantic mechanics could see their association with Team Penske flashing before their eyes. Since it was only a few days until to the last qualifying sessions, any damage could have precluded the racer from making the starting field.

Improbable as it sounds, the "trailer queen" went on to make Indy history. After Unser wheeled the Cummins Holset Turbos Special to victory, it went to Cummins Diesel headquarters in Columbus, Indiana, for "Cummins/Al Unser Day" festivities. In fact, it went back on display.

Opposite page: Mario Andretti lauds his crew, winners of the pre-race pit-stop competition (top left). Roger Penske and Chrysler boss Lee Iacocca meet before the race (top right). When Danny Ongais was hurt in a crash, Penske needed a new second car and a new driver. A show-circuit racer (bottom) and Al Unser, Sr., fit the bill. *This page:* A frequent visitor to the Speedway but never a competitor there, stock-car racing's "King Richard" Petty chats with Bobby Rahal (above). Paul Newman (below) attracts a crowd, though not just because he's a co-owner of Andretti's car. The pace car leads the tightly bunched field on a parade lap (right).

leads Guerrero by nearly 15 seconds. Arie Luyendyk is third and Danny Sullivan fourth.

Lap 70: Giving up the lead only when he makes routine stops, Andretti cruises in front. Only Guerrero and Sullivan are still on the same lap.

Meanwhile, defending winner Rahal's day ends with unresolved electrical problems, and Mears soon suffers a similar fate.

Lap 131: Tony Bettenhausen loses a wheel in Turn 3, and Guerrero hits it head-on at full speed, knocking the nose cone off his March. The loose wheel flies over the safety fence and strikes a spectator in the top row of the stands. He is the first spectator to die at the Speedway since 1960.

Guerrero loses a lap when he pits for a new nose cone but retains second place. Al Unser, Sr., is third and Sullivan fourth, both also a lap down.

Lap 151: Andretti, who leads 143 of the first 150 laps, pits under yellow without giving up first place. Al Unser, Sr., beats Guerrero out of the pits to take second, with both still a lap in arrears.

Lap 173: Third-place Unser makes what should be his final stop under green. Andretti still leads. Guerrero is right behind him, though still one lap down.

Lap 177: The crowd erupts in disbelief as Andretti slows on the front straight and pulls to the inside, permitting Guerrero to roar by, back onto the lead lap. Andretti rolls slowly around the oval and comes into the pits with electrical problems as Guerrero zooms into the lead.

Unser is second, but in danger of being lapped by the charging Guerrero, who has yet to make his last fuel stop.

Lap 182: Guerrero comes in for a splash of fuel to finish the race and stalls as he tries to leave. His crew push-starts him, but, with the huge crowd on its feet, he stalls a second time as Unser sweeps by to grab the lead.

Guerrero finally gets going, but before he can get up to speed, Unser passes him again to put the Colombian a lap down.

Lap 190: Guerrero passes Unser to get his lap back, and a lap later the yellow flag comes out when Andretti stalls on the course.

Finish: When racing resumes with four laps to go, there are six cars between Guerrero and Unser. Guerrero gets by four but runs out of laps and finishes 4.5 seconds behind Unser, who joins Foyt as a four-time winner.

The circumstances leading to Unser's win are amazing. He gets the ride after the first weekend of qualifying because of Ongais's injury. The car is one of last year's models (it was on display at a Pennsylvania hotel before being recalled to active duty), and it uses a Cosworth engine, rather than the Chevy V-8 Penske spearheads.

At 47, Unser is the oldest winning driver. He leads just 18 laps to give him a total of 613 lead laps, breaking Ralph DePalma's record of 612 set in 1921. Unser's 20th starting position is the furthest back for a winner since Rutherford came from 25th in 1974.

For Andretti, it is another heartbreak to finish ninth after leading 170 laps. For Guerrero, it is also a heartbreak to see victory slip away so close to the finish, though he will have more chances to win than the older Andretti.

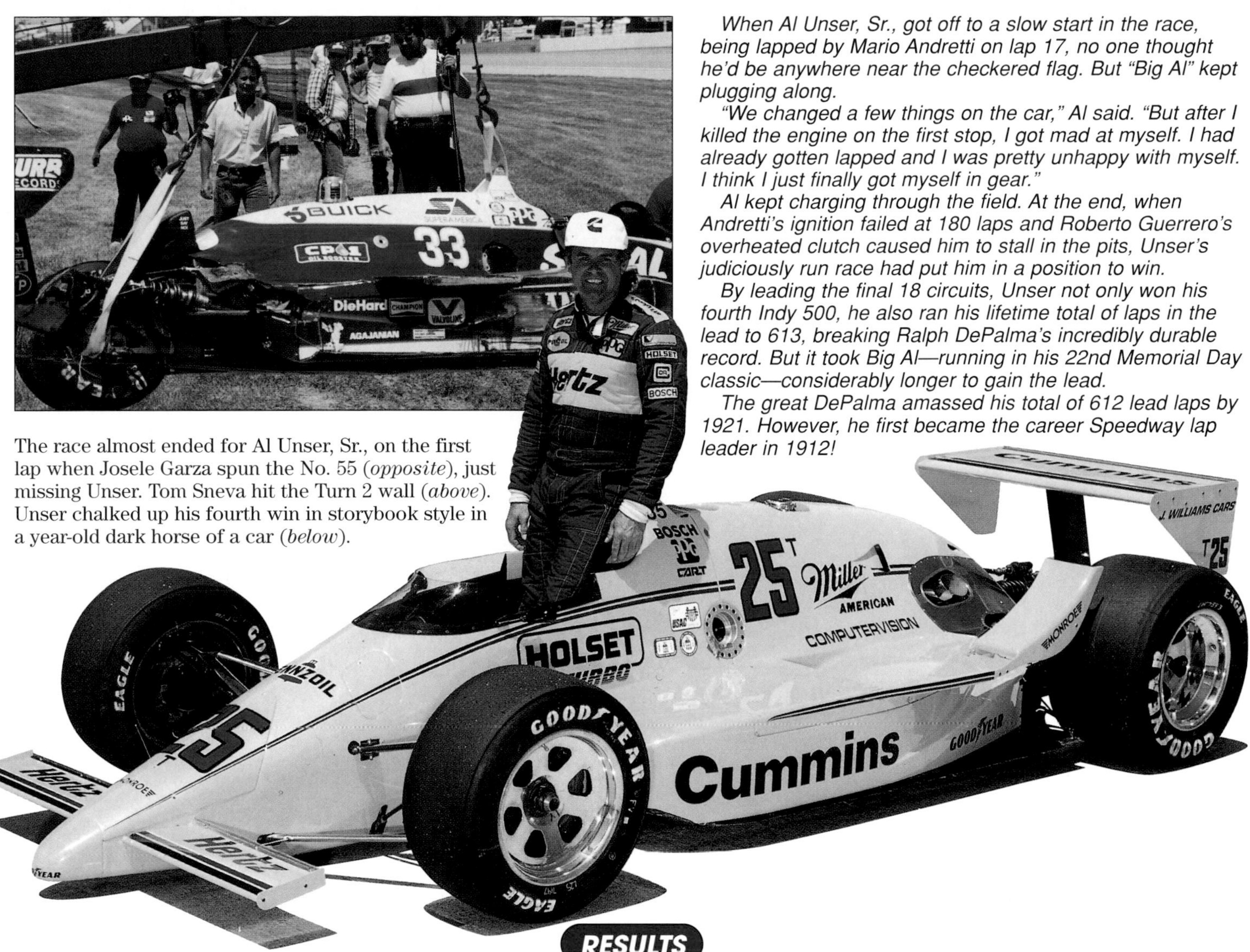

When Al Unser, Sr., got off to a slow start in the race, being lapped by Mario Andretti on lap 17, no one thought he'd be anywhere near the checkered flag. But "Big Al" kept plugging along.

"We changed a few things on the car," Al said. "But after I killed the engine on the first stop, I got mad at myself. I had already gotten lapped and I was pretty unhappy with myself. I think I just finally got myself in gear."

Al kept charging through the field. At the end, when Andretti's ignition failed at 180 laps and Roberto Guerrero's overheated clutch caused him to stall in the pits, Unser's judiciously run race had put him in a position to win.

By leading the final 18 circuits, Unser not only won his fourth Indy 500, he also ran his lifetime total of laps in the lead to 613, breaking Ralph DePalma's incredibly durable record. But it took Big Al—running in his 22nd Memorial Day classic—considerably longer to gain the lead.

The great DePalma amassed his total of 612 lead laps by 1921. However, he first became the career Speedway lap leader in 1912!

The race almost ended for Al Unser, Sr., on the first lap when Josele Garza spun the No. 55 (*opposite*), just missing Unser. Tom Sneva hit the Turn 2 wall (*above*). Unser chalked up his fourth win in storybook style in a year-old dark horse of a car (*below*).

RESULTS

NO.	DRIVER	CAR	ENTRANT	ENGINE	CYL	DISP	CHASSIS	COLOR	QUAL SPD	START	FIN	LAPS / SPEED / REASON OUT
25	Al Unser, Sr.	Cummins-Holset Turbos	Penske Racing, Inc.	Cosworth	8	160	'87 March	yelo, blue, blk	207.423	20	1	200-162.175
4	Roberto Guerrero	True Value/STP	Vince Granatelli Racing	Cosworth	8	161	'87 March	red	210.680	5	2	200-162.109
12	Fabrizio Barbazza	Arciero Winery	Arciero Racing Teams	Cosworth	8	160	'87 March	red	208.038	17	3	198-flagged
30	Al Unser, Jr.	Domino's Pizza	Shierson Racing	Cosworth	8	161	'87 March	red, wht, blue	206.752	22	4	196-flagged
56	Gary Bettenhausen	Genesee Beer Wagon	Brothers Racing	Cosworth	8	158	'86 March	red	204.504	15	5	195-flagged
22	Dick Simon	Soundesign Stereo	Dick Simon Racing	Cosworth	8	160	'87 Lola	blue, wht, red	209.960	6	6	193-flagged
41	Stan Fox	Kerker Exhaust/Skoal	A. J. Foyt Enterprises	Cosworth	8	160	'86 March	red	204.518	26	7	192-flagged
11	Jeff MacPherson	Team MacPherson	Galles Racing	Judd-Honda	8	161	'87 March	blue, wht, yelo	205.688	12	8	182-flagged
5	Mario Andretti	Hanna Auto Wash	Newman-Haas Racing	Ilmor Chevy	8	161	'87 Lola	red, yellow	215.390	1	9	180-ignition
16	Tony Bettenhausen	Nationwise Auto Parts/Payless	Bettenhausen Racing	Cosworth	8	160	'86 March	red, white	203.892	27	10	171-engine
21	Johnny Rutherford	Vermont American	Alex Morales, Co., Inc.	Cosworth	8	161	'87 March	red, white	208.296	8	11	171-flagged
91	Scott Brayton	Amway/Autostyle/Livingwell	Hemelgarn Racing, Inc.	Cosworth	8	161	'87 March	blue, wht, red	205.647	13	12	167-engine
3	Danny Sullivan	Miller American	Penske Racing, Inc.	Ilmor Chevy	8	161	'86 March	red, white	210.271	16	13	160-engine
33	Tom Sneva	Skoal Bandit	Mike Curb	Buick V-6	6	208	'87 March	green, white	207.254	21	14	143-accident T2
77	Derek Daly	Scheid Tire/Superior/Metro Link	B.C. Pace Racing	Buick V-6	6	208	'87 March	wht, blue, red	207.522	19	15	133-engine
20	Emerson Fittipaldi	Marlboro	Patrick Racing, Inc.	Ilmor Chevy	8	161	'87 March	white, red	205.584	33	16	131-engine
55	Josele Garza	Bryant/Schaefer/Mach. Union	Schaefer/Mach. Union Racing Team	Cosworth	8	160	'87 March	wht, blue, red	205.692	25	17	129-flagged
71	Arie Luyendyk	Living Well/Provimi/WTTV	Hemelgarn Racing, Inc.	Cosworth	8	159	'87 March	black, white	208.337	7	18	125-flagged
19	A. J. Foyt, Jr.	Copenhagen-Gilmore	A. J. Foyt Enterprises	Cosworth	8	159	'87 Lola	blk, red, gold	210.935	4	19	117-oil seal
81	Rich Vogler	Byrd's KFL/Living Well/VALPAK	Hemelgarn/Byrd Racing	Buick V-6	6	208	'87 March	red, white	205.887	11	20	109-rocker arm
98	Ed Pimm	Skoal Classic	Mike Curb	Cosworth	8	160	'86 March	blue, red, wht	203.284	30	21	109-turbo
2	Gordon Johncock	STP Oil	American Racing Series	Buick V-6	6	208	'86 March	blue, red, wht	207.990	18	22	76-valve
8	Rick Mears	Pennzoil Z-7	Penske Racing, Inc.	Ilmor Chevy	8	161	'86 March	yelo, red, blk	211.467	3	23	75-coil wire
15	Geoff Brabham	Team Valvoline	Galles Racing	Judd-Honda	8	161	'87 March	blue, wht, red	205.503	14	24	71-oil pressure
87	Steve Chassey	United Oil/Life of Ind.	Linda Laughrey	Cosworth	8	160	'87 March	blue, wht, red	202.488	32	25	68-engine
1	Bobby Rahal	Budweiser	Truesports Company	Cosworth	8	160	'87 Lola	red	213.316	2	26	57-ignition
29	Pancho Carter	Hardee's	Int. Assoc. Mach. & Aerospace Workers	Cosworth	8	160	'87 March	red, wht, orng	205.154	29	27	45-valve
44	Davy Jones	Skoal/Gilmore/UNO	A. J. Foyt Enterprises	Cosworth	8	160	'86 March	blk, wht, gold	208.117	28	28	34-engine
18	Michael Andretti	Kraco/STP	Kraco Enterprises	Cosworth	8	160	'87 March	yellow, blue	206.129	9	29	28-CV joint
23	Ludwig Heimrath, Jr.	MacKenzie/Horton	Dick Simon Racing	Cosworth	8	161	'87 Lola	blue, silver	207.591	10	30	25-spin
7	Kevin Cogan	Marlboro	Patrick Racing, Inc.	Ilmor Chevy	8	161	'87 March	white, red	205.999	24	31	21-oil pump
24	Randy Lewis	Toshiba-Altos	Leader Cards, Inc.	Cosworth	8	160	'87 March	white, blue	206.209	23	32	8-gearbox
84	George Snider	Calumet Farm-Copenhagen	A. J. Foyt Enterprises	Chevy V-6	6	207	'86 March	red, blue	203.192	31	33	0-fuel leak

1988

72nd Race • May 29, 1988

USAC reduces turbocharger boost by two inches, and it is now 45 inches for racing engines and 55 for stock blocks. In another shot at promoting naturally aspirated production-based engines, USAC raises the displacement limit from 355 cubic inches to 390.

Owner-driver Dale Coyne is the only one who takes the bait on naturally aspirated stock blocks, and he fails to qualify a 390-cubic-inch Chevy.

Porsche, a company that built its reputation in racing, comes to the Speedway for the first time with a new 161-cubic-inch turbocharged V-8 for Teo Fabi, who won the pole five years earlier as a rookie.

Two former winners—Bobby Rahal and Tom Sneva—switch to the Honda-based V-8, now called the Judd after engine builder John Judd. The Chevrolet-Ilmor V-8, Cosworth V-8, and Buick V-6 return. A turbocharged Chevy V-6 stock block that A. J. Foyt enters gives the starting field six different engines, the most variety in 20 years.

Lola is now the chassis of choice, with 18 starters choosing this British brand. March has 12 cars in the field, and the three-car Penske team, which won with a March last year, uses its own PC-17.

Five rookies make the show, and there are some familiar names among the newcomers: John Andretti, Mario's nephew and Michael's cousin; and Bill Vukovich III, son of Bill, Jr., and grandson of the 1953-54 winner.

The purse, which was $2.8 million just four years ago, escalates to $5 million for 1988.

PRACTICE AND QUALIFYING

TUESDAY, MAY 10: Despite this year's lower turbo boost, former winners Rick Mears and Mario Andretti shatter the unofficial speed record today. Andretti just misses 220 mph with a speed of 219.995, and Mears does a late-afternoon lap of 220.048. Track officials clock Andretti at 232 on the straightaways. Both drivers use the Chevy-Ilmor V-8.

WEDNESDAY, MAY 12: The Rick and Mario duel continues, and Andretti's Lola zips around the Brickyard during "happy hour" in just 40.62 seconds, 221.565 mph. Mears is close behind at 220.967 in his Penske.

FRIDAY, MAY 12: On the last day before the run for the pole, the battle between Mears and Andretti ends in a draw. Both run laps of 221.456 mph, though Andretti does it in cool conditions and Mears posts his in hot sun. →

STARTING LINEUP

Average Field Qualifying Speed: 210.188

Numbers in flags indicate finish position

POLE POSITION
Qualifying Speed: 219.198

Al Unser, Sr.

Arie Luyendyk

Derek Daly

Roberto Guerrero

Phil Krueger

Danny Sullivan

Al Unser, Jr.

Emerson Fittipaldi

Randy Lewis

Tom Sneva

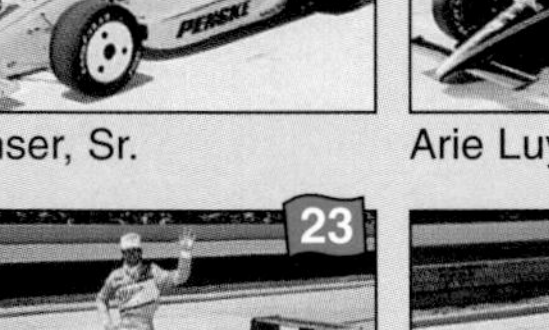

Rick Mears

Mario Andretti

Scott Brayton

Michael Andretti

Kevin Cogan

The Oldsmobile Cutlass Supreme coupe was reconfigured into a convertible to pace the 1988 Indy 500 field (*opposite*). General Motors's 138-cubic-inch "Quad-4" engine (*left*), a four-cylinder with dual-overhead camshafts, was turbocharged, intercooled, and fitted with custom heads, pistons, and cams to produce 250 horsepower. Retired Air Force General Chuck Yeager (*below*) was the driver for the second time.

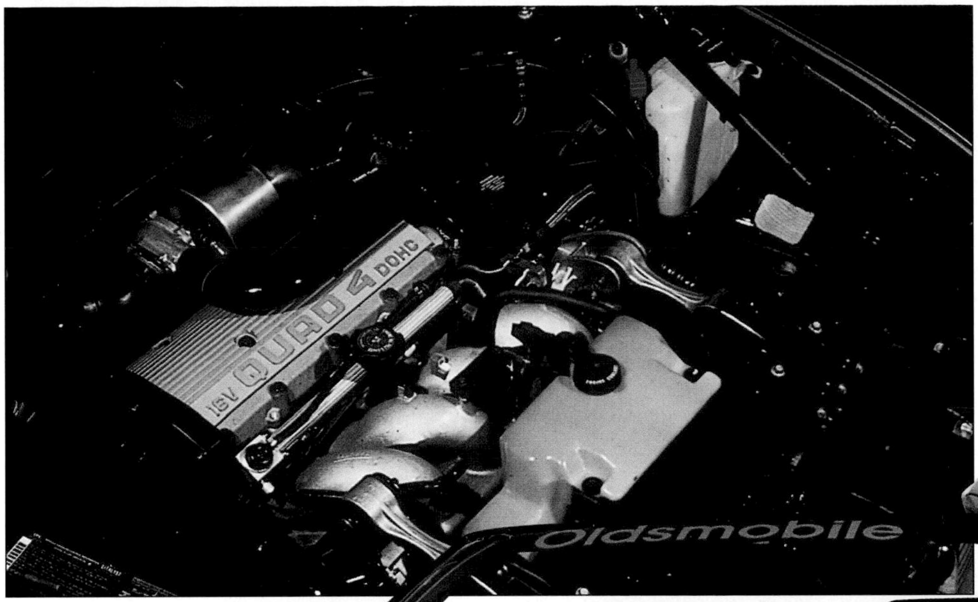

Jim Crawford · Dominic Dobson · Tony Bettenhausen · John Andretti · Johnny Rutherford · Howdy Holmes

Teo Fabi · Raul Boesel · Billy Vukovich III · Steve Chassey · Stan Fox · Rich Vogler

Dick Simon · Bobby Rahal · A. J. Foyt · Tero Palmroth · Rocky Moran · Ludwig Heimrath, Jr.

SATURDAY, MAY 13: On a hot, sunny Pole Day, Mario Andretti is the first to qualify, and a crowd of 200,000 buzzes with anticipation as he takes the green flag. Andretti's first lap is a disappointing 217 mph, and his next three are slower, averaging just 214.692. Andretti blames a patch of oil-drying powder in Turn 4 for slowing him down.

Al Unser, Sr., is the first of the Penske drivers to qualify, and he knocks Andretti off the pole at 215.27. Teammate Danny Sullivan is even faster, averaging 216.214 while setting a single-lap record of 217.7.

Mears goes out half an hour later and shatters the single-lap record the first time around at 220.453. The next three laps are slower, but Mears averages a record 219.198 to capture his fourth pole, tying A. J. Foyt and Rex Mays in that department.

Team Penske occupies the entire front row, and all three cars qualify with unique solid wheels instead of the usual spoke design. Andretti's speed is good enough for the inside of row two, and Al Unser, Jr., is next door, giving Chevy the first five spots. Arie Luyendyk's Cosworth is sixth fastest. →

To say Roger Penske's team dominated the month of May 1988 is one of the biggest understatements in Indianapolis 500 history.

First, Penske drivers Rick Mears, Danny Sullivan, and Al Unser, Sr., took the front row starting positions. This marked the first time teammates had filled the front row.

Second, among them, Team Penske's three chargers led all but eight laps of the race. (The remainder belonged to Jim Crawford in a Lola-Buick.) It was the first time since 1981, when Pat Patrick's fleet consisted of Mario Andretti, Gordon Johncock, and Gordon Smiley, that three teammates led the same race.

Bobby Rahal, the '86 winner, and four-time champ Al Unser, Sr., engage in some "bench racing" before the 500 (*top*). Rick Mears was the driver to beat after he won his fourth pole in the No. 5 Penske-Chevy (*above*). Howdy Holmes squeaked into the field as the slowest qualifier (*opposite top*). Goodyear Tire racing director Leo Mehl meets with Chief Steward Tom Binford (*opposite, middle left*); Mehl is in the blue shirt. Gordy Johncock is interviewed by ABC-TV's Jack Arute after getting bumped (*opposite center*). Owen Snyder, chief mechanic for Galles Racing, checks the instruments on Al Unser, Jr.'s, March (*opposite, middle right*). Danny Sullivan, goes one-on-one with Roberto Guerrero's No. 2 car in the annual pit stop competition (*opposite bottom*).

21
"JIFFY"
GOODYEAR
HOLMES
PPG
STARCRAFT

USAC

STP
abc
VALVOLINE
Gordon Johncock
GOODYEAR

footjoy
GALLES

Miller
STP

SUNDAY, MAY 22: On Bump Day, three-time winner Johnny Rutherford qualifies a Lola-Buick for his 24th race. Rich Vogler is the final driver to make the field and displaces two-time 500 champ Gordon Johncock. Average speed for the 33 cars is 210.188 mph, three mph faster than the previous year.

THE RACE

Start: Danny Sullivan noses ahead of Rick Mears at the green flag and slips in front as they dive into Turn 1. As the field roars through Turn 2, Scott Brayton spins and collects Roberto Guerrero, and both crash into the outside wall. When Tony Bettenhausen slows to avoid the accident, he spins into the wall. All three are out of the race.

During the caution period that follows, Stan Fox's Chevy V-6 drops out with a broken halfshaft.

Lap 6: When racing resumes, leader Sullivan and second-place Mears pull away from the pack, while Unsers senior and junior duel for third. Mears soon starts to fall back.

Lap 23: Mears, who has been slow for several laps, drops to seventh as Mario Andretti charges past the Unsers into second. When Mears pits a few laps later, he gets fuel, four new tires on regular wheels instead of the solid type, plus a new wickerbill on the rear wing and a front wing adjustment—in just 18 seconds.

Lap 30: Sullivan pits for the first time, giving the lead to teammate Al Unser, Sr. When Unser stops three laps later, Sullivan goes back in front. Mario Andretti pits with smoke coming off the back of his Lola. He returns one lap later for an extended stop for transmission repairs.

Lap 32: Tom Sneva, in second place after a flurry of pit stops, skids into the outside wall and caroms across the track, where he hits the inside wall and stops at the pit entrance. Sneva is unhurt.

Lap 40: Racing resumes with Sullivan leading Arie Luyendyk by 10 seconds. Unser, Sr., is third and Unser, Jr., is fourth. Mears falls a lap down to eighth.

Lap 58: A. J. Foyt crashes into the outside wall in Turn 2. He escapes injury, but his 31st race is over. On the restart, Luyendyk rear-ends another car and loses time getting repairs in the pits.

Lap 83: Al Unser, Jr., running second to Sullivan, breaks a CV joint exiting the pits and falls out of contention getting a new one. Jim Crawford's Buick V-6 moves into second when Al Unser, Sr., pits for duct tape to secure his front wing and falls to third. Mears is fourth, still a lap down.

Lap 92: As Sullivan laps Michael Andretti, Mears slips by his teammate to get back on the lead lap. The next lap, the yellow flag comes out for debris on the track, allowing Mears to close up behind the leaders.

Lap 94: When Sullivan and Unser pit under yellow, Crawford takes over first and Mears is second. Penske teammates Sullivan and Unser line up third and fourth behind Mears when racing resumes on Lap 96.

Lap 102: Crawford still leads, and Mears is closing in when Sullivan clips the wall in the south short chute twice before →

When the gates open at 5 A.M., the large crowd waiting to enter the track rushes in to select prime parking and picnic spots in the infield (*top*). Team Penske occupied the entire front row (*opposite*), with Rick Mears on the pole, Danny Sullivan in the middle, and Al Unser, Sr., outside. Porsche's first crack at the 500 ended in disappointing fashion when a wheel came off Teo Fabi's Quaker State car, causing him to crash on pit lane (*left*). Emerson Fittipaldi in the No. 20 March-Chevy slips by Bill Vukovich III on his way to second place (*above*). Vukovich wheeled his March-Cosworth into 14th place at the finish and was Rookie of the Year.

he grinds to a stop. The 1985 winner is out after dominating the first half of the race by leading 91 laps.
The top three cars pit under yellow, and Al Unser, Sr., emerges as the leader. Mears is second. Crawford stops a second time to plug a leaky transmission and falls to third, but he stays on the lead lap.

Lap 113: Mears, at one point in danger of falling two laps down, snatches the lead from teammate Unser.

Lap 117: Johnny Rutherford's last race ends in a Turn 1 crash that rips the right side wheels off his car, though the three-time winner is unscathed.

Lap 140: Mario Andretti's car stalls on the track, and the yellow comes out while he gets a tow to the pits. During a round of pit stops by the leaders, Mears winds up a full lap ahead of Unser and Crawford. Emerson Fittipaldi and Michael Andretti are fourth and fifth, also one lap back.

Lap 168: Just after Mears turns the fastest lap of the race, 209.5 mph, rookie Rocky Moran blows an engine on the front straight, bringing out the 12th caution of the day. Fittipaldi and Michael Andretti beat Mears out of the pits to get back on the lead lap.

Mears remains the leader and Crawford moves back into second.

Lap 175: Rich Vogler scrapes the wall between Turns 1 and 2 and continues to the pits as the yellow flag comes out again. Vogler gets fresh tires but as he tries to rejoin the field, his steering breaks and he crashes again in Turn 3, out of the race.

Lap 180: Mears pulls away and builds a 15-second lead while Fittipaldi and Crawford scrap for second place, still on the lead lap.

Lap 195: Crawford gives up third place when he pits for fuel and tires. A balky wheel nut extends his stay and drops him to sixth. Second-place Fittipaldi trails Mears by 20 seconds.

Finish: Michael Andretti, running fourth, causes the 14th caution of the day on Lap 197 when a sidepod flies off his car and lands on the track near the flag stand. The race ends under yellow.

Mears runs a patient race while his crew solves handling problems to claim his third victory and the fourth in the last five years for owner Roger Penske. Team Penske drivers lead all but eight laps to dominate the race and give the Chevy-Ilmor engine its first win, ending a 10-year Cosworth streak.

Fittipaldi is second and Al Unser, Sr., third, also with Chevy V-8s. Michael Andretti's exposed March-Cosworth finishes fourth, and Bobby Rahal is fifth with a Judd V-8. The Buick V-6 leads eight laps at the hands of Crawford, who ends up sixth.

Rookie Rocky Moran leads four-time starter Rich Vogler through a curve (*above*). Raul Boesel gets fresh rubber and fuel for the Domino's Pizza Lola-Cosworth (*above right*). Al Unser, Sr. (*right*), shooting for a record fifth win, led for 12 laps, but fell a lap down to teammate Rick Mears. Unser finished third, the same position in which he'd started. Mears (*opposite top*) fell a lap down early himself and patiently waited for his crew to cure handling problems during pit stops as he battled back to the front (*opposite, bottom left*). The win was Mears's third (*opposite, bottom right*) and car owner Roger Penske's fourth in five years and seventh overall. Mears won $809,853 of the $5 million purse.

RESULTS

NO.	DRIVER	CAR	ENTRANT	ENGINE	CYL	DISP	CHASSIS	COLOR	QUAL SPD	START	FIN	LAPS / SPEED / REASON OUT
5	Rick Mears	Pennzoil Z-7	Penske Racing, Inc.	Chevy Indy	8	161	'88 Penske	yelo, red, blk	219.198	1	1	200-144.809
20	Emerson Fittipaldi	Marlboro	Patrick Racing, Inc.	Chevy Indy	8	191	'88 March	white, red	212.512	8	2	200-144.726
1	Al Unser, Sr.	Hertz	Penske Racing, Inc.	Chevy Indy	8	191	'88 Penske	yelo, blk, blue	215.270	3	3	199-flagged
18	Michael Andretti	Kraco	Kraco Enterprises, Inc.	Cosworth	8	191	'88 March	yelo, blue, red	210.183	10	4	199-flagged
4	Bobby Rahal	Budweiser	Truesports Company	Judd	8	159	'88 Lola	red	208.526	19	5	199-flagged
15	Jim Crawford	Mac Tools	Kenny Bernstein	Buick V-6	6	208	'87 Lola	yelo, wht, red	210.564	18	6	198-flagged
30	Raul Boesel	Domino's Pizza	Douglas Shierson Racing Team	Cosworth	8	161	'88 Lola	red, wht, blue	211.058	20	7	198-flagged
97	Phil Krueger	CNC Systems/Taylor	R. Kent Baker Racing, inc.	Cosworth	8	161	'86 March	pink, wht, blue	208.212	15	8	196-flagged
22	Dick Simon	Uniden/Soundesign	Dick SImon Racing, Inc.	Cosworth	8	161	'88 Lola	blue, wht, red	207.555	16	9	196-flagged
7	Arie Luyendyk	Provimi Veal	Dick Simon Racing, Inc.	Cosworth	8	160	'88 Lola	black, white	213.611	6	10	196-flagged
11	Kevin Cogan	Schaefer/Playboy	Int. Assoc. Mach. & Aerospace Workers	Cosworth	8	161	'86 March	red, wht, blue	209.552	13	11	195-flagged
21	Howdy Holmes	Jiffy Mixes	Alex Morales Company, Inc.	Cosworth	8	160	'88 March	red, blue, wht	206.970	33	12	192-flagged
3	Al Unser, Jr.	Valvoline/Stroh's	Rick Galles Corporation	Chevy Indy	8	161	'88 March	blue, wht, red	214.186	5	13	180-flagged
56	Bill Vukovich III	Genesee Beer/E-Z Wider	Gohr Distributing Company	Cosworth	8	161	'88 March	blue, white	208.545	23	14	179-flagged
24	Randy Lewis	Toshiba/Oracle/Altos/Priam	Leader Cards, Inc.	Cosworth	8	161	'88 Lola	white, red	209.774	11	15	175-flagged
48	Rocky Moran	Skoal/Trench Shoring	A. J. Foyt Enterprises	Cosworth	8	161	'86 March	black, red	207.181	28	16	159-engine
29	Rich Vogler	Byrd's/Pepsi/Bryant	Jonathan Byrd/Mach. Union	Cosworth	8	161	'87 March	red	207.126	32	17	159-accident T3
92	Dominic Dobson	Moore Ind./Columbia Helicopters	Dobson Racing	Cosworth	8	161	'87 Lola	silver, red	210.096	21	18	145-low coolant
23	Tero Palmroth	Bronson/Neste/Editor	Dick Simon Racing Inc.	Cosworth	8	160	'87 Lola	blue, wht, red	208.001	25	19	144-engine
6	Mario Andretti	Amoco Ultimate/Kmart	Newman/Haas Racing	Chevy Indy	8	161	'87 Lola	wht, blk, blue, red	214.692	4	20	118-electrical
98	John Andretti	Skoal	Mike Curb Motorsports, Inc.	Cosworth	8	161	'88 Lola	green, white	207.894	27	21	114-engine
17	Johnny Rutherford	Mac Tools	Kenny Bernstein	Buick V-6	6	208	'87 Lola	yelo, wht, red	208.442	30	22	107-accident T1
9	Danny Sullivan	Miller High Life	Penske Racing, Inc.	Chevy Indy	8	161	'88 Penske	gold, wht, grn	216.214	2	23	101-accident T1
35	Steve Chassey	Trout Mtrsprts/Kasle Recycling	Gary Trout Motorsports	Cosworth	8	161	'87 March	blue, yelo, red	207.951	26	24	73-accident T4
71	Ludwig Heimrath, Jr.	MacKenzie Group	Hemelgarn Racing, Inc.	Cosworth	8	161	'88 Lola	blue, silver	207.215	31	25	59-accident T4
14	A. J. Foyt, Jr.	Copenhagen/Gilmore	A. J. Foyt Enterprises	Cosworth	8	161	'87 Lola	black, red	209.696	22	26	54-accident BS
81	Tom Sneva	Pizza Hut/WRTV-6	Hemelgarn Racing, Inc.	Judd	8	159	'88 Lola	red, blue, wht	208.659	14	27	32-accident T4
8	Teo Fabi	Quaker State/Porsche	Porsche Motorsports NA	Porsche	8	161	'88 March	green, white	207.244	17	28	30-accident pits
10	Derek Daly	Raynor Garage Doors	Raynor Motorsports Group	Cosworth	8	161	'88 Lola	wht, red, blk	212.295	9	29	18-gearbox
84	Stan Fox	Copenhagen/Calumet Farm	A.J. Foyt Enterprises	Chevy V-6	6	207	'86 March	black, red	208.578	29	30	2-half shaft
91	Scott Brayton	Amway Spirit	Hemelgarn Racing, Inc.	Buick V-6	6	208	'88 Lola	blue, wht, pink	212.624	7	31	0-accident T2
2	Roberto Guerrero	STP/Dianetics	Vince Granatelli Racing, Inc.	Cosworth	8	161	'88 Lola	red	209.633	12	32	0-accident T2
16	Tony Bettenhausen	Sony/Scot Lad Foods/Hardee's	Bettenhausen Racing & Assoc., Inc.	Cosworth	8	161	'87 Lola	orange, white	208.342	24	33	0-accident T2

1989

73rd Race • May 28, 1989

The Speedway repaves the entire track for the first time in 12 years, giving drivers a smooth new surface that promises higher speeds. Entries increase to 107 for the 73rd running of the 500, the most in five years.

The once-dominant March chassis accounts for just four of the 33 starters, versus 24 Lolas and five Penskes. More starters use Cosworth engines than any other (14), but there are seven Chevrolet-Ilmor V-8s, six Buick V-6s, five Judd V-8s, and a single Porsche.

Cosworth, shut out of the top three finishers last year, counters with an updated version of its V-8 with a shorter stroke and new valve arrangement for 1986 winner Bobby Rahal and Arie Luyendyk.

Porsche's operation is now in the hands of Derrick Walker, formerly the manager of Team Penske. Walker succeeds Al Holbert, who died in a plane crash the previous fall.

Popular driver Roberto Guerrero misses the race this year after five straight starts because he is under contract to drive a new Alfa Romeo engine, which is not ready for prime time.

Michael Andretti joins the Newman-Haas stable for his sixth 500 to team with papa Mario, creating the first father-son team. The elder Andretti makes his 24th start and 20th since his only win.

PRACTICE AND QUALIFYING

SUNDAY, MAY 7: Snow cut short practice the day before, but today is clear and cool—and hot on the track. Two-time world driving champ Emerson Fittipaldi hits 221.3 mph in a Penske PC-18-Chevy. Michael Andretti comes close at 220.9, and Al Unser, Jr., is third at 219.5.

MONDAY, MAY 8: Rick Mears shows he is a threat to win a record fifth pole by blazing around the Speedway in just 39.87 seconds, good for an unofficial record speed of 225.733 mph. Michael Andretti, Fittipaldi, and Al Unser, Sr., top 224.

THURSDAY, MAY 11: Team Penske driver Danny Sullivan does a full spin and crashes hard in Turn 3 when the engine cover flies off his car. The 1985 winner breaks his right forearm, ending his chance to run for the pole and perhaps knocking him out of the race. →

The 20th anniversary Pontiac Firebird Trans Am was the pace car for 1989 (*opposite page*), and it was powered by General Motors's turbocharged 231-cid V-6—the same engine that was the basis for the stock-block Buick engines that powered six racers in the field. The street version was rated at 250 horsepower. All three pace cars used by the Speedway were selected at random from the 1500-unit production run of the anniversary specials; 65 of them are lined up for a publicity photo (*above*). Only safety modifications were made for duty at the track. Three-time winner Bobby Unser was the driver during the race.

STARTING LINEUP

Average Field Qualifying Speed: 216.588

Numbers in flags indicate finish position

Emerson Fittipaldi

Scott Brayton

Raul Boesel

John Andretti

Arie Luyendyk

Al Unser, Sr.

Mario Andretti

Al Unser, Jr.

Randy Lewis

Gary Bettenhausen

POLE POSITION
Qualifying Speed: 223.885

Rick Mears

Jim Crawford

Bobby Rahal

A. J. Foyt

Teo Fabi

While one seldom sees a brand-new engine design take center stage from established racing power plants, that's exactly what happened with Chevrolet's Chevy Indy V-8. A large share of the powerful turbocharged overhead-camshaft engine's success was due to the prodigious testing efforts of Team Penske.

In 1989, the 500 fell to Emerson Fittipaldi in a Penske PC-18-Chevy Indy. Then the potent engine, built in England by Ilmor Engineering, carried "Emmo" to the season title.

In fact, between 1986 and 1989, the Chevy V-8 powered the winner in 32 of 58 races, which equates to a winning percentage of .552. Even more staggering was its reliability rate of 95 percent during the '89 season. In 93 separate starts in USAC and CART competition, the design suffered only five engine-related failures, an unprecedented measure of excellence.

Ludwig Heimrath, Jr.

Michael Andretti

Derek Daly

Kevin Cogan

Billy Vukovich III

Rich Vogler

Scott Pruett

Bernard Jourdain

Gordon Johncock

Danny Sullivan

Dominic Dobson

Pancho Carter

Tero Palmroth

Didier Theys

Tom Sneva

John Jones

Rocky Moran

Davy Jones

FRIDAY, MAY 12: Mears sets another unofficial record of 226.3 mph, and teammate Al Unser, Sr., nearly matches it at 225.7. Jim Crawford cranks up the Buick V-6 in his 1987 Lola to 226, adding his name to the list of possible pole winners.

SATURDAY, MAY 13: Rain postpones Pole Day.

SUNDAY, MAY 14: Unser, Sr., the first to qualify, breaks Mears's single-lap record by more than three mph with a speed of 223.803 mph and the four-lap record with an average of 223.471.

Michael Andretti qualifies at 220.94, but USAC finds his car is underweight and voids the effort. He gets shuffled back to the line for second-day qualifiers and starts in 21st position. Mario Andretti does 220.486, fast enough for a second-row start.

Mears goes a record 224.254 on his third lap and averages 223.885, also a record. Mears moves teammate Unser off the pole, but Crawford rolls out with a new Buick V-6 in his Lola.

Crawford's run includes a fast lap of 222 and he averages 221.45, third fastest so far. Fittipaldi then knocks Crawford off the front row with a run of 222.3.

Pole Day ends with Mears winning a record fifth pole, and the entire front row has Penske chassis and Chevy-Ilmor power for a second straight year.

THURSDAY, MAY 18: Jim Crawford escapes serious injury when the suspension breaks on his Lola-Buick and slams the Turn 3 wall. His crew says it hopes to fix the badly damaged car so Crawford can start from the second row.

SATURDAY, MAY 20: Danny Sullivan, his right arm in a cast, qualifies at 216 mph to secure a spot in the ninth row.

SUNDAY, MAY 21: Rich Vogler bumps three-time winner Johnny Rutherford. With two minutes left in qualifying, Rutherford makes another attempt in a car A. J. Foyt owns. He roars to a first lap of 217 mph, but the Cosworth engine cooks on the second lap, and Rutherford fails to make the show a 25th time. The average speed for the field climbs 6.4 mph to 216.588.

THE RACE

Start: Emerson Fittipaldi, starting from the outside of row one, wins the dash to Turn 1 and leads the first lap, with Rick Mears and Al Unser, Sr., in pursuit.

Lap 2: Coming on to the front straight, Kevin Cogan suddenly spins left and crashes into the inside retaining wall. Parts fly off his car as it hits a new steel barrier on the inside of the →

Mario Andretti's Newman-Haas Lola is weighed by USAC (*opposite*) to make sure it is legal. Roger Penske confers with Rick Mears (*top left*). Mears won the pole for a record fifth time and was favored to win a fourth race. *Left:* Mears's father, Bill, talks with A. J. Foyt, left, and Al Unser, Sr., right. Arie Luyendyk qualified for his fifth start in Dick Simon's No. 9 Lola (*top right*). Mears, acknowledging applause at the annual pre-race drivers' meeting (*second from top, right*), is ringed by a 500 Who's-Who: clockwise from the upper left are Al Unser, Sr., Mario Andretti, Al Unser, Jr., A. J. Foyt, Bobby Rahal, and Jim Crawford. With the field set, Raul Boesel's name is painted onto the pit wall (*above*).

pit wall, and the cockpit tub slides to a stop in the pits. Cogan miraculously crawls out of the wreckage on his own and walks away without assistance.

Lap 15: Fittipaldi leads when racing resumes, and Mario Andretti zips by Mears for second.

Lap 25: Fittipaldi leads Andretti by three seconds as Al Unser, Jr., gets by Mears for third place. Two laps later, Al Unser, Sr., passes Mears for fourth as the defending winner struggles.

Lap 34: Fittipaldi surrenders the lead to Andretti when he pits and regains it when other front runners make their stops. Mario Andretti runs second, Michael Andretti is third, and Mears moves back up to fourth.

Lap 41: Danny Sullivan drops out with clutch problems.

Lap 68: Al Unser, Sr., who has been running in the top five, rolls slowly into the pits. A broken clutch claims a second Team Penske car.
Fittipaldi leads Michael Andretti, Unser, Jr., Mears, and Mario Andretti, the only cars still on the lead lap.

Lap 85: Fittipaldi runs the fastest race lap ever, 222.469 mph, as he extends his lead over Michael Andretti and Unser. Mears still runs fourth and Mario Andretti is fifth.

Lap 88: When Fittipaldi pits, Michael Andretti moves into the lead—the first time a father and son lead the same race. Mario Andretti, meanwhile, lingers nearly four minutes in the pits with electrical problems, dropping out of contention.

Lap 99: When Michael Andretti makes his stop, Fittipaldi goes back in front and then puts Unser, Jr., a lap down. Halfway home, Fittipaldi leads Andretti, the only other car on the same lap, by 21 seconds. Unser is third and Mears is fourth, both a lap down.

Lap 112: Fittipaldi makes a routine stop for fuel and tires, and Michael Andretti inherits first place. →

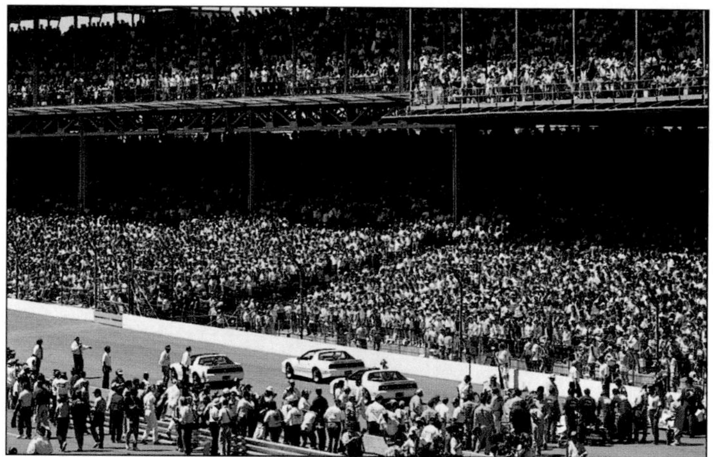

While the Speedway usually treated former 500 winner Danny Sullivan with kindness, the stubborn old track was anything but cordial to him in '89.

Sullivan had been turning some sensational laps during practice when his racer suddenly jumped into the outside wall. Danny received a broken right arm in the crash, and he seemed a doubtful starter for the 73rd Indy 500.

But after undergoing surgery to place a steel plate and screws in his arm, Sullivan qualified on the second weekend at 216.027. The run earned him the 26th starting spot on the grid.

Even with Danny's determination, 500 miles is a long way. Geoff Brabham would be waiting in the wings should Sullivan need relief. But the tough veteran shrugged off the idea.

"If we were running anywhere else, I'd be more concerned," Danny said. "But Indy is one of the smoothest places we race."

All the speculation went for naught, though, when Sullivan's clutch failed on lap 41, stopping his gallant run in 28th place.

The front row (*top*) had two former winners and one soon-to-be. Two-time Formula 1 champ Emerson Fittipaldi of Brazil was on the outside, Al Unser, Sr., held down the middle, and Rick Mears sat on the pole. Despite their similar livery, Fittipaldi and Unser weren't teammates. Fittipaldi—a 500 regular since 1984—drove for Patrick Racing, while Unser was Mears's mate in the Penske stable. Still, all three cars used Penske chassis with Chevrolet-Ilmor V-8s for power. The crowd and race crews stand eager for the command to start engines (*opposite middle*). With most of the 33 starters up and running, the pace car takes them around for an orderly start (*opposite bottom*). One racer, seen to the right of the scoring pylon, has already pitted with a problem. An aerial view (*left*) shows the immensity of the 2.5-mile oval and the excellent vantage point enjoyed by the Goodyear Blimp. By the time this picture of the teeming race course was taken, the Indianapolis 500 was already well-known as the largest one-day, single-site sporting event in the world.

One lap later, Mears pulls into the pits with smoke trailing his blown Chevy engine. After leading 192 laps the previous year, the three Team Penske drivers are out of the race without leading a lap.

Lap 124: Andretti stops for fuel and tires, and Fittipaldi is back in command. Andretti falls a lap down, joining third-place Unser.

Lap 139: The yellow flag comes out for Arie Luyendyk's blown engine, and when Fittipaldi pits, Andretti and Unser move back onto the lead lap.

Lap 154: Michael Andretti powers past Fittipaldi on the backstretch for the lead, the first time someone passes him on the track. Unser, Jr., follows nearly 15 seconds behind in third.

Lap 162: As Andretti passes the start-finish line in front of the main grandstands, his Chevy engine blows in a cloud of smoke. Andretti's crowd-pleasing run ends after he leads a total of 35 laps.

Lap 167: When the green flag returns, Fittipaldi pulls away to a 15-second lead over Unser. Third-place Raul Boesel is behind by five laps.

Lap 181: Tero Palmroth loses a wheel in Turn 4 but keeps his car off the wall and limps to the pits, bringing out the yellow flag.
Fittipaldi ducks into the pits for a splash of fuel, but Unser stays on the track, hoping he has enough fuel to make it to the finish. Though Fiitipaldi holds onto the lead, Unser lines up right behind him as they slowly circle the track under yellow.

Lap 186: Fittipaldi gets through traffic quicker than Unser on the restart and holds a 1.8-second lead.

Lap 192: Unser turning laps over 220 mph, closes to within half a second.

Lap 195: Unser is breathing down Fittipaldi's neck as they slip underneath Mario Andretti in Turn 1. Unser finally catches and passes Fittipaldi on the backstretch.

Finish: Unser leads by less than car length on Lap 199 as they head into Turn 1, but Fittipaldi catches up on the back straight.

Fittipaldi goes low into Turn 3 and almost pulls even with Unser when he starts to slide up the track. A small puff of smoke signals contact between the two speeding cars, and Unser spins 180 degrees and skids backwards into the outside wall, ending a thrilling duel that almost goes to the wire.

The pace car comes out and escorts Fittipaldi to the finish, the second race in a row that ends under yellow. Unser isn't hurt, and he gives Fittipaldi a thumbs-up salute as the Brazilian cruises by to victory.

Fittipaldi leads 158 laps in a commanding performance that earns him the first $1 million payday in Speedway history. He is the first foreigner to win since Graham Hill in 1966, and he gives owner Pat Patrick his first victory since 1982.

Unser's day ends after 198 laps (five as the leader), yet he still finishes second. Third-place goes to Brazilian Raul Boesel, who leads one lap and finishes six laps down with a Judd-powered Lola. Seven laps down are Mario Andretti in fourth and A. J. Foyt in fifth, his best finish since second place in 1979. Boesel's lead lap is the only one the Chevy-Ilmor engine does not lead.

Al Unser, Jr. (*top*), almost became the third member of his family to win the 500. He finished second despite crashing in Turn 3 on the 199th lap. The ninth row of John Jones, Danny Sullivan, and Kevin Cogan is ready to rumble (*above*). Cogan walked away from a fearsome crash very early in the race. Arie Luyendyk lasted 123 laps until his engine blew (*below*). John Andretti gets sideways in the pits in the No. 70 Lola-Buick (*opposite top*). He later retired with engine problems. Winner Emerson Fittipaldi (*opposite bottom*) survived a literal wheel-to-wheel duel with young Unser. He was the first to collect $1 million in prize money.

RESULTS

NO.	DRIVER	CAR	ENTRANT	ENGINE	CYL	DISP	CHASSIS	COLOR	QUAL SPD	START	FIN	LAPS / SPEED / REASON OUT
20	Emerson Fittipaldi	Marlboro	Patrick Racing, Inc.	Chevy Indy	8	160	'89 Penske	white, red	222.329	3	1	200-167.581
2	Al Unser, Jr.	Valvoline-Stroh's	Galles Racing Corp.	Chevy Indy	8	161	'89 Lola	blue, red, wht	218.642	8	2	198-accident T3
30	Raul Boesel	Domino's Pizza	Douglas Shierson Racing, Inc.	Judd	8	159	'89 Lola	red, wht, blue	218.228	9	3	194-flagged
5	Mario Andretti	Kmart/Havoline	Newman-Haas Racing	Chevy Indy	8	161	'89 Lola	blk, wht, red	220.486	5	4	193-flagged
14	A. J. Foyt, Jr.	Copenhagen-Gilmore	A. J. Foyt Enterprises, Inc.	Cosworth	8	161	'89 Lola	black, red	217.136	10	5	193-flagged
22	Scott Brayton	Amway-Speedway	Dick Simon Racing, Inc.	Buick V-6	6	208	'89 Lola	blue, wht, pink	220.459	6	6	193-flagged
50	Davy Jones	Euromotorsport/UNO	A. Ferrari/Euromotorsport Racing	Cosworth	8	160	'88 Lola	white, red	214.279	31	7	192-flagged
29	Rich Vogler	Byrd's Cafeteria-Bryant	Jonathan Byrd/Mach. Union	Cosworth	8	160	'88 March	red, white	213.239	33	8	192-flagged
69	Bernard Jourdain	Corona-Monarch	Andale Racing	Cosworth	8	160	'89 Lola	blue, red, wht	213.105	20	9	191-flagged
3	Scott Pruett	Budweiser	Truesports Company	Judd	8	158	'89 Lola	red	213.955	17	10	190-flagged
65	John Jones	Labatt's	Protofab Racing Partners	Cosworth	8	161	'89 Lola	blue, wht, gold	214.028	25	11	189-flagged
81	Bill Vukovich III	Consani-Sierra	Hemelgarn/Consani Racing	Judd	8	159	'88 Lola	red, white	216.698	30	12	186-flagged
71	Ludwig Heimrath, Jr.	MacKenzie	Hemelgarn Racing	Judd	8	159	'88 Lola	blue, silver	213.878	18	13	185-flagged
33	Rocky Moran	Skoal Bandit	A. J. Foyt Enterprises, Inc.	Cosworth	8	161	'86 March	black, red	214.212	28	14	181-flagged
10	Derek Daly	Raynor Garage Doors	Raynor Motorsports Group	Judd	8	160	'89 Lola	silver, red	214.237	24	15	167-flagged
56	Tero Palmroth	Neste-Rotator-Nanso	Gohr Distributing, Co., Inc.	Cosworth	8	161	'88 Lola	blue, yelo, wht	214.203	16	16	165-spindle
6	Michael Andretti	Kmart/Havoline	Newman-Haas Racing	Chevy Indy	8	161	'89 Lola	black, wht, red	218.774	21	17	163-engine
86	Dominic Dobson	Texaco Havoline Star	Bayside Mtr Sprts-Bruce Levin	Cosworth	8	161	'88 Lola	blk, wht, red, gld	213.590	29	18	161-flagged
15	Jim Crawford	Mac Tools-Planters	Kenny Bernstein-King Mtrsprts	Buick V-6	6	208	'87 Lola	yelo, wht, red	221.450	4	19	135-drive train
12	Didier Theys	Arciero Wines	Acriero Racing Teams	Cosworth	8	161	'88 Penske	red	213.120	19	20	131-engine
9	Arie Luyendyk	Provimi/Dutch Boy	Dick Simon Racing, Inc.	Cosworth	8	161	'89 Lola	black, gold	214.883	15	21	123-engine
24	Pancho Carter	Hardee's	Leader Cards, Inc.	Cosworth	8	160	'89 Lola	black	214.067	32	22	121-electrical
4	Rick Mears	Pennzoil Z-7	Penske Racing, Inc.	Chevy Indy	8	161	'89 Penske	yelo, red, blk	223.885	1	23	113-engine
25	Al Unser, Sr.	Marlboro	Penske Racing, Inc.	Chevy Indy	8	160	'89 Penske	white, red	223.471	2	24	68-clutch
70	John Andretti	Tuneup Masters	Vince Granatelli Racing, Inc.	Buick V-6	6	208	'88 Lola	red	215.611	12	25	61-engine
18	Bobby Rahal	Kraco Car Stereos	Kraco Enterprises, Inc.	Cosworth	8	161	'89 Lola	yellow, blue	215.611	7	26	58-valve
7	Tom Sneva	STP	Vince Granatelli Racing, Inc.	Buick V-6	6	208	'88 Lola	red	218.396	22	27	55-pit fire
1	Danny Sullivan	Miller High Life	Penske Racing, Inc.	Chevy Indy	8	161	'89 Penske	gold, wht, grn	216.027	26	28	41-rear axle
28	Randy Lewis	Toshiba-Oracle	TEAMCAR International,Inc.	Cosworth	8	160	'89 Lola	white, red	216.494	11	29	24-wheel bearing
8	Teo Fabi	Quaker State/Porsche	Porsche Motorsports	Porsche	8	159	'89 March	green, white	215.564	13	30	23-ignition
91	Gordon Johncock	STP-Pizza Hut	Hemelgarn Racing	Buick V-6	6	208	'88 Lola	yellow	215.072	23	31	19-engine
11	Kevin Cogan	Schaefer-Playboy	Int. Assoc. Mach. & Aerospace Workers	Cosworth	8	161	'88 March	red, wht, blue	214.569	27	32	2-accident FS
99	Gary Bettenhausen	ATEC Environmental	Mann Motorsports	Buick V-6	6	208	'87 Lola	orange, yellow	215.230	14	33	0-valve

1990

74th Race • May 27, 1990

Major changes occur in senior management following the death of longtime Speedway executive Joe Cloutier in late 1989. Tony Hulman George, the 30-year-old grandson of the late Tony Hulman, becomes the new president and CEO. His mother, Mari Hulman George, is now chairman, and Hulman's widow, Mary Fendrich Hulman, becomes chairman emeritus.

A record purse of $6.3 million attracts 97 entries, and new rules reduce the size of ground effects tunnels underneath the cars—the latest stab at slowing them down after 1989's record qualifying speeds.

The skyline at the Speedway changes with construction of 38 new suites behind the pits. The Tower Suites include plush accommodations inside, seats for 80 guests outside, and a great view of action in the pits and on the front straight.

Italian automaker Alfa Romeo returns after a 42-year absence with a new turbocharged V-8 for a two-car team. Four-time winner Al Unser, Sr., and Roberto Guerrero drive the Alfas for Patrick Racing. Defending winner Emerson Fittipaldi replaces Unser on the Penske team. Porsche enters a second car this year for John Andretti, who teams with Teo Fabi.

Another Andretti arrives on the scene. Rookie Jeff, the younger son of Mario, tries to join Dad, brother Michael, and cousin John to form a family quartet. Though Jeff qualifies, he gets bumped on the final day.

PRACTICE AND QUALIFYING

SUNDAY, MAY 6: New Team Penske driver Emerson Fittipaldi guns for two wins in a row with a fast time of 222.6 mph. Arie Luyendyk, driving a Lola-Chevy, is second at 221.1.

MONDAY, MAY 7: Despite the new rules regarding ground effects, speeds are climbing. Rick Mears is quickest at 224.4 mph, and Fittipaldi, Luyendyk, and Mario Andretti go over 222.2.

WEDNESDAY, MAY 9: While the 1990 chassis cope well with the new ground-effects restrictions, the "diffusers" that reduce downforce appear to make older cars a handful. Johnny Rutherford wrecks his 1989 Lola for the second time in three days, the sixth crash involving a pre-1990 car. Rutherford nearly gets airborne when he smacks the Turn 3 wall and ➔

STARTING LINEUP

Average Field Qualifying Speed: 217.437

Numbers in flags indicate finish position

Arie Luyendyk

Mario Andretti

Danny Sullivan

Randy Lewis

Kevin Cogan

Rick Mears

Michael Andretti

A. J. Foyt

Dominic Dobson

Eddie Cheever

POLE POSITION
Qualifying Speed: 225.301

Emerson Fittipaldi

Bobby Rahal

Al Unser, Jr.

John Andretti

Tony Bettenhausen

By qualifying for the 74th running of the Indy 500, A. J. Foyt made the starting field for the 33rd time, just four races short of half the entire number of races held. Since first turning up at the Brickyard in 1958, he had won four times and been in the top 10 on 12 other occasions. While A. J. is seldom happy with finishing anywhere but first, his sixth-place finish in 1990 put a gleam of satisfaction in his eye.

"I had a problem with the car bottoming out the whole race with a full fuel load," the 55-year-old legend explained. "It was especially bad in turns one and three."

"I'm very proud of A. J.," team owner Jim Gilmore said. "We did the very best we could."

But Foyt had already won a victory of sorts. Two days before the race, Rose-Hulman Institute of Technology presented him with an honorary doctorate in engineering.

Chevrolet cooked up a special version of its Beretta for this year's pace car (*opposite page*), a convertible with an integral hoop over the interior that provided the upper mounting points for the front seatbelts and bore a signal light intended to make the car more visible to racers during caution periods. The pace car was supposed to be a preview of a production convertible, but plans for the mass-market version were nixed before the race because prototypes did not meet Chevrolet's rigidity and quality standards. Chevy General Manager Jim Perkins (*top*), who had some racing experience, drove the Beretta on race day. Because the convertible was never offered for sale, Chevrolet instead built 4500 Beretta coupes as pace-car replicas. About 1500 were yellow, like the pace car; the rest were turquoise (*left*).

Gary Bettenhausen

Scott Goodyear

Dean Hall

Stan Fox

Al Unser, Sr.

Rocky Moran

Raul Boesel

Didier Theys

Teo Fabi

Scott Brayton

Jim Crawford

John Paul, Jr.

Tero Palmroth

Geoff Brabham

Pancho Carter

Tom Sneva

Roberto Guerrero

Billy Vukovich III

suffers a concussion and bruised knee.

FRIDAY, MAY 11: Jim Crawford loses control of his 1989 Lola-Buick in Turn 1 and spins backwards into the outside wall. The car becomes airborne and sails down the south short chute about 12 to 15 feet off the ground, doing a half spin before it lands right-side up and slides onto the grass. Somehow, Crawford escapes without major injuries.

Speeds continue to climb on the newer cars. Al Unser, Jr., emerges as a pole contender with a practice lap of 228.5 mph, an unofficial record. Fittipaldi is second quickest at 227.2 and Mears is next at 226.6.

SATURDAY, MAY 12: Rain washes out Pole Day for the second year in a row.

SUNDAY, MAY 13: Rain delays the first qualifying run until 4:34 P.M., and Emerson Fittipaldi makes it worth the wait. Fittipaldi breaks Rick Mears's single-lap mark the first time around at 225 mph and goes faster each subsequent lap until he finishes at 225.575. He posts a record four-lap average of 225.301—requiring less than 40 seconds per trip around the Brickyard.

Penske teammate Rick Mears, who already owns five poles, starts his run with a "slow" lap of 223.6. His last three circuits are at more than 224, but his average of 224.215 is more than one mph slower than Fittipaldi's speed.

Bobby Rahal is third fastest qualifier for the day at 222.694. When the 6 P.M. gun sounds, several cars are still in line to run for the pole, but they have to wait until next Saturday.

SATURDAY, MAY 19: It is still Pole Day when qualifying resumes, and Arie Luyendyk runs four consistent laps to average 223.304 mph and bump Bobby Rahal off the front row. The last threat for the pole is Al Unser, Jr., and he fizzles. Unser averages just 220.9 to line up seventh, next to four-time winner A. J. Foyt.

When Pole Day finally ends, Fittipaldi wins the prize, and Mears and Luyendyk share the front row. Chevy-Ilmor V-8s power the first three rows. The fourth row has Porsche, Cosworth, and Buick engines.

Among second-day qualifiers, Al Unser, Sr., and Roberto Guerrero place their Alfa Romeo-powered cars on the 10th row.

SUNDAY, MAY 20: For the second straight year, Johnny Rutherford gets bumped from the lineup on the last day. When the final gun ends qualifying, the average speed of the 33 starters creeps up nearly one mph over last year to 217.437 mph.

THE RACE

Start: Emerson Fittipaldi darts in front of Rick Mears into the first turn and leads the first lap. Arie Luyendyk moves into third.

Lap 8: Leader Fittipaldi, running at a record pace, laps four slower cars. As the leaders pick their way through traffic, Luyendyk and Bobby Rahal pass Mears. Rahal then takes second from Luyendyk as Mears falls back. →

The Andretti clan's presence at the Speedway grew again in 1990 with the arrival of Jeff, second from right, youngest son of Mario, right. Though Jeff qualified, he later was bumped from the field. Mario, making his 25th start, and son Michael, left, were teammates in the Newman-Haas stable and started next to each other on the second row. Neither led a lap nor finished the race. The fourth racing Andretti, Mario's nephew John, started from the fourth row with a Porsche V-8, but he, too, failed to finish. Michael placed 20th, John 21st, and Mario 27th—hardly a vintage year for the Andrettis.

The turbocharger pop-off valve on Rocky Moran's Lola-Buick is installed (*top left*). The Granatellis were big on Buick V-6s this year (*top right*); Vince Granatelli had three in the race. Rich Vogler hit the Turn 3 wall during practice (*second from top, left*). With the Beretta chosen as the pace car, Chevrolet had a chance to parade its pacers of yore, including the 1955 Bel Air (*left*). A. J. Foyt (*second from top, right*), making his 33rd start at the age of 55, showed he could still cut it with a sixth-place finish. "Flying Dutchman" Arie Luyendyk (*above*) had lots of speed in practice and qualified on the front row.

Lap 20: A rear wheel bearing breaks on Danny Sullivan's Penske, sending the 1985 winner into a full spin before he hits the outside wall. After the leaders pit under yellow, Fittipaldi still leads, Rahal is second, and Mario Andretti comes out third.

Lap 26: Rahal challenges for the lead when racing resumes, but Fittipaldi holds him off and pulls away again. Al Unser, Jr., snatches fourth place from Arie Luyendyk.

Lap 45: The second caution period, for a stalled car, lets the leaders pit under yellow again. Fittipaldi still leads, with Rahal and Unser, Jr., running 2-3.

Lap 58: Fittipaldi puts eighth-place Mears a lap down as he extends his lead over Rahal. Two laps later, Mario Andretti's engine blows, bringing an early end to his 25th 500 appearance.

Lap 91: Fittipaldi has yet to surrender the lead, and he runs this lap at a record 222.574 mph. Rahal holds onto second, about five seconds behind in a battle of former winners.

Lap 92: When Fittipaldi and Rahal pit under green, it looks like third-place Michael Andretti will inherit the lead, but he slows in Turn 4 with smoke coming off his right rear wheel. Andretti pulls into the pits with a fried wheel bearing.
Luyendyk moves into first instead and leads laps 93 and 94. Fittipaldi resumes command when Luyendyk stops for fuel and tires.

Lap 100: After 250 miles, Fittipaldi is cruising at a record 174.192 mph with a 15-second lead. Unser, Jr., is second, Rahal third, and Luyendyk fourth. Foyt runs fifth, a lap down, with Mears close behind.

Lap 117: Fittipaldi stops for fuel and four fresh tires, giving the lead to Rahal for the first time. A few laps later, Rahal and second-place Luyendyk make their stops. The lead reverts to Fittipaldi, but Rahal, Luyendyk, and Unser, Jr., are still on the lead lap. ➔

Defending winner Emerson Fittipaldi (*row above, left*) was a strong threat to repeat after winning the pole at record speed for his new employer, Roger Penske. Fittipaldi became the first to average less than 40 seconds a lap by qualifying at 225.301 mph—picking up a hefty bonus for his efforts (*row above, middle*). The jet dryers (*left*) were called out during the rainy first qualifying weekend. The "driving suit" on this "RoboCop" lookalike (*above*) appears to be fire- *and* dent-resistant. In contrast to qualifying, race day was warm and sunny and attracted the usual full house (*opposite, top row*). Arie Luyendyk contemplates the 500 miles ahead before the start of the 74th race (*opposite middle*). Tony Bettenhausen leads Raul Boesel and brother Gary Bettenhausen into Turn 1 shortly after the start (*opposite bottom*).

There were very few drivers in the race who didn't suffer some form of tire problems. Most of the trouble was caused by unseasonably cool weather. The tires just didn't work properly at the lower temperatures.

At one point, Bobby Rahal appeared to have the fastest car in the race.

"In the mid part of the race, the car ran beautifully," Bobby said. "But then right at the end with the last set of tires, the balance just changed on us."

Rahal's difficulty seemed to occur after his final pit stop. Team manager Barry Green decided to go back to a set of tires already run in the first part of the race, when Bobby was really flying.

"We tried to correct an understeer problem and we used the same set of tires," Rahal said. "In retrospect, it might have been a mistake. Finally, we made a couple of other adjustments and got the car back to running 220. But it was too late."

Lap 135: Fittipaldi makes an unscheduled stop when his tires blister, allowing Rahal to take over first and Luyendyk to move up to second.

Lap 141: John Andretti nicks the wall in Turn 4, bends his suspension, and spins to a halt in Turn 1. The yellow flag comes out for only the fourth time. Rahal and Luyendyk pit without losing their positions to Fittipaldi, who still runs third.

Lap 152: Stopping a third time in 35 laps, Fittipaldi again needs fresh tires because of blistering. He falls to fourth, a lap down. Rahal still leads at a record pace of nearly 180 mph, but Luyendyk starts closing the gap.

Lap 162: Luyendyk matches Fittipaldi's record lap of 222.574 mph and closes to within a second of leader Rahal.

Lap 167: After failing to wrest away the lead on successive laps, Luyendyk steers low into Turn 3 underneath Rahal and finally bolts into first on the north short chute.

Lap 171: Rahal makes his final pit stop, and two laps later Luyendyk comes in for his. He gets back up to speed before Rahal closes the gap.

Lap 180: Luyendyk stretches his lead to 3.2 seconds over Rahal and increases his average speed to a record 183.239 mph. Al Unser, Jr., clings to the lead lap in third place, 32 seconds behind.

Finish: Luyendyk, consistently lapping at 216 mph and faster, builds a lead of nearly 11 seconds to keep Rahal comfortably at bay and handily wins the fastest 500 ever.

Luyendyk is truly the Flying Dutchman today. He goes the distance in a little more than two hours, 41 minutes and averages 185.981 mph—more than 15 mph faster than Rahal's 1986 winning speed that was the previous record. Only four caution flags for a total 26 laps slow his progress.

Fittipaldi, who leads 128 laps, squeezes back onto the lead lap near the end and comes in third behind Rahal. Unser, Jr., is fourth, a lap down. Fifth-place Mears and sixth-place Foyt round out a top-six sweep for the Chevy-Ilmor engine, which wins for the third year in a row.

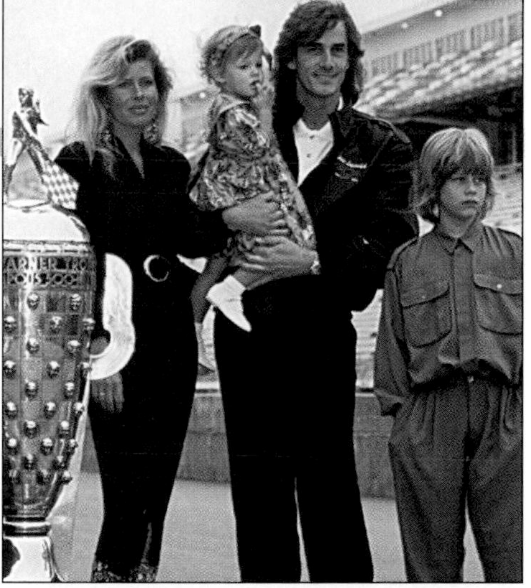

Opposite page: The familiar voice of longtime track announcer Tom Carnegie (top left) kept fans informed. Roberto Guerrero escaped injury when he wrecked his March-Alfa Romeo (top right). Bobby Rahal (bottom left) led for 35 laps. Al Unser, Jr., finished fourth in the Valvoline Lola (bottom right). *This page:* Talk about fast delivery. Winner Arie Luyendyk (far left) ran the quickest 500 miles in Indy history, putting smiles on the faces of his family (left) and the Doug Shierson Domino's Pizza team (below).

RESULTS

NO.	DRIVER	CAR	ENTRANT	ENGINE	CYL	DISP	CHASSIS	COLOR	QUAL SPD	START	FIN	LAPS / SPEED / REASON OUT
30	Arie Luyendyk	Domino's Pizza/Shierson	Douglas Shierson Racing, Inc.	Chevy Indy	8	160	'90 Lola	red, wht, blue	223.304	3	1	200-185.981
18	Bobby Rahal	STP-Kraco Chevy Lola	Galles-Kraco Racing	Chevy Indy	8	161	'90 Lola	yelo,blue,red	222.694	4	2	200-185.772
1	Emerson Fittipaldi	Marlboro Penske	Penske Racing, Inc.	Chevy Indy	8	160	'90 Penske	white, red	225.301	1	3	200-185.183
5	Al Unser, Jr.	Valvoline Chevy Lola	Galles-Kraco Racing	Chevy Indy	8	161	'90 Lola	blue, wht, red	220.920	7	4	199-flagged
2	Rick Mears	Pennzoil Z-7 Penske	Penske Racing, Inc.	Chevy Indy	8	160	'90 Penske	yellow	224.215	2	5	198-flagged
14	A. J. Foyt, Jr.	Copenhagen/Gilmore/Calumet	A. J. Foyt Enterprises	Chevy Indy	8	161	'90 Lola	black	220.425	8	6	194-flagged
22	Scott Brayton	Amway/Speedway Winning Spirit	Dick Simon Racing	Cosworth	8	160	'90 Lola	blue, wht, red	215.028	26	7	194-flagged
25	Eddie Cheever	Target/Mobil 1	Chip Ganassi Racing Teams	Chevy Indy	8	161	'89 Penske	red, white	217.926	14	8	193-flagged
11	Kevin Cogan	Tuneup Masters	Vince Granatelli Racing, Inc.	Buick V-6	6	208	'89 Penske	red	217.738	15	9	191-flagged
28	Scott Goodyear	Mackenzie Financial	O'Donnell Racing	Judd	8	158	'89 Lola	blue, white	213.622	21	10	191-flagged
70	Didier Theys	Tuneup Masters/RCA	Vince Granatelli Racing, Inc.	Buick V-6	6	208	'89 Penske	red	214.033	20	11	190-flagged
23	Tero Palmroth	Hoechst Celanese/Neste-Rotator	Dick Simon Racing	Cosworth	8	160	'90 Lola	white, blue	217.423	16	12	188-flagged
40	Al Unser, Sr.	Miller High Life	Patrick Racing International	Alfa Romeo	8	160	'90 March	wht, gold, red	212.087	30	13	186-flagged
12	Randy Lewis	AMP/Oracle/Samsung	Arciero Racing Teams	Buick V-6	6	208	'88 Penske	red	218.412	12	14	186-flagged
15	Jim Crawford	Glidden Paints	Menard, Inc.	Buick V-6	6	208	'89 Lola	red, orng, yelo	212.200	29	15	183-flagged
93	John Paul, Jr.	ATEC Environmental	Mann Motorsports	Buick V-6	6	208	'89 Lola	red, blk, orng, blue	214.411	32	16	176-radiator
39	Dean Hall	[insight] Lola	Dale Coyne Racing	Cosworth	8	161	'90 Lola	blue	216.975	24	17	165-suspension
4	Teo Fabi	Foster's Quaker State	Porsche Motorsports	Porsche	8	159	'90 March	white, blue	220.022	23	18	162-transmission
21	Geoff Brabham	Mac Tools/Truesports	Truesports Company	Judd	8	158	'89 Lola	yelo, wht, red	216.580	19	19	191-flagged
3	Michael Andretti	Kmart/Havoline	Newman/Haas Racing	Chevy Indy	8	161	'90 Lola	blu, wht, red	222.055	5	20	146-vibration
41	John Andretti	Foster's Quaker State	Porsche Motorsports	Porsche	8	159	'90 March	white, blue	219.484	10	21	136-spin T1
86	Dominic Dobson	Texaco-Havoline Star	Bruce Leven	Cosworth	8	160	'90 Lola	black	219.230	11	22	129-engine
20	Roberto Guerrero	Miller High Life	Patrick Racing International	Alfa Romeo	8	160	'90 March	wht, gold, red	212.652	28	23	118-suspension
81	Billy Vukovich III	Hemelgarn Racing	Hemelgarn Racing	Buick V-6	6	208	'88 Lola	yellow	211.389	31	24	102-engine
46	Rocky Moran	Gohr Racing/Glidden	Gohr Racing, Inc.	Buick V-6	6	208	'89 Lola	white	211.076	33	25	88-engine
16	Tony Bettenhausen	AMAX Lola	Bettenhausen Motorsports	Buick V-6	6	208	'89 Lola	blk, wht, red	218.368	13	26	76-engine
6	Mario Andretti	Kmart/Havoline	Newman/Haas Racing	Chevy Indy	8	161	'90 Lola	blu, wht, red	220.025	6	27	60-engine
19	Raul Boesel	Budweiser	Truesports Company	Judd	8	159	'89 Lola	red	217.381	17	28	60-engine
29	Pancho Carter	Hardee's	Leader Cards, Inc.	Cosworth	8	160	'90 Lola	blue	213.156	22	29	59-accident T4
9	Tom Sneva	RCA	Vince Granatelli Racing, Inc.	Buick V-6	6	208	'89 Penske	red	216.142	25	30	48-CV joint
51	Gary Bettenhausen	Glidden Paints	Menard, Inc.	Buick V-6	6	208	'89 Lola	orange, red	217.264	18	31	39-wheel bearing
7	Danny Sullivan	Marlboro Penske	Penske Racing, Inc.	Chevy Indy	8	160	'90 Penske	white, red	220.310	9	32	19-accident T1
97	Stan Fox	Miyano/CNC Systems/Baker	R. Kent Baker Racing, Inc.	Buick V-6	6	208	'87 Lola	pink	213.812	27	33	10-gearbox

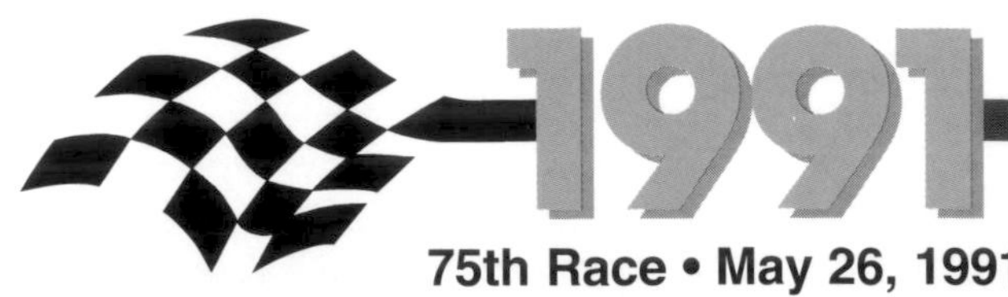

75th Race • May 26, 1991

Four-time winner A. J. Foyt announces before the 75th running of the 500 that his 34th race will be his last. As he prepares for his final appearance, a pair of rookies pursue significant firsts.

Willy T. Ribbs, a winner in the Trans-Am and IMSA series, tries to be the first African-American to qualify, and former Toyota Atlantic champ Hiro Matsushita tries to become the first Japanese to make the show.

Porsche withdraws from Indy-car competition, but there are still five brands of engines on the entry list: the dominant Chevrolet-Ilmor V-8, the Buick V-6, and the Cosworth, Alfa Romeo, and Judd V-8s, all turbocharged. The March chassis, which four years earlier was the choice of 28 starters, also disappears from the scene. Lola is now most popular.

The Truesports team enters a car of its own design with the Judd engine for drivers Geoff Brabham and Scott Pruett, who qualify the first American-made chassis since 1985. Penske again fields its own chassis, reserving the latest model for its two-car team of Rick Mears and Emerson Fittipaldi.

Ex-Team Penske manager Derrick Walker, who ran Porsche's Indy effort in 1990, forms his own team and fields a Lola-Cosworth for Ribbs. During the first week of practice, Walker switches to the Buick engine, delaying Ribbs's attempt at passing the rookie test until the second week. While Ribbs eventually gets his first Indy ride, four-time winner Al Unser, Sr., fails to secure one, ending a string of 21 straight starts.

PRACTICE AND QUALIFYING

TUESDAY, MAY 7: Rick Mears is fastest so far at 226.569 mph. Michael Andretti is next at 226; 1990 winner Arie Luyendyk and Mario Andretti just miss 225—all with Chevy engines. Gary Bettenhausen gets a Buick V-6 up to 224.9.

WEDNESDAY, MAY 8: Bobby Rahal, the 1986 winner, is fastest today at 226 mph. Jim Crawford is second at 225.6 with a Buick.

THURSDAY, MAY 9: On a cool, cloudy day, two more drivers join the 226-mph club. Emerson Fittipaldi runs 226.512, nearly matching teammate Rick Mears's top speed of the month. Kevin Cogan then blasts past both Penske drivers at 226.677 with a Lola-Buick V-6.

FRIDAY, MAY 10: Team Penske has a roller-coaster day. Mears spins in Turn 1 and hits the wall for the first time in his 14 years at the Speedway. He goes to the hospital to treat a minor foot injury. Fittipaldi sets fast speed of the month at 226.7 mph. Mears returns to the track in the late afternoon and turns a lap at 226.557 in his backup car.

➔

STARTING LINEUP

Average Field Qualifying Speed: 218.590

Numbers in flags indicate finish position

Mario Andretti

Al Unser, Jr.

Danny Sullivan

Scott Goodyear

Emerson Fittipaldi

A. J. Foyt

Michael Andretti

Jim Crawford

Jeff Andretti

Arie Luyendyk

POLE POSITION
Qualifying Speed: 224.113

Rick Mears

Bobby Rahal

John Andretti

Eddie Cheever

Gary Bettenhausen

While Willy T. Ribbs will go down in racing history as the first African-American driver in the Indianapolis 500, he wasn't the first black driver considered for a chance at the 500.

One May in the early Fifties, Eddie Anderson, who played Rochester on the Jack Benny's radio and television shows, came to Indy. Eddie hit it off with many racing dignitaries, including Wilbur Shaw and Tony Hulman.

When Anderson learned that Joie Ray, a black driver in the sprint car ranks was a licensed AAA competitor, Eddie made it his business to meet the young racer. A popular regular on the Midwest sprint circuit, Ray had a great following, and was known as a daring charger. The two men got along well, and Anderson contracted Andy Granatelli to build an Indy car for Ray. The story began to surface that Joie Ray had a solid deal for the 500.

However, the project fell through when Anderson's finances were tapped for a family emergency. The race car was never completed and Ray never got his shot at Indy. But a season or two later, Joie did the next best thing. He drove a sprint car owned by Mari Hulman George.

The Dodge Viper RT/10 was a last-minute choice as the pace car (*opposite* and *above right*). The Speedway announced the Dodge Stealth (*above left*), a clone of the Mitsubishi 3000GT, would pace the field. However, there was enough objection to a Japanese-built car that Dodge agreed to rush a prototype Viper into service, well before the car went into production. The 400-horsepower V-10 Viper was in the capable hands of retired race driver Carroll Shelby on race day. Willy T. Ribbs (*middle*) became Indy's first African-American driver, a distinction that almost belonged to sprint car driver Joie Ray (*top*) in the Fifties.

Mike Groff

Bernard Jourdain

Hiro Matsushita

Scott Pruett

Dominic Dobson

Gordon Johncock

Stan Fox

Tony Bettenhausen

Buddy Lazier

Tero Palmroth

Willy T. Ribbs

Pancho Carter

Kevin Cogan

Scott Brayton

Geoff Brabham

John Paul, Jr.

Roberto Guerrero

Randy Lewis

Rookie Mark Dismore suffers multiple leg and arm injuries when he spins in Turn 4 and tatoos the outside wall before sliding across the track into the inside wall. He then hits both the inside and outside pit walls before it is over.

SATURDAY, MAY 11: A. J. Foyt is the first to qualify on Pole Day, and he gets a loud cheer with a run of 222.443 mph, though most doubt it will be fast enough to win the pole. However, Mario Andretti, Jim Crawford, Bobby Rahal, and Michael Andretti, all of whom were quicker in practice, fail to knock Foyt off the pole.

Mears, in his backup car, finally tops Foyt with a four-lap average of 224.113. Teammate Fittipaldi is next, and he runs three laps in the 223-224 range before owner Roger Penske aborts the attempt. Penske decides to try again later in the day under cooler conditions.

Penske's plan backfires when rain ends qualifying before Fittipaldi and contenders Arie Luyendyk and Gary Bettenhausen get a shot. Mears wins a record sixth pole on a day in which only 12 cars qualify. Foyt and Mario Andretti join Mears on the front row. Michael Andretti is on row two, his cousin John is on row three, and rookie Jeff, Michael's younger brother, lines up on row four—the first family foursome in the 500.

SUNDAY, MAY 12: Gary Bettenhausen, denied a chance to run for the pole because of rain, qualifies faster than pole-winner Mears at 224.468 mph. It is the first time in 10 years the fastest qualifier does not sit on the pole. Luyendyk runs 223.881, quick enough to be on row one, but he joins Bettenhausen and Fittipaldi on row five, which averages one mph faster than the front row.

MONDAY, MAY 13: Walker Racing finally solves its engine gremlins long enough for Willy T. Ribbs to pass his rookie test. Ribbs gets his Lola-Buick up to 213 mph in practice.

FRIDAY, MAY 17: Ribbs gets up to 213 mph again before his Buick V-6 blows after 24 laps.

SATURDAY, MAY 18: Hiro Matsushita qualifies at 218.141 mph to become the first Japanese driver in the 500. American Buddy →

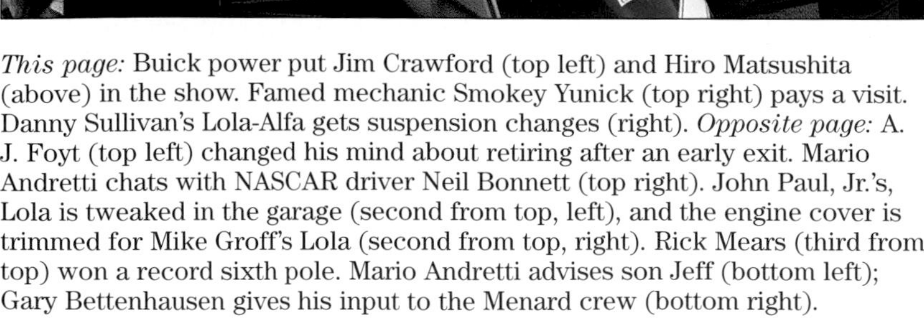

This page: Buick power put Jim Crawford (top left) and Hiro Matsushita (above) in the show. Famed mechanic Smokey Yunick (top right) pays a visit. Danny Sullivan's Lola-Alfa gets suspension changes (right). *Opposite page:* A. J. Foyt (top left) changed his mind about retiring after an early exit. Mario Andretti chats with NASCAR driver Neil Bonnett (top right). John Paul, Jr.'s, Lola is tweaked in the garage (second from top, left), and the engine cover is trimmed for Mike Groff's Lola (second from top, right). Rick Mears (third from top) won a record sixth pole. Mario Andretti advises son Jeff (bottom left); Gary Bettenhausen gives his input to the Menard crew (bottom right).

GILMORE
BOSCH
14

AC-Delco
KONI
Havoline

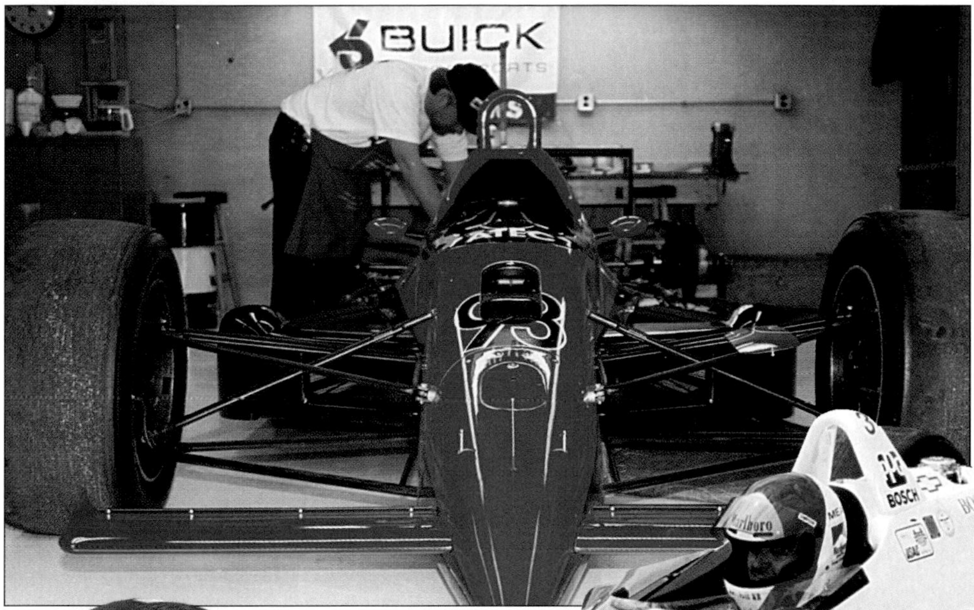

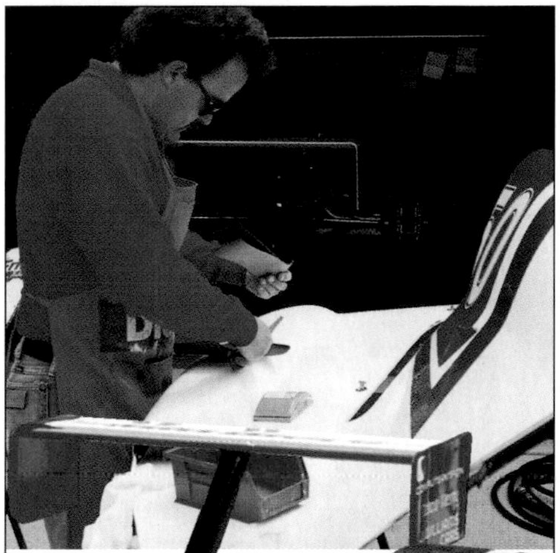

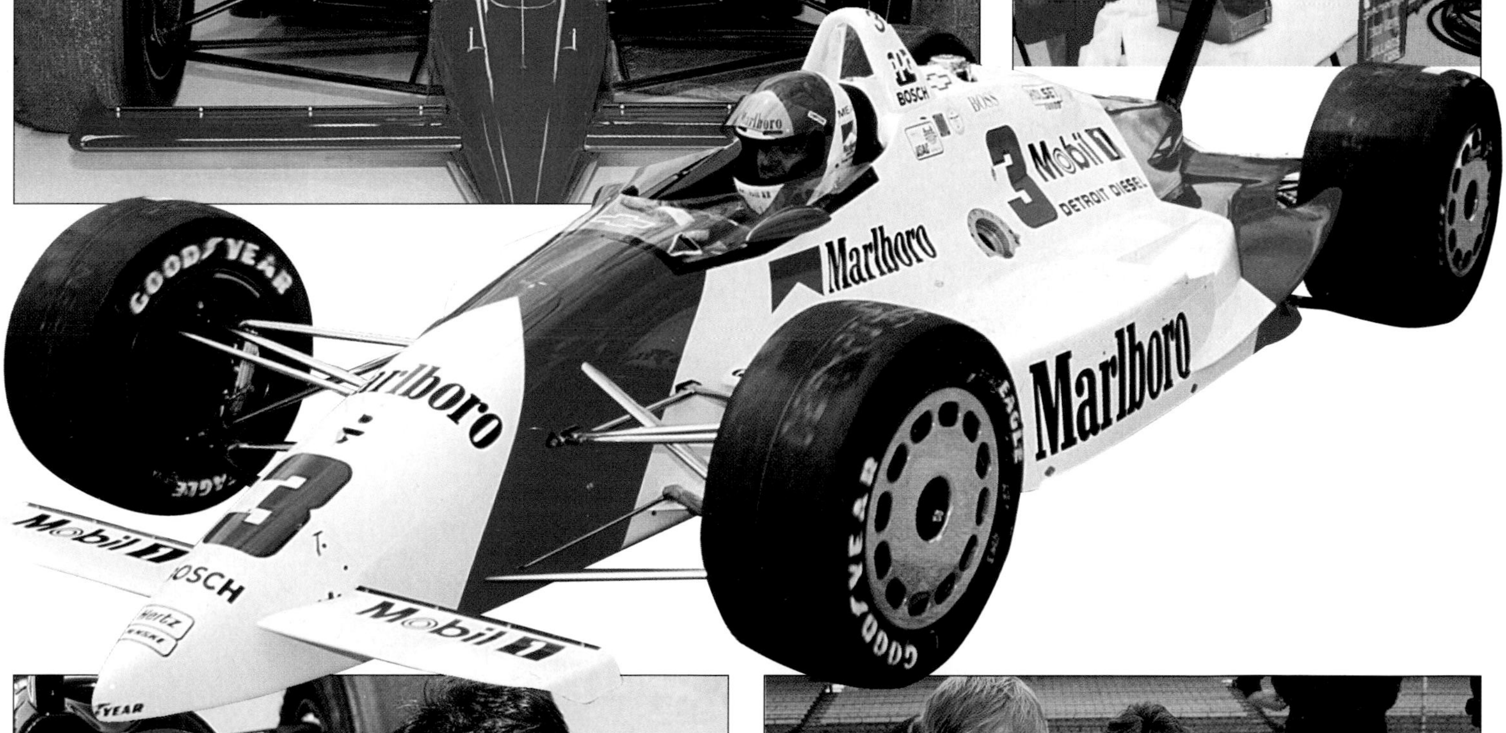

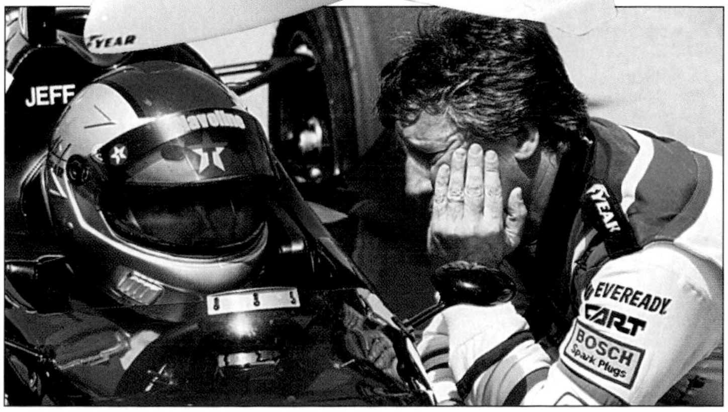

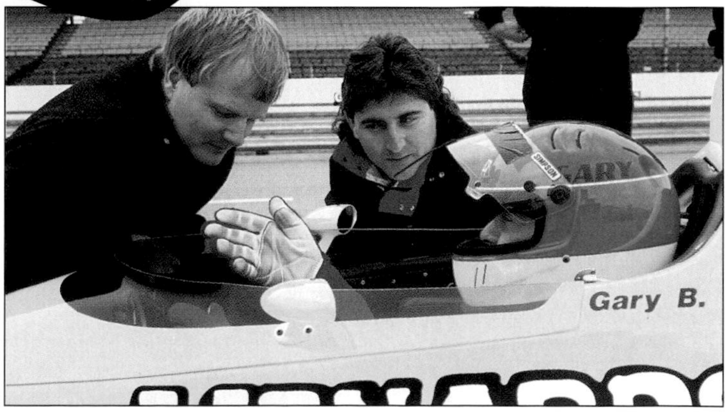

Lazier, however, gets in at 218.692 to be the fastest rookie. Ribbs suffers another setback when his new Buick V-6 breaks a valve during practice.

SUNDAY, MAY 19: Early on bump day, two-time winner Gordon Johncock squeaks into the field at 213.812 mph. Late in the day, Ribbs, using his fourth engine of the month, averages a solid 217.358 to bump Tom Sneva and become the first black driver in the Indy 500.

THE RACE

Start: Rain delays the race about 45 minutes, and when the green flag drops, Rick Mears charges into the lead as Mario Andretti moves into second. From the second row, Michael Andretti zooms around A. J. Foyt and Al Unser, Jr., to grab third.

Back in the field, Gary Bettenhausen does a half-spin to the inside of Turn 1, then recovers, but rookie Buddy Lazier locks his brakes and spins into the outside wall. Bettenhausen continues without damage, while Lazier nurses his damaged car around to the pits, where he calls it a day after one lap.

Lap 6: With the field back under green, Willy T. Ribbs pulls slowly into the pits with a blown engine.

Lap 12: Mario Andretti gets inside of Mears and shoots into the lead going into Turn 1. With his car pushing in the corners, Mears loses second to Michael Andretti a few laps later.

Lap 24: Kevin Cogan and Roberto Guerrero tangle in Turn 1 and crash hard into the outside wall. Guerrero is okay, but Cogan suffers a broken thigh and arm. Debris from the wreck damages the suspension on A. J. Foyt's car, knocking him out early from his 34th race.

Defending winner Arie Luyendyk drops a lap down during the yellow while he gets eight fresh spark plugs.

Lap 34: When racing resumes, it's father vs. son, Andretti-style, as Michael beats Mario into Turn 1 to take the lead and pull away. Teammates Bobby Rahal and Al Unser, Jr., run third and fourth.

Lap 55: After a round of green-flag stops by the leaders, Michael Andretti is still first, 12 seconds ahead of Unser and pulling away. Mario Andretti is third and Rahal fourth.

Lap 73: Michael Andretti is in command and about to put the fifth- and sixth-place cars of Emerson Fittipaldi and Mears a lap →

Rick Mears comes to rest after hitting the wall during practice (*top*). Randy Lewis wrecked in qualifying (*above*), but put a backup car in the race. Chairman Emeritus Mary Fendrich Hulman checks the weather at opening ceremonies (*below left*). Motorsports ambassador Linda Vaughn catches up with Gary Bettenhausen (*below middle*). Bobby Rahal (*below right*) is happy to have qualified on the second row. Jim Crawford logs practice time (*opposite top*). So do Bettenhausen, in No. 51, and A. J. Foyt, in No. 14 (*opposite, bottom left*). The sun comes up on another day at the Speedway (*opposite, middle left*). Fresh from leading forces in Persian Gulf combat, General Norman Schwarzkopf greets the crowd with his wife in pre-race pomp. With a couple of balky cars in the pits, the rest of the starters warm up behind the pace car (*opposite, bottom right*).

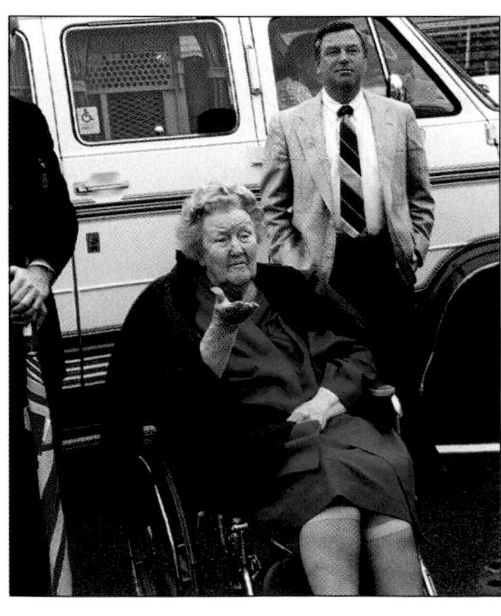

In 1990, A. J. Foyt suffered the worst wreck of his career on the road course at Elkhart Lake, Wisconsin. They said he'd never walk again, that he'd probably live out his days in a wheelchair. Certainly his driving days were over.

"I'm going to drive at least once more at Indianapolis," he told everyone.

Sure enough, during practice for the 1991 race, A. J. walked through the pit gate to cheers and eased himself into the cockpit of his famous No. 14. His qualifying average put him in the front row. In the race, a stray tire from the Kevin Cogan-Roberto Guerrero accident smashed his left front suspension, but there was no denying one thing: A. J. was back!

down, but suddenly his car gets loose in Turn 1 and the tail slides out of the groove. He catches it in time to stay off the wall and stay in front.

Lap 79: Andretti pits early under green. He gets three fresh tires and a front wing adjustment to correct the loose handling. After he leaves the pits, his crew finds the real cause of his handling problem—a punctured left rear tire that was slowly losing air. For the next 30 laps, Andretti wrestles with understeer, but still regains the lead.

Lap 89: Fastest qualifier Gary Bettenhausen, struggling to crack the top 10, drops out with a leaky radiator.

Lap 100: Michael Andretti leads Fittipaldi by two seconds. Rahal is third, five seconds back, and Mario Andretti is fourth, six seconds back.

Lap 109: Michael Andretti pits for fuel and a wing adjustment, giving the lead to Fittipaldi for the first time. Fittipaldi pits three laps later, but reclaims the lead after his stop and builds a 12-second cushion over Andretti.

Lap 148: The yellow comes out when Scott Brayton's engine blows, allowing second-place Andretti and third-place Mears to close up behind Fittipaldi.

Lap 153: Andretti zips inside of Fittipaldi on the restart and surges past Fittipaldi in Turn 1 for the lead.

Lap 166: When Andretti comes in for fuel and fresh rubber, Fittipaldi moves back into first.

Lap 169: Fittipaldi makes his last scheduled stop and blows his transmission as he charges out of the pits, ending his race after leading 46 laps. Andretti inherits an eight-second lead over Mears, the only other car on the lead lap.

Lap 182: Andretti leads Mears by more than 15 seconds when Danny Sullivan's Alfa Romeo detonates and covers the front straight with athick plume of smoke, bringing out the yellow. Andretti ducks into the pits for a splash of fuel, while Mears stays out and moves in front. Andretti lines up right behind Mears on the track.

Lap 187: When the green comes out, Andretti executes a daring pass in Turn 1, darting around the outside of Mears in traffic to grab the lead.

Lap 188: This time Mears smokes Andretti in Turn 1, using a similar move around the outside, and opens up breathing room on the backstretch.

Lap 191: With Mears leading Michael by two seconds, Mario Andretti's engine blows at the south end of the track. He coasts around to the north end and stops at the pit entrance. The yellow comes out, setting up a trophy-dash finish.

Finish: Mears has too much power and too much grip for Andretti when the green flag comes out. Mears runs 221.746 mph on Lap 196, his fastest of the day, and pulls away to a three-second victory.

At the age of 39, Mears ties A. J. Foyt and Al Unser, Sr., with four wins. He achieves in 14 years a feat that took Foyt 20 and Unser 22. Mears earns $1.2 million of a $7 million purse, both records.

The Andretti clan has a big day. Michael leads 97 laps in posting his best finish in eight tries. John is fifth, Mario is seventh, and Jeff is named Rookie of the Year. Once again, however, the big prize eludes the family.

After his early exit and disappointing 28th-place finish, Foyt hints he may be back next year.

Scott Pruett, in No. 19, and Bobby Rahal, in No. 18, log some mutual practice time (*top*). On race day, both retired with mechanical problems. Al Unser, Jr., gets fuel (*middle*) on his way to fourth place. Danny Sullivan's day ends with a turbocharger failure (*above*). The Pennzoil crew gives John Andretti the full-service treatment (*opposite, top left*). Buddy Lazier is pushed to the garage after a first-lap accident (*opposite, bottom left*). Rick Mears signifies that this trip to victory lane is his record-tying fourth visit (*opposite right*).

RESULTS

NO.	DRIVER	CAR	ENTRANT	ENGINE	CYL	DISP	CHASSIS	COLOR	QUAL SPD	START	FIN	LAPS / SPEED / REASON OUT
3	Rick Mears	Marlboro Penske	Penske Racing, Inc.	Chevy Indy	8	161	'91 Penske	red, white	224.113	1	1	200-176.457
10	Michael Andretti	Kmart Havoline	Newman/Haas Racing	Chevy Ilmor	8	161	'91 Lola	black, white	220.943	5	2	200-176.402
1	Arie Luyendyk	RCA/UNO	Vince Granatelli Racing, Inc.	Chevy	8	161	'91 Lola	red	223.881	14	3	199-flagged
2	Al Unser, Jr.	Valvoline Chevy Lola	Galles-Kraco Racing	Chevy	8	161	'91 Lola	blue,red, wht	219.823	6	4	198-flagged
4	John Andretti	Pennzoil Special	Hall/VDS Racing	Chevy Indy	8	161	'91 Lola	yellow	219.059	7	5	197-flagged
92	Gordon Johncock	Jack's Tool Rental/Bryant	Hemelgarn-Byrd Racing	Cosworth	8	160	'90 Lola	red	213.812	33	6	188-flagged
6	Mario Andretti	Kmart Havoline	Newman/Haas Racing	Chevy Ilmor	8	161	'91 Lola	black, white	221.818	3	7	187-engine
91	Stan Fox	Jonathan Byrd's/Bryant	Hemelgarn-Byrd Racing	Buick V-6	6	208	'91 Lola	red	219.501	17	8	185-flagged
16	Tony Bettenhausen	AMAX	Bettenhausen Motorsports, Inc.	Chevy Indy	8	208	'90 Penske	blk, wht, red	218.188	20	9	180-flagged
20	Danny Sullivan	Miller Genuine Draft	Patrick Racing International	Alfa Romeo	8	160	'91 Lola Alfa	black, gold	218.343	9	10	173-turbo
5	Emerson Fittipaldi	Marlboro Penske	Penske Racing, Inc.	Chevy Indy	8	161	'91 Penske	red, white	223.064	15	11	171-gearbox
19	Scott Pruett	Budweiser/Truesports 91C	Truesports Company	Judd	8	159	'91 Truesports	red	214.814	27	12	166-transmission
66	Dominic Dobson	Coors/Kroger/Rally's	Burns Racing Team, Inc.	Judd	8	159	'89 Lola	red, yellow	215.326	30	13	164-flagged
39	Randy Lewis	AMP/Orbit/Jenn-Air	Dale Coyne Racing	Cosworth	8	160	'90 Lola	yellow	214.565	31	14	159-flagged
86	Jeff Andretti	Texaco-Havoline Star	Bruce Leven	Cosworth	8	160	'91 Lola	black	217.632	11	15	150-engine
7	Hiro Matsushita	Panasonic Lola	Paragon Motorsports/Dick Simon	Buick V-6	6	208	'91 Lola	blue, yellow	218.141	24	16	146-flagged
22	Scott Brayton	Amway/Hoechst Celanese	Dick Simon Racing, Inc.	Chevy	8	161	'91 Lola	blue, wht, pink	218.627	19	17	146-engine
48	Bernard Jourdain	Monarch/A. J. Foyt	A. J. Foyt Enterprises	Buick V-6	6	208	'90 Lola	black	216.683	21	18	141-gearbox
18	Bobby Rahal	STP-Kraco	Galles/Kraco Racing	Chevy	8	161	'91 Lola	yelo, red, blue	221.401	4	19	130-engine
21	Geoff Brabham	The Mac Tools Distributors	Truesports Company	Judd	8	159	'91 Truesports	yelo, wht, red	214.859	22	20	109-electrical
12	Pancho Carter	Arciero/Alfa-LavalL/Doc's	Arciero Racing Teams	Buick V-6	6	208	'89 Lola	red	214.012	32	21	94-engine
51	Gary Bettenhausen	Glidden Paints Special	Menard, Inc.	Buick V-6	6	208	'91 Lola	orng, yelo	224.468	13	22	89-radiator
23	Tero Palmroth	Neste-Rotator Lola	Paragon Motorsports, Inc.	Cosworth	8	160	'90 Lola	white, blue	215.648	26	23	77-engine
50	Mike Groff	Fendi-Haw Tropic-Rohopac-Iema-Slam	Euromotorsport Racing, Inc.	Cosworth	8	160	'91 Lola	white, red	219.015	18	24	68-water leak
93	John Paul, Jr.	ATEC Environmental	D.B. Mann Motorsports, Inc.	Buick V-6	6	208	'90 Lola	purple, pink	217.952	25	25	53-oil leak
26	Jim Crawford	Quaker State	Kenny Bernstein's King Motorsports, Inc.	Buick V-6	6	208	'91 Lola	green, white	218.947	8	26	49-engine
15	Scott Goodyear	Mackenzie Financial	UNO Racing	Judd	8	159	'91 Lola	blue, white	216.751	12	27	38-engine
14	A. J. Foyt	Gilmore/Copenhagen	A. J. Foyt Enterprises	Chevy	8	161	'91 Lola	black	222.443	2	28	25-suspension
9	Kevin Cogan	Glidden Paints	Menard, Inc.	Buick V-6	6	208	'91 Lola	yelo, orng	222.844	16	29	24-accident T1
40	Roberto Guerrero	Sharp's Patrick Racing	Patrick Racing International	Alfa Romeo	8	160	'91 Lola	black, gold	214.027	28	30	23-accident T1
8	Eddie Cheever	Target/Scotch Video	Chip Ganassi Racing	Chevy	8	161	'91 Lola	black, red	218.122	10	31	17-electrical
17	Willy T. Ribbs	Cosby/Walker	Walker Motorsports, Inc.	Buick V-6	6	208	'90 Lola	red, yellow	217.358	29	32	5-engine
71	Buddy Lazier	Vail Beavercreek	Hemelgarn-Byrd Racing	Buick V-6	6	208	'90 Lola	white	218.692	23	33	1-accident SS

1992

76th Race • May 24, 1992

Ford returns to the Brickyard for the first time in 20 years with a new engine that threatens Chevrolet's four-year win streak. The new turbocharged Ford-Cosworth V-8 is about 90 pounds lighter and more powerful than the Chevy engine, and its smaller size allows tailoring the Lola chassis to a more aerodynamic design. Two teams enter the 500 with the Ford-Cosworth engine: Newman-Haas, for drivers Mario and Michael Andretti; and Ganassi Racing, for '90 winner Arie Luyendyk and ex-Formula 1 driver Eddie Cheever.

Chevrolet counters with a trimmer, more potent V-8 of its own—the Chevy-Ilmor B—but only Team Penske drivers Rick Mears and Emerson Fittipaldi have the latest version. Fifteen other drivers qualify with the older Chevy-Ilmor A engine.

Alfa Romeo drops out of Indy competition and the old Cosworth V-8 fades away after 16 years, including 10 straight wins before the Chevy engine took over. With the Cosworth gone, more teams turn to the production-based Buick V-6, a less-expensive engine that still gets more turbo boost under USAC rules (55 inches versus 45 on the smaller racing engines). Twelve Buicks qualify, the most so far.

On the chassis side, 27 starters use Lolas. There also are three Penskes, one Truesports, and two Galmers—a new chassis that owner Rick Galles enters for 1985 winner Danny Sullivan and Al Unser, Jr.

Seven rookies make the show, the most in 10 years, including road-racing champ Lyn St. James, the second woman to qualify. She finishes 11th to be Rookie of the Year.

PRACTICE AND QUALIFYING

SATURDAY, MAY 2: On the first day of practice, Jim Crawford sets an unofficial lap record of 229.6 mph with a Lola-Buick. Brazilian rookie Nelson Piquet, a three-time Formula 1 champion, is second at 225.9, and veteran Roberto Guerrero is third at 225.2, also with Buicks.

MONDAY, MAY 4: Three drivers top 230 mph in a stunning display of speed that forecasts a record-setting Pole Day. Crawford is fastest at 233.4. Michael Andretti is next at 230.8 with the new Ford V-8, and Guerrero places third at 230.4.

WEDNESDAY, MAY 6: Four-time winner Rick Mears →

STARTING LINEUP

Average Field Qualifying Speed: 223.479

Numbers in flags indicate finish position

POLE POSITION
Qualifying Speed: 232.482

Mario Andretti

Michael Andretti

Rick Mears

Al Unser, Jr.

Eric Bachelart

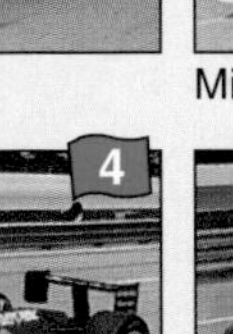

Eddie Cheever

Gary Bettenhausen

Danny Sullivan

Emerson Fittipaldi

John Andretti

Roberto Guerrero

Arie Luyendyk

Scott Brayton

Bobby Rahal

Stan Fox

Goodyear displayed its latest line of "soft goods" at the Speedway (*opposite top*). Tom Binford (*above left*) returned for his 19th year as chief steward. Lyn St. James (*above right*) became the second woman to qualify for the 500 and finished 11th to win Rookie of the Year. The Allante roadster was the pace car (*below* and *opposite bottom*), letting Cadillac show off its new Northstar V-8 engine.

Over the years, the Andrettis and Unsers have made many firsts at Indianapolis as far as father/son/ brother combinations are concerned. Al Unser, Jr., came up with a unique family record in the 1992 race.

While three generations of Vukovichs, two Parsonses, several Bettenhausens, and Mario, Michael, Jeff, and John Andretti have been among the numerous racing families at Indy, nothing like "Little Al's" mark came to pass until his initial victory in 1992. And it took him 10 starts before he could turn the trick. He had been close in 1989, when he finished second, as had Bill Vukovich, Jr., in 1973 and Michael Andretti in '91, who did likewise. But in 1992, Al Unser, Jr., finally became the first second-generation driver to win the Indy 500.

John Paul, Jr.

Jim Crawford

Buddy Lazier

Lyn St. James

Tom Sneva

Scott Goodyear

Scott Pruett

Jeff Andretti

A. J. Foyt

Brian Bonner

Dominic Dobson

Ted Prappas

Philippe Gache

Paul Tracy

Al Unser, Sr.

Raul Boesel

Jimmy Vasser

Gordon Johncock

sprains his right wrist and fractures his left foot in a Turn 2 crash that causes heavy damage to his backup car. The crash is caused when Mears spins into the outside wall when water from his own car leaks onto the track.

Mario Andretti is the fourth driver to top 230 in practice, running 231.1 mph with his Lola-Ford. Three others are faster today: Michael Andretti and Guerrero go 231.5, and Crawford is swiftest again at 233.2.

THURSDAY, MAY 7: Piquet's rookie effort ends when he crashes hard into the Turn 4 wall and suffers serious fractures to his feet and legs. The next day, team owner John Menard announces four-time winner Al Unser, Sr., will replace Piquet.

FRIDAY, MAY 8: Ford drivers Mario Andretti and Arie Luyendyk are fastest the day before Pole Day. Andretti hits 233.2 mph and Luyendyk 232.6. Guerrero and Crawford get their Buicks over 231 mph.

SATURDAY, MAY 9: Rain delays qualifying until 4 P.M., and the first driver out rewrites the single- and four-lap records. Luyendyk's fastest lap is 229.305 mph, and he averages 229.127 with his Lola-Ford.

Gary Bettenhausen sets a new one-lap record of 229.317 with a Lola Buick, but his average of 228.932 fails to knock Luyendyk off the pole. Roberto Guerrero, however, runs four consistent laps with his Lola Buick, topping out at 232.618 and averaging 232.482 to rewrite the records again and stake a strong claim to the top spot. Guerrero runs out of fuel after his last lap.

Mario Andretti qualifies late in the day at 229.503 to move Luyendyk to the outside of the front row. Mears, always a threat for the pole but still sore from his crash, averages less than 225. Four drivers are still in line for a shot at the pole when 6 P.M. rolls around.

SUNDAY, MAY 10: Eddie Cheever survives a pit-road collision with another car and qualifies his Lola-Ford at 229.639 mph, second fastest and enough to push teammate Arie Luyendyk to the second row.

Pole Day ends with three former Formula 1 drivers on row one: Roberto Guerrero's Buick is on the pole, Cheever's Ford is in the middle, and Mario Andretti's Ford is on the outside. Buick and Ford fill row two as well, and the first Chevy is Danny Sullivan's in the middle of row three.

Two four-time winners qualify on the eighth row. Al Unser, Sr., makes his 26th race and A. J. Foyt his 35th straight appearance.

FRIDAY, MAY 15: Filipino rookie Jovy Marcelo becomes the first driver to die at the Speedway in 10 years when he spins and slams into the Turn 1 wall, suffering massive head injuries.

USAC announces a new race-day procedure in which the pits will not open during caution periods until the field bunches up behind the pace car.

SUNDAY, MAY 17: Tom Sneva and Gordon Johncock qualify on the last day to increase the number of former winners in the field to a record 10. Rookie Ted Prappas is the slowest and last driver to qualify, and he bumps Scott Goodyear. However, Goodyear replaces teammate Mike Groff in a car that Groff qualified earlier and starts 33rd. The average speed climbs 4.9 mph to a record 223.479.

THE RACE

Start: On this chilly, overcast day, Roberto Guerrero tries to warm his tires on the parade lap. When he guns his engine, →

Opposite page: Indy is the backdrop for an Unser reunion (top), from left, "Little Al," Bobby, and "Big Al." The cars of Scott Goodyear and Gordon Johncock visit the Valvoline fueling station (second from top). Hiro Matsushita broke his leg when he crashed in qualifying (third from top). Jim Crawford's No. 26 Lola-Buick (bottom) was the fastest second-day qualifier. *This page:* Rookie Paul Tracy hits the wall in practice (right). Pancho Carter failed to qualify the No. 81 Hemelgarn entry (below). The Menard team (below right) had, from left, Gary Bettenhausen and former winners Al Unser, Sr., and Tom Sneva. Roberto Guerrero's No. 36 Buick (bottom left) took the pole at a record speed (bottom right). Guerrero picked up some extra cash for the feat (third from top, right).

his Lola-Buick spins off the track on the back straight and runs into the inside wall, knocking the polesitter out of the race before the green flag.

When the race starts, Mario Andretti gets around Eddie Cheever, and Michael Andretti zips by both from the second row to grab the lead in the first turn and pull away.

Lap 12: Following the first caution flag, former winner Tom Sneva loses control on the restart in Turn 4 and crashes into the outside wall, bringing out the second yellow. Most drivers pit during the first two cautions, but Scott Goodyear stays on the track and jumps from last place to seventh. Cheever beats Michael Andretti out of the pits to lead under yellow.

Lap 21: Michael Andretti roars by Cheever on the restart and pulls away from the pack to resume the lead.

Lap 67: When the green flag comes out after another caution, rookie Philipe Gache catches the Turn 1 wall, spins, and gets hit by Stan Fox. Neither is injured.

Michael Andretti still leads and Cheever is second, both in Lola-Fords. Emerson Fittipaldi moves up to third in a Penske-Chevy, the last car on the lead lap.

Lap 75: The combination of cold tires on a cold track results in yet another accident that claims three cars, two of them driven by former winners. Jim Crawford starts it when he spins in the south short chute. Rick Mears has nowhere to go and they crash into the outside wall. Penske teammate Fittipaldi slows down as he approaches the wreck, but does a half spin into the Turn 1 wall. All three suffer minor injuries.

Lap 82: On the restart, Mario Andretti loses it in Turn 1 

Roberto Guerrero is on pole on the parade lap (*above*), but on the hook after he crashes on the back straight (*left*) before the green flag flies. Guerrero teammate Jim Crawford spins and collects the Marlboro car of Rick Mears (*bottom row, this page and opposite*). Scott Brayton's Buick engine lets go on lap 93 (*opposite, top left*). Danny Sullivan pits (*opposite, top right*). Crashes claim Jimmy Vasser (*opposite, second from top left*), Gary Bettenhausen (*opposite, second from top right*), and Stan Fox (No. 91), who hits a spinning Phillippe Gache (*opposite, third from top*).

MOLSON
KRACO
STP
18

91
GOODYEAR

and smacks the outside wall head-on, another victim of cold tires. He breaks toes on both feet in the accident.

Lap 115: Jeff Andretti runs into the Turn 2 wall when his right rear wheel hub breaks. Gary Bettenhausen spins and crashes trying to avoid Andretti, who suffers serious injuries to his feet and legs.

Michael Andretti still leads, and his Lola-Ford pulls away from second-place Arie Luyendyk when racing resumes. Cheever is third and Al Unser, Jr., fourth in a Chevy, but the dominant Andretti is close to lapping him.

Lap 136: Luyendyk, running second to Michael Andretti, tries to go inside of A. J. Foyt, but is tapped by the Texan, who has lost his left-side mirror. As a result, Luyendyk bangs the outside wall in Turn 4 and becomes the sixth former winner to drop out of the race and the fifth to crash. Only 16 cars are still running.

Unser, Jr., moves into second place and Cheever trails in third. Al Unser, Sr., is fourth in a Buick-powered Lola, and Goodyear is fifth. All are on the lead lap.

Lap 166: Andretti runs the fastest lap of the day, a record 229.118 mph. Al Unser, Jr., falls to third after a pit stop, and Goodyear moves up to second. Al Unser, Sr., is fourth, but still on the lead lap.

Lap 173: Michael Andretti pits for the last time, taking on four tires and enough fuel to go the distance. Goodyear still runs second, ahead of Unser, Jr., after they make their final stops.

Lap 188: Unser, Jr., passes Goodyear in traffic to grab second place, although still more than half a lap behind leader Andretti.

Lap 189: Andretti's Lola-Ford, dominant since the start, suddenly slows, and he coasts to a stop on the backstretch. After leading 160 laps and with victory in sight, a broken fuel-pump belt adds another heartbreak to the Andretti family's misery. Michael immediately leaves the Speedway to visit his injured father and brother.

As the yellow comes out so Andretti's car can be retrieved, Unser, Jr., inherits the lead with Goodyear right behind. Unser, Sr., and Cheever run third and fourth, also on the lead lap.

Finish: When racing resumes on Lap 194, Goodyear hounds Unser lap after lap in a thrilling dash to the wire. Goodyear manages to catch up as they exit Turn 4 but can't keep pace on the front straight.

As they roar out of Turn 4 on the last lap, Unser's car gets a little loose and he lifts momentarily, letting Goodyear dive inside as they sprint to the finish line. Goodyear hugs the pit wall and pulls alongside, but Unser holds him off to win by half a car length—.043 seconds—in the closest finish in 500 history.

After three straight top-four finishes, "Little Al" finally earns a spot on the Borg-Warner trophy, raising the Unser family's victory total to eight. He leads just 25 laps and averages 134.477 mph, the slowest since 1958. Goodyear loses by an eyelash but wins widespread recognition for his relentless charge from the 33rd starting position. At the age of 52, "Big Al" Unser comes in third to give the Buick V-6 its highest finish ever. Fourth-place Eddie Cheever has the highest finishing Ford-Cosworth engine, which leads 171 laps.

This is the last race for four former winners, including four-time champs Foyt and Mears, two-time winner Gordon Johncock, and 1983 winner Tom Sneva.

An early caution brings the leaders into the pits (*top*) and sets up a dash for track position. The yellow flag waved 13 times. Al Unser, Jr., addresses the crowd (*above*) after nipping Scott Goodyear in a heart-pounding race to the wire. The next day, he poses for pictures with his crew (*opposite top*) and accepts the keys to the Cadillac Allante pace car (*opposite bottom*).

RESULTS

NO.	DRIVER	CAR	ENTRANT	ENGINE	CYL	DISP	CHASSIS	COLOR	QUAL SPD	START	FIN	LAPS / SPEED / REASON OUT
3	Al Unser, Jr.	Valvoline Galmer	Galles-Kraco Racing	Chevy Indy-A	8	161	'92 Galmer	blue, wht, red	222.989	12	1	200-134.477
15	Scott Goodyear	MacKenzie FInancial	Walker Motorsports, Inc.	Chevy Indy-A	8	161	'92 Lola	blue, silver	221.801	33	2	200-134.477
27	Al Unser	Conseco Special	Team Menard, Inc.	Buick V-6	6	208	'92 Lola	yelo, orng, red, blue	223.744	22	3	200-134.375
9	Eddie Cheever	Target-Scotch Video	Chip Ganassi Racing Teams, Inc.	Cosworth XB	8	160	'92 Lola	black, red	229.639	2	4	200-134.374
18	Danny Sullivan	Molson/Kraco/STP	Galles-Kraco Racing	Chevy Indy-A	8	161	'92 Galmer	blue, wht, red	224.838	8	5	199-flagged
12	Bobby Rahal	Miller Genuine Draft	Rahal/Hogan Racing	Chevy Indy-A	8	161	'92 Lola	blk, yelo, red	224.158	10	6	199-flagged
11	Raul Boesel	Panasonic/Sega	Dick Simon Racing, Inc.	Chevy Indy-A	8	161	'92 Lola	blue, yelo, red	222.434	25	7	198-flagged
8	John Andretti	Pennzoil Special	Hall/VDS Racing, Inc.	Chevy Indy-A	8	161	'92 Lola	yelo, blk, red	222.644	14	8	195-flagged
14	A. J. Foyt, Jr.	Copenhagen	A. J. Foyt Enterprises	Chevy Indy-A	8	161	'92 Lola	black	222.798	23	9	195-flagged
93	John Paul, Jr.	D. B. Mann/Buick	D. B Mann Motorsports	Buick V-6	6	208	'90 Lola	blue, pink	220.244	18	10	194-flagged
90	Lyn St. James	Agency Rent-A-Car/JC Penney	Paragon Motorsports, Inc.	Chevy Indy-A	8	161	'91 Lola	blue, wht, red	220.150	27	11	193-flagged
68	Dominic Dobson	Tobacco Free America	Burns Racing Team, Inc.	Chevy Indy-A	8	161	'91 Lola	black, red	220.359	29	12	193-flagged
1	Michael Andretti	Kmart/Texaco	Newman/Haas Racing	Cosworth XB	8	160	'92 Lola	black, white	228.169	6	13	189-fuel pressure
21	Buddy Lazier	Leader Cards/Lola	Leader Cards, Inc.	Buick V-6	6	208	'91 Lola	red, yelo, blue	222.688	24	14	139-engine
6	Arie Luyendyk	Target-Scotch Video	Chip Ganassi Racing Teams, Inc.	Cosworth XB	8	160	'92 Lola	black, red	229.127	4	15	135-accident T4
31	Ted Prappas	Say No To Drugs/P.I.G.	Norman C. Turley	Chevy Indy-A	8	161	'91 Lola	blk, orng, red	219.173	32	16	135-gear box
51	Gary Bettenhausen	Glidden Paints	Team Menard, Inc.	Buick V-6	6	208	'92 Lola	yelo, red, orng	228.932	5	17	112-accident BS
48	Jeff Andretti	Gillette/Carlo/Texaco	A. J. Foyt Enterprises	Buick V-6	6	208	'91 Lola	black	219.306	20	18	109-accident T2
39	Brain Bonner	Applebee's/Danka	Dale Coyne Racing	Buick V-6	6	208	'91 Lola	green, white	220.845	26	19	97-accident T4
7	Paul Tracy	Mobil 1	Penske Racing, Inc.	Chevy Indy-B	8	161	'91 Penske	wht, blue, red	219.751	19	20	96-engine
47	Jimmy Vasser	Kodalux	Hayhoe-Cole Racing, Inc.	Chevy Indy-A	8	161	'91 Lola	blk, wht, yelo	222.313	28	21	94-accident T1
22	Scott Brayton	Amway/Northwest Airlines	Dick Simon Racing, Inc.	Buick V-6	6	208	'92 Lola	blu, wht, red	226.142	7	22	93-engine
2	Mario Andretti	Kmart/Texaco	Newman/Haas Racing	Cosworth XB	8	160	'92 Lola	black, white	229.503	3	23	78-accident T4
5	Emerson Fittipaldi	Marlboro	Penske Racing, Inc.	Chevy Indy-B	8	161	'92 Penske	white, red	223.607	11	24	75-accident T1
26	Jim Crawford	Quaker State	Kenny Bernstein's King Motorsports	Buick V-6	6	208	'92 Lola	green, white	228.859	21	25	74-accident T1
4	Rick Mears	Marlboro	Penske Racing, Inc.	Chevy Indy-B	8	161	'92 Penske	white, red	224.594	9	26	74-accident T1
91	Stan Fox	Jonathan Byrd's/Bryant	Hemelgarn/Byrd Racing	Buick V-6	6	208	'91 Lola	red	222.867	13	27	63-accident SS
44	Philippe Gache	Formula Proj.-Rhone Poulenc Rorer	Formula Project/Dick Simon	Chevy Indy-A	8	161	'91 Lola	blue, wht, red	221.496	16	28	61-accident T1
92	Gordon Johncock	STP/Jacks Tool	Hemelgarn/Runyan Racing	Buick V-6	6	208	'91 Lola	red	219.288	31	29	60-engine
10	Scott Pruett	Budweiser	Truesports Company	Chevy Indy-A	8	161	'92 Truesports	red, white	220.464	17	30	52-engine
59	Tom Sneva	Glidden Paints/Menards	Team Menard, Inc.	Buick V-6	6	208	'91 Lola	yelo, red, orng	219.737	30	31	10-accident T4
19	Eric Bachelart	Royal Oak/Mi-Jack	Dole Coyne Racing	Buick V-6	6	208	'90 Lola	red	221.549	15	32	4-engine
36	Roberto Guerrero	Quaker State	Kenny Bernstein's King Motorsports	Buick V-6	6	208	'92 Lola	green, white	232.482	1	33	0-DNS, accident BS

1993

77th Race • May 30, 1993

After last year's record qualifying speeds and rash of injuries, the Speedway takes new steps to slow the cars and make the track safer. New warmup lanes for entering and leaving the pits replace the aprons that some drivers used to run deeper into the corners. The turns are narrower and rumble strips on the inside of the corners prevent drivers from running below the white line. The different arc through the turns makes it less likely cars will spin directly into the outside wall. USAC also trims the wings on the cars, which reduces cornering speeds.

After Michael Andretti's dominating performance the previous year with the Ford-Cosworth V-8, several teams adopt this engine, setting up a stronger assault on the Chevrolet-Ilmor V-8 that has won the last five races.

Andretti misses this race after nine consecutive starts attempting to follow in his father's footsteps by competing in Formula 1. Replacing him on the Newman-Haas team is 1992 Formula 1 champion Nigel Mansell, and the British driver quickly becomes the center of attention. Mansell joins three other former world driving champs in the field: Newman-Haas teammate Mario Andretti and Brazilians Emerson Fittipaldi and Indy rookie Nelson Piquet.

With four-time winner Rick Mears retiring the previous December, Team Penske reverts to a two-car effort for Fittipaldi and Paul Tracy.

Bobby Rahal arrives with a new business partner, Carl Hogan, and a new chassis, the Rahal-Hogan (an update of the 1992 Truesports chassis). Most of the 102 entries list either Lola or Penske chassis.

Though the Buick V-6 is still available, the car company reduces its involvement. Team owner John Menard steps in to continue developing the stock-block engine under his own name.

PRACTICE AND QUALIFYING

SUNDAY, MAY 9: Speeds are indeed lower than last year. Paul Tracy is quickest at 223.9 mph in a Penske-Chevy, and Mario Andretti is right behind at 223.5 in a Lola-Ford.

TUESDAY, MAY 11: Nineteen-ninety winner Arie Luyendyk posts the fastest practice speed so far, 225.9 mph, in a Lola-Ford. Roberto Guerrero hits 224.5 in a Lola-Chevy, and Emerson Fittipaldi tops 222 in a Penske-Chevy.

WEDNESDAY, MAY 12: Nigel Mansell makes a grand

STARTING LINEUP

Average Field Qualifying Speed: 219.692

Numbers in flags indicate finish position

Raul Boesel

Stefan Johansson

Emerson Fittipaldi

Danny Sullivan

Stephan Gregoire

Mario Andretti

Al Unser, Jr.

Nigel Mansell

Scott Brayton

Kevin Cogan

POLE POSITION
Qualifying Speed: 223.967

Arie Luyendyk

Scott Goodyear

Paul Tracy

Roberto Guerrero

Nelson Piquet

The newest edition of the Chevrolet Camaro Z28 paced the field (*above*). It used a stock 350-cubic-inch V-8. Chevy also provided the driver, division General Manager Jim Perkins, and the official truck (*opposite*). Carl Haas, co-owner of the Newman-Haas team, draws for qualifying position the day before the run for the pole (*top right*). Al Unser, Jr.'s, No. 3 Lola leads a group of cars out of Gasoline Alley on Pole Day (*left*).

17 Gary Bettenhausen

25 Lyn St. James

10 John Andretti

23 Dominic Dobson

21 Willy T. Ribbs

16 Eddie Cheever

9 Teo Fabi

31 Stan Fox

12 Al Unser, Sr.

18 Hiro Matsushita

26 Geoff Brabham

22 Didier Theys

29 Jeff Andretti

13 Jimmy Vasser

20 Tony Bettenhausen

27 Robby Gordon

15 Davy Jones

24 Jim Crawford

entrance to the Brickyard. A back injury delays his arrival, but he breezes through the Speedway rookie test in a couple of hours before posting a practice lap of 218.6 mph, 10th fastest of the day. Raul Boesel has the day's best speed, 224.5, and Tracy is next at 224.1.

THURSDAY, MAY 13: Luyendyk raises the top practice speed to 226.2 mph, and Andretti is second quickest at 225.4. Mansell is one of four drivers who top 224.

FRIDAY, MAY 14: Boesel has his best speed of the week, 225.6 mph, and Mansell comes in second at 224.9. The run for the pole the next day appears to be wide open.

SATURDAY, MAY 15: Rookie Robby Gordon, driving for A. J. Foyt, bangs the wall in morning practice on Pole Day. Gordon escapes injury, and Foyt—who is considering taking a shot at making his 36th straight race—instead takes a slow parade lap in his familiar No.14 and announces his driving days are over. He is now officially a full-time owner.

Mario Andretti is the first to qualify, and his average of 223.414 mph looks like it could hold up as the temperature climbs. Scott Goodyear does 222.344, but Raul Boesel soon tops him by just .035 mph.

As shadows cool the track at 5 P.M., Arie Luyendyk knocks Andretti off the pole with a run of 223.967. Three more drivers top 220—Mansell, Swedish rookie Stefan Johansson, and Fittipaldi, but no one tops Luyendyk, who wins the pole. Andretti and Boesel fill out a front row made up entirely of Lola-Fords.

SUNDAY, MAY 16: Al Unser, Sr., qualifies for his 27th race with a Lola-Chevy and Bobby Rahal makes his 11th with his own chassis and a Chevy engine. Both look vulnerable to bumping with speeds in the 217 mph range.

SUNDAY, MAY 23: It is bump day, and Rahal is on the bubble. With 15 minutes left, Eddie Cheever bumps Rahal with a four-lap average of 217.599. Rahal goes out in his backup car at 5:59 P.M. but manages only 216.342, well short of the speed he needs to make the field. The 1986 winner finds his venture into chassis design a humbling experience.

The average speed of the field drops 3.787 mph to 219.692, but just 6.7 mph separates the fastest and slowest cars.

THE RACE

Start: From the outside of row one, Raul Boesel dives in front of Arie Luyendyk at the first turn for the lead as Mario Andretti drops to third.

Lap 12: Boesel's Lola-Ford still leads, but Andretti passes Luyendyk for second in Turn 1.

Lap 16: Jim Crawford spins in Turn 2 but keeps his car off the wall. When the yellow comes out, most of the front runners pit. Rookie Stephan Gregoire's Buick leads a lap, and then gives way to Kevin Cogan's Chevy.

Boesel, in third before the yellow, gets a one-lap penalty for passing Andretti on the warmup lane, dropping him to the rear of the field.

Lap 23: Back under green, Al Unser, Sr., passes Cogan for the lead. Unser, who turned 54 the previous day, is the oldest driver to lead a 500.

Lap 30: Danny Sullivan crashes in Turn 3, and Unser and Cogan pit, giving the lead to Andretti. Luyendyk runs second →

Top: A. J. Foyt (left) was happy with his new driver, rookie Robby Gordon. That is, until Gordon hit the wall in the No. 41 Lola (*middle*). Al Unser, Sr., who qualified for his 27th 500, visits with Johnny Rutherford, a veteran of 24 starts (*above*). Jeff Andretti's car catches fire in the pits during practice (*opposite top*). He was unhurt. Raul Boesel tries out the track's new deceleration lanes (*opposite, middle*). Arie Luyendyk wins the pole in the No. 10 Target/Scotch car (*opposite, bottom left*); Jimmy Vasser practices for his second 500 (*opposite, bottom right*).

During morning practice prior to the first day of qualifying, A. J. Foyt turned several effortless laps in the 221-222 mph range. As it turned out, this may have been quick enough to have put him in the front row for a 36th consecutive start at Indy. But when Foyt saw his young protégé and teammate, Robby Gordon, crash into the wall, he decided he was through. A. J. took one farewell lap by himself, waved to the fans, and announced his retirement. He addressed the crowd in an emotion-choked voice.

"This is the place that made A. J. Foyt," he said. "And this was the place to quit. I love you fans," he said, waving to the crowd. "I drove for you all every time out."

On his way back to the garage area, Foyt paused to shake hands with fans. "That's okay, darlin'," Foyt drawled when a young girl asked for his signature on a program. "I'm in no hurry today."

and Emerson Fittipaldi third. Nigel Mansell is fourth, but on the restart, Teo Fabi blows by him to take the position.

Lap 47: When Andretti slows to negotiate traffic, Luyendyk slips by into the lead. Mansell takes third place from Fittipaldi, closes up behind teammate Andretti, and then moves inside in Turn 1 to grab second place.

Lap 58: The front runners pit under green, and the lead becomes a hot potato. Unser, Sr., regains the lead for five laps. When he stops, John Andretti, rookie Robby Gordon, and Scott Goodyear each lead two laps. After the flurry of pit stops, Mansell passes Andretti to take the lead and builds a 10-second cushion.

Lap 91: When the leaders pile into the pits during a caution period, Mansell overshoots his pit and drops from first to seventh. Mario Andretti emerges as the leader, with Unser, Sr., and his son running second and third, and Luyendyk fourth.

Lap 96: Paul Tracy, racing Scott Brayton for fifth place, crashes in Turn 3. Brayton escapes without damage.

Lap 102: Andretti builds a lead of almost half a lap over Al Unser, Jr. Scott Brayton runs third, Luyendyk fourth, and Mansell fifth. Al Unser, Sr., falls back, his Chevy engine overheating.

Lap 128: Jeff Andretti and Roberto Guerrero tangle in Turn 3 and crash. Just as the yellow comes out, leader Mario Andretti is pulling into the pits. USAC rules that Andretti entered the pit when it was closed and assesses a stop-and-go penalty. Andretti drops to second and defending winner Al Unser, Jr., leads for the first time. Unser's father remains a factor in third place, and Brayton and Fittipaldi are fourth and fifth. Only six cars are out at this point.

Lap 152: Andretti finally catches and passes Unser, Jr., for the lead, and Fittipaldi closes up behind Unser in third. →

This page: Paul Newman (left) is the better-looking half of the Newman-Haas partnership. Lyn St. James models the latest in racewear (above). Jim Nabors belts out *Back Home Again in Indiana* (right). Formula 1 champ Nigel Mansell tours the track (below). *Opposite page:* Front-row cars roll toward the start (top). Raul Boesel wins the dash to the first turn (bottom left). Robby Gordon gets a big splash of fuel (middle right). Comedian Jay Leno visits the Brickyard (bottom right).

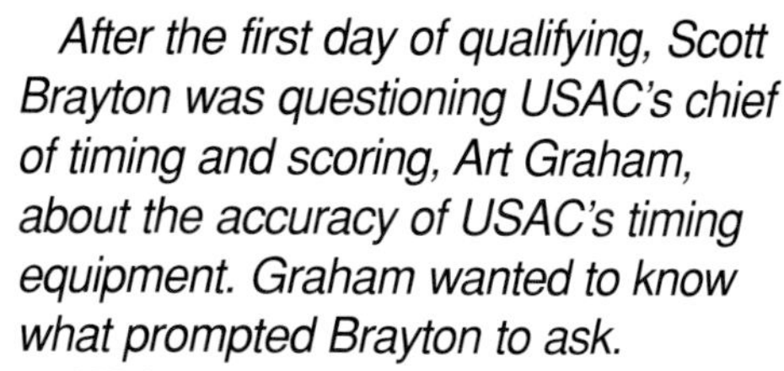

After the first day of qualifying, Scott Brayton was questioning USAC's chief of timing and scoring, Art Graham, about the accuracy of USAC's timing equipment. Graham wanted to know what prompted Brayton to ask.

"Well, it has to do with Roberto's total time," he replied in reference to Roberto Guerrero.

Guerrero had averaged 219.645 mph for his run, while Brayton recorded 219.637, good for 10th and 11th starting positions, respectively. Their times were only seven thousandths of a second apart after four laps.

"Huh? I must have scrubbed off some speed somewhere," Brayton said.

Energizer
6
Gillette
BASF
TEXACO
uniden
10
RAYOVAC
Scotch
igloo
START

BOSCH

Lap 174: Following a caution, Andretti leads Fittipaldi and Mansell on the restart, but Mansell makes a daring outside pass around both into Turn 1 to snatch the lead. Andretti falls back with tire problems as Fittipaldi closes up on Mansell.

Lap 185: A stalled car at the entrance to the pits brings out another caution. Mansell leads, and Fittipaldi and Luyendyk sit next in line as the cars gather behind the pace car. As they take the green flag, Fittipaldi shoots inside of Mansell on the front straight, and just before Turn 1, Luyendyk zips around the outside of Mansell, dropping him to third.

Lap 193: Fittipaldi stretches his lead to four seconds over Luyendyk when Mansell gets too high in coming out of Turn 2 and bangs the outside wall, bringing out the yellow. Mansell decides to stay out on the track to hold on to third place.

Finish: As they approach the restart on Lap 196, Fittipaldi slows drastically in the north short chute, forcing Luyendyk and Mansell to back off. Fittipaldi then blasts off toward the green flag before his pursuers get back on the throttle and can catch him.

On Lap 198, Fittipaldi runs the fastest lap of the race, 214.8 mph, and pulls away to a 2.9-second margin over Luyendyk. Fittipaldi earns his second win, team owner Roger Penske notches his ninth, and the Chevy-Ilmor captures its sixth straight.

Mansell comes in third despite hitting the wall and is the first rookie since Donnie Allison in 1970 to complete 500 miles. Fittipaldi leads just the last 16 laps. Twelve different drivers lead during the day, and there are 23 lead changes in an entertaining and highly competitive race. Twenty-four cars are still running at the finish, 10 of them on the lead lap.

Jeff Andretti in the No. 21 Lola-Buick and Roberto Guerrero in the No. 40 Lola-Chevy get too close in Turn 3 (*top*) and wind up in the wall (*above*). *Right:* Emerson Fittipaldi, in the No. 4 Marlboro Penske, has Arie Luyendyk on his tail and Nigel Mansell close behind soon after Fittipaldi snatched the lead from Mansell on a restart late in the race. Twelve drivers swapped the lead 23 times during the race. Fittipaldi streaks across the finish line (*opposite top*) for his second win in five years and the ninth win for owner Roger Penske. Fittipaldi (*opposite bottom*) led just 16 laps in his Penske-chassis car powered by the latest-version Chevy-Indy engine and earned a $1,155,304 paycheck for the day's work.

RESULTS

NO.	DRIVER	CAR	ENTRANT	ENGINE	CYL	DISP	CHASSIS	COLOR	QUAL SPD	START	FIN	LAPS / SPEED / REASON OUT
4	Emerson Fittipaldi	Marlboro	Penske Racing, Inc.	Chevy Indy-C	8	161	'93 Penske	white, red	220.150	9	1	200-157.207
10	Arie Luyendyk	Target/Scotch	Chip Ganassi	Cosworth XB	8	160	'93 Lola	black, red	223.967	1	2	200-157.168
5	Nigel Mansell	Kmart/Texaco-Havoline	Newman/Haas Racing	Cosworth XB	8	160	'93 Lola	black, white	220.255	8	3	200-157.149
9	Raul Boesel	Duracell/Mobil 1	Dick Simon Racing	Cosworth XB	8	160	'93 Lola	black, copper	222.379	3	4	200-157.142
6	Mario Andretti	Kmart/Texaco-Havoline	Newman/Haas Racing	Cosworth XB	8	160	'93 Lola	black, white	223.414	2	5	200-157.133
22	Scott Brayton	Amway/Byrd's/Bryant	Dick Simon/Jonathan Byrd	Cosworth XB	8	160	'93 Lola	blue, wht, red	219.637	11	6	200-157.117
2	Scott Goodyear	MacKenzie Financial	Walker Motorsport, Inc.	Cosworth XB	8	160	'93 Lola	blue, silver	222.344	4	7	200-157.099
3	Al Unser, Jr.	Valvoline	Galles Racing International	Chevy Indy-C	8	161	'93 Lola	blue, wht, red	221.773	5	8	200-157.070
8	Teo Fabi	Pennzoil	Hall/VDS Racing, Inc.	Chevy Indy-C	8	161	'93 Lola	yelo, blk, red	220.514	17	9	200-156.968
84	John Andretti	Foyt/Copenhagen/Marmon Wasp II	A. J. Foyt Enterprises	Cosworth XB	8	160	'93 Lola	black	221.746	24	10	200-156.964
16	Stefan Johansson	AMAX Energy & Metals	Bettenhausen Motorsports	Chevy Indy-C	8	161	'93 Penske	blk, wht, red	220.824	6	11	199-running
80	Al Unser, Sr.	Budsweiser	Kenny Bernstein's Budweiser King Racing	Chevy Indy-C	8	161	'93 Lola	red, white	217.453	23	12	199-running
18	Jimmy Vasser	Kodalux/STP	Hayhoe-Simon Racing	Cosworth XB	8	160	'93 Lola	black, yelo	218.967	19	13	198-running
11	Kevin Cogan	Conseco Special	Galles Racing International	Chevy Indy-C	8	161	'93 Lola	blue, white	217.230	14	14	198-running
50	Davy Jones	Agip-Andrea Moda-ETI-Marcelo	Euromotorsport Racing, Inc.	Chevy Indy-A	8	161	'93 Lola	black, yelo	218.416	28	15	197-running
59	Eddie Cheever	Glidden/Menard	Team Menard, Inc.	Buick V-6	6	208	'93 Lola	yellow	217.599	33	16	197-running
51	Gary Bettenhausen	Glidden Paint	Team Menard, Inc.	Menard V-6	6	208	'93 Lola	yelo, red, orng	220.380	18	17	197-running
15	Hiro Matsushita	Panasonic Special	Walker Motorsport, Inc.	Cosworth XB	8	160	'93 Lola	blue, yelo	219.949	26	18	197-running
36	Stephan Gregoire	Formula Proj/Maalon/GSF/Safeway	France Info Formula Product	Buick V-6	6	208	'92 Lola	red, blk, grn, yelo, blu	220.851	15	19	195-running
76	Tony Bettenhausen	AMAX Energy & Metals	Bettenhausen Motorsports	Chevy Indy-C	8	161	'93 Penske	blk, wht, red	218.034	22	20	195-running
75	Willy T. Ribbs	Bill Cosby/Service Merchandise	Walker Motorsport, Inc.	Cosworth XB	8	160	'92 Lola	white, red	217.711	30	21	194-running
92	Didier Theys	Delta Faucet/Kinko	Hemelgarn Racing, Inc.	Buick V-6	6	208	'92 Lola	purple	217.752	32	22	193-running
66	Dominic Dobson	Coors Light/Indy Parks	Burns Motorsports	Chevy Indy-A	8	161	'92 Galmer	black, red	218.776	27	23	193-running
60	Jim Crawford	Budsweiser	Kenny Bernstein's Budweiser King Racing	Chevy Indy-C	8	161	'93 Lola	red, white	217.612	31	24	192-running
90	Lyn St. James	JC Penney/Nike	Dick Simon Racing	Cosworth XB	8	160	'93 Lola	blk, wht, red	218.042	21	25	176-gearbox
27	Geoff Brabham	Glidden/Menard	Team Menard, Inc.	Menard V-6	6	208	'93 Lola	yelo, blu, red	217.800	29	26	174-engine
41	Robby Gordon	A. J. Foyt Copenhagen Racing	A. J. Foyt Enterprises	Cosworth XB	8	160	'93 Lola	black	220.085	25	27	165-gearbox
40	Roberto Guerrero	Budsweiser	Kenny Bernstein's Budweiser King Racing	Chevy Indy-C	8	161	'93 Lola	red, white	219.645	10	28	125-accident T3
21	Jeff Andretti	Interstate Batteries/Gillette/Taesa	Pagan Racing	Buick V-6	6	208	'92 Lola	black, yelo	220.572	16	29	124-accident T3
12	Paul Tracy	Marlboro	Penske Racing, Inc.	Chevy Indy-C	8	161	'93 Penske	white, red	220.298	7	30	94-accident T3
91	Stan Fox	Delta Faucet/Jacks Tool	Hemelgarn Racing, Inc.	Buick V-6	6	208	'91 Lola	purple	218.765	20	31	64-engine
77	Nelson Piquet	ARISCO/STP	Team Menard, Inc.	Menard V-6	6	208	'93 Lola	red	217.949	13	32	38-engine
7	Danny Sullivan	Molson	Galles Racing International	Chevy Indy-C	8	161	'93 Lola	blue	219.428	12	33	29-accident T3

1994

78th Race • May 29, 1994

Engines dominate the pre-race news. Roger Penske drops a bombshell when he announces in April his team will use a new turbocharged Ilmor-built Mercedes-Benz engine that threatens to blow competitors into the weeds. Penske takes advantage of a USAC rule change the year before that says pushrod engines no longer have to be based on production engines. Instead of starting with an off-the-shelf passenger-car engine like the Buick V-6, Ilmor builds a new pushrod V-8 with a single in-block camshaft specifically for the 500.

As a "stock-block" engine, the Ilmor-Mercedes V-8 gets more displacement than the multi-cam Ford-Cosworth engine (209 cubic inches instead of 162) and 55 inches of turbo boost instead of 45. The result is an estimated 1000 horsepower, about 150 more than the Ford, previously the most potent. However, the 500 will be the first race for the unproven Mercedes engine.

Penske also hires 1992 winner Al Unser, Jr., to join two-time winner Emerson Fittipaldi and Paul Tracy on his team. Fittipaldi logs 880 practice laps at Indy during May, while the team simultaneously conducts engine durability tests at Penske's Michigan track.

Honda becomes the first Japanese manufacturer to launch a factory engine effort at Indy. Honda supplies its new multi-cam V-8 to the team of 1986 winner Bobby Rahal—who returns after missing the 1993 show because of an uncompetitive chassis—and Mike Groff.

Chevrolet drops out of the Indy-car engine business, but the V-8 that formerly wore the bow-tie emblem lives on as the Ilmor. In the continuing search for a competitive advantage, several teams switch to the new British-made Reynard chassis.

Michael Andretti is back after a difficult year on the Formula 1 circuit, while father Mario announces this is his final year.

PRACTICE AND QUALIFYING

SUNDAY, MAY 8: Speeds are higher than last year the first day cars hit the track. Scott Brayton is fastest of the day at 227.658 mph with a Menard V-6, and Roberto Guerrero is second at 225.558 with a Buick V-6.

MONDAY, MAY 9: Emerson Fittipaldi runs 226.5 mph with the new Mercedes pushrod V-8 in a Penske chassis that sports a larger rear wing that other teams try to copy. Michael Andretti, however, is quicker at 227 with the new Reynard chassis and Ford engine.

TUESDAY, MAY 10: Raul Boesel surprises many with today's fast time of 230.4 mph in a Lola-Ford, but lurking very close behind him are Team Penske drivers Paul Tracy →

STARTING LINEUP

Average Field Qualifying Speed: 223.270

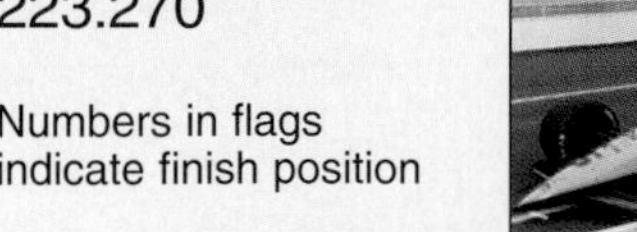

Numbers in flags indicate finish position

Emerson Fittipaldi

Lyn St. James

Mario Andretti

Dominic Dobson

Dennis Vitolo

Raul Boesel

6
Michael Andretti

18
Arie Luyendyk

Eddie Cheever

Hideshi Matsuda

POLE POSITION
Qualifying Speed: 228.011

Al Unser, Jr.

2
Jacques Villeneuve

22
Nigel Mansell

10
John Andretti

Stan Fox

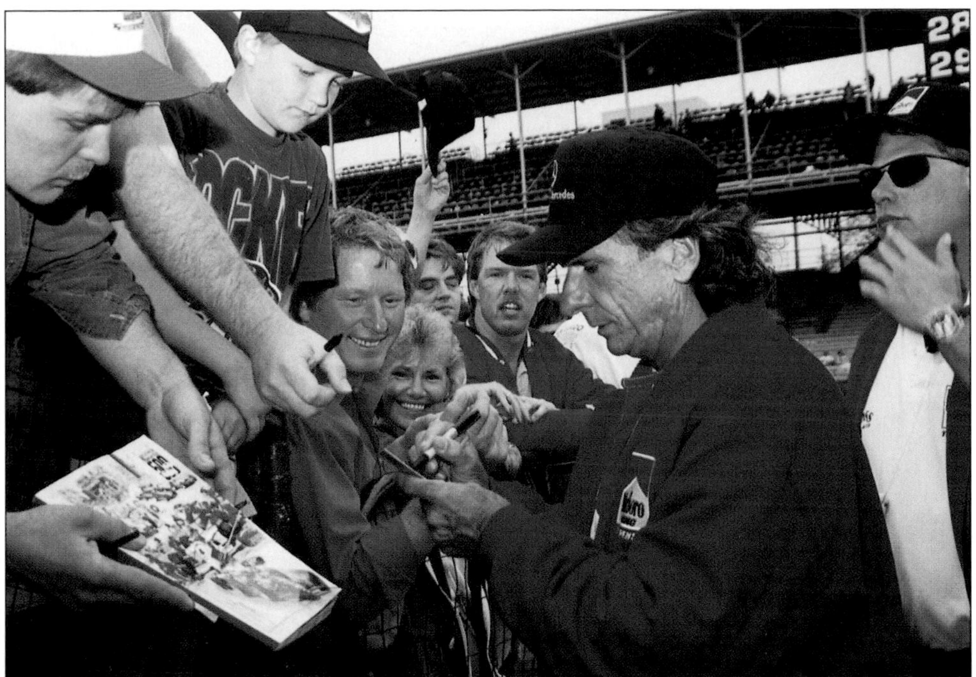

Thirty years after the original Mustang paced the starting field, the latest version was chosen to lead the '94 field (*opposite*). It took its place alongside the Mustang pace cars from 1979 and 1964 (*below*). Defending winner Emerson Fittipaldi draws plenty of autograph seekers (*right*).

Hiro Matsushita

Brian Till

Teo Fabi

Stefan Johansson

John Paul, Jr.

Scott Goodyear

Scott Sharp

Roberto Guerrero

Scott Brayton

Adrian Fernandez

Mauricio Gugelmin

Marco Greco

Jimmy Vasser

Robby Gordon

Bryan Herta

Paul Tracy

Bobby Rahal

Mike Groff

and Fittipaldi, both of whom top 229.

FRIDAY, MAY 13: For the second day in a row, Fittipaldi's Mercedes is fastest at more than 230 mph and teammate Tracy is next at 228-plus. Tracy later spins in Turn 3 and winds up smacking the outside wall in Turn 4, suffering a concussion that knocks him out of Pole Day participation.

SATURDAY, MAY 14: Rain delays the start of qualifying more than an hour, and Raul Boesel is the first to make a serious bid for the pole. His Ford averages 227.618 mph. Canadian rookie Jacques Villeneuve makes an impressive debut with a run of 226.259 in a Reynard-Ford.

Al Unser, Jr., is the first in a Penske-Mercedes to make an attempt, and his first lap of 225.722 upholds his reputation as a so-so qualifier. Laps two and three surpass 228, however, and his fourth nearly reaches 229.5 for a four-lap average of 228.011, good enough to take the pole away from Boesel.

Among other qualifiers, Lyn St. James makes her third straight race at 224.154, slightly faster than the cocky Nigel Mansell and quick enough for row two. Rookie Hideshi Matsuda becomes the second Japanese driver on the grid, joining Hiro Matsushita. Bobby Rahal and Mike Groff both qualify the new Honda engine, but at the two slowest speeds so far. The day ends with eight cars still eligible for the pole, including that of Emerson Fittipaldi.

SUNDAY, MAY 15: It is warm and sunny when Fittipaldi makes his run for the pole, and he is slower than teammate Unser at 227.303 mph. No one else is close, and Unser chalks up his first Indy pole, while Boesel and Fittipaldi fill out the front row.

TUESDAY, MAY 17: The biggest news is off the track. Al Unser, Sr., who has four wins, 27 starts, and a record 644 lead laps on his illustrious resume, unexpectedly announces his retirement. He has been struggling to get up to speed with a new team, Arizona Motor Sports.

Bobby Rahal announces he is acquiring 1993 Penske-Ilmor cars for himself and teammate Mike Groff as insurance in case their underpowered Lola-Hondas are bumped.

SATURDAY, MAY 21: Three-time winner Johnny Rutherford, who hasn't qualified for the 500 since 1988, announces his retirement.

Rahal and Groff withdraw their qualified Lola-Hondas, and both safely make the field at higher speeds with year-old Penske-Ilmors.

SUNDAY, MAY 22: Rookie Marco Greco is the only driver to qualify on the final day, and he bumps Scott Goodyear. Teammate Davy Jones gives up his seat, and for the second time in three years, Goodyear starts 33rd in a car another driver qualifies.

Greco's car is the sixth to qualify that Dick Simon either owns or prepares for the race. Nine rookies are in the race, the most since 1982. The average speed of the 33 cars climbs more than 3.5 mph to 223.270, just under the 1992 record.

THE RACE

Start: Al Unser, Jr., and Emerson Fittipaldi pull ahead of Raul Boesel on the front straight, and Unser darts in front of Fittipaldi to reach Turn 1 first and take the lead. Michael Andretti moves up to third as Boesel drops back.

Lap 21: Roberto Guerrero spins into the Turn 2 wall and is the first car out of the race. When the leaders pit underyellow, Fittipaldi takes over the lead, Michael Andretti →

Teo Fabi (*top*) is secured in the Pennzoil Reynard. Cousins Michael and John Andretti (*above*) finished in the top 10. Michael's dad, Mario (*left*), contemplates his final Indy start. Jacques Villeneuve's Player's crew goes against John Paul, Jr.'s, team in the pit-stop competition (*below*). Robby Gordon and Willy T. Ribbs (*opposite top*) teamed up for Walker Racing, but Ribbs, right, couldn't find the speed to make the field. Emerson Fittipaldi heads out at "happy hour" (*opposite middle*). A wider pit lane and new scoring pylon were the most visible improvements to the venerable Speedway (*opposite bottom*).

On the first day of qualifications in 1994, a heavy rain delayed the program for one hour, 15 minutes. When time trials began, it was obvious the track had lost a good deal of speed.

But no one told Hideshi Matsuda. Not only was his four-lap qualifying average of 222.545 mph a new record for rookie qualifiers, but for most of the afternoon, it appeared Matsuda might start on the front row. Eventually, Matsuda was pushed back to the 14th starting position. But he was still on cloud nine. "This is the happiest moment of my life," he kept saying.

Race day proved his qualification run was no fluke. At one point, Matsuda was running in seventh place. But reality has a way of settling in at Indianapolis. On lap 91, Matsuda lost control in Turn 2 and smacked the wall hard.

A surprisingly quick study, Matsuda had fallen in love with Indy when he covered the 500 as an analyst for Japanese television. It was during a broadcast that he announced to his countrymen, "I want to do that!"

moves into second, and Unser falls to third.

Mario Andretti, comes into the pits in fourth place but never comes out. His 29th and final race (second only to A. J. Foyt's 35) ends with fuel system problems. Andretti retires with just one victory but 556 laps as the leader, third overall and one more than Foyt.

Lap 30: Back under green, Mike Groff and Dominic Dobson make contact in Turn 1 and crash into the outside wall. As other cars slow to avoid the wreck, Lyn St. James rear-ends Scott Goodyear. Groff, Dobson, and Goodyear are out of the race, but St. James gets back in after a long stop for repairs.

Fittipaldi's Mercedes still leads with the field under yellow, and Unser is second. Eddie Cheever is third and Michael Andretti fourth.

Lap 50: Fittipaldi pulls away to a 3.6-second lead over Unser, with John Andretti in third, 10 seconds back. Michael Andretti falls to 16th, a lap down, after making a green-flag stop to replace a cut tire.

Lap 70: It is still a Team Penske show, with Fittipaldi hogging the spotlight. After a round of green-flag pit stops, he leads teammate Unser by nearly 16 seconds. Rookie Jacques Villeneuve is third, the only other car still on the lead lap.

Lap 95: As most of the field heads for the pits during a caution period, rookie Dennis Vitolo runs over a wheel on John Andretti's car and lands on top of the rear of Nigel Mansell's car. Mansell, who was running third before the yellow, and Vitolo are out. John Andretti continues on and finishes 10th. Afterwards, he flies to Charlotte, North Carolina, to compete in a 600-mile NASCAR stock-car race the same evening, the only driver to accomplish that feat.

Lap 100: When racing resumes, Fittipaldi still leads and 

The fifth row of, from left, Dennis Vitolo, Hideshi Matsuda, and Stan Fox (*opposite top*) fires its engines for the start. Florence Henderson sings the national anthem (*opposite, bottom left*). Historic race cars tour the track as part of pre-race activities (*opposite, bottom right*). The pace lap creates order from apparent chaos (*top*). Mike Groff, in car No. 10, tangles with Dominic Dobson's No. 17 (*above*) in Turn 1 on the 30th lap. Scott Goodyear, in the No. 40 Budweiser Lola, runs over debris from the accident (*second from top, right*) and damages his suspension. Safety crews direct traffic around the disabled cars during the ensuing yellow (*right*).

pulls away from Unser. Villeneuve trails in third, the only other car on the lead lap.

Lap 170: Giving up the lead only when he pits for fuel and tires, Fittipaldi builds a commanding lead of 31 seconds—about three-quarters of a lap—over Unser, though he may have to stop for fuel once more to go the distance. Michael Andretti works his way back up to third, still a lap down, with Villeneuve fourth and Bobby Rahal fifth.

Lap 180: Fittipaldi passes Unser to put his teammate a lap down. Three laps later, Unser jumps back in front of Fittipaldi on the front straight.

Lap 185: Fittipaldi is still trying to lap Unser, and as the cars shoot out of Turn 4, Fittipaldi gets too high and whacks the outside wall, shattering what looks like a cinch third victory. Unser roars away down the front straight into first place.

Finish: With enough fuel to finish the race, Unser stays on the track during the yellow for his teammate's wreck. Second-place Villeneuve, on the same lap as the leader, does likewise.

When racing resumes, Unser's Mercedes engine lets him power away from Villeneuve. On Lap 197, the caution flag comes out again when Stan Fox crashes in Turn 1, and the race ends under yellow.

Unser wins for the second time in three years, and it comes on his father's 55th birthday. Al, Sr., joins "Junior" for a victory lap around the Brickyard, where the Unser family has now won nine times. Unser, Jr., earns a record $1,373,813.

Team owner Roger Penske wins for the 10th time and does so in dominating fashion. Fittipaldi leads 145 laps and Unser 45. However, USAC rewrites the engine rules for 1995, and the short life of the pushrod Ilmor-Mercedes V-8 ends after one successful outing.

Villeneuve leads seven laps, and the 23-year-old Canadian wins Rookie of the Year for his second-place finish, the highest for a rookie since Roberto Guerrero did likewise in 1984.

Eddie Cheever slips by John Andretti on the inside of the track (*top left*). Cheever finished eighth and Andretti 10th. Rookie Hideshi Matsuda's No. 99 Lola-Cosworth whacks the Turn 1 wall (*top right*), putting him out in 24th place. When Emerson Fittipaldi's No. 2 Penske (*left*) hits the wall while he is leading, his misfortune brings joy to Al Unser, Jr.'s, crew (*above*) because their driver takes over first. "Little Al" and family celebrate his second victory and the ninth for the Unser clan (*opposite, top left*). A Penkse chassis with a Mercedes-Benz pushrod engine did the trick for Unser (*opposite, bottom*). The fans take away great memories—and leave behind mounds of trash (*opposite, top right*).

RESULTS

NO.	DRIVER	CAR	ENTRANT	ENGINE	CYL	DISP	CHASSIS	COLOR	QUAL SPD	START	FIN	LAPS / SPEED / REASON OUT
31	Al Unser, Jr.	Marlboro	Penske Racing, Inc.	Merc-Benz	8	209	'94 Penske	white, red	228.011	1	1	200-160.872
12	Jacques Villenueve	Players LTD	Forsythe/Green Racing, Inc.	Cosworth XB	8	161	'94 Reynard	blue, white	226.259	4	2	200-160.749
4	Bobby Rahal	Miller Genuine Draft	Rahal/Hogan Racing	Ilmore-D	8	161	'93 Penske	blk, gold, red	224.094	28	3	199-running
18	Jimmy Vasser	Conseco/STP	Hayhoe Racing	Cosworth XB	8	161	'94 Reynard	blue, white	222.262	16	4	199-running
9	Robby Gordon	Valvoline/Cummins	Walker Racing	Cosworth XB	8	161	'94 Lola	blue, wht, red	221.293	19	5	199-running
8	Michael Andretti	Target/Scotch	Chip Ganassi Racing Teams, Inc.	Cosworth XB	8	161	'94 Reynard	black, red	226.205	5	6	198-running
11	Teo Fabi	Pennzoil	Hall Racing, Inc.	Ilmor-D	8	161	'94 Reynard	yelo, red, blk	223.394	24	7	198-running
27	Eddie Cheever	Quaker State	Team Menard, Inc.	Menard V-6	6	208	'93 Lola	grn, red, orng, yelo	223.163	11	8	197-running
14	Brain Herta	A. J. Foyt/Copenhagen	A. J. Foyt Enterprises	Cosworth XB	8	161	'94 Lola	black, red	220.992	22	9	197-running
33	John Andretti	A. J. Foyt/Byrd's/Bryant	Jonathan Byrd/A. J. Foyt Racing	Cosworth XB	8	161	'94 Lola	red	223.263	10	10	196-running
88	Mauricio Gugelmin	Hollywood Indy Car	Chip Ganassi Racing Teams, Inc.	Cosworth XB	8	161	'94 Reynard	red, blue, wht	223.104	29	11	196-running
19	Brian Till	The Mi-Jack Car	Dale Coyne Racing	Cosworth XB	8	161	'93 Lola	yellow, red	221.107	21	12	194-running
91	Stan Fox	Delta Faucets/Jacks Tool	Hemelgarn Racing, Inc.	Cosworth XB	8	161	'94 Reynard	purple, yellow	222.867	13	13	193-accident T1
22	Hiro Matsushita	Panasonic/Duskin	Dick Simon Racing, Inc.	Cosworth XB	8	161	'94 Lola	blue, red, yelo	221.382	18	14	193-running
16	Stefan Johansson	Alumax Aluminum	Bettenhausen Motorsports	Ilmor-D	8	161	'93 Penske	blue, red	221.518	27	15	192-running
71	Scott Sharp	PacWest Racing	PacWest Racing Group	Cosworth XB	8	161	'93 Lola	blue, wht, red	222.091	17	16	186-running
2	Emerson Fittipaldi	Marlboro	Penske Racing, Inc.	Merc-Benz	8	209	'94 Penske	white, red	227.303	3	17	184-accident T4
28	Arie Luyendyk	Indy Regency Racing-Eurosport	Indy Regency Racing	Ilmor-D	8	161	'93 Penske	blue, wht, red	223.673	8	18	179-engine
90	Lyn St. James	Spirit of Amer./JC Penney/Rebook/Lee	Dick Simon Racing, Inc.	Cosworth XB	8	161	'94 Lola	blk, wht, red	224.154	6	19	170-running
59	Scott Brayton	Glidden Paint	Team Menard, Inc.	Menard V-6	6	208	'93 Lola	red, orng, yelo	223.652	23	20	116-engine
5	Raul Boesel	Duracell Charger	Dick Simon Racing, Inc.	Cosworth XB	8	161	'94 Lola	black, copper	227.618	2	21	100-water pump
1	Nigel Mansell	Kmart/Texaco-Havoline	Newman/Haas Racing	Cosworth XB	8	161	'94 Lola	black, white	224.041	7	22	92-hit by #79
3	Paul Tracy	Marlboro	Penske Racing, Inc.	Merc-Benz	8	209	'94 Penske	white, red	222.710	25	23	92-turbo
99	Hideshi Matsuda	Beck/Simon	Beck Motorsports/Simon	Cosworth XB	8	161	'93 Lola	silver	222.545	14	24	90-accident T1
45	John Paul, Jr.	ProFormance Tm Losi/Cybergenics	ProFormance Motorsports	Ilmor-D	8	161	'93 Lola	blue, white	222.500	30	25	89-accident T3
79	Dennis Vitolo	Hooligans/Carlo/Charter Amer.	Dick Simon Racing, Inc.	Cosworth XB	8	161	'93 Lola	red	222.439	15	26	89-accident T3
25	Marco Greco	Int. Sports LTD	Arciero Project Indy/Simon	Cosworth XB	8	161	'94 Lola	blk, wht, red	221.216	32	27	53-electrical
7	Adrian Fernandez	Tecate/Quaker State	Galles Racing International	Ilmor-D	8	161	'94 Reynard	red, grn, wht	222.657	26	28	30-suspension
17	Dominic Dobson	PacWest Racing	PacWest Racing Group	Cosworth XB	8	161	'94 Lola	blue, wht, red	222.970	12	29	29-accident T1
40	Scott Goodyear	Budweiser	Kenny Bernstein's Budweiser King Racing	Cosworth XB	8	161	'94 Lola	red	223.817	33	30	29-suspension
10	Mike Groff	Motorola	Rahal/Hogan Racing	Ilmor-C+	8	161	'93 Penske	blue, wht, red	221.355	31	31	28-accident T1
6	Mario Andretti	Kmart/Texaco-Havoline	Newman/Haas Racing	Cosworth XB	8	161	'94 Lola	black, white	223.503	9	32	23-fuel system
21	Roberto Guerrero	Interstate Batteries	Pagan racing, Inc.	Buick V-6	6	208	'92 Lola	black, green	221.278	20	33	20-accident T1

1995

79th Race • May 28, 1995

The Hulman family marks its 50th year as owners of the Speedway. In more ways than one it is one of the most eventful months of May in track history.

Firestone returns to the Brickyard for the first time since 1974, and the tire company that won 43 straight races from 1920 to 1966 tries to break Goodyear's lock on the 500.

The pushrod Mercedes-Benz V-8 that won last year for Team Penske in dominant fashion disappears as USAC reduces the turbocharger boost for this quasi-stock-block engine. Mercedes is back, however, with a new dual-cam racing V-8, an evolution of the Ilmor engine. Penske's is among the teams that use the new Mercedes engine.

Honda, shut out of last year's 500, renews its efforts with a more powerful turbocharged V-8, and Ford-Cosworth upgrades its XB turbo V-8. Car owner John Menard continues refining the Buick-based, stock-block Menard V-6, which still is allowed 55 inches of turbo boost under USAC rules, compared to 45 inches for the pure racing engines.

Tom Binford, chief steward the last 22 years, announces he will step down after this year to become commissioner of the new Indy Racing League that Speedway President Tony George will launch in 1996. Keith Ward will succeed Binford.

In contrast to recent races when as many as four Andrettis are in the field, there is only one this year—Michael. Mario retires, John moves on to NASCAR, and Jeff is still recovering from injuries.

PRACTICE AND QUALIFYING

SATURDAY, MAY 6: Practice opens with a loud roar from the Menard V-6. Nineteen-ninety winner Arie Luyendyk unofficially tops Roberto Guerrero's 1992 qualifying record with a lap at 233.281 mph. Menard teammate Scott Brayton is nearly as fast at 232.408. Second-year driver Jacques Villeneuve is next at 226.3 with a Ford-Cosworth.

MONDAY, MAY 8: Luyendyk runs the fastest practice lap ever—234.107 mph—on just his third circuit. Brayton is next at 232.859 to give the Menard team the two fastest cars for the third day in a row. Paul Tracy's Ford-Cosworth is a close third at 231.315.

THURSDAY, MAY 11: Team Menard raises the standard again as Pole Day nears. Luyendyk goes 234.332 mph, but Brayton tops ➔

STARTING LINEUP

Average Field Qualifying Speed: 226.912

Numbers in flags indicate finish position

POLE POSITION
Qualifying Speed:
231.604

Scott Goodyear

Mauricio Gugelmin

Jimmy Vasser

Andre Ribeiro

Teo Fabi

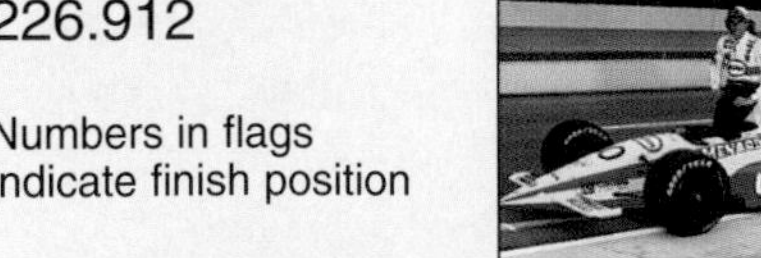

Arie Luyendyk

Jacques Villeneuve

Scott Pruett

Stan Fox

Eddie Cheever

Scott Brayton

Michael Andretti

Robby Gordon

Hiro Matsushita

Roberto Guerrero

A collection of racing helmets (*top two rows, this page and opposite*) shows the amount of art and science that goes into their splashy appearance and aerodynamic details. The helmets are designed to improve air flow over the car and reduce the wind buffeting that can affect the driver. Warner Brothers cartoon characters drum up business for Kodak's Mini Indy display at the new infield Fan Fest (*opposite bottom*). The Chevrolet Corvette was invited back for a return engagement as the pace car (*left*), and Chevy General Manager Jim Perkins returned for his third stint as the driver. The 'Vette's 300-horsepower 350-cubic-inch V-8 required no modification for pace-car duty, and the car received only the required safety equipment and decals before it was ready for the Brickyard.

Danny Sullivan

Bobby Rahal

Eliseo Salazar

Christian Fittipaldi

Scott Sharp

Bryan Herta

Alessandro Zampedri

Hideshi Matsuda

Buddy Lazier

Eric Bachelart

Carlos Guerrero

Davy Jones

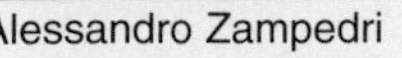

Paul Tracy

Gil de Ferran

Raul Boesel

Adrian Fernandez

Lyn St. James

Stefan Johansson

him at 234.656. Six other drivers top 230. Scott Goodyear cranks his Honda up to 232.246 to be third fastest, and Robby Gordon's Ford is fourth at 231.8.

FRIDAY, MAY 12: For the seventh day in a row, Team Menard is fastest. Luyendyk sets another unofficial record at 234.913 mph, and Brayton follows at 234.473. Michael Andretti's Ford-Cosworth is third at 233.724. Ten other drivers exceed 230, and records seem sure to fall on Pole Day.

SATURDAY, MAY 13: Rain delays the start of qualifying until late afternoon, and Arie Luyendyk makes the first serious claim to the pole with a run of 231.031 mph in his Lola-Menard, more than 1.4 mph shy of the record.

Not long after, Scott Brayton averages 231.604 mph, also short of the record but fast enough to bump teammate Luyendyk off the pole.

Michael Andretti is the last to qualify today, and his 229.294 is fast enough to be on the front row. Several others are still in line when the 6 P.M. gun sounds, leaving the pole undecided until Sunday.

SUNDAY, MAY 14: Scott Goodyear mounts the final challenge for the pole with a Reynard-Honda, and his 230.759 mph is fast enough to bump Michael Andretti off the front row.

Scott Brayton wins the pole in his 14th start, and Menard V-6s start first and second. Honda becomes the first Japanese engine manufacturer to qualify, and Scott Goodyear gives Firestone tires a front-row start.

MONDAY, MAY 15: Team Penske continues to struggle after skipping first weekend qualifying. Defending winner Al Unser, Jr., climbs out of his Penske chassis and borrows a Reynard in a search for more speed.

THURSDAY, MAY 18: Team Penske appears ready to bail out of its uncompetitive chassis. The Rahal-Hogan team, which made the 1994 race with help from Roger Penske, returns the favor by letting Penske borrow one of its backup Lola-Mercedes.

FRIDAY, MAY 19: Penske driver Emerson Fittipaldi gets his borrowed Lola up to 227.8 mph in practice, well above the 225 necessary to make the field. Teammate Unser continues to struggle with the Penske chassis and fails to reach 220.

SATURDAY, MAY 20: After running practice laps at more than 227 mph, Unser is the first Penske driver to try to qualify. His Lola does only 224 mph on the first two laps, and Penske waves off the attempt.

➔

A. J. Foyt delivers emphatic instructions (*top*) to his new driver, Scott Sharp, during qualifying. Marco Greco (*middle*) wasn't speedy enough to make the 500 a second time after cracking the field as a rookie in 1994. Fellow Brazilian Andre Ribeiro went hard into the Turn 3 wall on Pole Day (*above*), but suffered only bruises. He came back the following weekend to qualify a Reynard-Honda in 12th position for his first Indianapolis start. Canadian Jacques Villeneuve, 1994 Rookie of the Year, damaged his backup Reynard-Ford-Cosworth in practice (*left*) and suffered a bruised foot. Villeneuve regrouped and put his car on the second row.

Emerson Fittipaldi makes his first run a while later and posts lap speeds of 225, 225.4, and 226 before Penske waves off, even though it looks fast enough to make the field. Unser goes out again and reaches 225.4 before his Mercedes V-8 gives up. All the practice laps earlier in the day burned out his qualifying engine.

SUNDAY, MAY 21: It is do or die for Team Penske. Fittipaldi squeaks his Lola into the field at 224.907 mph, but looks vulnerable on the bubble. On his third and final attempt, Al Unser, Jr., can muster only 224.101—too slow to make the field. Unser, who sat on the pole in 1994, becomes the first defending winner who fails to qualify. The Unser family fails to make the race for the first time since 1962.

Stefan Johansson is the last to qualify, and his speed of 225.547 easily bumps Fittipaldi. Team Penske, winner of 10 races and three of the last four, suffers a humbling defeat by failing to place a car in the field.

The 33 starters average a record 226.912 mph, and just 6.58 mph separates the fastest car from the slowest.

THE RACE

Start: Both Goodyear and Firestone lead the first lap. Scott Goodyear's Firestone-shod Honda gets around the Menard V-6s of Scott Brayton and Arie Luyendyk at the green flag. It is the first time a Japanese engine leads the 500, and the first time since 1973 that Firestone tires lead.

Further back, Stan Fox goes low into Turn 1 and loses control when something breaks at the rear of his car. Fox bangs into Eddie Cheever and gets airborne before hitting the wall head on, his car splitting open at the cockpit. Carlos Guerrero, Eric Bachelart, Gil de Ferran, and Lyn St. James also get caught in the wreck, and all are out of the race by lap six. Fox suffers severe head injuries, but recovers months later.

Lap 10: Luyendyk's Menard V-6 blows by Goodyear's Honda for the lead on the restart, and Michael Andretti then gets by to drop Goodyear to third.

Lap 17: Andretti grabs the lead from Luyendyk, giving a Ford-powered car the lead for the first time.

Lap 36: Jacques Villeneuve inherits the lead when others pit, but neither he nor his crew realizes he is in first place when the yellow flag comes out a lap later. Instead of falling in behind the pace →

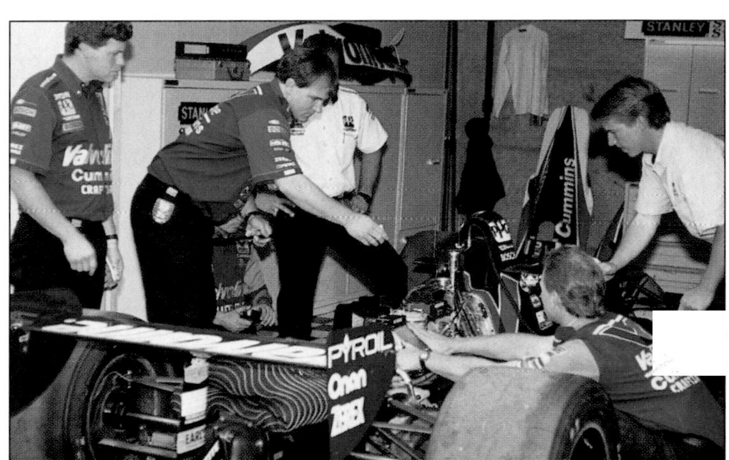

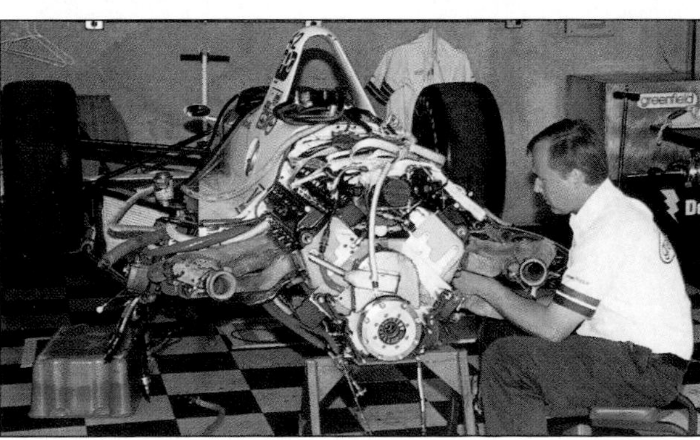

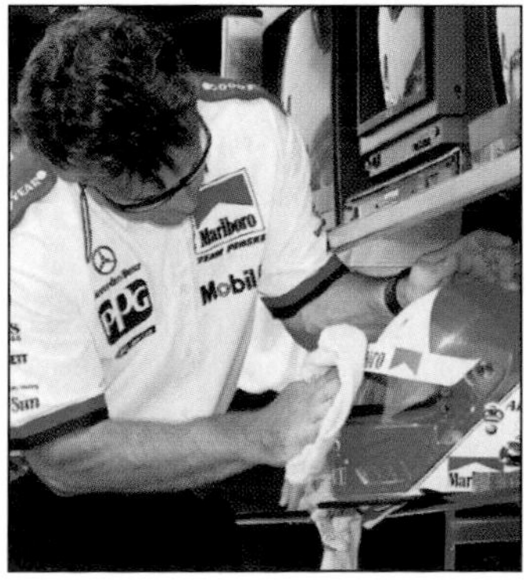

Chilean rookie Eliseo Salazar (*top left*) started from the outside of row eight and finished fourth. The Walker Racing crew (*top right*) works on the Ford-Cosworth engine in Robby Gordon's Reynard. Stefan Johansson (*above left*), driving for Tony Bettenhausen's team, gives his crew feedback during practice. The USAC testing lab in the garage area (*above*) checked parts for safety and performance standards. Michael Greenfield's entry (*far left*) had a pushrod engine developed by his father, Peter. A crash kept him out of the field. Al Unser, Jr.'s, helmet is kept at the ready (*left*).

car, Villeneuve passes it twice. USAC hits Villeneuve with a two-lap penalty for passing the pace car, dropping him to 24th place and seemingly out of contention.

Lap 45: When racing resumes, Andretti leads and pulls away by more than 16 seconds ahead of Goodyear. Mauricio Gugelmin is third.

Lap 77: When Gugelmin slows to enter the pits, Andretti goes around him in Turn 4, but his Lola slides too high and scrapes the outside wall. After leading 45 laps, Andretti climbs out of his car, suspension damage ending another shot at victory.

Goodyear inherits the lead, but loses it to Gugelmin when he pits three laps later.

Lap 117: Gugelmin pits under green, giving the lead to Goodyear, who pits two laps later.

Lap 123: The leaders having stopped under green, Villeneuve gets back onto the lead lap, and when the caution flag comes out, he pits under yellow.

Gugelmin regains the lead when racing resumes, and Goodyear chases in second. Robby Gordon is third.

Lap 156: When the leaders pit under green, Villeneuve stays on the track and takes over first place. Scott Pruett is now second, Goodyear third, and Gordon fourth. Gugelmin drops to fifth with handling problems.

Lap 163: Leader Villeneuve is heading for the pits when Davy Jones hits the Turn 2 wall, bringing out the yellow. Villeneuve steers back onto the track at the last moment, averting a possible pit violation penalty.

When the pits open, the leaders come in except for Jimmy Vasser, who inherits first place and becomes the eighth different driver to lead. Villeneuve stalls as he tries to leave the pits and winds up behind Pruett and Goodyear in fourth place.

Lap 170: Racing for the lead, Pruett slips underneath Vasser in Turn 3. As Vasser moves higher to give Pruett room, his Reynard loses grip and slides into the outside wall.

Lap 176: With the field bunched up behind the pace car, Goodyear gets a run on Pruett when the green flag comes out and takes over first place on the front straight.

Three laps later, Goodyear runs the fastest lap of the race, 224.009 mph, but can't shake Pruett, who clings to his tail. →

Opposite page: Team Menard put two of its American-built, Buick-based V-6s (top right) in Lola chassis (bottom left) on the front row. Arie Luyendyk (top left) qualified third fastest and Scott Brayton (second from top, right) won the pole. Brayton gives the thumbs-up signal with owner John Menard and team manager Larry Curry (bottom right). *This page:* Team Penske's Al Unser, Jr. (top left), and Emerson Fittipaldi (top right) both failed to qualify. Roger Penske (middle row, left) shows the strain of a difficult month. Football star Joe Montana (center) was an interested spectator. Jay Leno visits with 500 driver Robby Gordon and NASCAR ace Jeff Gordon (middle row, right). Mary Fendrich Hulman (above) ordered the engines started on race day. The drivers took care of the rest (right).

Lap 185: Second-place Scott Pruett makes a run at Goodyear, but gets too high in Turn 2, clips the outside wall, and skids hard into the inside wall.

No leaders pit during the ensuing yellow. Goodyear lines up first behind the pace car, with Villeneuve second and rookie Christian Fittipaldi third.

Lap 190: Anticipating the green flag, Goodyear roars past the pace car before it leaves the track. Villeneuve—penalized earlier for the same infraction—slows to avoid passing the pace car as Goodyear accelerates up the front straight.

Lap 193: Starter Duane Sweeney waves the black flag at Goodyear, ordering him to pit for a stop-and-go penalty for passing the pace car. Goodyear ignores the summons and keeps going.

Finish: Goodyear still runs at the front of the pack, but USAC stops scoring him after Lap 195. Villeneuve becomes the leader and cruises to victory, 2.48 seconds ahead of rookie Fittipaldi. Bobby Rahal is third for the second race in a row.

Villeneuve struggles back from a two-lap penalty to become the first Canadian winner and completes 505 miles before anyone else does 500. Villeneuve leads just 15 laps but wins $1.3 million of a record $8 million purse. He gives the Ford-Cosworth engine and Reynard chassis their first victories and stretches Goodyear tire's win streak to 24 years.

In his first two races, Villeneuve completes every lap—and then some—and finishes first and second. The next season, he moves on to Formula 1 competition and an eventual world championship in 1997.

Scott Goodyear, who came so close to winning in 1992, blows an almost certain victory by being too eager on the last restart. His gaffe also deprives Honda of its first visit to victory lane. Ten different drivers swap the lead 24 times. Despite the six-car wreck on the opening lap, 18 cars are still running at the finish, seven on the lead lap (not including Goodyear).

Only seconds after the field took the green flag on race day, Stan Fox's racer went out of control, triggering a five-car accident in the first turn. On the way to the wall, Stan's machine collected Eddie Cheever's car. Sandwiched between Fox's car and the unforgiving concrete, Cheever took quite a shot. But it was nothing compared to the ride Fox took. After bouncing off Cheever's racer, Fox hit the wall head-on. The force was so tremendous, the bodywork literally exploded from the crumpled machine. Cheever was the first to arrive at Fox's destroyed Reynard 915, but there was little assistance he could offer the critically injured veteran. Stan faced many months of hospital care and rehabilitation. Eventually he would totally recover from this near-fatal accident.

Friends and others told Cheever he was just in the wrong place at the right time. Eddie said little about the accident, until the following evening at the annual victory banquet.

While nearly every other driver voiced hope for Stan's recovery, Cheever, who was obviously very concerned about his fellow driver, spoke his mind. "If my job was to help make Stan's impact a little softer," Cheever said, "then I was glad to be there."

Stan Fox (*top*) was making his eighth start when his No. 91 Reynard unexpectedly darted toward the wall on the first lap. His airborne racer split open, Fox is precariously exposed in the multi-car accident (*left*). He survived, but there was little car left for safety crews to collect (*above*). Arie Luyendyk (*opposite, top left*) led seven laps and was the only one of three Menard cars to go the distance, finishing seventh. Jacques Villeneuve, in just his second start, became the first Canadian winner when countryman Scott Goodyear roared by the pace car and was penalized for ignoring a black flag. Villeneuve (*opposite, top right and bottom*) won the season championship, then departed for Formula 1.

RESULTS

NO.	DRIVER	CAR	ENTRANT	ENGINE	CYL	DISP	CHASSIS	COLOR	QUAL SPD	START	FIN	LAPS / SPEED / REASON OUT
5	Jacques Villeneuve	Player's LTD	Team Green	Ford/Cos XB	8	161	'95 Reynard	blue, white	228.397	5	1	200-153.616
15	Christian Fittipaldi	Marlboro Chapeco	Walker Racing	Ford/Cos XB	8	161	'95 Reynard	grn, yelo, blue	226.375	27	2	200-153.583
9	Bobby Rahal	Miller Genuine Draft	Rahal Hogan Racing	Merc-Benz	8	161	'95 Lola	blk, gold, red	227.081	21	3	200-153.577
7	Eliseo Salazar	Cristal/Mobil 1/Copec	Dick Simon Racing, Inc.	Ford/Cos XB	8	161	'95 Lola	grn, wht, yelo	225.023	24	4	200-153.553
5	Robby Gordon	Valvoline/Cummins	Walker Racing	Ford/Cos XB	8	161	'95 Reynard	wht, red, blue	227.531	7	5	200-153.420
18	Mauricio Gugelmin	Hollywood/PacWest	PacWest Racing Group	Ford/Cos XB	8	161	'95 Reynard	red, wht, blue	227.923	6	6	200-153.392
40	Arie Luyendyk	Glidden Special	Team Menard, Inc.	Menard V6	6	208	'95 Lola	red, orng, yelo	231.031	2	7	200-153.067
33	Teo Fabi	Combustion Eng./Indeck	Forsythe Racing, Inc.	Ford/Cos XB	8	161	'95 Reynard	red, white	225.911	15	8	199-flagged
17	Danny Sullivan	VISA/PacWest	PacWest Racing Group	Ford/Cos XB	8	161	'95 Reynard	wht, blue, red	225.496	18	9	199-flagged
25	Hiro Matsushita	Panasonic Duskin YKK	Arciero Wells Racing	Ford/Cos XB	8	161	'95 Reynard	blue, red, yelo	226.867	10	10	199-flagged
34	Alessandro Zampedri	The Mi-Jack Car	Payton/Coyne Racing	Ford/Cos XB	8	161	'94 Lola	yellow, red	225.753	17	11	198-flagged
21	Roberto Guerrero	Upper Deck/General Comp.	Pagan Racing	Merc-Benz	8	161	'94 Reynard	white	226.402	13	12	198-flagged
4	Bryan Herta	Target/Scotch Video	Target/Chip Ganassi Racing	Ford/Cos XB	8	161	'95 Reynard	blk, red, yelo	225.551	33	13	198-flagged
24	Scott Goodyear	LCI/Motorola/CNN	Tasman Motorsports Group	Honda FGH	8	161	'95 Reynard	yelo, blk, red	230.759	3	14	195-flagged*
54	Hideshi Matsuda	Taisan/Zunne Group	Beck Motorsports	Ford/Cos XB	8	161	'94 Lola	black, silver	227.818	20	15	194-flagged
16	Stefan Johansson	Team Alumax	Bettenhausen Motorsports, Inc.	Ford/Cos XB	8	161	'94 Reynard	blue, red	225.547	31	16	192-flagged
60	Scott Brayton	Quaker State/Glidden	Team Menard, Inc.	Menard V6	6	208	'95 Lola	grn, red, orng, yelo	231.604	1	17	190-flagged
31	Andre Ribero	LCI Int./Honda	Tasman Motorsports Group	Honda FGH	8	161	'95 Reynard	blue, red, yelo	226.495	12	18	187-flagged
20	Scott Pruett	Firestone Patrick	Patrick Racing	Ford/Cos XB	8	161	'95 Lola	red, wht, blue	227.403	8	19	184-accident T2
11	Raul Boesel	The Duracell Charger	Rahal Hogan Racing	Merc-Benz	8	161	'95 Lola	blk, yelo, red	226.028	22	20	184-oil line
10	Adrian Fernandez	Tecate/Quaker State	Galles Racing International	Merc-Benz	8	161	'95 Lola	red, green	227.803	25	21	176-engine
12	Jimmy Vasser	Target/STP	Target/Chip Ganassi Racing	Ford/Cos XB	8	161	'95 Reynard	blk, red, yelo	227.350	9	22	170-accident T3
77	Davy Jones	Jonathan Byrd's/Bryant	Jonathan Byrd/Dick Simon	Ford/Cos XB	8	161	'95 Lola	red	225.135	32	23	161-accident T2
3	Paul Tracy	Kmart/Budweiser	Newman/Haas Racing	Ford/Cos XB	8	161	'95 Lola	red, white	225.795	16	24	136-electrical
6	Michael Andretti	Kmart/Texaco Havoline	Newman/Haas Racing	Ford/Cos XB	8	161	'95 Lola	blk, wht, red	229.294	4	25	77-suspension
41	Scott Sharp	Copenhagen Racing	A. J. Foyt Enterprises	Ford/Cos XB	8	161	'95 Lola	red, black	225.711	30	26	74-accident T4
80	Buddy Lazier	Glidden/Quaker State	Team Menard, Inc.	Menard V6	6	208	'95 Lola	grn, red, orng, yelo	226.017	23	27	45-fuel system
19	Eric Backelart	The AGFA Car	Payton/Coyne Racing	Ford/Cos XB	8	161	'94 Lola	red	228.875	26	28	6-mechanical
8	Gil de Ferran	Pennzoil Special/Hall	Hall Racing, Inc.	Merc-Benz	8	161	'95 Reynard	yellow	225.437	19	29	1-accident T1
91	Stan Fox	Delta Faucet/Bowling	Hemelgarn Racing, Inc.	Ford/Cos XB	8	161	'95 Reynard	purple	226.588	11	30	0-accident T1
14	Eddie Cheever	Copenhagen Racing	A. J. Foyt Enterprises	Ford/Cos XB	8	161	'95 Lola	red, black	226.314	14	31	0-accident T1
90	Lyn St. James	Whitlock Auto Supply	Dick Simon Racing	Ford/Cos XB	8	161	'95 Lola	yellow, red	225.346	28	32	0-accident T1
22	Carlos Guerrero	Herdez-Viva Mexico	Dick Simon Racing	Ford/Cos XB	8	161	'95 Lola	wht, grn, yelo	225.831	29	33	0-accident T1

*Stopped scoring on Lap 195.

1996

80th Race • May 26, 1996

After decades of evolution, the advent of the Indy Racing League brings revolution to the Brickyard. Speedway President Tony George creates the IRL as an oval-track series with key goals of lowering the cost of racing and providing more opportunity for American drivers.

George makes a controversial decision to reserve 25 of the 33 starting positions at Indy for teams that compile the most points in the first two IRL races at Orlando, Florida, and Phoenix, Arizona. The only caveat is that the top 25 teams qualify at a minimum 220 mph.

Championship Auto Racing Teams, which has provided the bulk of the cars and drivers for the 500 since 1979, objects to the new qualifying rule and boycotts the race, except for two members—Galles Racing and Walker Racing. CART stages a competing 500-mile race the same day at Michigan International Speedway.

With most of last year's competitors at the CART race, the Speedway sees its biggest freshman class in more than six decades. A diverse mixture of rookies and veterans walks the garage area in search of rides.

The rules governing the cars are the same as last year's, but the track gets a new, glass-smooth asphalt surface that promises record speeds. The number of entries drops to 77 from 104 the previous year, and most use the Ford-Cosworth V-8 or Menard V-6 and its Buick forerunner. Galles's two entries for veteran driver Davy Jones are the only ones with Mercedes-Ilmor V-8s. Chassis are divided between Lola and Reynard. This is the last year for the current formula because the IRL will field completely new chassis and production-based, naturally aspirated 4.0-liter V-8s in 1997.

PRACTICE AND QUALIFYING

MONDAY, MAY 6: After two days of rain, only rookies try out the track today. Tony Stewart immediately becomes the center of attention by setting an unofficial record of 237.3 mph with his Lola-Menard. Menard teammate Mark Dismore is a distant second at 228.6, and Michel Jourdain, Jr., is third with a Lola-Ford at 228.2.

TUESDAY, MAY 7: Veterans join rookies on the track today, but that fails to intimidate Stewart, who is fastest again at 236.1 mph. Teammates Eddie Cheever and Scott Brayton are right behind at 236 and 235.8, respectively. Former winner Arie Luyendyk has the fastest Ford, good for 233.6. ➔

In a year of tumultuous change at the Speedway, some things remained constant, including the deep voice of track announcer Tom Carnegie (*above*) coming over the PA system. Carnegie marked his 50th year at the Speedway with such familiar pronouncements as "He's on it" during qualifying runs. *Opposite:* The change was attributed to Speedway President Tony George, who made the 500 part of his new all-oval Indy Racing League series. George, right, talks with Brad Calkins, one of the new wave of car owners who embraced the IRL concept.

STARTING LINEUP

Average Field Qualifying Speed: 227.807

Numbers in flags indicate finish position

Eliseo Salazar

Roberto Guerrero

Buzz Calkins

Michele Alboreto

Richie Hearn

Davy Jones

Buddy Lazier

Michel Jourdain, Jr.

Mike Groff

Mark Dismore

POLE POSITION
Qualifying Speed: 233.100

Tony Stewart

Eddie Cheever, Jr.

Alessandro Zampedri

Davey Hamilton

Stephan Gregoire

Lyn St. James

Scott Sharp

Paul Durant

Johnny Parsons

Hideshi Matsuda

Danny Ongais

John Paul, Jr.

Arie Luyendyk

Robbie Buhl

Brad Murphy

Johnny O'Connell

Scott Harrington

Johnny Unser

Jim Guthrie

Marco Greco

Racin Gardner

Fermin Velez

Joe Gosek

THURSDAY, MAY 9: Luyendyk runs the fastest lap so far, 237.774 mph, with his Reynard-Ford. Stewart leads Team Menard with a lap of 237, and Brayton and Cheever both top 234. Buddy Lazier is fifth fastest at over 233 in a Reynard-Ford. The fastest five ride on Firestone tires.

FRIDAY, MAY 10: The day before the pole goes up for grabs, Luyendyk turns an even faster lap, 239.26 mph, and looks like the driver to beat. Stewart leads the Menard cars at 236, and Scott Sharp, driving a Lola-Ford for A. J. Foyt, posts his fastest lap of the week, 235.7.

SATURDAY, MAY 11: Pole Day qualifying starts late because of showers, but records still fall like rain. Davy Jones is the first to outdo Roberto Guerrero's 1992 qualifying speeds, setting a one-lap mark of 233.082 mph and a four-lap mark of 232.882 in his Lola-Mercedes.

A short time later, Tony Stewart knocks Jones off the pole with new records of 233.179 for a single lap and 233.1 for four in his Lola-Menard. Four drivers in a row challenge Stewart, including Guerrero, Eliseo Salazar, and Menard teammates Eddie Cheever and Scott Brayton, but none tops the rookie's speeds—until Luyendyk finally makes a run late in the day after replacing two engines.

Luyendyk does a first lap of 231.756, but cranks his Ford up each succeeding lap until he hits 234.742 his last trip around to average 233.39, a record performance that ends Stewart's claim to the pole.

Team Menard refuses to surrender. Minutes later, owner John Menard withdraws Brayton's Lola, which sits securely on the second row. Brayton jumps into his backup car and runs four laps in a row at faster than 233, averaging a record 233.718, a scant .328 mph faster than Luyendyk to win his second straight pole in gutsy fashion.

Post-qualifying inspection reveals that Luyendyk's car is seven pounds underweight, and USAC throws out his speeds. When Pole Day ends, teammates Brayton and Stewart are first and second with Menard V-6s, and Jones is third with a Mercedes V-8.

SUNDAY, MAY 12: Luyendyk bounces back from Saturday's debacle to set record speeds of 237.498 mph for one lap and 236.986 for four, marks likely to stand for years because slower cars are coming in 1997. As a second-day qualifier, he starts from the seventh row.

FRIDAY, MAY 17: Just six days after Brayton makes his memorable run for the pole, the 37-year-old veteran of 14 starts at the Speedway dies in a tragic accident during practice. Brayton spins in Turn 2 when one of his rear tires deflates. The left side of his Lola crashes hard into the outside wall, and Brayton absorbs the full impact.

SUNDAY, MAY 19: Joe Gosek, a star on the modified circuit,

In bygone days, rookies of the year and other front-running Indy drivers often ventured back to their hometown tracks, the small, sometimes out-of-the-way venues that set them on the road to the 500.

But in more modern times, fewer Indy standouts ever returned to their roots, even for a personal appearance. That changed—at least for one year—with '96 Rookie of the Year Tony Stewart.

When the 25-year-old Stewart went back to his roots, he went all the way back. On the Fourth of July 1996, he returned to his home track in Rushville, Indiana, where he'd won his very first race seven years before. Welcomed home with a tremendous ovation from the fans, Tony won the feature race of the evening, a three-quarter midget-car event held on the ⅙-mile Rushville Fairgrounds dirt track.

Rookie Tony Stewart (*top left*) and '90 winner Arie Luyendyk (*left*) were favored early. Lyn St. James's Lola-Cosworth gets attention (*above*). The IRL hired three-time winner Johnny Rutherford (*opposite, top right*) to advise newcomers. With a new engine formula due in '97, the Menard V-6 (*opposite, second from top right*) had its last run at the 500. Buddy Lazier (*opposite, top left*) was fast in practice. Jim Guthrie (*opposite, middle left*) made his first 500. Four-time winner Al Unser, Sr., counsels nephew Johnny Unser (*opposite, middle right*). Johnny Parsons hits the wall in Pole Day practice (*opposite bottom*).

Many people voiced concern over the huge group of rookies with little or no Indy-car experience entered in the first Indy Racing League-sanctioned 500. But many of the 17 newcomers who started were impressive in the skill and good judgment they showed.

One driver, Racin Gardner, had no trouble with Indy's high speeds. Racin—his real name—started and finished 25th, but he was the "fastest" rookie in the race. That's not to say he had the fastest speed of the rookie class of '96; that honor went to polesitter Tony Stewart. To say Racin was the fastest rookie at Indy requires looking past his times on the track.

In 1994, Gardner drove the Green Monster jet-engine car in the Nevada desert at more than 500 mph. That's what made him the fastest driver at Indianapolis.

qualifies at 222.793 mph to bump Billy Boat and become the final driver to make the fastest 500 field ever. The 33 starters average 227.807, beating the record set a year earlier by nearly one mph.

Rookie Gosek drives one of seven cars that Team Scandia, led by engineer Dick Simon, places on the grid. Sixteen other drivers are making their first start, the most rookies since 1930, when there were 19.

Team Menard announces that Danny Ongais, whose last start was in 1986, will replace the late Scott Brayton in car No. 32. Ongais starts 33rd. Menard teammate Tony Stewart moves over to become the first rookie since Teo Fabi in 1983 to start from the pole. Davy Jones is now in the middle and Salazar moves up to the outside of row one.

THE RACE

Start: Rookie Johnny Unser pulls into the pits on the pace lap with gearbox problems that knock him out of the race before it starts. At the green flag, Tony Stewart pulls ahead to take the lead, becoming only the third rookie to lead his first lap. Eliseo Salazar gets around Davy Jones to move into second place.

Lap 10: Stewart runs 234.421 mph, the fastest lead lap ever. Arie Luyendyk, who starts 20th, is up to eighth place.

Lap 11: Paul Durant blows his engine and spins in his own oil in Turn 3, bringing out the yellow. Danny Ongais also spins in Turn 3, but stays off the wall and continues to the pits.

Lap 21: Back under green, leader Stewart pulls away to a cushion of more than five seconds, while Roberto Guerrero passes Salazar for second.

Lap 32: Stewart makes his first pit stop under green, giving the lead to Guerrero. After the other leaders make their stops, Stewart is back in front and leads Salazar by 11 seconds.

Lap 54: Stewart, whose Menard V-6 appears to be losing power, pits under yellow and gives the lead to Guerrero. Salazar, who was second, also pits, stalls his car twice, and falls out of the top five.

Lap 70: When the leaders stop under yellow, Guerrero's crew has trouble attaching the fuel hose, and then he kills the engine when he tries to leave. Guerrero falls out of the top five. Davy Jones takes the lead and Buddy Lazier moves into second. Stewart, struggling for power, falls to third, and Luyendyk moves up to fourth.

Lap 78: Eddie Cheever, running 16th after a long pit stop, posts the fastest race lap ever at the Speedway, 236.103 mph, with his Lola-Menard. ➔

Rookie Richie Hearn (*opposite, top left*) finished third, running on the lead lap in the No. 4 Reynard-Cosworth. Dan Drinan's hopes for his first start ended with a heavy crash in practice (*opposite, bottom left*). The Team Menard garage that housed Scott Brayton's car is closed the day after his fatal accident, as fans and members of the racing community express their sympathies with flowers (*opposite right*). A morning rain on race day brought out the fleet of Dodge safety trucks to dry the track (*right*). The start was delayed only 15 minutes. When the green flag came out, Tony Stewart nosed ahead of Eliseo Salazar into Turn 1 to become only the third rookie in history to lead the first lap of an Indy 500 (*below*). Stewart qualified second, but inherited the pole when teammate Brayton was killed in practice. He led 44 laps before his engine blew.

Lap 82: Stewart pulls into the pits with a burned piston, ending his day. He leads 44 laps in his first race, a feat that garners Rookie of the Year honors. Jones still leads, Lazier is second, and Luyendyk third.

Lap 98: Luyendyk is second when he pits under yellow and stalls trying to leave his pit. He then gets sideswiped by Salazar in the acceleration lane, and Luyendyk's Reynard requires an extended stop for repairs, knocking him out of contention. Salazar comes back in to replace a flat tire and falls a lap down. Jones leads at 250 miles, Lazier is second, and Guerrero is third.

Lap 120: Jones and Guerrero pit, but Lazier stays out and takes over the lead. Alessandro Zampedri moves into second.

Lap 134: When Lazier stops under yellow, Guerrero regains the lead. Jones is now second, Richie Hearn third, and Lazier fourth.

Lap 159: Jones grabs the lead from Guerrero, who pits under green and gets doused with methanol when the fuel hose malfunctions. In the ensuing confusion, a crewman tries to pull Guerrero from the car, disabling his radio. Guerrero goes a lap down.

Lap 162: Lyn St. James and Scott Harrington tangle at the south end of the track and skid into the outside wall. St. James suffers a broken wrist.

Lap 169: When racing resumes, leader Jones rides just behind Salazar, who is still a lap down. As Jones tries to pass on the inside, Salazar moves over twice to block him. The second time, Jones scrapes the inside wall. As Jones slows to maintain control, Zampedri—Salazar's teammate—zips by into the lead. Lazier runs third.

Lap 190: Despite handling problems after his brush with the wall, Jones catches and passes Zampedri in Turn 4 for the lead. Third-place Lazier is hooked up and closing on Zampedri.

Lap 191: Lazier blasts by Zampedri on the back straight for second place and closes in on leader Jones.

Lap 193: Lazier zooms around the inside of Jones on the front straight to grab the lead and pulls away.

Lap 196: Scott Sharp spins in Turn 2 and hits the outside wall. As the cars circle behind the pace car under yellow, Michel Jourdain, Jr., is between leader Lazier and second-place Jones.

Finish: Lazier has a clear track ahead when the green comes out with one lap to go. By the time Jones passes Jourdain on the backstretch, Lazier's Reynard-Ford is too far ahead to catch. Lazier, enduring excruciating back injuries from a racing accident two months earlier, beats Jones to the finish line by just 0.695 seconds, the third closest finish to date. He gives Firestone tires its first victory in 25 years.

As Lazier takes the checkered flag, Guerrero loses control in Turn 4 and tangles with Salazar and Zampedri. All three hit the wall, and Zampedri gets airborne and lands upside down on the straightaway. Zampedri, who finishes fourth, suffers severe leg and foot injuries.

Rookie Hearn finishes third, about seven seconds behind Lazier and the last car on the lead lap. Ten caution periods for 59 laps slow the race average to 147.956 mph, but the lead changes hands 16 times among five drivers in a competitive race that goes to the wire.

The turbocharged era ends with Ford-Cosworth V-8s capturing five of the top six spots. (Jones's lone Mercedes-Ilmor takes second.)

A group of front-runners dices for position on the front straight early in the race (*opposite top*). Buddy Lazier is on the outside (*opposite, bottom left*) as Eddie Cheever (No. 3) and Arie Luyendyk (No. 5) run side-by-side past the flag stand. Roberto Guerrero's topsy-turvy day ended in the pits, where he came to rest after the last-lap crash that destroyed his No. 21 Reynard (*opposite, bottom right*). He still finished fifth. Alessandro Zampedri and Eliseo Salazar were also involved in the incident that took place just as the race was ending. Winner Lazier, smiling through the pain of his injured back, hoists the traditional jug of milk in victory lane (*left*) after beating Davy Jones by just 0.695 seconds. Car owner Ron Hemelgarn is on the left. Lazier led 43 laps, and his Reynard-Cosworth (*below*) was fastest when it counted most---at the end.

RESULTS

NO.	DRIVER	CAR	ENTRANT	ENGINE	CYL	DISP	CHASSIS	COLOR	QUAL SPD	START	FIN	LAPS / SPEED / REASON OUT
91	Buddy Lazier	Delta Faucet-Montana	Hemelgarn Racing, Inc.	Cosworth XB	8	161	'95 Reynard	purple	231.468	5	1	200-147.956
70	Davy Jones	Delco/Futaba	Galles Racing International	Merc-Benz	8	161	'95 Lola	black, white	232.882	2	2	200-147.948
4	Richie Hearn	Ralph's Food 4 Less/Fuji	Della Penna Motorsports	Cosworth XB	8	161	'95 Reynard	black, yellow	226.521	15	3	200-147.871
8	Alessandro Zampedri	Mi-Jack/AGIP/Xcel	Team Scandia	Cosworth XB	8	161	'95 Lola	red	229.595	7	4	199-accident T4
21	Roberto Guerrero	WavePhore/Pennzoil	Pagan Racing	Cosworth XB	8	161	'95 Reynard	white, yellow	231.373	6	5	198-accident T4
7	Eliseo Salazar	Cristal/Copec/Mobil	Team Scandia	Cosworth XB	8	161	'95 Lola	green, white	232.684	3	6	197-accident T4
32	Danny Ongais	Glidden/Menards	Team Menard, Inc.	Menard V-6	6	208	'95 Lola	red, yelo, orng	233.718	33	7	197-running
52	Hideshi Matsuda	Team Taisan/Beck	Beck Motorsports	Cosworth XB	8	161	'94 Lola	black, red	226.856	30	8	197-running
54	Robbie Buhl	Original Coors/Beck	Beck Motorsports	Cosworth XB	8	161	'94 Lola	black, red	226.217	23	9	197-running
11	Scott Sharp	Conseco	A. J. Foyt Enterprises	Cosworth XB	8	161	'95 Lola	blue, wht, red	231.201	21	10	194-accident T2
3	Eddie Cheever	Quaker State	Team Menard, Inc.	Menard V-6	6	208	'95 Lola	grn, red, orng, yelo	231.781	4	11	189-running
14	Davey Hamilton	A. J. Foyt/Copenhagen	A. J. Foyt Enterprises	Cosworth XB	8	161	'95 Lola	black, red	228.887	10	12	181-running
22	Michel Jourdain, Jr.	Herdez/Quaker State/Viva Mexico!	Team Scandia	Cosworth XB	8	161	'95 Lola	grn, wht, red	229.380	8	13	177-running
45	Lyn St. James	Spirit of San Antonio	Zunne Group Racing	Cosworth XB	8	161	'94 Lola	pink, black	224.594	18	14	153-accident T1
44	Scott Harrington	Gold Eagle/Mech. Laund./Harrington/LP	Della Penna Motorsports	Cosworth XB	8	161	'95 Reynard	black, yellow	222.185	32	15	150-accident T1
5	Arie Luyendyk	Byrd's/Bryant	Jonathan Byrd/Treadway Racing	Cosworth XB	8	161	'95 Reynard	red, white	236.986	20	16	149-contact south warmup
12	Buzz Calkins	Bradley/Hoosier Lottery	Bradley Motorsports	Cosworth XB	8	161	'95 Reynard	red	229.013	9	17	148-rear brakes
27	Jim Guthrie	Team Blueprint Racing	Team Blueprint Racing	Menard V-6	6	208	'93 Lola	yelo, red, blk	222.394	19	18	144-engine
30	Mark Dismore	Quaker State/Menards	Team Menard, Inc.	Menard V-6	6	208	'95 Lola	grn, red, orng, yelo	227.260	14	19	129-engine
60	Mike Groff	Valvoline/Cummins/Craftsman	Walker Racing	Cosworth XB	8	161	'95 Reynard	wht, blue, red	228.704	11	20	122-fire
34	Fermin Velez	Scandia/Xcel/Royal Purple	Team Scandia	Cosworth XB	8	161	'95 Lola	blue, wht, yelo	222.487	28	21	107-engine fire
43	Joe Gosek	Scandia/Fanatics Only/Xcel	Team Scandia	Cosworth XB	8	161	'94 Lola	red	222.793	31	22	106-radiator
10	Brad Murphy	Hemelgarn/Delta Faucet	Hemelgarn Racing, Inc.	Cosworth XB	8	161	'94 Reynard	purple	226.053	26	23	91-suspension
20	Tony Stewart	Menards/Glidden/Quaker State	Team Menard, Inc.	Menard V-6	6	208	'95 Lola	grn, yelo, red, orng	233.100	1	24	82-engine
90	Racin Gardner	Scandia/Slick Gardner	Team Scandia	Cosworth XB	8	161	'94 Lola	red	224.453	25	25	76-suspension
41	Marco Greco	A. J. Foyt Enterprises	A. J. Foyt Enterprises	Cosworth XB	8	161	'94 Lola	black, red	228.840	22	26	64-engine
9	Stephan Gregoire	Hemelgarn/Delta Faucet	Hemelgarn Racing, Inc.	Cosworth XB	8	161	'95 Reynard	purple	227.556	13	27	59-coil pack fire
16	Johnny Parsons	Team Blueprint Racing	Team Blueprint Racing	Menard V-6	6	208	'93 Lola	yellow, red	223.843	27	28	48-radiator
75	Johnny O'Connell	Mechanics Laundry	Cunningham Racing	Cosworth XB	8	161	'95 Reynard	white	222.361	29	29	47-fuel pickup
33	Michele Alboreto	Rio Hotel/Perry Ellis/Royal Purple	Team Scandia	Cosworth XB	8	161	'95 Reynard	red	228.229	12	30	43-gear box
18	John Paul, Jr.	V-Line/Earl's Perform./Crowne Plaza/Keco	PDM Racing, Inc.	Menard V-6	6	208	'93 Lola	black, red, yelo	224.757	17	31	10-ignition
96	Paul Durant	Manaras/Simu/Glenmark/Miller Eads/Fortune Tech.	ABF Motorsports, LLC	Buick V-6	6	208	'92 Lola	white	225.404	24	32	9-engine
64	Johnny Unser	Ruger-Titanium	Project Indy	Cosworth XB	8	161	'95 Reynard	black, red	226.115	16	33	0-transmission

1997

81st Race • May 25-27, 1997

New engines and new chassis for the Indy Racing League's second season lower the cost of admission for race teams and lower speeds for the drivers, fulfilling two of the IRL's original goals.

The screaming turbocharged V-8 racing engines and pushrod V-6s of previous years are out, and throatier naturally aspirated V-8s from Oldsmobile and Nissan are in. Most of the 64 entries list Oldsmobile's Aurora V-8, which wins the two IRL races prior to the 500, and a handful use Nissan's Infiniti V-8. Under the new IRL formula, both are production-based, 4.0-liter engines with dual-overhead camshafts and four valves per cylinder. Any team can buy one starting at $75,000 assembled.

Familiar chassis brands such as Lola and Reynard also are gone. Instead, two new chassis are available to all teams for a uniform price of $263,000, the Italian-made Dallara and British-built G Force. Each type wins an IRL race before the 500.

Amid all the changes, the Speedway continues the controversial "25/8" rule instituted the previous year, reserving 25 of the 33 starting positions for the top performers in earlier IRL races. The 25 cars with the most IRL points cannot be bumped if they qualify at a minimum 206 mph. The entry list includes 13 rookies, and all qualify to join nine second-time starters on the grid.

PRACTICE AND QUALIFYING

SUNDAY, MAY 4: Only a handful of rookies are on the track today, and Italian Formula 1 vet Vincenzo Sospiri is fastest at 212 mph with a Dallara-Aurora.

Off the track, Team Menard makes a surprise announcement that it is switching from Firestone to Goodyear tires for drivers Tony Stewart, last year's top rookie, and Robbie Buhl.

TUESDAY, MAY 6: Veterans get on the track, and Arie Luyendyk, the fastest qualifier last year, shows he wants to repeat that performance. Luyendyk is fastest at 218.7 mph, and NASCAR regular Robby Gordon is second at 215.5. Stewart, defending winner Buddy Lazier, and Scott Sharp top 214. Lazier is the only one with an Infiniti V-8.

WEDNESDAY, MAY 7: Luyendyk is fastest again, this time hitting 220.297 mph in his G Force. Sharp is second fastest at 217.4, but a few laps after hitting his high note for the day, Sharp spins in Turn 4 and whacks the outside wall. The car sustains heavy damage, but Sharp walks away with a bruised knee. ➔

Three-time winner Johnny Rutherford (*above*) drove the Oldsmobile Aurora pace car (*opposite bottom*), the first four-door to lead the way since the 1947 Nash Ambassador. Speedway President and IRL founder Tony George (*left*) launched a new era of production-based V-8 engines for the 500. Roberto Guerrero's car (*opposite, top left*) was one of a handful that used the Nissan Infiniti engine. Team Hemelgarn switched to the Olds Aurora V-8 (*opposite, top right*) for defending winner Buddy Lazier just before Pole Day, joining the majority of the entries for this year's race.

STARTING LINEUP

Average Field Qualifying Speed: 212.286

Pole Position Qualifying Speed: 218.263

Vincenzo Sospiri

Jim Guthrie

Eliseo Salazar

Robby Gordon

Kenny Brack

Mike Groff

Tony Stewart

Scott Goodyear

Davey Hamilton

Eddie Cheever

Affonso Giaffone

Dr. Jack Miller

Arie Luyendyk

Robbie Buhl

Jeff Ward

Buddy Lazier

Stephan Gregoire

Buzz Calkins

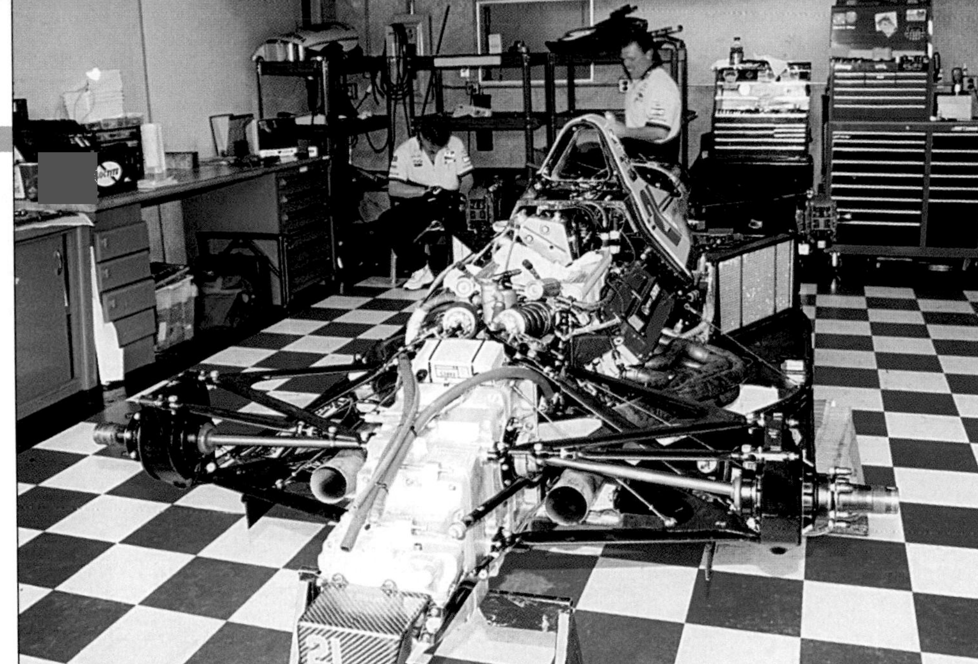

Robbie Groff | Billy Roe | Marco Greco | Greg Ray | Paul Durant

Steve Kinser | Sam Schmidt | Tyce Carlson | Fermin Velez | Claude Bourbonnais | Johnny Unser

Roberto Guerrero | Billy Boat | Mark Dismore | Dennis Vitolo | Alessandro Zampedri | Lyn St. James

Second-year driver Jim Guthrie, who drove his low-budget Blueprint Racing Dallara to an upset win at Phoenix in March, is third fastest at 216. Gordon and Stewart are close behind.

THURSDAY, MAY 8: Team Menard ends its four-day experiment with Goodyear tires and returns to Firestone. Stewart and Buhl are slightly quicker, 215.8 and 215.7 mph, respectively, on the Firestones.

Luyendyk—who also uses Firestones—is top gun again, however, at 217.3. Later in the day, the 1990 winner spins twice in the south short chute and grazes the wall, damaging the nose of his G Force.

Lyn St. James gets her Infiniti-powered Dallara up to 212.5, fourth quickest for the day.

FRIDAY, MAY 9: Luyendyk completes the sweep for the week, posting a best time of 218.3 mph. Menard teammates Stewart and Buhl get closer, however, with speeds of 217.3 and 216.9, respectively.

Two drivers suffer injuries in separate crashes. John Paul, Jr., breaks a leg and heel when he spins into the outside wall in Turn 4. Sharp, driving an A. J. Foyt entry, also hits the Turn 4 wall and suffers a concussion that sidelines him on Pole Day.

SATURDAY, MAY 10: Several cars qualify early in the day, but it is nearly 3:30 P.M. when Luyendyk makes the first serious run for the pole with a four-lap average of 218.263 mph—nearly 19 mph slower than his record a year ago.

Indy rookie Sospiri mounts a surprising challenge with a run of 216.822, but it is the next attempt that makes Luyendyk hold his breath.

Tony Stewart takes just .183 second longer than Luyendyk to complete four laps and averages 218.021, barely missing the pole. Despite a first lap faster than 217, teammate Robbie Buhl waves off a second run. Buhl returns shortly before 6 P.M. and settles for 216.102, fourth fastest for the day.

Luyendyk wins his second pole and earns $100,000 for his effort. Stewart and Sospiri join him on the front row. A total of 21 cars qualify on Pole Day, including 1996 winner Buddy Lazier, who trades in the Infiniti engine for an Aurora and is 10th fastest. Teammate Lyn St. James has the fastest Infiniti, and her speed of 210.145 is good for 16th on the grid.

TUESDAY, MAY 13: A. J. Foyt announces veteran sports-car racer Johnny O'Connell will drive the No. 1 car instead of Scott Sharp, who is still recovering from his concussion. PDM Racing replaces the injured John Paul, Jr., with rookie Tyce Carlson.

FRIDAY, MAY 16: Just three days after replacing Sharp in the No. 1 Foyt car, O'Connell hits the outside wall at the south end of the track and suffers a dislocated foot that will keep him out of the race. Foyt has to find another driver.

Off the track, IRL Executive Director Leo Mehl announces the "25/8" qualifying rule will be dropped for 1998, saying the car owners agree "it's time to move on."

SUNDAY, MAY 18: Two starting spots are still open on bump day. Johnny Unser fills one at 209.344 mph with a Dallara-Infiniti, and rookie Greg Ray fills the other at 213.760 with a Dallara-Aurora.

Shortly after noon, second-year driver Paul Durant climbs into Foyt's No. 1 G Force for the first time, runs just 12 practice laps, and goes out to qualify. Durant averages 209.149 to bump Alessandro Zampedri, the slowest qualifier who lacks a guaranteed spot under the 25/8 rule.

Rookie Claude Bourbonnais qualifies at 210.523, bumping Unser, who also lacks a guaranteed starting spot. Zampedri, battling back from severe injuries suffered in last year's race, jumps into a Team Scandia backup car and averages 211.757 in a light rain to bump Lyn St. James, the next slowest qualifier without one of the 25 guaranteed spots.

Second-year driver Scott Harrington makes the final qualifying attempt in a Dallara-Aurora the Johansson/Immke team obtains ➔

Alessandro Zampedri, badly injured in '96, returned in Team Scandia's No. 34 Dallara (*top*). Teammate and fellow Italian Vincenzo Sospiri, a rookie, qualified third in the No. 8 car (*middle*). Dennis Vitolo's Dallara-Infiniti is weighed at trackside (*above*). Fermin Velez (*opposite, top left*) was another member of Scandia's five-car team. Indy veteran Robby Gordon (*opposite, top right*) took time out from NASCAR to run the 500. Roberto Guerrero does a burnout during pit-stop practice (*opposite middle*). Johnny O'Connell, replacing the injured Scott Sharp, crashed in A. J. Foyt's No. 1 Conseco car (*opposite, bottom left*), which the team dubbed "Christine." Foyt confers with Billy Boat (*opposite, bottom right*), who finished seventh.

Running in the Indianapolis 500 was always in the back of Steve Kinser's mind. But being a sprint-car ace in the Nineties wasn't likely to earn a trip to the Brickyard, even for a 14-time champ on the tough World of Outlaws circuit who'd won more than 400 features. However, the advent of the Indy Racing League—and a lot of help from his friends and sponsors—put Steve in the big show. It's doubtful that any driver in the field received as loud and long an ovation as the Bloomington, Indiana, native did when his name was announced on race day.

Kinser was running well when he was involved in a late-race accident. Typically, he took the blame. "I feel like I let everybody down," he said solemnly. Then his countenance brightened as he spoke about the first time he came to Indy. Heads turned and eyebrows were raised among the reporters and hangers-on, none of whom could recall Steve's "other time" at Indy.

It was in 1981, a thrown-together deal headed by Gary Stanton, and utilizing an old Penske chassis and a used Cosworth engine. Kinser sailed through the rookie test and practiced within a fraction of a mile per hour of making the field. But a brush with the wall ended their hopes.

It's only a little more than an hour from Bloomington to Indianapolis, but some roads take a little longer. Steve Kinser had finally made the trip.

at the 11th hour from Foyt. Harrington tops 214 on his first lap, but loses control in Turn 2 on the second and crashes into the wall.

Qualifying ends with two well-known names—St. James and Unser—victims of the 25/8 rule. St. James's speed of 210.145 mph and Unser's 209.344 are faster than those of seven drivers with reserved spots. After a quick huddle by IRL officials, Mehl announces, "We must start the 33 fastest cars, so we will add the two bumped cars." The field expands to 35 cars, the most since 1979. St. James and Unser, both with Infiniti-powered Dallaras, start from the 12th row. Twenty-nine starters use the Aurora engine.

THE RACE

Rain delays pre-race activities more than an hour on May 25, and the cars grid under threatening skies. Less than 20 minutes before the start, a downpour sends the cars back to Gasoline Alley. Track officials announce at 1:30 P.M. that the race will run the following day, the first postponement in 11 years.

Start: There is again a threat of rain as the field circles in formation on the pace lap. Two cars on row five come together in Turn 4 and collect the third. All three drivers—Stephan Gregoire and rookies Affonso Giaffone and Kenny Brack—point fingers at each other, but the result is they are all out of the race. Alessandro Zampedri pulls into the pits with a broken timing chain, and rookie Sam Schmidt soon follows with a blown engine. Five cars are out before the first green flag.

When the green flag drops, Tony Stewart streaks ahead of polesitter Arie Luyendyk from the middle of row one to grab the lead. Robby Gordon, who starts 12th, charges up to fifth on the first lap.

Lap 11: With the field under caution for Claude Bourbonnais's blown engine, light rain starts to fall. Four laps later, the red flag flies when it begins to pour. The race is postponed again for another day.

Restart: The sky is clear and the temperatures cool as the 29 remaining cars run three laps in single file under yellow. Leader Stewart pulls away from Luyendyk when racing resumes, and Gordon closes on Robbie Buhl for third.

Lap 20: Gordon suddenly slows and pulls off the track in Turn 3. He jumps out of his car and rolls in the wet grass trying to put out a methanol fire. Fuel leaks into the cockpit of his G Force, where it is ignited by heat, and Gordon suffers burns on his arms and legs.

The leaders pit under yellow and Stewart gets out first. Buhl beats Luyendyk out of the pits to take second, and defending winner Buddy Lazier jumps up to fourth.

Lap 24: As the field gets ready to go green, rookie Steve Kinser rear-ends Eliseo Salazar on the front straight. In the scramble that follows, Mark Dismore spins and hits the wall, and Roberto Guerrero damages his front suspension. Both drop out. Kinser gets a new nose cone and Salazar gets emergency suspension repairs; both get back in the race.

Lap 29: When racing resumes, Stewart builds a comfortable lead while Menard teammate Buhl fights off Luyendyk for second. Lazier runs fourth and rookie Jeff Ward fifth.

Lap 63: Luyendyk gets around Stewart to lead for the first time. Buhl holds third and Lazier is fourth. Luyendyk leads 44 of the next →

Jeff Ward turned in one of the finest non-winning drives in Indy history in 1997. Starting seventh, he was never out of touch with the leaders. He even led as late as lap 192 before Scott Goodyear and Arie Luyendyk got around the youngster, who was named Rookie of the Year. But Ward hung on for a well-deserved third.

His car owner and teammate, Eddie Cheever, was ecstatic. "When everybody was telling me Jeff was a shoo-in for Rookie of the Year, I said, 'This guy doesn't want to mess around with Rookie of the Year; he wants to win this race,'" Cheever said.

Jeff admitted to one miscue when he was in the lead. "The pace car was on the warm-up lane and I was on the track. I thought he was going to stay there, and then he came across. The next thing I know, I see the fender of an Aurora. I thought, 'Here I am leading the race, and I'm going to hit the pace car!'"

Team Menard driver Robby Buhl (*opposite, top left*) qualified the second row. Tony Stewart won the prize for consistency (*opposite, top right*), but Arie Luyendyk earned the big check for the pole (*opposite, bottom left*). Florence Henderson and Jim Nabors were back for their annual pre-race performances (*opposite, bottom right*). A downpour on the scheduled race date (*second from top, left*) sent cars back to the garages and fans scurrying for cover (*right*). The weather improved slightly on Memorial Day, when the raised arms of crew members signaled started engines (*top*), and the Aurora pace car led the field to a green flag (*second from top, right*). It took a third day before the race could be completed. That's when Eliseo Salazar got sideways after being rear-ended by Steve Kinser (*opposite, third from top*).

47 laps, surrendering first place only during a green-flag pit stop.

Lap 114: Lazier leads when Billy Roe and Paul Durant tangle in Turn 3 and crash hard into the wall. Roe escapes injury, but Durant breaks his pelvis.

Buhl takes over first place when Lazier pits and drops to sixth. Stewart moves into second and Ward takes third. Luyendyk falls to fourth, having pitted just before the yellow.

Lap 138: Dr. Jack Miller crashes at the north end of the track, and Mike Groff spins to avoid the wreck. The "Racing Dentist" is out, but Groff continues.

When most of the leaders pit under yellow, Ward stays out and becomes the leader. Stewart winds up second. Luyendyk and teammate Scott Goodyear are third and fourth, and Lazier and Buhl complete the top six, all on the lead lap.

Lap 188: Ward still leads and Goodyear is second when Luyendyk attempts to snatch third place from Stewart. Luyendyk catches Stewart in Turn 2 and tries to pass him on the back straight, but Stewart pinches to the left and blocks him. Luyendyk gets two wheels on the grass and backs off.

Lap 189: Kinser dips low going into Turn 4 and nicks Buzz Calkins, who is heading to the pits with a broken half shaft. Kinser ricochets across the track in front of Lyn St. James and slams the wall. St. James spins and also hits the wall. Neither is hurt, but both are out.

Lap 192: After leading 49 of the last 51 laps, Ward makes a splash-and-go fuel stop under yellow and surrenders first place to Goodyear, who stays on the track. Luyendyk lines up directly behind his teammate in second.

Lap 194: When the green comes out, Luyendyk catches Goodyear on the back straight and slips underneath in Turn 3 to take the lead.

Lap 196: The yellow light flashes when one of Lazier's mirrors flies off his Dallara and lands on the track. Luyendyk still leads.

Lap 198: Back under green, Luyendyk leads Goodyear down the front straight when Stewart gets too high coming off Turn 4 and brushes the wall to bring out another caution.

Stewart apparently suffers no damage and stays out as the safety crew scours the track for debris. Luyendyk leads, and teammate Goodyear is right behind him on the track.

Finish: Still under caution, the field approaches the flagstand for the final lap. The green flag unexpectedly waves, catching most drivers off guard, but the yellow caution lights remain on around the track, adding to the confusion.

An alert Luyendyk jumps on the throttle before Goodyear does and roars away. Goodyear closes the gap slightly on the backstretch but runs out of track to catch up.

Luyendyk wins for the second time by just .57 of a second, the third closest finish in history. He leads 61 laps in his G Force-Aurora to give Oldsmobile its first victory at the Speedway and Firestone a second straight for its tires. The Aurora engine dominates, claiming the first 11 positions and leading all 200 laps.

It takes three days to complete 500 miles because of rain, but seven drivers swap the lead 19 times in an entertaining and engaging race. Luyendyk collects $1,568,150 of the $8,642,450 purse, both record amounts. Goodyear, runner-up in two of Indy's three closest finishes, gives owner Fred Treadway a 1-2 sweep. Ward comes in third and is named Rookie of the Year, and Lazier nurses his ailing Aurora engine to fourth. Stewart leads the most laps, 64, and salvages fifth place in the last car on the lead lap.

Early action finds Mark Dismore leading Roberto Guerrero, Billy Boat, and Greg Ray (*opposite top*). Billy Roe, in the No. 50 Dallara-Aurora, and Paul Durant in the unlucky No. 1 G Force-Aurora, crashed in Turn 3 (*opposite, second from top*). Durant broke his pelvis. Eliseo Salazar survived a bump to the rear in the No. 7 Dallara, but later dropped out when the brakes failed (*opposite, third from top*). Robby Gordon was an early victim of a fuel leak that forced him to bail out into the wet grass to douse a methanol fire (*opposite bottom*). Either milk-chugging Arie Luyendyk forgot about his 1990 victory, or he is signaling that he is No. 1 again (*right*). Luyendyk's second win (*below*) ushered in the IRL's new era of naturally aspirated V-8s, giving Oldsmobile its first 500 victory.

RESULTS

NO.	DRIVER	CAR	ENTRANT	ENGINE	CYL	DISP	CHASSIS	COLOR	QUAL SPD	START	FIN	LAPS / SPEED / REASON OUT
5	Arie Luyendyk	Wavephore/Sprint PCS/Miller/Provimi/Nortel	Treadway Racing LLC	Aurora	8	244	G Force	wht, blue, red	218.263	1	1	200-145.827
6	Scott Goodyear	Nortel/Sprint PCS/Quebecor	Treadway Racing LLC	Aurora	8	244	G Force	white, blue	215.811	5	2	200-145.820
52	Jeff Ward	FirstPlus	FirstPlus/Team Cheever	Aurora	8	244	G Force	red, wht, blue	214.517	7	3	200-145.779
91	Buddy Lazier	Delta Faucet/Montana	Hemelgarn Racing, Inc.	Aurora	8	244	Dallara	purple	214.286	10	4	200-145.705
2	Tony Stewart	Glidden/Menards	Team Menard, Inc.	Aurora	8	244	G Force	red, yelo, orng	218.021	2	5	200-145.490
14	Davey Hamilton	Powerteam Racing	A. J. Foyt Enterprises	Aurora	8	244	G Force	white, red	214.484	8	6	199-running
11	Billy Boat	Conseco	A. J. Foyt Enterprises	Aurora	8	244	G Force	blue, wht, red	216.299	22	7	199-running
3	Robbie Buhl	Quaker State	Team Menard, Inc.	Aurora	8	244	G Force	grn, yelo, red, orng	216.102	4	8	199-running
30	Robbie Groff	Alfa-Laval/Team Losi	McCormack Motorsports, Inc.	Aurora	8	244	G Force	white	207.792	21	9	197-running
33	Fermin Velez	Old Navy/Royal Purple/Alta/Xcel	Team Scandia	Aurora	8	244	Dallara	blue, wht, red	206.512	29	10	195-running
12	Buzz Calkins	Bradley Food Marts	Bradley Motorsports	Aurora	8	244	G Force	red	209.564	16	11	188-running
10	Mike Groff	Byrd's/Visionaire/Bryant	Jonathan Byrd-Cunningham Racing LLC	Infiniti Indy	8	244	G Force	red, white	208.537	18	12	188-running
90	Lyn St. James	Lifetime TV/Cinergy/Delta	LSJ Racing/Hemelgarn Racing, Inc.	Infiniti Indy	8	244	Dallara	purple, wht, red	210.145	34	13	186-accident T4
44	Steve Kinser	One Call/Menards/Quaker State/St. Elmo's	Sinden Racing	Aurora	8	244	Dallara	red, wht, blue	210.793	20	14	185-accident T4
54	Dennis Vitolo	SmithKilne Beecham/Kroger	Beck Motorsports	Infiniti Indy	8	244	Dallara	purple, blue	207.626	28	15	173-running
22	Marco Greco	Side Play/Int'l Sport/Alta/Xcel	Team Scandia	Aurora	8	244	Dallara	red	210.322	27	16	166-drive shaft
8	Vincenzo Sospiri	Old Navy/Royal Purple/Alta/Xcel	Team Scandia	Aurora	8	244	Dallara	blue, wht, red	216.822	3	17	163-coil
9	Johnny Unser	Delta Faucet/Montana/Cinergy	Hemelgarn Racing, Inc.	Infiniti Indy	8	244	Dallara	purple,red	209.344	35	18	158-engine
18	Tyce Carlson	Klipsch/Tnemec/Plye/V-Line/Earl's	PDM Racing, Inc.	Aurora	8	244	Dallara	black	210.852	26	19	156-accident T2
40	Dr. Jack Miller	Crest/Trane/Spot-On	Arizona Motorsports	Infiniti Indy	8	244	Dallara	wht, blue, red	209.250	17	20	131-accident T3
1	Paul Durant	Conseco	A. J. Foyt Enterprises	Aurora	8	244	G Force	blue, white	209.149	33	21	111-accident T3
50	Billy Roe	Sega/Prog. Elect./Keco/UJT	Eurointernational, Inc.	Aurora	8	244	Dallara	white, black	212.752	24	22	110-accident T3
51	Eddie Cheever	FirstPlus	FirstPlus/Team Cheever	Aurora	8	244	G Force	red, wht, blue	214.073	11	23	84-timing chain
7	Eliseo Salazar	Copec/Cristal	Team Scandia	Aurora	8	244	Dallara	white, grn, red	214.320	9	24	70-brakes
97	Greg Ray	Tobacco Free Kids	Thomas Knapp Motorsports/Genoa	Aurora	8	244	Dallara	black	213.760	30	25	48-water pump
27	Jim Guthrie	Jacuzzi/Armour Golf/Ertl	Blueprint Racing, Inc.	Aurora	8	244	Dallara	blue, wht, red	215.207	6	26	43-fuel pressure
21	Roberto Guerrero	Pennzoil	Pagan Racing	Infiniti Indy	8	244	Dallara	yellow	207.371	19	27	25-suspension
28	Mark Dismore	Mechanics Laundry/Bombardier/Grainger	PDM Racing, Inc.	Aurora	8	244	Dallara	blk, red, white	212.423	25	28	24-accident T4
42	Robby Gordon	Coors Light	Team Sabco	Aurora	8	244	G Force	silver, blu, red	213.211	12	29	19-fire
72	Claude Bourbonnais	Jacuzzi/Armour Golf/Ertl	Blueprint Racing, Inc.	Aurora	8	244	Dallara	blue, wht, red	210.523	32	30	8-engine
77	Stephan Gregoire	Estridge/Miller Eads	Chastain Motorsports	Aurora	8	244	G Force	blue, wht, red	213.126	13	31	0-accident T4
17	Affonso Giaffone	General Motors	Chitwood Motorsports	Aurora	8	244	Dallara	purp, yelo, red, grn	212.974	14	32	0-accident T4
4	Kenny Brack	Monsoon	Galles Racing	Aurora	8	244	G Force	red, wht, blk	211.221	15	33	0-accident T4
16	Sam Schmidt	HOPE Prepaid Fuel Card	Blueprint Racing, Inc.	Aurora	8	244	Dallara	purple, yelo, wht	215.141	23	34	0-engine
34	Alessandro Zampedri	Mi-Jack/Royal Purple	Team Scandia	Aurora	8	244	Dallara	yellow, red	211.757	31	35	0-oil leak

1998

82nd Race • May 24, 1998

Practice drops from the usual two weeks in May to just six days, and qualifying is now one weekend instead of two in the first major schedule change since 1952. Indy Racing League founder and Speedway President Tony George compresses the schedule to cut costs for the teams and boost fan interest in the scramble for starting positions. Also, the 11-race IRL series gains a title sponsor, the Pep Boys auto parts stores.

Seventy-three entries are received. Most use the dominant Oldsmobile Aurora engine; the Infiniti V-8 is the choice of only three entrants. The new Indianapolis-built Riley & Scott chassis joins the returning British G Force and Italian Dallara.

After a rash of injuries in 1997, new IRL safety rules require energy-absorbing headrests and foam padding around the driver's seat. A lighter, redesigned transmission comes in a new case intended to crush more easily on impact.

Eight rookies make the show, Americans all. Among them is 46-year-old short-track star Jack Hewitt, the all-time USAC Silver Crown winner and the oldest rookie ever. Robby Unser, youngest son of three-time winner Bobby, becomes the sixth member of his family to qualify for a 500.

Mary Fendrich Hulman, Tony Hulman's widow, dies on April 10 at the age of 93. When Speedway Chairman Mari Hulman George gives the command for drivers to start their engines, the order goes out to an all-male field for the first time since 1991. Lyn St. James fails to qualify for a seventh straight start when her Infiniti-powered G Force falls short on Bump Day.

PRACTICE AND QUALIFYING

SUNDAY, MAY 10: On the opening day of practice, four drivers top Arie Luyendyk's 1997 pole speed of 218.263 mph. Team Menard's Robbie Buhl leads the way at 219.3. Luyendyk and Scott Sharp also top 219. Late in the day, rookie Jimmy Kite bangs the Turn 4 wall, damaging the right side of his Dallara.

MONDAY, MAY 11: Reigning IRL champ Tony Stewart, slowed by engine problems the day before, posts an unofficial lap record of 223.7 mph at 11:34 A.M. Sharp is second fastest at 222.1. Second-year drivers Kenny Brack and Billy Boat, running A. J. Foyt's entries, also top 222.

Veteran Danny Ongais, 55, briefly loses consciousness when he spins in Turn 3 and clobbers the outside wall.

TUESDAY, MAY 12: Stewart laps the Brickyard at 223.691 mph during "happy hour" to be fastest again. Brack is second at 221.6, Sharp is third at 220, and Boat is fourth, also at 220. Greg Ray gets his unsponsored car on the track for the first time and is fifth fastest at 219.9. All five are in Dallara-Auroras.

IRL medical director Dr. Henry Bock says that Ongais suffered a concussion in his crash and will not be cleared to drive.

THURSDAY, MAY 14: Stewart is back on track after Team Menard spent the previous day chasing engine gremlins. Stewart runs 223.4 mph just before 6 P.M. for the day's top speed, edging Brack's 223.2. Greg Ray's shoestring operation (one chassis, two engines) gets another boost with the third-highest speed, 222.7.

Kite crashes for the second time this week when an oil leak sends his Dallara spinning backwards into the Turn 4 wall. Kite escapes injury again, but his primary car takes heavy damage.

FRIDAY, MAY 15: Fifty-five cars hit the track the day before the run for the pole. Team Menard's Stewart has the top speed for the third time, 223.8 mph—the fastest practice speed so far. Brack and Boat are next, at 223.4 and 221.7 respectively, setting up a duel for the pole between Menard's and A. J. Foyt's drivers. Boat's fast lap comes in his backup Dallara after he wrecks his primary car in Turn 3.

SATURDAY, MAY 16: Sam Schmidt is the second to qualify on Pole Day, and he easily tops Luyendyk's 1997 pole run with a four-lap average of 219.982 mph. Robbie Buhl is next out, and he moves Schmidt aside with a run of 220.236. Menard teammate Tony Stewart follows and is faster still at 220.386. At high noon, with the sun heating up the track, Kenny Brack averages 220.982 to knock Stewart off the pole. ➔

Opposite: Golfer Greg Norman prepared to drive the Corvette pace car (top left), but shoulder surgery forced him to withdraw. Parnelli Jones drove the pace car on race day. A. J. Foyt squeezed into the car that bore him to his first victory in 1961 (bottom left) as part of a salute to former winners, and Bill Camarano showed off Walt Faulkner's No. 98 from 1950 that he restored (top right). Race week activities included a hot-air balloon race (middle right) and displays from the track museum (bottom right).

STARTING LINEUP

Average Field Qualifying Speed: 218.305

Numbers in flags indicate finish position

POLE POSITION
Qualifying Speed: 223.503

Kenny Brack

Sam Schmidt

Roberto Guerrero

Mark Dismore

Dr. Jack Miller

Greg Ray

Robbie Buhl

Davey Hamilton

Buddy Lazier

Marco Greco

Billy Boat

Tony Stewart

Scott Sharp

Scott Goodyear

J. J. Yeley

Buzz Calkins

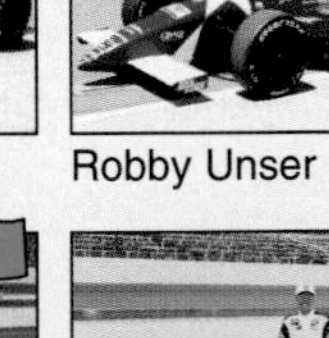

Robby Unser

Donnie Beechler

Jeff Ward

Raul Boesel

Billy Roe

Eddie Cheever, Jr.

Jim Guthrie

Steve Knapp

Jimmy Kite

Stan Wattles

Mike Groff

John Paul, Jr.

Andy Michner

Jack Hewitt

Johnny Unser

Arie Luyendyk

Stephan Gregoire

Some 45 minutes later, Brack's teammate, Billy Boat, electrifies the crowd with a first lap of 224.573. He averages 223.503 to set a new standard for the IRL's naturally aspirated engines.

Foyt's drivers sit first and second until 5:15 P.M., when crowd favorite Greg Ray cranks up his Dallara to 221.125, squeezing between Boat and Brack onto the front row. Boat's pole-winning run is the first for Foyt since becoming a full-time owner.

Twenty-six cars are in the field, and the seven fastest are Dallaras. Among those who don't qualify are Kite, who hits the wall for the third time this week, and Eliseo Salazar, who spins in Turn 1 and cracks the outside wall. Neither is hurt.

SUNDAY, MAY 17: Two notables qualify early on Bump Day. Jeff Ward, 1997 Rookie of the Year, averages 219.086, and two-time winner Arie Luyendyk, slowed by engine problems Saturday, puts last year's winning car in at 218.935 mph.

Two drivers who crashed Saturday bounce back to qualify. Salazar gets his Riley & Scott in at 216.259—second slowest so far—and Kite is fastest of the day at 219.29. Veteran Mike Groff bumps Billy Roe, slowest of the Pole Day qualifiers, but Roe jumps into his backup car and ousts Salazar.

THE RACE

Start: Rain delays the start 40 minutes, and when the green flag waves, polesitter Billy Boat beats Greg Ray and Kenny Brack into the first turn.

Back in the pack, Eddie Cheever gets sideways in Turn 1, pinching rookie J. J. Yeley onto the grass. Yeley spins across the track, narrowly missing Cheever and three others, and stops just short of the outside wall. Yeley, Cheever, and Jack Hewitt all pit for fresh tires under yellow and fall to the rear.

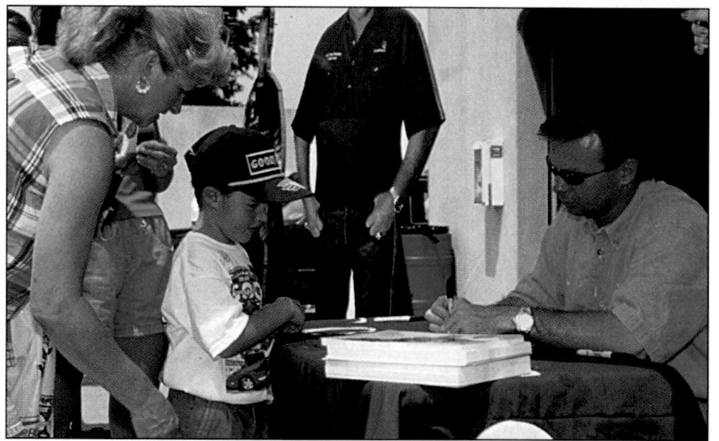

Lap 3: On the restart, Boat hangs on to the lead with Ray on his tail. Menard teammates Tony Stewart and Robbie Buhl get around Brack for third and fourth place.

Lap 13: In the first lead change, Ray slips inside of Boat in Turn 3, holds him off down the front straight, and then pulls away.

Lap 17: As Buddy Lazier pits for a wing adjustment, Stewart gets around Boat for second place and closes on leader Ray.

Lap 21: Stewart catches Ray in traffic on the front straight and blows by him in Turn 1 for the lead.

Lap 22: Stewart's Aurora engine starts smoking as he heads into Turn 1. He stops in the south short chute next to the outside wall, angrily tossing his steering wheel as he climbs out. A pre-race favorite, a blown engine makes him the first one out.

The leaders pit under yellow. Ray comes out first, followed by Brack, Davey Hamilton, and Scott Goodyear. Boat falls to 11th after an extended stop for tires and suspension adjustments.

Lap 32: Ray slows dramatically on the backstretch, and Brack rushes by into the lead. Meanwhile, Cheever—29th after his early pit stop—works back into the top 10.

Lap 35: Under caution due to Donnie Beechler's blown engine, Boat pits again for a wing adjustment; he falls from sixth to 19th. Brack still leads, with Buhl second and Hamilton third.

Lap 41: After racing resumes, Cheever continues his charge to the front. He passes Buhl on the front straight for fourth, dusts Scott Sharp for third the next time around, and gets by Hamilton for second a lap later. →

Opposite page: Eliseo Salazar demolishes his Riley & Scott chassis in a Turn 1 crash on Pole Day (top). Jimmy Kite clips the wall in the No. 7T Scandia Dallara the same day (second from top). Billy Boat autographs a photo for a young fan (third from top). Kite, the youngest driver in the field at 21, enjoys a visit from contestants in the annual 500 Festival queen competition (bottom). *This page:* Boat put his Conseco-sponsored Dallara (top) on the pole at 223.503 mph, nearly 2.4 mph faster than Greg Ray. The front row (middle right) was composed entirely of second-time starters, from left, Ray, Boat, and Kenny Brack. Boat won $100,000 and a Harley-Davidson motorcycle (above left) for taking the pole. Mike Groff settles into his "work environment" (middle left). Scott Goodyear's Pennzoil crew takes part in the annual pit-stop competition (above right), which it won.

Lap 44: Buhl slows in the south short chute and pulls off the track on the backstretch with a punctured radiator. Both Team Menard cars are out. When most of the front runners pit, Buzz Calkins leads and '96 winner Lazier moves into second.

Lap 49: As the field roars by on the restart, Boat slows on the front straight, smoke trailing from his transmission.

Further up the backstretch, as a pack of cars heads into Turn 3, Sam Schmidt and Davey Hamilton are side-by-side when Schmidt loses control and spins across the track into the outside wall. Hamilton slips by, as does Cheever, but six others get caught up. Jim Guthrie runs over Schmidt's rear wing, which lands on the track, and slams into the outside wall nearly head-on. Guthrie breaks his right elbow and right leg and cracks some ribs.

The crash sidelines Schmidt, Guthrie, Stan Wattles, Billy Roe, and Mark Dismore. Roberto Guerrero suffers minor damage and Marco Greco stalls his engine, but both continue.

Lap 63: After a long caution to clean up the Turn 3 accident, Brack leads, Cheever is second, and Sharp is third when racing resumes. They pull away from the rest of the pack.

Lap 68: Cheever darts underneath Brack for the lead in Turn 1 after dogging him for two laps. John Paul, Jr., gets around Sharp for third. A lap later, Arie Luyendyk, who starts 28th, goes by Sharp to grab fourth.

Lap 85: The leaders pit under the green. When Cheever comes in, he locks up his right front tire; when he starts to leave, his fuel hose is still connected, but his crew stops him in time.

Lap 88: Brack is leading when he pulls into the Turn 3 warmup lane and slowly coasts around the north end of the track to his pit stall near Turn 1, out of fuel. Angry car owner Foyt takes out his frustrations on a laptop computer that was supposed to keep precise track of fuel mileage. All six starters from the first two rows are either out of contention or out of the race.

Lap 98: With the field under yellow, Cheever gives up the lead to top off his tank and falls to seventh. Paul moves in front, Hamilton is second, and rookie Robby Unser is third. Former winners Luyendyk and Lazier round out the top five.

Lap 114: When Paul pits under green, Hamilton is the 10th driver to lead. Luyendyk runs second, Cheever third, Lazier fourth.

Lap 147: During another round of green-flag stops, Paul pits from first place, handing the lead to Luyendyk.

Lap 150: Luyendyk pits, giving the lead to Cheever. As he heads out of the pits, Luyendyk slows to a crawl, a blown clutch ending his bid for a third win and bringing out the yellow. When racing resumes on lap 156, Cheever leads, Lazier is second, rookie Steve Knapp is third, and Paul is fourth.

Lap 176: The leaders make their final pit stops under yellow. Cheever beats Lazier and Knapp back onto the track.

Lap 182: Two cars are between Cheever and second-place Lazier as the field approaches the green flag. Lazier gets by both before reaching Turn 1 and closes to within four car lengths of Cheever.

Lap 191: Greco's engine blows at the north end of the track, bringing out the 12th caution flag of the day. After building a 3.5-second lead, Cheever now finds Lazier lurking behind his rear wing as they follow the pace car.

Finish: On the restart on lap 194, Cheever swerves to the inside of the front straight to try to break the draft, but Lazier stays close going into Turn 1. Nearly scraping the wall as he exits the turns, Cheever stretches his lead a little on the backstretch.

Cheever tops 213 mph as he pulls away and finishes 3.19 seconds ahead of Lazier to become the 58th different winner in 500 history. He earns $1.4 million of the $8.7-million purse, and as the owner of his own car, avoids arguments over the driver's share. The 40-year-old Cheever leads 76 laps.

Lazier's second-place finish gives him three straight in the top four. Knapp comes in third on the lead lap to earn Rookie-of-the-Year honors.

This page: Fans spill out onto Georgetown Road after the race (left). An elusive stray dog dashes down the front straight prior to the start (above). *Opposite page:* Speedway Chairman Mari Hulman George gives the command to start engines (top left). Within moments of the start (top right), J. J. Yeley spins in Turn 1 (second from top). The crowd reacts to a dejected Tony Stewart (third from top) after his engine blew while he was leading. Jim Guthrie slams backwards into the Turn 3 wall in a seven-car wreck (third from top). Stephan Gregoire scrapes the wall late in the race (bottom).

Qualifying week was rough sledding for 46-year-old rookie Jack Hewitt. After 25 years of rough-and-tumble racing on America's short tracks, the sprint-car legend from Troy, Ohio, had finally won a shot at Indy in 1998. The last of the rookies to pass his driver's test, Hewitt's week consisted of mechanical problems, high-speed spins, and accidents that threatened to derail his chances of qualifying.

But with the determination that had always marked his career, Jack qualified his Parker Machinery entry 21st. On race day, he made a solid run, finishing 12th.

After the 500, Jack dedicated his inspired drive to his father. A journeyman driver in the sprint car and supermodified ranks, Don Hewitt was the first driver to turn a lap at the storied Eldora Speedway. But he never made it to Indy. Eleven months before Jack made the field at Indy, Don Hewitt died of burns suffered in a welding accident. "Dad was right there with me all day," Jack said. "He was riding right along with me. I hope I made him proud."

Owner-driver Eddie Cheever (*below*) overcame an early pit stop that put him near the back of the field to win by 3.19 seconds over Buddy Lazier in his Dallara-Aurora. "I don't know what I'm supposed to say," the usually loquacious Cheever stammered in victory lane (*left*). After a gulp of milk and a ride in the Corvette pace car, Cheever addresses the crowd (*above*) while accompanied by Manny, Moe, and Jack, mascots of the Pep Boys, official sponsor of the IRL.

RESULTS

NO.	DRIVER	CAR	ENTRANT	ENGINE	CYL	DISP	CHASSIS	COLOR	QUAL SPD	START	FIN	LAPS / SPEED / REASON OUT
51	Eddie Cheever	Rachel's Potato Chips	Team Cheever	Aurora	8	244	Dallara	black, blue	217.334	17	1	200-145.155
91	Buddy Lazier	Delta Faucet/Coors Light	Hemelgarn Racing, Inc.	Aurora	8	244	Dallara	purple, yellow	218.288	11	2	200-145.118
55	Steve Knapp	Primadonna Resorts/Miller Milling	ISM Racing	Aurora	8	244	G Force	orange, black	216.445	23	3	200-145.076
6	Davey Hamilton	Reebok	Nienhouse Motorsports	Aurora	8	244	G Force	orng, slvr, blk	219.748	8	4	199-running
52	Robbie Unser	Team Cheever	Team Cheever	Aurora	8	244	G Force	red, wht, blue	216.534	21	5	198-running
14	Kenny Brack	PowerTeam A. J. Foyt Racing	A. J. Foyt Enterprises	Aurora	8	244	Dallara	wht, red, yelo	220.982	3	6	198-running
81	John Paul, Jr.	Team Pelfrey	Team Pelfrey	Aurora	8	244	Dallara	red, wht, blk	217.351	16	7	197-running
17	Andy Mitchner	Konica/Syan	Syan Racing	Aurora	8	244	Dallara	white, blue	216.922	19	8	197-running
44	J. J. Yeley	One Call/Quaker St./Menards	SRS	Aurora	8	244	Dallara	grn, blue, yelo, orng, red	218.044	13	9	197-running
12	Buzz Calkins	Int. Star Registry/Bradley	Bradley Motorsports	Aurora	8	244	G Force	red, white	217.197	18	10	195-running
7	Jimmy Kite	Royal Purple/Synerlec	Team Scandia	Aurora	8	244	Dallara	purple, yellow	217.477	26	11	195-running
18	Jack Hewitt	Parker Machinery	PDM Racing, Inc.	Aurora	8	244	G Force	yelo, red, black	216.316	22	12	195-running
35	Jeff Ward	Tabasco/Superflo/Prolong	ISM Racing	Aurora	8	244	G Force	red, blk, green	219.086	27	13	194-running
16	Marco Greco	Int. Sports, Ltd.	Phoenix Racing	Aurora	8	244	G Force	red, black	217.953	14	14	183-engine
10	Mike Groff	J.Byrd's/VisionAire/Bryant	Jonathan Byrd/Cunningham Racing LLC	Aurora	8	244	G Force	red, wht, blue	216.704	32	15	183-running
8	Scott Sharp	Delphi Auto Systems	Kelley Racing	Aurora	8	244	Dallara	red, yellow, blk	219.910	7	16	181-gear box
77	Stephan Gregoire	Blue Star/Tokheim/Estridge/Miller-Eads	Chastain Motorsports	Aurora	8	244	G Force	blue	217.036	31	17	172-running
97	Greg Ray	Texas Mtr Spdwy/TNN/Tr. Value/Dixie Chopper	Thomas Knapp Mtrsprts/Genoa Racing	Aurora	8	244	Dallara	black	221.125	2	18	167-gear box
30	Raul Boesel	Beloit/Fast Rod/Tm Losi/TrnsWrld Divers.	McCormack Motorsports	Aurora	8	244	G Force	white, black	217.303	30	19	164-running
5	Arie Luyendyk	Sprint PCS/Rd. Shack/Qualcomm	Treadway Racing, LLC	Aurora	8	244	G Force	blk, white, red	218.935	28	20	151-gear box
40	Dr. Jack Miller	Crest Racing	Crest Racing/SRS	Infiniti Indy	8	244	Dallara	red, white, blue	217.800	15	21	128-running
21	Roberto Guerrero	Royal Spa/Pagan/Dallara-Olds	Pagan Racing	Aurora	8	244	Dallara	red, wht, black	218.900	9	22	125-running
11	Billy Boat	Conseco A.J. Foyt Racing	A. J. Foyt Enterprises	Aurora	8	244	Dallara	green	223.503	1	23	111-drive line
4	Scott Goodyear	Pennzoil Panther	Panther Racing, LLC	Aurora	8	244	G Force	yellow, black	218.357	10	24	100-clutch
9	Johnny Unser	Delta/Hemelgarn	Hemelgarn Racing, Inc.	Aurora	8	244	Dallara	purple, yellow	216.316	25	25	98-engine
99	Sam Schmidt	Best Western Gold Crown Special	LP Racing, Inc./PCI	Aurora	8	244	Dallara	yellow, red	219.982	6	26	48-accident T3
28	Mark Dismore	Learjet/Valvoline/Delphi	Kelley Racing	Aurora	8	244	Dallara	red, wht, black	218.096	12	27	48-accident T3
19	Stan Wattles	Metro Racing/NCLD	Metro Racing Systems	Aurora	8	244	Riley & Scott	black	217.477	29	28	48-accident T3
53	Jim Guthrie	Delco Remy/Goodyear/Aurora	ISM Racing	Aurora	8	244	G Force	blk, red, white	216.604	20	29	48-accident T3
33	Billy Roe	Royal Purple/ProLink/Scandia	Team Scandia	Aurora	8	244	Dallara	purple, orange	220.386	33	30	48-accident T3
2	Robbie Buhl	Johns Manville/Menards	Team Menard, Inc.	Aurora	8	244	Dallara	blue, yelo, orng, red	220.236	5	31	44-radiator
98	Donnie Beechler	Cahill Auto Racing	Cahill Auto Racing, Inc.	Aurora	8	244	G Force	black	216.357	24	32	34-engine
1	Tony Stewart	Glidden/Menards Special	Team Menard, Inc.	Aurora	8	244	Dallara	yelo, orng, red	220.386	4	33	22-engine

INDEX

INDIANAPOLIS
MOTOR
SPEEDWAY